A HISTORY
of the
TOWN *of* UNION

in the
County of Lincoln, Maine,
to the
Middle of the Nineteenth Century

with a
Family Register
of the
Settlers Before the Year 1800, and of Their Descendants

John Langdon Sibley

MEMBER OF THE MASSACHUSETTS HISTORICAL SOCIETY

"*E minimis maxima.*"

HERITAGE BOOKS
2011

HERITAGE BOOKS
AN IMPRINT OF HERITAGE BOOKS, INC.

Books, CDs, and more—Worldwide

For our listing of thousands of titles see our website
at
www.HeritageBooks.com

A Facsimile Reprint
Published 2011 by
HERITAGE BOOKS, INC.
Publishing Division
100 Railroad Ave. #104
Westminster, Maryland 21157

Originally published:
Benjamin B. Mussey and Co.
Boston, 1851

—Errata—

On pages 2 and 20, for "1707" read *1607*; p. 9, for "July" read *May*; p. 111, for "bolt" read *bolter*; p. 133, for "Jane" read *James*; p. 318, for "Freeman Luce Daggett" read *John S. Daggett*; p. 323 for "John Hawes" read *John Brown*; p. 360, for "sergeant-major" read *major*; p. 390, for "windward" read *leeward*.

The inaccuracy of the different records which have been transcribed has led to inconsistency in regard to several names; the middle name of the same individual in some instances being omitted, and in others retained.

— Publisher's Notice —

In reprints such as this, it is often not possible to remove blemishes from the original. We feel the contents of this book warrant its reissue despite these blemishes and hope you will agree and read it with pleasure.

International Standard Book Numbers
Paperbound: 978-0-7884-5147-8
Clothbound: 978-0-7884-8645-6

ERRATA.

On pages 2 and 20, for 1707 read 1607; p. 9, for "July" read *May;* p. 111, for "bolt" read *bolter;* p. 133, for "Jane" read *James;* p. 318, for "Freeman Luce Daggett" read *John S. Daggett;* p. 323 for "JOHN HAWES" read JOHN BROWN; p. 360, for "sergeant-major" read *major;* p. 390, for "windward" read *leeward.*

The inaccuracy of the different records which have been transcribed has led to inconsistency in regard to several names; the middle name of the same individual in some instances being omitted, and in others retained.

FOREWORD

John Langdon Sibley wrote, in the last chapter of his *History of the Town of Union*, that a town history should be accurate and complete, just and truthful. In the years since Sibley's book was published in 1851, scholars, local and state historians, and residents of this community in the St. George's River valley have found his town history valuable for precisely those qualities.

John Sibley was assistant librarian at Harvard when he wrote his *History of the Town of Union*, but there are other credentials which need to be considered to understand why this local history is superior. Details of the daily life in a pioneer settlement are recorded and documented because Sibley knew and listened to the stories of those who cleared the land.

Pioneers suffered hardships. Sibley gathered information from the lips of the participants, so that his Union history is a valuable source of everyday life and methods of doing. These experiences had parallels in other settlements but are missing from many town histories.

Military musters, time set aside for militia units to gather and maneuver, were required by law but often were holidays with social, political and economic influences. Sibley's descriptions of young boys trailing the troops appear to give the feelings he had himself as a lad. The details of these military affairs as recorded by Sibley have been incorporated in other local histories.

Growing up in a community which had been settled only twenty-eight years before his birth gave John Sibley first hand knowledge of Union's history. Leaving home to study at Phillips Exeter Academy and then at Harvard University provided Sibley with a perspective of rural Maine life missing in many records where it was assumed that everyone knew and would recall the early struggles.

Sibley's parents deserve credit for encouraging their son's studies and for supplying information about Union while Sibley was in Cambridge.

Dr. Jonathan Sibley and his wife Persis Morse Sibley came to Union from New Hampshire in September of 1799.

Unable to afford college, Jonathan Sibley had studied medicine with Dr. Carrigain of Concord, New Hampshire and been examined and admitted to the New Hampshire Medical Society in January of 1799. Eight months later he was a farmer and physician in the town of Union, Maine.

Throughout his lifetime, Dr. Sibley was interested and active in town affairs, especially those concerned with education and history. The exchange of letters between father and son provided primary source information for the *History of the Town of Union* and so did the lectures on history given by Dr. Sibley at the winter lyceums.

In 1862, John Langdon Sibley asked the trustees of Phillips Exeter Academy to accept the legacy he had inherited from his parents, funds accumulated through rigid economy and self-denial. In this same document Sibley states his parents lamented the poverty which prevented them from continuing their educations and that he wants their savings to go to the institution which accepted him and gave him financial aid. In addition to this gift, Sibley made other contributions for the support of meritorious and needy students, gifts which amounted to more than $34,000 before he was prevailed upon in 1872 to divulge this support to the school which had given him his start.

Sibley began working in the library when he entered Harvard as a "president's freshman" and graduated in 1825 free of debt and with high scholarship. In 1829, Sibley graduated from divinity school and was ordained as a pastor of a church in Stow but after four years he returned to Cambridge. In 1841 Sibley was appointed assistant librarian at Harvard and in 1856 he became librarian, a position he held until his retirement because of poor health in 1877.

At Harvard Sibley was, and still is, known for his careful research and literary accuracy. His *Biographical Sketches of Graduates of Harvard University* was the first work of its kind published in America and is a major contribution to the early history of New England.

In 1866 John Sibley married Charlotte Augusta Langdon Cook. Upon his death in 1885, Sibley's estate was to be used by his wife during her lifetime and then to be given to the Massachusetts Historical Society to be invested as a permanent fund with the income devoted to the publication of biographical sketches of Harvard graduates.

John Langdon Sibley spent his boyhood in a rural community where he witnessed virgin forests being cleared for farms. He attended a one-room schoolhouse, trapped foxes, had personal conversations with first settlers and their descendants, studied the hand-written records of town meetings, and corresponded with individuals writing other town histories. Then, through his studies and library work at Harvard, Sibley developed skills in researching facts and documenting materials.

Ben Ames Williams used Sibley's *History of the Town of Union* and records of surrounding villages when he wrote *Come Spring*, his fictionalized version of the settling of Union. Williams walked the land to get a feel for distances and time because he wanted historical accuracy.

John Langdon Sibley's section on animals and the details of everyday life—lives of his contemporaries and their parents—helped make Williams' novel valuable as historical fiction. Sibley's objective viewpoint from the Harvard Library, woven together with his personal boyhood memories and his father's reports on politics, education and economics, made *History of the Town of Union* a fine record of Maine history in 1851. No one could write such a history today. Reprinting this fully written town history makes the wealth of Sibley's years of research available to readers again.

October 1986   A. CARMAN CLARK
                            Union Historical Society

JOHN L. SIBLEY
J. H. Buffords, Lith.

CONTENTS.

CHAPTER I.

GEOGRAPHY. — Situation. Boundaries. Rivers and Brooks. Ponds. Soil. Climate. Freshets. Hail and Frogs. Lightning. Health and Longevity. Scenery. 1

CHAPTER II.

ANTE-PLANTATION HISTORY. — Muscongus or Waldo Patent. Disputed Territory. St. George's River proposed as a Boundary. Indians. Hart's and Boggs's Escape from them. Dické and the Comet. 22

CHAPTER III.

PLANTATION HISTORY. — 1772, 1773: First Settlers. The Anderson Party. 1774, Plan of Anderson's Lot. Purchase of the Township by Dr. John Taylor. His Arrival with the Butlers and others. First Public Act of Devotion. Frightened Moose. Occupation of the Anderson Camp. Clearing commenced. High Words with the Anderson Party. Taylor's Return to Massachusetts. Deed to Taylor. 1775: Taylor in Congress. Butlers again at Work. First Rye sowed. Butlers go West. Taylor comes back and labors. Butlers return: are hired out to Benjamin Packard. Packard's Log-house. Timber for Taylor's Buildings. Privations. Butler and the Bear. . . 27

CHAPTER IV.

PLANTATION HISTORY, *continued.* — 1776: Philip Robbins's Purchase. David Robbins's the first Family. Richard Cummings. Taylor again. First Frame House. First Crop of Rye. Raising of a Barn. Log-houses of Richard Cummings and David Robbins. Arrival of the Families of Philip Robbins and Richard Cummings. Crowded House. Timber House. Barn. Taylor's Mills. 36

CHAPTER V.

PLANTATION HISTORY, *continued.* — 1777: Phinehas Butler enters the Army. Purchases by Abijah Hawes; by Ezra Bowen; by Jonathan Amory; by Joel Adams, Jason Ware, and Matthias Hawes. Settlement of John Butler. 1778: Suchfort the Hessian. Blacksmithing. Calamitous Fire. Suffering for Food. 41

CONTENTS.

CHAPTER VI.

PLANTATION HISTORY, *continued.* — 1779: Wheaton's Purchase. Settlement of Joel Adams, Matthias Hawes, and Jason Ware. Woodward. Fairbanks. Settlement of Moses Hawes. Ebenezer Robbins. 1780: Jennison's Purchase. 1781: First Wedding. Jessa Robbins. 1782: Settlement of Phinehas Butler. Elisha Partridge. Taylor's Conveyance to Reed. 45

CHAPTER VII.

PLANTATION HISTORY, *concluded.* — 1783: Log-house. Bride. Bride's Dower. Jessa Robbins. 1784: Amariah Mero. 1785: Josiah Robbins. Gillmor. Cat-and-clay Chimney. Royal Grinnell. Elijah Holmes. 1786: Arrival of the Families of Josiah Robbins; of Samuel Hills. Samuel Martin. Organization of the Plantation. 51

CHAPTER VIII.

INCORPORATION HISTORY. — 1786, Petition for Incorporation. Act of Incorporation. Number and Names of the Inhabitants. 60

CHAPTER IX.

SETTLERS AFTER THE INCORPORATION. — 1787: Levi Morse. Oliver Leland. William Hart. 1788: The Maxcys. 1789: The Daggetts. Seth Luce. Christopher Butler. Ichabod Irish. Barnabas Webb. 1793: Casualty to the Maxcy Family. Remarks on the Early Settlers. 64

CHAPTER X.

POPULATION. — Census, Aug. 1, 1790. Abstracts from Censuses. Hawes's Census in 1826. State Census, March 1, 1837. 73

CHAPTER XI.

POPULATION IN 1850. — Census, June 1, 1850, with Names and Ages. . . . 77

CHAPTER XII.

MINERAL AND ARBORAL PRODUCTS. — Minerals. Timber. Felling of Trees. Burning of Cut-downs. Shingles. Benjamin Speed. Lakin. Boards and Saw-mills. Lime-casks. 97

CHAPTER XIII.

AGRICULTURAL AND HORTICULTURAL PRODUCTS. — Barley and Rye. Indian Corn. Wheat. Potatoes. Fruit. Peaches and Plums. Apples. . . 105

CHAPTER XIV.

MANUFACTURES AND TRADE. — Spinning Wheels. Looms. Home-made Clothing. Fulling Mills. Carding Machines. Factories. Paper Mills. Tanneries. Potash. Iron Works. Fossetts' Mills. Stores. Carting Goods to Boston in the War of 1812. Canals. 108

CONTENTS. V

CHAPTER XV.

MUNICIPAL HISTORY. — Town Meetings. Notifications. Places of holding them. Town Officers. Oath of Office in 1787. Town Clerks. Selectmen. Assessors. Constables. Collectors. Treasurers. Tithingmen. Fish Wardens. . 114

CHAPTER XVI.

TOPOGRAPHICAL HISTORY. — First Burial Place. Old Burying Ground. First Private Burying Ground. Second Private Burying Ground. East Union Burying Ground. Hearses. Common. Pound. Town House. . . . 130

CHAPTER XVII.

FIRST MEETING-HOUSE. — Early Efforts for a Meeting-house. Spot selected. Location changed. Contracted for. Porch. Raising. Enclosed. Pillars. Pulpit Window. Outside to be finished. Temporary Seats. Pews. Roof to be painted. Sale of Pews. Names of Owners. Lock voted. Description of the House. Pews built in the Gallery. Repairs. Stove. Decay and Desecration of the House. Taken down. Associations with it. Customs. Marriage Publishments. Dogs and Dog Whippers. 143

CHAPTER XVIII.

ECCLESIASTICAL HISTORY. — 1779 to 1806: Going to Meeting at St. George's. John Urquhart. Isaac Case. Nine Pounds raised for Preaching. William Riddel called. Aaron Humphrey. Two hundred Dollars raised. Mode of dividing the Money. Abraham Gushee called. Jabez Pond Fisher called. Jonathan Gilmore. Henry True called and settled. 161

CHAPTER XIX.

ECCLESIASTICAL HISTORY, *continued.* — Organization of the First Congregational Church. Mr. Huse's Account of the Proceedings. Conduct of Samuel Hills and the Rev. Messrs. Sewall, Bayley, and others. Articles of Faith. Covenant. Signers' Names. Opposition by the Hills Party. Hills's "Ex Parte" Council, Sept. 10, 1806. Conduct of the Hills Party about the Ordination. Hills censured. Council, June 29, 1808. Hills's "Ex Parte" Council, Feb. 15, 1809. Second Congregational Church organized. Mr. Huse's Letter concluded. 171

CHAPTER XX.

ECCLESIASTICAL HISTORY, *continued.* — 1807 to 1819: Proceedings of the Town to pay Mr. True. Remission of Ministerial Taxes. Signers to the Methodists; to the Friends; to the Baptists. Movements to dissolve the Town's Contract with Mr. True. Incorporation of the First Congregational Society. Dissolution of the Town's Contract. 192

CHAPTER XXI.

ECCLESIASTICAL HISTORY, *continued.* — 1816 to 1825: Attempts to raise Money. Dissolution of Mr. True's Pastoral Connection with the Church and Society.

a*

CONTENTS.

Page.
Result of the Council. Proposals for uniting the Congregational Churches. Obstacles to a Union. Union effected. 204

CHAPTER XXII.

ECCLESIASTICAL HISTORY, *continued.* — 1825 to 1850: Preachers after the Union. Freeman Parker. George W. Fargo. Ordination and Dismission of Oren Sikes. Meeting-house. Ordination and Dismission of Uriah Balkam. Samuel Bowker's Ordination. 214

CHAPTER XXIII.

ECCLESIASTICAL HISTORY, *continued.* — METHODISTS AND BAPTISTS. — Methodist Church and Society. First Methodist Preaching. Circuits and Districts. Organization. Places of Worship. Meeting-house. Camp Meetings. Parsonage. Preachers. Baptist Church and Society. Central Baptist Church. 217

CHAPTER XXIV.

ECCLESIASTICAL HISTORY, *concluded.* — UNIVERSALISTS. — First Universalist Preaching. Organization. Maine Association. John Bovee Dods. Constitution. Preachers. Meeting-house. Bell. 222

CHAPTER XXV.

DELUSIONS AND SUPERSTITIONS. — Signs and Omens. Witchcraft. Bewitched Horse. 227

CHAPTER XXVI.

POLITICAL HISTORY. — Voting. Separation of Maine from Massachusetts. Harmony and Diversity of Sentiment. Embargo. Petition to the President of the United States. Reply. Remonstrance. Petition to the Legislature of Massachusetts. Celebration, July 4, 1810. Celebration in 1814. Ode and Hymn. 230

CHAPTER XXVII.

POLITICAL HISTORY, *concluded.* — Members of Congress. Governors. Lieutenant-Governors. Town Representatives. Justices of the Peace. Coroners. Post Offices and Postmasters. 239

CHAPTER XXVIII.

FINANCIAL HISTORY. — Taxes. Early Apportionment of Taxes. Controversy with Warren. Petition to the Legislature in 1780. Petition to the Legislature in 1783. Plantation Taxes. Taxes since the Incorporation. Taxes paid in Produce. Exemption of Philip Robbins, jun. Table. Adams's Petition to the Legislature in 1794. State of the Finances in 1795. Dollars and Cents. Taking the Valuation. Payment of Taxes. . . . 256

CHAPTER XXIX.

FINANCIAL HISTORY, *concluded.* — Reed's Case. Surplus Revenue. Paupers. Warning out of Town. Maintenance of the Poor. 266

CONTENTS.

CHAPTER XXX.

HIGHWAYS. — Early Difficulties in Travelling. Moss. Paths. Spotted Trees. Exposure of Matthias Hawes. First Roads. First Highway Districts. Character of the Roads. Corduroy Roads. Boating and Visiting. Ox Sleds. First Teaming to Neighboring Towns. 273

CHAPTER XXXI.

HIGHWAYS, *concluded.* — Surveyors and Commissioners. Taxes. Compensation. Time for doing the Work. Breaking Roads in Winter. Comparative Value of Money and Labor. 279

CHAPTER XXXII.

BRIDGES. — Log Bridges. Lower, or True's Bridge. Middle Bridge, at Bachelor's Mills. South Union Bridge. Upper Bridge, at Hills' Mills. Report on Bridges in 1805. Appropriations. 287

CHAPTER XXXIII.

EDUCATIONAL HISTORY. — Earliest Schools and Teachers. Schools at a later Period. School Children in Summer. Drink. Recess. Josiah. Complaints and Punishments. Girls' Work in School. Reading. Spelling. Noontime and Dinners. Winter Schools. Severer Punishments. Intermissions in Winter. Studies. Evening Schools. 294

CHAPTER XXXIV.

EDUCATIONAL HISTORY, *concluded.* — School Districts. School Houses. School Committees. School Agents. School Children. School Money. High Schools. Lyceum. Libraries. 302

CHAPTER XXXV.

PROFESSIONAL HISTORY. — College Graduates. Lawyers. Physicians. Indian Doctor. Urine Doctor. Singing Masters and Singing Schools. Brass Band. 318

CHAPTER XXXVI.

MILITARY HISTORY. — Revolutionary Soldiers. Loyalist. Incidents in the Revolutionary War. French War. Military Appropriations. Powder House. Military Spirit. 327

CHAPTER XXXVII.

MILITARY HISTORY, *continued.* — Infantry Officers. Light Infantry. Its Organization and Dress. Its Officers. Rifle Company. Its Organization and Dress. Rifles. Its Officers. Disbandment. 338

CHAPTER XXXVIII.

MILITARY HISTORY, *continued.* — War of 1812. Pay voted by the Town. Drafts. Alarm. Companies ordered out. Parade on Sunday. March to

CONTENTS.

Camden. Peace. Soldiers from Union in the Army. Texan War. Mexican War. 343

CHAPTER XXXIX.

MILITARY HISTORY, *continued.* — Difficulty with the Waldonian Officers. The Dinner. Waldonian Influence in the Field. Election of Lieut.-Col. Bachelder. Precedence of Rank on the Field. Remoteness of Musters. Pecuniary Considerations. Indignation at a Military Election. Acts of the Legislature. Excitement. 350

CHAPTER XL.

MILITARY HISTORY, *continued.* — Violent Rain-storm. The Companies at Waldoborough Meeting-house. Uncomfortable Feelings. Burial of the Colonel under Arms. Uneasiness. Anecdotes. Line formed. Irregular March to the Muster-field. Rogue's March. Unsuccessful Attempt to stop the Music. Orders misunderstood. Confusion. Desertion. Hurrah. 354

CHAPTER XLI.

MILITARY HISTORY, *continued.* — Col. Avery Rawson. Charges against him stopped. Charges against Officers in Union. Trial of Lieut.-Col. John Bachelder. Trial of Capt. Lewis Bachelder. 361

CHAPTER XLII.

MILITARY HISTORY, *continued.* — Trial of Capt. John P. Robbins. Objections and Protest. Charges and Specifications. Result. 366

CHAPTER XLIII.

MILITARY HISTORY, *continued.* — Evasion of the Laws. John Chapman Robbins becomes Clerk. Loss of the Company Roll. Muster near Trowbridge's, in Warren. Lieut. Ebenezer Cobb. "A good time." Horsemen ride about the Muster-field. Robbins gives Orders. Unsuccessful Attempts to arrest him. Notes for Fines burnt as Wadding. 370

CHAPTER XLIV.

MILITARY HISTORY, *continued.* — Orders to elect Officers. Movements to Re-elect Capts. Bachelder and Robbins. Nathan Bachelder chosen Captain. Pardon Robbins and the Cabbage. Re-election of Capt. Noah Rice. He is cashiered. Voluntary Trainings and Muster. Aroostook War. Rifle Company disbanded. Philo Thurston. Ebenezer Ward Adams chosen Captain. His Trial and Imprisonment. 373

CHAPTER XLV.

MILITARY HISTORY, *continued.* — Two Companies of Infantry. Election of Officers at Amos Walker's. March to the Common. 379

CONTENTS.

CHAPTER XLVI.

MILITARY HISTORY, *concluded.* — Qualifying Remarks. Extension of the Unmilitary Spirit. Change of Public Sentiment. Military Musters. . . . 382

CHAPTER XLVII.

ZOOLOGICAL HISTORY. — Early Hunting and Hunters. Boggs. Anderson. Davis and the Tortoise. Dické. The dogs Tuner and Lion. Laws about Deer and Moose and Deer-reeves. Deers. Moose. Their Haunts. Time and Manner of hunting them. Their Yards. Transportation of Moose Beef. Dressing and cooking it. Moose in Summer. One killed in Seven-tree Pond. 386

CHAPTER XLVIII.

ZOOLOGICAL HISTORY, *continued.* — Bears. Bear Traps. Setting Guns. Bears caught by David Robbins and Jessa Robbins. Baited and killed by Ezekiel Hagar. Love Rum. Taken to Boston and shot. Encounters on Seventree Pond; on Hart's Hill; on Hills Point; on Simmons's Hill; on the Robbins Neck. Adam Martin. Jason Ware and his Dog Sambo. Fate of Sambo. Mrs. Hart and the Bear Trap. 395

CHAPTER XLIX.

ZOOLOGICAL HISTORY, *continued.* — Wolves. Wolf-hunt. Cat-vaughan. Foxes. Personal Experience. Fox seized by Asa Messer. Beavers. Raccoons. Musquash. Minks, Sables, and Loup-cervier. Weasel. 406

CHAPTER L.

ZOOLOGICAL HISTORY, *continued.* — Ducks. Wild Pigeons. Loons. Crows and Blackbirds. Hunting Matches. 413

CHAPTER LI.

ZOOLOGICAL HISTORY, *concluded.* — Fish Laws. Salmon. Alewives. Fishhawks and Eagles. Eels. Smelts. Trout and Pickerel. Other Fish. . 418

CHAPTER LII.

CONCLUSION. — Design. Sources of Information. Changes since the Settlement. Possibilities and Responsibilities. 425

FAMILY REGISTER 429
GENERAL INDEX 519

HISTORY OF UNION.

HISTORY OF UNION.

CHAPTER I.

GEOGRAPHY.

Situation. — Boundaries. — Rivers and Brooks. — Ponds. — Soil. — Climate. — Freshets. — Hail and Frogs. — Lightning. — Health and Longevity. — Scenery.

SITUATION.

THE town of Union, in the county of Lincoln and State of Maine, is situated in about 44° 15′ north latitude, and 7° 50′ east longitude from the city of Washington. The Common, or principal village, is twenty-eight miles east-south-east of Augusta, eight miles from the head of the tide-waters of St. George's River at Warren, and twelve miles from the State Prison in Thomaston.

BOUNDARIES.

The town is bounded on the south and south-west by Warren and Waldoborough; on the west by Medomac River, which separates it from Washington; and on the north and north-east by Appleton and Hope and Camden, till at its eastern extremity it makes with Camden and Warren an angle on the north-west side of Mount Pleasant, near its summit.

RIVERS AND BROOKS.

ST. GEORGE'S RIVER, formerly the Segochet, Segohquet, or Segocket, enters the town through Sunnybec Pond on the north. After running about a mile and a half, in which it passes Hills' Mills and Bachelor's Mills, it flows in a westerly and southerly direction into Round Pond. Thence it runs east into Seven-tree Pond. Its course afterwards is southerly through Warren, towards the Atlantic Ocean.[1]

The PETTENGILL STREAM runs from the Cedar Swamp in Appleton, across a corner of Union, by

---

[1] Belonging to the splendid library of John Carter Brown, of Providence, R.I. is a manuscript, copied from the "Mus. Brit. Bibl. Sloan. No. 1622." It is the "historie of Trauaile into virginia Britania .... gathered & observed as well by those who went first thither, as collected by William Strachey, Gent." In a detailed account of the unsuccessful attempt to plant a colony at "Sachadehoc," the name of this river is incidentally introduced and spelled Segohquet. Capt. John Smith, in his "Generall Historie," spells it Segocket. David Crockett, Esq. of Rockland, who has had much intercourse with the Penobscot Indians for sixty or seventy years, thinks they did not give the name Segocket to any part but the branch which rises in Cushing, and, pursuing a north and west course, joins the main river near the dividing line of Union and Warren. He says, moreover, that Governor Neptune, of the Penobscots, told him Jorgis, or Chorchis, as the word is pronounced by them, is the Indian word for George's, and that the meaning is "delightsome" or "delightful." Governor Sullivan, in a Topographical Description of Thomaston, in the Collections of the Massachusetts Historical Society, vol. iv. says "its Indian name was Georgekee, from whence was probably derived its present name of George's." May not the governor be mistaken in spelling the word Georgekee, instead of Georgekeag; and the terminal syllable have been used to mean the same as in Wessaweskeag, another place in the vicinity; and the Indians have prefixed the word George's, which was in use by the whites after the river was discovered?

In 1605, Capt. George Weymouth, probably in honor of the patron-saint of England, gave the name St. George's to an island, which, according to Rosier's description, agrees with Monhegan. St. George's now is the name of a cluster of islands. St. George's Island Harbor, at the mouth of St. George's River, is probably the place which Weymouth visited, and named Pentecost Harbor. There can be but little doubt that the river derived its name from the island mentioned by Rosier. The five Indians seized and carried off by Weymouth, it is supposed, were taken from this river. That there was an Indian village on the river seems probable from Capt. John Smith's map, on which he assigns to a village the name Norwich, given by Prince Charles, afterward King Charles the First. May not this village have been at the fishing-ground by the head of the tide in Warren?

The Strachey MS. states, that, when Popham was on the way to Sagadahock in 1707, he anchored near "St. George his Island," and " found a Crosse sett vp, one of the same wch Capt. George Weymou .... left upon this Island." On Sunday, Aug. 7, " the chief of both

Fossett's Mills; and enters Medomac River, about two miles southerly of the north-west corner of the town.

MUDDY BROOK conveys the water of Muddy Pond from the north-west into Round Pond. It carries a stave-mill.

BOWKER BROOK, or CASHMAN BROOK, as it is frequently called from a family which resided near it early in the nineteenth century, runs southerly, and enters St. George's River about half a mile above Round Pond.

SEVEN BROOK rises in Appleton, east of Sunnybec Pond, and enters Seven-tree Pond at its north end.

CRAWFORD'S RIVER, commonly called the MILL STREAM by the early settlers, and afterward MAXCY'S MILL STREAM, runs west from Crawford's Pond to Seven-tree Pond. Its water is comparatively warm in winter, and, being uncommonly pure, is very valuable for manufacturing purposes. The Indian name, which was known to the early settlers, is lost. On this stream is the village of South Union.

MILLER'S BROOK, sometimes called the DANIELS BROOK, rises in Hope, and, taking a southerly direction, passes through the farms of John Payson, Nathan Daniels, and others, and enters Crawford's Pond near Miller's Point.

EASTERN STREAM, sometimes called LERMOND'S STREAM, rises in Hope, passes through "The Lakes," and, after a south-south-west course, in which it carries several mills, flows into Crawford's Pond.

FISH'S STREAM, rising in Barrett's Pond near Hope Corner, runs in a southerly direction, and passes

---

the shipps wth the greatest part of all the Company landed on the Island where the Crosse stood . . . . and heard a Sermon delivered unto them by Mr Ri: Seymour."

Rosier's account of Weymouth's Voyage in "Purchas his Pilgrimes," iv. 1659, and Coll. Mass. Hist. Soc. 3d series, viii. Holmes's Annals, i. 123. Map in Smith's Description of New England. Smith's "Generall Historie of Virginia," &c. 205. Belknap's American Biography, ii. 137, 146. Williamson's History of the State of Maine, i. 192.

through Fish's Pond. There is another stream, which rises in Grassy Pond, and runs south-south-westerly. These two unite in Crawford's Meadow, whence their waters flow by Hilt's Mills, and enter Crawford's Pond at its south-east corner. Both streams carry mills before and after they are united.

Some of the small streams, Seven Brook for instance, are occasionally dry or nearly so in summer, though it was not the case when the town was first settled. Some persons think this is caused by the soil washed in from the ploughed and cultivated banks, and by the clearing up of the forests, which overhung the springs by which they were fed.

PONDS.

SUNNYBEC POND, situated partly in Hope and partly in Union, is 198 rods wide, on the Hope and Union line. There is a tradition, that several Indians came from the East on a hunting and fishing excursion. At the harbor in Lincolnville they caught some ducks, and called the place Duck Trap. They proceeded with their ducks to Camden, which they called Megun-ti-cook,[1] because there they began to cook them. On arriving at Friendship, they broke their cooking pot, and called the place Me-dun-cook.[2] Proceeding up the St. George's, they came to Sunnybec Pond, which they named Sunny-bake, because they were obliged to cook their fish and food in the sun on the rocks. In the earliest document in which it is mentioned, it is spelled Sunnyback. If Sunnyback be the correct orthography, there is room for conjecture that it was so called because the sidehill back of the pond is particularly exposed to the rays of the sun. Vegetation there comes forward much earlier than in

[1] It is more probable that the word is Indian, and means large bay, or place of great swells of the sea.

[2] By some said to mean "a sandy, gravelly, poor place, or poor country." D. Crocket says, *cook*, in a compound word, means haven or harbor; and the other part of the compound word designates something which is peculiar or distinctive in the harbor.

other places. Governor Neptune, and some others of the Penobscot tribe of Indians, are not able to give the meaning of the word Sennebec. A year or two ago, David Crocket suggested, diffidently, that Soony-bach or Soony-bech might mean the *appearance* presented by an enclosure of water, or of water almost surrounded with woods and hills; and that, from this general appearance, the name may have been derived. Recently, he made inquiries of the Indian doctor of the Penobscot tribe, who intimated that "*soony* meant shady, and that *bec* meant a place where other water comes in across the main channel," as the Androscoggin, or, more properly speaking, the Ameriscoggin, comes into the Kennebec, and thus furnishes part of the name to the latter river. Perhaps one or more of the streams which enter the pond were much larger, and the entrance more noticeable by the Indians, when the whole town was covered with a forest than since it has been cleared.

ROUND POND, which is about three quarters of a mile in diameter, is called LITTLE POND on a plan of a survey of the Mill Farm, at South Union, dated May 13, 1774. It probably derives its present name from its circular shape. If a person stands on the ice in the middle of it, he will hardly perceive a difference in the distance to any part of the shore.

MUDDY POND, covering from fifty to one hundred acres, and having a cranberry meadow, is situated a little more than a mile north-west of Round Pond.

SEVEN-TREE POND is about three miles long, and extends into Warren. It derives its name from seven trees, which grew on the only island in it when the first settlers came to the place. Several of these trees were standing thirty or forty years ago. They have fallen, till now only one of the smaller of them remains. They were very large, and must have derived their nourishment mainly from the water, which was reached by the fibres of the roots extending down to it through the crevices of the rocks. The island has so little soil, that it is doubtful whether trees, if planted, could now be made to live.

CRAWFORD'S POND, situated in the south-easterly part of Union and in Warren, is 150 rods wide where it is crossed by the line which divides the towns. It derives its name from John Crawford, a native of Stirling in Scotland, who lived about a quarter of a mile above the village in Warren. Col. Samuel Waldo, son of the Brigadier-General, gave to the Scotch settlers the use of all the meadows in the vicinity, which had not been previously laid out for the inhabitants of Warren. Crawford took the meadow on the east side of the pond which bears his name. Having cleared a sled-road to it about the year 1764, he went to Thomaston, made application to Waldo for the meadow, and called for a bowl of punch on the occasion. Waldo took a draught " To Crawford's Meadow," and told him that it should thenceforth bear that name.[1]

SOIL.

By competent judges, the soil of Union is considered as good as that of Farmington and Winthrop, which are generally regarded as the best farming towns in the State. Some persons think it superior. For many years after the settlement, there was early in summer a luxuriance of vegetation and a beauty unsurpassed in the county. The primitive soil had not been worn. It consisted of leaves and vegetable mould, which had been accumulating for centuries. Perhaps one of the richest spots in town is on the north side of Crawford's River, near the outlet. It is said to be the only place where any corn ripened in the cold season of 1816. Immense quantities of alewives had been carted on for manure, the situation was warm, there was a good crop, and the inhabitants went to the owner to procure the corn for seed the next year.

[1] D. Dické, of Warren.

CLIMATE.

Of course there is no essential difference between the climate of Union and that of Maine in general. The warm season commonly begins two or three weeks later, and the cold weather a little earlier, than in Massachusetts. In an old account-book[1] of Matthias Hawes are various memoranda; and, to gratify those who are curious to make comparisons between the weather many years ago and at the present time, the following are extracted: — "1780, March 5. Moderate weather, and wind southwardly. The ponds begin to break up at the edges. April 16. The first of our going down the river by water. April 23. The river is almost broke up. 1781, Nov. 9. The first snow this fall. 1782, June 7. A frost which killed some of our sauce. Sept. 1. Last week a light frost. Sept. 12. The first frost this fall. Oct. 31. The first snow. Nov. 17. A slight snow on the ground. 1783, April 2. The river open so as to pass with a float. 1784, April 17. The snow almost gone in open land. The pond broken up at the edges. 1785, April 2. Snow three feet deep. 1786, April 2. Snow came knee deep. Last Sunday the river open so as to pass down to Mr. Philip Robbins's. At that time the snow almost gone in open lands."

Josiah Robbins harvested rye in July, 1786. The crop was raised on new burnt ground, south and east of the Old Burying Ground. It was protected by the forest on the summit of the hill, and the sun poured its rays into the blackened field. But it was the only time that Robbins or any man has ever been able to do it in July.

Governor Sullivan writes in 1794, for the "Collections of the Massachusetts Historical Society," vol. iv.: "The prevailing winds, during the winter season, are from the north-west. Snows generally fall on a level to the depth of three or four feet. Frosts are fre-

[1] For the loan and free use of this book, the writer is indebted to the kindness of Mr. Noyes P. Hawes, of California.

quently discoverable in September, and in October ice in considerable quantities is made. The snow and ice generally lie till April, when the sun is so high as to melt and carry it away. . . . In July and August, the heat is oftentimes more intense than in Boston; but the evenings and mornings are much cooler."

Gen. Knox, in his "Advertisement of Land for Sale," dated June 15, 1799, says: "The ground is generally covered with snow from the middle of December to the last of March. . . . Although the spring season may be rather later, the winters do not set in earlier than at Boston."

Samuel Hills[1] wrote: "28 January, 1797, rain the first time since November 22d, being sixty-seven days, and very cold, there being but three days that it thawed out of the sun. . . . Oct. 26, 1827. Seven-tree Pond crossed on the ice, believed to be the earliest for forty years past. . . . Pond open between the Eyes, 15 March, 1828. Pond open down to David Robbins, 1 April, 1828. Seven-tree Pond free of ice on the 4th, if not on the 5th."

Forty yoke of oxen hauled a one and a half story dwelling-house from the Colonel Hawes Place across Seven-tree Pond on the ice to the hill south of South Union, April 4, 1844. The pond broke up three days afterward. The circumstance that the ice was so strong, and continued so late in the season, was a subject of much remark. Some of the old inhabitants did not recollect that it had ever occurred before. Once in the present century, the winter set in on the 23d of November.

It is generally thought that there has been considerable change in the climate since the first settlement. The wind, since the hills have been laid bare, may be as bleak, and the snows nearly as deep, as they were seventy-five years ago; but, since the forests have

---

[1] As Samuel Hills kept a journal, and made copious notes during his lifetime respecting nearly all the important events in town, it is greatly regretted that they were not preserved. Most of his papers were placed in a garret to which children had access, and all except a few fragments of interleaved almanacs were destroyed.

been cleared and the land cultivated, the average temperature, it is said, has become milder. Snows are less frequent; and, instead of remaining on the ground as formerly, and making good sledding for months in succession, their duration is uncertain. In some winters, but little snow falls, sometimes hardly enough to enable the farmer to do by sledding the work appropriate to the season; though, early in January, 1851, the snow on an average was about two and a half feet deep. The fathers of the town speak in strong language of the severity of the early winters. As, however, a series of metereological observations has never been made here, the truth as to change of climate cannot be settled by incontestable data. It is not known that there are in existence any memoranda of consequence on the subject, except those which have been given; and they are very incomplete and unsatisfactory.

FRESHETS.

In the spring of 1832, the town was visited by heavy rains. "From the 18th of July to the 10th of June, we had not one fair day. The sun would appear but for an hour or two in the middle of the day, when it appeared at all; and then it would be obscured by thick clouds. Most of the days during this time, it was not seen: when it did shine, it produced but little effect, being obstructed by fog and broken clouds. On the 19th, 20th, and 21st days of May, it rained. On the 20th (Sunday and Sunday night), it fell in cataracts. The rain was terrible: it came down as though the 'windows of heaven were opened.' Our roads were like rivers, and the natural rivers overflowed their banks like the Nile. There were bayous or sluices which carried off the water from the main channel of the river into the valleys. The view at Bachelor's Bridge was awfully grand. The face of the earth looked as if the fountains of the great deep were broken up. An avalanche slipped off the mountain near our powder-house, in a south-west direction.

carrying rocks with it weighing several tons. A rivulet of running water followed after. In this town the water was higher than ever it was known to be before by our oldest inhabitants. There was a ferry-boat plying over the lowlands between Waldoborough and Warren. Great damages have been sustained in this country from the loss of bridges, mills, &c. In this town, two principal bridges over the St. George's River have been carried away, together with one saw-mill, one bark-mill, the old factory, and several other buildings, great and small. Many of our farmers have ploughed up their cornfields, and sowed them with barley and oats. Now the season seems to be favorable for all things, except corn." [1]

On the east side of the stone dam at the Middle Bridge was a saw-mill, and over it a machine-shop. The bulkhead of the flume, being rotten, gave way; and, consequently, the lower end of the saw-mill tipped down. The dam was washed off, and the stones were deposited a short distance below in the eddy, the bottom of which previously could not be reached with a long pike-pole. The roof of the saw-mill having been tipped under the bridge, it carried it off on its back, stopped with it about thirty rods below, and laid it across the fence on the line between Robbins and Gillmor. The saw-mill and machine-shop went twenty-five or thirty rods further, and landed near the pine-tree on Robbins's corn-land. So quietly were they carried down, that the chimney and bricks in the machine-shop were undisturbed, and the gouges and chisels lay on the turning-lathe, ready for use.

During this freshet, the water crowded into the Robbins Meadow. Little's Meadow, at the head of Seven-tree Pond, was also flooded. The water pressed so hard from the Robbins Meadow, that a little digging, perhaps fifteen minutes', would have opened a passage across the road, where it was stopped mainly by the dirt crowded out of the ruts. Thus, from

[1] Dr. Sibley's Letter, June 14, 1832.

Bachelor's Mills to the head of Seven-tree Pond, a new channel for the river might have been opened nearly in the course of the canal.

HAIL AND FROGS.

"July 21, 1820, there was a tremendous shower of hail at Sennebec. A few large ragged pieces of ice fell at my house. Hail fell during two hours, and it was thought by some that it would have been a foot deep, if it had not melted on the ground. The crop of corn is entirely destroyed. Grain, potatoes, and other articles much injured. Ninety squares of glass were broken in Esquire M'Lean's house, and as many more in Lemuel Lincoln's house. Yesterday morning, the pastures on the east side of Appleton Ridge appeared white with ice, when viewed by the inhabitants of the town of Hope. Last night, a man told me that he dug down through the hail where it had rolled in a heap under the fence near Andrew Suchfort's (thirty hours after it had fallen), and found it ten inches deep. I have my information from the sufferers; but I think some allowance ought to be made for their injured feelings.

"August 6th. Seventy-two hours after the hail, I visited the place to see the ruins. I passed from Sennebec Pond to Appleton Ridge, where the hail had made the greatest havoc. The whole face of nature was changed. The verdure of the fields was taken away, and the earth appeared as though it had been covered several days with snow. The corn, grain, beans, peas, and garden vegetables, were totally destroyed, and there was but a small hope of potatoes. The people were gathering up their [corn?] and mowing their wheat for fodder. A place was shown to me by the inhabitants where the hail had drifted by wind and rain to the top of a wall, and was supposed to have been four feet deep. It was not all melted. I saw a drift of hail in another place six inches deep, and ten or fifteen feet long on the north side of a wall, and have been told that it remained two or three days

GEOGRAPHY.

longer before it was melted. Much glass was broken. Some herds of cattle fled to the woods, and whole broods of young geese and turkeys were killed. The hailstones were shaped like a small watch, with the addition of what appeared to be small round hailstones congealed to the edges of the larger ones. The circumference of one stone that had been measured was $5\frac{3}{8}$ inches.

"No sooner was the hail dissolved than the frogs appeared. They were like the grasshoppers for multitude. Various were the conjectures of the people about their origin. Some supposed that they fell from the clouds with the hail. Others accounted for them different ways; but their origin is now clearly ascertained to have been a mill-pond in Cedar Swamp, west of Appleton Ridge. An old Quaker told me that he was at the mill-pond, piling up boards, about the first of July, and that the shore was covered with small frogs, hatched the present year; that the largest of them left the water first, and that the smaller ones followed after; that they travelled west of the pond into the wilderness, and east of the pond towards St. George's River. The frogs that took an easterly direction had to pass about half a mile through the woods (where they covered the ground) to the west end of the grass fields on Appleton Ridge. When they entered the cleared land, they fed on grasshoppers, and appeared to travel faster than in the woods.

"The old Quaker said he liked to have them come, as they did no harm at all, but evidently thinned off the grasshoppers where they went. These frogs pursued uniformly the course in which they set out. One man observed that they could not be whipped back again toward their mill-pond. On the 1st instant I was on Appleton Ridge. The inhabitants have had a plantation meeting, and chosen a committee to apprize the damage done by the hail, and intend to apply to the neighboring towns, or to the Legislature of the State, for means of subsistence through the winter. They have sown much turnip-seed and some buckwheat in their corn-fields. The potatoes are sprouting up, and give hopes of a small crop. The apples which had not been beaten from the trees by the hail were so bruised on the upper side, that that side had ceased to grow; while the other side grew as fast as though there had been no hail. There was not a mess of green sauce to be had in all the neighborhood. I saw the frogs. They appeared to be pursuing an easterly course, and had progressed to within about fifty rods of St. George's River, where I saw many of them hopping on the west side of a wall, by which they had been obstructed in their course. They were green and speckled, and of a small size. Yesterday, a man told me that their number was greatly diminished. He supposed they had died."[1]

LIGHTNING.

June 29, 1815. During a terrific thunder shower in the morning, James Lermond, aged about forty, living in the house with his brother William, at the east part of the town, was killed by lightning. Being at work on the highway, he went home to get shelter. After hanging up his hat, he stood at a table, with his face towards the window. The lightning came down the stud of the window about as low as his breast, then leaped to his breast, passed down his body, made a hole through the floor, and threw him backwards towards the fire. The ashes were scattered over his face. He was killed instantly. By the same stroke of lightning, the front door and the studs were thrown out, and the mouldings above and the window were thrown in. Glass in the several windows around the house was broken out. A stud from the west side was carried across the chamber, and hurled several rods through a window on the east side. The second story of the house was torn in pieces. The lightning ran in every direction. From careful observations, it was evident that its course had often been upward.

" August 8, 1819. Four weeks ago, we had a fright-

[1] Letter of Dr. J. Sibley.

ful tempest. The lightning struck a large barn belonging to Ephraim Boggs, in Warren[1] (half a mile south of Moses Morse's), and burnt it to the ground. The same day the lightning struck a balm-of-Gilead tree near Moses Morse's house, and a stump in his fence, which it set on fire. William Hart's barn was also struck at the same time, and Mr. Metcalf's[2] cow-yard fence. The next Saturday after Mr. Boggs's barn was burnt, he had another barn of the same size on the same ground finished, doors all swinging; and I am told that thirty men dined together on the barn-floor. The old barn had in it about ten tons of old hay. The new barn was built almost entirely by charity.

"Last Sunday, we had another shower; the lightning burnt Noah Rice's barn, containing much hay. Obadiah Morse's barn, with forty tons of hay, was set on fire by the lightning; but the fire was extinguished.[3] The same day, lightning struck in many places elsewhere. Last Monday, our people were all in motion, declaring that they would do equal to what Warren had done. Teams driving through all the town with timber and lumber for Capt. Rice. Wednesday, phœnix-like, the barn began to rise from the ashes, and before night it was covered with boards. It is very large, and makes a fine appearance. I am told it contains ten tons of hay, which has been given to Capt. Rice.

"P. S. Aug. 9. Alas! this is not all. Yesterday, the lightning visited us again, and burnt a barn filled with hay for Lemuel Wentworth,[2] struck Christopher Newbit's house,[2] and killed a child belonging to Jotham Davis.

"Within four weeks, I have seen three large barns with much hay burnt to the ground by lightning; and the fire in another barn kindled by lightning has been

---

[1] Near Union line. [2] In Hope.

[3] Mr. Morse hastened to the barn, rolled up the hay, and trod on it, and thus smothered the fire; but his hands were badly burnt.

extinguished, and a child killed, and all within three miles of the place where this is written.

"Lemuel Wentworth had a load of hay on his wagon to carry to Capt. Rice, when his barn was burnt. It stood in the old barn; new barn burnt. Hay unloaded."

"On Sunday morning, May 25, 1823, at 5 o'clock, a chimney in the dwelling-house of Jason Ware was struck by lightning. The chimney and house were injured, and a brick was removed from the hearth. Mrs. Ware and a son, though sitting one in each corner of the fireplace, were not hurt. Mr. Ware, being in the act of placing a backlog, was struck on the head with the fluid, which burnt and broke the thick woollen coat on his right shoulder and arm, destroying the principal part of the sleeve above the elbow, setting on fire his cotton shirt, burning his flannel waistcoat, ripping both seams in the leg of the boot, and breaking and burning the foot of it. His hair and eyebrows were singed; and the injury, which was of the compound nature of a bruise and a burn, extended down the right side of the neck, over the shoulder and arm, and down the thigh, leg, and foot [and perforated his boot near the heel]. He fell instantly, and was apparently dead. Cold water was thrown into his face [friction was resorted to], and he exhibited signs of life. He was then held erect, and cold water poured upon him profusely. Applications of poultices, and subsequently of plasters, were made to the wounded parts; and shortly the skin, which to a considerable extent was entirely dead and black, was removed in large pieces. In a fortnight he was able to walk, and in a reasonable time recovered a comfortable state of health, though not so good as before. The shock appeared to add something to the infirmities of age.

"The same stroke of lightning tore a large timber from the roof of the barn of Matthias Hawes, about 25 rods distant; while several cattle in the stall below did not receive any injury. Some persons said they perceived, both at the house and the barn, a strong smell of brimstone; others compared it to gunpowder."[1]

Aug. 25, 1840. The lightning struck the store of Henry Fossett, in the north-west part of the town. Robert Rokes, of Appleton, sitting on the counter, was killed. On a bench below him, which was placed along against the counter, sat, on one side of him, John Rokes, of Hope. He was stunned, and so injured that he did not recover for many weeks. On the same bench, but on the other side of Robert Rokes, sat Jacob Sibley, leaning forward. He was stunned, and carried home in a wagon. His burns were so deep, that he did not become even tolerably well till the following spring; and the state of his physical system, and the large scars and ridges, which resemble the twists in ropes, make it obvious that the effects will be seriously felt through life. Thomas Fossett and Robert Pease were stunned, and slightly injured, but shortly recovered. Paul Lincoln was stunned, and so seriously injured, that for some time his life was despaired of; but after some months he recovered. Henry Fossett, the only person in the store who was not hurt, and but for whose escape the store and all the persons in it would undoubtedly have been burnt, was behind the counter at the time, and threw out the cotton batting which had been ignited. The wounds would not have been so deep, if, amid the confusion, water had been thrown upon the clothes, which continued to burn for a long time after the sufferers were struck down.

HEALTH AND LONGEVITY.

"People never die in Union" was the remark of a native of Thomaston; and probably there are not many towns in Maine, in which the deaths are fewer or the sickness less, in proportion to the number of inhabitants. This, however, like other towns, has had seasons of extensive mortality. In 1792–3, the throat

[1] Dr. J. Sibley's Letters.

distemper, as it was commonly called, carried off a very large number of the children, and spread a general mourning through the small population. In 1826 the dysentery was very prevalent and fatal.

Consumption, too, has called off one after another from some families, till but very few members remain to mourn over the departed. In such cases, it is not unnatural for those who are fast wasting away, eagerly to adopt any suggestion for relief from the destroyer. Accordingly, in 1832 and 1833, a few persons put in practice the proverb, that the burning of the lungs of relatives who died of consumption would cure that disease in the living. One body was exhumed several months after death, and the vital parts were burned near the grave, which was in the Old Burying Ground. The theory seemed to be, that the disease, being a family disease, would thus be burned out or exterminated. But death still claimed the fair and the beautiful as his own.

Some idea of the general healthfulness of the place may be formed from the following memoranda by the Rev. Mr. True, which purport to notice all the deaths in town, inclusive of infants, for the several years to which they relate: —

1807	11	1813	9	1819	6	1825	18
1808	5	1814	9	1820	6	1826	25
1809	7	1815	11	1821	8	1827	9
1810	6	1816	11	1822	13	1828	21
1811	10	1817	9	1823	17	1829	16
1812	7	1818	3	1824	16	1830	22

When the census was taken in 1830, there were 17 males and 16 females above 70 years of age; and in 1840 there were 15 males and 24 females. In 1835 there were 26 or more persons who were as much as 75 years of age. It is thought that the oldest person who has died in town was the widow Abigail Messer, probably 99.

Without attempting an analysis of the causes of the healthfulness of the place, it may be observed, the water is in general uncommonly pure. The relative position of the hills and valleys favors a brisk circulation of air through all parts of the town, and particularly in the direction of north and south. Though the elevations are not mountainous, there is comparatively little low ground; and the fog, which lies in the valleys and along the river almost every morning in summer, while it favors vegetation, is not found to produce debility or disease. The agricultural employments of the inhabitants are highly conducive to vigor and strength. Indolence and luxury are almost unknown. Men, women, and children wear the hue of health. From thirty to forty years ago, it was a common remark of strangers, that there was more female beauty in Union than in any other town in the county or State. The fresh countenance, the clear or brilliant eye, the natural, uncompressed form, were testimonials to the generally good habits and customs of the people, as well as to the healthfulness of the town.

SCENERY.

It would be unjust to the town not to allude to its scenery. By some visitors, at the season of the year when the earth is in its richest attire, it is said to be the most beautiful which they have ever beheld. Hills and valleys, ponds and streams, the romantic and the picturesque, are combined in the prospects. On a bright June morning, a ride in almost any direction affords a rich enjoyment to people of taste and admirers of nature. One person might be pleased to leave the beaten road, and stroll along the river below the bridge at South Union, and watch the water tumbling over and among the rocks overhung with bushes, and threading its way down to the pond. Another, of a more pensive turn, might stand by the large rock in the Old Burying Ground. On all sides are graves. There sleep the fathers and the mothers of the town, at rest from worldly anxiety, suffering, and toil. Around them are gathered many of their children and children's children. On the east lies a placid lake. To the north-west opens a bright, sunny landscape, winning the thoughts away from the clouds and storms and melancholy of this life, and directing them to higher and holier scenes.

For a broader view, ascend the summit of the hill near the Common. About one hundred rods north of it is a snug house, almost hidden by trees; and beyond it, for a long distance, the ground is nearly a plain, but varied with pleasing undulations. On the right, near the foot of the hill, glides Seven Brook; and on the left, twenty or thirty rods distant, is St. George's River. Beyond these, and circumscribing them from the east around to the west, the rise of land is not unlike an elongated amphitheatre. On this extensive hillside may be seen farms above farms, covered with cattle and sheep, and dotted over with houses and barns. The rows of corn and potatoes, two or three miles distant, are so regular that with a good eye it seems as if they may be counted. Flitting clouds throw their racing shadows, and wave chases wave, over the surface of the bending fields of grain.

Immediately at the foot of the hill on the south is the green Common, surrounded with neatly painted houses and shops, which extend to the west till they meet the mills carried by the St. George's. On the rise of land 150 or 200 rods distant in the south-southwest, the back part of the Old Burying Ground juts out from behind a hill, and exposes to view the marble gravestones which have been placed there by the hands of friendship and affection. A little to the east of south lies Seven-tree Pond, so clear that in it may be seen mirrored, two or three miles distant, the trees and fields on its southern banks. And east of this pond is a moderate swell of land intersected by Crawford's River, which drives the spindles, the shuttles, the hammers, and the saws of the busy little village of South Union.

There are still broader views. Barrett's Hill to the north-east, and the swell of land on the west, command extensive prospects of Kennebec County; and,

in very clear weather, a glimpse of the White Hills of
New Hampshire, about one hundred miles distant. In
the south-east part of the town is Mount Pleasant, the
highest of the eminences, known to all seamen on
the coast, for nearly three hundred years, as the Penobscot or Camden Hills. From its summit, a short
distance beyond the town-line, may be seen below, as
on a map, a great part of Penobscot Bay with as
many islands as there are days in the year; and far to
the east the apparently unbounded Atlantic Ocean.
How often, before a European had removed trees for
the first building-spot in the vast wilderness of New
England, was this summit welcomed by Smith,[1] Pop-

[1] In 1603, Martin Pring, according to "Purchas his Pilgrimes,"
iv. 1654, "fell in with a multitude of small Ilands, in the latitude of
43 degrees, the —— of June, which Ilands were found very pleasant
to behold. Here we found an excellent fishing for Cods. . . . We
sayled to the South-west end of these Ilands, and there rode with our
ships vnder one of the greatest. One of them we named *Foxe Iland*,
because we found those kind of beasts thereon. So passing through
the rest with our Boates to the mayne Land, which lieth for a good
space North-east and South-west, we found very safe riding among
them in sixe, seven, eight, ten, and twelve fathomes. At length, com-
ming to the Mayne in the latitude of 43 degrees and an halfe, we
ranged the same to the South-west."
In 1604, Champlain was for some time among the islands; and, in
September, went up the Penobscot River twenty-five leagues to a
small stream, not far above which were falls. He speaks of Cape
Bedabedec, which, according to Jeffery's Atlas, is Owl's Head. He
was probably the first white man who explored the river. He gives
minute directions for entering it. The edition of his voyages published
by Jean Berjon at Paris, in 1613, of which there is a copy in the
library of Harvard University, contains many passages omitted in
later editions.
Rosier, in Weymouth's Voyage, already alluded to on page 2, states,
that from "S. George's Iland we might discern the main land from
the west-south-west to the east-north-east, and a great way (as it then
seemed, and we after found it) up into the main we might discern
very high mountains, though the main seemed but low land," &c.
Williamson, History of Maine, i. 193, states that the place where
they went ashore and amused themselves in hunting, June 12, 1605,
was Penobscot, now Camden, Hills.
The Strachey MS. in the details of the voyage of the Popham party
to Sagadahock, in 1707, states, "there be three high mountaynes that
lie in on the Land, the Land called Segohquet, neere about the River
of Penobscot," and gives drawings of their appearance from different
points of view.
In 1614, Capt. John Smith, whose history, in connection with

ham, Weymouth, Champlain, Pring, and the seamen, who, for half a century or more before them, sailed along the coast to fish and to trade with the Indians! How many thoughts crowd the mind respecting those times, and the changes which have since taken place! Though no thrilling events, to command the attention of the general reader, have ever occurred in the town, there are around it associations with olden time, which give additional interest to scenery which it would require a poet and a painter properly to describe.

Pocahontas, is familiar to every school-child, spent several months exploring the coast in an open boat with eight men. In 1616, he published his Description of New England, accompanied with a map. On page 24, he says, "North-west of Penobscot," meaning only Penobscot Bay, " is *Mecaddacut*, at the foot of a high mountain, a kind of fortresse against the *Tarrantines*, adjoining to the high mountaines of *Pennobscot*, against whose feet doth beat the Sea: But over all the Land, Iles, or other impediments, you may well see them sixteen or eighteen leagues from their situation. *Segocket* is the next: then *Nuscongus*, *Pemmaquid*," &c. Mecaddacut, on Smith's map, is called Dunbarton or Dunbarte. From its situation at the south of the range of hills and east-north-east of one or two other eminences, it is not improbable that Smith meant to locate the Indian village at Camden, on the Megunticook, or perhaps a little further south. Indian territories were not distinctly bounded. Bedabedee may have designated the coast, and included the Penobscot Hills and Owl's Head. When it is considered that Indians, giving to the consonants a soft or obscure sound, do not enunciate them distinctly, that Smith gives the name as it sounded to his English ears, and Champlain as it sounded to the French, it is not improbable that Bedabedec and Medambattec and Mecaddacut are meant to represent the same Indian word.

It is somewhat remarkable that the accounts of the early explorations of the coast of Maine have not been more carefully examined. Many of the harbors, headlands, and islands, as laid down on Smith's map, are easily identified, by recurring to page 205 of his "Generall Historie of Virginia, New England," &c. published in 1626, where the Indian names stand side by side with the English names given by Charles the First, while Prince Charles. Smith was here in the summer. He speaks with enthusiasm of the country. In 1616 he published his book and his map, for the purpose of prevailing on people in England to form a colony. If his project had been carried out successfully, some spot in this vicinity, and not Plymouth, would have been chronicled as the birthplace of New England. The settlers, however, would have been adventurers in quest of pelf, rather than the sturdy pilgrims who fled from persecution to enjoy religious liberty. They probably would not have given the Pilgrim-leaven to the character of New England, and more or less to that of the whole world. And it may therefore be considered fortunate, perhaps, that his plan did not succeed.

CHAPTER II.

ANTE-PLANTATION HISTORY.

Muscongus or Waldo Patent. — Disputed Territory. — St. George's River proposed as a Boundary. — Indians. — Hart's and Boggs's Escape from them. — Dické and the Comet.

MUSCONGUS OR WALDO PATENT.

UNION was part of the tract of land called the Muscongus Patent, which was a grant made March 2, $16\frac{29}{30}$, by the Plymouth Council to John Beauchamp, of London; and Thomas Leverett, then of Boston in England, and subsequently of Boston in New England. Afterwards this tract was called the Waldo Patent.

DISPUTED TERRITORY.

Union is in the territory over which, for more than a century, the French and the English alternately claimed jurisdiction; and, if there had been any inhabitants, they would have been constantly harassed by the conflicting parties and by the Indians. The changes of the governments, and the quarrels and hostilities connected therewith, do not claim special notice, as the beginning of a settlement on the soil of this town had not then been made.

ST. GEORGE'S RIVER PROPOSED AS A BOUNDARY.

In 1711 or 1712, it was proposed to make St. George's River the boundary between the English and the French.[1] If this had been effected, the inhabitants

---

[1] Mémoires des Commissaires du Roi et de Ceux de sa Majesté Britannique, sur les Possessions et les Droits respectifs des deux Couronnes en Amérique, ii. 382, 4to, Paris, 1755. Memorials of the English and French Commissaries concerning the Limits of Nova Scotia or Acadia, i. 420-5, 4to, Lond. 1755. Remarks on the French Memorials concerning the Limits of Acadia, p. 58, 8vo, Lond. 1756. Histoire et Description Générale de la Nouvelle France, &c. par le

on the west side of the river might now have been subject to the President of the United States, and part have been doing homage to the Queen of England. On the one side of the river the fugitive slave would be liable to be returned to his master, while on the other he would be as secure as in Canada.

INDIANS.

There is no evidence that this was a place much resorted to by Indians, though the Wawenocks[1] inhabited the country from Sagadahock to St. George's River. It is obvious, however, that they were here occasionally. It is said that during the French war several lived along Crawford's River, and between Seven-tree Pond and Round Pond, near the latter. Stone hatchets, chisels, and other Indian implements, have been found near the Upper Bridge, in the vicinity of which was a good place for fishing at the waterfall. About half-way between Nye's Corner and Sunnybec Pond, very near the spot where the school-house now stands, two Indian skeletons were ploughed up in repairing the road some twenty-five years since. Hatches, arrow-heads, &c. were found by the early settlers near the mouth of Crawford's River. A brass kettle, as large as a pail, was also found there. At the

P. De Charlevoix, ii. 236, 4to, Paris, 1744. [Jeffery's] Conduct of the French with Regard to Nova Scotia, p. 39, 8vo, Lond. 1754.

In this connection may be inserted an extract from a letter of the historian, William Gordon, to Arthur Lee, then in Congress. It is dated at Jamaica Plain, in Roxbury, Massachusetts, April 2, 1783. It is among the manuscripts of Arthur Lee, in the library of Harvard University : —

"What may have been sent you from France, I know not; but you may DEPEND upon the following information.

"The British would not allow the boundaries of Nova Scotia to terminate at St. Croix, but demanded Kennebec at first, and afterwards insisted upon Penobscot as their ultimatum, until Mr. Adams produced the records of the Massachusetts, and the authorities of Shirley, Pownal, Bernard, and Hutchinson, as well as the original grant of Nova Scotia by James the First to Sir William Alexander, and invited the British minister to state a written claim of Kennebec or Penobscot as the boundary of Nova Scotia, that it might be answered in writing, which brought him to reason."

[1] Williamson's Maine, i. 468.

present day, various Indian implements are occasionally turned up by the plough on the farm of Joseph Gleason. There are holes on the Robbins Neck, near the outlet of Round Pond, and on the ridge near the head of Seven-tree Pond on its east side, and in other places. By some it is conjectured that Indians dug them for the purpose of burying their provisions, and by others for concealing, as far as practicable, fires which might be wanted for cooking or for comfort. Another supposition is that they are Indian cellars.

In the archives of the State of Massachusetts[1] is a journal of a scouting party, which may contain an allusion to the place when a wilderness. It has been suggested that it was probably the journal of Capt. Matthias Remely.[2] "Oct. 13, 1757, I went out myself to a place called Sterling,[3] which is about nineteen miles up the river, divided my men into small scouts; some went up the river sundry miles, others towards the back of Broad Bay."

David Dické, of Warren, says that an Indian was

---

[1] MS. vol. 38, A, p. 297.

[2] For this suggestion, and for important information, the reader is indebted to Cyrus Eaton, Esq. of Warren; who, though laboring under the misfortune which called forth one of the most admirable apostrophes of Milton, has made a valuable collection of materials, which, by the assistance of a dutiful daughter in delicate health, have been put together so as to make an important work respecting the settlements on St. George's River, and particularly respecting the town of Warren.

In the American Quarterly Register, xiii. 162, is an account of Lutherans in Waldoborough. There are sketches of some of the towns in Maine in different "Historical Collections." There are no town histories which make separate volumes but the following:— William White's History of Belfast, 12mo; Belfast, 1827, pp. 120. George Folsom's History of Saco and Biddeford, 12mo; Saco, 1830, pp. 331. William Willis's History of Portland, 2 vols. 8vo; Portland, 1831 and 1833, pp. 243, 355. Jonathan D. Weston's History of Eastport and Vicinity, 8vo; Boston, 1834, pp. 61. Charles Bradbury's History of Kennebunk Port, 12mo; Kennebunk, 1837, pp. 301. Thomas Parker's History of Farmington, 8vo; Farmington, 1846, pp. 136. William Allen's History of Norridgewock, 12mo; Norridgewock, 1849, pp. 252. J. W. Hanson's History of Norridgewock and Canaan, 12mo; Boston, 1849, pp. 372.

[3] The Sterling here alluded to was part of Warren.

buried on Seven-tree Island, some time before the settlement of the town; and because earth was scarce, or because he was an Indian of consequence, a mound or pile of stones, chiefly flat, was placed over the remains. The stones, he adds, were carried away, and used at South Union, in building a chimney or an oven, which was put up, either by the first or the second party of settlers, for the purpose of cooking. Phinehas Butler, of Thomaston, has no recollection of it, and thinks it certainly could not have been so.

Not any Indians were living here when the first settlers came. They often visited the town afterwards, " hunted along almost every year," and were on friendly terms with the inhabitants. " The white children and the pappooses slid down hill and played together like school children."[1] The Indians sometimes solicited the whites to accompany them in hunting. Once, Philip Robbins went, in accordance with an Indian's request; and they killed two old bears and either one or two cubs, which they found under the root of a tree that had been blown down. In the year 1777, a company of six encamped between Philip Robbins's and the river. " One of the Indians punished his child for stealing (or carrying off from about the house where he had found it) the broken bowl of an iron spoon."[2] Samuel Boggs had been to Sunnybec to make tree-nails, and there his mare died in foaling. The Indians were exceedingly straitened for food, and called the flesh very good moose-beef.[3] They also brought away some of the foal, and it was all the food they had when they came.

During one winter, some Indian families were encamped near the head of Seven-tree Pond; and during another there were several near the brook between Jessa Robbins and Moses Hawes. None, however, resided a long time in the town.

[1] Mrs. Dunton.   [2] H. True, M.D.   [3] Jessa Robbins.

HART'S AND BOGGS'S ESCAPE.

There is a story that Stephen Hart, uncle of William Hart, when stationed at the fort in Thomaston, was in a float with Samuel Boggs, trapping in Crawford's Pond. They discovered Indians on Miller's Rocky Point at the north end of the Pond, and immediately directed their course homeward. The Indians, supposing they would naturally go down the St. George's, ran to intercept them on their way to Seven-tree Pond. The hunters, anticipating this movement, instead of taking the route, hastened towards the south end of Crawford's Pond. As they passed the point at the extremity of the island, they saw seven Indians on the western shore. They plied their paddles with increased vigor. Having thrown their traps overboard, they landed on the south shore, and, with the adroitness of hunters, fled towards their home. The Indians, having discovered their mistake, pursued them. The parties crossed each other's tracks two or three times. Hart and his companion, however, succeeded in getting safely into the fort, though they were fired upon just before they arrived there. This adventure may have occurred in the Old French or Seven Years' War; or it may have been later, as the Indians were jealous of the white hunters, and sometimes disposed, even in peace, to wreak vengeance on them as intruders.[1]

DICKE' AND THE COMET.

The only other incident, known to have occurred here before the settlement by the whites, was communicated in the following words: "In 1769, William Dické went up to Union alone to hunt for beaver. Night and storm coming on, he landed on Seven-tree Island, sheltered himself from the rain beneath his inverted float, and slept till the tempest abated and the clouds broke away. Then, looking out, he beheld for the first time the comet of that year, with its long, fiery, fan-shaped train, glaring in all its sublimity.

[1] Fisher Hart and John F. Hart.

Being but seventeen years of age, quite illiterate, and wholly ignorant of the cause or even the existence of such phenomena, we may well imagine the surprise and terror it gave him. Being told it was a sign of war, and finding it verified by the revolutionary contest, he became unalterably fixed in the belief; and, when a similar one appeared in 1811, he confidently and successfully predicted the war with Great Britain, which followed the next year."

CHAPTER III.

PLANTATION HISTORY, 1772—1775.

1772, 1773, First Settlers. — The Anderson Party. — 1774, Plan of Anderson's Lot. — Purchase of the Township by Dr. John Taylor; his Arrival with the Butlers and others. — First Public Act of Devotion. — Frightened Moose. — Occupation of the Anderson Camp. — Clearing commenced. — High Words with the Anderson Party. — Taylor's Return to Massachusetts. — Deed to Taylor. — 1775, Taylor in Congress. — Butlers again at Work. — First Rye sowed. — Butlers go West. — Taylor comes back and labors. — Butlers return: are hired out to Benjamin Packard. — Packard's Log-house. — Timber for Taylor's Buildings. — Privations. — Butler and the Bear.

1772, 1773.

THE first white people who located themselves in town, probably came in September or October, 1772. Archibald Anderson and James Anderson, from the part of Warren called Stirling;[1] James Malcom, from

[1] The name is derived from the Stirling in Scotland, from which the settlers originated. Although the records commonly spell Sterling, Sterlington, and Sterlingtown, with an *e*, it is evidently wrong, as the place in Scotland is spelt with an *i*. Lord Stirling, a general in the American army in the Revolution, who made claim to the earldom of Stirling (which he was believed to have legally established, but against which the House of Lords decided), spelled his name in the same way. See Sedgwick's Life of William Livingston, 214,

Cushing; and John Crawford, jun. from the upper part of Warren Village, ascended St. George's River, to "take up" land. All of them were natives of Scotland, and came to this country in childhood with the Stirling colony which settled in Warren. In their hunting and lumbering excursions, they had undoubtedly become well acquainted with the value of the lumber and the nature of the soil. On a knoll eight or ten rods from Seven-tree Pond, about forty rods west of the ledge in Joseph Gleason's field, and thirty rods north of the outlet of Crawford's River, from which the knoll was then separated by low, wet ground, they built a camp, the cellar belonging to which has been recently filled. On the top of the camp were a few boards which they brought from Warren. Here James Malcom and Archibald Anderson intended to reside. James Anderson and John Crawford, jun. took possession of the Robbins Neck, and ran a possession-fence from the head of Seven-tree Pond to the St. George's, a short distance below Bachelor's Mills. The four residents lived together in the camp.[1]

1774.

There seems to have been some understanding between these men and Thomas Flucker, who represented the Waldo heirs, that they should become owners of the Mill Farm on Crawford's River. The Mill Farm was surveyed, and on the plan it is called "Mr. Archibald Anderson's Lot." The description which is written on the plan contains names supposed by some to have been of later origin. It is probably the oldest document in existence, of which it can be said there is no doubt that it has particular reference to this town.

---

and Sparks's Writings of Washington, iii. 235. It may be added, that the claim was confirmed to the Stirling family about the year 1833. Before Union was incorporated, it was called Taylortown as often as Stirlington.

[1] David Dické, of Warren.

"Lincoln, ss. St. George's River, May 13th, 1774. — Then surveyed this lot of land for Mr. Archibald Anderson, at a place called Seven-tree Pond, on St. George's River, without the bounds of any town; but in the county of Lincoln and province of the Massachusetts Bay in New England; beginning at a white oak-tree standing on the eastern side of said Seven-tree Pond, said tree marked on four sides; and from thence running east two hundred and twenty poles to a red oak-tree marked on four sides; and thence running south two hundred poles to a stake and heap of stones standing on the west side of Crawford's Great Pond, said stake is marked on four sides; and then running west one hundred and eighty poles to an elm-tree standing on the east side of said Seven-tree Pond, said tree is marked on four sides; then running northerly by the side of said pond, as the shore layeth to the bounds first mentioned; to contain two hundred and twenty-four acres and one hundred square poles, as appears by this actual survey taken by me, Nathaniel Mesarvy, sworn surveyor of lands."

The plan, which is not very exact, is on a scale of forty poles to one inch. From the appearance of Seven-tree Pond, the survey seems to have been made when the low ground on its borders was covered with water and frozen over. The south line of the mill-lot crosses Crawford's River from west to east near the falls, perhaps a very little south of them; the north line appears to coincide nearly with the south line of John F. Hart's land. The Mill Farm, or mill-lot, included the farms now owned by Messrs. Vaughan, McGuier, Daniels, and Alden, on the south side of Crawford's River, and on the north side all to John F. Hart's southern line.

In the spring of 1774, when this survey purports to have been made, Dr. John Taylor, of Lunenburg, Mass. entered into a negotiation with Flucker, for the entire gore of unappropriated land, of very irregular shape, which lay between the lands belonging to the "Twenty Associates, called the Lincolnshire Company," and the towns of Waldoborough, Warren, and Camden. Taylor raised the objection of pre-occupancy by the Anderson party. Flucker is said to have replied, that they had not fulfilled their agreement;

they had been cutting lumber and making staves, but had not paid any thing, nor done any thing towards clearing the land or introducing settlers. In their justification, it has been said they did not then know it was practicable to get a crop of rye or Indian corn from burnt ground. Flucker agreed to protect Taylor from harm; and the bargain was concluded, as some of the aged inhabitants say, for about ninepence an acre. Dr. Taylor soon sailed to Sheepscot, with one Capt. Decker, in a slaver so filthy that the smell was almost intolerable, as it had just returned from a voyage for negroes. He was accompanied by John Butler and Phinehas Butler,[1] two young men who were bound out to him till they should be twenty-one years of age. For their services they were to receive one every-day suit and one handsome suit of clothes, and one hundred acres of the land which Taylor had purchased. Besides these, were Thomas Wright, from Lunenburg, Samuel Searles, and Stephen Wyman. According to an agreement of Decker with the captain of a fishing-schooner, the party was carried to the St. George's, and landed at the Lower Rips, or Miller's Landing, on Saturday, July 16, 1774. John McIntyre, who kept a ferry, sold a ferry-boat to Dr. Taylor. On Monday, the boat, baggage, provisions, axes, agricultural implements, &c. were carried across the neck from Boggs's Landing to the river above Starrett's Bridge. The company rowed up the St. George's. They landed near the mouth of Crawford's River, on the north side of it, expecting to find and occupy the Anderson camp. But, as it was sunset, and too late to search for it in a wilderness where they were all strangers, the boat was drawn up with a view to their camping down where they were. Dr. Taylor then said to his companions, that, as they had been wonderfully preserved by a kind Providence during their voyage and journey, they ought to return

---

[1] Phinehas Butler, of Thomaston, who furnished a great part of the information in this chapter.

thanks for the protection of Heaven. Accordingly, he stood up by a majestic tree in this wilderness, and began his devotions. Suddenly, the party was started by the rustling of leaves and crackling of limbs. Their excitement was not diminished either by the awful stillness and solitude of the place, or by the darkness which was fast gathering around them. The doctor paused. Every one looked eagerly for the cause of the noise. Their fears, however, were soon quieted. There came rushing by them a frightened moose. The doctor resumed and finished the prayer. This was probably the first public act of devotion ever performed by a white man within the limits of the town. Such were the peculiar circumstances and the spirit in which the pioneers began the arduous work of settling Union. The serious and the ludicrous were comically combined.

Dr. Taylor and his companions passed the night in the open air. Early the next morning, they discovered the camp within a very few rods of their resting-place. They took possession of it. It was the only shelter they had during the season. The same day, Tuesday, July 19, they began to cut down trees near the ledge in Joseph Gleason's field. Accordingly, this may be regarded as the day on which the first blow was struck with a view to a settlement of the town. As the persons who came previously did not make a permanent establishment, this is the day which should be kept in remembrance for centennial celebrations.

Before a week elapsed, the Anderson party came and claimed the place. High words passed between them and Taylor. The doctor told them he had bought the land, and should at all events make a settlement on the mill-lot, where he then was; but that each of them might have a hundred-acre lot in any other part of his purchase. They indignantly rejected the offer, and went off.

Dr. Taylor's party continued to labor through the season. They felled the trees on several acres, principally on the north side of the river, beginning at Seven-tree Pond, and working towards Crawford's

Pond. In the fall they went away. Taylor hired out John Butler and Phinehas Butler in Thomaston, where they passed the winter. Upon going to Massachusetts, Taylor got the following deed[1] executed:—

"KNOW ALL MEN by these presents, that we, Thomas Flucker, of Boston, in the county of Suffolk, Esq. and Hannah Flucker his wife, Isaac Winslow, of Roxbury, in said county of Suffolk, Esq. and Francis Waldo, of Falmouth, in the county of Cumberland, Esq. all of the province of Massachusetts Bay, in New England, in consideration of the just sum of one thousand pounds, lawful money, to us in hand paid before the delivery hereof by John Taylor, of Lunenburg, in the county of Worcester and province of Massachusetts Bay aforesaid, physician, the receipt whereof we do hereby acknowledge, have given, granted, bargained, and sold, and do by these presents give, grant, bargain, sell, alien, and fully, freely, and absolutely convey and confirm unto him the said John Taylor, his heirs and assigns for ever, a certain tract or parcel of land lying on St. George's and Madomock Rivers, in the county of Lincoln and province aforesaid, being a township containing thirty-four thousand five hundred and sixty acres of good land, bad land, and water, butted and bounded as followeth: to wit, beginning at a birch-tree marked, which is the north-east corner of Waldoborough; thence running south seven degrees east by said Waldoborough, two miles and an half to a hemlock-tree marked; thence due east across Seventree Pond and Crawford's Pond, so called, six miles and two hundred and fifteen rods to a stake and stones at the line of the township called Camden, belonging to the Twenty Associates, called the Lincolnshire Company; thence northwest by north crossing Sunnyback Pond, so called, by the land of said Twenty Associates, eleven miles and eighty rods; thence south-west by west[2] five miles and twenty-four

---

[1] The copy of the deed, and several abstracts of other deeds, have been furnished through the kindness of the Rev. Uriah Balkam, of Wiscasset.

[2] Among the papers of the late T. L. Jennison, M.D. of Cambridge, Mass. is a memorandum purporting to be by David Fales, Esq. of Thomaston, "that the western line of Dr. Taylor's township was not run in its proper place when the town was laid out, and that the courses given in the deed were according to the direction of the magnetic needle, and not on a true meridian."

rods; thence south three miles and two hundred and eighty rods to a spruce-tree marked, which is the north-west corner of the town of Waldoborough; thence easterly by said Waldoborough three miles and one hundred and sixty rods to the bound first mentioned.

"To have and to hold the said granted and bargained premises, together with all their appurtenances, free of all encumbrances whatsoever, to him the said John Taylor, his heirs and assigns, as an absolute estate of inheritance in fee simple for ever. And we, the said Thomas Flucker, Hannah Flucker, Isaac Winslow, and Francis Waldo, for ourselves, our heirs, executors, and administrators, do hereby covenant to warrant and defend the afore-granted premises unto the said John Taylor, his heirs and assigns for ever, against the lawful claims and demands of all persons.

"In witness whereof, we, the said Thomas Flucker, Hannah Flucker, Isaac Winslow, and Francis Waldo, have hereunto set our hands and seals this thirtieth day of September, anno Domini one thousand seven hundred and seventy-four, and in the fourteenth year of his majesty's reign.

"THOS. FLUCKER, and a seal.
"HANNAH FLUCKER, and a seal.
"ISAAC WINSLOW, and a seal.
"FRAS. WALDO, and a seal.

"Signed, sealed, and delivered in presence of us,
"DANL. HUBBARD.
"DAVID GREENE.

"Suffolk, ss. Boston, Nov. 17, 1774. — Then the above-named Thomas Flucker, Hannah Flucker, Isaac Winslow, and Francis Waldo, personally appeared and owned this instrument to be their act and deed.

"JOHN AVERY, Just. Pacis."

1775.

In September, 1774, while Taylor and his men were felling trees in the forest of Maine, and beginning the settlement of a town, the first Continental Congress was in session at Philadelphia. On the 19th of April, 1775, was the battle of Lexington and Concord; and on the 17th of June, that of Bunker Hill. The war of the

American revolution was begun in earnest. Dr. Taylor was an ardent whig, and one of the leading members of the Massachusetts Provincial Congress.[1] He was too much interested in political affairs to return immediately. Accordingly, in April, he sent Thomas Wright, who, with the two Butlers, again took possession of the camp, and went to work on the Mill Farm. Wright was soon taken sick, and returned to the West-

---

[1] Dr. Taylor was born about the year 1734, probably in Townsend, Mass. He was a physician and trader in Lunenburg, when he purchased the plantation of Stirlington. He was married, by Rev. Wm. Emerson, to Mrs. Rebecca Prescott, of Concord, Aug. 28, 1766. She died March 3, 1772. July 16, four months afterward, he was married, by Rev. Nathaniel Merrill, to Mrs. Anna Dole, of Dunstable, N.H. She died Feb. 1774. He married, July 6, 1777, Ruth, second daughter of John Hunt, Esq. of Watertown; and she died Nov. 30, 1778. He was also once published without being married. After he left Lunenburg, he resided at Pomfret, Ct. and subsequently at Douglas, Mass. He had a son John, born Jan. 1, 1768, and a daughter Betsey. The latter married Josiah Reed. By his second wife, he had a son Daniel, who lived for a time in Belchertown, Mass. was called Doctor, had at least a son and two daughters, and probably moved to the State of New York. According to Phinehas Butler, Dr. Taylor, when a young man, cared little for religious subjects, " till he had a dream about the resurrection. After that he appeared to believe in God and a Saviour." From the Lunenburg town-records, it appears he was one of the selectmen and assessors of that town in 1771, 1772, and 1773. In 1772, he was chosen representative to the Legislature by the towns of Lunenburg and Fitchburg. When he was elected in 1774, these towns, May 20, voted to him patriotic instructions. He was member of the Massachusetts Provincial Congress, which convened at Cambridge, Feb. 1, 1775, adjourned Feb. 16, met at Concord, March 22, and continued in session till its adjournment, April 15. It is said to have been through his influence that the adjournment to Concord was effected. Being convened at Concord, April 22, the Provincial Congress adjourned, and met the same day at Watertown, where it was dissolved, May 29, 1775. In the meantime, the battle of Lexington was fought. Dr. Taylor was one of the prominent men of the Congress, on which devolved very solemn and weighty responsibilities. On the journals, his name occurs oftener than that of any man, except Gen. Ward. On the important committees he was associated with Col. Prescott, of Bunker Hill memory, Governor Brooks, of Massachusetts, Vice-President Gerry, and Governor Gill. He was on the committee which drew up the reply to Gen. Gage's proclamation of June 12, 1775, promising pardon to all except Samuel Adams and John Hancock; and was one of the committee to take depositions, after the battle of Lexington and Concord, to be forwarded to Dr. Franklin, in England. He was also a member of the Massachusetts Council, elected May 28, 1777.

ward, as Massachusetts and even New Hampshire were called then, and for a long time afterward. The two young men continued to work through the summer. More trees were cut, principally but not entirely on the north side of the stream. By the labors in the present and the preceding years, a clearing was made from Seven-tree Pond to Crawford's Pond. Towards autumn the felled trees were burnt. Oxen were then hired of William Boggs, of Warren, and ten bushels of rye were sown. This was the first grain ever sown in Union.

The Butlers had toiled in solitude. To them the Lord's Day and the week-day were the same. With each morning they rose to provide or prepare their food and chop trees. It is not to be wondered at that they felt no particular attachment to this mode of life. Accordingly, when they had sowed the grain, they went to Massachusetts. After their departure, Taylor came, hired Germans and others, lived in the old camp, sowed rye on the remainder of the cleared land, and returned to Massachusetts. Having been absent about two months, during which John Butler lived with Col. Willard, of Lancaster, and Phinehas with Dr. Taylor's father, in Townsend, the two young men returned to Union. It was late in the fall. Taylor hired them out to Benjamin Packard for the winter.

In the course of this season, Benjamin Packard, of Cushing, who came from Bridgewater, Mass. had built a log-house. It was the first house of any kind ever built within the limits of the town, unless some are disposed to dignify by the name of *house* the shanty or camp which had been put up at the Mill Farm. It was about twenty feet long and eighteen feet wide. It had one room, a cat-and-clay chimney, a stone chimney-back, but no jambs. It was about fifty rods north-west of the island in Seven-tree Pond. Of the three knolls there, the cellar is still visible on the one nearest to the island. Stones were dug out of the cellar-hole in September, 1848. It is supposed they belonged to the chimney, as the cellar probably was not stoned. In the winter of 1775–6, Packard and the Butlers lived here, getting out lumber for Taylor's buildings at the Mill Stream. The pine-timber was taken chiefly from the west side of Seven-tree Pond, and the oak from the east side, some of it even from the island in Crawford's Pond. Their fare was poor. Packard was a poor provider, and the Butlers suffered with hunger. In the course of the winter, while at work on the island in Crawford's Pond, Phinehas Butler saw by the side of a log something which excited his curiosity. He went to the log, and, as he stooped to see what was there, a bear suddenly thrust his nose up into his face. Butler settled his axe into Bruin, and despatched him forthwith. " After that," says he, " we lived like princes."

CHAPTER IV.

PLANTATION HISTORY, 1776.

Philip Robbins's Purchase. — David Robbins's the first Family. — Richard Cummings. — Taylor again. — First Frame House. — First Crop of Rye. — Raising of a Barn. — Log-houses of Richard Cummings and David Robbins. — Arrival of the Families of Philip Robbins and Richard Cummings. — Crowded House. — Timber House. — Barn. — Taylor's Mills.

WITH the year 1776 came a change. Several persons agreed with Philip Robbins, of Walpole, Mass. to take farms, if he would come east and purchase a tract of land. Accordingly, Robbins made an agreement with Dr. Taylor for about 7,500 acres, at fifty cents an acre. He also agreed to introduce a specified number of settlers. Subsequently, Robbins, in consequence of a misunderstanding with Taylor as to the price, did not take so much. The deed was executed August 1, 1777; in which John Taylor, of Stirlington, conveys to Philip Robbins, of Stirlington, for £1,200 lawful money, a tract of land " in said Sterlingtown, containing near 4,000 acres more or less, bounded thus: Beginning at a hemlock-tree marked, by Seven-tree Pond, so called, which is part of St. George's River; thence running west, by the line of the town of Warren 596 rods to a hemlock-tree marked, at Waldoborough line; thence north 7° west, two miles and a half by said line to a birch-tree marked, at the north-east corner of said Waldoborough; thence east, two miles and ninety-six rods to St. George's River, near the mouth of Bowker Brook, so called; thence southerly, by said St. George's River as it runneth, and by Round Pond and Seven-tree Pond as they lie, to the bound first mentioned."[1]

David Robbins, Philip Robbins's oldest son, had been living two years at Thomaston, on what is called the Kelsey Farm, situated on the west side of the Meadows, and had there built a small log-house. His father offered to give him one hundred and fifty acres more or less, in Union, if he would settle on it; and his

[1] Mrs. Mero says, the two parties agreed in the fall that the papers should be made out by Dr. David Fales, of Thomaston. Accordingly, after laboring on his land in the year 1776, and inducing some settlers to come here, Robbins departed for the Westward for the purpose of bringing down his family. The day before he expected to sail, he called on Fales, according to agreement, to sign the papers; but Taylor had gone. Under the circumstances, Robbins hesitated what course to pursue. However, as he had already done much on the land, and there was hardly a doubt that Taylor would abide by his agreement, Robbins concluded to proceed. The next year, Taylor insisted on having about one dollar an acre. Robbins finally took the tract above described. He gave particular charge to his agent at Walpole to pay his debt to Taylor on the very day that it became due; but a violent storm came on, and he did not arrive at Taylor's till the following day. Then, as continental bills had depreciated, Taylor insisted on having specie. Finally, according to Jessa Robbins, Taylor told Philip Robbins he should pay specie, or he would sue him to the farthest court. Robbins told him he would not pay him specie, if he sued him to h—l, and got the d——l for his attorney. The result was a lawsuit. Robbins "scraped together" some money, besides what he got for his farm at Walpole. After the execution was out, Taylor hesitated to take the pay. The attorney applied to the Judge and Clerk to receive the continental money. It was counted out; Robbins's lawyer had in his hands a demand against Taylor, which amounted to more than the execution; a writ was immediately served, and the money secured to Taylor's creditor.

wife fifty acres more, if she would come and cook for him and his hired men. David Robbins could not get a deed, or any security for one, of the person who had sold to him in Thomaston; for he had gone off, it was said, as a tory. Accordingly, his father's proposition to him and his wife was accepted. With their children they came in May, 1776, and occupied the log-house built by Packard, who, in consequence of the Robbins purchase, was obliged to go off. This was the first family which moved into Stirlington. Before the decease of David Robbins, there was standing in Warren or Thomaston only one house, built before he came here. At the time of his coming, there was not another family above Boggs's in Warren. None of the land between them was cleared. There was no road, not even a footpath. Mrs. Robbins[1] did not see the face of a woman from the time of her arrival in May till the following autumn. To this day, people speak of her excessive joy when another female came to reside with her.

At the same time with David Robbins came Philip Robbins and his sons, Jessa and Ebenezer. Philip Robbins settled west and north of the island in Seven-tree Pond, on the place where Stephen Hawes now lives. He brought six men to assist him in clearing his land. During the season he cut down and burned over about twenty acres.

Richard Cummings, from Stoughton, came the same spring in May, cleared a small spot on the farm now owned by Henry Seiders, sowed some spring grain, tarried a short time, and returned to Massachusetts.

In the spring of the same year, Dr. Taylor again visited his township. Having hired Col. Benjamin Burton, afterward an officer in the revolutionary war, Nathaniel Fales, of Thomaston, and others, he built the first frame-house in the place. It was about

---

[1] Probably the first white females ever in the place were two young women of somewhat suspicious character, who, in the spring before the arrival of Mrs. Robbins, came by themselves from Warren in a boat to the Mill Farm, and returned on the same day.

eighteen feet by twenty, and stood on the spot now occupied by Joseph Gleason's house. Gleason's kitchen is over the old cellar, and Taylor's well furnishes the water now used by Gleason's family. This was the only frame-house in Union till some years after the town was incorporated. The boards were brought on the ice from Lermond's Mills, at Oyster River, by Phinehas Butler.

This year, the Butlers, Jessa Robbins, and others, reaped the rye, of which the Butlers had sowed a considerable part in the preceding year. It was the first grain ever harvested in town.

In the course of the same summer, Taylor erected a barn, measuring about thirty-four by forty feet. The posts, beams, and rafters were of oak. The entire male population of Stirlington, consisting of six men and two lads, one seventeen and the other nineteen years old, were present at the raising. The timber was so large and heavy, and the gang, of which Philip Robbins is said to have been the captain, was so small, that two days were required to put up the frame. The flesh was scraped from the arms, and the gang so exhausted by lifting and straining as to be hardly able to work for nearly a week.

It was some time in the course of the year that Richard Cummings built a log-house. Except Packard's, it was the first in town. It was situated about midway between the road and the pond. In the fall of the same year, or in the spring of the next, David Robbins built the next log-house on land now owned by the heirs of his son David. It was between the present house and the pond, so near to the latter — perhaps fifteen rods distant — that the water used by the family was brought from it. The top of the house was covered with slabs brought from Mill River in Thomaston. "The house," says Mrs. Dunton, "was caulked with moss. The chimney was on the outside of the house. Mother baked all the bread-by the fire, but the next year got along comfortably, as we had a clay oven out of doors."

In the fall, Philip Robbins went to Walpole, and returned with his family. On arriving at the Fort Wharf in Thomaston, they were met by their friends, and came up the river to Stirlington.[1]

In the vessel with the family of Philip Robbins came Richard Cummings and his family. They landed from Seven-tree Pond, Nov. 2. Before this, Philip Robbins lived with his son David in the Packard House. When his family came, all for a short time lived together. There were fourteen persons dwelling together in this small log-house. The first fall, three low bedsteads were set up in the garret. It was necessary to lay the fourth bed on the floor of the garret, so as to crawl over it to get to the others. The ascent to the garret was by steps cut into a log which stood by the side of the fireplace. Another bed, with a trundle bed under it, was in the room below, which was also the kitchen, reception-room, parlor, &c. The members of the household who were unprovided for lay on the floor. This house Philip Robbins and his family occupied probably about four years. Thus the fathers and mothers of the town found it necessary to live and to lodge.

In this year Philip Robbins put up a timber-house. The timbers, twelve by twenty inches in size, were dovetailed, or locked in, at the ends. The roof was covered, but there were no doors or windows; nor

---

[1] Mrs. Susan Mero says, that, when they arrived at the Fort Wharf, her uncle Gregory, of Camden, met them, and insisted on carrying her, then a girl eight years old, to his home. Accordingly, she mounted his horse behind him. On the way they went through an almost impassable swamp, in which the horse sometimes sank two or three feet. After a week's visit, her uncle brought her to Taylortown. Guided by spotted trees, they came up on the east side of Seven-tree Pond. The bushes and limbs were so thick that she frequently was in imminent danger of striking her feet, and being turned and thrown from the horse. At Crawford's River, there being no bridge, Taylor's men were hailed across the stream. They went to the pond, and rowed round its mouth instead of crossing it. The boat was then rowed back, though at first she hesitated about "getting into a thing that looked so much like a hog's trough." Shortly afterwards, she was carried across the pond, about five-eighths of a mile, to her father's.

was it inhabited for three or four years. "It was so built that the Indians could not shoot through it." Into this the family put their effects when they came in November.

In the fall of this year, Philip Robbins got out a frame for a barn, which he put up in 1777.[1] It was in this year also that Taylor put up the frame of a sawmill, a little below the present mills on Crawford's River. A grist-mill was afterwards put under the sawmill.

CHAPTER V.

PLANTATION HISTORY, 1777, 1778.

1777, Phinehas Butler enters the Army. — Purchases by Abijah Hawes; by Ezra Bowen; by Jonathan Amory; by Joel Adams, Jason Ware, and Matthias Hawes. — Settlement of John Butler. — 1778, Suchfort the Hessian. — Blacksmithing. — Calamitous Fire. — Suffering for Food.

1777.

In February, 1777, Phinehas Butler, who was acting as Taylor's agent, enlisted in Stirlington under Col. Benjamin Burton,[2] and joined the army.

In June came Abijah Hawes, the first settler from Franklin, Mass. He had received continental bills in payment for services in the revolutionary war. The bills were depreciating, and he resolved to purchase a farm with them. In order to save his means and buy

---

[1] Col. Burton's bill shows the value of labor at the time: —

Nov^{br.} 22 1776 St Georges
PHILIP ROBINS *Dr*
To Hughing of a fraim for a Barn O. T. [Old Tenor] £22	10	0
To 9 Days work of Myself and Brother at 3£ per Day 27	00	0
To one Two year old Heffer *a* 12 Dollars . . . 27	00	0
To 13 Days Work at 37/6 24	6	6
100	16	6

[2] Col. Burton died in Warren, May 24, 1835, aged 86.

as many acres as possible, he performed the journey from Franklin to Stirlington on foot and alone. He selected the farm now owned by his son, Whiting Hawes, on the west side of Seven-tree Pond, supposing that it would be the more salable from the circumstance that David Robbins had settled on the one side of it, and Ezra Bowen, who, after having worked for Taylor a year or two, had the same month selected the farm on the other side. Bowen's is now owned by Capt. John Pearse Robbins, and is next to Warren line. Hawes and Bowen began to chop the trees on their respective lots on the same day.

July 4, a deed was executed by which "John Taylor, of a new plantation called Sterlingtown, in consideration of the sum of £2,000 lawful money, conveys to Jonathan Amory, of Boston, merchant, a tract of land in Sterlingtown, with a dwelling-house, barn, grist-mill, and saw-mill thereon standing, containing about 6,500 acres more or less, bounded thus: Beginning at a maple-tree marked, at the most south-westerly corner, which is on the line between the town of Warren and said plantation; thence east by said town-line, till it comes to Camden line; thence by said Camden line north-westerly, till that line strikes St. George's River; then on the east side of said river, till it comes to the first-mentioned bounds."

By this deed, and the one to Philip Robbins, Taylor disposed of all the land in Stirlington east of St. George's River, and south of the line which ran westerly from the mouth of the Cashman Brook.

At the time of Burgoyne's surrender, Oct. 17, 1777, it is said there were but three families in Stirlington. They must have been the families of Philip Robbins, David Robbins, and Richard Cummings.

From a plan drawn by David Fales, and dated Thomaston, Nov. 15, 1777, it appears that in this year Joel Adams bought of Philip Robbins the tract of land which was divided between himself, Jason Ware, and Matthias Hawes. Ware and Hawes probably visited this town at the same time and returned.

John Butler was married this year, though it is not known when he moved his wife into Stirlington.[1] After living seven years at the Mill Farm, he settled on the farm subsequently owned by Capt. Nathaniel Bachelor, and resided there till the spring of 1791, when he moved to Thomaston.

1778.

In the fall of 1778, Philip Robbins introduced from Boston Andrew Suchfort, a German, who was captured at Stillwater. It is said that he was a very strong man, and once brought two bushels of rock-salt on his back from Waldoborough. When Philip Robbins moved from the Packard House, which was probably in the fourth summer after he came here, Suchfort became the occupant. He lived in it till after the town was incorporated. He settled in Appleton, near the head of Sunnybec[2] Pond, on its west side, and died at an advanced age in Washington, where he was living with his son.

For several years there was no blacksmith in Stirlington. The inhabitants occasionally employed Caleb Howard, of Waldoborough. In December of this year he made his annual visit. He brought nails and the number of shoes which the settlers sent word to him would be wanted. There being no floor, an ox was "cast" on the ground in the barn of Philip Robbins. From an iron pot, placed for the blacksmith's convenience in the lean-to, on a stump which had not been dug up, the sparks rose through the poles, of which a scaffold-floor was always made in those days, set the hay and grain on fire, and the barn was immediately enveloped in flames. The fire spread so rapidly, that the fowls were burnt, and "the ox was singed nearly

---

[1] He purchased all Dr. Taylor's furniture. Among the items on the bill of sale, which is dated July 23, 1777, is "Mr. Willard on the Catechism, £3. 0. 0." It was the first folio printed in British America, and is now in the possession of his son, Charles Butler, of Thomaston.

[2] By the Indians probably pronounced *Soony-bech*.

half over." Mrs. Mero says, that, as her mother, Mrs. Robbins, was hastening to the burning barn, the children following her, she observed to them, " It is of no use to go, we will all go back." Upon entering the house, they found that also on fire. In the hurry the door had been left unlatched, or the wind had blown it open. The draft, which was very strong when it came up from the pond, had carried fire into the ends of the logs, which had been cut off to admit a stone for a chimney-back. All the water used was brought from the pond, and there was none in the house. The snow was very deep, and consequently abundant; but it was not practicable to apply it to the interstices between the logs. Mrs. Robbins immediately attached a rag to the end of a stick, and kept dipping it in the snow and applying it to the fire till she extinguished it. As the logs were dry spruce, it is probable that the house would have been burnt, if the discovery of the fire had occurred five minutes later, or if Mrs. Robbins had not adopted this expedient to put it out. Her hands were severely burnt.

The loss of the barn was a grievous calamity. The people generally stacked their hay, and built small log-hovels to cover their cattle. With the exception of the barn on the other side of the pond, where nobody lived but in the Taylor House, this was the only one in the plantation. It contained the rye of Philip Robbins raised on twenty acres, besides all the other grain on the west side of the river, and about twenty tons of hay. Thirty bushels of wheat, belonging to Richard Cummings, were burnt. Several tons of the hay were saved by throwing snow upon it; but the " cattle kept lowing about, and would not eat it, because it was smoked." Philip Robbins saved one bushel of rye. Mr. Porterfield, of Thomaston, gave him one bushel of corn, which, it being winter and no boating, he and Suchfort " backed up " to Stirlington from Lermond's Mills on Oyster River. This was all the grain Robbins had till the spring opened, which was late. Then, with depreciated continental paper, he bought a hogshead of Indian corn, for which he paid twenty-five dollars a bushel.

The barn was burnt on Friday. On Saturday a shelter for the cattle was put up. To add to the misfortunes, on Sunday a yoke of oxen broke through the ice and was drowned, on the way to bring home hay from the Round Pond Meadows. In consequence of this fire, ten head of cattle died during the winter. It was probably after this that David Robbins's family, consisting of the parents and three children, were reduced to such extremities, that, for fourteen days, they subsisted on "two quarts of rye-meal, which they ate with birch-sap, in which was put a little pickle. A few boxberry leaves and buds finished the daily repast."[1] There is said to have been a time when David Robbins, after having planted the seed-ends of potatoes, dug them up, and cut off for food all but the eyes.

CHAPTER VI.

PLANTATION HISTORY, 1779—1782.

1779, Wheaton's Purchase. — Settlement of Joel Adams, Matthias Hawes, and Jason Ware. — Woodward. — Fairbanks. — Settlement of Moses Hawes. — Ebenezer Robbins. — 1780, Jennison's Purchase. — 1781, First Wedding. — Jessa Robbins. — 1782, Settlement of Phinehas Butler. — Elisha Partridge. — Taylor's Conveyance to Reed.

1779.

"JANUARY 2. John Taylor conveys to Mason Wheaton land in Sterlingtown, containing 1,000 acres, bounded as follows: Beginning at Bowker Brook near where it empties into St. George's River; thence west by land sold to Philip Robbins 436 rods; thence north 240

---

[1] Mr. Noyes P. Hawes, who several years ago prepared notices of the town, which he has generously permitted to be freely used, as may be seen from the extracts credited to him.

rods; thence east 682 rods to St. George's River; then southerly by said river about 240 rods; then west 214 rods to the first bound."[1] Col. Wheaton resided here a short time, but did not move his family from Thomaston. He raised a barn in July, 1780. He returned to Thomaston, and was the first representative from that town to the Legislature of Massachusetts.

May 15. Joel Adams, Matthias Hawes, and Jason Ware, three unmarried men from Franklin, Mass. came and settled on the north-west side of Round Pond. Their land, which had been bought by Joel Adams, was divided into three farms of different sizes. Lots were drawn for choice, and each obtained the farm he preferred. Hawes had 255 acres, Ware 230, and Adams took two lots making 410 acres. They lived together in a log-house which they built on Ware's land, below the present Hawes House, and near the pond. Their oven was on a ledge near their house. Becoming rather dissatisfied with their mode of life, they hired Jemima Robbins, who began to keep house for them, June 29, 1780. Here they continued till the "Royal Mess," as they called themselves, was broken up. Each member contributed his share of the provisions, and their accounts are still preserved. Joel Adams settled on the farm south of Muddy Brook, now owned by the Rev. Mr. Irish. Jason Ware settled on the north side of the same brook, where his son, Vinal Ware, now lives; and Matthias Hawes immediately north of him, on land now in the possession of his descendants.

With these persons came Nathan Woodward, who did not settle in town. He began to clear the farm north of Matthias Hawes. It is now owned by Nathan D. Rice. Having a great aversion to hemlock-trees, he hired a man to girdle all on the farm, and they have been dead many years.

A man named John Fairbanks, from Franklin, came at the same time; but he did not settle. He lived for

---

[1] Abstract from the deed recorded at Wiscasset.

a while on the farm now owned by Benjamin Litchfield, went back, and kept a store in Roxbury, Mass.

In the same year came Moses Hawes, also from Franklin. He settled on the farm now owned by his son, Col. Herman Hawes.

Amos Lawrence, from Franklin, a young man who had served in the revolutionary war, came probably this year. He exchanged the Simmons Farm on the hill back of Mr. Seiders for one in Warren.

Ebenezer Robbins, from Walpole, a half-brother of Philip Robbins, " had made a beginning" at Fox Islands. The exposed situation of the islands on the seacoast during the war led most of the inhabitants to abandon them. Ebenezer Robbins came to Stirlington soon after the battle of Biguyduce or Penobscot. He settled on the place more recently owned by Asa Morse. His children were Bela, Philip, Zilpah, Azubah, and Molly.

1780.

"July 19. John Taylor, of Pomfret, Conn. conveys to William Jennison, of Brookfield, Mass. land in Sterlingtown, bounded thus: Beginning at the northeast corner of Waldoborough; then east 256 rods on land of Philip Robbins to the south-west corner of Mason Wheaton's land; then north 697 rods and 14 links to the north-east corner of said tract; then west 4 miles 96 rods to the west line of Sterlington, being north-west corner of said tract; then south by said line 697 rods 14 links to north-west corner of Waldoborough and south-west corner of said tract; then east by Waldoborough line 3½ miles to first bound."[1]

---

[1] Abstract from the deed recorded at Wiscasset.

In this transaction, Dr. Taylor agreed to take Dr. Jennison's real estate, consisting of three farms, with their improvements, and wild land in Douglas, Mass. The consequence was quarrels, lawsuits, and executions, till the end of Taylor's life. According to Jessa Robbins, Dr. Jennison, in endeavoring to dispose of some of his land here to one Tucker, recommended it upon the strength of what Taylor had said. Taylor also wanted to sell to Tucker, and said to him, "Buy of me, and get good land: it will take 1,000 acres of Jennison's land to keep

1781.

In this year there does not appear to have been any new settler or any important occurrence. The "Royal Mess" underwent a change. Before the middle of

a red squirrel alive." Upon being questioned, he said he had made to Jennison substantially the same statement. Jennison told Tucker that "Taylor was a thief and a liar, and not fit to keep gentlemen's company," and not only refused to retract when called upon, but repeated the charges publicly. Taylor prosecuted him, and Jennison gained the case by proving that Taylor had taken a bag of wheat from a mill without leave, and an ox which he sold to a commissary in the revolutionary war. Several actions were brought by the parties against each other. Jennison brought one in March, 1781. After various law operations, Taylor was committed to jail in Worcester, March 12, 1784, on Jennison's execution, "for about £900 lawful money." Taylor, in a communication published March 18, 1784, in the *Worcester Spy*, speaks of having sold farms "to the amount of several thousand pounds silver money value, and loaned the money arising therefrom, a part to this Commonwealth [Massachusetts], but principally to the United States, taking their promise to return the same within three years, with interest;" but adds, that he had not to that "day received one farthing of the principal, and but a small part of the interest." The rest of the communication is taken up with abusing Jennison, and demanding settlement of and with all his creditors. Jennison replied in detail, April 8; and this drew out a long rejoinder, April 22. Taylor was in some way released, and was a delegate from Douglas to the Massachusetts Convention held in January and February, 1788, "for the purpose of assenting to and ratifying the Constitution recommended by the Grand Federal Convention." It seems, however, that he was recommitted to jail. There he occasionally gave festive entertainments, remarking that he could afford to do it with the interest of Jennison's money. Many other things were done to irritate Jennison, who took measures to have him watched. Taylor went across the street to buy some tempting fruit, and, in doing it, broke his bonds for the liberty of the jail-yard. At last, according to some, he took rum and opium in anticipation of being recommitted to jail by the persons who had been his bondsmen. By others, it is said he "had been on a spree for a number of days; and, having no rum or brandy, went to looking over his bottles of medicine, and came to some laudanum, and drank a dram of it, whether by mistake or otherwise not known. An emetic was administered, and he was ordered to walk out of doors in the open air;" but he died the same day, April 27, 1794, at Douglas, in the sixtieth year of his age.

The part taken by Dr. Taylor in the Convention for adopting the Federal Constitution may be understood from the "Debates, Resolutions, and other Proceedings of the Convention," reported by Benjamin Russell, and printed in Boston in 1788. From this it appears that he was in favor of annual instead of biennial elections to the

September, Joel Adams married Jemima, daughter of Philip Robbins. The ceremony was performed by Col. Mason Wheaton, of Thomaston. He disappointed them at the time fixed for the wedding; but, not long afterward, he married them in the log-house which was occupied by the " Royal Mess." The ceremony being over and the company seated, the mother of the bride observed, " Mr. Justice, you have but half done your work." " Why not ? " said he. " Why, you have not pronounced them man and wife." With some confusion he asked them to rise again, and the ceremony was satisfactorily concluded. It was the first wedding in town, and it is said that it was the first at which Col. Wheaton ever officiated.

Mrs. Adams did not move from the log-house where she had been employed. The " Royal Mess " still continued; each member contributing provisions, and

House of Representatives, and of a larger representation than was proposed. The senatorial term of six years seemed to him very objectionable. He also expressed some apprehension lest the two branches of Congress might "play into each other's hands," advocated the doctrine that members should be paid by the State Legislatures rather than by the United States, raised some objections to a Federal City, and entered into the discussions respecting proposed amendments. When the question of ratifying the proposed Constitution was finally put, it was carried by a majority of only nineteen; 187 voting in its favor, and 168 against it. Shortly afterward, Dr. Taylor rose, and said that " he had uniformly opposed the Constitution; that he had found himself fairly beaten; and expressed his determination to go home, and endeavor to infuse a spirit of harmony and love among the people."

To this long note it may be added, that Dr. William Jennison was probably born in Salem, Mass. where his father was a clergyman. He had a good education, and studied medicine with Dr. Prentice, of Lancaster. He resided at Mendon, now Milford, where he married Mary Staples; also at Douglas, Sudbury, and Brookfield. At the age of sixty-six, he died at Brookfield, May 8, 1798, in consequence of a fall from his horse. He was a man of great activity and energy, and during the Revolution was a prominent whig. His children were —
1. William; 2. Samuel, a lawyer; 3. John, a lawyer, settled in Boston, and died of lung fever; 4. Timothy Lindall, M.D. of Cambridge, Mass.; also Ebenezer, who lived for some time in Union, was surveyor, married in Boston, and died a few years since at Dixmont, where he was postmaster. There were also Mary, who married Jonathan Whipple, father of the late William J. Whipple, Esq. of Cambridge; and Abigail, who is still living.

the unmarried members paying for the services rendered by Mrs. Adams. Adams and his wife, in the fall, visited Massachusetts.

This year Jessa Robbins began to clear the farm south of Round Pond, where he now lives with his son, Jason Robbins.

1782.

"January 15. Mr. Adams gone down to George's, after his things he brought from the Westward; likewise to help Mr. Butler up with his lady's goods."[1] Mr. Phinehas Butler, having completed his term of service in the army, returned to Thomaston, and there married, Oct. 18, 1781, Milea, daughter of Oliver Robbins. She was the first white female born in Thomaston, east of Mill River. Jan. 17, 1782, he moved into a log-house in Stirlington, which he built on the farm now owned by James Grinnell, on the west side of the St. George's, about half-way from the Middle to the Upper Bridge. He returned to Thomaston, Nov. 14, 1785, where he and his wife are now both living.

"Sabbath-day, April 28, 1782. Last week, Mr. Elisha Partridge moved upon Col. Wheaton's farm in this place."[1] He came from Franklin, and was a tenant under Col. Wheaton. The place was afterwards bought by the Daggetts. His log-house was probably very near the spot now occupied by Nahum Thurston's house.

"May 16. John Taylor conveyed to Josiah Reed land in Sterlingtown, bounded as follows: Beginning on the western side of Sunnybeck Pond in a side line of Camden; thence north-west by north on Camden line to the north-west corner of the township the grantor purchased of Thomas Flucker and others, Sept. 30, 1774; thence south-west by west and southerly, on the most western line of said township, till it comes to the six-thousand-acre lot sold to William Jennison; then easterly and southerly, by said six-thousand-acre lot, to the most north-westerly corner of

[1] Matthias Hawes's Account-book.

a thousand-acre lot sold to Mason Wheaton; thence easterly, on the northern line of said thousand-acre lot, to St. George's River; then northerly, by said river to the first bounds, containing by estimation upwards of 14,000 acres."

This was the last of the land owned by Dr. Taylor. It is said, that, in consequence of the lawsuit with Dr. Jennison, and to avoid attachments by his creditors, he put his property into the hands of his son-in-law Reed, who never restored it.

Another change was made in the "Royal Mess." "Nov. 4. Mr. Adams moved out of this house, and Mr. Ware moved in with his wife.... Nov. 22. I brought up my boards for my house from the mill.... Dec. 7. I raised the roof of my house.... Dec. 25. I moved into my house."[1]

CHAPTER VII.

PLANTATION HISTORY, 1783—1786.

1783, Log-house. — Bride. — Bride's Dower. — Jessa Robbins. — 1784, Amariah Mero. — 1785, Josiah Robbins. — Gillmor. — Cat-and-clay Chimney. — Royal Grinnell. — Elijah Holmes. — 1786, Arrival of the Families of Josiah Robbins; of Samuel Hills. — Samuel Martin. — Organization of the Plantation.

1783.

JAN. 1, Matthias Hawes married Sarah Payson, in Warren; and on the 16th " moved home and began to keep house;"[1] and thus another family was added to the population. According to Mrs. Hawes, the house which Mr. Hawes had begun was by some considered "a little more stylish" than any other of the log-houses in the plantation. No other house in Stirlington was shingled. This was covered with shingles made by Mr. Hawes himself. It contained a kitchen,

[1] Matthias Hawes's Account-book.

bedroom, buttery, and had a good cellar. The logs of which the walls were made, instead of being rough, were hewed both inside and outside. There was a regularly laid floor; but, as the boards were not nailed down, considerable care was requisite, in drawing up the table for a meal, to prevent it from being upset. On the west end was a place designed for a chimney. For a flue, boards were stuck up endwise, ten or twelve feet apart at the bottom, to secure them from taking fire, and tipped inward toward the top, so as to leave a comparatively small opening for the passage of the smoke. The fire was built on the ground, and a flat stone used for a chimney-back. The only window was made by a wooden slide. This was closed when it stormed, and then the newly-married couple saw by means of the light which came down the chimney. As the ground on which the fire was built was lower than the floor, the occupants, when it was cold, sat on the ends of the boards, and suspended their feet in front of the fire. A crane was made by extending a pole across the fireplace, and resting the ends in the crotches of sticks which were driven into the ground, one on each side of the fire. These were the accommodations when Mr. Hawes "moved home and began to keep house." He made bricks and put up a chimney in the spring. In the fall he went to Boston, where he procured glass, and made two small windows. Some of the other people in Stirlington used mica or "isinglass." Oiled paper was also in use.

Commonly a log-house had but one room. Sometimes two rooms were made by suspending a bedquilt from the ceiling. In Mr. Hawes's house, besides the indispensable requisites for housekeeping, was a large spinning-wheel. There was also a loom, which, large as looms were then made, must have occupied a very important portion of the room. Log-houses, however, were easily built, and when finished were commonly tight, well caulked with moss, sometimes with clay, and were very warm. Trees were growing at the doors; and the settlers, desiring to get rid of them that they might have the land for cultivation, rolled into the fireplaces huge logs, six or eight feet in length, and piled them up as long as they would lie upon each other.

As a description has been given of the house into which a bride and bridegroom moved, it may not be amiss for the present luxurious generation to know something about a lady's dower in the early settlement of the town. The mother of Mrs. Hawes had three daughters to fit out, and she divided her furniture as equitably as she could among them. The following was what Mrs. Hawes had: One coverlet, one pair of sheets, one feather-bed; three white kitchen-chairs; one white chest with one drawer, the legs of which she colored with an indigo bag; one looking-glass, about eight by ten inches, with flowers running up the sides; one tea-kettle; one spider; two pewter porringers, holding about one pint each; three knives, three forks; three flowered cups, three saucers, three plates, taken from a set of crockery; three pewter plates, and two or three wooden trenchers to eat upon, which were kept neat with much care, and occasionally boiled in lye; also an old-fashioned loom and a great spinning-wheel. After a while the knives were broken, and her husband took some broken scythes to the blacksmith, and had shanks drawn out, which he inserted into wooden handles made by himself. To this may be added what belonged to her husband, viz.: One sea-chest, one straw-bed, one pair of woollen blankets, and one iron pailful-pot, exceedingly annoying, because, in boiling, the fat, if not the food, almost invariably escaped through the broken side of it. In this manner one of the most worthy couples in the place began housekeeping. Mrs. Hawes was subsequently confined; and then, to meet expenses, she was obliged to part with her wedding gown of home-made linen. Afterward Mr. Hawes broke his leg, and his wife was obliged to take charge of the outdoor and indoor work, and cut the wood for cooking; but he was able to assist her by entertaining the twin children. When haying time came, he was obliged to part with his wedding garment.

In the fall of the year 1783, Jessa Robbins began housekeeping.

1784.

In September, 1784, Amariah Mero came from Stoughton, and bought the farm now owned by his son, Spencer Mero. Afterward, he settled on the farm and lived in the house with Philip Robbins, whose daughter he married. At this time there were thirteen families.

1785.

In the spring of 1785, Josiah Robbins, brother of Philip Robbins, came to Stirlington, and began to clear the Robbins Neck.[1] This name is given to the peninsula, the neck of which is intersected by a line running north-westerly from the north end of Seventree Pond to the St. George's, a little below the Middle Bridge. Josiah Robbins, with David Gillmor, senior, of Franklin, Mass. bought the entire peninsula, containing about two hundred and seventy acres. Gillmor never came to Union to reside. His son Rufus came in 1787, improved the south part of the Neck, and cleared the True Farm, or Fuller Farm, as it is sometimes called, now owned by Mr. Charles Fogler. His house was on the west side of the road, a little below Mr. Fogler's, and very near the foot of the hill. Robbins built his house on the brow of the hill, between the house now owned by his grandson, Willard Rob-

---

[1] A few years after Josiah Robbins moved to town, there was a gathering to raise a barn for him. Bread was very scarce; and rum, in those days considered almost indispensable on such occasions, commanded an exorbitant price. But, as there were fish in abundance and some meat, it was concluded, instead of the ordinary refreshment, to have a supper. David Cummings, then a boy, was sent on an errand from the barn to the house, where he saw Mrs. Robbins taking bread from the oven. Watching his opportunity, he broke off a piece, and ran. He often spoke of it when he became a man, and added that this was one of the richest meals he ever ate; for his dinner that day had consisted of nothing but boiled beech-leaves.

bins, and the pond. The old cellar may still be seen. A cat-and-clay chimney was made by driving into the ground four crotched sticks, for the four corners of the fireplace. Bars were laid in the crotches; and on these bars, which were high and commonly of wood, was laid a mixture of clay and chopped straw. Lengthwise in this mixture was laid a stick, about an inch in diameter; and this was also covered with it. Thus the sides of the chimney were built. In a few days, the clay was hardened by the heat. Flat stones were placed against the logs of the house, to prevent them from taking fire. The door was opposite the side of the fireplace. Long back-logs were slipped in under the bars on which the cat-and-clay chimney rested.

In May came Royal Grinnell, with his family. At that time there were fifteen families. It is said that there was not probably a washtubful of grain in the place.[1] He lived on the Mill Farm two or three years,

[1] There have been seasons of so great scarcity, that some of the most prosperous inhabitants occasionally subsisted on alewives and milk. This was the case with Samuel Hills and family. When Mrs. Matthias Hawes was about fifteen years old, and resided with her parents in Warren, she fared thus for three weeks, and became so exhausted that she often laid her head down upon the loom where she was weaving, and shed tears. And, even when there was grain, it was difficult to get it ground. The millstones at Taylor's mills were small and poor. Often there was want of water. Oftener the mill was out of order. Then it was customary to put corn into a hole made in the end of a log, which was sometimes hooped with iron, and to crack it with a wooden pestle, either held in the hands, or attached to an apparatus like a pump-handle. Thus a family obtained hominy. For finer meal, the cracked corn was sifted through holes made in birch-bark with heated fork-tines. Sometimes it was considered advisable to take a grist to mill. Then it was carried to Oyster River, to Molineux's mills in Camden, or to Wessaweskeag in Thomaston. The bags were boated to the Carrying Place in Warren. There they were left till the carrier went to the head of the tide, about two miles distant, hired a horse, and returned for them. They were then transported across the Carrying Place, put into another boat, and the horse was returned to its owner. In this way, by water and by land, the grist was borne forward to the mill. The same tedious process was repeated in returning. For each grist, it was necessary six times to cross the Carrying place in Warren.

Sometimes the grain was carried on horseback the entire distance from Union. Then it was necessary to walk by the horse all the way. The bushes, fallen trees, old logs, gulleys, were so numerous, and the

and had charge of the mills. Mrs. Grinnell was in the habit of assisting her husband in setting the mill-logs, and marking the boards. On an emergency, she took an ox-chain, wound it over her shoulders and back, and carried it to the blacksmith-shop of Samuel Hills, to be mended. After living at South Union three years, Mr. Grinnell, with his wife[1] and children,

path, which was designated by spotted trees, was so bad, that frequently the bags were taken off and replaced twenty times during the journey.

Jessa Robbins says he has hauled grain on a hand-sled to Seven-tree Pond, carried it on his back the two miles at the crossing place in Warren, and rowed it to Lermond's. His mill being a tide-mill, and the water frequently low, he oftener had to go on with it to Coombs's, at Wessaweskeag. The journey always required two, and sometimes three days.

In a time of scarcity, the owners, on their return, frequently loaned the greatest part of the meal to the needy. The earliest crop of rye was harvested and ground as soon as possible, in order to relieve the inhabitants, perhaps for a week, till other crops were ripe. If any one had a suitable piece of ground, he sowed barley, as it ripened earlier. When Royal Grinnell was miller at South Union, he frequently ground the poor man's peck or half-bushel of grain, without taking the toll.

[1] Mrs. Grinnell and Nathaniel Robbins, Esq. have dwelt much upon the annoyance from the small black flies, with which the woods swarmed when they came here. Though they have now almost wholly disappeared, the common black flies cannot in number be compared with them. If it were practicable to count them, they could be reckoned only by millions. Their bodies were about half as large as mosquitos. They bit, and drew blood instantly. This was followed by an inflammation and swelling, which continued several days. If a child went to the door for a minute or two, it would return covered with them, and with the blood running down its face, hands, and legs. Haymakers, choppers, and laborers in general, covered their faces with handkerchiefs in self-defence. The annoyance was indescribable. When night came, they ceased from their bloody work. But it was only to give place to mosquitos, which then began in turn their attacks. During the warm season, the inhabitants had no peace, either by night or by day. The only partial remedy lay in building large fires, and raising a dense smoke before the doors of the log-houses; and, if the smoke filled the houses, it was considered vastly preferable to the mosquitos.

Dr. Thaddeus William Harris — whom Professor Agassiz does not hesitate to pronounce "*decidedly* the best entomologist in the world" — in his Treatise on Insects, p. 405, calls the small black fly, or gnat, *Simulium molestum*, and says: "These little tormentors are of a black color; their wings are transparent; and their legs are short, and have a broad, whitish ring around them. The length of the

settled on the farm which was in possession of Phinehas Butler before he moved to Thomaston.

Aug. 25. Elijah Holmes, from Sharon, married in Stirlington Dorcas Partridge, from Franklin. He took up his residence on the place subsequently owned by the late Obadiah Morse, and now by James Adams Ulmer, of Thomaston. He cut the logs of his house, " backed " them together, put up the walls before any one knew it, and then announced to the family of Capt. Adams, with whom he boarded, that he had a house. He also lived on the farm now owned by Philo Thurston, and afterward near Capt. Tobey, on the farm since owned by Deacon Morse. Not many years passed before he moved to Rockland, and became an extensive landowner.

1786.

In 1786, Josiah Robbins moved his family from Franklin. On the Lord's Day before their departure for the wilderness, where they would be beyond the sound of the gospel, the sons and daughters were led by their parents to the front of the pulpit, and " in the presence of the large congregation received the ordinance of baptism and the apostolic blessing of that venerable man," the Rev. Dr. Emmons. After this consecration, they took their departure. They landed

body rarely exceeds one-tenth of an inch. They begin to appear in May, and continue about six weeks, after which they are no more seen. . . . They are followed, however, by swarms of midges, or sand-flies, *Simulium nocivum*, called no-see-'em by the Indians of Maine on account of their minuteness. So small are they, that they would hardly be perceived were it not for their wings, which are of a whitish color, mottled with black. Towards evening, these winged atoms come forth, and creep under the clothes of the inhabitants, and by their bites produce an intolerable irritation, and a momentary smarting, compared, in Gosse's Canadian Naturalist, to that caused by sparks of fire. They do not draw blood; and no swelling follows their attacks. They are most troublesome during the months of July and August." It is very likely that these animals caused part of the sufferings alluded to; but, as the inhabitants in Union were not naturalists, and had not a very correct idea of these insects, it is probable that oftentimes they did not distinguish the midges from the gnats which immediately preceded them.

at Wheaton's, afterwards called Green's Wharf, in Thomaston, about two hundred rods west of the Knox Mansion. They went up the river in a gondola to the head of the tide. Then their luggage, furniture, &c. because of the falls, were hauled across the Carrying Place to a landing opposite Isaac Starrett's. Here they were met by Philip Robbins and David Robbins from Stirlington, who came down the river in log-canoes. Boards were laid across the canoes, the goods were put on, and all embarked for the place of destination. They landed on Philip Robbins's farm, near the island, May 17, 1786, after a journey of seventeen days, having waited in Boston fourteen days for a wind.

In the vessel with Josiah Robbins came Samuel Hills, the first blacksmith, with his wife. An older brother, a painter, had lived with Oliver Robbins in Thomaston, and died there. Hills came down to look after his brother's effects, and thus found his way to Union. In 1785 he had cleared Hills Point. He settled, lived, and died near Seven-tree Pond, on the east side of it, below Crawford's River. The farm is now owned by Nathaniel Robbins.

At the time of the arrival of Robbins and Hills, there was no house or settlement on the east side of the St. George's, except on the Taylor farm.

Besides the persons who have been named, there was, when Robbins and Hills moved to Stirlington, another person here, the year of whose coming is not known. Samuel Martin, from Bristol, who had lost the sight of one of his eyes, resided below Sunnybec Pond, at the saw-mill, which then stood thirty or forty rods above the present Upper Bridge. He afterward moved to Hope.

The names of all the settlers in Stirlington Plantation, and the places on which they lived, have now been given. Occasionally, in Mr. Hawes's Account-book, mention is made of the arrival and departure of other persons. They were obviously, for the most part, visitors. Some came to see their friends in the wilderness; others, perhaps, to look at the country with a view to settlement; and a few may have worked a short time with the settlers. But none, except those who have been named, ought to be reckoned among the settlers in town before it was incorporated. The period covers seventeen years since Dické, on Seven-tree Island, saw the comet; fourteen years since the Anderson party built their camp near Crawford's River, and twelve since the first arrival of Dr. Taylor.

ORGANIZATION OF THE PLANTATION.

In 1786, Stirlington, or Taylortown, was organized as a plantation. In connection with its organization is the following document. It is the earliest entry on any of the town-books: —

" Lincoln, ss. — To Philip Robbins, gent. a principal inhabitant of the plantation called Sterlington, in said county of Lincoln, greeting :

" In obedience to a precept from William Lithgow, Esq. treasurer of the county aforesaid, to me directed ; — These are to require you forthwith to notify and warn the inhabitants of your said plantation, being freeholders, to meet at the dwelling-house of Capt. Philip Robbins, in said plantation, on Monday the twelfth day of June next, at ten of the clock in the forenoon, in order that such of the inhabitants of the said plantation [as] shall then assemble shall and do choose a moderator and clerk, and also assessors and collector or collectors for said plantation's proportion of all such taxes as have [been] or may be assessed upon the same county, either for soldiers' bounty-money or for defraying the necessary charges of the said county, until other assessors and collectors shall be chosen in their stead at the annual meeting of said plantation in March next; such clerk, assessors, and collectors to be sworn by the moderator of said meeting [to] the faithful discharge of their respective trust[s]; and the assessors, so to be chosen and sworn, thereupon to take list of the ratable polls and a valuation of said estate of the inhabitants of said plantation, for to make such assessments, and to judge of the qualifications of voters in meetings of such inhabitants thereafter to be holden, until other

valuation shall be made; and to make return of the names
of the collector or collectors, with the sum committed to
him or them to collect, as soon as may be, to the said
William Lithgow, Esq. or his successor in said office of
treasurer; and make return of this warrant, with your doings
thereupon, unto said meeting.

"Given under my hand and seal at Thomastown, in said
county, May 3, 1786.

"MASON WHEATON, Justice of Peace.

"Sterlington County Tax £2 11 10
"Soldiers' Bounty . . . 1 12 4¾

"A true copy.
"MOSES HAWES, Plantation Clerk."

CHAPTER VIII.

INCORPORATION HISTORY, 1786.

Petition for Incorporation. — Act of Incorporation. — Number and Names of the Inhabitants.

IN consequence of the preceding warrant, the inhabitants made a movement to obtain an Act of Incorporation. The petition, which is the second document on the town-records, was drawn up within a fortnight after the plantation-meeting, and signed by Moses Hawes, Joel Adams, and Samuel Hills, "Committee of the Plantation of Sterlington." It is not probable that it was presented. There is not any copy of it in the office of the Secretary of the Commonwealth of Massachusetts; and filed with the Act of Incorporation, as belonging to it, is the following petition, which undoubtedly led to the granting of the Act:—

"To the Honorable Senate and House of Representatives of Massachusetts, in General Court assembled.

"The petition of the inhabitants of the plantation known by the name of Sterlington humbly showeth, — That they have for a long time past and still continue to experience many and great inconveniences arising from the want of roads, bridges, &c. to and from this place, and [of] other privileges which incorporated towns enjoy; and whereas the Honorable Court have seen fit to lay a tax of sixty-five pounds upon us, which, under our present low and distressed circumstances, we are unable to pay without great difficulty and inconvenience in the manner prescribed, as four-fifths of the land belongs to non-resident proprietors, and there being no roads laid out to this place; we therefore pray that the Honorable Court would permit us to lay out said tax in defraying charges of a bridge now a building of one hundred and ten feet long, and in opening and making roads, and building another bridge of one hundred and seventy feet long; which bridge must be built before there will be any passing by land or water to or from this place. [And] If, in their wisdom and justice, [they] shall think reasonable and fit, [that they will] incorporate a certain tract of land, containing thirty-two thousand acres, including twelve thousand acres, which was deducted when the last purchase was made, for ponds and waste land, on which land is settled twenty-five polls, and upwards of seventy women and children; which land was purchased by the once honorable John Taylor, Esq. of the late Secretary Fluker, into a township by the name *Lindall*,[1] which is bounded as followeth, viz.: Southwardly on the town of Warren, westwardly on Waldoborough, northwardly on land supposed to belong to this Commonwealth, and eastwardly on land belonging to the heirs of the late Brigadier-General Waldo, till it comes to first bounds mentioned, that we may receive and enjoy all those privileges which corporate towns are by law entitled to; and your petitioners, as in duty bound, shall ever pray. By order of the Committee,

"Moses Hawes, Clerk.

"Sterlington, Sept. 12, 1786."

---

[1] The word *Lindall*, on the manuscript-petition, is written in a back hand, and appears to have been inserted to fill a blank. As Dr. Jennison was connected with the Lindall family, it may have been done through his influence. There is a tradition, pretty well authenticated, that, when the subject was under consideration, the uncommon harmony and union among the people were spoken of; and it was suggested and urged at the Legislature, that *Union* would be appropriate, and it was readily acceded to.

INCORPORATION HISTORY.

The preceding petition was followed by —

"An Act for Incorporating the Plantation called Sterlington, in the county of Lincoln, into a town by the name of Union.

"Whereas it appears to this Court that it would be productive of public good, and for the benefit of the inhabitants and proprietors, that the plantation called Sterlington, in the county [of] Lincoln, should be incorporated into a town:

"Be it enacted by the Senate and House of Representatives, in General Court assembled, and by the authority of the same, — That the plantation called Sterlington, and included within the boundaries described in this Act, together with the inhabitants thereof, be, and they are hereby, incorporated into a town by the name of Union, beginning at the south-easterly corner thereof, being a stake and stones; thence bounding easterly on land belonging to Waldo's heirs, by a line running north-west by north, eleven miles and eighty rods; thence bounded northerly by land supposed to belong to the Commonwealth, by a line running south-west by west, five miles and twenty-four rods; thence westerly by lands supposed to belong to said Waldo's heirs, by a line running south, three miles and two hundred rods; thence on the same land, east, three miles and an half; thence south, two miles and an half and twenty rods; thence bounded west on the town of Warren by a line running east, six miles and two hundred and fifteen rods, to the bounds first mentioned;[1] and the said town is hereby vested with all the

---

[1] In consequence of a precept from the General Court of Massachusetts, the inhabitants moved, during the years 1794–96, to have a survey of the town. The plan was made by Ebenezer Jennison, Esq. and is now in the office of the Secretary of the State of Massachusetts. It is not very exact. There have been unsuccessful movements of late years for a new survey. If there were a good plan, a map would have accompanied this volume. The part of the town west of Medomac River was set off to Putnam, when that town was incorporated by an Act passed Feb. 27, 1811. In June, 1817, "all that tract or gore of land lying between the towns of Waldoborough and Union" was annexed to the latter. Consequently, the town is smaller and the boundaries are different from what they were originally.

Though there has not been a survey, the town-lines have been perambulated. Oct. 2, 1823, this was done between Union and Waldoborough, from Medomac River to Warren line, by John Gleason, attended by John W. Lindley and Herman Hawes. In 1840, Sept. 8,

ACT OF INCORPORATION.

powers, privileges, and immunities, which towns within this Commonwealth are entitled to, or by law enjoy.

"And be it further enacted by the authority aforesaid, — That Waterman Thomas, Esq. be, and he hereby is, empowered to issue his warrant to some principal inhabitant of the said town, requiring him to warn the inhabitants thereof to meet at such time and place as he shall therein set forth, to choose all such officers as towns are required and empowered by law to choose in the month of March or April annually.[1]

"This act passed Oct. 20, 1786."

At the time of the incorporation, the town contained the following families;[2] the figures denoting the number of members : —

Willard Robbins and others perambulated the line between Union and Appleton; Jan. 13 and 14, 1841, between Union and Warren; and Jan. 25 and 26, between Union and Hope. In April, 1841, the town "voted that suitable stone-monuments be put up between said towns, provided the adjoining towns will be at their proportion of the expense." Sept. 12, 1844, Ebenezer Blunt, selectman of Union, and George Pease, selectman of Appleton, perambulated the line between the towns, and "set up stone-monuments at the corners, and where the line crossed the highways, and near the banks of all the ponds and rivers which said line crossed." The same was done Nov. 9, 1844, on the line between Union and Hope by Ebenezer Blunt, and by Josiah Hobbs, one of the selectmen of Hope. June 10, 1843, the town "voted that the selectmen be a Committee to petition to the Supreme Court to have the line run between the county of Lincoln and Waldo." This is of importance, as Union is a border town.

[1] At the end of the manuscript Act of Incorporation, in the State House at Boston, is the following memorandum : — "In the House of Representatives, Oct. 12, 1786. This bill, having had three several readings, passed to be engrossed. — Sent up for concurrence.
"ARTEMAS WARD, Speaker."

On the back of the bill is the following : — "In Senate, Oct. 18, 1786. This bill, having had two several readings, passed a concurrence to be engrossed with an amendment at A. — Sent down for concurrence. "SAMUEL PHILLIPS, jun. President."

"A, dele from A to B, and insert *thereof that the Plantation called Sterlington, in the county of Lincoln.*"

"In the House of Representatives, Oct. 19, 1786. — Read and concurred. "ARTEMAS WARD, Speaker."

The words to be erased in the first paragraph were, " A *of said plantation that the same* B."

[2] N. P. Hawes's MS.

Joel Adams	5	Amariah Mero	2
Ezra Bowen	5	Elisha Partridge	5
John Butler	5	Bela Robbins	2
Richard Cummings	6	David Robbins	9
Royal Grinnell	4	Ebenezer Robbins	3
Abijah Hawes	3	Jessa Robbins	2
Matthias Hawes	4	Josiah Robbins	5
Moses Hawes	5	Philip Robbins	3
Samuel Hills	2	Jason Ware	5
Elijah Holmes	2		

CHAPTER IX.

SETTLERS AFTER THE INCORPORATION,
1787—1793.

1787, Levi Morse; Oliver Leland; William Hart. — 1788, The Maxcys. — 1789, The Daggetts; Seth Luce; Christopher Butler; Ichabod Irish; Barnabas Webb. — 1793, Casualty to the Maxcy Family. — Remarks on the Early Settlers.

1787.

AMONG the settlers who came soon after the incorporation was Levi Morse. He was hired "for forty shillings a month, and found," by Dr. Jennison, then of Brookfield, to chop for him *three* or *six* months, as Morse should choose. Having received one dollar to pay his passage by water, he left Sherburne for Boston, April 23, 1787. "April 26, sailed for St. George's River; arrived there, 29th.... 1788, May 5, came [from Sherburne] to Boston; sailed Wednesday morning; arrived [at] St. George's River, May 8th; went up to Union the 9th." From other memoranda left by him, it appears that he returned from Sherburne to Union every spring for several years; spending the winters, as many of the early settlers did, in Massachusetts. In 1789, he brought with him John Locke, son of a former President of Harvard University. The agreement with Locke was to pay him, for six months, "six pounds twelve shillings in good rye at the market price in" Sherburne, besides furnishing him with a passage, provisions, washing, and mending, from the time of his sailing from Boston. For a considerable part of the time before his marriage, Morse cooked his own food, occasionally employing Mrs. Josiah Robbins to bake his bread. He settled on the farm now owned by his sons, Levi Morse and George B. Morse.

With Morse also came Oliver Leland from Sherburne. He began to clear the farm next to Morse's, on the south. After a year or two, he lost his thumb by the bursting of a gun while hunting near Crawford's Pond, and went back to Sherburne.

William Hart, from Sherburne, came with Morse. Both of them seem to have been under the patronage of Mr. Amory, who, being desirous of introducing settlers, offered to give Hart either of the lots of land which did not border on the pond. He selected the one north of the mill-lot. It differed but little in value from what were then considered the best; for its western boundary was but a few rods from the water. The farm is now owned by his son, John Fisher Hart. At one time, Morse, Hart, and Gillmor boarded with Josiah Robbins, for which they worked two days in each week.

1788.

The Maxcys came from Attleborough, Mass. Joseph Maxcy came first in 1788, settled on the farm since known as the Gay Farm, on the west side of the brook, more than a mile east of the Common; and he built a frame-house, the second in town. With Joseph Maxcy came Joseph Guild. At one time, either alone or in company with Joseph Maxcy, he owned the Gay Place. Josiah Maxcy came with his father, Lieutenant Benjamin Maxcy, and his father's family, in 1791. They lived in the Taylor House. Mrs. Daggett says that her father brought two cows, a yoke of oxen, and an ox-wagon. This wagon was the first in town. He loaded his goods upon it, and drove it up. It was an object of such interest, that the people, as he passed, came out to look at it. In about six weeks the lieutenant died. Joseph Maxcy then moved to South Union, and his mother and her children to the Gay Place. Joseph Maxcy built another small frame-house, the third in town; and then the family, with Josiah, moved back to the Taylor House.

1789.

The Daggetts, says Brotherton Daggett, being strongly inclined to move from Martha's Vineyard, sent Thomas Daggett, jun. to Albany and the vicinity, in New York, to look up a farm. He was not a judge of land, and returned without finding one to suit him. Thomas Daggett, sen. came along the coast, went back from Camden into the woods, and with some others was about to purchase the whole of Appleton Ridge, except the proprietors' reserved lots. On going to the rear of the Ridge, and seeing the Cedar Swamp, his courage failed him, and he went home without concluding a bargain. A year or two afterwards, Thomas Daggett, jun. and Aaron Daggett came to Union. They purchased the place since owned by Olney Titus, cleared a piece, and sowed rye. In the fall, they took, as a specimen, a box of soil from the land now owned by Nahum Thurston, returned to Martha's Vineyard, and spent the winter. Their father, Thomas Daggett, sen. was prevailed on to accompany them to Union in the following May. He bought 700 acres of land of Col. Wheaton, divided it into lots of about 100 acres each, sold some, and gave the others to his sons. He returned to Martha's Vineyard, and came with his family in August. He landed at Warren. Every thing seemed different from what it was in May. He was a nervous man; and, finding himself here for life, he exclaimed, "I am completely undone." The forests looked formidable: "it was too woody for him." This was probably in 1789. The family came up from Warren in boats, as Josiah Robbins's had done three years before, and as William Hart did when he moved his wife and furniture in October, 1793.

About the same time with the Daggetts came Seth Luce and family, also from the Vineyard, and settled in the west part of the town.

Christopher Butler, with his family, also from Martha's Vineyard, came in 1789. He bought the place on which Oliver Leland had made a beginning. It is on the north side of the road which runs east from the Common, and at the intersection of it with the road to Warren on the east side of the Pond.

Ichabod Irish, a cooper of wooden ware, came to Union, from Little Compton, R.I. Sept. 17, 1789. The good Quaker resided first on the west side of the river, near the Middle Bridge. The small stock of provisions which he brought was soon exhausted; and, in the great scarcity of the following winter, his family experienced much suffering. They killed their fowls, because they had not the means to keep them alive. They made an effort, however, to winter their geese, because feathers were very valuable. But, before spring, the starving geese were observed to peck the under bark of the white birch firewood at the door. After this, the family shaved and broke the bark into small pieces for them, and thus kept them from dying.

One morning, Mr. Irish, being at the house of Capt. Adams, was invited to sit down to breakfast. He declined; he could not eat while his children were without food at home. Mrs. Adams immediately gave him half the loaf she had baked from meal procured from her brother, Jessa Robbins; enjoined on him the strictest secresy, lest she should be censured for giving away her brother's gift; and sent him home to his wife and children rejoicing, and shedding tears. At another time, Mrs. Matthias Hawes gave him a portion of dough which she was kneading, and he carried it home in a towel. The children, "hungry all the time," were constantly gnawing the under bark of the white birch, and eating it, till it brought on constipation and disease.

In the spring, Royal Grinnell gave to the Rev. Cornelius Irish, then a boy, a long white potato, familiarly called a "Bunker potato." He "ran home as pleased as if he had got fifty dollars." The potato was forthwith thrust into the fire to be roasted, and shared among the children. But so long had they lived without such a luxury, that they could not wait for it to be cooked. They took it out, and cut off the outside as fast as it was roasted, till the whole was devoured. Meal was dealt out almost as sparingly as medicine; and, when enough could be obtained, the family luxuriated on water-porridge. With the opening of the spring came some relief. Leaves and "longtongue" were picked, and, being boiled, were eaten as greens. Shortly afterward came fish, particularly salmon, and starvation ceased to be so terribly formidable as it had been.

Mr. Irish was respected for his integrity and worth. His business increased. He manufactured wooden ware, and, when there was snow, carried it about for sale on a hand-sled. In the winter of 1790–91, he took some of it to Barretts Town. It was bartered for three bushels of rye. As he was returning, a snow-storm came on. He was obliged to abandon his load while on Sunnybee Pond; and, though he succeeded in returning home, it was with extreme difficulty. So vivid is the recollection of his distress when he entered the house, that his children to this day cannot speak of it but with deep emotion.

While in this state of poverty, Mr. Irish was solicited to take a child three or four years old, and was promised fifty acres of land if he would keep him a specified time. As this seemed to open the only way by which he could obtain land, he accepted the proposal. The child was introduced to the family, wore dresses colored with hemlock-bark, as the other children did, and shared in their trials and poverty. Mr. Irish kept him till he secured the land. Thus he became owner of the farm in the Daggett neighborhood, to which he moved from Bachelor's Mills. The lad had good principles instilled into his mind, and had worthy examples to imitate. He afterward went to sea, and became a successful sea-captain. Any person wishing to know more about him may consult Capt. Barnabas Webb, a man of worth and wealth in Thomaston.

1793.

May 13, Amy, widow of Benjamin Maxcy, and her daughters, Lydia and Sally Maxcy, with Chloe, wife of Joseph Maxcy, crossed Seven-tree Pond, to attend the funeral of Esther Cummings, at the house of her uncle, Jessa Robbins, where she died. After the funeral, they, with Simeon Wellman of Attleborough, who was an apprentice to Joseph Maxcy, and William Montgomery, got into a boat to return. As it was leaky and overloaded, the water soon poured in faster than it could be baled out. At a short distance from Hills Point, between it and the house of Philip Robbins, the boat settled down into the water. All on board instinctively rose. Their screams were heard on both sides of the pond, and as far as Christopher Butler's. The boat did not sink, but rolled over. All except Lydia succeeded in getting hold of it. To her, Sally was extending her hand, when Wellman, exceedingly frightened, sprang upon the boat. All again lost their hold; and the females, except Sally, were drowned. By the buoyancy of her clothes, by her repeated and persevering struggles to put her hand on the boat, which was constantly on the roll and often rolled over her, and by breathing from time to time as she got her head above water and her hand on the boat, she succeeded in saving herself, though she sank once. Finally, the two men got hold of one side, and she of the other; and then they sustained themselves till another boat came to their relief,[1] and Capt. Joel Adams took Sally out of the water into it.

[1] The information respecting this distressing event was obtained several years since at an accidental interview with the only surviving female. Since the above was written, her son, the Hon. John Dag-

On the small population of Union at the time, this tragical event left an indelible impression. It is often spoken of to this day by the elderly people in a manner which indicates the deep feeling which it created. It stands out more prominently in the history of the town than any other casualty before or since. After gett, author of the History of Attleborough, has by particular request furnished a copy of the touching and excellent letter which his mother wrote immediately afterward. It was penned when opportunities for good education were few, by a girl about fourteen years old, in deep affliction, just after being rescued from drowning, and with the corpse of a sister before her.

"Union, May 16, 1793.

"Honored Uncle and Aunt, — It is with great sorrow that I take my pen in hand to inform you of the sudden and unexpected death of my near and dear mamma, and sister Chloe, and sister Lydia. We went to the funeral of one of my dear mates; and, when we were coming back, there were six in the float, viz. my mamma, sister Chloe, and sister Lydia, Simeon Wellman, William Montgomery, and myself. We set out from the shore, expecting to arrive to our house; but, when we got into the middle of the pond, the wind blowed very hard and the float leaked, and she being loaded very heavy, so that every wave that came ran over the stern into the float, and directly she filled with water, and sunk down even with the water, and turned us all out. Then, oh! the dismal shrieks, the dying groans, which were then heard piercing the ears of many of my kind neighbors, who all ran to arrest us. But all in vain to some; for mamma, and sister Chloe, and sister Lydia, were floating on the water; they were soon took into the float, all possible care taken and methods tried to bring them to, but all in vain; for vain is the help of man without God's blessing.

"Could I collect my thoughts, I would try to acquaint you further of this solemn transaction. The two men and myself were hold of the float. Sometimes the float was over me, and I got hold again. Through the distinguishing goodness of God, our lives were ransomed from the deep waters.

"Oh! my dear uncle and aunt, how can I paint these lines with grief equal to my conception! My dear mamma and dear sister Chloe were laid by my dear daddy yesterday [in] the house appointed for all living. Lydia wan't found until this day — is now a corpse before me. Oh! my dear uncle and aunt, can you forbear mourning with me, though at a distance? Do pray for me; for I am a sinner, and need the prayers for all God's people. I think my grief being redoubled would sink me as deep as I was sunk in the water, if my heavenly Father did not support me. My daily prayer is to God that I may make a right improvement of all God's dealing with me. You cannot in any measure conceive of the distressed circumstances of this family; my kind brother, bereaved of his nearest and dearest connection — myself, with Hervey and Ama, left without father or mother, full of grief. May God support us, and enable us to be fol-

this event, Joseph Maxcy sold the Gay Place, so called, to Gay. In the autumn of 1793, Sally Maxcy returned to Attleborough.

REMARKS ON THE EARLY SETTLERS.

The account of the early inhabitants has now been brought down to a time when it is inexpedient to continue details respecting them. Most of the men had been in the revolutionary war. They had strong arms and stout hearts, and were well qualified to make a beginning in a wilderness. Many of them were devout, practical Christians, who feared God and eschewed evil. Deprivations and trials developed in them and their children a character which is perceptible in the present population. They were strangers to luxuries. In consequence of their isolated situation and the pressure of outward circumstances, they became deeply interested in each other's welfare. Hospitality was unlimited. The guest of one family was by all the others welcomed as a particular friend. The bonds of union were strengthened by many family ties among them. There were common interests in clearing the ground and raising crops, common sufferings when provisions were scarce, and common apprehensions of danger from the enemy at Biguyduce. They hunted and fished, and every one was alive to every other one's successes and perils. So strong was the sympathy, that the little community for many years may be regarded more as one large family than a few scattered inhabitants.

If any one had a delicacy — and, in those days, delicacies meant things substantial — if any one killed a bear, an ox, a hog, or a calf, he shared it, by loan or

lowers of Christ, and bear our affliction with patience, as he left us the example; so I conclude myself your sorrowful niece.
    Though distant graves divide our dust,
    Yet pray the Lord our souls may meet among the just.
"Kind uncle, if you please, send me a word of comfort; for my nearest and dearest friends cannot.
                                "SALLY MAXCY

otherwise, with his neighbors. Wherever sickness came, all were as ready to serve and to watch, as with a brother or sister. In any misfortune or affliction all sympathized. When there was a death, each family felt the shock. Every one who could went to the funeral; and in general sorrow, as if a near and dear friend were taken away, the remains were borne to their final resting-place.

In winter, the solitude was broken by the sound of the axe. The wind soughed through the pines. The moon's rays were reflected with a glare from the surface of the pond, which, as the ice cracked, sent forth rumblings during the long night. The fox barked. The owl hooted mournfully. The wolf howled hideously. Neighbors called on each other in the evenings, related their experience in the old French war and the revolutionary war, and their adventures from day to day in hunting moose, bears, and other game. An importance was attached to many incidents which would scarcely demand a passing notice in a different state of society.

And, as they talked, huge fires were kept burning; and on the glowing back-logs it was easy for the imagination to discover animals and men, and a multitude of creatures which never had existence. The well-caulked and heated log-houses excluded the pinching cold. The people, rough and coarse in manners and language, but with warm hearts, were unacquainted with the artifical wants of the present day. They subsisted on their coarse fare, and had better appetites and greater happiness than are found with kings and queens in gorgeous palaces.

CHAPTER X.

POPULATION.

Census, Aug. 1, 1790. — Abstracts from Censuses. — Hawes's Census in 1826. — State Census, March 1, 1837.

When the census was taken in 1790, Henry Dearborn was marshal of the District of Maine. The other United States marshals gave details. He gave only summary statements. Accordingly, all that was to be learned from his return is that, Aug. 1, 1790, Union contained two hundred inhabitants. Perhaps this was but little more than conjecture.

The following statements are from subsequent returns: —

AGE.	1800.		1810.		1820.	
	Males.	Females.	Males.	Females.	Males.	Females.
Under 10 years	121	102	252	221	234	218
10 and under 16	37	47	87	81	132	130
16 and under 26	55	43	111	119	131	123
26 and under 45	61	57	149	124	130	132
45 and upwards	29	21	61	61	80	81
	303	270	660	603	707	684
		303		660		*707
All other free persons, except Indians, not taxed.		573 2		1266		1391
Total		575				

Subsequently the details were more minute.

* Including 32 males between 16 and 18 years of age. In 1820, there were 291 persons engaged in agriculture, 7 in commerce, and 59 in manufactures.

AGE.	1830.		1840.	
	Males.	Females.	Males.	Females.
Under 5 years	128	120	143	135
5 and under 10	129	104	145	125
10 and under 15	104	103	106	116
15 and under 20	103	90	93	90
20 and under 30	155	142	146	144
30 and under 40	67	76	104	99
40 and under 50	60	69	63	65
50 and under 60	53	41	42	55
60 and under 70	16	19	46	28
70 and under 80	15	15	13	19
80 and under 90	2	1	2	5
	832	780	903	881
		832		903
Total		*1612		†1784

In 1826, Mr. Noyes P. Hawes prepared the following document, giving the name and number of members of each family, and the number of houses, classified according to school districts:—

SCHOOL DISTRICTS. — No. I.

John Little	6		Josiah F. Day	9
Daniel F. Harding	3		Bradley R. Mowry	10
Rufus Gillmor	6		Joseph Vaughan	13
Marcus Gillmor	4		Susman Abrams	4
Elisha Harding	5		Spencer Walcott	6
Abner Pitts	6		John Drake	9
Zaccheus Litchfield	8		Jesse Drake	12
Elisha Bemis	8		Abiel Gay	5
Ebenezer Alden	10		David Gay	6
Amos Barrett	5		Elijah Gay	4
Levi Morse	11		Amos Walker	9
Gorham Butler	6		David Bullen	6
John Butler	9		Aaron Young	8
John S. Bartlett	5		Nathan Daniels	10
Betsey Richards	3		John Payson	4

* Of whom two were blind.

† Including two insane or idiots at private charge. In 1840, according to the census, there were 330 persons engaged in agriculture, 13 in commerce, 93 in manufactures and trades, 7 in navigation, 7 in the learned professions and engineering; and 4 were revolutionary pensioners.

HAWES'S CENSUS.

No. II.

Ezra Bowen	3	Jason Robbins		4
Oliver Bowen	2	John Chapman Robbins		16
Abijah Hawes	6	Herman Hawes		10
David Robbins	4	Walter Adams		5
David Robbins, jun.	11	Henry True		5
John L. Robinson	5	Nathaniel Robbins		9
Andrew Robinson	2	John Jones		6
David Cummings	10	Obadiah Harris		4
Jessa Robbins	3	John Dods Bovee		4

No. III.

Moses Simmons	7	Marlboro' Packard		5
Ziba Simmons	6	Leonard Barnard		5
Leonard Wade	5	John Pearce Robbins		6
John W. Lindley	8	Suell Cummings		7
Benjamin Litchfield	9	Obadiah Morse		10
Adam Martin	6	Joseph Cushman		6
Amariah Mero	5	James Shibles		2
Spencer Mero	8	Noah Rice		10
Bela Robbins	2	Samuel Jameson		5
Ebenezer Robbins	7	Allen Stone		6
Joseph Clark	6			

No. IV.

Phinehas Butler	13	Charles Titus		9
John Butler	8	Abraham Brown		7
Ichabod Maddocks	3	Royal Grinnell		4
John Thompson	10	Alpheus Collamore		11
Otis Bills	8	Reuben Hills, jun.		8
Cyrus Nye	4	Nathan Hills		11
James Maxfield	7	Samuel Hills, 2d		9
Thomas Nye	9	Josiah Hills		7
Charles Hitchborn	5	Lewis Robbins		9
Caleb Maddocks	4	Reuben Hills		2
Asaph Lucas	5	George Silloway		6
William Libbey	7	Josiah Hills		9
Ebenezer Cobb	6	Jonathan Eastman		9
Walter Blake	10	Jonathan Sibley		4
John Burkett	11	Patrick Tenney		4
Olney Titus	6			

No. V.

Joel Adams	3	Samuel Daggett		3
Cornelius Irish	8	Ebenezer Daggett		7
Ebenezer W. Adams	10	William Daggett		8
Jason Ware	2	Nahum Thurston		5
Vinal Ware	4	Philo Thurston		6
Matthias Hawes	6	James Grinnell		7
Sarah Brown	3	Robert Dickey		8
David Stimpson	8	Nathaniel Bachelor		10
Bailey Grinnell	7	John Bachelder		6
William Shepard	7	George R. Allen		3
Nathan D. Rice	11	David Carriel		2

POPULATION.

No. VI.

Edmund Daggett	7	Daniel Shepard		
Lewis Bachelder	6	Daniel Shepard, jun.		
Benjamin Walker	11	Thaddeus Shepard		
Nehemiah Adams	4	Joseph Morse		4
Thomas Mitchell	5	Jonathan Morse		5
Samuel Daggett, jun.	5	Joshua Morse		6
John Walker	9	Samuel Fuller		6
John Burns	12	Thaddeus Luce		11
Daniel Walker	6	Seth Luce		4
Solomon Hewes	3	Jonathan Breck		6
Rowland Cobb	4	Calvin Gleason		9
Rachel Mitchell	5	Isaac Townsend		13
Cyrus Robbins	6	John Tobey		9
John Stevens	7	Nathaniel Tobey		8
David Law	9			

No. VII.

Nathan Bachelder	6	William Coggan	6
William Lawrence	6	Robert Thompson	6
Ichabod Irish	7	Timothy Stewart	4
Reuben Alford	5	Thomas Butler	4
Judson Caswell	2	Elkanah Morton	7
Edward Brown	3	Henry Blunt	2
Thomas A. Mitchell	4	Ebenezer Blunt	5
John Gowen	8	Jacob Sibley	11
Reuben Packard	7	Penty Walcott	9
Henry Fossett	10	Jonathan Carriel	8
Charles Hall	3	Jonathan Carriel, jun.	3
Brotherton Daggett	13	Isaac Booth	8
Isaac Upham	8	Samuel Norwood	5
Rachel Stone	3	Luther Bryant	5
Samuel Stone	5	William Bryant	4
Jeremiah Mitchell	8	James Bryant	5
Asa Messer	9	Judith Clark	5
Thomas Messer	6	—— Whedon	2
Joseph Bryant	2		

No. VIII.

Joseph Miller	12	Willard Gay	5
James Littlehale	7	Johnson Pilsbury	14
Simon Fuller	6	Obadiah Gardner	8
Caleb Howard	8	Life Boggs	5
Christopher Young	5	William Boggs	3
James Sinclair	11	Sally Cooper	2
Daniel Linniken	6	Joseph Robbins	8
Daniel Howard	5	Abel Walker	12
William Lermond	7	Silas Walker	3
Jason Davis	5	Samuel Quiggle	7
Sterling Davis	5	Joel Robbins	8
Lemuel Rich	9	John Hemenway	13
John Lermond	7	Alexander Skinner	7

No. IX.

John Whiting	12	John Swan		8
John Fogler	6	Charles R. Hunnewell		2
Samuel Hills	3	Polly Gleason		8
Sanford Hills	7	Fisher Hart		2
Moses Morse	6	John M. Thorndike		8
Nathan Daniels, jun.	4	Phillips C. Harding		5
Robert Foster	10	Aaron Hart		4
Mrs. Wingate	3	William Hart		2
Benjamin Dow	4	John F. Hart		5
Leonard Follansbee	8			

No. X.

Ezekiel Hagar	4	Martin Sidelinger	9
Samuel Hagar	8	Leonard Bump	8
Benjamin L. Law	9		

Inhabitants, 1,550; families, 238; houses, 215; scholars, 715.

A census of the inhabitants in town, March 1, 1837, was taken by William Gleason, Esq. in conformity with an Act of the Legislature requiring it before the town could receive its proportion of the "surplus revenue." At that time, the number of persons under 4 years of age was 230; from 4 to 21 years of age, 742; and there were 782 persons who were more than 21 years of age, — making a total of 1,754.

CHAPTER XI.

POPULATION IN 1850.

Census, June 1, 1850, with Names and Ages.

THE following census was also taken by William Gleason, Esq. At the time, particular attention was not given to the spelling, and probably several of the names are not printed as commonly written. Members of the same family not unfrequently spell the name differently, and there are some cases in which a person does not always observe uniformity in spelling his own name. The order in which the names were entered on the census-book is preserved, as it often indicates the neighborhood and locality. The first column of figures denotes the number of the houses; the second, the number of the families. The other figures designate the ages.

1. 1	Robert McGuier	52		Mary A. Vaughan	10
	Caroline McGuier	41		Wm. H. H. Vaughan	9
	Mary A. McGuier	18		Martha Ann Vaughan	4
	Orison McGuier	15		George Vaughan	2
	Caroline A. McGuier	14		Charles A. Vaughan,	8 mo.
	Edwin C. McGuier	7	9.10	Joseph Vaughan	74
2. 2	Moses Morse	65		Hannah Vaughan	68
	Hannah Morse	61		Susan Vaughan	31
	Dexter P. Morse	26		Augustus Vaughan	25
	Hannah P. Morse	22		Lucy L. Jones	28
3. 3	Edward P. Morse	33	10.11	Levi Morse	45
	Martha A. Morse	24		Eliza Morse	45
	Quincy A. Morse	2		Caroline E. Morse	15
	Nathaniel K. Aglar	15		Edwin L. Morse	12
	Caroline F. Stone	16		Levi R. Morse	7
4. 4	Ambrose Leach	47		John A. Morse	5
	Julia Leach	38		Mary D. Taylor	10 mo.
	James L. Leach	18		Mansfield Richards	16
	Frances E. Leach	15	10.12	Nathan D. Payson	25
	Ambrose A. Leach	8		Frances A. B. Payson	23
	Lucy A. Sayward	22		Clarissa Post	45
5. 5	Nathan Daniels, jun.	49		David Y. Post	18
	Mehitable Daniels	46		Mary C. Post	15
	Mary E. Daniels	24		Joseph White	19
	Joel Daniels	16	11.13	George W. Morse	36
	Levi Daniels	12		Mary H. R. Morse	33
6. 6	Charles A. Hawes	31		Leslie M. Morse	7
	Angeline S. Hawes	29		Sarah A. Morse	3
	Llewellyn K. Hawes	12		Harriet E. Morse	1
	Ellen A. Hawes	10	12.14	Gorham Butler	40
	Eliza M. Hawes	7		Catherine Butler	30
	Martha M. Hawes	5		Albion D. P. Butler	8
	Harriet R. Hawes	3		John G. Butler	3
	Colin Hawes	1		Adeline A. Gallop	12
7. 7	Amos Drake	44		Marcus Roakes	16
	Melancy Drake	42		John O'Connor	55
	Oramel L. Drake	20	13.15	Daniel F. Harding	64
	Mary O. Drake	16		Harriet Harding	57
	Statira M. Drake	14		Amos B. Harding	24
	Amos L. Drake	4		Henry F. Harding	23
8. 8	Benjamin B. Hills	29		Daniel Harding	21
	Amelia H. Hills	25		Harriet Harding	18
	Sylvia A. Hills	1 mo.	14.16	John Butler, 2d	37
8. 9	William Vaughan	36		Ann M. Butler	33
	Abigail H. Vaughan	31		Gorham W. Butler	12

UNITED STATES CENSUS.

	Name	Age
	Simeon N. Butler	9
15.17	John N. Fairbanks	56
	Martha Fairbanks	54
	Eunice Dean	25
	Henry Fairbanks	18
	George Fairbanks	15
16.18	Wesley Butler	32
	Sally Butler	63
17.19	Christopher Butler	30
	Sarah Butler	24
	Elizabeth Butler	6
	Lydia A. Butler	3
	William O. Butler	1
17.20	John Butler	69
	Hannah Butler	70
18.21	Luther Gould	22
	Sarah Gould	31
	James Gould	5
19.22	Thurston Whiting	42
	Lydia G. Whiting	36
	Frederic P. Whiting	6
	Mary B. Whiting	4
	Ralph W. Rising	11
	Orren Davis	15
20.23	Simeon Noyes, jun.	29
	Elizabeth T. Noyes	22
	Georgiana Noyes	2
	George Fred. Noyes, 1 mo.	
	Achsah Chase	51
	Edward L. Whitney	25
21.24	John Hemenway, jun.	38
	Harriet N. Hemenway	35
	Ann Fogler	65
22.25	Nathaniel Robbins	45
	Harriet Robbins	40
	Frances A. Robbins	18
	Ann E. Robbins	16
	Lovey W. Robbins	15
	Edward K. Robbins	11
23.26	Gilb. M. Blackington	47
	Lois Blackington	41
	Benj. B. Blackington	23
	Gilb. M. Blackington	21
	Selina Butler	22
	Jacob W. Butler	15
	Cordelia Briggs	15
24.27	Samuel Quiggle, jun.	38
	Clem'tine Q. Quiggle	37
	Gilford W. Quiggle	9
	Sarah A. Quiggle	7
	Margaret A. Quiggle	5
	Samuel Quiggle	78
25.28	Silas Walker	46
	Rachel Walker	30
	Silas S. Walker	17
	Joseph Walker	23
	Harriet Walker	14
	Olinda Walker	11
	Betsey Walker	4
26.29	Minot Tolman	27
	Harriet A. Tolman	24
	John B. Robbins	42
	Henry Tolman	15
27.30	David Hull	52
	Mary N. Hull	47
	Emily F. Hull	14
	Ann A. Hull	18
	Caroline E. Hull	12
	George Evans Hull	5
28.31	Calvin Hemenway	32
	Louisa Hemenway	28
	Calvin Hemenway	6
	Alfred Davis	18
29.32	Miles Hemenway	40
	Mary A. Hemenway	29
	Julia A. Hemenway	14
	Hiram B. Hemenway	10
	Addison Hemenway	9
	Rufus L. Hemenway	3
30.33	John Hemenway	69
	Mehitable Hemenway	62
31.34	Danf. Blackington	43
	Louisa Blackington	33
	Rufus Blackington	15
	Ellis G. Blackington	12
	Charles Blackington	8
	Esth. A. Blackington	2
32.35	Mark Young	31
	Jane P. Young	27
	William A. Young	6
	Leurissa Young	5
	Harriet Young	23
33.36	John Briggs	53
	Eliza Briggs	43
	Lewis B. Briggs	13
	William J. Briggs	7
	Gilbert B. Briggs	5
	Ann E. Briggs	3
	John Walker Briggs	1
34.37	Abel Walker	71
	Polly Walker	69
	Alanson Walker	30
	Marcus Walker	26
	Elzira Walker	22
	Martha M. Walker	14
35.38	Samuel Haskell	33

POPULATION.

	Adeline Haskell	34	42.47	Erastus St. Clair	36
	Mary Haskell	9		Sarah E. St. Clair	29
	Flotillah Haskell	7		William B. St. Clair	13
	Delia Ann Haskell	2		John L. St. Clair	8
	Laura Haskell	2 mo.		Eliza E. St. Clair	5
36.39	Josh. W. Wentworth	35		Henry F. St. Clair	1
	Beulah Wentworth	36		James St. Clair	73
	Laura E. Wentworth	8		Sarah S. St. Clair	71
	Marcus E. Wentworth	4		Caleb P. Butler	21
	Marcellus Wentworth	2	43.48	William Hilt	42
36.40	Calvin Boggs	40		Emeline Hilt	34
	Adeline Boggs	40		Mary A. Hilt	14
	Amelia Boggs	15		Martha J. Hilt	13
	Matilda Boggs	15		John L. Hilt	8
	Martha Boggs	9		Elsie G. Hilt	11
	Henry Boggs	7		William E. Hilt	3
	Mary Boggs	7		Lusena D. Hilt	2
	Lucinda Boggs	6		Henry Peabody	16
	Sally Cooper	79	44.49	Sterling Davis	46
36.41	Diana Robbins	74		Betsey Davis	44
37.42	David E. Gardner	39		Lusena C. Davis	21
	Diana S. Gardner	41		Joseph M. Davis	16
	Hannah S. Gardner	9		Henry Robbins	31
	Ellis S. Gardner	6	45.50	John W. Lermond	36
	Abigail Rollins	71		Sabra Lermond	41
38.43	Wilbur Davis	43		Andrew J. Lermond	19
	Rosanna Davis	41		Lucy Lermond	70
	Oscar Davis	20		Artemas Howard	30
	Benjamin B. Davis	18	46.51	Jason Davis	49
	Dexter Davis	15		Chloe Davis	53
	Elisha H. Davis	15		Jane Davis	19
	Edwin Davis	13		Roxana Davis	14
	Sarah E. Davis	10		Chloe A. Davis	13
	Emily Davis	8		Elvira Davis	8
	Alice J. Davis	7		William Davis	17
	Marshall W. Davis	1		Josiah A. Maxcy	9
39.44	Henry D. Fuller	41		Ebenezer Robbins	40
	Eliza Fuller	35	47.52	Fisher A. Daniels	41
	Charles Fuller	15		Julia A. Daniels	41
	Oliver K. Fuller	13		Obadiah G. Daniels	16
	Nelson Fuller	11		Amanda N. Taylor	10
	Henry E. Fuller	9	48.53	Joseph Daniels	43
	Antoinette L. Fuller	4		Sarah Daniels	37
	Paulina Newcomb	11		Edwin R. Daniels	19
40.45	John Heisler	28		Lucy R. Daniels	16
	Rachel Heisler	21		Sarah E. Daniels	14
	Mary E. Heisler	5		Zilpah E. Daniels	11
	Sarah E. Heisler	9 mo.		Lois A. Daniels	6
41.46	John Newcomb	48		Frances E. Daniels	1
	Nancy Newcomb	32	48.54	Nathan Daniels	79
	Lucretia Newcomb	15		Lavinia Daniels	27
	Eliza Newcomb	8	49.55	John Payson	58
	Orrett Newcomb	2		Lois Payson	52

UNITED STATES CENSUS.

	John Ellis Payson	23
	George W. Payson	22
	Eliza A. Payson	19
	James M. Payson	14
	Fisher D. Payson	10
50.56	Milton Daniels	47
	Nancy Daniels	32
	Lewis R. Daniels	19
	Lucy A. Daniels	13
	Laura M. Daniels	8
51.57	Aurel. P. Lawrence	26
	Huldah Lawrence	30
	Aurel. L. Lawrence	2
52.58	Levi V. Hastings	34
	Abigail Hastings	32
	Laura M. Hastings	5
	Thaddeus Hastings	27
53.59	John Lermond	40
	Hannah Lermond	38
	Adelbert Lermond	12
	John F. Lermond	10
	Eliza E. Lermond	8
	Frederic Lermond	4
	Ansel Hastings	24
	Geo. W. Thompson	25
	Charles Pratt	27
	Clarissa Webster	18
53.60	Nancy Lermond	77
54.61	E. G. D. Beveridge	35
	Martha Beveridge	24
	George W. Beveridge	26
	Martha F. Beveridge	22
	Llew'd M. Beveridge	1
55.62	Elbridge Lermond	37
	Huldah Lermond	32
	Ephraim Lermond	16
	Julia Lermond	11
	Albert S. Lermond	10
	Elbridge G. Lermond	8
	Huldah E. Lermond	5
	Frank J. Lermond	4
56.63	Nathaniel Lothrop	28
	Mary H. Lothrop	26
	Manford N. Lothrop	2
	Edwin N. Lothrop	2 mo.
	Charles Murphy	18
57.64	Lewis Andrews	40
	Sarah Andrews	35
	Angelina Andrews	16
	Adelia Andrews	13
	Amanda Andrews	8
	Virginia Andrews	6
	Lewis F. Andrews	1
	James W. Spear	18
58.65	Winslow B. Hastings	32
	Martha J. Hastings	27
	Le Forest Hastings	2
	Daniel Titus	21
59.66	William H. Gowen	29
	Louisa A. Gowen	22
60.67	Emery Thomas	28
	Eliza A. Thomas	28
	William C. Thomas	4
	Emery F. Thomas	2
61.68	Edward V. Collins	59
	Sarah Collins	57
	John T. Collins	27
	Tryphena Moore	26
	Albert D. Moore	28
	Almina J. Collins	19
	Leonidas E. Collins	16
62.69	Lydia Skinner	53
	Henry Skinner	30
	Joseph Skinner	22
	Sanford Skinner	20
	Lois Skinner	18
	Sylvia J. Skinner	16
	Lydia Skinner	11
	Louisa Skinner	20
63.70	Jane Davis	77
64.71	Mark Davis	74
	Betsey Davis	71
	Mary Davis	38
65.72	George S. Littlehale	34
	Jane W. Littlehale	26
	James R. Littlehale	7
	George A. Littlehale	4
	Carol. M. Littlehale	1
	Susan Littlehale	64
	Maxcy Davis	24
	Joseph Durgin	15
66.73	Horace Miller	37
	Miriam H. Miller	36
	Martha S. Miller	14
	Dudley Miller	10
	Mary O. Miller	3
66.74	Joseph Miller	72
	Betsey Miller	66
67.75	Charles Miller	39
	Lucy Miller	41
	George A. Miller	15
	Julia D. Miller	14
	John A. Miller	10
	Sarah A. Miller	5
	Charles A. Miller	4
	Mary E. Miller	2

POPULATION.

68.76	Wm. H. Burroughs	42
	Frances Burroughs	35
	Henry Burroughs	2
69.77	Amos Walker	72
	Judith Walker	69
	Joel A. Walker	28
	Isaac Walker	26
70.78	John Drake	70
	Margaretta Drake	42
	Samandel Drake	20
	George Drake	16
	Lydia Drake	23
	Charles Drake	22
71.79	Jesse Drake	68
	Polly Drake	61
	Millard G. Drake	28
	Josiah Drake	19
	Mary F. Gay	14
72.80	John M. Thorndike	66
	Betsey Thorndike	56
	Wm. H. Thorndike	34
	Abigail C. Thorndike	29
	Mary Thorndike	23
	George W. Thorndike	21
	John E. Thorndike	18
	Sarah B. Thorndike	15
	Lucy E. Thorndike	10
73.81	John S. Dunton	33
	Joanna Dunton	42
	John C. Gay	22
	Olive D. Gay	19
	James Gay	17
	Sarah W. Gay	16
	F. Ellen Dunton	10
	Lucy E. Dunton	7
	Gavanus Dunton	6
	Charles R. Dunton	4
	Sophia J. Dunton	3
	Lauretta A. Dunton	1 mo.
	Martha H. Gay	21
	John Curtis	84
74.82	Luther Drake	35
	Abigail P. Drake	30
	Lusena A. Drake	11
	Melvina O. Drake	9
	Louisa J. Drake	6
	Luther Drake	4
	Almond G. Drake	2
	Albert R. Drake	1 mo.
	Julia A. Davis	19
75.83	Ebenezer Alden	75
	Patience Alden	68
	Augustus Alden	34
	Margaret Alden	35
	Patience G. Alden	6
	George A. Alden	2
	Edward Alden	28
76.84	Christopher Young	55
	Nancy Young	50
	Robert T. Young	23
	Mary Rollins	17
77.85	John Jones	59
	Abigail Jones	58
	William H. Jones	25
	Abigail Jones	21
	John E. Jones	19
	Augustus Jones	17
	Eugene Jones	7
78.86	Benjamin L. Jones	31
	Jane M. Jones	24
	Louise Jones	3
	Celeste Jones	2
79.87	Andrew Libbey	29
	Aroline E. Libbey	27
	Martha J. Libbey	3
80.88	Samuel Bowker	36
	Elizabeth E. Bowker	28
	Charles I. Bowker	5 mo.
81.89	Joshua S. Greene	40
	Sarah H. Greene	44
	William Greene	6
	Charles Greene	4
82.90	John W. C. Lord	39
	Priscilla Lord	39
	George F. Lord	14
	Lucy O. Lord	12
	Cyrus W. Lord	11
	Ellen V. Lord	9
	Martha P. Lord	7
	Priscilla G. Lord	6
	Ann Lord	3
	John E. Lord	4 mo.
83.91	Ebenezer Cobb	56
	Patience M. Cobb	53
	David B. Cobb	16
	Marcellus L. Cobb	13
	Elizabeth Lermond	26
	Ambrose Wellman	20
83.92	Rufus Gillmor	80
	Sarah Gillmor	80
	Lusena Crowell	57
	Darius Bump	21
84.93	Zuinglius Collins	38
	Julia A. Collins	28
	Leroy Z. Collins	5
	Azelia M. Collins	2

UNITED STATES CENSUS.

	Name	Age
	Elkanah Wingate	32
	Helen Wingate	22
	Loammi Cummings	20
	Samuel G. Hills	20
	Ziba Simmons	19
	James Stevens	21
	Frank Stevens	26
	Peter Adams	16
	Ebenezer Handay	29
	Harriet Bachelder	22
85.94	Samuel Cummings	41
	Paulina Cummings	25
	Vilet. A. Cummings	11
	Elv. P. Cummings	1 mo.
	Benjamin Achorn	40
86.95	Jesse W. Payson	34
	Abigail H. Payson	27
	Matilda H. Payson	5
87.96	Asa Messer	35
	Hannah A. Messer	36
	Caroline M. Messer	5
	Caroline Messer	20
88.97	Isaac Flitner	40
	Clem'te S. Flitner	29
	Georga. A. Flitner	7
	George F. Flitner	3
89.98	Nathan B. Robbins	34
	Abigail C. Robbins	31
	Levi M. Robbins	6
	Edgar M. Robbins	4
	Nathan D. Robbins	1
90.99	Ward Adams	37
	Martha O. Adams	36
	Martha M. S. Adams	11
	Wesley F. Adams	9
	Olivia C. Adams	7
	Elverton W. Adams	2
	Harriet Young	24
91.100	Nelson Cutler	45
	Love T. Cutler	39
	John E. Cutler	19
	Mary C. Cutler	16
	Caroline M. Cutler	13
	Charles H. Cutler	11
	Frank M. Cutler	8
	Clara A. Cutler	4
	Coraella Cutler	6 mo.
92.101	Edward Hills	34
	Almena D. Hills	25
	Hiram A. Hills	2
	Helen M. Hills	6 mo.
	Samuel Hills, jun.	22
93.102	William E. Cobb	26
	Elvira E. W. Cobb	26
	William Adams	30
	Warren Wentworth	28
	Andrew Benner	30
	Joseph Morse	35
	Joseph O. Cobb	23
	Sarah Lehr	24
	Rufus Prescott	16
94.103	Elijah Vose	43
	Mary B. Vose	30
	Helen A. Vose	6
	Mary T. Vose	5 mo.
	Elijah V. Haskell	12
95.104	Nathl. K. Burkett	38
	Polly Burkett	35
	Isaac H. Burkett	14
	Oscar A. Burkett	13
	Mary A. Burkett	10
	Ellen M. Burkett	8
	Elias Burkett	1
96.105	Lewis Robbins	67
	Phebe Robbins	63
	Lewis Robbins, jun.	33
	Matilda Robbins	22
	Roscoe B. Robbins	3
	Charles Robbins	1
	Johnson Miller	18
97.106	Fisher Hart	66
	Matilda Hart	45
	Adelph. L. Bartlett	17
	Fostina M. Bartlett	20
	Martha Cromett	13
98.107	Samuel Hills	70
	Israel Hills	31
	Sarah Hills	20
	Laura A. Brown	19
99.108	Josiah Sterling	53
	Caroline Sterling	50
	William Sterling	21
	Jane Sterling	17
	George W. Sterling	19
	Martha A. Sterling	15
	Caroline R. Sterling	13
	Thurston J. Sterling	7
	Eliza B. Jameson	18
100.109	Joshua Morse	48
	Reliance Morse	48
	Clara Morse	23
	Elijah Morse	26
	Louisa Morse	21
	Reliance Morse	19
	Delora Morse	17
	Susanna Morse	15

POPULATION.

	Harriet Morse . .	13
	Celestia Morse . .	12
	Anthony A. Morse	9
	Chester L. Morse .	7
101.110	Horatio N. Clouse	28
	Olive Clouse . .	56
102.111	Nathan Hills . .	65
	Polly Hills . . .	62
	Silas Hills . . .	23
	Matilda Hills . .	19
	Reuben Dickey .	18
103.112	William Caswell .	47
	Eunice Caswell .	39
	Ethelbert Caswell.	13
	Augustus Caswell	11
	Elmira Caswell .	18
	Amos Caswell . .	9
	Melinda Caswell .	7
	Hannah M. Caswell	4
	Nathaniel Caswell	2
	Oscar Caswell .	8 mo.
104.113	George Silloway .	57
	Charles Stearns .	12
	Amelia Fuller . .	10
	Pardon Robbins .	21
104.114	Eunice Hart . .	35
	Diantha Hart . .	13
	Martha Hart . .	11
105.115	Josiah Hills . . .	61
	Mehitable Hills .	56
	Joel Hills . . .	20
	Enoch Hills . .	20
	Minerva Hills . .	13
	Stephen Hills . .	32
106.116	Jonathan Eastman	63
	Nancy Eastman .	56
	Nancy Eastman .	31
	Elvira Eastman .	29
	Joseph Eastman .	27
	Benjamin Eastman	23
	Louisa Eastman .	21
	Eveline Eastman .	19
	Aug'tine Eastman	17
	Austin Lawrence .	15
107.117	Jonathan Sibley .	77
	William C. Sibley.	43
	Mary McCurdy .	57
	Sarah K. McCurdy	17
	Franklin Fairbanks	16
108.118	Willard Robbins .	50
	Deb'h W. Robbins	49
	Nancy E. Robbins.	26
	Deb'h M. Robbins	21
	Wm. M. Robbins .	19
	Wd. Robbins, jun.	17
	Nathl. A. Robbins	15
	Adelbt. P. Robbins	13
	Augusta A. Robbins	9
	Edwin L. Robbins .	6
109.119	Sylv's H. Peabody	28
	Harriet Peabody .	27
	Lauraette Peabody	3
	Fancina E. Peabody	1
	Cyrenus Peabody,	3 mo.
110.120	Micajah G. Morse .	31
	Elizabeth U. Morse	31
	Helen L. Morse .	5
	Ann E. Morse .	2 mo.
	Jonathan Morse .	74
	Margaret Demuth .	65
111.121	John Little . . .	74
	Sarah Little . .	72
	Lydia Little . .	50
	John M. Little . .	25
112.122	Charles Fogler . .	40
	Martha Fogler . .	47
	Cyrus N. Fogler .	15
	Mary F. Fogler .	13
	John F. Fogler .	11
	Martha Ann Fogler	9
	Edward T. Nye .	24
113.123	Silas Hawes . . .	28
	Margaret Hawes .	24
	Emma F. Hawes	5 mo.
114.124	Isaac C. Hovey .	31
	Roxana N. Hovey	24
	Harriet L. Hovey .	5
	Sarah Hovey . .	2
	James Barker . .	21
115.125	George Fossett .	38
	Sarah Fossett . .	32
	James Fossett . .	9
	George M. Fossett	5
	Abigail Keene . .	19
	Caroline Keene .	20
116.126	John Burkett . .	69
	Abigail Burkett .	63
117.127	Bradley R. Mowry	54
	Rhobe G. Mowry .	49
	Harriet R. Mowry	23
	Emeline H. Mowry	21
	Ann M. Mowry .	21
	Augustus Mowry .	18
	Irene Mowry . .	16
	Oscarene Mowry .	16
	Mortim. H. Mowry	14

	Josephine Mowry .	10
118.128	Ambrose Linniken	24
	Lois A. Linniken .	23
	Ann E. Linniken, 11 mo.	
	Heman Achorn .	15
119.129	Church Burton .	42
	Ann Lewis Burton	39
	Nancy Burton . .	14
	Benjamin Burton .	11
	Mary A. Burton .	9
	Isabel Burton . .	7
	Estella Burton . .	4
	John C. Burton 6 mo.	
	Warren Hills . .	18
	Elizabeth Gay . .	29
120.130	Asa Andrews . .	37
	Selina Andrews .	27
	John H. Andrews.	6
	George A. Andrews	5
	Sarah L. Andrews	2
	Car. A. Andrews, 8 mo.	
	Charles W. Post .	21
	Arav. C. Andrews	20
121.131	Daniel R. Ryan .	19
	Cordelia R. Ryan .	19
	John W. Ryan . 7 mo.	
122.132	John F. Hart . .	54
	Mary Hart . . .	54
	Willard Hart . .	30
	Lucy Ann Hart .	24
	Avery S. Hart . .	23
	Abigail S. Hart .	20
	William Hart . .	16
	John A. Hart . .	14
	Edwin H. Hart .	11
	Miriam Hart . .	82
	Luther Hart . .	75
123.133	Saml. M. Howland	35
	Lydia T. Howland	38
	Abby I. Howland .	12
	Saml. D. Howland	9
	Osgood Howland .	5
124.134	George H. Jones .	34
	Caroline A. Jones .	32
	Caroline S. Jones .	1
125.135	Barzil. G. Whiting	35
	Nancy Whiting .	68
126.136	Jo. Vaughan, jun.	38
	Joanna Vaughan .	37
	Lewis Vaughan .	15
	Celest. A. Vaughan	13
	Helen Vaughan .	11
	Edwin M. Vaughan	9
	Jo. Alb. Vaughan .	6
	Mary F. Vaughan .	4
	Hewet C. Vaughan, 4 mo.	
127.137	John Pardoe . .	36
	Mary Pardoe . .	37
	M. Ellen Pardoe .	6
	John Pardoe, jun. .	5
	Marcus Pardoe . .	3
	Nancy Butler . .	53
128.138	James P. Davis .	22
	Lydia S. Davis . .	17
	Catharine Davis .	52
129.139	Asa Pitcher . . .	43
	Paulina Pitcher .	42
130.140	Lyman Alden . .	41
	Sarah Eliz. Alden .	39
	Helen L. Alden .	13
	Eugene B. Alden .	11
	Lyman M. Alden .	7
	Henry E. Alden .	3
131.141	John Williams . .	36
	Sarah Williams .	34
	George F. Williams	6
	Aug. E. Williams .	3
	Chas. F. Williams .	17
132.142	Phillips C. Harding	50
	Parney Harding .	59
	Francis Harding .	26
	John Harding . .	25
	Abigail C. Harding	21
	Harriet Harding .	19
	Oren Harding . .	22
	John Whittemore .	42
133.143	Joseph Gleason .	48
134.144	Saville Metcalf . .	41
	Lois Metcalf . .	41
	Caroline P. Metcalf	10
	Hannah E. Metcalf	10
	Stephen L. Metcalf	9
	Saville D. Metcalf .	5
	James C. Metcalf .	1
135.145	James B. Morse .	27
	Mary A. Morse .	26
136.146	Edmund Crowell .	43
	Jane W. Crowell .	37
	Edmd. Crowell, jun.	2
	Delia Crowell . .	1
	Mary Martin . .	18
	Albert Tobey . .	15
137.147	Philo Thurston, jun.	30
	Olive Thurston .	31
	Willis E. Thurston, 7 mo.	
138.148	William Gleason .	44

POPULATION.

	Lydia Gleason	43
	Abigail C. Gleason	19
	Micajah Gleason	15
	Hannah I. Gleason	11
	Helen E. Gleason	8
	Edward Gleason	6
139.149	Spencer Walcott	43
	Esther P. Walcott	44
	Hannah Walcott	19
	Loana M. Walcott	14
	Mary A. Walcott	13
	Sanf'd H. Walcott	11
	Joseph D. Walcott	9
	M'tha C. Walcott, 10 mo.	
	Hannah Walcott	75
	Spencer W. Hills	25
140.150	Charles Young	43
	Betsey Young	36
	Rosanna A. Young	15
	George A. Young	6
141.151	Noah S. Rice	37
	Augusta D. Rice	30
	Caroline L. Rice	8
	Henry Clay Rice	6
142.152	James Grinnell	52
	Sarah Grinnell	53
	John Grinnell	26
	Julia M. Grinnell	21
	Royal Grinnell	18
	James A. Grinnell	15
	Laurette Grinnell	9
143.153	Benjamin Walker	62
	Elizabeth Walker	64
	Eliz'th M. Walker	33
144.154	Simon M. Thompson	42
	D. W. P. Thompson	16
145.155	Phinehas Butler	62
	Silence Butler	57
	Phinehas W. Butler	16
146.156	Charles Sumner	58
	Nancy Sumner	53
	Hannah F. Sumner	30
	Wm. O. Sumner	28
	Eliz'th M. Sumner	26
	James S. Sumner	24
	Jane R. Sumner	22
	Irene V. Sumner	19
	Charles J. Sumner	17
	Priscilla D. Sumner	13
	Lucy A. Sumner	11
	Geo. F. D. Sumner	8
147.157	John Kimball	44
	M'garet J. Kimball	41
	Nathl. M. Kimball	14
	John L. Kimball	11
	Banning P. Kimball	8
	Myra A. Kimball	4
148.158	George W. Butler	41
	Eleanor Butler	41
	Susan R. Butler	17
	Mary Ann Butler	15
	Hosea C. Butler	13
	John S. Butler	11
	Albert E. Butler	8
149.159	Matthias Butler	25
	Liana E. Butler	19
	Amina C. Butler	3
	Azelia M. Butler	1
150.160	Sarah Butler	54
	Harriet Morton	11
	Ephraim U. Butler	20
151.161	Israel Barker	47
	Mary Barker	43
	Marston Barker	14
	Mary E. Barker	11
	Wm. H. H. Barker	9
	Julia M. Barker	6
152.162	Story Thompson	33
	Hannah Thompson	33
	Elias R. Thompson	10
	Julia A. Thompson	7
	Gilb. M. Thompson	3
	C. S. Thompson	1
	William Harriman	44
	Amb'se Thompson	20
	John Thompson	57
	Martha Thompson	62
153.163	James Thompson	46
	Harriet Thompson	41
	Solomon Thompson	20
	Erast. C. Thompson	16
	Aug'tine Thompson	14
	Lucy E. Thompson	11
	Martha J. Thompson	10
	Lewis Thompson	7
154.164	Nathan Whitney	50
	Clarissa Whitney	39
155.165	Thomas C. Nye	37
	Amanda J. Nye	30
	Emma A. Nye	8
	Vienna C. Stetson	23
	Anna Nye	73
156.166	Charles F. Blake	35
	Jane Blake	65
	Emily R. B. Dorman	40
	Theron Blake	27

UNITED STATES CENSUS.

157.167	Caleb Maddocks .	49
	Nancy Maddocks .	57
	Geo. L. Maddocks .	23
	Angeline Maddocks	17
	Ira Maddocks . .	19
	Aaron Maddocks .	18
	Nancy Maddocks .	15
	Susan'h Maddocks	13
158.168	Henry Butler . .	38
	Mary Butler . .	40
	Thomas J. Butler .	11
	Rhoda Butler . .	5
	Huldah T. Butler, 3 mo.	
	Geo. L. Maddocks	22
159.169	Moses Hawes . .	33
	Lucinda Hawes .	30
	Elizabeth Libbey .	67
	Sarah Jackson . .	15
	Rosanna Fuller .	4
160.170	Abigail Stewart .	65
161.171	Oren O. Stewart .	30
	Mary A. Stewart .	30
162.172	Waldron S. Butler	49
	Harriet Butler . .	32
	O. Nelson Butler .	9
	Eben. Ed. Butler .	8
	Thomas Butler .	1
	Jeruel Butler . .	47
163.173	Thomas Butler . .	80
164.174	Ebenezer Blunt .	54
	Susan Blunt . .	52
	Mary A. Blunt . .	19
	Martha Blunt . .	17
	Betsey Blunt . .	16
	Oscar Blunt . .	7
165.175	Jacob Sibley . .	73
	Abigail Sibley . .	71
166.176	Ebenezer B. Sibley	32
	Melea Sibley . .	24
	Lucy A. Sibley .	4
	Franklin E. Sibley	3
	E. Florena Sibley, 7 mo.	
	Dudley Farnham .	20
167.177	Thomas J. Blunt .	25
	Nancy Blunt . .	21
	Eliza F. Blunt . .	2
	Martha A. Blunt .	1
	Daniel Clark . .	20
168.178	Wm. D. Stewart .	42
	Maria Stewart . .	40
	Harriet Stewart .	15
	Sarah Stewart . .	12
	Cyrus G. Stewart .	10
	Wm. M. Stewart .	7
	Ann M. Stewart .	1
169.179	Eunice Lincoln .	50
	Lemuel Lincoln .	17
	Alvan Lincoln . .	14
	Berthana Lincoln .	12
	Joshua Lincoln .	10
	Eldora G. Lincoln .	2
170.180	Willard Lucas . .	44
	Anna Lucas . . .	40
	Mary F. Lucas . .	20
	Austin Lucas . .	18
	Amanda Lucas .	16
	Martha A. Lucas .	13
	Eliza F. Lucas . .	11
	Harrison F. Lucas .	4
171.181	Ebenez. McPheters	42
	Sarah McPheters .	30
	Albert McPheters, 9 mo.	
	Ellen Jameson . .	5
172.182	John Lanfest . .	28
	Lavinia Lanfest .	21
	Matilda A. Lanfest	1
173.183	Andrew P. Gilman	40
	Sarah Gilman . .	35
	Andrew Gilman .	17
	Nathl. P. Gilman .	15
	Alexander Gilman	8
	Mary E. Gilman .	5
	Flora Gilman . .	2
174.184	Stillman Nye . .	27
	Emily B. M. Nye .	21
175.185	Obadiah Harris .	54
	Mary Harris . .	54
	Herman Harris .	22
	Wm. S. Harris . .	20
	Isaac S. Harris . .	14
176.186	Ziba Simmons . .	60
	Hannah Simmons .	49
	Hervey B. Simmons	21
	Mary Wentworth .	15
	Martha J. Jameson	8
177.187	Mary Simmons . .	54
	Moses L. Simmons	25
	Luther L. Simmons	23
	Angenon Simmons	17
178.188	Herman Mero . .	29
	Electa A. Mero .	25
	Arthur L. Mero .	2
179.189	John Lindley . .	38
	M'garet L. Lindley	38
	Catharine J. Lindley	13
	Rienzi M. Lindley	11

POPULATION.

	Name	Age
	Ada A. Lindley	9
	Wm. L. Lindley	6
	John W. Lindley	2
	Eliza Lindley	1 mo.
180.190	John W. Lindley	67
	Lucy W. Lindley	66
	Charles Walter	24
181.191	Isley Martin	44
	Eliza Martin	45
	George Y. Martin	13
	Sarah Martin	11
	Adam Martin	75
	Mary Martin	67
	Francis Sennott	19
182.192	Spencer Mero	57
	Esther Mero	53
	Elisha H. Mero	23
	Spencer Mero, jun.	20
	Sarah F. Mero	17
	Anson Mero	14
	Chester Mero	9
183.193	Benj. Litchfield	68
	Nancy Litchfield	58
	Alden Litchfield	19
	Silas C. Litchfield	16
	Helen A. Coombs	11
	John H. Coombs	9
	Nancy A. Coombs	7
	Hannah Libbey	16
184.194	Marlboro' Packard	46
	Mary A. Packard	42
	Nathan Packard	17
	Benaiah Packard	14
	Martin Packard	12
	Mary C. Packard	10
	Franklin C. Packard	8
	Wm. Allen Packard	5
	Edward T. Packard	3
	Selinda S. Packard	1
	Emily A. Decoster	21
185.195	Seth Miller	52
	Mary Miller	43
	Love Miller	8
	Laura Miller	7
	Lewella Miller	6
	Roscoe Miller	3
	Granville Miller	1
186.196	Joseph Cushman	56
	Eleanor Cushman	59
	Henry T. Cushman	28
	Daniel B. Cushman	22
	Alma F. Cushman	16
	Ezra W. Curtis	11
187.197	Seth M. Cushman	32
	Lucy A. Cushman	21
	H'riet V. Cushman	6 mo.
	H'riet M. Sidelinger	12
188.198	Jedidiah Morse	34
	Rebecca B. Morse	28
	Alenzer F. Morse	3
189.199	Sarah Rice	66
190.200	Edward Clary	
	Nancy Clary	
	Caroline Clary	5
	Josephine Clary	4
	Silas H. Clary	8 mo.
	Betsey Tuck	58
191.201	Leonard Barnard	49
	Nancy Barnard	49
	Charles A. Barnard	25
	Ira Barnard	23
	Clarissa Barnard	20
	Delora Barnard	18
	Edward Barnard	15
192.202	Michael N. Filer	33
	Sarah C. Filer	28
	Mary C. Filer	2 mo.
193.203	Suell Cummings	61
	Sophia Cummings	50
	Lydia M. Cummings	25
	Maria Cummings	20
	Delana Cummings	18
	Nancy Cummings	16
	Suell Cummings	13
	Wm. A. Cummings	8
194.204	Joseph Irish	33
	Cordelia Irish	32
	Milton Irish	9
	Mary E. Irish	3
	George A. Irish	9 mo.
195.205	Cornelius Irish	68
	Polly Irish	68
196.206	Ebenez. W. Adams	62
	Mima Adams	58
	Olivia D. Adams	31
	Esther A. Adams	23
	Maryan D. Adams	22
	Polly Ripley	60
197.207	Otis Hawes	57
	Elsie Hawes	53
	Philander Hawes	22
	Cyrene Hawes	17
	Laurinda Hawes	14
	Edwin Hawes	10
	Charles B. Hawes	8
	Julia Hawes	20

UNITED STATES CENSUS. 89

198.208	Sarah Hawes	85
	Julia Hawes	52
199.209	Moses Luce	35
	Sarah Luce	35
	Seth Luce	9
	Elizabeth M. Luce	7
	Remember Luce	60
	Almond Thompson	24
200.210	Caleb Howard	70
	Betsey Howard	51
	George Howard	23
201.211	Richard Sayward	67
	Eliza Sayward	68
	Richd. K. Sayward	30
	Perez B. Sayward	25
	Christiana Mitchell	19
	Henry Mitchell	13
202.212	Daniel Shepard	74
	Alice Shepard	75
	John A. Shepard	45
	Eliza Shepard	43
	Wm. Shepard	41
	Elsie Shepard	34
	Daniel Shepard	33
	Amanda Shepard	30
203.213	Albert Fuller	36
	Nancy Fuller	37
	Isaac F. Fuller	11
	Mary E. Fuller	9
	Lucy Fuller	7
	James C. Fuller	5
	Albert J. Fuller	1
204.214	Geo. W. Sidelinger	28
	Eliz. J. Sidelinger	26
	Jacob Sidelinger	4
	Sarah J. Sidelinger	2
	Ara. W. Sidelinger	1
	Edw.A.Sidelinger,	1 mo.
205.215	Moses Sidelinger	35
	Jane A. Sidelinger	29
	Angelet. Sidelinger	10
	Mary J. Sidelinger	7
	M'garet Sidelinger	5
	Ever't B. Sidelinger	3
	C'line L. Sidelinger	1
	Martha Ripley	13
	George Ripley	23
206.216	Daniel Sidelinger	62
	Caroline Sidelinger	18
	E. A. G. Sidelinger	16
	SimonM.Sidelinger	14
	H'rietM.Sidelinger	13
	Mary E. Sidelinger	9
	Henry F.Sidelinger	7
	Hez. H. Sidelinger	4
207.217	Daniel Ripley	57
	Gardner Ripley	21
208.218	John Hagar	33
	Jane Hagar	27
	Emily J. Hagar	8
	Ann S. Hagar	6
	John E. Hagar	4
	Edwin L. Hagar	2
	Samuel Hagar	9 mo.
209.219	Martha Philbrook	34
	Charles Philbrook	4
	Jos. F. Philbrook,	10 mo.
210.220	Lewis Law	33
	Lydia Law	26
	Norris M. Law	3
211.221	Sewell Hagar	56
	Eleanor Hagar	44
	Mary Hagar	14
	Ezekiel Hagar	11
	Martha Hagar	9
	George A. Hagar	7
	Franklin Weever	20
212.222	Ebenez. Sidelinger	46
	C'harine Sidelinger	47
	Sarah Sidelinger	24
	Robt. M. Sidelinger	23
	Andrew Sidelinger	21
	Spencer Sidelinger	19
	L'ciusH.Sidelinger	17
	James Sidelinger	15
	Ann M. Sidelinger	13
	Daniel Sidelinger	10
	Manuel Sidelinger	8
	Miles Sidelinger	6
	Ira Sidelinger	2
213.223	Benjamin L. Law	67
	Esther Law	61
	Charles P. Law	39
	Benjamin Law	37
	Franklin Law	33
	Stephen Law	28
	Henry Law	26
	Harriet Law	22
	Rebecca Law	19
214.224	Ebenezer Daggett	52
	Salome Daggett	45
	Charles M. Daggett	16
	C'tine C. Daggett	14
	Darius Daggett	12
	Harriet D. Daggett	10
	Lucius C. Daggett	7

POPULATION.

	Angelia Daggett	3		Almatia W. Robbins	17
215.225	E. N. Butler	41	225.235	Reuben Hagar	41
	Mary Butler	44		Nancy Hagar	36
	Susan M. Butler	16		Chester Hagar	9
	Harriet P. Butler	14		Westford Hagar	7
	George A. Butler	12		Norris Hagar	5
	Mary E. Butler	10		Eldon Hagar	1
	Wm. H. H. Butler	8	226.236	Thaddeus Shepard	71
	Amelia M. Butler	6		Susan Shepard	61
	Charles Tripp	33		Noah E. Shepard	28
	Catharine Butler	73		James E. Shepard	15
216.226	John Burns, jun.	44		George Shepard	11
	Lucy Burns	8		Mary Shepard	9
	Thomas Hagar	29		Nathan Shepard	60
	Esther Hagar	22	227.237	Thad. S. Shepard	37
	Mercy Jones	62		Sarah S. Shepard	30
	Llewellyn Burns	16		George Howard	21
217.227	Alfred Adams	60	228.238	Mace Shepard	40
	Esther Page	52		Martha J. Shepard	41
	Ruth Adams	45		Martha J. Shepard	8
	Jas. Orson Adams	33	229.239	Daniel D. Law	49
	Joel Adams, jun.	11		Jane L. Law	37
218.228	Thaddeus Luce	67		Mary P. Law	14
	Lavinia Luce	64		Frederic Law	7
	Maria Luce	28		Jas. Thomas, jun.	19
	Rosilla Luce	23	230.240	Silas P. Law	33
	Sullivan B. Luce	21		Sarah Law	33
	Ann C. Gleason	3 mo.		Albert Law	10
219.229	Abigail Cole	51	231.241	Stephen Carriel	47
	Mary A. Cole	14		Jane Carriel	48
	Joseph E. Cole	9		Sylvester B. Carriel	22
220.230	Robert Dickey	27		Leander T. Carriel	19
	Sarah A. Dickey	21		Adelia W. Carriel	17
	Joseph K. Dickey,	7 mo.		Augustus G. Carriel	10
	Isaac Rackliffe	14		Albion D. Carriel	6
221.231	Vinal Ware	60	232.242	John Stevens	56
	Lavinia A. Ware	49		Mary Stevens	39
	Harriet M. Ware	17		Armina Pease	15
	Erastus Ware	15		Sumner Pease	13
	Lucy Tuck	70		Gilbert Pease	12
	Sarah Brown	65		Mary J. Stevens	3
	Emeline Crabtree	24		Harriet Stevens	19
222.232	David Seavey	38		John S. Stevens	17
	Sarah A. Seavey	32	233.243	Nathl. G. Lothrop	46
223.233	Nathan D. Rice	64		Betsey E. Lothrop	46
	Eliza Carriel	46		Julia A. Lothrop	13
	James Kieff	22		Harriet E. Lothrop	11
	Dennie Stetson	16		Elijah Lothrop	10
224.234	Cyrus Robbins	51		Sarah Lothrop	9
	Olivia Robbins	56		Alden Lothrop	6
	Eber A. Robbins	23	234.244	Parker Messer	49
	Olivia V. Robbins	20		Eliza Messer	45
	Laurilla A. Robbins	18		Robert M. Messer	21

UNITED STATES CENSUS. 91

	Charles H. Messer	17
	Ambrose Messer	14
	Eliza E. Messer	2
235.245	Nancy Bryant	47
	Jacob S. Bryant	21
	Joseph Bryant	18
	Nancy J. Bryant	16
	Abby M. Bryant	10
	John F. Bryant	9
236.246	Daniel Walker, jun.	37
	Lydia Walker	41
	Jason Walker	14
	George P. Walker	12
	Catharine Walker	10
	Lucinda Walker	7
	Martha A. Walker	4
	Levi Walker	2
237.247	Danford Carriel	40
	Harriet N. Carriel	35
	Rachel H. Carriel	3
	Flora R. Carriel	1
	Jonathan Carriel	67
	Sybil Carriel	63
238.248	Martha Carriel	56
	Olive Carriel	46
239.249	John Walker	74
	Sarah Walker	72
	John Walker, jun.	33
	Eliz'th B. Walker	27
	John C. Cromett	8
240.250	Cyrus Robbins, jun.	27
	Margaret Robbins	27
	Eldred Robbins	4 mo.
	Nelson Burns	17
	Joel Burns	12
	Lucinda Burns	23
	Augustus Burns	21
	Henry Burns	19
	John Burns	72
	Margaret Burns	62
241.251	Daniel Walker	76
	Fanny Walker	71
	Fanny Achorn	46
	Eliz'th B. Achorn	18
	Elisha Achorn	20
	Jacob B. Achorn	13
	Daniel Achorn	6
242.252	George Cox	27
	Fanny Cox	23
	Mary M. Cox	6
	John W. Cox	3
	Wm. A. J. Leach	3
243.253	John Taylor	42
	Maria Taylor	37
	Frances O. Taylor	16
	Elsie G. Taylor	14
	Lindall R. Taylor	12
	George B. Taylor	10
	Sarah M. Taylor	1
244.254	Samuel Fuller, jun.	34
	Eliza Fuller	22
	Wm. E. Fuller	5
	Abigail A. Fuller	4
	Flora I. Fuller	2
	M'garet A. Fuller	2 mo.
245.255	Samuel Fuller	62
	Jemima Fuller	58
	Sarah J. Fuller	22
	Rhoda Fuller	21
	Fisher H. Fuller	27
	Charles Fuller	15
	Lewis Law	6
246.256	Pond Davis	46
	Betsey Davis	42
	Wm. L. Davis	19
	Angeline M. Davis	16
	Helen E. Davis	13
	Elsie A. Davis	10
	Ada F. Davis	7
	Mercy D. Davis	5
	Hannah A. Davis	2
	Jacob P. Davis	83
247.257	Asaph Lucas	65
	Hannah Lucas	64
	John O. Lucas	10
	Hannah Grinnell	43
248.258	Edwin Lucas	43
	Phebe Lucas	30
	Willard Lucas	12
	John O. Lucas	10
	Armeda A. Lucas	6
	Auga. Blake Lucas	4
	Mary A. Lucas	8 mo.
249.259	Olney Titus	77
	Abigail Titus	75
250.260	Philo Thurston	55
	Julia M. Thurston	51
	Nathan'l Thurston	23
	Jo. D. Thurston	20
	Harl. W. Thurston	13
	Darwin Thurston	7
251.261	Albert Thurston	26
	Lavinia Thurston	25
	Chas. A. Thurston	1
	Rhoda Fuller	21
252.262	Hugh Gordon	40

POPULATION.

	Margaret Gordon	27
	Angelia S. Gordon	16
253.263	Nathan Bachelder	49
	Jane Bachelder	49
	Nath. A. Bachelder	22
	Llew. F. Bachelder	21
	Ama. E. Bachelder	17
	Austin E. Bachelder	15
	L'cius F. Bachelder	13
	Adelaide Bachelder	11
	Electa Bachelder	9
	George Bachelder	2
	Edward Taylor	27
	Mary Taylor	23
254.264	Amos Barrett	70
	Harriet R. Barrett	42
255.265	Benj. Bachelder	29
	Ann Bachelder	26
	Ann R. Bachelder	4
	Rachl. N. Bachelder	2
	Sarah A. Bachelder	21
256.266	Jesse Arnold	32
	Mary J. Arnold	31
	Thomas E. Arnold	8
	Alfred E. Arnold	4
	Helen Arnold	2
257.267	Nathaniel Clark	44
	Betsey A. Clark	42
	Harriet A. Clark	17
	Sarah P. Clark	15
	Martha E. Clark	14
	Octavius L. Clark	10
	Julia F. Clark	8
	Nathl. S. Clark	2
258.268	Japheth Gove	44
	Nancy Gove	42
	Williston F. Gove	23
	Antoinette Gove	21
	James Gove	18
	Olivia Gove	15
	Charles Gove	10
	George Gove	3
	Harriet Young	24
	Edward McLean	19
	Joseph Carkin	19
259.269	John Bachelder	59
	Julia Bachelder	53
	H'riet L. Bachelder	24
	John M. Bachelder	21
	F'ces V. Bachelder	18
	Chas. G. Bachelder	16
	Eliza M. Bachelder	14
	Mary C. Bachelder	12
260.270	Franklin Rice	32
	Patience M. Rice	28
	Albert A. Rice	5
	Helen E. Rice	1
	Wm. M. Robbins	19
261.271	Josiah Shepard	30
	Statira Shepard	23
	Susan C. Shepard	1
262.272	Nathan M. Gleason	44
	Charles Gleason	17
	Sarah A. Gleason	15
	Eliza M. Gleason	11
	Maria Gleason	1
263.273	David N. Oakes	69
	Mary Oakes	62
	Mary Oakes	36
	Nancy Oakes	34
	Martha Oakes	21
	David N. Oakes	19
	C. Sumner Oakes	27
264.274	William Coggan	46
	Mary Coggan	39
	Ethelda Coggan	20
	Emily B. Coggan	16
	Deborah M. Coggan	13
	Esther F. Coggan	10
	Alanson M. Coggan	9
	William Oxton	23
	William Thompson	42
265.275	Robert Thompson	50
	Charity Thompson	40
	Jedidah Thompson	21
	M'cellus Thompson	18
	Ellen A. Thompson	17
	Laura E. Thompson	16
	H'riet A. Thompson	9
266.276	Charles Hibbard	44
	Lydia P. Hibbard	40
	Daniel Hibbard	18
	Hollis Hibbard	16
	Cyrus Hibbard	13
	Chas. W. Hibbard	11
	Parker M. Hibbard	7
	James R. Hibbard	3
267.277	Alexr. Suchfort	29
	Mary Suchfort	23
	Hannah Suchfort	3
	John G. Suchfort, 1 mo.	
	Elizabeth Coombs	15
268.278	John Proctor	53
	Clarissa Proctor	48
	Philander Proctor	12
	Adelbert Proctor	10

UNITED STATES CENSUS.

	Elvira Proctor	16
	Mary Proctor	19
	Sarah Roakes	27
269.279	Rebecca Metcalf	58
270.280	Judson Caswell	53
	Mercy Caswell	38
	Hannah Caswell	18
	John C. Caswell	16
	Lemuel Caswell	14
	Lozeah Caswell	11
	Mary O. Caswell	8
	Christiana A. Caswell	6
	Caroline E. Caswell	3
271.281	Elias Skidmore	51
	Priscilla Skidmore	52
	Elias Skidmore	25
	Gardner Skidmore	23
	Emily F. Skidmore	16
	Thos. W. Pinkham	14
	Roderic G. Newhall	6
272.282	Walter W. Clark	54
	Joanna Clark	44
	Ellen A. Clark	20
	Henry D. Clark	18
	Ezra B. Clark	16
	Isaac M. Clark	14
	James A. Clark	9
273.283	Alpheus Collamore	68
	Chloe Collamore	57
	Richard Collamore	23
	Mary Collamore	20
	Andrew J. Collamore	17
	Elias A. Collamore	1
	Elmina P. Roakes	21
274.284	John Jones, 2d	53
	Sally Jones	49
	Martha M. Jones	25
	William M. Jones	24
	John F. Jones	23
	Albert M. Jones	20
	Leander Jones	17
	Licona Jones	15
	George M. Jones	12
	Benson G. Jones	10
275.285	Samuel Norwood	33
	Sibyl Norwood	30
	Lysander Norwood	10
	Sarah Norwood	8
	Lucretia Norwood	6
	Orlando Norwood	3
	Llewellyn Norwood	1
276.286	Henry M. Collier	35
	Mahala Collier	30
	Helen M. Collier	1
	James Upham	12
277.287	Robert M. Pease	52
	Sarah Pease	51
	Zilpah H. Pease	19
	Lucy A. Pease	17
	Austin L. Pease	15
	Helen A. Pease	5
278.288	Benjamin Frye	46
	Nancy Frye	46
	Job Frye	42
279.289	James Roakes	26
	Lois Roakes	26
	Susan Roakes	1
280.290	Asa Gowen	39
	Hannah Gowen	38
	Harriet Ellen Gowen	14
	Abby Electa Gowen	9
	Hannah A. Gowen	4
	William Stevens	5
	Benjamin Dow	87
281.291	John Gowen	69
	Rebecca H. Gowen	69
282.292	David Fossett	42
	Martha A. Fossett	33
	Henry M. Fossett	12
	Mary E. Fossett	9
	Sarah Fossett	6
	Julia Fossett	2
	George Miller	62
283.293	Samuel Fossett	29
	Mary A. Fossett	26
	Isaac H. Fossett	4
	Caroline M. Fossett	2
284.294	Nathan Knowlton	31
	Mary Knowlton	27
	Leonora Knowlton	1
285.295	Henry Fossett, jun.	34
	Amanda Fossett	23
	Oscar Fossett	3
	Mary E. Fossett	1
286.296	Enoch Weeks	25
	Ruth A. Weeks	19
287.297	Henry Fossett	67
	Thomas C. Fossett	38
	Abigail Fossett	33
	Ellen Fossett	1
288.298	Josiah Simmons	27
	Rachel Simmons	30
	James H. Simmons	8
	Hannah D. Simmons	4
	Ra. M. Simmons, 8 mo.	
	Eliza Jane Davis	20

289.299	Oliver Townsend	30			Francis M. Adams	6
	Nancy Townsend	22			Samuel S. Adams	2
	Georgiana Townsend	2			Jerh. W. Mitchell	15
	R. O. Townsend, 7 mo.			301.311	Minot Messer	45
290.300	Samuel Stone	63			Lydia Messer	41
	Elizabeth Stone	50			John B. Messer	23
	Elmira A. Stone	17			Caroline H. Messer	21
	Roscoe Stone	11			Samuel L. Messer	19
	Augusta Stone	9			Thomas G. Messer	16
291.301	Job C. Simmons	34			Vinal Messer	14
	Clarissa Simmons	36			Lydia A. Messer	11
	Harriet Simmons	9			Hannah M. Messer	11
	George Simmons	7			Eliza Messer	10
	Henry Simmons	5			Margaret M. Messer	8
	James Simmons	3			Emeline Messer	5
	Sarah E. Simmons	1			Aravilla B. Messer	1
	A. M. Simmons, 8 mo.				Phebe Messer	79
292.302	George M. Fossett	32		302.312	Ebenezer S. Messer	37
	Sarah A. Fossett	26			Nancy S. Messer	38
	Stephen H. Fossett	5			Laura Messer	13
	Margaret M. Fossett	2			Charles H. Messer	11
	Martha F. Fossett	1			Emma P. Messer	9
293.303	Zebedee Simmons	23			Mary Messer	6
	Margaret Simmons	30			Amanda Messer	1
	John E. R. Simmons	1			John Brown	19
	C. A. Z. Simmons, 2 mo.				Hannah Messer	75
294.304	George B. Daggett	25			Hannah Messer	41
	Mary J. Daggett	25		303.313	Nathaniel B. Gowen	27
	Amelia Burns	9			Elizabeth H. Gowen	21
295.305	Isaac Upham	70		304.314	Sarah A. Hart	12
	Eliza T. Upham	60			Richard Moody	32
	Eliza F. Upham	19			Sarah Moody	30
296.306	John Upham	30			William Moody	8
	Mary A. Upham	27			Mahala Moody	5
	Euphemia A. Upham	1			Eldora Moody	9 mo.
	Warren C. Upham	14			Harriet Moody	11
	Abigail Bruce	61		305.315	Benjamin Clark	57
297.307	Joseph M. Gleason	41			Eliza Clark	49
	Frances Gleason	42			Chandler Brackett	20
	Jane A. Gleason	11		306.316	Silas Carriel	41
	William C. Gleason	9			Sally Carriel	37
	Martha A. Gleason	3			Woodbury Carriel	9
	Harris Lanfest	23			Martha Carriel	8
298.308	Rufus Stone	24			Aldana Carriel	6
	Silvia G. Stone	24		307.317	James Bryant	50
	William Caswell	16			Charlotte Bryant	55
299.309	John Oakes	39			Silas C. Bryant	23
	Ellen Oakes	46			David Bryant	20
	Sanford Mero	15			Arvilla Bryant	16
	Maria Jameson	11		308.318	Joseph Wheaton	60
300.310	John Adams	31			Mary Wheaton	60
	Rachel Adams	29		309.319	Aaron Bryant	42
	Thomas M. Adams	8			Emeline Bryant	42

UNITED STATES CENSUS.

	Wm. H. Bryant	17
	Mary E. Bryant	15
	Delphina G. Bryant	14
	Sarah Bryant	13
	Phebe J. Bryant	11
	Martha A. Bryant	9
	Julia E. Bryant	5
	James F. Bryant	2
310.320	Nathan Clark	47
	Mary M. Clark	46
	Elizabeth O'Meira	17
	Gilbert Pitman	43
	Edson S. Stevens	3
	Enoch B. Evans	25
311.321	Isaac Townsend	69
	Sarah Townsend	66
	Caroline Townsend	19
	Martha Townsend	26
312.322	Isaac Townsend	32
	Fanny Townsend	31
	Mary O. Townsend	3
	E. E. Townsend,	9 mo.
313.323	John Robinson	57
	Harriet Robinson	43
	Darius Robinson	18
	Stillman Robinson	16
	Horatio Robinson	14
	Elvina Robinson	15
	Delano Robinson	9
	Alonzo Robinson	7
	Oramil Robinson	5
314.324	Orris Blood	39
	Maria Blood	40
	Delora A. Blood	11
	Josiah Drake	19
	Jesse Drake	7
	Miriam H. Blood,	8 mo.
	Lewis Robbins	16
315.325	Cyrus Morton	45
	Sally Morton	38
	James G. Morton	18
	C. Roscoe Morton	13
	Sarah F. Morton	11
	Ann M. Morton	6
	John C. Morton	8
	Nancy J. Morton	2
316.326	Calvin Gleason	35
	Abigail S. Gleason	29
	Helen C. Gleason	8
	Moses S. Gleason	6
	John A. Gleason	3
	John Brown	18
	Cyrenus Daggett	19
317.327	Sally Gleason	67
	Caroline McKinney	16
318.328	James Townsend	35
	Mary F. Townsend	28
	Aldana S. Townsend	11
	Geo. W. Townsend	9
	F. L. Townsend	7
	Jas. A. Townsend	4
	Oceana M. Townsend	1
319.329	Artemas Shepard	73
	Martha Shepard	50
	Benjamin Smith	18
320.330	Leonard Wade	77
	Sally Wade	70
	Sarah Daggett	43
	Mary E. Daggett	6
321.331	John Tobey	82
	Melicent Tobey	52
	Elkanah M. Wingate	28
	Helen M. Wingate	22
322.332	N. Thurston, jun.	25
	Ann E. Thurston	25
	Ella M. Thurston	1
	Nahum Thurston	58
	Martha Thurston	61
	Caroline A. Thurston	21
	Martha A. Thurston	23
323.333	George Luce	39
	Patience Luce	36
	Frances M. Luce	10
	Charles B. Luce	8
	Joseph F. Gleason	16
324.334	Robert Dickey	74
	Mary Dickey	64
325.335	Madan K. Payson	26
	Abigail A. Payson	28
	Lauriston M. Payson	3
	Matilda L. Payson	1
326.336	John P. Robbins	56
	Mary Robbins	58
	Almina Robbins	17
327.337	Jason Robbins	50
	Lucy Robbins	51
	Clementine Robbins	17
	Alphonso Robbins	14
	Jason Robbins	11
	Lycurgus Robbins	6
	Jessa Robbins	91
328.338	George Cummings	50
	Avis Cummings	50
	Loam. D. Cummings	20
	Geo. E. Cummings	18
	Plympton Cummings	12

96   POPULATION.

	Rosanna Cummings	73		Martha Rollins	17
	Hannah Hills	22	335.345	Napoleon Bemis	40
329.339	Henry Seiders	51		Fairezina Bemis	40
	Mary S. Seiders	42		Elizabeth A. Bemis	8
	Mary Jane Seiders	21		John Robinson	18
	Margaret S. Seiders	16	336.346	Joseph G. Cummings	35
	Joseph Seiders	14		Margaret Cummings	32
	Edward Seiders	13		Amos Cummings	9
	Emerson Seiders	11		Avis M. Cummings	5
	Sarah L. Seiders	8		Samuel L. Cummings	3
	G. Melvin Seiders	6		S. E. Cummings, 9 mo.	
	Frederic A. Seiders	2	337.347	Stephen S. Hawes	40
330.340	Waterm. M. Robbins	27		Alzina Hawes	41
	David Robbins	62		Aravesta M. Hawes	19
	Hannah E. Robbins	29		Aravilla A. Hawes	19
	Nancy M. Robbins	23		Marietta B. Hawes	8
	Caroline M. Robbins	22		Abigail S. Hawes	1
	Maxcy Robbins	20	338.348	Lewis Bachelder	53
	Ermina G. Robbins	18		Hannah Bachelder	53
	Lydia A. Robbins	14		Edwin A. Bachelder	16
331.341	Whiting Hawes	56	339.349	Benjamin Bryant	45
	Julia Hawes	52		Betsey Bryant	45
	Nancy Hawes	66		Benjamin Bryant	16
	Norman L. Crockett	13		John Bryant	14
332.342	William G. Hawes	39		Lucy Bryant	10
	Roxana Hawes	38		Llewella Bryant	8
	Herbert A. Hawes	11		Thomas Bryant	6
	Henry A. Hawes	9		Maria Bryant	4
	Edwin R. Hawes	7		Mary Bryant	1
	Phebe R. Hawes	1		Mary Bryant	25
	Emery R. Hawes	4		Elizabeth M. Hills	11
	James O'Meira	19		Abner Bills	26
	Julia A. McAllister	16		Timothy Alexander	23
333.343	Herman Hawes	66		John Thompson	31
	Abigail Hawes	67		Lucretia Rice	20
334.344	Manning Walcott	37		Catharine Robbins	18
	Mary Walcott	35		Lysander Daggett	19
	Herman H. Walcott	12		Emeline Hills	30
	Edgar H. Walcott	8		Nathl. Q. Bachelder	23

Total number of inhabitants, 1,970; including 1 blind, 5 idiots, 6 insane, 3 paupers, 139 mechanics, 430 farmers. There are no colored persons.

Maine is the birthplace of nearly all the inhabitants. The following are exceptions: Nova Scotia, 1; New Brunswick, 2; Ireland, 2; England, 1; New Hampshire, 36; Vermont, 1; Massachusetts, 115; Rhode Island, 5; Connecticut, 3; New York, 2; Kentucky, 1.

CHAPTER XII.

MINERAL AND ARBORAL PRODUCTS.

Minerals. — Timber. — Felling of Trees. — Burning of Cut-downs. — Shingles. — Benjamin Speed. — Lakin. — Boards and Saw-mills. — Lime-casks.

MINERAL PRODUCTS.

There has never been a mineralogical or geological survey of the town worthy of even a passing notice. What treasures may lie buried here can only be known when greater attention is given to the subject. It is certain, however, that there are quarries of limestone, some of which is white and fine grained; but large pieces, free from defects and veins, have not hitherto been obtained. The burning of lime never has received much attention. There are also quarries of granite. Sulphureous iron ore, from which are derived sulphur, alum, copperas, sulphuric acid, &c. is found in immense quantities, particularly in the eastern part of the town. A web of cloth, which had been laid upon the ground to be whitened, was buried under an autumnal snow; and, when it was dug out some time afterward, it had acquired a beautiful copperas color. East of Crawford's Pond, on the land of Christopher Young, is a mineral spring which blackens leaves at its bottom; and crystallized copperas is formed on logs which lie in it. In surveying the county line a few years ago, the magnetic needle was so much disturbed for a mile or two on Appleton Ridge that it was of little or no use.

ARBORAL PRODUCTS.

Timber. — When the first settlers came, the land, particularly the section of it which lies east of Seventree Pond, was covered with an uncommonly heavy growth of timber. Pine, hemlock, spruce, fir, grew abundantly on what was called by the early settlers the "black land" or low ground; and on the ridges or higher ground were beech, red oak, birch, maple, ash, &c. There was but little white oak, and that was on the intervales. There was no walnut or chestnut. With the early settlers, it was a great object to obtain land for cultivation. Lumber was so abundant that "it would not half pay the expense of getting it out." Consequently, trees were recklessly and wantonly destroyed, and forests of as good timber as ever grew were burnt on the ground.

FELLING OF TREES. — Among some of the early settlers, there was a custom of girdling large trees and cutting out large chips beneath the bark, which was removed. The smaller growth of wood and the underbrush were cleared out, so that the land could be cultivated; and the girdled trees were left to die, and to fall as they decayed. This mode of clearing was not common.

Another mode was generally adopted by persons who felled trees by the acre. The chopper observed the direction in which they leaned and could be made to fall advantageously. He selected a range, at the head of which was a large tree, a little elevated, with branching, heavy limbs, to be used as a "driver." The trees were then cut about half through, and the chips so taken out, that, when the trees fell, the tops would lie in an angular direction towards each other along the whole range. The "driver," being then cut through, fell upon the next trees, and these in turn upon the next, and so on till the whole range came down with a tremendous crash. Thus half the labor was saved, and the tops were brought together in a favorable position to be burnt.

BURNING OF CUT-DOWNS. — After the trees had been left to dry through a considerable part of the season, the "cut-down," or "fell-piece," was set on fire. The smoke gathered over the burning materials, and the fire raged till an immense black cloud hung over the spot and rolled off, indicating for many miles the destruction which was going on. In one place, the fire, when it encountered a pile of dry limbs and leaves, might be seen suddenly starting up to a great height; and, in another, climbing to the summit and wreathing itself around tall trees which had been left standing, or penetrating hollow pines and darting its fiery tongues through the sides and holes which time had opened. And as the sea of fire was surging, eddying, and rolling, it scattered cinders and ignited limbs to a great distance. Sometimes it spread its ravages through forests; or, as if determined to riot on the ruin it made, and to bid defiance to man and the elements, it would run over dry grass-fields faster than a horse would gallop, destroy cattle, barns, dwelling-houses, and even human life. It would diffuse its peculiar odor into remote States, darkening the air, reddening the sun, and alarming the ignorant and superstitious at the distance of hundreds of miles from the scene. Nothing but a deluging rain could subdue it.[1]

And even when such ravages were not made,— and there never were such in Union,— the fire continued to burn in the "cut-down" for many days. As soon as the heat would admit, the laborers began to cut, and with the aid of oxen and chains to put into piles, the blackened and imperfectly burnt logs. This business they followed, covered with smut, till the new piles, compactly put together, were in a condition to be reburnt. After all, many firmly-rooted stumps, large blackened logs, and dead limbless trunks, remained. In subsequent years, when time and alternating storm and sunshine had weakened the strength of the stumps and dead trunks and opened cavities in them, these were again set on fire, and threw a brilliant light to a great distance over the cleared fields, in the night; or they were uprooted and piled with logs yet to be consumed.

[1] A fire of this kind occurred in Lebanon and vicinity in 1761, and in Alna and vicinity in September, 1823. A striking account of such a fire is narrated by J. J. Audubon, in his Ornithological Biography, ii. 397. See also Cooper's Novels.

This kind of havoc, vigorously begun, was continued to some extent in town for half a century. Still there was some reservation even at the first. The best trees, or some of them, particularly if they grew near rivers or mills, were used for valuable purposes. Tall pines, which had been swayed by the breeze for centuries, and whose graceful trunks sometimes rose to the height of ninety feet before being marred by a limb or a knot, were often converted into masts; or, being cut into mill-logs, were rolled into the ponds and streams to be floated to the places of their destination.

SHINGLES. — The manufacture of shingles was begun early, and for some time it increased with the decrease of lumber. The only mode of making them, before the invention and introduction of shingle-mills, twenty or thirty years ago, was by sawing logs into pieces of suitable length, splitting the pieces, and shaving the shingles by hand. Sometimes, in the course of a winter, there were collected on the Common huge piles, which the storekeepers purchased of the inhabitants of this and the neighboring towns. Many were made in the part of Union now included in Washington. Of the makers in the early part of the present century, the best was Benjamin Speed. In what he manufactured, there were a beauty and a finish which entitled him to the appellation of a scientific shingle-maker. There was also engaged in the business a family named Lakin, from Groton, Mass. The husband and the wife, in the winter season, would go into the woods, and, one at each handle of a long saw, work hard through the day, cutting trees into blocks. It may be doubted which of the two was the most expert in splitting and finishing them. And often has the wife come to the Common — eight miles — on horseback, with a child in her arms, and a heavy bunch of shingles on each side of her horse, balanced by means of ropes and withes across the beast's back. Under the ropes and withes, to prevent them from cutting the horse, was a bag of hay. To all these was superadded a meal-bag, containing a jug for rum or molasses, or some other article then deemed necessary for a family. At the present time, shingle-mills are so common that rift and shaved shingles, though much better, are seldom made.

BOARDS AND SAW-MILLS. — The sawing of lumber into boards has always been an important item in the business of the town. One of the first acts of the proprietor, Dr. Taylor, was to erect a saw-mill. Not long afterward, another saw-mill was built by Josiah Reed. It stood below Sunnybec Pond, several rods above the present location of Hills' Mills.

Four or five years before the present century, when, except Jonah Gay's, there was no house in town east of the road on the east side of Seven-tree Pond, a saw-mill was built on the stream which runs into Crawford's Pond. Lermond of Warren came early in the week, and went into the woods. There he labored regularly, about a fortnight at a time, remote from all inhabitants. On the Saturday at the end of the fortnight, towards evening, he emerged from the forest to spend the night at William Hart's. On the next morning, he took his boat, proceeded down the St. George's, procured a supply of provisions and other necessaries, returned the same evening or the next morning to Hart's, and then buried himself again for a fortnight in solitude. In this way he labored till the work was done. He was not a joiner by trade, and the mill had but four braces, and those were "cut in with a post-axe." The log, in the sawing, was run back by putting the feet upon pegs or pins in a wheel. Before the close of the eighteenth century, other saw-mills were built. In 1826 there were six in operation; in 1840 and in 1843 there were eight. In 1845 it was estimated that at least twenty-seven saw-mills had been built or re-built, and seven of them were then used. This would not be remarkable on rivers as large as the Kennebec or the Penobscot; but it deserves notice in connection with a river no larger or longer than the St. George's, which does not admit of logs being floated from a great distance in the interior.

In the early part of this century, the mills were continually in operation. Lumber accumulated at the mill-yards, and rafts and logs floated on the rivers and ponds. By day and by night, at home and abroad, the ears were constantly greeted with the busy, hurrying sound of saws, working as if they were alive and their cravings could never be satisfied.

LIME-CASKS. — The first person who gave his attention particularly to the manufacture of lime-casks was John Little. This was early in the nineteenth century. Within twenty-five years afterward, there was a cooper-shop at almost every man's door. From August 15, 1794, the casks were to contain 100 gallons each, and to be made of well-seasoned oak or ash staves, with ten hoops on each cask, well driven, and sufficiently secured with nails or pins. Afterward they were reduced to 75, and in 1810 to 50 gallons. Now they will hold about 28 gallons. At first they were made of rift staves, and the price for putting them together was twenty cents each. The highest sum for which they were sold at Thomaston was sixty cents. Now they are sold for about thirteen cents; sixteen and seventeen cents being considered high, though they can hardly be afforded at that price. About the year 1818, when the price was thirty-two or thirty-three cents, the coopers, who could make twelve in a day, were dissatisfied because their wages were reduced to twelve and a half cents. Not many years after the commencement of the business, the demand was so great that casks were put together hastily; and there was seldom a load from any part of the country carried to Thomaston, in which some were not crushed on the way. Legislation has been resorted to frequently; but the laws are often willingly evaded both by makers and purchasers, and there is difficulty in enforcing them.

The introduction of stave-machines within twenty-five or thirty years — of which there are now nine or more in the town — enables the inhabitants to work up almost every kind of lumber, which would otherwise be worthless. The facilities for putting together the materials, which are now bevelled by machinery, save a great amount of labor. The number made cannot be ascertained. In 1826 it was estimated at 30,000.[1] Considerable inquiry has been made of coopers and carters; and it is not unreasonable to say that at the present time there are not less than one hundred thousand, and it is not improbable that there are one hundred and fifty thousand made annually in Union alone.

Not far from the year 1840, a few shrewd traders about the Common, during one winter, purchased all the lime-hogsheads which were brought to them, and paid for them in goods at the Thomaston prices. They were heaped up till the Common appeared almost as if covered with one huge pile. The store-keepers made contracts to supply purchasers in Thomaston at a fixed price. Thus the prices, which fluctuated daily according to the number in the market or the number immediately wanted, assumed a firmness which it is said was on the whole favorable to the makers, to the Union traders, and to the Thomaston lime-burners.

When hogsheads were first made, the number carried to Thomaston in a load was comparatively small. About the year 1817, it had increased to sixty. The roads were so bad that this was as large a load as four oxen could draw. Now the casks are smaller, the roads better, and four oxen will carry two hundred; and a load of one hundred and sixty is common. Formerly these were placed on their ends in long erect racks built for the purpose. Three tiers, one above the other, numbering ten in each tier, presented thirty lime-casks to view on either side. Now the tops of the racks are wider than the bottoms, and of course the loads spread at the top and are not so high.

For many years, after letting their oxen rest on the Lord's Day, the farmers started them at sunset, and, driving during the night, arrived at Thomaston on the

---

[1] N. P. Hawes's MS.

following morning. Now, horses are frequently substituted for oxen; and the plan is to drive on Friday night, so as to give teams rest on the Lord's Day, after their return, before putting them to the regular week's work. But neither Saturday nor Monday has ever been exclusively the market-day. The manufacturers or carters go when it is most convenient or advantageous; and, instead of being limited to Thomaston, as they were thirty years ago, they now dispose of the greater part of their hogsheads at East Thomaston, or Rockland, which has grown up since that time, and to which is a road through the Camden Hills by Mount Pleasant.

If no more were carried to Thomaston annually than the one hundred or one hundred and fifty thousand from Union, it would be an item of value in trade. But on some mornings, thirty, forty, or perhaps fifty loads of various sizes, containing from twenty to one hundred and sixty lime-casks each, are seen at the market. They are brought from the country nearly fifty miles back; from Hope, Appleton, Searsmont, Montville, Liberty, Palermo, Washington, Jefferson, &c. The farmer, on rainy days, goes into his cooper-shop, and, in the course of a summer, has time to manufacture one or more loads. The hired laborer, easily taught, thus makes his rainy days and leisure hours profitable to his employer.

Having carried a load or more to market, the man, in comfortable, if not affluent circumstances, brings home flour, groceries, and other necessaries, or money to pay taxes, or he lays up something for sickness or declining years. The team returns leisurely northward on Saturday afternoon, bringing the teamster reposing at full length on the bottom of his rack, with his feet in an opposite direction from the sun. His hat is pulled over his face to exclude the sun's beams from his eyes, and his body vibrates from side to side, as either wheel strikes and passes over a stone or plunges into a hole. A barrel of flour is on the end of his rack, and a bag of groceries is suspended from a chain across the top. It seems as if such must be a hard life. But it is free from the anxiety which sometimes, every night, week after week, drives sleep from the man of extensive business; it is favorable to health, vigor, and independence; and, when to these are added moral and intellectual cultivation, it may well be doubted if there is, with all its hardships, any life so happy as the farmer's.

CHAPTER XIII.

AGRICULTURAL AND HORTICULTURAL PRODUCTS.

Barley and Rye. — Indian Corn. — Wheat. — Potatoes. — Fruit. — Peaches and Plums. — Apples.

BARLEY AND RYE. — Neither rye nor any grain but barley was raised on the St. George's when Union was settled. "It was thought a stupid thing for Philip Robbins to go back into the country to get a living on a farm." When he mentioned to Anderson of Warren his intention of raising rye, Anderson scouted the idea. Robbins is said to have told him, "I mean to get a living off of my farm; I shall raise rye, and you may have to come and buy of me yet;" — a prediction that was fulfilled in a season of scarcity which followed.[1] The first grain put into the ground by any one in town was rye. Within two years after Philip Robbins settled here, twice as much rye was raised on his and the Mill Farm as along the whole of the St. George's. The common kind was the winter rye. It was sown in autumn upon burnt ground, — a mode not known to the settlers of Warren, who supposed the soil, in order to produce grain, must be ploughed, as

[1] Jacob Robbins.

in their native country. Since the woods have been cut off, the summer rye has been introduced, and the sowing of this kind is generally preceded by ploughing. In 1840, according to the town-valuation, 559 bushels were raised; according to the United States census, 1,443.

INDIAN CORN was planted on burnt ground. By some of the early settlers, the ground was ploughed before the grain was put into it. This mode of cultivation was inconvenient among the roots, stumps, logs, and knolls, which abounded in every new field; and experience soon taught the lesson that corn came to maturity sooner when planted in the warm black mould than in the ploughed soil. In 1840, according to the town-valuation, 3,151 bushels were raised; according to the United States memoranda, 4,960.

The year 1831 was the most remarkable for corn which has ever been known in Maine. It flourished like weeds, and ripened very early. Ezekiel True, of Montville, harvested one hundred bushels on the last day of August. It seemed as if every kernel grew which was dropped anywhere on the ground.[1] Success, however, with Indian corn is uncertain. An early frost has often ruined the crop.

WHEAT is raised; but the people commonly prefer to buy flour, and to give their attention to other kinds of produce. Ten or twelve years ago, much interest was taken in wheat. In 1840, according to the town-valuation, there were raised 3,013 bushels; according to the United States census, 2,658. In 1837 the crop was 4,249 bushels.

POTATOES were a very important article of culture, till "the rot" prevailed extensively in 1846. Since that time, comparatively little attention has been given to them, and the whole State has been obliged to abandon the cultivation of the agricultural product most important for subsistence or for export. In 1840 the town-valuation states that 44,075 bushels were raised;

---

[1] N. Robbins, Esq.

and the United States census, that there were 44,960 bushels.

PEAS, BEANS, TURNIPS, CARROTS, BEETS, ONIONS, PARSNIPS, CABBAGES, yield abundant crops.

FRUIT. — There are several kinds of fruit. And if each man would give a little attention to the subject, and plant a few fruit-trees, and graft or bud them, he might have the luxury of a rich repast at almost any season of the year.

PEACHES AND PLUMS. — The climate is so cold that peaches cannot be raised. But there might be an abundance of garden plums. Whenever their cultivation has been properly attended to, there has been great success.

APPLES. — There were but few apples till after the beginning of the nineteenth century. Among the items of property belonging to Matthias Hawes, very soon after his arrival, is recorded " a box of apple-trees." Philip Robbins and David Robbins, before they had been here long, probably did something in the way of raising them. A memorandum made by Levi Morse, Nov. 12, 1793, says, " Set fifteen apple-trees. . . . Nov. 17 and 18, 1794, set fifty apple-trees. . . . Nov. 12, 1797, first fifteen apple-trees I set bore ten apples. . . . Our orchard bore about one bushel of apples this year — 1798." This orchard, and those of Philip Robbins and David Robbins, were probably the first in town. In the year 1800, Dr. Sibley had one or two quarts of apple-seeds, picked out of pomace, brought to him on horseback from Hopkinton, N.H. They were planted, and the trees disposed of among the inhabitants. Orchards have since become common and large. In 1826, it was estimated that there were one hundred,[1] which produced on an average 10,000 bushels annually. According to the valuation of 1840, the quantity was 9,546 bushels. But the interest once felt in raising them for the purpose of making cider has diminished in consequence of the progress of temperance.

[1] N. P. Hawes's MS.

CHAPTER XIV.

MANUFACTURES AND TRADE.

Spinning Wheels. — Looms. — Home-made Clothing. — Fulling Mills. — Carding Machines. — Factories. — Paper Mills. — Tanneries. — Potash. — Iron Works. — Fossetts' Mills. — Stores. — Carting Goods to Boston in the War of 1812. — Canals.

MANUFACTURES.

SPINNING WHEELS. — The old spinning-wheel, turned by hand and doling out its single thread, was in use from the first settlement of the town. It was considered indispensable to every household. The spindle was made to revolve by means of a band connecting it with a large wheel. Notwithstanding the facilities for manufacturing yarn at the present day, it is still occasionally used in many families. The only improvement in it is the "patent head," which is merely the addition of an intervening wheel between the large one and the spindle.

LOOMS. — The old-fashioned loom, more costly than the spinning-wheel, was not so common. The shuttle was thrown through the warp with the hand. The fly-shuttle, introduced about the year 1812 or 1815, was considered a great improvement.

HOME-MADE CLOTHING. — By means of the spinning-wheel and the loom, the inhabitants were able to provide themselves with woollen garments. The fleece was made into rolls by the tedious process of carding by hand. By the industrious housewife the rolls were spun on the large wheel, which in winter was brought up before the kitchen fire, — the only fire in the house, except when there was company. The yarn was then woven, and the cloth taken to the clothier, dressed and returned, having been dyed Holland-brown or smoke-color. Cloth for striped frocks, and for some other purposes, was made and worn without being sent to the fulling-mill. A tailoress was commonly employed to cut and sometimes to baste the garments, which were subsequently made by the wife and daughters.

The foot-wheel converted into linen the flax which was raised on the farm. Winter evenings, when there were not more pressing duties, were spent by the females around a rousing wood-fire, in knitting stockings, mittens, and leggins, from home-made yarn. Thus was every family practically in favor of domestic manufactures.

FULLING MILLS. — The first fulling-mill was built on Crawford's River in 1799, by Micajah Gleason, from Framingham, Mass. There have been four since, though there are none now.

CARDING MACHINES. — The first machine for carding wool was built by Ebenezer Alden in 1806. There have been four, of which two are now in operation.

FACTORIES. — In 1809, a cotton-factory was built on the west side of St. George's River, just below the Middle Bridge. Its operations were never very extensive. The building was carried away by a freshet in 1832. The Farmers' Woollen Factory was built near the Upper Bridge in 1814, and owned in shares of ten dollars each. Wool was carded there as recently as 1843, though no cloth was dressed during the two or three previous years. In 1843, William Gleason converted into a woollen-factory the building which had been used for a paper-mill at South Union.

PAPER MILLS. — Several years ago, the manufacture of paper was carried on extensively. The water in Crawford's River is peculiarly good for the purpose. On this river, in 1810, was erected a paper-mill, which was burnt in 1818. Another building was put up in 1819; but no paper was made there after 1837. Immediately above the Middle Bridge was another paper-mill, which was burnt early on the morning of June 11, 1843. The machinery, said to have cost $3,000, and unwrought stock valued at more than $2,000, were destroyed. The paper was saved. Insured at Worcester, Mass.

MANUFACTURES.

TANNERIES. — Richard Cummings was the first person who tanned hides. He abandoned the business after a few years, and the people traded for leather at Warren. In 1826, there were three tanneries; one owned by Joseph Beckett, south-south-west of the Methodist Meeting-house; another by Susman Abrams, a Jew,[1] a few rods below the Middle Bridge; and another on the east side of the St. George's above the Upper Bridge. In 1840, there were four in town.

POTASH. — Soon after the incorporation of the town, Edward Jones made potash, in small quantities, near the Lower Bridge. For several years in the early part of the nineteenth century, Ebenezer Alden manufactured five or six tons annually in a building which he erected for the purpose, on a rivulet at the brow of the hill east of Seven Brook, on the south side of the road.

[1] Susman Abrams was from Hamburg. In early life he travelled as a pedler, and traded in old clothes. To save expense, he lived on bread and butter, carrying his butter with him in a covered pewter porringer. It is supposed he fled for some misdemeanor, embarked on board a vessel, and was concerned in the sinking of it. After a residence in Waldoborough, and subsequently in Thomaston, he came to Union. Here he carried on the business of coopering and tanning. He was never very successful in the accumulation of property. His accounts were always kept in the Hebrew characters, and were read from the right to the left. Not being able, as he said, to translate from the Hebrew into our language, he first translated into the German, and then from the German into the English. He was very observant of his written or printed prayers; but in his conduct there was much of the inconsistency which was laid to the charge of the Jews by our Saviour. On one occasion a Jew came to keep the Passover with him. The iron vessels, before being used, were heated red hot, that no leaven might by any possibility remain attached to them. Being very fond of eels, Abrams allowed his appetite to get the better of his religious scruples, and ate a hearty meal, to the great horror of his brother Jew, from whom he received a very severe rebuke for the unrighteous deed. Although he professed faith in Judaism only, and not in Christianity, he was a constant attendant on public worship. On Saturday, which is the Jewish sabbath, he abstained from hard labor, but took occasion to ride about and transact business. Not recognizing any obligation to keep sacredly the first day of the week, he often worked in secret at his tan-yard, and once fell into a vat and was nearly drowned. He was never much liked by the men, and was generally hated by the women. Nov. 29, 1810, he was married to the widow Mary Jones, of Friendship. He died, without issue, Oct. 6, 1830; aged, it is supposed, about eighty-seven years.

IRON WORKS. — In June, 1843, an iron-foundery was established at South Union. Here "are made all kinds of country castings." In August, 1844, business was commenced in the edge-tool factory of Vaughan and Pardoe. Nearly four thousand axes are made annually; also ship-tools to the value of about $1,500, and cooper's tools to about the same amount. March 12, 1850, J. Vaughan and Co. commenced business in their shovel-factory. The manufactures at all these establishments are regarded as of a very superior quality; as well as the tool-work of Bradley R. Mowry, at the Middle Bridge.

FOSSETTS' MILLS. — The most extensive mill establishment was the Fossetts', at North Union. It was completed in December, 1848, at an expense of about $10,000. Under one roof were a saw-mill, a gristmill with "three run of stones," besides a corn-cracker, stave-machine, shingle-machine, lath-machine, threshing-machine, cleanser, and bolt, — all carried by steam. They were destroyed by fire, June 21, 1850.

TRADE.

STORES. — Brotherton Daggett says, that, though there had been a store on St. George's River, there was not any when he came in 1789. Edward Jones, near the Lower Bridge, afterward kept a few articles, which were mostly bartered for ashes. It was the largest collection which had been brought to Union for sale. In 1801, Ebenezer Alden sold goods at his dwelling-house. He put up a frame near his potash, and boarded it. John Little bought it, moved it to the Common, clapboarded it, and finished the interior in 1802, and furnished it. The building is now occupied as a store by Asa Messer and Israel Hills, the second story having been added. Ebenezer Alden and Nathaniel Robbins formed a partnership in the fall of 1803. Afterward came Mallard and Chase; and subsequently, from Spencer, Mass. came Charles Pope and William Pope. Major Robert Foster, upon moving into town from Newburyport or the vicinity, during the war of 1812, opened a store at South Union, on the place now owned by Joseph Vaughan. It was the only store in town at the time. Not long afterwards, Alden and Robbins had separate stores. There have been several others since that time, some in the remote parts of the town. In 1840 there were six, in 1843 there were eight, and in 1849 twelve stores. Barter is carried on extensively by the storekeepers. The inhabitants sell to them produce; and much more business is done than is common in country towns which are not larger. As Thomaston and Rockland are extensively engaged in making lime, the farmers find there a good market for every thing which they raise, though not unfrequently the agricultural produce and the meat are carried to Belfast; and the storekeepers sell butter, cheese, &c. at Boston.

CARTING GOODS TO BOSTON. — During the war of 1812, when the British had possession of all the United States territory east of Penobscot River, many goods were carted from Hampden and Frankfort to Boston by residents in Warren and the vicinity. Isaac Hills and John Burkett, of Union, engaged in this business in 1814 and 1815. One load, previously contracted for, was carried from Union to Boston, after the arrival of the news of peace. Duties were high. A man on the British side of the Penobscot, according to an agreement previously made, sent goods to another on the American side. A third person seized them as smuggled property, and had them prized. The person to whom they were sent then gave bonds for the whole amount for which they were prized, sent them to Boston, and paid the bonds, the amount of which was less than the duties would have been. The journey to and from Boston required about two months, and travelling fifteen miles was considered a good day's work. A load generally contained two and a half tons. It was drawn by six oxen, for eighty dollars a ton, in wagons covered with boards.

CANALS. — To facilitate trade, an Act was passed March 9, 1793, authorizing Charles Barrett, within six years, to cut a canal from Barretts Town, beginning "twenty-five miles above the head of the tide in George's River, ... to communicate with the sea at the mouth of said river," and, with his heirs and assigns, to "have the exclusive right of making locks and canals upon the said river," for seventy years; "provided," &c. The toll was one shilling and sixpence for every ton "transported in boats or other vessels through the locks and canals at the Upper Falls in said river, at the mouth of Senebec Pond," or "through the locks and canals by the Lower Falls in said George's River, near the head of the tide." The same toll was to be levied "for every thousand feet of boards, and in the same proportion for plank and square timber, and every other species of lumber, whether transported on rafts or otherwise." Every boat or other vessel, not loaded, was to "pay at the rate of one shilling for every ton weight it was capable of conveying."

The canal was opened only from Round Pond. General Knox, of Thomaston, became the principal or sole owner before it was completed. Its construction, during part of the time at least, was superintended by a French engineer, sent by him from Philadelphia. It was used for several years; but the great profits expected from it were not realized. Before the general's death in 1806, it was neglected; and any one who went down the river with lumber, on applying to the lock-keeper, was told to "lock" it himself. A petition for doubling the toll was presented to the Legislature. It was dated at Union, May 21, 1802, and signed by Amos Barrett, Ebenezer Alden, John Dickey, Robert Dickey, Eleazar Dickey, Nathan Blake, Amariah Mero, Nathaniel Robbins, Josiah Robbins, Edward Jones, and Ichabod Maddocks. Still the canal continued to be unprofitable, and was allowed to go to decay.

The population of the towns on the St. George's having increased, another canal, in 1846, was laid out from Thomaston to Searsmont. It was urged that there would be a good dividend from the tolls for produce and kiln-wood. The opening of it to Sunnybec Pond was noticed in the "Thomaston Recorder," immediately after its completion in the fall of 1847. It has already been leased for several years. A steamboat has been on the canal, and once went into Sunnybec Pond.

CHAPTER XV.

MUNICIPAL HISTORY.

Town Meetings. — Notifications. — Places of holding them. — Town Officers. — Oath of Office in 1787. — Town Clerks. — Selectmen. — Assessors. — Constables. — Collectors. — Treasurers. — Tithingmen. — Fish Wardens.

TOWN-MEETINGS.

NOTIFICATIONS. — The inhabitants, at different times, have voted that the notifications for town-meetings[1] should be posted up at private dwelling-houses,

[1] The earliest record of the mode of notifying the inhabitants is dated April 2, 1787; when it was "voted that the constable should set up two notifications, one at Mr. Joel Adams's and the other at Mr. Philip Robbins's, and that should be sufficient notice to warn town-meetings." In 1789, one notice was to be "set up at Mr. Joel Adams's, and the other at Mr. Woodcock's grist-mill." In 1796, they were to be posted up "in the most public places in town, and where meetings are held on Sundays, when there is any." April 2, 1798, "on the front of the meeting-house twelve days prior to the day the meeting is to be." This mode was continued till 1805, when they were to "be posted up in Messrs. Alden and Robbins's store." In 1806, on the meeting-house; besides which, in 1807, there was to be one "at Jason Ware's, or where the Methodist meeting is held; also one at James [Rice's] seven days prior to the meeting." In 1808, the third notice was to be at Starrett's Mills, in what is now Washington. In 1811, at each of the two meeting-houses; and, in 1817, an additional one at the school-house near Sterling Davis's, ten days previous to the meeting. In 1818 at each of the two meeting-houses fourteen days, and in 1819 at each of the three meeting-houses twelve days, previously. In 1820, notifications were to be put up two sabbaths before the meeting. In 1834, the places designated were the Methodist Meeting-house, John Little's, John Lermond's grist-mill; and, in 1838, the Post Office, Lermond's mills, and Fossett's store. In 1848, at the last three places,

stores, mills, school-houses, meeting-houses, and the post-offices. This has been done fourteen, twelve, or ten days, or two sabbaths, before the meeting. Occasionally the time has been only seven days for a notification sent to a remote part of the town.

Sometimes notices were added at the bottom of the warrant: " Dec. 18, 1788. All those that have any demands on the town, who are inhabitants, are desired to bring in their accounts to the selectmen." " Oct. 4, 1790. The inhabitants are requested to bring a list of all the children born in this town that are not recorded, and also the deaths, so as the clerk may make a record, as they will avoid the penalties in the law."

PLACES OF MEETING. — The first meeting on record was the plantation-meeting held at the log-house of Philip Robbins, June 12, 1786, in regard to an Act of Incorporation. The first meeting after the incorporation was at the same place, Jan. 15, 1787, for organization and for the election of town-officers for the first time. Here, too, March 5, 1787, was held the first regular March meeting. The meetings were continued at private houses till Aug. 29 and Oct. 26, 1791. On these two days, they were in the school-house which had been recently built near Moses Hawes's, after which they were again held in private houses or barns.[1] The first time the meeting-house was used for

and at the Methodist Meeting-house ; and, in 1849, at the same places as in 1848, with the addition of one at the East Union Post Office.

[1] Town-meetings were also held as follows : — In Moses Hawes's house, April 2, 13, 20, March 19, May 30, Nov. 19, 1787 ; March 8, April 5, May 26, June 25, Oct. 4, 1790; March 7, April 4, May 23, 1791; April 1, Dec. 2, 1793 ; Nov. 3, 1794 ; March 2, 1795 ; also in his barn, May 7, 1792. Rufus Gillmor's house, Sept. 4, 1789 ; March 6, 1797 ; and in his barn, July 8, 1793 ; Feb. 1, 1799, the meeting was adjourned from his house to the meeting-house. Richard Cummings's house, Jan. 4, 1790. Philip Robbins's house, Nov. 5, 8, 12, 1790 ; Jan. 3, 10, 25, 1791. Jonathan Newhall's house, April 2, 1792. Capt. George West's house, Nov. 2, 1792 ; March 4, 1793 ; March 3, April 7, 1794 ; Jan. 16, March 7, April 4, 1796. Edward Jones's house, Sept. 1, 1794 ; April 6, 1795. Josiah Robbins's, Nov. 7, 1796 ; Feb. 6, 1797 ; March 5, 1798. John Little's, Nov. 7, 1814, where a moderator was chosen, and the meeting adjourned to a future day at the meeting-house.

the purpose was May 6, 1795. Here the town-meetings were ordinarily held afterward. The inclemency of the weather, however, the house not being warmed, sometimes compelled the people to adjourn to dwelling-houses; and once, March 5, 1804, to the store of Alden and Robbins. Feb. 6, 1809, Major Maxcy and Mr. Pope, who were chosen moderators, having declined serving, Nathaniel Robbins consented to discharge the duties, the town having "voted that Esq. Robbins have leave to wear his hat." March 2, 1812, an unsuccessful attempt was made to have the town-meetings held half the time at the Methodist Meeting-house. April 2, 1838, was the last day of assembling for town-business in the Old Meeting-house. The next meeting, held Sept. 10, 1838, was in the Methodist Meeting-house, when it was "left with the selectmen to procure a suitable place." Oct. 29, 1838, it was in "Bachelder's new building, near his mill;" April 1, 1839, in "Ebenezer Cobb's new barn;" and April 16, at the Methodist Meeting-house. The first meeting in the Town House was April 6, 1840.

TOWN-OFFICERS.

OATH OF OFFICE. — April 13, 1787, a warrant was issued for a meeting, in order to swear the officers chosen at the annual meeting in the March preceding, agreeably to an Act passed March 10, 1787. The meeting was adjourned to April 20, when each of the town-officers subscribed and took the following oath of office: —

"I do truly and sincerely acknowledge, profess, testify, and declare, that the Commonwealth of Massachusetts is, and of right ought to be, a free, sovereign, and independent State; and I do swear that I will bear true faith and allegiance to the said Commonwealth, and I will defend the same against traitorous conspiracies and all hostile attempts whatsoever; and I do renounce and abjure all allegiance, subjection, and obedience to the king, queen, or government of Great Britain (as the case may be), and every other foreign power whatsoever; and that no foreign prince, persons, pre-

TOWN-CLERKS AND SELECTMEN. 117

late, state, or potentate hath or ought to have any jurisdiction, superiority, pre-eminence, authority, dispensing or other power, in any matter, civil, ecclesiastical, or spiritual, within this Commonwealth; except the authority and power which is or may be vested by their constituents in the Congress of the United States; and I do further testify and declare, that no man or body of men hath or can have any right to absolve or discharge me from the obligation of this oath, declaration, or affirmation; and that I do make this acknowledgment, profession, testimony, declaration, denial, renunciation, and abjuration, heartily and truly, according to the common meaning and acceptation of the foregoing words, without any equivocation, mental evasion, or secret reservation whatsoever. So help me God."

TOWN-CLERKS.

Moses Hawes, as plantation-clerk, signed the warrant for the plantation-meeting, June 12, 1786. At that meeting he was again elected plantation-clerk; and, Jan. 15, 1787, town-clerk. From that time the office has been held as follows: —

1787–1793.	Moses Hawes.	1823–1828.	Henry True.
1794–1802.	Edward Jones.	1829–1830.	Nathl. Robbins.
1803–1806.	Stephen March.	1831–1836.	Jno. Bachelder.
1807.	Edward Jones.	1837–1846.	Cyrus G. Bachelder.
1808.	Jona. Sibley.		
1809–1811.	Nathl. Robbins.	1846 (June 8)–1850.	Zuinglius Collins.
1812.	John Little.		
1813–1822.	Nathl. Robbins.	1851.	Andrew Libbey.

SELECTMEN.

1787. Jan. 15. Philip Robbins, Joel Adams, Jason Ware.
1787. March 5. Philip Robbins, Joel Adams (in whose place was chosen, April 13, Jason Ware), Ezra Bowen.
1788. Josiah Robbins, Jason Ware, Joel Adams.
1789. Jason Ware, Josiah Robbins, Joel Adams.
1790. Jason Ware, Josiah Robbins, Moses Hawes.
1791. Joel Adams, Joseph Guild, Samuel Daggett.
1792. Joel Adams, Amariah Mero, Joseph Maxcy.
1793. Amariah Mero, Moses Hawes, Josiah Maxcy.
1794. Amariah Mero, Josiah Maxcy, Jason Ware.

MUNICIPAL HISTORY.

1795. Edward Jones, Ebenezer Jennison, Joel Adams.
1796. Amariah Mero, Edward Jones, Joel Adams.
1797. Amariah Mero, Edward Jones, Joel Adams.
1798. Edward Jones, Rufus Gillmor, Joel Adams.
1799. Rufus Gillmor, Ebenezer Jennison, Josiah Maxcy.
1800. Edward Jones, Rufus Gillmor, Josiah Maxcy.
1801. Moses Hawes, Joseph Maxcy, Thomas Mitchell.
1802. Joseph Maxcy, Edward Jones, Rufus Gillmor.
1803. Joseph Maxcy, Rufus Gillmor, Nathan Blake.
1804. Joseph Maxcy, Rufus Gillmor, Joseph Morse.
1805. Rufus Gillmor, Joseph Morse, Nathaniel Robbins.
1806. Joseph Maxcy, Nathaniel Robbins, Joseph Morse.
1807. Joseph Morse, Matthias Hawes, Marlboro' Packard.
1808. Joseph Morse, Matthias Hawes, Marlboro' Packard.
1809. Nathaniel Bachelor, Joel Adams, William Hart.
1810. Nathaniel Bachelor, Nathan Blake, Joel Adams.
1811. Nathaniel Robbins, John Lermond, Joel Adams.
1812. John Lermond, Joseph Morse, Matthias Hawes.
1813. John Lermond, Joseph Morse, Micajah Gleason.
1814. John Lermond, Joseph Morse, Micajah Gleason.
1815. Nathl. Bachelor, Micajah Gleason, Nathan Daniels.
1816. Nathl. Bachelor, Micajah Gleason, John Lermond.
1817. Micajah Gleason, John Lermond, Thomas Mitchell.
1818. Micajah Gleason, John Lermond, John W. Lindley.
1819. Micajah Gleason, John Lermond, John W. Lindley.
1820. Micajah Gleason, John Lermond, John W. Lindley.
1821. Micajah Gleason, John Lermond, John W. Lindley.
1822. John W. Lindley, Herman Hawes, James Littlehale.
1823. John W. Lindley, John Lermond, Herman Hawes.
1824. John Lermond, John W. Lindley, Joseph Morse.
1825. John Lermond, Nathaniel Robbins, Noah Rice.
1826. John Lermond, Nathaniel Robbins, Noah Rice.
1827. John Lermond, Nathaniel Robbins, Samuel Stone.
1828. John Lermond, Nathaniel Robbins, Samuel Stone.
1829. John Lermond, Samuel Stone, Spencer Mero.
1830. John Lermond, Samuel Stone, Herman Hawes.
1831. Herman Hawes, Samuel Stone, John Payson.
1832. Herman Hawes, John Lermond, Peter Adams.
1833. Herman Hawes, Peter Adams, James Littlehale.
1834. John Lermond, Peter Adams, John W. Lindley.
1835. John Lermond, John W. Lindley, Jonathan Carriel.
1836. J. W. Lindley, Jonathan Carriel, Phillips C. Harding.
1837. J. W. Lindley, Phillips C. Harding, Nath. Bachelder.

ASSESSORS.

1838. John Lermond, Peter Adams, Phillips C. Harding.
1839. Peter Adams, John W. Lindley, Willard Robbins.
1840. John W. Lindley, Willard Robbins, Wm. Coggan.
1841. John W. Lindley, John Payson, Nathan Hills.
1842. John W. Lindley, Ebenezer Blunt, Willard Robbins.
1843. Ebenezer Blunt, Phillips C. Harding, Wm. G. Hawes.
1844. Ebenezer Blunt, Phillips C. Harding, Wm. G. Hawes.
1845. P. C. Harding, George Cummings, Jo. M. Gleason.
1846. Ebenezer Blunt, Geo. Cummings, Elbridge Lermond.
1847. Ebenezer Blunt, Geo. Cummings, Elbridge Lermond.
1848. Ebenezer Blunt, Wm. G. Hawes, Elbridge Lermond.
1849. William G. Hawes, Elbridge Lermond, Wm. Coggan.
1850. Ebenezer Blunt, William G. Hawes, John Lermond.
1851. Ebenezer Blunt, William G. Hawes, John Lermond.

SELECTMEN'S COMPENSATION. — April 4, 1791, " Voted the selectmen's work may be allowed as highway-work that is done in laying out roads the year ensuing." With this exception, there is no record of the compensation to the selectmen till " April 5, 1802: allowed Thomas Mitchell, $5.50; Capt. Joseph Maxcy, $4; Moses Hawes, $12.84; all three for serving as selectmen the year. . . . Voted the selectmen be allowed one dollar a day." This compensation continues to the present time, the selectmen bearing their own expenses when on duty.

ASSESSORS.

1786. Jason Ware, Josiah Robbins, Samuel Hills.
1787. Jan. 15. Samuel Hills, Josiah Robbins, Jason Ware.
1788. Jason Ware, Josiah Robbins, Moses Hawes.
1789. The Selectmen.
1790. The Selectmen.
1791. Barnard Case, Josiah Robbins, Joseph Maxcy.
1792. The Selectmen.
1793. David Robbins, Jason Ware, Josiah Robbins.
1794. Moses Hawes, Samuel Hills, Joseph Maxcy.
1795. The Selectmen.
1796. Edward Jones, Joel Adams, Moses Hawes.
1797. Matthias Hawes, Josiah Maxcy, Edward Jones.
1798. Edward Jones, Waldron Stone, Christopher Butler.
1799. The Selectmen.

1800. The Selectmen.
1801. Ebenezer Jennison, Josiah Robbins, Henry Blunt.
1802. Josiah Maxcy, John Tobey, Nathaniel Robbins.
1803. Nathaniel Robbins, Josiah Maxcy, Samuel Daggett.
1804. Nathaniel Robbins, Josiah Maxcy, Samuel Daggett.
1805. Josiah Maxcy, Samuel Daggett, Joel Adams.
1806. Josiah Maxcy, Nathan Daniels, Joel Adams.
1807. Josiah Maxcy, Samuel Daggett, Timothy Stewart.
1808. Josiah Maxcy, Edward Jones, Joel Adams.
1809. Josiah Maxcy, Ebenezer Alden, John W. Lindley.
1810. Simeon Butters, Timothy Stewart, Nathan Daniels, Edward Jones.
1811. The Selectmen.
1812. John Little, Timothy Stewart, Spencer Walcott.
1813. Timothy Stewart, John W. Lindley, Herman Hawes.
1814. Spencer Walcott, Bailey More, Henry Blunt.
1815. Henry Blunt, Herman Hawes, John W. Lindley.
1816. Spencer Walcott, Thomas Mitchell, Nathl. Robbins.
1817. The Selectmen.
1818. Thomas Mitchell, Herman Hawes, William Boggs.
1819. Thomas Mitchell, Herman Hawes, Sterling Davis.
1820. Herman Hawes, Thomas Mitchell, John Butler 1st.
1821. Thos. Mitchell, John W. Lindley, John Butler 1st.
1822. Spencer Walcott, Samuel Stone, John Lermond.
1823. Thomas Mitchell, Spencer Mero, James Littlehale.
1824. Herman Hawes, Calvin Gleason, James Littlehale.
1825. Calvin Gleason, Ziba Simmons, James Littlehale.
1826. Calvin Gleason, James Littlehale, Ziba Simmons.
1827. James Littlehale, Calvin Gleason, Ziba Simmons.
1828. John W. Lindley, James Littlehale, Herman Hawes.
1829. James Littlehale, Calvin Gleason, Noah Bartlett.
1830. James Littlehale, Calvin Gleason, Noah Bartlett.
1831. Calvin Gleason, Sterling Davis, Ziba Simmons.
1832. Thomas Mitchell, James Littlehale, Ziba Simmons.
1833. Henry Blunt, Christopher Young, John W. Lindley.
1834. Thos. Mitchell, Phillips C. Harding, Herman Hawes.
1835. Phillips C. Harding, William Coggan, Nathan Hills.
1836. Phillips C. Harding, William Coggan, Nathan Hills.
1837. The Selectmen.
1838. William Coggan, Nathan Hills, Sterling Davis, jun.
1839. Ebenezer W. Adams, Isley Martin, Jo. Vaughan, jun.
1840. John Gowen, Joseph Vaughan, Leonard Barnard.
1841. James Littlehale, Jo. M. Gleason, Stephen S. Hawes.

1842. Joseph M. Gleason, Stephen S. Hawes, Elbridge Lermond.
1843. Joseph M. Gleason, Stephen S. Hawes, Elbridge Lermond.
1844. Joseph M. Gleason, Orson Cromett, Sterling Davis, jun.
1845. Sterling Davis, jun., Cyrus Gowen, Elijah Vose.
1846. Willard Robbins, William Gleason, Nelson Cutler.
1847. The Selectmen.
1848. Moses Hawes, Sterling Davis, jun., Charles Fogler.
1849. Wm. G. Hawes, Elbridge Lermond, Wm. Coggan.
1850. Ebenezer Blunt, William G. Hawes, John Lermond.
1851. Ebenezer Blunt, William G. Hawes, John Lermond.

ASSESSORS' COMPENSATION. — The assessors have commonly been chosen by ballot; but sometimes, as March 8, 1790, the town has voted that the selectmen should be the assessors for the year.

The compensation has not been uniform. 1793, April 1, " Voted, for making taxes, to Capt. Joel Adams, £1. 14s.; to Lieut. Maxcy, £1. 4s.; to Amariah Mero, £1. 12s." 1794, April 7, " Voted to allow Mr. Jason Ware £1. 14s. for taking valuation and making taxes." 1802, April 5, "Allowed the following accounts, viz.: Josiah Robbins, $10.50; Henry Blunt, $7.50; Ebenezer Jennison, $16.75; all for taking valuation and making taxes the year passed." 1796, April 4, " Voted the assessors have 83 cents a day for 1795 and 1796." In 1797 and 1798, the compensation was $1.17 a day. In 1800 it was $1 a day, and so continued till 1847, when it was fixed at $1.25; but, in 1848, it was again restored to $1 a day. No extra compensation is allowed for board, lodging, or travel. The assessors divide such expenses by entertaining each other at their respective dwelling-houses, while making the taxes.

CONSTABLES.

1787, Jan. 15. David Robbins.
1787, March 5, 1788. Abijah Hawes.
1789–90. Samuel Hills. — 1791–1802. Amariah Mero.

1803. Moses Hawes. — 1804–6. Amariah Mero.
1807. Spencer Walcott. — 1808. Jabez N. Mitchell.
1809. John Drake. — 1810. Thomas Mitchell, jun.
1811. Thomas Mitchell, jun., Rufus Gillmor.
1812. Thos. Mitchell, jun. — 1813–17. Eben. W. Adams.
1818–19. Rufus Gillmor. — 1820. John Chapman Robbins.
1821. Herman Hawes. — 1822. Rufus Gillmor.
1823. Nathan D. Rice. — 1824. Thomas Mitchell.
1825–28. Isaac Hills. — 1829. John Chapman Robbins.
1830. Samuel Daggett, jun. — 1831. Nathan Hills.
1832–33. Nelson Cutler. — 1833, Oct. 28. Wm. Caswell.
1834. Robert Thompson, jun. — 1835–39. Nathan Hills.
1840. Christopher Young, Nathan Hills, Thomas C. Fossett, Elbridge Lermond, Thurston Whiting.
1841. Nathan Hills, Thos. C. Fossett, Christopher Young.
1842. Elisha E. Rice.
1843. Christopher Young, Nathan Hills, Elisha E. Rice, Thomas C. Fossett, Joseph M. Gleason, Robert Thompson, jun.
1844. Christopher Young, Nathan Hills.
1845. Christopher Young, Nathan Hills, Ebenezer Blunt.
1846. Christopher Young, Nathan Hills, Ebenezer Blunt, George Jones.
1847. Christopher Young, Ebenezer Blunt, Edward Hills, Charles Fogler.
1848. Edward Hills, Christopher Young, Ebenezer Blunt.
1849. Edward Hills, William Caswell, Christopher Young, Charles A. Hawes, Nathan Hills, J. W. Payson, Samuel Haskell, Thomas C. Fossett.
1850. Edward Hills, William Caswell, Joseph M. Gleason, Danford Blackington, Nathan Hills, William Gleason, Nathan Whiting, Christopher Young.
1851. Edw. Hills, Christopher Young, Joseph M. Gleason.

CONSTABLES' COMPENSATION. — May 20, 1799, it was "voted to allow Amariah Mero eight dollars for eight years' service as constable." April 5, 1802, "Voted to allow the constable one dollar a year." Oct. 28, 1833, "Voted to set up the office of constable to the highest bidder." It was taken by William Caswell at five dollars and seventy-five cents. April 7, 1834, it was bid off by Robert Thompson, jun. at fifteen dollars.

COLLECTORS

1786. David Robbins.
1787. Jan. 15. David Robbins.
1787. April 2. Joel Adams, at . . 0s. 6d. per pound.
1788. March 3. Richard Cummings 0s. 10d. per pound.
1788. April 7. Amariah Mero . . 0s. 10d. per pound.
1789. Ebenezer Jennison . . . . 0s. 11d. per pound.
1790. Ebenezer Jennison . . . . 1s. 10d. per pound.
1790. Nov. 8. Joel Adams . . . 2s. 0d. per pound.
1791. David Robbins . . . . . 1s. 11d. per pound.
1792. Samuel Hills . . . . . . 1s. 0d. per pound.
1793. Edward Jones . . . . . 1s. 7d. per pound.
1794. Timothy Stewart[1] . . . . 0s. 7d. per pound.
1794. David Robbins[2] . . . . 1s. 10d. per pound.
1795. Josiah Robbins . . . . . 1s. 7d. per pound.
1796. Richard Cummings . . . . 1s. 0d. per pound.
1797. Richard Cummings . . . . 1s. 4d. per pound.
1798. Thomas Mitchell . . . . 1s. 4d. per pound.
1799. March 5. Edward Jones, who was excused . . . . . 1s. 4d. per pound.
1799. April 1. Nathaniel Robbins . 1s. 8d. per pound.
1800. Thomas Mitchell . . . . 1s. 4d.[3] per pound.
1802. Spencer Walcott . . . . 0s. 8d.[3] per pound.
1803. Spencer Walcott . . . . 8 cents per pound.
1804. Jabez N. Mitchell . . . . 2c. 5m. per dollar.
1805. Spencer Walcott . . . . 8c. 0m. per pound.
1806. Jabez N. Mitchell . . . . 8c. 0m. per pound.
1807. Josiah Robbins . . . . . 7c. 5m. per pound.
1808. Jabez N. Mitchell . . . . 8c. 0m. per pound.
1809. John Drake . . . . . . 7c. 0m. per pound.
1810. Thomas Mitchell, jun. . . . 10c. 0m. per pound.
1811. Thomas Mitchell, jun. . . . 3c. 0m. per dollar.
1812. Thomas Mitchell, jun. . . . 5c. 9m. per pound.
1813. Ebenezer W. Adams . . . 6c. 8m. per pound.
1814. Ebenezer W. Adams . . . 6c. 9m. per pound.
1815. Ebenezer W. Adams . . . 5c. 9m. per pound.
1816. Jeremiah Mitchell . . . . 7c. 0m. per pound.
1817. Ebenezer W. Adams . . . 1c. 9m. per dollar.
1818. Rufus Gillmor . . . . . 2c. 5m. per dollar.
1819. Rufus Gillmor . . . . . 2c. 5m. per dollar.

[1] For the inhabitants.   [2] For non-residents.   [3] Lawful money.

1820. John Chapman Robbins ... 3c. 0m. per dollar.
1821. Herman Hawes ..... 2c. 5m. per dollar.
1822. Herman Hawes ..... 3c. 0m. per dollar.
1823. Nathan D. Rice ..... 2c. 8m. per dollar.
1824. Thomas Mitchell .... 2c. 7m. per dollar.
1825. Isaac Hills ...... 2c. 5m. per dollar.
1826. Isaac Hills ...... 1c. 9m. per dollar.
1827. Isaac Hills ...... 2c. 9m. per dollar.
1828. Isaac Hills ...... 2c. 9m. per dollar.
1829. John C. Robbins (April 6) . 1c. 0m. per dollar.
1829. Saml. Daggett, jun. (Sept. 14) 2c. 8m. per dollar.
1830. Samuel Daggett, jun. ... 0c. 9m. per dollar.
1831. Nathan Hills, *giving* for the privilege ...... 0c. 4m. per dollar.
1832. Nelson Cutler ..... 1c. 0m. per dollar.
1833. Nelson Cutler ..... 0c. 8m. per dollar.
1834. The Treasurer ..... (no record.)
1835. Nathan Hills ...... 0c. 4m. per dollar.
1836. Nathan Hills ...... 0c. 5m. per dollar.
1837. Nathan Hills, *giving* ... 0c. $1\frac{1}{10}$m. per dollar.
1838. Nathan Hills ...... 0c. 9m. per dollar.
1839. Nathan Hills, *giving* ... 0c. 7m. per dollar.
1840. Nathan Hills ...... 0c. 1m. per dollar.
1841. The Treasurer ..... (no record.)
1842. Elisha E. Rice ..... (no record.)
1843. Ebenezer Cobb ..... 1c. 5m. per dollar.
1844. Ebenezer Cobb ..... 1c. 5m. per dollar.
1845. Ebenezer Blunt ..... 1c. 0m. per dollar.
1846. Ebenezer Blunt ..... 1c. 0m. per dollar.
1847. Ebenezer Blunt ..... 1c. 5m. per dollar.
1848. Ebenezer Blunt ..... 1c. 5m. per dollar.
1849. Joseph M. Gleason .... 1c. 5m. per dollar.
1850. Joseph M. Gleason .... 1c. 5m. per dollar.
1851. Joseph M. Gleason .... 1c. 5m. per dollar.

COLLECTORS' COMPENSATION. — Against the preceding names are placed the terms on which the taxes were collected in the different years. The office has generally been "set up at vendue," and undertaken by the lowest bidder. The first record of this proceeding is dated April 2, 1787; and the assessors were instructed "to add sixpence a pound on the next tax," this being the rate at which the collecting was undertaken. In 1846 and since, a collector has been regularly chosen, the terms on which he would undertake the business being understood before his election.

If a collector fails to procure satisfactory bondsmen, or to do the duty, or resigns, a substitute is chosen. Nov. 3, 1794, it was voted to allow to John Butler 1s. 6d. on the pound for collecting No. 3 tax; and an order of the same date was accordingly issued to pay him £4. 0s. 4d. The No. 3 tax was the one for the third year from the incorporation of the town, and Butler may have discharged part of the duty of collecting it.

The collector is held accountable for the whole amount of the taxes committed to him, whether they are against responsible persons or not. The risk he thus assumes is not great. A very poor person is seldom taxed, lest he should thus gain a residence in the town, and the people become liable for his support. If, after reasonable efforts, it is considered impracticable to collect any one's tax, the amount is remitted by an act of the town[1] in town-meeting, and thus the collector's liability ceases. But it must be apparent that the collector has made reasonable exertion to obtain it. Jan. 4, 1790, an article was brought forward "to see if the town will allow John Butler such taxes as he cannot collect on the tax-bills committed to him to collect, for the reasons that he can produce;" but "the town voted that they supposed he had not tried sufficiently."

The rates for collecting taxes sometimes have depended in part on the additional duties or privileges of the collectors. In 1839, it was voted that the person who "bid them off" should "have the constable's berth." In April, 1843, a vote was passed to choose a collector by ballot; but it was immediately recon-

---

[1] April 6, 1829, when the subject of abatement of taxes came before the town, it was "voted that the selectmen should abate such taxes as they might think proper."

sidered, and the selectmen were instructed to receive proposals and report at an adjourned meeting. At the adjourned meeting, it was "voted that the collection of taxes be put up at auction to the lowest bidder, he having the privilege of being constable, and doing the business of the town gratis."

TREASURERS.

1787–95. Matthias Hawes.	1834–35. Nathl. Robbins.
1795–1800. Jason Ware.	1836. Amos Drake.
1801–10. Levi Morse.	1837. Ebenezer Cobb.
1811–18. Spencer Walcott.	1838–43. Amos Drake.
1819–28. Ebenezer Alden.	1844. Bradley R. Mowry.
1829–31. Danl. F. Harding.	
1832. Nathl. Robbins.	1845–50. Elijah Vose.
1833. John Little.	1851. Spencer Walcott.

The name of the town-treasurer for 1792 and 1793 is not on record; but it was undoubtedly Matthias Hawes. He was regularly elected also in 1795, but soon declined, and was succeeded by Jason Ware, May 6, 1795.

TREASURER'S COMPENSATION. — May 20, 1799, "Voted to allow Mr. Jason Ware twenty-four dollars for four years' services as treasurer." April 5, 1802, " Voted to allow the treasurer six dollars a year." The same allowance was made in 1804 and 1805, and has been continued to the present time.

TITHINGMEN.

1787. John Butler. — 1788. Samuel Hills.
1789. Amos Lawrence. — 1790. David Woodcock.
1791. Jason Ware. — 1792. Richard Cummings.
1793. Christopher Butler, Seth Luce.
1794. George West, Bailey Grinnell.
1795. George West, Edward Jones.
1796. Jessa Robbins, Levi Morse.
1797. Bailey Grinnell, Joseph Butler.
1798. David Snell, Thomas Daggett.
1799. Christopher Butler, Matthias Hawes.
1800. Matthias Hawes, Christopher Butler.

TITHINGMEN.

1801. Jason Ware, Rufus Dyer.
1802. Matthias Hawes, Jason Ware.
1803. Rufus Dyer, Daniel Walker.
1804. Joel Adams, Abel Walker. — 1805. Amos Walker.
1806. Danl. Walker. — 1807. Danl. Walker, Abel Walker.
1808. Jessa Robbins, Samuel Daggett.
1809. (March) David Robbins, Wm. Boggs, Edward Jones.
1809. (April) Joel Adams, Thomas Mitchell, Samuel Hills.
1810. George Bowes, Israel Leavitt.
1811. Jason Ware, Christopher Butler, Abijah Hawes.
1812. Samuel Hills 1st, Thaddeus Luce, Jessa Robbins.
1813. Simeon Butters, Jessa Robbins.
1814. Solomon Hewes, Susman Abrams.
1815. Jonathan Carriel, Solomon Hewes, Simeon Butters, Joseph Morse, Samuel Hills, Richard Cummings, Aaron Young, George Wellington, Jacob Ring, Abel Walker, Thomas Mitchell, and Zebulon Sargent. The latter chosen May 8, in the place of Otis Bills, excused.
1816. Sterling Davis, Simon Fuller, Spencer Walcott, not sworn; Abijah Hawes, Jessa Robbins, Solomon Hewes, Cornelius Irish, Amos Walker, Simeon Butters, Jeremiah Stubbs, John Butler 1st, Benjamin Walker, Samuel Hills, sworn.
1817. Cornelius Irish, Samuel Hills 1st, Simon Fuller, Jessa Robbins, Calvin Gleason, Thaddeus Luce, Abijah Hawes.
1818. Jessa Robbins, Daniel Walker, Joel Adams.
1819. Daniel Walker, Bela Robbins, Simeon Butters.
1820. Daniel Walker, John Walker, Abel Walker.
1821. Samuel Hills, Simeon Butters.
1822. John Kieff, Simeon Butters, Phinehas Butler.
1823. Daniel Walker, Simeon Butters.
1824. Daniel Walker, Simon Fuller, John Butler.
1825. Daniel F. Harding, James Maxfield, Abel Walker.
1826. Edward Brown, John Hemenway, Reuben Hills.
1827. Zaccheus Litchfield, Roland Cobb, James St. Clair.
1828. Johnson Pilsbury, James Maxfield.
1829-41. (No record.)
1842. Joseph Irish, Obadiah Harris, Prince Luce.
1843. Robt. Thompson, jun., Elisha E. Rice, Nath. Whitney.
1844. George W. Butler, David Hill, Ebenezer W. Adams.
1845. Nathan Whitney, Walter Blake, Nathan Hills, jun.

1846. Horace Titus, Walter Blake, Nathan Hills 2d.
1847. Abel Walker, William Shepard, Oren O. Stewart, Thaddeus Luce, Nathan Walker.
1848. Abel Walker, William A. Thayer, Samuel Bowker, Isley Martin, Charles Kahler.
1849. Obadiah Harris, William Caswell, Calvin Boggs, Nathan D. Rice.
1850. William Shepard, Hugh Gordon, George M. Fossett, James Davis, David Blackington.
1851. Hugh Gordon, Ebenezer W. Adams, Nathan Whitney, Samuel Howland.

In 1815, the law for prosecuting violators of the Lord's Day was vigorously enforced. As the complainant was entitled to one-half of the fine, it is not to be supposed that he was always indifferent about the fee, or that he was actuated solely by a desire to check the profanation of the day.

On one occasion, a teamster, who had been carting goods to Boston, arrived at Waldoborough on Saturday. Being very unwilling to spend Sunday on the road, he took his departure about midnight for his home in Union. One of his oxen was thus overtasked, and he was delayed. For this delinquency he was complained of by a vigilant tithingman, whose house he was obliged to pass, and was fined.

On another occasion, a citizen of Boston, having heard of the dangerous illness of an intimate friend, was hastening home, and tarried at the tavern overnight. He rose very early on Sunday morning, and quietly departed with his family in his carriage, while many of the neighbors were yet asleep. But his departure did not escape the vigilance of a tithingman, who entered a complaint, though he did not himself see him.

All persons were permitted to enter complaints; and sometimes ill-will was gratified. A young man went to spend the Lord's Day with a relative, whose nearest neighbor he disliked. During the day, the neighbor went into the field to look at his cattle or sheep. Accordingly, on Monday, a complaint was entered against him for violating the Lord's Day. There were similar proceedings in other towns. They show the practical operation of the law.

FISH-WARDENS.

1787. David Robbins, Amariah Mero, John Butler.
1788. Royal Grinnell, John Butler, David Robbins.
1789. Jessa Robbins, Amariah Mero, Royal Grinnell.
1790. David Woodcock, Josiah Robbins, Philip Robbins.
1791. John M. Wight, Samuel Hills, Thomas Daggett, jun. Levi Morse, David Robbins.
1793. Edward Jones, David Robbins, Christopher Butler, Samuel Hills, Levi Morse.
1794. David Robbins, Josiah Hart, William Hart.
1795. Rufus Gillmor, Philip Robbins, Jessa Robbins, Christopher Butler, Josiah Maxcy.
1796. Royal Grinnell, Nathaniel Robbins, Christopher Butler, David Robbins.
1797. David Robbins, Christopher Butler, Moses Hawes, David Gillmor, Rufus Gillmor.
1798. Olney Titus, Josiah Maxcy, Christopher Butler, David Gillmor, Nathaniel Robbins.
1799. David Robbins, David Gillmor, Thomas Nye, Jeremiah Mitchell, Matthias Hawes.
1800. Thomas Nye, Rufus Dyer, Olney Titus, George Washington West, Royal Grinnell.
1801. David Gillmor, Edward Jones, Nathaniel Robbins, Matthias Hawes, Thomas Nye.
1802. Olney Titus, Rufus Dyer, Edward Jones, Edward Oakes, Jesse Rogers.
1803. A. Mero, John Butler, Nich. Smith, Tho. Nye, R. Gillmor; April 4, Rufus Dyer, in the place of T. Nye.
1804. Abel Walker, Royal Grinnell, Nicholas Smith, John Clark, Benjamin Eastman.
1805. David Robbins, John Clark, Calvin Morse.
1806. Jonathan Daggett, Ezekiel Hagar, Amos Barrett.
1807. Spencer Walcott, Thomas Nye, Christopher Butler, David Robbins, Royal Grinnell.
1808. Edward Jones, William Hart, James Rice, Nathan D. Rice, Richard Grinnell.
1809. Timothy Stewart, Thomas Nye, Zelotes Tucker.
1823. Eben. W. Adams, John Butler 1st, Phinehas Butler.

CHAPTER XVI.

TOPOGRAPHICAL HISTORY.

First Burial Place. — Old Burying Ground. — First Private Burying Ground. — Second Private Burying Ground. — East Union Burying Ground. — Hearses. — Common. — Pound. — Town House.

BURIAL-PLACES.

FIRST BURIAL PLACE. — Fourteen[1] persons were buried in David Robbins's field, on the point of land which juts into the west side of Seven-tree Pond. The only adults were Elisha Partridge and Jessa Robbins's first wife.

OLD BURYING GROUND. — Who owns the Old Burying Ground? This question is often asked, and from the town-records will now be given all the information respecting it which they contain.

Nov. 8, 1790, Matthias Hawes, Ezra Bowen, and David Woodcock, were chosen a committee "to look out a plat of ground and procure the same for a burying-place," and "to settle with David Robbins in regard of the inhabitants that had been buried on his land." David Woodcock[2] died Dec. 9, and was the first person buried in the Old Burying Ground. March 7, 1791, the "report of the [other members of the] Committee on the spot for a burying-place at the north end of the spot for the meeting-house," was accepted by the town. At the same time it was "voted that Mr. Philip Robbins shall clear and improve the

---

[1] N. P. Hawes's MS.

[2] Mr. Woodcock lived at South Union. The road around the head of Seven-tree Pond was so bad that it was hardly passable. The pond was frozen so as to prevent crossing with boats, and yet the ice was not thick. The funeral procession went to the pond; and the people, two by two, passed along on the margin very near the shore, at great distances from each other, lest the cracking ice should give way beneath their feet.

spot for a burying-place, till it be subdued according to his proposal." Aug. 29, 1791, "Chose two sextons to attend the graveyard, viz. Rufus Gillmor and Nathaniel Robbins." It was expected that the meeting-house would be erected near the place selected for burials. When it was determined to build the house on the Common, the inhabitants continued to bury where there had already been several interments.

There is no other record on the subject till Jan. 16, 1796, when it was voted to fence the burying-ground and measure it, — a vote which was reconsidered April 4. May 20, 1799, Rufus Gillmor, for twenty-five dollars, agreed to put round it "a good five-rail fence, with a decent gate in the front," by the last of June; and David Robbins, Amariah Mero, and Thomas Mitchell, were chosen a committee to see that it was done according to agreement. April 7, 1806, the selectmen were directed to fence it with boards and pine-posts. April 4, 1808, upon an article "to see if the town will request Mr. Robbins to pasture the burying-ground with sheep and horses only, or act and do any thing relative thereto," it was "voted that the selectmen be a committee to contract with some person or persons to fence" it, and report at the May meeting. In May, 1809, Amariah Mero took at auction, for thirteen dollars, the job "to make a new fence on the north side, . . . similar to that now standing by the road, and to have the remainder of the old fence repaired well." The records make no further mention of the subject till Sept. 10, 1827, when it was "voted that the selectmen make or repair the fence about the burying-ground, to the best advantage." Nov. 7, 1836, "voted that the selectmen see that the burying-ground near Willard Robbins's be fenced as soon as may be for the interest of the town, and with such materials as they may think most suitable."

There is no record of any purchase or agreement respecting the land. It is doubtful if any record was made. Mr. Robbins, the owner of the land, gave the place to be used as a burying-ground; it being understood that the town should fence it, and that he should pasture it with sheep or such cattle as would not injure the graves or grave-stones. "The town," according to the late Nathaniel Robbins, Esq. "has generally been negligent about fencing it." In April, 1842, William Gleason, Calvin Gleason, and Samuel Stone, were chosen a committee to examine the condition of the fence; and, upon their making a report, Aug. 27, it was "voted that the building of said fence be left in the hands of the selectmen." Probably nothing was done; for, Sept. 29, 1845, the town voted to allow "Willard Robbins's bill for repairs done on graveyard-fence from 1834 to 1845."

At the meeting in April, 1842, when the subject of the fence was brought forward, it was "voted that the selectmen procure a deed of said ground in behalf of the town." A deed was not obtained. Sept. 29, 1845, when Willard Robbins's bill for repairs was allowed, an article was brought forward "to see if the town will allow any person to pasture the town burying-ground;" whereupon Walter Blake, Nathan Hills, and Elijah Vose, were chosen a committee "to ascertain what right, if any, the town had to said burying-ground, and report at the next town-meeting." Their report is not recorded. In July, 1846, Nathaniel, son of Josiah Robbins, not knowing, and not being able to ascertain from his father's deed, whether he had any title to it or not, gave a quit-claim deed of the Old Burying Ground to his son Willard.

The situation of this ground is very beautiful; and if trees, shrubbery, and flowers were planted, it would be one of the most interesting spots in Union. Here, too, is the only monument in town. It is of marble, and was placed over the grave of Nathaniel Robbins, Esq. Dec. 4, 1850, in memory of him and his wife Lovey, who is buried by his side.

FIRST PRIVATE BURYING GROUND. — The warrant calling a town-meeting, July 4, 1820, contains an article "to hear the report of the selectmen relative to buying a piece of land for a burying-ground;" and it was "voted that the selectmen be a standing committee, and make further report respecting the burying-ground in the west part of the town." May 7, 1821, the selectmen were authorized to purchase a piece of land of Samuel Daggett, provided they could obtain a sufficient quantity for a sum not exceeding twenty-five dollars. The next mention of the subject bears date April 5, 1830, when Calvin Gleason, Henry Fossett, and Henry Blunt, were chosen a committee "to make such inquiries as they think proper, as to purchasing a piece of land for a burying-ground." The town voted not to accept their report, which was made Sept. 13. Individuals then took up the subject, and a justice's warrant for incorporation was granted Nov. 22, 1830; at which time ground was bought in the corner of the field made by the two roads, about 100 rods north-east of the present graveyard. The funeral of Mrs. Jane Bryant, the only person buried here, was Jan. 14, 1831. The ground was so wet that the coffin rose, and the body was removed, April 16, 1831, to the present burying-ground, which was purchased by a committee chosen Dec. 30, 1830, and was accepted Jan. 22, 1831. The burial of Mrs. Jonathan Morse was the next. There were fourteen removals from other places, most of them from the Old Burying Ground. Henry Fossett, Ebenezer Blunt, Brotherton Daggett, and Thomas Mitchell, had each of them one child, and Calvin Gleason, Nahum Thurston, and John Tobey, had each of them two children, reburied here. Beside these were Jonathan Carriel; also Philip Grinnell and wife, who were removed from Liberty in 1834; and a child of Nathan D. Rice, Nov. 18, 1835, which was re-interred at the time he buried another. The records were remarkably well kept, giving the ages, and also the time of all the burials, by Samuel Daggett, the sexton and clerk, till his decease in the fall of 1846.

SECOND PRIVATE BURYING GROUND. — A justice's warrant was issued Nov. 1, 1841, and a meeting held and proprietors incorporated Nov. 8, at which time may be dated the opening of the Second Private

Burying Ground. The deed of the land probably is
of a later date. Formerly the spot was the northern
part of the Rev. Mr. True's orchard. In April, 1844,
the town voted to pay half the expense of building the
fence between it and the Old Burying Ground. It is
divided into family lots, cornered by marble posts. The
first person buried in it was David Cummings, who
died the 24th, and not, as the grave-stone states, the
17th of March, 1842. Several bodies in the Old Burying
Ground were disinterred, and reburied here. Here
are the only tombs in the town. The first was built
in the north-east corner of the ground, in the autumn
of 1846, to be a temporary receiving tomb when the
ground is frozen. Before this time, graves were dug
during the winter. The first person whose remains
rested here temporarily was the wife of Dr. Jonathan
Sibley. A few weeks afterward, the tomb was again
opened to receive the remains of Mrs. Reed, who was
the second tenant, and who with the first was interred
in the spring of 1847. In the autumn of 1848, two
contiguous tombs were built by Ebenezer Alden and
John Little, who owned adjoining lots. Some of the
proprietors have ornamented their squares with trees.

EAST UNION BURYING GROUND. — July 4, 1820,
John W. Lindley, Micajah Gleason, and Reuben Hills,
were chosen a committee " to examine and report on
the petition for a burying-ground in the east part of
the town." Nov. 6, the town accepted a report " to
purchase a piece of land of John Lermond at twenty-five
dollars an acre, and one dollar per rod for the wall
standing thereon." This land was about 100 rods, in
a north-easterly direction, from the present private
burying-ground, and near a large rock. Ephraim
Bowley and four (?) children were buried here; but
the ground was so wet, that it was voted, Sept. 11,
1826, that "the treasurer be authorized to exchange
deeds with John Lermond," for another spot "more
suitable." The spot obtained was north of this, on
the north side of the river, near the mills. Sept. 8,
1828, it was "voted that John Lermond build the

fence, to the best advantage to the town." Several persons were buried here; but the ground was so rocky, that nearly all the inhabitants in the vicinity united in purchasing the spot now known as the East Union Private Burying Ground. The first burial in this yard was of Sarah G. Collins, who died Feb. 27, 1846. As early as Aug. 17, 1846, sixteen bodies, mostly from the second place selected, had been reinterred. The ground is the property of individuals, and divided into lots.

HEARSES.

For many years, the remains of the dead[1] were carried to the grave on biers, which were borne on men's shoulders, sometimes two or three miles. There were commonly eight bearers; four to relieve the other four at short distances. Subsequently, when horse-wagons came into use, the custom was introduced of removing the body of a wagon, and "strapping" or cording the coffin to the axle-trees. May 1, 1817, and Sept. 27, 1822, the selectmen were authorized "to procure a good decent hearse for the use of the town." There was none in town before this time. Dec. 20, 1823, Abiel Gay, for $23.50, bid off the job of building a hearse-house, sixteen feet by eight, and seven feet high, and agreed to have it done to the acceptance of the selectmen in June. Sept. 13, 1824, it was voted to purchase a pall, paint the hearse-house, and repair the fence. April, 1845, P. C. Harding was authorized to purchase two hearses, with palls for the same, and to dispose of the old one. April, 1846, it was voted that the town provide a hearse for the bury-

---

[1] Of course, when there were but few families, a death was immediately known by all in town. Now it is generally announced by the bell. Within a few hours after a death, the bell is rung in the usual manner, — unless it be in the night, when the ringing is deferred till the following morning. Then, for a male, the bell is struck three strokes in rapid succession three times, there being between each three strokes an interval of one two or minutes. For a female, it is the same, except that the strokes are three times two. After this the age is tolled, — one stroke for each year.

ing-ground at East Union. One for the First Private
Burying Ground was voted in May. In April, the
selectmen were authorized to purchase two harnesses
to accompany the hearses; also, in May, another for
the hearse at the West Burying Ground.

COMMON.

The Common also has been a topic of much discussion. The earliest record alluding to the subject bears date April 5, 1790. "Voted that boars and rams shall not have the liberty of going on the Common." Voted that "hogs shall have liberty of going on the Common at large."[1] Jan. 16, 1796, Josiah Robbins, Timothy Stewart, Amariah Mero, Samuel Hills, and David Robbins, were chosen a committee "to apply to David Gillmor for a deed of two acres for a meeting-house lot, and to measure the same." There does not seem to have been any action upon the subject immediately; for, Nov. 5, 1798, the town voted not to accept the report of a committee chosen to lay out the Common round the meeting-house, but "to have the Common as surveyed by Mr. Waldron Stone." It was somewhat rough at this time, as we may infer from an article in the warrant for May 27, 1801, "to see if the town will clear out the stumps and stone out of the Common, so as it may be fit for training

---

[1] Votes of a similar nature were frequently passed. Hogs were privileged characters each year afterward till 1794. From 1794 to 1799, votes were annually passed that "swine be allowed to run at large, being yoked and ringed as the law directs." With the exception of the year 1804, they have never since been allowed their liberty, not even if subjected to the ignoble yoke on the neck and wire-ring in the nose. Several movements have been made in their behalf; but their friends have been so disconcerted in town-meetings at having their articles always "dropped," that it is many years since they have given up in despair all attempts to procure for them the rights and privileges which they enjoy in some of the streets of large cities.

The general principle of choosing all men hog-reeves who have been married in the course of the preceding year has not always prevailed here. Unmarried persons have sometimes attained to the distinguished honor, though there is no record that the honor has been conferred on any one since April 4, 1825, when it was "voted to choose no hog-reeves."

for the town-soldiers." The same warrant contained an article "to see if the town will accept of a deed of land for a Common, for a training-field, from Mr. David Gillmor." The town "voted the selectmen be a committee to apply to Mr. David Gillmor for a deed of the Common in the best manner they can get it for the town, and to postpone the clearing until a deed is procured."

April 4, 1808, upon an article to see if the town will survey the Common, it was "voted that the selectmen look up the deed of the Common, and put it on record as soon as convenient." On the 2d of May following, it was "voted that the selectmen survey the Common, and compromise with Capt. [Rufus] Gillmor, and David his brother, by giving up the old deed, and taking a new one on the terms proposed by Capt. Gillmor, and get the deed recorded." Accordingly, the following deed was obtained:—

"KNOW ALL MEN by these presents, that I, David Gillmor, of the Plantation No. Two, in the county of Hancock, and State of Massachusetts, gentleman, in consideration of one hundred dollars, well and truly paid by Nathaniel Bachelor, Joel Adams, and William Hart, selectmen of the town of Union for the year A.D. 1809, and their successors in said office as selectmen of Union, the receipt whereof I do hereby acknowledge, do hereby give, grant, sell, and convey unto the said Bachelor, Adams, and Hart, and their successors in the office of selectmen of said Union, for ever, a certain tract of land lying in Union aforesaid, and is bounded as follows, viz.: Beginning at a stake and stones standing west thirty-three degrees south seven rods and five links from the south-west corner of Capt. Rufus Gillmor's dwelling, at the northerly corner of said tract; thence south seven degrees east [west?] fourteen rods to a stake and stones; thence east fifteen degrees south twenty-three rods to a stake and stones; thence east seventeen degrees north thirteen rods and five links to a stake and stones; thence east twenty-six degrees north eight rods to a stake and stones; thence north seven degrees west four rods and sixteen links to a stake and stones; thence west fourteen degrees north forty rods and twenty links to the bound first mentioned, be the same more or less ; and the above premises are to be occupied for the sole purpose for a Common for the use of the town of Union, to have and to hold the afore-granted premises to the said Bachelor, Adams, and Hart, or their successors, to their use and behoof for ever.

"And I do covenant with the said Bachelor, Adams, and Hart, that I am lawfully seized in fee of the afore-granted premises; that they are free of all incumbrances; that I have good right to sell and convey the same to the said Bachelor, Adams, and Hart, or their successors in office; and that I will warrant and defend the same premises to the said Bachelor, Adams, and Hart, for ever, against the lawful claims and demands of all persons.

"In witness whereof, I, the said David Gillmor, have hereunto set my hand and seal, this fifteenth day of June, in the year of our Lord one thousand eight hundred and nine.

"DAVID GILLMOR, and seal.

"Signed, sealed, and delivered in presence of us,
"RUFUS GILLMOR.
"NATHL. ROBBINS.

"Lincoln, ss. June the 15, A.D. 1809. Then the above-named David Gillmor personally acknowledged the above instrument to be his free act and deed before me,

"NATHL. ROBBINS, Justice of Peace."

1809, April 3, the town "voted that cattle shall not be allowed to run loose on the Common on public days." Sept. 25, 1809, David Robbins, Nathaniel Robbins, and Amos Barrett, were chosen a committee to keep the Common clear of incumbrances.

1830, April 5, an unsuccessful proposition was brought forward "to see if the town would pay Daniel F. Harding and John Little for the powder already expended, and necessary to be expended, in removing the ledge on the Common."

1838, Sept. 10, an article was "dropped," which requested the town to "authorize the treasurer to release to D. F. Harding, and the subscribers associated with him, for building a Congregational Meeting-house, the land on which the Old Meeting-house stood, including that portion of the Common below Ebenezer Cobb's line and the road leading from said Cobb's new building to Zaccheus Litchfield's house." This was at the beginning of an excitement in regard to the location of the meeting-houses. At different times, several votes were passed, the object of some of which may have been to test the feelings of the town as to how far they meant to allow the Common to be trespassed upon. The deed was obscure; and, Nov. 29, 1838, it was " voted that the selectmen survey, or cause to be surveyed, the Common, and erect suitable monuments at every angle and corner, and ascertain the right said town has to it, if any." April 1, 1839, an application was made by the Universalists " to see if the town would allow Nathaniel Bachelor, and such others as may be associated with him, to build a free meeting-house near where the old house stood, blow the rock, and level the ground in front of the contemplated free meeting-house. . . . Voted that they be allowed to blow out the rock and level off the spot in front." An application came from the other party, April 16, 1839, " to see if the town would allow Joseph Vaughan and others to blast rocks and remove them from the ledge on the Common for the use of a meeting-house. . . . Voted that they be allowed to blow out and remove the rock from the Common."

Upon recurring to the deed, it was found impossible, by pursuing the courses marked out in it, to arrive at the point of departure ; and it was concluded that the word *east* meant *west*. April 29, 1839, the town " voted that the selectmen survey the Common as now holden, and [that] durable monuments [be] erected at the angles of the same, and a plan thereof made and filed in the clerk's office." From this plan, it appears that the Universalist Meeting-house projects somewhat upon the Common.

Several articles have been brought forward in town-meetings, during the last eight years, respecting incumbrances and pasturing cattle on the Common, —

designed probably by a few individuals to tease each other, or for sport.

POUND.

Of course, the cattle of the early settlers grazed in meadows and browsed in woods in the summer, and were fed principally on meadow-hay in the winter. Cow-bells and sheep-bells were fastened to the necks of the leaders of the herds and flocks, so that they might be the more easily found. From an early period, owners have left with the town-clerks records of the marks of their cattle. "Thomas Daggett's mark for his cattle, sheep, &c. is half a crop on the foreside of the left ear, and the end of the right ear cut off. Entered Aug. 28, 1790." Another entry, dated March 27, 1840, "is a swallow's tail on both ears, and a notch in the underside of both ears." Among the early settlers it seemed desirable that this or some other mode of identifying the cattle and sheep should be adopted, by which, in case of their straying or doing damage, the owners might be known. April, 1824, a vote was passed "that cattle shall not run at large the present year." Similar votes have generally been adopted at the annual April meetings since that time.

The subject of a pound was brought up June 20, 1803, but voted down. March 3, 1806, "Voted to build a pound, and set it near the Common." It was to be of pine, forty feet square, and to be completed by the first of June. William Boggs undertook the job for forty-six dollars. It was erected on the west end of the Common, and occupied the spot where the store of N. Cutler, Esq. now stands. Robert Bunting was annoyed; and, May 2, 1808, obtained leave of the town to move it "to some suitable place near the dwelling-house of James Rice," who lived by the Methodist Meeting-house on the farm now owned by Nathan D. Rice.

April 1, 1822, the selectmen were chosen "a committee to examine the pound, and to report their opinion at the next meeting on the necessity of building a new one." Sept. 9, 1822, it was voted to build one " in some convenient spot on Rufus Dyer's land; the same to be built of rocks, four feet thick at the bottom, and two feet thick at the top; the wall to be six feet high with rocks, with timber on the top; three square good posts for to hang the door to, with a good door well hung with iron hinges and well secured with a good lock; the whole to be done in a workmanlike manner, and to be twenty-five feet square within the wall." The building of it was put up at auction, Nov. 4, and taken by Nathaniel Robbins for twenty-eight dollars.

TOWN-HOUSE.

As early as March 3, 1806, the warrant for a town-meeting contained an article " to see if the town would build a town-house." The subject was not again brought forward till July 1, 1837. The east and the west parts of the town became divided. Some of the people wanted to have it at Barrett's Corner, north-west of the Middle Bridge. Some wanted it near the Methodist Meeting-house, on land which would be given by Nathan D. Rice; and others near the Common, where Ebenezer Cobb was willing to have it erected " east of his new building, without expense to the town for land." Each of these places was approved by the town at one or another of the meetings. Plans were also adopted, and committees were chosen and authorized to make contracts for the building. Even a deed for the land was obtained of N. D. Rice. The whole population became excited; at one meeting reconsidering votes passed at a preceding meeting, or in the earlier part of the same meeting. The people often met, and the discussion was continued till June 17, 1839, when the whole town rallied; and it was voted, yeas 157, nays 146, " to reconsider all votes formerly passed." This being done, it was " voted that we build a town-house, to be located near the powder-house; and that it be built according to the blue plan, 40 by 48 feet, as accepted at a former meeting; that the selectmen be a committee to superintend the building of said house, and give directions as to the height of the posts and finishing said house. And the treasurer be authorized forthwith to enter into bonds with Ebenezer Cobb to build the same for the sum of six hundred dollars; one-half to be paid by the first day of April, 1840, the other half by the first day of September, 1840, when said house is finished; said Cobb to furnish land and other materials suitable for said house."

July 1, 1839, an attempt was made to procure another reconsideration of the votes; but the town, 143 to 73, "voted not to reconsider," and the selectmen were appointed " a committee to locate the town-house in the vicinity of the powder-house, and agree with Mr. Cobb for a piece of land suitable for the same." The house was built, and thus ended the struggle. A stove was voted April 7, 1845. Further details[1] would be uninteresting, except as they might illustrate the orderly manner in which town-affairs are conducted, when hundreds of people are exceedingly zealous in matters considered favorable or prejudicial to their interests and convenience.

[1] In April, 1844, it was voted that the building should "be used only for political purposes;" but, April, 1845, the letting of it was "left discretionary with the selectmen." April 7, 1845, voted that Ebenezer Cobb take care of the Town-house. April 6, 1846, the selectmen were authorized to lease the upper part of it "to John W. Lindley and his associates, with a privilege for the purpose of finishing a hall; provided they shall get and keep the Town-house insured so long as they shall occupy the same, reserving the right to rescind the lease upon paying a full compensation for their expenditures." The building has often been used for public worship, for justices' courts and courts of reference, and by the band when practising music.

CHAPTER XVII.

FIRST MEETING-HOUSE.

Early Efforts for a Meeting-house. — Spot selected. — Location changed. — Contracted for. — Porch. — Raising. — Enclosed. — Pillars. — Pulpit Window. — Outside to be finished. — Temporary Seats. — Pews. — Roof to be painted. — Sale of Pews. — Names of Owners. — Lock voted. — Description of the House. — Pews built in the Gallery. — Repairs. — Stove. — Decay and Desecration of the House. — Taken down. — Associations with it. — Customs. — Marriage Publishments. — Dogs and Dog Whippers.

The present generation knows but little about the efforts of the fathers of the town to provide a place for worship. The country had not recovered from the exhaustion consequent on the revolutionary war. The burden of building a meeting-house was heavy. The people were poor. They were also embarrassed by the wants and inconveniences always incident to new settlements. But, in their day, a meeting-house was considered nearly as important to a town as a dwelling-house to a family. Accordingly, in showing the patience and perseverance of the inhabitants from the beginning to the completion of the house, more details will be given than can be generally interesting.

1787.

The first recorded notice occurs April 2, the year after the incorporation. Then, every house in town, except the Taylor House, was made of logs. Philip Robbins, Matthias Hawes, Josiah Robbins, Ezra Bowen, Joel Adams, Moses Hawes, and Abijah Hawes, were chosen a committee "to look out and find the most convenient spot to set a meeting-house, and procure a deed of the same." Philip Robbins was " to see if Mr. Jonathan Amory would give a lot of land for the support of the gospel, and get a deed of it. . . . [The town] would not do any thing in

regard to clearing a spot, [or] hiring preaching."
Nov. 19, the committee reported that the most convenient spot was "on the line between Josiah Robbins's and the land of David Gillmor. Bounds: South corner; north thirty-six degrees east, sixteen rods; thence north forty-two degrees west, twenty rods; thence south thirty-six degrees west, sixteen rods; thence south forty-two degrees east, twenty rods." This spot was on the hill now known as the Old Burying Ground. Samuel Hills, Moses Hawes, and John Butler, were chosen a "committee to write a letter to Mr. Amory for a deed for the same."

1788-90.

April 7, 1788, " Voted that the town will clear up a spot to set a meeting-house." May 28, " Set up at vendue, to be cleared by the lowest bidder. Bid off by Amariah Mero, who is to clear and fence, and seed to grass for the first crop, and to have the improvement till the town call for it for the above use; he keeping the brush down and fence in good order." July 14, the town "voted that they would build," and "that a tax of £110 be assessed and collected, in boards, shingles, or any thing that is necessary to build a meeting-house, and that it be paid in by the last of May, 1789." Messrs. Woodcock, Josiah Robbins, and Moses Hawes, were chosen a committee to receive and prize the lumber. The work, however, progressed slowly. The time for payment was extended to June 1, 1790. An unsuccessful attempt was made to reconsider the vote passed July 14, 1788.

1791.

March 7, the town "chose Josiah Robbins, Joel Adams, Thomas Daggett, Philip Robbins, and Joseph Maxcy, a committee to receive and prize the lumber;" and the time for payment was "lengthened to 1½ months from the date of this meeting. . . . Voted the thanks of the town be given to the committee for services done in procuring a bond for a deed of Mr.

Woodcock in behalf of Mr. Jonathan Amory for a [spot] to set a meeting-house."

1792.

April 2, " Voted to set the meeting-house on the north side of the road from Capt. West's to Christopher Butler's, and on the east of the road to Senebec Pond, in the crotch by Mr. Gillmor's new field."[1] Josiah Robbins, Joel Adams, Philip Robbins, Bela Robbins, Seth Luce, Joseph Maxcy, Samuel Daggett, Joseph Guild, and Capt. George West, were chosen a committee " to look out the most convenient spot near where it now is " voted, and to " agree with Mr. Gillmor for the spot, and make their report at the next meeting." It was voted that the house should be forty feet by fifty,[2] and that Matthias Hawes, Joseph Maxcy, and Amariah Mero, should be a committee " to inquire of a suitable person, of the cost and plan of such a house." May 7, the town chose Capt. George West " chairman of the town's committee," to which they added Mr. Thomas Daggett. At the same time they accepted the " spot the committee looked out to set a meeting-house on," and chose Joseph Maxcy, Amariah Mero, and Edward Jones, " a committee of three to draw a plan and prize produce to pay the £110 tax that was granted."

More than five years had thus passed away. Dec. 12, 1792, effectual measures were taken for making a beginning. It was voted to put up at auction the job of furnishing a frame of the following dimensions : —

Two sills, 50 feet long, 12 inches square, oak.
Five sills, 40 feet long, 12 inches square, oak.
Two plates, 50 feet long, 8 inches by 12, pine.
Six beams, 42 feet long, 12 inches by 14, pine.

---

[1] At the same time, Ebenezer Robbins and his estate were " set off to Thomaston to do duty and to receive privilege in building a meeting-house and supporting the gospel — at his request."

[2] At the next meeting, the size was reconsidered, and it was voted to build forty feet square. This vote was again reconsidered Nov. 2, and the house was built forty feet by fifty.

Two gallery girths, 40 feet long, 12 inches square, pine.
One gallery girth, 30 feet long, 12 inches square, pine.
Sixteen posts, 25 feet long, 12 inches at the foot, oak.
Ten beams, 12 feet long, 10 inches by 12, pine.
Six girths, 13 feet long, 8 inches by 10, oak.
Four girths, 12 feet long, 8 inches by 10, oak.
Six girths, 10 feet long, 8 inches by 10, oak.
Twelve rafters, 28 feet long, 8 inches square at head, ten of them pine, and two oak.
Four kingposts, 20 feet long, 10 inches by 12, oak.

The contract was taken by Josiah Robbins for £32, the lumber to be " on the spot by the first of June, all but the slit-work, and that by the first of May." " Voted there shall be a committee to take the taxes, and deduct out £40 to pay for the getting of the timber, and average the remainder on the inhabitants and non-residents, to be paid in materials as follows: Boards, shingles, joists, or slit-work, at prices set by a committee heretofore chosen. And this committee shall examine the lumber so delivered, and give orders on the collector, which shall pay so much of their taxes."

1793.

March 4, an assessment of £50 was voted[1] for framing, raising, and inclosing the house; and Philip Robbins, Rufus Gillmor, and George West, were chosen a committee to procure workmen. Uriah Coffin bid off at auction a contract to furnish, for £4, sixty sleepers hewed on two sides, eight inches thick, oak or hemlock. April 1, " Voted to build a porch, and there should be 168 feet of square timber and 76 feet hewed on two sides for sleepers, and that application should be made to Mr. Bosworth[2] for the dimensions of the same." Bid off by C. Butler for £1. 14s. Thirty pounds were voted, Dec. 2 and on the seventh of the following April, " towards finishing " the house.

[1] At the same time, it was voted "to give Mr. Ebenezer Robbins his meeting-house tax, as he is old, and nearly past his labor."

[2] Mr. Bosworth, of Warren, " was the master-builder, and almost the only man who knew how to do such work."

In autumn the frame was completed. The day for raising it must have been one of extraordinary interest. The hearts of the people were gladdened at the prospect of obtaining what had been the subject of many prayers and a great deal of anxiety and Yankee calculation for more than six years. A "raising," too, in those days, was very laborious. Rigging and machinery were seldom used. The timber was commonly large and heavy. Pike-poles and men's arms were the means by which a frame was put up. In raising so large a building as a meeting-house, it was necessary to look to neighboring towns for assistance.

Accordingly, on Wednesday, Oct. 3, when the sun rose above the forests and shone on the few cultivated fields, it requires no great stretch of the imagination to picture the moving of most of the population of Union, and of many persons from Warren and Thomaston, and of some perhaps from Waldoborough, towards a common centre. Some were in boats on the pond and river. Others were on horseback. The greater part were on foot, wending their way through the woods, among stumps, stones, and holes, and over corduroy roads. As they passed by the humble dwellings, — for, with very few exceptions, the habitations were log-houses, — they were hailed with loud, sharp voices and a hearty welcome to "come in and take some refreshment, or something to eat." On the tables were placed the best of every thing which could be furnished from the herds, flocks, fields, and barn-yards.

By Philip Robbins a corner-stone had been previously taken out of the river near Bachelor's Mills. It was laid by means of a compass east and west, without any other ceremony. As it was always customary for all who attended a "raising" to labor gratuitously and to be furnished with refreshments, "Rufus Gillmor got a barrel of rum, and the men took their eleven o'clock and their four o'clock in good shape." Amariah Mero applied to the heavy timbers some rigging which he had previously borrowed at Warren. The band of the frame on the east end was raised by fastening the rigging to the limbs of a native oak, which was near it. One piece of timber, and then another, was slowly and tediously lifted, till all were put in their places. After two days, or perhaps three, of excessive labor, the raising was completed. It is said, that, to the eyes and imaginations of some of the inhabitants, it seemed almost as if they were to have a Solomon's Temple. A general enthusiasm prevailed among the population, which was then so small[1] that nearly one-half of the persons who assisted in the raising were from the neighboring towns.

Upon hearing the report of the building committee, Dec. 2, it was "voted that the time for getting lumber for the meeting-house be prolonged till the middle of the next March." Afterward, little by little, for many years, additions and improvements were made according to the inclinations and ability of the people.

1794.

April 7, thirty pounds were granted toward finishing the house. Sept. 1, it was voted that twenty pounds should be immediately assessed and worked out " on the highway, in the room of the twenty pounds granted by the General Court to be worked out on the highways, and to appropriate the said twenty pounds in cash towards inclosing[2] the meeting-house." The proceedings of the year concluded with a vote, Nov. 3, that "the committee procure pillars to be turned for the meeting-house."

---

[1] At this time, says Mrs. William Hart, the only families in town, on the east side of Seven-tree Pond, were those of Samuel Hills, Joseph Maxcy, Josiah Maxcy, William Hart, Spencer Walcott, Christopher Butler, Levi Morse; and on the road to the east part of the town lived Jonah Gay. On the west side lived Ezra Bowen, Abijah Hawes, David Robbins, Richard Cummings, Moses Hawes, Amariah Mero, Edward Jones, Rufus Gillmor, and Josiah Robbins. On the south of Round Pond lived Jessa Robbins; and on the west of it were Joel Adams, Jason Ware, and Matthias Hawes. Besides these there were, in other parts of the town, Seth Luce, Bailey Grinnell, George West, Royal Grinnell, William Lewis, Thomas Daggett, Thomas Daggett, jun., Samuel Daggett, and Aaron Daggett.

[2] That is, boarding and shingling the roof.

1795.

May 6, the town voted not to grant more money, and that "the money in the hands of the several collectors of the taxes granted for building the meeting-house be first expended for the purpose of inclosing the same." At the same time, Ebenezer Jennison, Rufus Dyer, and David Gillmor, and subsequently Amariah Mero, in place of E. Jennison, who declined, were chosen a committee to draw a plan of the groundwork, to prize the pews, and report at the next meeting.

1796.

In the "dead of winter," Jan. 16, a town-meeting was held; and it was voted to raise by tax "sixty pounds, or two hundred dollars, to procure lumber for the meeting-house, so that it may be seasoned and fit to work the ensuing summer; . . . and that the tax be assessed in the course of a fortnight," according to the valuation taken for the preceding May. David Gillmor, Rufus Gillmor, and Joseph Maxcy, were chosen a committee to receive such lumber as was suitable; and it might be brought in until April. April 4, the committee were instructed to enlarge the pulpit-window as they may think best. May 5, it was voted to finish the outside of the meeting-house, and that the job should " be set up at vendue to the lowest bidder, all but setting the glass." It was to be done "like the Warren Meeting-house, and in a workmanlike manner, by the first day of November; all, except the window-sashes and doors, which were to be done by the last day of June, 1797." The materials were required to be on the ground in two months, or by the 25th of July. The contractor was to "enter into bonds with sufficient bondsmen," and " to have one-half the pay when the clapboarding was done, viz. by the first of November, and the other half when the remainder of the work was done." The bid was taken by Capt. George West, at one hundred and ninety-four dollars. He seems to have thought it an unprofitable job; for, Nov. 5, 1798, he made an unavailing application for more compensation. At the same time the subject of pews was taken up. The meeting-house was never dedicated. As soon as it was covered, and the floor laid, religious services were held in it. Temporary seats were made by loosely placing the ends of long planks or boards on blocks or on the buts of beams or logs.

The committee chosen May 6, 1795, delayed their report from one town-meeting to another till Nov. 7, 1796. Then it was voted to accept the plan of Amariah Mero, and not to accept the prices affixed to his plan. A committee was chosen upon the spot to re-apprize the pews, and to report before the meeting dissolved; and their report was accepted. An article had been inserted in the warrant in relation to the selling of the pews. It was voted to put them up at auction, the bids to be for choice. The terms of payment were one-fifth in ten days, two-fifths in six months, and the other two-fifths when the work was finished. "Nothing short of half a dollar" was to be bid, and "nothing to be considered a bid unless it was above the apprizement." No persons were allowed to bid but the inhabitants and such non-residents as owned land in the town. No. 18 was reserved by the town as a minister's pew. No record is made of the success of the sale; but it was "voted to adjourn selling the remainder of the pews until March meeting" in the next year.

1797.

Feb. 6, it was "voted to procure materials, and to go on with finishing the house;" and Josiah Robbins, Amos Barrett, and David Gillmor, were chosen the committee. They were "instructed to purchase boards and such other lumber as was necessary to finish the lower part" of it. This seems to have been the extent to which it could be expected to carry the finishing.

When the March meeting was held, it was "voted to sell the remainder of the pews this day, upon the same terms as before; the time for payment to be dated from this meeting." Aug. 28, the town instructed the treasurer " to call on those who had not paid for their pews nor given security, to settle with him and give him security, or pay the money in one month from this time, viz. by the 28th of September; but, upon failure thereof, the pews to be again the property of the town and at the town's disposal."

1798.

Pews were probably built this year. March 5, a new committee was chosen " to go on with finishing the meeting-house." It consisted of Rufus Gillmor, Christopher Butler, and David Gillmor. April 2, the committee were "instructed to inquire into the state of the moneys belonging to the meeting-house, to see what is due to the town for pews, and what is due from the town for work. If there be money sufficient for that and other purposes, the committee are to paint the roof of the meeting-house, and to act further, according to their discretion in the business."

Some of the pews which had .been sold were not paid for: they reverted to the town, and it was voted to sell them at the May meeting. The sale was deferred till Nov. 5. Then the selectmen were chosen a committee to report conditions in fifteen minutes. The report required the purchaser " to pay two dollars earnest, or give a note on demand therefor; to pay one-fifth (including the two dollars) in ten days," two-fifths in two months, and two-fifths in six months, and to give notes to the town-treasurer to that effect. If any one did " not keep the pew after bidding it off, he was to forfeit the two dollars earnest " money. Four pews only were sold, when it was found necessary to postpone the sale.

At this meeting, measures were taken to confirm the titles. The town voted " to have the numbers of the pews, together with the prices paid for them, recorded on the town-book, which was to be considered as a sufficient title thereto ; a certificate to be given by the clerk to the purchasers, if required." Accordingly there is the following record, which probably includes those sold subsequently:—

	No.	Price.		No.	Price.
Nathl. Robbins	1	$41.50	Olney Titus	21	$25.50
Philip Robbins	2	41.00	David Gillmor	22	27.00
David Robbins	3	36.00	Moses Hawes	23	27.00
Rufus Gillmor	4	35.50	David Robbins	24	27.50
—— ——	5	00.00	Edward Jones	25	26.00
Philip Robbins	6	35.50	Bailey Grinnell	26	25.50
Joel Adams	7	35.00	David Robbins	27	26.00
Jessa Robbins	8	36.50	Josiah Robbins	28	30.00
Amariah Mero	9	31.50	Samuel Hills	29	23.00
William Lewis	10	29.50	Abijah Hawes	30	22.50
Matthias Hawes	11	29.50	David Cummings	31	24.00
Amariah Mero	12	29.50	Moses Hawes	32	24.00
Capt. Geo. West	13	25.00	Amariah Mero	33	24.50
Thomas Daggett	14	20.50	Waldron Stone	34	24.00
Timothy Stewart	15	20.00	Chris. Butler	35	20.00
David Gillmor	16	40.50	David Robbins	36	21.00
Richd. Cummings	17	28.50	Thomas Butler	37	21.00
Clergyman's	18	00.00	John Tobey	38	21.00
—— ——	19	30.00	—— ——	39	20.50
Seth Luce	20	32.00	Rufus Gillmor	40	19.50

1799.

April 1, instead of forcing the sales, it was "voted to keep the pews for the present for those persons to sit in who have none." Also "voted to choose a person to take care of the meeting-house, to sweep the same once a month, to set up the same to the lowest bidder. Bid off by David Robbins at one dollar and fifty cents."

1801.

April 6, "The selectmen to provide a lock, and put it on the front door."

1803.

March 7, Rufus Gillmor appointed by the town to take charge of the meeting-house, keep the key, &c.

1804—1813.

The history of the house has been given from the beginning to the time when it probably received the last stroke ever given by the town toward making it a convenient place for public worship. In this condition it remained for several years. The shingles were put on the roof, and the clapboards on the walls, with wrought nails, — cut nails not having come into use. The ceiling was the only part which was plastered. Through this, in the south-east corner of the house, was an opening to the garret, in which for many years the town's powder was kept. The wainscot, rising as high as the window-sill, was of planed boards. Above this, rough boards, with the points of clapboard-nails sticking through them, were visible between the beams and studs. The pews were square, and contained seats on three sides. There were three body-pews on each side of the broad aisle, and three back of them; and these twelve pews were separated by an aisle from the wall-pews, which extended entirely round the building, except where they were interrupted by the pulpit and the single place for entrance to the house. None of the seats in the pews were nailed down, very few were hinged, and all could be turned up edgewise. At the beginning of a prayer, not a little noise was made by the universal practice of carelessly turning them up; and, on concluding it, the building rang with the clattering sound as they were slammed down. The upper part of each pew, instead of being panel-work, consisted of small trunnels, fancifully wrought with a lathe, and placed almost but not quite far enough apart for the children to put their heads through; reminding one of sheep-racks. The fronts of the galleries rested on square pillars covered with planed boards, at the upper part of which was something probably meant to be an entablature. Around the gallery, loosely laid on refuse ends of joists and beams, extended two sets of plank-seats, the rear range being a little higher than the other. In front of the preacher sat the singers. On his left sat the girls, and on his right the boys, who sometimes by their improprieties attracted the attention of the congregation below. Large holes, where the braces were not closely fitted into the beams, were sometimes occupied by bats, which occasionally squealed in the time of divine service. In the garret was a large number of them. The plaster, in one or more places, dropped from the ceiling; and, soon after it was repaired, its downward tendency would be renewed, to the great annoyance of any who might sit under it.

1814—1823.

Such was the state of things, Jan. 5, 1814, when it was "voted that Capt. Amos Barrett and his associates be allowed the east and west galleries in the easterly meeting-house, for the purpose of building twenty pews therein to be owned by them; and, in consideration thereof, to finish off the whole of the inside of the house in a neat and workmanlike manner, without any expense to the town." This was done. Two ranges of square pews, with an intervening aisle, were built in the east and west galleries, and one range back of the singers' seats, before May 17, 1815; when "the proprietors and owners of the pews in the gallery met in said house, and, on examination, found but nineteen pews subscribed for; and they voted, that, if any one or more would pay for the remaining pew, they should have their choice." Rufus Gillmor and Nathaniel Robbins took the remaining pew, selecting No. 9. The other nineteen were disposed of by draft.

Names.	No.	Names.	No.
Fogler and Little	1	Elisha Bennett	11
Maxcy and Eastman	2	John Drake	12
Nathaniel Robbins	3	Susman Abrams	13
David Robbins	4	Rufus Gillmor	14
Amos Barrett	5	Robert Foster	15
Ebenezer Alden	6	Joseph Miller	16
Mitchell and Mitchell	7	Micajah Gleason	17
Vaughan and Hart	8	Nathan Daniels	18
Gillmor and Robbins	9	Luce and Hawes	19
Jessa Robbins	10	Hart and Thorndike	20

1824—1833.

Nothing more was done to the meeting-house till May 3, 1824, when, from the consideration that it was used as a place to transact town-business, it was voted to shingle it, "to repair the jets and the plaster overhead, and to put it out to the lowest bidder." Voted liberty to lower the roof without expense to the town. Bid off by Nathaniel Robbins at $113, "including repair of jets and plaster."

Jan. 1825, "the first stove was put up," and "some of the men who put it in bound themselves that they would drink no rum for one year."

The house, however, had seen its best days. All efforts afterward to keep it in good condition were unsuccessful. In the course of time, the steps, which were hewed logs extending the whole length of the porch on each of its three sides, began to decay and settle, so that it was difficult to get into the house and out of it. Parts of the floor became uneven, and exhibited marks of age. The doors were often ajar. The wind rattled the loose windows, and whirled the snow through the crevices. A board was nailed over a part of the pulpit-window to prevent the storms from driving through the broken panes of glass. The carpenter stored lumber and window-sashes in the house, and the saddler found it convenient to dry his hair in the porch. An old horse, which was going at large on the Common, was mischievously led into it by some one, and ranged there and was fed for several days. Some of these evils were removed, and others remedied in part, by the different denominations which occasionally worshipped there. But the improvements were only temporary. Neither the town nor individuals felt interest enough to preserve the building, which was not worth repairing.

1834—1839.

April, 1834, a proposition "to see if the town will sell the Old Meeting-house or purchase the pews of such pew-owners as may wish to sell the same, or do any thing relative thereto," was dropped; as likewise was an article, April 18, 1836, "to hear the report of a committee upon the Old Meeting-house, and take such further measures as the town may think proper on said report." Nov. 20, 1837, an article "to see if the town will make repairs on the Old Meeting-house" drew out a vote, "that the selectmen make such repairs on the Old Meeting-house as they may think [proper], not to exceed five or six dollars." Several Universalists joined the Congregational Society, and the house was finally demolished in 1838. This act caused some excitement. Sept. 12, 1838, Walter Blake and Nathan Hills were chosen a committee "to ascertain whether the town had any right in the Old Meeting-house, and to report at the next meeting." At the next meeting, Nov. 29, the report was re-committed. Legal counsel was asked of Hon. Samuel E. Smith, ex-governor of Maine, in a communication dated March 28, 1839. The committee mention, as reasons for thinking the house belonged to the town, several circumstances in its history which have already been noticed, and conclude by stating that "the Congregational Society never claimed any exclusive right to the house until the year 1838, at which time it was taken down by their authority, after an apprizement of the pews by a committee appointed by the Congregational Society, without notice to the pew-owner or the town." Mr. Smith's opinion bears date April, 1839. In accordance with it, the report to the town, made April 16, states, "Your committee are clearly of opinion, that the town, as such, had, at the time the said house was taken down, no title to or interest in the same." The report was laid on the table. This was the end of the house.

It may be added, that there were many persons in Union who felt regret when it was pulled down. Some were living who had been familiar with all the struggles, in the poverty of the town, to have it erected. Others had sat around the Lord's table, not only in the best days of the house, but when the beams and rafters and rough boards were in plain sight; happy in having any place, however humble, where they could meet to worship God. They had enjoyed more in this building than many do in splendid cathedrals. Here, too, some had consecrated themselves and their children to God at the baptismal font; and the remains of dear friends and relatives had been placed in front of the pulpit, while the last service was performed before they were committed to their final resting-place. Almost every person in town had some interesting associations with the building.

How many, even in middle life, recollect some of the habits of the time! The husband came to meeting on horseback, with his wife on a pillion behind him, and stopped at a long log, on the west side of the house. One end of this crotched log, which had been cut from a large tree near the canal in Robbins's Meadow, was "canted up," so that the wife could alight without inconvenience; the other was hewed so thin that she walked ten or twelve feet down an inclined plane to the ground. The husband, without dismounting, rode away to the withe-and-stake board-fence, in the rear of the house, to tie his horse. One venerable, excellent old man, always at church, though he lived some miles distant, stood during prayer with his arms folded, and face to the wall; while his queue, carefully tied with a leathern string or an eel-skin, projected over his coat-collar, and hung down between his shoulders. The horses — a long row — "were hitched" to the fence during the service. Of vehicles of any kind there were but few. In winter might be seen a light sled, and in summer a light cart, in which a very fleshy woman, drawn by a pair of steers, was generally brought to meeting, as late even as the year 1814. To the close of the last century, while the country was new, there were customs which now would create great sensation. On stormy days, women wore their husbands' hats and great-coats. Mrs. Moses Hawes and Mrs. Snell, not having bonnets, for years wore handkerchiefs on their heads. Thomas Daggett, sen., Captain Nicholson, and Ebenezer Daggett, consulting their own convenience and comfort, were in the habit, even in meeting, of wearing cotton caps, which rivalled the snow in whiteness. As most of the mothers had nobody to leave their small children with at home, and were very desirous of going to meeting, they often took them; and sometimes their juvenile concerts attracted more attention than the minister or the music of the choir. In the intermissions, before mails were so common and intercourse so easy as they now are, the people usually took a small lunch from their pockets, a few doughnuts, or "fried cakes" as they were ordinarily called, or a few apples, if they had them; and, as they were eating them, collected in groups in front of the house to hear and retail the gossip and the news. The women, as now, were grouped in pews in different parts of the house, through which might be heard the pleasant murmuring sounds of their happy voices; while the younger portion of the fair sex stood in the entry or strolled away, three or four at a time, to get a draught of water, or to look at the gravestones in the Old Burying Ground, or to enjoy the prospect from the summit of the hill. From Thanksgiving Day to Fast Day, when there was but one service on a Sunday, before people had become as effeminate as now, the inhabitants came several miles and sat in the cold, when this, like all meeting-houses of the time, was not provided with fire, and the only protection from the storm and cold without was one thickness of boards and clapboards. If, before or after the season for a single service, a cold day came, the rousing wood-fire at John Little's barroom, and the warm rooms of the neighbors, were ever ready to give the worshippers welcome; and they went to them as freely as to their own dwellings.

Publishments for marriage, too, are associated with the Old Meeting-house. Very seldom were they posted, as they are now. Occasionally, a very modest couple, or the lady to whom a public annunciation would be unpleasant, had the intention posted up in the porch. But commonly, just after the benediction by the minister in the forenoon, and sometimes immediately before the service in the afternoon, the town-clerk, with the preface "Please to take notice," proclaimed aloud the names of the persons and their intentions.

On one occasion, the town-clerk, being called away, requested his son to put up in the porch a written notification for a marriage. The lad, fifteen or sixteen years old, feeling confidence in his ability to perform the duty according to the common mode, assumed the responsibility of deviating from his father's instructions, and, with some degree of animation and gesticulation, but without any other preface than what was used by his father, amused some and distressed others by crying the intention aloud.

There is another interesting association with the Old Meeting-house. In those days, dogs were nowise remarkable for good manners. Occasionally, they would intrude into the aisles, and trot round the meeting-house during public worship. Two men, David Robbins and Jessa Robbins, who had long whips, and who sat in convenient pews, were by the town chosen dog-whippers.[1] Considerable skill was necessary on their part to discharge their duty effectually, and in such a way that their constituents, or at least all those who were at the meeting, should have ample auricular evidence from the dogs themselves that the dog-whippers were faithful guardians of the rights and privileges of the people who came to worship. Accordingly, when a dog, following the praiseworthy example of his master, walked into the house, one of the dog-whippers, generally David Robbins, whose pew was about half-way from the door to the pulpit, would get up with the stillness and caution of an old hunter, carefully raise his whip, holding it so

[1] Dog-reeves, March 3, 1800, Amariah Mero, David Robbins, Rufus Dyer; March 2, 1801, David Robbins, Rufus Dyer, Jessa Robbins, Daniel McCurdy.

that it would have free sweep along the broad aisle, watch his opportunity as the dog was passing, and bring it down upon him with unmerciful energy. The yelping was unmusical, awakened undevout feelings through the congregation, and disturbed

> "Both mongrel, puppy, whelp, and hound,
> And curs of low degree,"

everywhere on the Common, and set them all to barking. Even when David Robbins was old and infirm, his zeal and fidelity did not abate. Not being able, without great pain, to rise from his seat, he would then strike and pommel the dogs with his crutches.

The preceding statements do not all apply exclusively to Union. They illustrate the customs and habits of people in new settlements. The contrast at the present day is so striking, that it is hard to believe some of them could have been true here, even so late as half a century since. The Old Meeting-house, around which are clustered a multitude of early associations, has been demolished. The old pew and the seat among the singers are gone. The locks of the venerable man who spake the words of warning and of exhortation have become silvery white, and he dwells far from the place of his pastoral labors. But, on many persons, impressions were made which can never be forgotten or effaced. Peace to the departed spirits who were wont to gather within the walls of the old house! The time will soon come when it will be said that "no one is living who saw the Old Meeting-house, which was erected with many prayers, struggles, and sacrifices."

CHAPTER XVIII.

ECCLESIASTICAL HISTORY, 1779—1806.

Going to Meeting at St. George's. — John Urquhart. — Isaac Case. — Nine Pounds raised for Preaching. — William Riddel called. — Aaron Humphrey. — Two hundred Dollars raised. — Mode of dividing the Money. — Abraham Gushee called. — Jabez Pond Fisher called. — Jonathan Gilmore. — Henry True called and settled.

1779—1781.

" SUNDAY, May 30, 1779, went to meeting at George's, and heard Rev. Mr. Auherd [Urquhart][1] hold forth.... Sunday, July 11, 1779, I went to meeting, and heard the Scotch minister preach.... Sunday, Sept. 17, 1780, Mr. Adams, Mr. Ware, and Mrs. Jemima Robbins, are gone to meeting this day.... Sunday, Sept. 16 [1781], Mr. Adams and his wife are gone to meeting; likewise Mr. Ware and Hills." These notices, taken from the old account-book of Matthias Hawes, are the earliest relating to attendance on public worship. Mr. Hawes makes similar memoranda respecting himself and his neighbors three times during the following two years. To go down the

---

[1] According to Greenleaf's "Sketches," the Rev. John Urquhart, a Presbyterian, came to this country in 1774, and was soon employed to preach at Warren. He was regularly removed from his charge there by the Presbytery convened at Salem, Mass., in September, 1783. The people were more desirous to get rid of him than he was to go. In the autumn of 1784, he was preaching at Ellsworth, and in the summer of 1785 at Topsham. In the fall of 1785, he commenced his labors at Union River; but was dismissed early in 1790. The name is sometimes pronounced Urcutt, and sometimes Orcutt. When he was at Union, Messrs. Jessa Robbins and Jacob Robbins say their father requested him to write his name. He wrote it Auquhart, with a piece of chalk over the fireplace, where it was legible for many years. He spelt and pronounced it with the broad Scotch accent; A-u—*awe*, q-u-a—*awe*, h-a—*awe*, r-t, thus giving the sound *awe* three times in spelling it.

river by water, and attend divine service a few times in a year at Warren or Cushing, — for Mr. Urquhart preached alternately in those places, — was as much as could reasonably be expected.

1782—1784.

Feb. 6, 1782, Mr. Hawes writes, " The Rev. Mr. Urquhart preached a sermon at Mr. Philip Robbins's." This was undoubtedly the first sermon ever preached in this town. Before Mr. Hawes moved to Stirlington, there were not people enough to make a congregation; and, as he was in the habit of noting events, particularly those that were of a religious nature, there is no good reason to doubt that he recorded the first meeting ever held in the place. There seems not to have been any more preaching till Mr. Hawes writes: " March 7, 1784. Last week, Mr. Case[1] was in this place, preaching with us." This is all that is known about the public worship before the town was incorporated.

1787—1791.

At the April town-meetings in 1787 and 1788, there were unsuccessful attempts to obtain a vote to hire preaching. March 30, 1789, the town voted to raise nine pounds to hire preaching part of the year. Samuel Hills, David Woodcock, and Abijah Hawes, were chosen a committee to hire the preachers and lay out the money. April 5, 1790, fifteen pounds were voted, and Thomas Daggett, Philip Robbins, and Josiah Robbins, were chosen the committee; but the vote was re-considered Jan. 10, 1791. With the exception of the nine pounds in 1789, it is not probable that any ministerial money was raised by the town for nearly twenty-five years from the time of the occupancy by the Anderson party.

---

[1] Rev. Isaac Case, then a young Baptist preacher at Thomaston, was lately living at Monmouth, and occasionally preaching, though probably more than ninety years old.

1796.

The inhabitants had been putting forth their energies to build a meeting-house. They were too poor to be doing much for the support of public worship. The next allusion to preaching is an article in the town-warrant for March 7, 1796, " to see if the town will hire Mr. Riddel to preach the ensuing summer; whereupon it was voted to hire him, if the committee could agree with him." The committee chosen were Thomas Daggett, Philip Robbins, Amos Barrett, Josiah Maxcy, and Edward Jones. The further consideration of the subject was deferred till April 4, when it was voted, 31 to 4, to give Mr. Riddel a call to settle in the ministry, with an annual salary of two hundred and fifty dollars, to be increased five pounds yearly till it amounted to one hundred pounds. The town-record states, that " the committee went to see him and give him a call; but he would not accept, and so went away and left us to take care of our own souls." The matter was brought to a close, May 5, by a vote to raise money to pay him[1] for his past services, and to pay his board; but not to raise any for preaching the ensuing summer.

[1] The Rev. William Riddel was born at Coleraine, Mass., Feb. 4, 1768, and graduated at Dartmouth College in 1793. He studied divinity a short time with Dr. Burton, of Thetford, Vt.; and afterwards pursued the study with the Rev. Dr. Emmons, of Franklin, Mass. He was ordained colleague-pastor with the Rev. Alexander McLean, of Bristol, Maine, in June, 1796, and was dismissed in the summer of 1804. He then labored some time in the employment of the Massachusetts Missionary Society in the State of New York, — the Western Home Missionary field at that time. He was afterwards twice settled in Vermont. He spent the last years of his life at South Deerfield, Mass., where he died Oct. 24, 1849. Sept. 4, 1797, he married Lucy, daughter of the Rev. Samuel Hopkins, D.D. of Hadley, Mass.: she died in December, 1813. They had three sons and four daughters. Two of the daughters and two of the sons died in infancy. The other son is the late Secretary of the American Education Society. — *American Quarterly Register*, xiii. 253, 259; *S. H. Riddel's MS. Memoranda.*

The same day on which his call was voted, the town " voted the committee be instructed to procure a lot of land of Messrs. Amorys for a ministerial lot; if they will give it, to accept it thankfully; if not, to purchase, if they can, on reasonable terms."

1797—1801.

Aug. 28, 1797, it was voted "to hire a Methodist preacher, and to raise one hundred dollars by tax, agreeable to law, to pay said preacher, — none to pay but such as are willing." Edward Jones, Amos Barrett, and Matthias Hawes, were chosen the committee; and they continued in office in 1798. Aaron Humphrey[1] was employed. July 16, 1798, the town voted to hear him another year, if the committee could agree with him "for half the time as heretofore."

April 1, 1799, an article proposing to re-hire Mr. Humphrey, and another to hire a Congregational preacher, were both dropped; as likewise was an article, May 20, to grant money for preaching.

In 1801, no money for preaching was granted. April 6, it was voted that the Congregational part of the town have the meeting-house half the time.

1802, 1803.

Feb. 8, 1802, Moses Hawes, Thomas Mitchell, and Samuel Hills, were chosen a committee "to procure a candidate to preach two or three sabbaths, to be paid by contribution." April 5, it was voted to hire preaching the ensuing summer, and to raise two hundred dollars by a tax, and that every man might pay his money for the support of preachers of his own religious sect or denomination. A ministerial committee to procure preaching was chosen, consisting of Stephen March, Rufus Gillmor, and Nathan Blake, Congregationalists; and Edward Jones, Joel Adams, and Christopher Butler, Methodists. The method of distributing the money agreeably to the spirit of the foregoing vote was acted upon in town-meeting, Nov. 1, and is recorded in the following words: —

---

[1] Rev. Aaron Humphrey subsequently joined the Episcopalians. He was preaching at Gardner in 1812. It is supposed he afterwards preached in Vermont and New York, and subsequently in Wisconsin. It may be added, in illustration of the religious spirit of the times, that Mr. Humphrey made a prayer at the raising of Mr. Cashman's barn.

"Voted to accept Mr. Blake's motion, as made in writing, respecting the division of money granted to hire preaching, viz.: In order that the money granted for ministerial use the present year may be distributed agreeable to the spirit and intention of the vote which made the grant, it is motioned that the following mode be adopted to effect the purpose, viz.: That the denomination of Christians called Methodist deliver to the selectmen a certificate in the words following (and signed by all who wish to have their money applied agreeable to said vote): —

"'This may certify, that we, the subscribers, do approve of and embrace the doctrine and church-discipline of the denomination of Christians called Methodist, and are of that sect.' And, as soon as the selectmen shall be notified by the Methodist Society, in writing, that any specific sum of money is due to any of their public preachers, it shall be the duty of the selectmen to order the same to such preacher, provided those who certify they are Methodist have paid the collector so much money of the grant for ministerial use. And any person or persons certifying to the selectmen in writing, that he or they embrace the doctrine and discipline of the Baptist Society, and certify that the money they are taxed in said grant is due to a public teacher of their denomination, the selectmen may order it accordingly, provided the same is paid to the collector.

"And whatever sum of money is due to Mr. Abraham Gushee for preaching, or others for boarding him, and certified to the selectmen in writing by such committee as the town may appoint for that purpose, may be ordered out of the above-said grant.

"And if any description of persons may think themselves aggrieved by this method of distributing the money, they may have opportunity to lay their case before the town for redress."

It seems, however, that this mode of proceeding did not give universal satisfaction; for, March 7, 1803, there was an unsuccessful attempt to re-consider part of the vote.

In the meantime the pulpit had been supplied by Mr. Abraham Gushee. He came to Union, July 3, 1802, and began his labors on the following day. July 29, a proposition to hire him to preach for two months was referred to the ministerial committee. Nov. 1, the day on which Mr. Blake's motion was accepted, it was voted to hire him on probation until after the March town-meeting. A change was made in the committee, which appears to have consisted subsequently of the three Congregational members only. March 7, 1803, the town voted to invite Mr. Gushee to settle in the ministry. At the same time it was —

"Voted to accept a motion made by Mr. Nathan Blake, which was expressed in the following words, viz.: Agreeably to the 16th article in the warrant, it is proposed to the town to invite Mr. Abraham Gushee to settle here as a minister of the gospel, and pastor of the Congregational Church which is now contemplated to be formed in this town; and that the town offer Mr. Gushee for his support an annual salary of $334, so long as he shall continue to be the minister of this town, and to commence on the day of ordination.

"And, as it is the opinion of this town that a minister cannot be useful to a society when a majority are dissatisfied with his ministration, therefore, to prevent the series of controversy and animosity which have often occurred in towns under those circumstances, it is proposed that the settlement be on the following conditions, viz.: That, if a major part of the supporters of Mr. Gushee shall become dissatisfied with his ministration, and shall, in a meeting for that purpose, state the cause of their uneasiness, and communicate the same to Mr. Gushee, and said cause shall continue six months after, then, in a legal meeting for that purpose, the major part of Mr. Gushee's supporters may vote his dismission. Or, if Mr. Gushee shall be dissatisfied, and shall state the cause thereof to the society, and said cause shall not be removed in the term of six months after, Mr. Gushee may make known to the society his wish to have the contract of his settlement dissolved; and said contract shall be dissolved in either case, and Mr. Gushee's salary paid up to said time.

"Voted that Josiah Robbins, Stephen March, Amos Barrett, Thomas Daggett, and Samuel Hills, with the selectmen, be a committee to confer with Mr. Gushee, respecting his settling among us as a minister of the gospel."

Mr. Gushee,[1] after receiving his call, made a visit to Massachusetts, returned in June, and gave a verbal answer in the negative. " One great and principal reason was, there was a respectable number of inhabitants of the town who were opposed to Congregationalists, — there were Methodists, Baptists, &c." He " had an idea that another person with prudence might somewhat further unite, or at least avoid the censure that fell upon one who first came among them."

On the 30th of June, after Mr. Gushee received his invitation to be settled, the town " voted to raise by tax five hundred dollars for ministerial use." A committee of five, including the selectmen, was chosen to agree with a candidate. Two of the selectmen declined; and the committee chosen consisted of Nathan Blake, Stephen March, Thomas Mitchell, Josiah Robbins, and Amos Barrett. Dec. 19, Mr. Fisher was employed to preach four sabbaths. At the same time, there was an unsuccessful attempt to get a vote " to exempt the Methodists from paying their ministerial tax to the collector."

1804.

Jan. 16, there was another attempt on a larger scale. It was designed to unite all the denominations but the Congregational. It was expected, that, at this meeting, Mr. Fisher would be invited to become the minister. If so, there were some who apprehended there might be difficulty about having their ministerial taxes paid to preachers of their own denomination; and there were others, who, fearful of heavy taxes, were not disinclined to worship where they would pay less. If the article had been voted to the letter, it would have opened the way for evasions of the ministerial tax. It was " to see if the town will set off all the people of different denominations that do not hold with or do

---

[1] Mr. Gushee was born in Raynham, Mass., Sept. 19, 1775, graduated at Brown University in 1798, studied divinity with the Rev. Mr. Fobes, of Raynham, and was licensed to preach by the Bristol County Association. He was ordained, Sept. 23, 1803, at Dighton, where he continues in the pastoral office. — *MS. Letter.*

not attend to the Congregational order, so that they may enjoy their own principles and pay their own preaching; so that the town shall not have any demands upon them as it respects raising money to support ministers or pay for preaching, or act or do any thing as the town may think proper." The town " voted that the society of Methodists be exempted from paying the last year's ministerial tax, they producing to the selectmen a satisfactory certificate that they ought to be excused by law."

At the same meeting, it was voted to invite Jabez Pond Fisher[1] to settle in the ministry, with an annual salary of four hundred dollars. The invitation was accompanied with the conditions which had been annexed to the call given to Mr. Gushee. Mr. Fisher did not accept the invitation.

April 2, Geo. Wellington, Stephen March, Thomas Mitchell, Abijah Hawes, and Samuel Daggett, were chosen the ministerial committee. July 9, an article being before the town-meeting in relation to giving Jonathan Gilmore[2] a call to settle, it was voted to hire him for six months; and a committee, consisting of Mr. Blake, Mr. Mitchell, and Mr. David Robbins, was chosen " to wait on him, and inform him that the town request the favor of his attendance." But there is no further record as to the proceedings.

---

[1] Mr. Fisher was born at Wrentham, Mass., Oct. 7, 1763; served in the war of the Revolution; graduated at Brown University in 1788; and, in February, 1790, was licensed to preach. " He received several calls to settle; one at Ashby, Mass., 1791, and another the same year at Pelham, N.H.; it is believed, another from Claremont, N.H.; and, not far from that time, one at Henniker, N.H." He was ordained at West Nottingham, now Hudson, N.H., Feb. 24, 1796; and dismissed in June, 1801. A lawsuit followed, which cost the town $1,500 or $2,000. He declined a call from the church in Washington, N.H. He was installed at Boothbay, Maine, June 29, 1809, and dismissed in 1816. Subsequently, he was employed by the New Hampshire Missionary Society four years. After this, he preached six or seven years at Deering, N.H.; and died there, Dec. 13, 1836.

[2] Mr. Gilmore was from Raynham or Franklin, Mass. He graduated at Brown University in 1800. After being at Union, he went back to Massachusetts, was married, and subsequently became a farmer in Starks, Maine.

1805, 1806.

March 4, 1805, the proposition, "to raise money to hire preaching the year ensuing," was dropped. But, April 1, Nathan Blake, Seth Luce, Amos Barrett, Jonathan Carriel and Samuel Daggett, were chosen a committee to "hire a candidate;" and they were instructed to send to "Mr. Fobes [of Raynham] or to Mr. Ripley [of Concord] for such candidate as they think proper."[1]

The next movement was Nov. 11, "to see if the town will give Mr. Henry True a call to settle in the work of the ministry in this town, agreeably to the request of the church." The call was voted, and Mr. True invited to settle "as a minister of the gospel and pastor of a Congregational church in this town," with "an annual salary of four hundred dollars, so long as he shall continue to be the minister of this town," to "commence on the day of his ordination." Coupled with the invitation, and in the same language as before, were Mr. Blake's conditions. Mr. True preached from September to December. He went to New Hampshire, and spent the winter; and, April 21, 1806, the church "voted renewedly to invite him to take the charge and oversight of the church as pastor thereof."

May 14, 1806, it was voted to add twenty cords of wood and twenty-five dollars annually to the salary, and "to allow Mr. True[2] four sabbaths in the year to visit his friends."

[1] April 1, 1805, upon an article continued from March 4, 1805, "to see if the town will allow the Methodists to have the use of the meeting-house a part of the time for the year ensuing," it was "voted that the Methodists and Baptists have the use of the meeting-house at all times when the town is not supplied with a candidate."

[2] The Rev. Henry True was born at Hampstead, N.H., May 20, 1770. His father, the Rev. Henry True, of Hampstead, born at Salisbury, Mass., Feb. 27, 1726, was a staunch whig. He would not drink any but "home-made" tea, and published, probably in a newspaper, a poem on Liberty Tea. He married, Nov. 30, 1753, Ruth, daughter of Deacon James Ayer, of Haverhill, Mass., who died Jan. 18, 1810, æt. 81. One of her uncles, it is said, was killed at the Indian attack on Haverhill. Mr. True's grandfather, James [?], belonged to Salisbury, Mass., where the early ancestors of the name settled, and died

Notwithstanding an opposition, which will be noticed in detail hereafter, Mr. True accepted the invitation. Measures were taken for the ordination. July 14, Capt. Amos Barrett, Mr. Nathan Blake, and Mr. McDowell,[1] were chosen a committee to join with the church in inviting the council. Major Maxcy, Capt. Barrett, Captain Gillmor, Mr. David Robbins, and Mr. Nathaniel Robbins, were chosen to make provision for the council. Major Maxcy, Capt. Bachelor, and Capt. Barrett, were chosen a committee "to put the galleries of the meeting-house in such order, by laying joists in the same, as will answer the temporary purpose of an ordination." The ordination took place Sept. 24, 1806. By a special vote of the church, six members present, the pastor elect was admitted to their fellowship and communion. The services were probably as follows: Prayer by Rev. Freeman Parker, of Dresden; reading the Scriptures by Rev. Mr. Cochran, of Camden; sermon by Rev. Hezekiah Packard, of Wiscasset; ordaining prayer by Rev. Mr. Johnson, of Belfast; charge by Rev. Manasseh Cutler, of Hamilton, Mass., an eminent divine and naturalist, and the pioneer from Massachusetts to Ohio; right hand of

at Hampstead about the time of the American Revolution. Mr. True's father died May 22, 1782. On Sunday, he preached and appointed a lecture for Thursday. On Tuesday, he attended family devotions in the morning, apparently well, and died before noon. Mr. True was fitted for college, partly at the academy in Atkinson, and partly with the Rev. Mr. Merrill, of Plaistow, whose house was just within the bounds of Haverhill. He graduated at Dartmouth College in 1796. He taught school five or six years in Salisbury, Beverly, Tyngsborough, and other places. He studied divinity, partly with the Rev. Mr. Laurence, with whom he boarded when teaching in Tyngsborough, and partly with Rev. Dr. Chaplin, of Groton. He preached some at Tewksbury and Dracut; one summer at Mr. Merrill's, in Plaistow; and, during one session of congress, for Rev. Manasseh Cutler, of Hamilton. He has been one of the trustees of Warren Academy for many years, also chaplain of a regiment, justice of the peace and quorum, and town-clerk; "none of the offices very profitable." He published a sermon delivered at Hampstead, Nov. 15, 1807. In the fall of 1849, he moved with his wife to Marion, Ohio, to reside with his son.

[1] Mr. McDowell, a Scotchman, settled in the part of Union which is now within the bounds of Washington.

fellowship by Rev. Jonathan Huse, of Warren; concluding prayer by Rev. Mr. Dow, of Upper Beverly, Mass., who was afterwards settled at York. The council was entertained at Capt. Barrett's. The meeting-house was thronged. The occasion was one of great interest and excitement. Ordinations were not common. This was the first in the town. Among the persons present were Major-General Henry Knox's family from Thomaston. The evening, as well as the day, was not without manifestations of much joy on the part of a great portion of the inhabitants.

CHAPTER XIX.

ECCLESIASTICAL HISTORY.
(*Continued.*)

Organization of the First Congregational Church. — Mr. Huse's Account of the Proceedings. — Conduct of Samuel Hills and the Rev. Messrs. Sewall, Bayley, and others. — Articles of Faith. — Covenant. — Signers' Names. — Opposition by the Hills Party. — Hills's "Ex Parte" Council, Sept. 10, 1806. — Conduct of the Hills Party about the Ordination. — Hills censured. — Council, June 29, 1808. — Hills's "Ex Parte" Council, Feb. 15, 1809. — Second Congregational Church organized. — Mr. Huse's Letter concluded.

An account of the organization and subsequent movements of the First Congregational Church may be given, in part, by an extract from a letter of the Rev. Jonathan Huse, of Warren, to the Rev. Hezekiah Packard, then of Wiscasset: —

"Warren, Feb. 20, 1818.
"Sir, — Agreeably to your request, I will attempt to state a number of circumstances and facts, which serve to prove the existence of a party, exclusive, and disorderly spirit in some clergymen in this district, who profess to be [of] our denomination. In doing this, I do not rely entirely on my own recollection: I made a minute of them soon after their occurrence.

"Some time about the commencement of the year 1803, application was made to me by several persons in the town of Union, adjoining this town, for assistance in forming a church in said town. I accordingly met them with a delegate from our church, proposed such questions to them as I thought proper, gave them some suitable advice, and exhibited to them a confession of faith and covenant for their subscription. After mature consideration and examination, they subscribed the articles of faith and covenant, and were acknowledged a sister-church. They appeared perfectly satisfied with each other, and united as a band of brothers and sisters. The sacrament of the Lord's supper was administered to them a few times the ensuing summer, and baptism to some of their children.

"In October, 1803, one man in the town, by the name of Hills, who wished to join the church, prevailed with the members to consent that the Rev. Messrs. Jotham Sewall, Kiah Bayley, and Jonathan Huse, should be invited to meet the church at Union, and see if it would be advisable to alter the covenant and articles of faith. They accordingly met. Messrs. Sewall and Bayley (who had seen the covenant before, and expressed their opinion to Mr. Hills) declared the covenant and confession of faith were not sufficiently explicit and orthodox; that Unitarians, and every denomination of Christians, might subscribe to them; that, in order that other orthodox churches might fellowship with them, especially their own, it was necessary there should be an alteration of the covenant and confession. I told these gentlemen and the church present, that our church would fellowship [with] them, and I presumed the major part of the Congregational churches in New England would do the same; that the confession and covenant were almost identically the same which our church, and the South Church in Andover [Mass.], had adopted. I thought them sufficiently explicit, scriptural, and orthodox, and did not think it expedient any alteration should be made, unless the church was dissatisfied and wished such alteration. Each member expressed his entire satisfaction with them, and said they had no wish for any alteration. Accordingly, nothing was done.

"The man (Mr. Hills), at whose request these gentlemen appeared at Union, was dissatisfied; and Messrs. Sewall and Bayley were disappointed. Hills was determined to have an alteration, and agreed with Mr. Sewall, who was then going east on a mission, to call on his return, and assist him in effecting his object. On Mr. Sewall's return, a few months afterwards, he went with Mr. Hills to the members of the church individually; and, by talking to them in a plausible manner, induced them to give a tacit consent to some alteration, in order, as was said, for the accommodation of Mr. Hills. The church was convened, re-examined, and approved by Sewall; and Hills admitted. These things were done without any previous notice being given to me. The covenant and confession were afterwards shown me, and I was asked if I could fellowship with the church upon their adoption of them. I answered in the affirmative, though I expressed my dissatisfaction with Sewall's interference, and thought the alterations unnecessary.

"It soon appeared that Hills, at whose importunity and for whose accommodation the alterations were made, was determined to rule the church. He attempted to bind them by obtaining their signatures to certain restrictive articles which he presented, the principal of which was to submit themselves to the control and superintendence of the association[1] to which Messrs. Sewall and Bayley belonged. He violently opposed almost every candidate they had. He was chiefly instrumental in preventing the settlement of one or two, to whom calls were presented. It ought to be noticed, that there was a constant communication kept up between Messrs. Sewall and Bayley, and Mr. Hills, by correspondence and by visiting. The latter did nothing without the advice of the former."

ARTICLES OF FAITH.

The following are the "Articles of Faith and Covenant agreed on by the Congregational Church of Christ in Union, at its embodying, March 3, 1803, and adopted, with additions," to accommodate Mr. Hills, "Feb. 6, 1804." The additions are in brackets; the other parts being what was adopted March 3, 1803.

---

[1] This association considered that the candidate should come "in the shadow of Bayley or Sewall, and that the church must not let the town employ a preacher; but the church did not feel bound by this rule." Hills insisted that this association alone should supply. The town employed Mr. True.

The form in which it was adopted, Feb. 6, 1804, for the purpose of accommodating Mr. Hills, was the one which continued to be used: —

"We, whose names are hereunto subjoined, that we may promote the growth of religion in our souls, and enjoy the ordinances of the gospel in a church-state, do now profess our faith, and covenant together in manner following, viz.: —

"1. We believe in one God, who is Father, Son, and Holy Ghost [and that the Son and Spirit are co-equal and co-eternal with the Father].

"2. We declare our faith in the divine inspiration of the Scriptures of the Old and New Testament, which we receive as the word of God, and profitable for doctrine, for reproof, for correction, for instruction in righteousness [and contain a perfect rule of faith and practice, and that no other writings ought to be received as a divine revelation].

"3. We believe in the fall of man, the [total] depravity of human nature [by which he exposed himself and all his numerous race to endless misery; and that, in consquence of Adam's fall, all his posterity came into the world in a state of condemnation and wrath.

"4. We believe] the redemption through the mediation, intercession, and atonement of [Jesus] Christ [by which God can, consistently with the honor of his law, pardon and save all who repent and believe].

"5. We believe the necessity of regeneration in order to salvation, and that this is effected by the exceeding greatness of God's [special] power, and [instantaneously] wrought in an ordinary way, through the instrumentality of means.

"6. [We believe that all things, visible and invisible, were created by God for his own glory, and that he governs them according to his eternal purpose].

"7. We believe the true church is founded on Christ, the chief corner-stone; and that the gates of hell cannot prevail against it, to its utter extirpation.

"8. [We believe that salvation is offered to all, but that none will accept and be brought to true repentance and faith in Christ, but those who are chosen through sanctification of the Spirit and belief of the truth according to God's eternal purpose.

"9. We believe that all who are united truly to Christ

are justified freely by grace, and kept by the mighty power of God through faith unto eternal salvation].

"10. We believe Christ hath appointed two special ordinances to be observed by every true believer in his name, viz. baptism and the [Lord's] supper.

"11. We believe the qualifications for these ordinances, in all adults, are sincere repentance towards God, and faith in our Lord Jesus Christ [without which no person can have any right to baptism, either for himself or his children, neither can he have any right to the solemn ordinance of the Lord's supper.

"12. We believe that God has appointed an order of men to preach the gospel, and administer the ordinances to suitable subjects.

"13. We believe that all offences of a public nature ought to be publicly confessed.

"14. We believe the church ought never to receive any person into their fellowship, whether he has been professor or not, until they are satisfied, in a judgment of charity, that he has been born again].

"15. We [also] believe the future existence [and immortality] of the soul, the resurrection of the bodies [both of the just and the unjust], and the day of future judgment, in which every one will receive a reward according to his works [that Christ will at the day of judgment receive the righteous into life eternal, and punish the wicked with everlasting destruction from the presence of the Lord and from the glory of his power. Amen]."

"THE COVENANT.

"And we do also humbly and penitently, asking the forgiveness of our sins through the blood of the great Redeemer, give up ourselves to God in an everlasting covenant, in our Lord Jesus Christ; and, as in the presence of God, do solemnly promise, that, by the assistance of the Divine Spirit, we will forsake the vanities of the present evil world [abstaining ourselves from all gaming, frolicking,[1] and do our endeavor to restrain all under our care from such sinful courses], and [so] approve ourselves the true disciples of

---

[1] For the words "gaming and frolicking," Mr. True, with the concurrence of the church, substituted the words "amusements and practices which are inconsistent."

Jesus Christ in all good carriage towards God and towards men. And we likewise promise to walk together in Christian communion, as members of the church of Christ, and to attend statedly upon the administration of the ordinances of the gospel [baptism and the Lord's supper, and the public worship of God on his holy day], when it can conveniently [with respect to health and opportunity] be done. And [we promise to sanctify the sabbath, to attend the worship of God daily in our families and closets], to watch over one another [according to scripture rule], and to submit to the discipline of the church now formed in this place [and, taking the gospel-rule of discipline for our directory, we engage to admit all to our holy communion who can give a rational scriptural evidence of a work of sanctifying grace upon their hearts, in a judgment of charity, whose lives correspond thereto. We do also covenant to devote our offspring to the Lord, doing our duty to them in religious instructions, training them up in the nurture and admonition of the Lord]; and finally, by daily prayer to God in the name of Christ, we will seek for grace to enable us to keep this covenant. [And may the merciful God pardon our many errors and imperfections, prepare us for, and at last receive us to glory, through the merits of the great Head of the church, to whom be praise for ever and ever. Amen.]"

When the church was organized by Rev. Mr. Huse, March 3, 1803, the articles and covenant, in the form in which he presented them, were signed by Thomas Daggett, Josiah Robbins, Abijah Hawes, Seth Luce, Margaret Hawes, and Dolly Law. On the 28th of August, the Rev. Mr. Johnson being chosen moderator, the church admitted Capt. John Nicholson and Sarah his wife, Mrs. Rebecca Daggett, Mrs. Sarah Robbins, Mrs. Jemima Robbins, Mrs. Dinah Mitchell, Miss Sally Boon, Samuel Walker, jun., Thomas Mitchell, and Stephen March; also, by letters of recommendation, Daniel Shepard and Sarah his wife. At the same meeting, or not long afterward, Mrs. Abigail Hills and Mrs. Martha Williams were admitted, and Abijah Hawes chosen deacon. Among those who subsequently joined it, with or without letters of recommendation, were Jonathan Carriel and his wife Sibyl, Tempe Briggs, Rebekah Gowen, Jedidah Daggett, Betsey Allen, Mary Tobey, Mary wife of Thos. Mitchell, Mercy wife of Jeremiah Mitchell, Rhoda Ellis, Sarah Barrett, John Millbanks [?], Jas. Rice, John Gleason and wife, David Robbins and his wife Mercy, Mary wife of Capt. Amos Barrett, Mary True, Harriet Barrett, William Daggett, George Wellington, Polly wife of Calvin Morse, Mrs. Mero, Thomas Hemenway and wife, Elizabeth Robbins, Daniel F. Harding, and Mrs. Rice.

"In the autumn of 1805," continues Mr. Huse, "the church and congregation invited Mr. Henry True to settle with them in the gospel-ministry. Mr. Hills, with two others, who were after him admitted into the church, opposed his settlement. They took every means in their power to prevent his giving an affirmative answer to the call. They made such representations to him as induced him to write a negative answer, which was to be read on a particular day. But his friends, finding what was done, took pains to convince him he had been deceived by the misrepresentations of these men. He was consequently prevailed with to suspend his answer, and afterwards gave it in the affirmative. The three disaffected members contended for their right to choose half the ordaining council. This privilege was not indulged them. The council was called, consisting of a representation from the churches in Hamilton, Beverly, Wiscasset, Dresden, Belfast, Camden, and Warren."

Aug. 19, the church voted "that three churches be sent to, in order to settle difficulties between us and Brothers Samuel Hills, Stephen March, and Amos Walker." The disaffected members, however, obtained an *ex parte* council before the ordination, of which the following is the record: —

"At an ecclesiastical council, convened, in consequence of letters missive from a minority of the church in Union, at the house of Mr. Samuel Hills, Sept. 10, 1806, — present, Rev. Messrs. John Sawyer, Jotham Sewall, Eliphalet Gillett; delegates, Mr. Benjamin Kelley, Mr. Moses Weymouth, —

chose Rev. John Sawyer moderator, Rev. Eliphalet Gillett scribe.

"Voted Mr. Isaac Robinson, deacon of the church in Hamden, Bangor, and Orrington, a member of the council.

"After prayer by the moderator for light and direction from God,—

"Voted that a letter be sent to Deacon Abijah Hawes, informing him and the church of our being convened in council, and requesting their attendance at the meeting-house at nine o'clock to-morrow morning; also a letter to Mr. True, requesting his attendance at the same time and place, in order that the council may have such information on the subjects of difference between some members of the church as to enable them to give such advice as the existing state of things may require. Adjourned to [to-]morrow morning.

"Sept. 11, 1806, met according to adjournment.

"Voted to proceed to the meeting-house at nine o'clock.

"After prayer by the moderator in the meeting-house, four articles[1] of grievance were submitted to the council by Mr. Samuel Hills, in behalf of the minority of the church. After attention to the subjects of difficulty, and receiving what light could be collected from the aggrieved members of the church and other gentlemen of the parish who

---

[1] The articles were the following: —

"1. We find ourselves aggrieved, that our brethren have declined to accept the offer of the Rev. Mr. Bayley to preach with us, we being destitute, and administer the Lord's supper according to a vote of the church; and a continued neglect of attending to that ordinance for several months.

"2. That our brethren have infringed the rights of the church, in deciding a question respecting the rights of the aggrieved in inviting a council to assist in the ordination of Mr. Henry True, which we think belongs exclusively to the church.

"3. That our brethren hold us under discipline, having never brought a specific charge against us, and decline to furnish us, according to promise, with a copy of a paper, purporting to be articles of accusation against Samuel Hills, Stephen March, and Amos Walker.

"4. We consider it of great importance to a people to have such a minister set over them as thereby the glory of God and the good of their souls may be promoted, and cannot but feel aggrieved that our brethren are disposed to urge forward the settlement of a person whom we do not consider calculated to answer these great and important ends; especially as we think that more than half of the brethren and sisters collectively are dissatisfied, and that he has not that share in the affections of the people at large, which is necessary to render his ministrations beneficial to them."

attended, the council retired to Mr. Spencer Walcott's, and drew up the following result: —

"'With respect to the first article of complaint, this council are of opinion, that the church were too inattentive to their vote to receive assistance from the Lincoln Association, and particularly so in neglecting the proposal of Mr. Bayley; that such neglect was calculated directly to hurt the feelings of the aggrieved brethren and sisters.

"'With respect to the second, this council are of opinion, that, if the church admitted the town-committee to vote with them, or use their influence in determining the right of some of the members, it is a just matter of grievance.

"'With respect to the third, this council do not see that there is sufficient evidence exhibited to prove that the church did formally or regularly hold the aggrieved brethren under discipline; yet there is too much reason to think that the church acted inconsistently in discovering a disposition to treat them so, and not doing any thing decidedly; and also exhibiting charges, and not affording the aggrieved an explicit statement of the same, that they might either clear themselves or plead guilty, appears to this council an unsuitable way of proceeding, and is calculated to give offence.

"'With respect to the fourth article, this council do not feel themselves authorized to determine any thing with respect to Mr. True's qualifications as a preacher of the gospel; but think the church ought to act with the greatest caution in so important an affair, and not rashly do any thing that would part asunder the mystical body of Christ in this place; carefully and tenderly consult the feelings and views of the aggrieved brethren and sisters, and mutually seek direction of God. And, if the aggrieved party do not obtain satisfaction as to Mr. True's qualifications as a gospel-minister before ordination, we advise them to lay their difficulties before the ordaining council.'

"The aggrieved members also submitted the following questions: —

"'Question 1. — Can there be a case in church-discipline, in which the first and second steps pointed out in the 18th of Matthew may be dispensed with?

"'Answer. — This council is of opinion, that, as it is evidently the design of gospel-discipline to preserve or restore peace and order to the church, and, as the directions of Christ, in the 18th of Matthew, are very explicit, it must be a very peculiar case to justify the omission of the first and second steps in dealing with an offender.

"'Question 2. — What is the right of the sisters of the church? and how far may they act, according to the Scripture, in the settlement of a minister, whether they belong to the town or not?

"'Answer. — We do not consider the sisters of the church as having any right to vote in settling a minister of the gospel. But, as they are members of the body of Christ, and are in mutual and solemn covenant with the brethren, they have right to the communion and fellowship of the church in the means of grace and special ordinances of the gospel. Therefore the sisters have a right to expect the church will conscientiously seek their Christian edification in settling a minister; and Christ will esteem it very offensive if any of his flock should be neglected or despised.

"'This council regret that the church could not feel so much of the condescending temper of Christ as to have attended the sitting of the council, and assisted them in obtaining that correct information which is so needful and desirable in determining matters of such importance. Feeling the importance of harmony and peace in the churches, the council exhort the friends of Christ in this place to look to Almighty God for the outpouring of his spirit, that they may adopt and pursue all their measures with wisdom, and walk in all the divine statutes and ordinances blameless.

"'Done in council unanimously at Union, on the tenth and eleventh of September, 1806.

"'JOHN SAWYER, Moderator.
"'E. GILLETT, Scribe.'"

The church, it seems, took no notice of the movement, it being evidently an *ex parte* affair. However, Sept. 17, they "voted to request Brothers Hill, March, and Walker to join in a mutual council to settle difficulties subsisting in the church, — the council to be called at some future day when the church may think proper."

To the council convened for ordination, continues Mr. Huse, —

"A memorial was presented by the three disaffected persons, purporting that Mr. True was not the man of their

MUTUAL COUNCIL.

choice, &c. After attending to the objections, and examining the candidate, the council unanimously voted, 'that the objections were obviated by Mr. True's confession of faith, and by answers he made to questions proposed to him.' Mr. True was ordained September, 1806. Hills, with the other two, continued their opposition to Mr. True; and Hills, in particular, made great exertions to disaffect the people toward him, especially such as he thought could be influenced by him. Hills was, after considerable time had elapsed, censured by the church[1] for some of his conduct relating to Mr. True and others."

A year and a half passed. March 23, 1808, the church voted to join in a mutual council. This council convened in Union, June 29. There were present

---

[1] The records upon this subject are as follows : —

Oct. 23, 1806, the church, being convened, " voted, We feel it a duty to notice the complaints laid before the church by Nathan Blake against Brother Samuel Hills." The church met again Oct. 30, and heard the charges and Mr. Hills's defence, and adjourned to Nov. 13. Then, " after assenting to articles of grievance brought by Deacon Hawes and Brother Mitchell, voted to add to the articles of grievance the taking down of the names of men not belonging to the Congregational Society." At the adjourned meeting, Nov. 24, it was voted. "That, on account of the articles of grievance and fault, which we have laid before Brother Samuel Hills, we cannot conscientiously commune with him, and do therefore suspend him from our communion till we obtain satisfaction."

The "taking down of names," just mentioned, needs a word of explanation. The charge seems to have been that Mr. Hills went to different persons, and, without intimating his purpose, elicited from them remarks or criticisms unfavorable to Mr. True, and then took down the names of these persons as objecting to him. The paper containing these names was brought to the pastor elect, on the evening preceding the day when he was to give a reply to the invitation to be settled. He immediately wrote an answer in the negative. At the intermission on the Lord's Day, on the afternoon of which the answer was to be read, the purport of it became known. Great indignation was expressed; and Mr. Huse, with whom Mr. True had an exchange, was persuaded not to read it. Some persons said they had been misunderstood by Mr. Hills, and others denied what they were charged with saying. Subsequently, as has already been mentioned in Mr. Huse's letter, Mr. True gave an affirmative reply. Mr. Hills sent to Mr. True a note, expressing an inclination to make some statements respecting affairs in town. Mr. Blake, thinking it not expedient for them to have an interview by themselves, accompanied Mr. True; but Mr. Hills declined saying any thing upon the subject in the presence of a third person.

the Rev. Messrs. Scott,[1] of Minot; Johnson, of Belfast; Jotham Sewall, of Chesterville; John Sawyer, of Boothbay (the last two missionaries); Packard, of Wiscasset; Huse, of Warren; and Bayley, of Newcastle, who was "put on" in place of Rev. Mr. Gillett, of Hallowell, who was invited, but did not attend.

The church, being convened on the same day, "voted, upon the concessions of Brothers Amos Walker, Stephen March, and Samuel Hills, before the mutual council, to forgive and restore them."

The record of the council, signed by Jonathan Scott[1] as moderator, and Hezekiah Packard as scribe, states that, —

"After adjusting the council to the satisfaction of the parties, the Rev. Mr. True was requested to exhibit the doings of the church in said town. Upon which the Rev. Mr. True produced articles of charge against their brethren, Samuel Hills, Stephen March, and Amos Walker; and, after reading the same, their reply and defence was called for and exhibited. The council resulted as follows, viz.: After a deliberate, patient, and impartial hearing and investigation of all matters of charge and grievance exhibited by the church against their brethren, Hills, March, and Walker, the council were happy to find, that, in consequence of explanations and concessions of the accused brethren, the church unanimously voted they were satisfied. The church, on their part, made such explanations and concessions with regard to the charges produced by said Hills, March, and Walker, as manifested a conciliatory disposition; and we lament, that,

---

[1] Mr. Scott was quartered on Capt. Barrett, with whom Mr. True boarded. It is said that the object was to afford Mr. Scott an opportunity to elicit Mr. True's heresies. The result, however, was different. Mr. Scott found there was but little difference of sentiment. Friendly letters passed between them afterward. In one dated Oct. 6, 1808, which Mr. Scott wrote to Mr. True, he observes, "I heard your character, as a minister of the gospel, often impeached before the council when I was with you, as you know, in such sentences as these: 'He is not fit to preach the gospel;' 'We cannot be fed by his preaching, &c. &c.' But, while there was nothing specified which exhibited the truth and evidence of the assertions, such impeachments did not influence my judgment against you, nor lessen my esteem for you, any at all, neither then when uttered, nor in any moment since."

although a full reconciliation was truly desirable, we have not the satisfaction of seeing all matters of difficulty done away." The result concludes with several apostolical exhortations to the members of the church to promote peace and harmony among themselves.

"Notwithstanding this result," continues Mr. Huse in his letter, "the three members continued restless and dissatisfied; and, in two or three weeks, they, with nine females, sent a request to the church to be dismissed, that they might join some other church, or form themselves into a new one.[1] The church thought themselves unauthorized to grant their request.[2] After a few months, the before-named Sewall came into town, preached several lectures in the town, and upon the borders of adjacent towns. And, while he was with these disaffected persons, a line was sent to Rev. Mr. True, to be communicated to the [church], signed by these persons, in which they protested against the 'conduct of the church, and declare that they withdraw from

---

[1] The request was in the following words: "Brethren, you must be sensible, that we, the undersigned, members of the Congregational Church of Christ in this place, have been for a long time much tried and grieved, that we cannot enjoy Christian communion in this church, agreeable to our desires; and, as we have made several attempts to have our grievances redressed, and as often failed, and now feel ourselves held as it were in bondage, therefore, brethren, we desire your consent, by vote, that we may withdraw our relation from this church, and have the liberty of joining some sister-church, or be formed into a new church, as we may think most expedient. Your compliance, we trust, will save us the trouble of another council, as we cannot feel content to remain in such a disagreeable and unhappy situation."

[2] It is not improbable, that the difficulties in Union led to the following determination in the ministerial association: "Warren, Aug. 24, 1808. Voted, that to promote a more perfect union among our churches, and to form a consistory for hearing and ending all questions of discipline, which shall not be settled in each separate church, that each of our churches be invited to send a delegate with the minister to form a consociation." This proposition being brought before the church at Union, Sept. 14, it was voted unanimously to accept the above invitation, and to assist in forming a consistory.

On the same day in which the church agreed to assist in forming a consistory, they voted, "We at present deem it improper to dismiss members of a church, without recommending them, at the same time, to some other church specified in the request." This was in accordance with the sentiments of Mr. Scott, who stated in his letter of Oct. 6, 1808, that it would be, "in effect, to unchurch them; and such proceeding has no precedent in the New Testament."

them, exhort them to repentance, and say they should rejoice to receive any of them who should see the error of their ways, repent, and reform.'

"Directly upon this, and while Mr. Sewall was with them, they proceeded to call an *ex parte* council; and, a few days previous to meeting of council, they gave Mr. True notice of what was done, requesting his attendance with the council."

RESULT OF THE COUNCIL.

"Agreeable to letters missive from the aggrieved brethren, formerly members of the church of Christ in Union, an ecclesiastical council was convened at the house of Mr. Samuel Hills, Feb. 15, 1809, for the purpose of attending to, and giving advice and counsel, in relation to difficulties, which have for some time past existed in the church.

"Present: Rev. Elders Kiah Bayley, John Sawyer, Jonathan Ward, Amasa Smith, Jotham Sewall, Samuel Sewall, and Jonathan Belden. Delegates: Ebenezer Haggett, Sewall Crosby, Moses Weymouth, Ezekiel Avery, Asa Chase, and Thomas Ring. Rev. John Sawyer was chosen moderator, and Rev. Jonathan Belden scribe.

"After prayer by the moderator, the letter missive from the aggrieved brethren was read, in which it was stated, that they had, after long waiting and many painful efforts to settle the difficulties subsisting between them and the majority of the church, finally remonstrated, protested, and withdrawn from them. Finding that the aggrieved had actually separated themselves from the church, the council proceeded to inquire into the grounds and reasons of their conduct in withdrawing. Upon inquiry, the council found that difficulties had existed in the church for more than two years and a half; that, on Sept. 10, 1806, an ecclesiastical council had been convened by the aggrieved, to give them advice respecting their difficulties; that the following articles of grievance were laid before the council for their consideration."

Here follow the four articles already printed in the note on page 178; after which, the narrative continues, —

"That no attention was paid to the advice of said council by the church.

"That, on Sept. 24, 1806, the aggrieved brethren presented to the council convened for the ordination of Mr. True, a remonstrance, expressing their dissatisfaction with his ministrations, and their apprehensions, that, if he was settled, they could not conscientiously attend his ministrations; and that the consequence would be an unhappy separation of the church; and that evil consequences, civil and religious, would result to this society.

"That, on Oct. 18, 1806, a complaint was brought by Mr. Blake, who was not a professor of religion, before the church, against Mr. Samuel Hills, containing several heavy charges.

"That, on Nov. 13, 1806, the church exhibited articles of complaint against Brothers March, Walker, and Hills; and, on Nov. 24, proceeded to suspend Brother Hills from their communion.

"That, after various fruitless efforts to obtain a mutual council to settle their difficulties, the following articles of complaint were, among others, exhibited by the aggrieved against their brethren, May 10, 1808: —

"1. That our brethren urged us to take measures to ascertain the opposition to Mr. True, and then blamed us therefor.

"4. In bringing and acting upon charges against the brethren, without sufficient evidence.

"8. In refusing to take a vote upon an acknowledgment of one of the church, although it had been presented nearly five months.

"9. In neglecting, for more than thirteen months, to prosecute the charges brought against some of the brethren.

"10. That our brethren have not been sufficiently cautious in admitting persons occasionally to the Lord's table."[1]

"That, on June 29, 1808, a mutual council was convened to attend to the difficulties existing in the church. That, after the council had heard the charges against the aggrieved, and some explanations were given, the church voted to restore Messrs. March, Walker, and Hills.

"That the matters of complaint exhibited by the aggrieved against the church were not settled by the council.

"That, on July 12, 1808, the aggrieved requested the church to let them withdraw their relation to the church; but were denied their request.

"That, on Sept. 29, 1808, the following articles of complaint were exhibited against the church: —

---

[1] The substance of the other articles is comprehended in the subsequent charges.

"*To the Rev. Henry True, to be communicated to the church.*

"We, the undersigned, beg leave to state, that we feel much wounded and aggrieved by the conduct of the church.

"1. That our brethren have, in open violation of their vote, refused to accept of the assistance of some of the Lincoln Association, and have treated, and continue to treat, them with cold neglect.

"2. That they have infringed the rights of some of the members of the church, in admitting a committee of the town to act with them on matters belonging exclusively to the church.

"3. That they have, in a hasty and inconsiderate manner, urged forward the settlement of Mr. True, contrary to the judgment and feelings of the major part of the brethren and sisters of the church.

"4. That our brethren have disobeyed the commands of Christ, in not taking the private steps in their discipline; —

"5. In bringing charges against some of the brethren that had no foundation in truth; —

"6. In allowing Mr. Blake to interfere in the discipline of the church, and using his influence with them, by pleading before them against some of their brethren; —

"7. In not consulting the church upon the propriety of coming to the Lord's table under existing difficulties; —

"8. In refusing to act upon business regularly brought before them; —

"9. In transacting important church-business before the hour appointed for church-meeting; several of the brethren not having arrived, and the said business not having been regularly opened to the church for their consideration, or they notified that such business was to be acted upon at a future meeting.

"Samuel Hills,
"St. March,
"In behalf of the aggrieved."

"That, on Nov. 12, 1808, the aggrieved presented a remonstrance against the conduct of the church, in not attending to their complaints.

"That, on Jan. 5, 1809, the aggrieved protested against the conduct of the church, and withdrew from their communion.

"That, for more than two years, the aggrieved have been deprived of gospel-ordinances; and that little or no pains have been taken with the sisters, either to give them satisfaction, or to convince them of their error, if they were in one.

"While the council were investigating the business, the Rev. Mr. True and some members of the church, at the special request of the council, attended, and very candidly offered many remarks and explanations and concessions, with a view to throw light upon the subject under consideration, for the information of the council.

"It was earnestly recommended, both to the church and the aggrieved, that they should make an effort to settle their difficulties. And the council conversed with each party separately to see if no method could be devised for their re-union, but could not discover any way to unite them on gospel-principles.

"All hope of obtaining an object so desirable being at an end, in the view of the council, after a deliberate and attentive review of the difficulties submitted for their consideration, the council voted unanimously as follows: —

"1. That, in the opinion of this council, the subjects of complaint presented by the aggrieved against the majority are matters of real grievance.

"2. That the articles of complaint were generally supported.

"3. That the covenant-relation between the minority and majority of the church in this place is dissolved, in consequence of the breach of covenant on the part of the majority, and the steps taken by the minority; — on this view of the subject, together with the consideration that the minority, upon close examination of their experiences and religious opinions, do appear to be qualified, agreeably to the rules of the gospel, to enjoy gospel-ordinances."

"And although many unhappy consequences may follow, yet this council feel themselves justified, and under indispensable obligation from Christ's command to feed his sheep and lambs, to assist them by forming them into a church.

"The council deeply deplore the evils that have arisen in this part of our Lord's vineyard, and lament that they should feel a necessity of taking such a painful step. They compassionate the deplorable state of that part of the church, whose general conduct, in relation to the subjects of complaint which have come before the council, they are constrained to disapprove. They ardently pray that God would give them repentance unto life; and they exhort and beseech them to turn to God with all their hearts, with supplication and prayer, and to amend their ways; to return to their brethren, and endeavor to heal the wounds they have occasioned, and build up the kingdom of Christ in this place.[1]

[1] According to Mr. Huse's letter, it seems that, in relation to this council, "Mr. True, with some of the church, met them, and assured them they did not mean to acknowledge them as a council. They proceeded, however, to examine the charges of grievance exhibited by these three disaffected members against the church. The charges were much the same as those laid before the mutual council. They all had some relation to the conduct of the church with regard to the

"The council would betray weakness and the want of gospel-impartiality, were they to decide that nothing wrong, in this long state of controversy and difficulty, had fallen to the lot of the minority. But, from a view of the whole of their proceedings, we consider them as having acted in the main agreeably to the directions of the gospel.

"And it is our decided belief, that, had the church been earnest for the maintenance of a just, equal, and faithful gospel-discipline, this very unhappy separation would not have taken place.

"*To the church now formed by their desire, and the approbation of this council.*

"Christian Brethren, — We acknowledge you as a church of Christ, and receive you into the fellowship of the churches of Christ. We wish you the presence and blessing of Jesus, the great Head of the church, and pray that he would establish and build you up in the faith and in love, and increase you abundantly. But, when we view your situation and prospects, we tremble for you. We therefore exhort you to be wise as serpents, and harmless as doves. Walk circumspectly towards those that are without, and let your light shine before others. Remember you are a city set upon a hill. Let the word of God dwell in you richly. Be much in prayer. Forsake not the assembling yourselves

---

settlement of Mr. True. Nothing intentionally wrong was proved against the church, except their persevering to settle Mr. True in opposition to the desire of the minority. It is worthy of notice, that three members of this *ex parte* council were on the preceding mutual council; and all, at least except one, assented to the result of said council. But, notwithstanding the mutual council resulted that 'the church, on their part, made such explanations and concessions with regard to the charges produced against them by their brethren, Hills, March, and Walker, as manifested a conciliatory disposition,' and exhorted them all to be at peace among themselves, this *ex parte* council resulted that 'the covenant-relation between the majority and minority of the church in Union is dissolved, in consequence of the breach of covenant on the part of the majority and the steps taken by the minority;' and that they 'feel themselves justified, and under indispensable obligation from Christ's command to feed his sheep and lambs, to assist them by forming them into a church.' They censured the conduct of the church, and expressed an ardent prayer 'that God would give them repentance unto life,' and exhorted and besought them 'to turn to God with all their hearts, with supplication and prayer, and to amend their ways, return to their brethren, and endeavor to heal the wounds which they have occasioned, and build up the kingdom of Christ in this place.'"

together; but be careful to meet statedly for the worship of God on the sabbath, and endeavor, as far as you can, to obtain the public ministrations of the word and ordinances of God. Hold fast the doctrines[1] of the uncorrupted gospel. Be attentive to the examination of those who are admitted to your communion. Watch over one another in the Lord. See that the discipline of God's house be duly executed, and that you fall not out by the way. Be not high-minded, but fear lest you bring a reproach upon yourselves and others, to the great injury of religion. We exhort you to keep together, and to strengthen each other's hands in every good work. Bring up your children for God. We charge you to live in love, and to cultivate peace and good understanding among yourselves; and we pray that the God of peace may dwell with you. And now, brethren, we commend you to God and the word of his grace, which is able to build you up, and to give you an inheritance among all them that are sanctified.

"The above result approved by the unanimous vote of council, this seventeenth day of February, 1809.

"JOHN SAWYER, Moderator.
"JONATHAN BELDEN, Scribe."

To continue Mr. Huse's letter:—

"Even before this separation, it was no uncommon thing for missionaries to go into Union, give advice to the disaffected party, preach public lectures, while Mr. True was preaching there on probation and after his ordination; — I

---

[1] One objection to Mr. True was, that the Rev. Mr. Ripley, of Concord, Mass., had sent him; and therefore he must be a Socinian. This charge was constantly made throughout his ministry, though Mr. Ripley had probably never heard of him till after he came to Union. The first sabbath Mr. True was here, "Mr. Sawyer, then of Boothbay, was present from the Lincoln and Kennebec Association to hold the ground. Mr. True supplied in the morning. He went to Warren in the afternoon to attend a funeral, and Mr. Sawyer preached in the meeting-house while he was gone." A system of opposition ran through all the veins of the Lincoln and Kennebec Association. Mr. Hills carried his opposition so far, that he " got Mr. True to his house one evening to examine his experience, while others were in a different room to listen and report according to his [Hills's] dictation." Hills and the Lincoln and Kennebec Association were identified in their spirit. When Mr. True was supported by subscription, and before dismission, Sewall, Belden, and others took possession of the

mean such missionaries as were under the influence of, and immediately connected with, the members of the before-mentioned party-council. Since the separation, the members of the council have considered this little party as under their immediate and exclusive care, and have taken pains to countenance and support them in their separate condition, by visiting them, preaching to them, administering the sacrament to them, and by often directing missionaries to them, who are of their particular sentiments in religion. They are countenanced by the Maine Missionary Society, particularly by the Lincoln and Kennebec Association, the most active and influential members of which societies composed the *ex parte* council.

"Mr. True is a modest, moderate Calvinist. No one pretends to find fault with his doctrines or moral conduct; only that he does not go far enough, and they cannot feel that he is a converted man. The majority of the church of which he is pastor are apparently serious, orthodox, and exemplary Christians. I have personally known them for many years. But they do not carry points of doctrine quite so far as some others, particularly as Mr. Hills, who is a disciple of Dr. Emmons; and they do not wish to be under the entire control of the Lincoln and Kennebec Association.

"Members of the *ex parte* council above mentioned, and missionaries under their influence, not only visit and preach to the party in Union, but many times preach in other towns where are settled ministers, barely at the request of an individual, male or female, boy or girl, over whom they have gained some ascendency. They make a practice of passing by settled ministers, and associating with those in parishes who are a little disaffected toward their own ministers. These things are done very frequently in this and other towns in this county."[1]

meeting-house. Even while Mr. True was a candidate, "Jotham and Samuel Sewall appointed lectures at the meeting-house and other places, without consulting him." It should be added, in justice to Rev. Mr. Mitchell, who afterward was settled in Waldoborough, that he did not sympathize with the opposers of Mr. True, "and invited Mr. True to take a mission from the Maine Missionary Society."

[1] The details given will enable those who wish it to judge of the merits of a controversy which kept the community in high excitement for many years, and of which the lamentable effects are felt to the present day. A lesson may be learned respecting the sectarian spirit of the time, not merely in Union, but in the State generally;

Such was the origin of the Second Congregational Church in this town. At the organization, Feb. 17, 1809, they adopted the articles of faith and the covenant which were then in use by the First Church, and which were adopted by them, Feb. 6, 1804, with the alterations then made to suit Mr. Hills. The only change of the language was in the substitution of the words, " We engage to admit to our holy communion such, and none but such, as give a rational, scriptural evidence," for the words, " We engage to admit to our holy communion all who can give a rational, scripture evidence," &c.

and, though the remaining part of Mr. Huse's letter does not pertain exclusively to Union, it is thought proper to add it: —
"The Maine Missionary Society, or rather Mr. Bayley, of Newcastle, its President, and the Lincoln and Kennebec Association, take the utmost pains to ascertain every vacant parish, where there is the least prospect of establishing a minister, and immediately send them one after their own heart, supported for a while by the society's funds, but accompanied with a letter to some individual in the parish, suggesting to him the propriety of their hiring him, at least for a while, after the term of his mission expires; and the good, unsuspecting people think they can do no less. By this means, they have sometimes succeeded in palming ministers of a particular complexion upon towns and societies in this quarter. In some instances they have established ministers, whose sentiments, when fully known, are very obnoxious to a great majority of the people.

"The ministers and missionaries from the Maine Society, or Lincoln Association, avoid other settled ministers, who do not belong to those societies. They do not allow their candidates to have any ministerial connection with those ministers, any further than to preach in their towns, not exchange. Nor do they allow the churches, over which they gain control, to invite the assistance of neighboring churches in ordinations, whose pastors are not of their number, or whose sentiments, they suspect, do not perfectly correspond with theirs. Two such instances have recently occurred in this immediate vicinity. I need not mention them to you. I am well acquainted with the members of a church in an adjoining town, where they have lately settled a minister, have often administered the ordinances to them, and am well convinced they are in fellowship with me and our church, and yet our church was not invited to assist at the ordination. One of the members frankly told me 'they did not send to all churches they wished, because they were under the Maine Missionary Society.' I must close my narration, though it might be protracted. You are at liberty to make any use of it you please.

"I am your brother in the ministry,
"JONA. HUSE."

The following are the names of the seceders who formed the Second Congregational Church:—

Samuel Hills	Abigail March
Stephen March	Sarah Nicholson
Amos Walker	Martha Williams
Abigail Hills	Huldah Blanchard
Mary Fogler	Sally Barnard
Hannah Walker	Sally Shepard.

To these were added, at the time of the organization, Feb. 17, 1809, —

John Clark, Judith Clark, Judith Walker.

There were subsequently added, —

David Starrett, June 11, 1810; Jane Kirkpatrick, Aug. 5, 1810; Sarah Tucker, Aug. 5, 1810; Daniel Walker, Nov. 18, 1810; James Starrett, March 5, 1815; Rev. James Ricker, July 2, 1815; and afterward, Jane Cutting.

CHAPTER XX.

ECCLESIASTICAL HISTORY, 1807—1819.

Proceedings of the Town to pay Mr. True. — Remission of Ministerial Taxes. — Signers to the Methodists; to the Friends; to the Baptists. — Movements to dissolve the Town's Contract with Mr. True. — Incorporation of the First Congregational Society. — Dissolution of the Town's Contract.

1807.

DURING these church-difficulties, the town was required each year to act on parochial affairs; for towns then discharged the duties which now devolve on parishes. Mr. True's opponents were not inactive. March, 1807, Jonathan Newhall, Nathaniel Robbins, Nathan Blake, Joel Adams, Simeon Butters, Oliver

REMISSION OF MINISTERIAL TAXES. 193

Pratt, and Marlboro' Packard, being two persons from each of the principal denominations in town, and one Quaker, were chosen a committee "to consider the aggrieved of all parties, to fix a compromise, and to report at the May meeting." May 11, the town accepted their report, —

"That all who are not of the Congregational Society, and who do not intermeddle with said society's affairs, or vote in town on ministerial matters, and will exhibit to the selectmen a certificate thereof signed by each person of their society who are subject to be taxed, and by a committee of three members of their church, in the month of June or July annually, shall have their ministerial taxes abated before the tax-bills are committed to the collector. And it shall be the duty of the selectmen and assessors to make said abatements, and form a list of said persons, and set the sums against each name so abated, and cross said ministerial tax, and deliver said list to the town-clerk, who shall make record of the same, and certify to the town-treasurer the amount of said abatement."

This principle was adopted also in 1808, 1809, and 1810. Thus, although the taxes were assessed regularly, those of the seceders were not called for by the collector; and it was virtually left optional with the societies, except the Congregational, to raise any thing or nothing for the support of religious worship among themselves.

1808.

March 7, the town voted "to relinquish so much of the ministerial tax of the Methodists for 1806 and 1807 as the selectmen may think proper to cross."[1] It was also "voted to relinquish the ministerial taxes assessed to the following names in the year 1807, viz.: Spencer Walcott, Oliver Pratt, Simon Fuller, Nathan

---

[1] At the same time it was voted to let the Methodists have the meeting-house the last sabbath in March. Sept. 17, it was voted to let the Baptists have the meeting-house the first sabbath in November.

Carver, Thomas Daggett, Sterling Davis, Zelotes Tucker, Marlboro' Packard, Barnabas Simmons, Ezra Bowen, Abel Walker, Mary Gay, Marble Alford, Jacob Ring, and Robert Thompson," who belonged to the Baptist denomination.

In accordance with the report accepted May 11, 1807, the town-records, under the year 1808, contain the following names of persons who did not belong to the Congregational Society, together with their ministerial taxes:—

METHODISTS.

Joel Adams	$4.43	Solomon Hewes	$1.54
Christopher Butler		Levi Irish	1.06
John Butler	6.54	Cornelius Irish	1.89
Gorham Butler		Edward Jones	2.77
Jonathan Brown	1.37	John Kieff	1.41
Thomas Butler	4.36	Asaph Lucas	1.26
Joseph Butler	4.40	Thaddeus Luce	1.65
Simeon Butters	3.05	Josiah Maxcy	6.05
Charles Butters	1.67	Hervey Maxcy	3.95
Alford Butters	1.02	Obadiah Morse	3.42
John Clarke	3.43	Bela Robbins	4.81
John Clarke, 2d	1.42	Nathan D. Rice	1.91
Joshua Collamore	1.96	Timothy Stewart	4.25
Alpheus Collamore	1.46	David Snell	4.06
Simon Drake	2.03	David Snell, jun.	1.13
Simon Chaffin	2.18	Jacob Severance	1.73
John Drake	2.55	James Thompson	4.25
Rufus Dyer	3.00	Olney Titus	2.78
Henry Esensa	3.26	Daniel Walker	2.77
Jonathan Eastman	3.71	John Walker	3.78
Royal Grinnell	4.45	Jason Ware	7.92
Richard Grinnell	1.54	Aaron Young	2.91
Bailey Grinnell	6.61	Aaron Young, jun.	2.36
Samuel S. Grinnell	1.53	Daniel Murray	1.00
Matthias Hawes	8.27	James Maxfield	1.00
Reuben Hills	13.27	Jeremiah Clough	1.00
Samuel Hills, 2d	1.86	Lewis Robbins, 2d	1.00
Nathan Hills	1.95	Isaac Carkin	1.00
Reuben Hills, jun.	1.86	Jeremiah Stubbs	1.00

FRIENDS.

Jonathan Newhall, $4.25; Ichabod Irish, $2.56; total, $6.81.

BAPTISTS.

Marble Alford . .	$1.81	William Lermond .	$3.46
Ezra Bowen . . .	3.61	James Lermond . .	2.49
William Boggs . .	3.40	Oliver Pratt . . .	5.76
Nathan Carver . .	2.39	William Peabody .	1.50
Thomas Daggett . .	4.22	Marlboro' Packard .	5.67
Sterling Davis . .	3.52	Barnabas Simmons .	6.41
Simon Fuller . . .	2.78	Daniel Shepard, jun.	1.70
Peter Fales . . .	3.55	Jacob Sibley . . .	2.92
Mary Gay	2.92	Zelotes Tucker . .	2.39
John Hemenway . .	1.86	Abel Walker . . .	1.58
Daniel Howard . .	1.38	George W. West . .	4.38
Edmund Luce . .	2.19	Spencer Walcott . .	5.87
John Lermond . .	7.24	Jacob Ring . . .	1.00

1809.

March 6, 1809, a committee, consisting of Amos Barrett, Nathan Blake, Congregationalists; Joel Adams, Edward Jones, Methodists; and Spencer Walcott, Oliver Pratt, Baptists, was chosen to inquire into the state of the treasury respecting ministerial money. The town accepted the report, May 1, in which they say, "So far as we can ascertain by the selectmen's book and other documents, there is a deficiency in the treasury, to complete Mr. True's salary to September, 1808, of the sum of $262.56, including orders of the assessors for Richard Cummings and others," — who stated that they belonged to some other society, — " and that Mr. True relinquished his right to twenty-five dollars' annual allowance in place of firewood," until such time as he might signify his want of it.

At the same time, it was voted to raise one thousand dollars for ministerial use; and Nathan Blake, Ebenezer Alden, and Charles Pope, were chosen a committee to treat with Mr. True. There is no record of the report of this committee.

The names of the signers to other societies, Nov. 1, 1809, with their several ministerial taxes, are on record as follows:—

METHODISTS.

David Snell*	$4.00	Rufus Dyer*	$3.13
Cornelius Irish*	3.03	Alpheus Collamore*	2.60
Obadiah Morse*	4.86	Joseph Butler	5.85
Edward Jones	3.94	Adam Martin	2.88
James Thompson	5.17	Joel Adams*	5.85
Solomon Hewes*	1.64	Bailey Grinnell*	6.83
Jocob S. Adams	1.23	Thaddeus Luce*	2.19
Matthias Hawes*	11.94	James Maxfield	1.99
Ebenezer Robbins	1.91	Isaac Carkin	1.23
Mace S. Grinnell*	1.23	Jeremiah Luce*	1.23
Jacob Sevrance	2.30	Ezra Bowen, jun.	1.23
Alford Butters	2.73	Samuel Hills, 2d*	2.68
Samuel Spurr	3.70	Jason Ware*	10.07
Gorham Butler*	2.94	Philip Robbins	0.32
Aaron Young*	2.20	Thomas Messer	3.39
Christopher Butler*	3.16	John Drake*	3.56
John Lermond*	9.74	Ichabod Maddocks*	3.17
Aaron Young, jun.*	3.41	Richard Grinnell*	1.80
Josiah Hills*	2.46	Simon Chaffin	2.96
Reuben Hills, jun.*	2.34	David Snell, jun.*	1.89
Nathan Hills*	3.01	Royal Grinnell*	6.98
Jonathan Eastman*	5.36	Bela Robbins*	6.28
Thomas Butler*	5.80	John Walker*	5.02
Jeremiah Stubbs	1.70	Reuben Hills*	16.09
Simon Drake*	3.18	Olney Titus	3.35
William Lermond	5.22	John Clark*	4.12
Joseph Miller*	4.64	John Kieff	1.76
Hervey Maxcy	5.60	Ezekiel Clark	1.62
Henry Esensa*	4.13	Nathan D. Rice	2.46
James Brown	1.72	Joshua Collamore*	2.28
Simeon Butters*	3.46	John Butler*	2.77
Timothy Stewart*	5.68	Isaac Booth*	1.23

* Under date July 18, 1811, these persons, with Alford Adams, Leonard Bump, Jesse Drake, David Grafton, Isaac Hills, James Littlehale, Lewis Robbins 2d, Shadrach Snell, Vinal Ware, and George W. West, are recorded as belonging to the Methodist Society.

BAPTISTS.

Jacob Demuth	. . $3.17	Jacob Sibley*	. .	$4.42
James Lermond*	. 3.80	Thomas Daggett*	.	6.67
Marble Alford	. . 2.90	Edmund Luce	. .	3.00
Abel Walker .	. . 2.04	Ezra Bowen*.	. .	4.87
James Sinclair*	. . 1.67	Richard Cummings*		8.78
Daniel Howard*	. 1.83	Abel Le Doit .	. .	1.23
Simon Fuller*	. . 3.85	Benjamin Buzzell	.	1.90
Nathan Carver*	. . 3.47	William Boggs* .	.	4.61
Marlboro' Packard*.	7.60	Spencer Walcott*	.	9.00
Barney Simmons*	. 9.49	James Littlehale .	.	3.96
Sterling Davis*	. . 4.65	Peter Fales	. . .	4.56
Jacob Ring* .	. . 1.23	Zelotes Tucker	. .	2.92
William Peabody	. 1.81	George W. West .	.	6.36
Oliver Pratt .	. . 6.36			

1810.

In May, and also in September, 1810, unsuccessful attempts were made to reconsider the vote relieving the Baptists and the Methodists from paying their taxes to the collector. Sept. 17, it was "voted to dismiss the Rev. Henry True as minister of the town of Union." Nov. 5, a similar idea was contained in an article "to see if the town will take measures, and what they shall be, to dissolve the contract between the Rev. Henry True and the inhabitants of this town of Union, or act or do any thing relative to ministerial or religious matters which may come before them." No action was taken till Nov. 19, when the town voted to "adopt measures to dissolve the contract, ... and to choose a committee of three to state their

---

* Together with Mary Gay, Aaron Gleason, John Hemenway, Ziba Simmons, and Simon Wingate, are entered on the town-records July 18, 1811, as belonging to the Baptists.

May 6, 1811, the town voted to allow Samuel Hills, Stephen March, Daniel Walker, Amos Walker, John Clark 2d, and Stephen Childs, to "have the appropriation of their ministerial money to the support of their own teacher." And, April 13, 1812, a certificate, signed by Samuel Hills and Stephen March, states that Samuel Hills, Daniel Walker, Amos Walker, John Clark, jun., Stephen Childs, John Whiting, John Whitney, Nathan Barnard, and Stephen March, are members of the religious society in Union, called the Second Congregational Society.

objections against him." The committee, viz. Edmund Mallard, Thomas Nye, and Herman Hawes, at an adjourned meeting, Nov. 19, made the following statement: —

"Your committee, after due deliberation, have unanimously agreed to report as follows: —

"From our own daily observation, and the repeated complaints of our friends and many others, supporters of the Rev. Henry True, we are led to believe that the said Henry True is unmindful of a large portion of his parishioners, and treats his congregation with great partiality. We are fully convinced that he, the said Rev. Henry True, treats some of his parishioners in a familiar and friendly manner, as a minister in our opinion ought to do; while many others are treated with great indifference, and, in some instances, with an apparent studied neglect. We are of opinion that the said Henry True's ministration and manner of instruction, for the reasons above stated, has [have] become unprofitable, and [are] rather calculated to scatter, divide, and wean the members of the Congregational Society in this town from each other, than to cherish that equality, harmony, and friendship, without which the said society will be soon broken up, and the great blessings resulting from such regulated and properly conducted societies wholly lost. We are fully convinced, that a large proportion of the said Rev. Henry True's supporters are dissatisfied, and the dissatisfaction is still increasing, which lessens the number of his supporters to that degree, that the ministerial tax on the few remaining is very burthensome, and in some instances peculiarly distressing. All which is humbly submitted."

The report was not accepted. The town adopted the motion made by Jonathan Sibley, as follows: —

"That it is the opinion of this town that the ministerial taxes have become too burthensome to be borne, and pray the Rev. Henry True to aid the town in taking such measures as will have a tendency to ease the town somewhat of the burden." Philip Robbins, Josiah Robbins, Henry Blunt, Jonathan Sibley, Walter Blake, Edmund Mallard, and Nathaniel Bachelor, were chosen "a committee to present the above to Mr. True, and try to treat with him on the above subject."

1811.

Jan. 7, 1811, the town voted[1] to accept the proposal made by the Rev. Henry True, "that his parishioners pay him the same tax upon the poll and the same valuation of property as they paid him the first year after said True's settlement."

The subject of dissolving the connection between the town and Mr. True was often brought up, and might have created much difficulty if he had insisted on his salary during the whole of his ministry; for the town would have been obliged to pay it. Consequently, the warrants frequently contain articles in relation to this subject. Many of them are substantially repetitions of others; but they show the difficulty attending a dissolution of the connection between pastor and people, and the inclination to have a legal adjustment.

1813.

June 19, 1813, the proposition was "to see if the town will choose a committee to compromise with the Rev. Henry True." They voted "to choose a committee to settle" with him. It consisted of Ebenezer Alden, Nathaniel Robbins, Joseph Morse, George Kimball, and Jonathan Sibley. The committee reported,—

"That Mr. True has received nothing for his services for his three last ministerial years; that his legal demand upon the town for said services is $1,273.44.

"That Mr. True makes the same proposition to the town now that he made in January, 1811, to wit: 'that his parishioners pay him the same upon the poll and the same tax upon the same valuation of property as they paid him the first year after his settlement;' or, in other words, if the society will pay him the amount of the sums already assessed for ministerial use, with the addition of $200 before the first of March next, he will give a receipt in full for his salary up

---

[1] At the same town-meeting it was "voted that the town consent to have the Methodist Society petition to the Legislature" "for an Act of Incorporation." Probably the petition was not sent.

to the present month; which sum of $600 already assessed with $200 added, amounting in the whole to $800, in the opinion of your committee, is about what Mr. True would have received the said three years, provided the said proposition of January, 1811, had been properly met and properly carried into effect.

"Your committee further report, that Mr. True will not make any further demand upon the town for his salary the year beginning the present month, from the strength of contract subsisting between him and the town, provided the town desired that he should continue his connection with his society that time, and that he will receive his salary by subscription.

"Your committee would recommend, that, on this present day, an order be drawn by the proper officers upon the treasurer for the sum of $600, and that the treasurer be ordered to give Mr. True a note of hand for the sum of $200, payable next March, that Mr. True may receipt for said sum of $800 agreeable to his proposal, which will bar all demands by Mr. True upon the town for salary, up to the last Wednesday in the present month.

"All which is respectfully submitted,
"Per order, EBENR. ALDEN.
"Union, Sept. 6, 1813."

The report was accepted, with the exception of the clause respecting the treasurer's giving to Mr. True a note of hand.

1814.

May 9, the question was again brought forward " to see if the town will dismiss the Rev. Henry True as a town-minister. . . . Motioned, that whereas the Rev. Henry True has repeatedly in the pulpit professed a readiness to dissolve the contract between the town of Union and himself as their pastor, whenever it was their desire, — Voted that it is the desire of the people of the town of Union, one of the contracting parties, that the said contract with the Rev. Henry True be dissolved, and expire at the expiration of six months; and that the town-clerk be ordered to serve the Rev. Mr. True with an attested copy of the above."

1815.

May 8, 1815, agreeably to an article inserted in the warrant, the town "gave their consent" to have the Congregational Society incorporated. Accordingly, the Massachusetts Legislature, Jan. 31, 1816, passed the following —

"Act to incorporate the First Congregational Society in the town of Union.

"Sec. 1. — Be it enacted by the Senate and House of Representatives in General Court assembled, and by the authority of the same, That Nathaniel Robbins, Rufus Gillmor, Ebenezer Alden, Robert Foster, Amos Barrett, John Little, Joseph Vaughan, Elisha Bennet, Moses Morse, Jonathan Carriel, jun., Calvin Morse, John Fogler, Abijah Hawes, David Robbins, James Rice, Seth Luce, Jessa Robbins, Herman Hawes, Amariah Mero, Thomas Mitchell, Nathan Daniels, Levi Morse, John P. Robbins, Nathaniel Bachelor, William Dougherty, Fisher Hart, Caleb T. Jacobs, William Hart, David Robbins, jun., Jonathan Carriel, Micajah Gleason, Whiting Hawes, John W. Lindley, Ebenezer W. Adams, Samuel Spear, John Tobey, David Carriel, Jeremiah Mitchell, Thaddeus Shepard, and Noah Rice, with such other inhabitants of the town of Union as do not belong to any other religious society, and such as may hereafter associate with them, with their polls and estates, be, and they hereby are, incorporated into a religious society, by the name of the First Congregational Society in Union; and the said society is hereby invested with all the powers and privileges, and subjected to the same duties and requisitions as other religious societies are invested and subjected to, according to the laws and constitution of this Commonwealth.

"Sec. 2. — Be it further enacted, That if any person living in said town of Union, who may at any time hereafter desire to become a member of said First Congregational Society, shall declare his or her desire and intention thereof in writing, and deliver the same to the minister or clerk of said society, and a copy of the same to the minister or clerk of the religious society to which he or she may at that time belong, such person shall, from the time of delivering such declaration, be considered a member of said First Congregational Society in Union.

"Sec. 3. — Be it further enacted, That when any member of the said First Congregational Society may think proper to secede therefrom, and to unite with any other religious society in the said town of Union, the same course and process, *mutatis mutandis*, shall be had and done as is presented in the second section of this Act. Provided, however, that in every case of secession from one religious society and joining another, every such person shall be held to pay his or her proportion or assessment of all parish or society taxes legally voted by the society, prior to his or her secession therefrom, in manner above pointed out.

"Sec. 4. — Be it further enacted, That any Justice of the Peace for the county of Lincoln, upon application therefor, is hereby authorized to issue his warrant, directed to some member of said Congregational Society, requiring him to notify and summon the members thereof to meet at such convenient time and place as may be appointed in said warrant, to organize the said society by the election of its officers.

"Approved by the Governor, Feb. 1, 1816."

The warrant was issued by Stephen March, Esq., Justice of the Peace, to Ebenezer W. Adams, one of the members of the First Congregational Society in Union; and the first meeting was held April 10, 1816.

1819.

After the incorporation of this society, parochial matters were not acted upon as town-business. But a settlement was yet to be made with Rev. Mr. True. Nothing seems to have been done till April 15, 1819, when Mr. True signed the following document: "I, the subscriber, hereby release the town of Union from all demands and claims whatever, and fully acknowledge that I have no claim or demands against them." Even this seems not to have been entirely satisfactory; for, May 8, the selectmen were chosen a committee to wait on him, "and in behalf of the town to dissolve the contract which was made with him at or about the time of his ordination." The following report, made at an adjourned meeting in May, was accepted: —

"Whereas the inhabitants of the town of Union, on the eleventh day of November, 1805, voted to pay the Rev. Henry True an annual salary of four hundred dollars, so long as he should continue to be the minister of said town; and whereas the said vote contains conditions to be performed by either party wishing a dissolution of the connection between said parties, antecedent to such dissolution; and whereas the said True did, in April, A.D. 1816, discontinue to be the minister of said town; and whereas doubts have arisen whether said vote or contract does not remain in force, — now, therefore, I, the said True, and we, Micajah Gleason, John Lermond, and John W. Lindley, in behalf of said town, chosen for that purpose, do hereby agree to dissolve said vote or contract, and all contracts subsisting between said town and said True; and we mutually agree to waive all right of notice which either party may have precedent to said dissolution; and I, the said True, for myself, my heirs, executors, administrators, and assigns, release said town from all contracts heretofore made to me by said town; and we, the said Gleason, Lermond, and Lindley, on the part of the said town as aforesaid, discharge the said True from all contracts and engagements which he may have heretofore entered into with said town.

"HENRY TRUE.

"MICAJAH GLEASON, }
"JOHN LERMOND, } Committee.
"JOHN W. LINDLEY, }

"Union, May 26, 1819."

By this act, Mr. True probably relinquished all that was due to him before the incorporation of the society.

The only other movement which the town as such afterward made about sustaining public worship was to "pass over an article," Sept. 8, 1823, "to see if the town would raise a sum of money, to be divided among the several denominations, to defray the expenses of preaching the gospel."

CHAPTER XXI.

ECCLESIASTICAL HISTORY, 1816—1825.

Attempts to raise Money. — Dissolution of Mr. True's Pastoral Connection with the Church and Society. — Result of the Council. — Proposals for uniting the Congregational Churches. — Obstacles to a Union. — Union effected.

CONGREGATIONAL SOCIETY.

The evils which existed while parochial business was transacted by the town were not obviated by the incorporation into a society. At the meeting, April 10, 1816, called for organization, the society " voted that $250 be raised by assessment for the support of the Rev. Henry True." Similar votes were passed in 1817 and in 1818. No money was voted in 1819. In 1820 it was " voted to raise money by subscription for ministerial use." In 1821, propositions, first to raise $200, and next $150, both failed; as did another to raise $200 in 1824. Mr. True, however, received but a small part of what was voted; a few presents were made to him by friends; and, during the latter part of his ministry, he received a small sum for preaching as a missionary in the vicinity.

After several indications of the necessity of a dissolution, the church, March 7, 1820, " voted unanimously that they did not wish the pastoral relation between them and the Rev. Henry True dissolved at present." But, Sept. 21, the church " met at Brother James Rice's, agreeably to previous notice; and it was mutually agreed that the pastoral relation between the Rev. Henry True and the church should be dissolved,[1] and the pastor choose the council and fix the time for effecting the object; and that the pastor may remove all relation from the church, if he should be desirous of

[1] This change in the purposes of the church was brought about by the manœuvring of Mr. Noah Emerson, then preaching in town.

it." The churches in Wiscasset, Dresden, and Warren, were sent to; but the Dresden church was not represented. The council met Oct. 25.

"After organization and prayer by the moderator, proceeded to business.

"Preparatory to the deliberations of the occasion, the church was requested to communicate the several results of council relating to ecclesiastical affairs of the town. After examining the documents exhibited, the council came to the following result: —

"1. The connection between pastor and church, minister and people, is peculiarly endearing and solemn and sacred, and has been, in all ages in the Christian church, instrumental in building up the Redeemer's kingdom. The council now convened deem this connection too sacred to be dissolved for trivial reasons; but they doubt not that causes may exist and circumstances occur which justify a separation.

"2. The council, finding that, at a regular meeting of the church, Sept. 21, 1820, it was mutually agreed that the pastoral relation between the Rev. Henry True and the church be dissolved, and that the pastor choose the council and fix the time for effecting that object, by the authority vested in them, declare said connection dissolved accordingly.

"3. The council are happy to find the church have passed the following vote: 'The church of Christ, of which the Rev. Henry True is pastor, voted, Oct. 25, 1820, that they highly esteem their pastor as a neighbor and friend, as a citizen and Christian; and that they regard and respect him as a conscientious and faithful minister of the Christ, and deeply lament that circumstances are such that a dissolution of his pastoral relation to them has become expedient. The church is still anxious for his welfare, and prays for his health and prosperity.' And the council cordially unite in giving him their approbation as a minister of Christ, and recommend him as such to the service of the churches, wishing him to administer gospel-ordinances as occasions may require."
[Then follow pertinent words of counsel and of sympathy with the pastor; after which the fourth section contains similar sentiments for the church.]

"5. The council think it their duty, before closing this result, to introduce the following statement of facts: —

"It appears from letters missive, calling an *ex parte* council, that those who were erected by that council into a church-state had, 'after long waiting and many painful efforts to settle difficulties subsisting between them and the majority of the church, finally remonstrated, protested, and withdrew.' And yet it appears from the result of the council which ordained Mr. True, that, in the unanimous opinion of said council, Mr. True's confession of faith, and the answers he gave to questions proposed to him by the council, obviated and did away all the objections brought against him by the professedly aggrieved. It appears also from the result of a mutual council, called in 1808, to adjust difficulties subsisting between the brethren of the church in Union, that the church manifested toward the disaffected a conciliatory disposition; and the council regretted, although a full reconciliation was truly desirable, that they had not the satisfaction to see all matters of difficulty done away. It appears likewise that the *ex parte* council, whose result has been carefully examined, 'exhort and beseech the church to repent and turn to God with all their heart, with supplication and prayer, and to amend their ways, and return to their brethren, and endeavor to heal the wounds they had occasioned.' And yet great exertions have been made from time to time, and even by members of the said *ex parte* council, to unite the two churches; thus expressing a wish to hold Christian fellowship with those whom they had severely censured and virtually discarded. Indeed, the council deem it proper distinctly to state, from the testimony before them, that the original objectors to the Rev. Mr. True have, in the opinion of the council, manifested unreasonable opposition to his labors and ministry in this place; and that their advisors have been wanting in that uniting and conciliatory spirit which is required in the disciples of Christ, and especially in them who are set for the preaching and defence of the gospel of peace.

"Voted that the scribe read this result in public.

"H. PACKARD, Moderator.
"D. F. HARDING, Scribe."

This was the termination of Mr. True's ministry. On the same day, the church chose the Rev. Jonathan Huse, of Warren, to act as moderator, " during the time of their destitution of a pastor."

About this time, measures were taken to effect a union of the First with the Second Congregational Church. Conversations were held; but there does not appear to have been any action till June 17, 1820, when, at a meeting of the two churches, the Rev. Amasa Smith was chosen moderator, and Daniel F. Harding scribe; and it was "voted that each church have a copy of" certain written "proposals" for a union. It was also voted to adjourn the meeting to July 6, which should "be observed as a day of public fasting and prayer; and that the Rev. Messrs. Ingraham, Mitchell, Huse, True, and Smith be requested to attend on that day." At the adjourned meeting, Mr. Huse was chosen moderator in the place of Mr. Smith, who declined; and the First Church "resolved that a union at that time was unadvisable."

In a communication to the Maine Missionary Society, extracts from which are published in their fourteenth annual report, appended to the anniversary sermon of the Rev. Benjamin Tappan, is the following language of Noah Emerson, who was engaged in preaching during the greater part of this year: —

"I labored in the place six weeks, with very little apparent success. But it then appeared that the Lord was there by the special influence of his Spirit. On the 24th of September, at the close of the public exercises of the sabbath, a meeting of religious inquiry was appointed for the benefit of those that might entertain a hope of renewing grace, and for that of others who might be under serious impressions. Eight such individuals attended the first meeting, which was solemn and interesting. One about fifty years of age appeared, and declared, as David, 'what the Lord had done for his soul.' One such meeting was held every week; and, in every meeting for six successive weeks, the number of convicted sinners and hopeful converts continued to increase; so that the cries of distressed souls and praises of renewing grace were alternately heard, which seemed on the one hand to increase the distress and deepen the conviction, while on the other to temper the joy and increase the thankfulness for saving mercy."

Oct. 25, 1820, the day when the council met to ratify the proceedings in regard to Mr. True's dismission, the following vote was passed by the church of which he had been the pastor: —

"Whereas no regular communication has been made from the Second to the First Congregational Church in this place, relative to a union; and whereas there are some members of the First Church whose feelings and wishes have not been consulted, and who have expressed an opinion that there is not a probability of a harmonious co-operation in ecclesiastical matters, if a union should take place between the churches, — therefore voted unanimously, that, if any members of this church cannot be reconciled to its proceedings, they shall have liberty to remove their relation from this church, and join any sister-church they may wish."

"Nov. 1, 1820, voted that the proposals presented by the Rev. Noah Emerson be read. Voted to acquiesce in said proposals, in case Mr. Samuel Hills withdraw his relation to the Second Church, and in case the sisters of the First Church acquiesce." The last vote was reconsidered Nov. 16, and it was "voted to invite the Second Congregational Church to return, agreeably to proposals of Rev. Mr. Emerson. . . . Nov. 23, voted by both churches unanimously to unite;" that "the proposals be read next sabbath, and the churches sit together. Voted to dismiss both moderators, viz. Rev. Jonathan Belden and Rev. Jonathan Huse."

The following were the " proposals : " —

"Considering that, several years ago, a number of our church (*i.e.* the First Congregational Church in Union) became dissatisfied, and, without our consent, were formed into a separate Congregational Church by an *ex parte* council; that, since the formation of this church, an unhappy division has existed, which has occasioned many party feelings, much to the dishonor of religion; that, while this division continues, we have but little reason to think that the ministrations of the gospel will be constantly supported among us; that a number of individuals, giving satisfactory evidence of piety, wish to join a Congregational Church and enjoy the privileges of the same, but, being much grieved by this unhappy division, are hence prevented from joining either church; considering also that a number of said separate church

UNION OF THE CHURCHES. 209

have of late manifested a disposition to join us again, — we, the First Congregational Church of Christ in Union, desirous of healing the unhappy division, and of restoring peace and prosperity to the church, feel it our duty and privilege to invite the said separate church to join us, and, as many of them as went out from us, to return to their former standing in our church, on the following conditions: —

"1. That we, Samuel Hills, Amos Walker, David Starrett, Daniel Walker, Abigail Hills, Sarah Barnard, Martha Williams, Judith Walker, Jane Cutting, Judith Clark, members of the said separate church, do confess to God and man whatever we have done amiss, and ask forgiveness of both.

"2. That we, John Gleason, Seth Luce, David Robbins, James Rice, William Daggett, Dorothy Law, Mary Mitchell, Mercy D. Mitchell, Anna Gleason, Mercy Robbins, Rhoda Ellis, Rebecca Gowen, Mary Tobey, Jedidah Daggett, Daniel Shepard, Sarah Shepard, members of the First Congregational Church in Union, do, on our part, confess to God and man whatever we have done amiss, and ask forgiveness of both.

"3. That we, said members of both churches, do now forgive each other, and do solemnly promise never to mention any past difficulties to the offence or grief of any member; and, should any one be so unhappy as to be overtaken in such a fault, he or she, thus in fault, shall immediately confess it, and be forgiven.

"4. That we, the First Congregational Church of Christ in Union, do now receive you, the said separate church, into our church in regular standing and in full communion, upon your giving renewedly your assent to our confession of faith and articles of covenant.

"5. This exhibition we make in public before all, that others also may fear. (1 Tim. v. 20.)"

[Accordingly], "on the following sabbath, the united church made a public exhibition of their union, which, after mutual confession and forgiveness of both churches, was effected by the First Church's receiving the Second into their church in regular standing and in full communion, as soon as the Second had given a public assent to their confession of faith and articles of covenant." [1]

Although by this act the two churches came together, there were some church-members who did not

---

[1] Mr. Emerson, in Appendix to the Rev. Dr. Tappan's Discourse.

join in it, and they considered themselves not bound by it. Dec. 28, there was chosen a committee who made an unsuccessful attempt to obtain the records of the First Congregational Church. Jan. 9, 1821, the committee was increased; and, "to make further exertions to obtain former church-records." Mr. True offered to meet the clerk, and let him copy all he wished; but he declined giving up the original records, as he desired to deliver them to his successor. Jan. 16, it was voted, "that the deacons and clerk be a committee to treat with Deacon Abijah Hawes and others respecting a communication received from them, and to try to effect a further union of churches." April 26, voted "that Brother James Rice deliver those church-vessels, now in his care, into Deacon Daniel Walker's hands for keeping." At the same meeting, a committee was chosen and "instructed to inform our dissenting brethren, that we expect them to accede to the articles of our union, or withdraw, or agree upon a mutual council, previous to our next communion." May 5, voted "that an address be presented to Deacon Hawes, to be communicated to our dissenting brethren." The address, which has not been found, drew out the following reply:—

"From the brethren and sisters who decline acceding to the articles of union of churches, to Mr. Daniel Walker, moderator of a church-meeting, held May 5, 1821 : —

"Taking into view the communications already passed on the subject of the union, we are constrained to conclude that your communication, containing only presumptuous accusations, inconsiderate assertions, and rash declamations, was purposely intended to terrify.

"We, however, wish you to examine circumstances impartially, and be undeceived respecting the votes referred to. The vote of the First Church, giving liberty to withdraw and join a sister-church, you have not correctly stated. And in no way does it impose on us any duty or obligation to avail ourselves of its privileges; and, until we do choose to avail ourselves of it, it is of no effect, and we stand in the same condition as if the vote had never passed.

"The 'vote of the same church at a subsequent meeting, to invite conditionally the Second Church to unite,' was not a vote of the church, but a vote of five members only, and the meeting irregularly and imprudently called. 'And the still later vote to receive them' was not a vote of the church, but a vote of five members at an adjournment of an irregular meeting. And they did not unite by any vote, but in compliance with certain extraneous articles of agreement.

"There has never been an actual reception of the Second Church into the First; but a part of the First have seceded, and united with the Second.

"We earnestly pray that we and you may be made to see the errors of our steps, that if possible we may be delivered from persecution, and stand by our covenant without intimidation; and, finally, that you may conduct with wisdom, and not be left to such measures as shall extend the mischiefs already created."

May 24, the church-records state: "Whereas the church has been charged with taking unlawfully certain articles of church-furniture, claimed as the property of Abijah Hawes, of Union, and are prosecuted by him for the same, —

"Voted that we consider the property ours; that we have a perfect right to it in law and equity; that we feel no fear of being unable to substantiate our claims before a proper tribunal; but, considering that we are on both sides the professed disciples of Christ, brother going to law with brother, we are willing, for the sake of peace and to avoid throwing a stumbling-block before the world, to relinquish our just rights, to give up said property, and pay what cost has accrued. Provided, however, this act of ours shall not be construed into an acknowledgment of the claim [of] Deacon Abijah Hawes and others who unite with him to be a church in any form.

"Voted that a committee of three be appointed to communicate the foregoing vote to Deacon Hawes, and endeavor to effect a settlement on the principles avowed in said vote.

"Voted that Brothers Daniel Walker, Thomas Mitchell, and David Robbins, be this committee.

"June 16. The committee appointed at our last meeting to settle with Deacon Hawes report and return a receipt of the settlement.

Sept. 6. "The brethren who consider themselves the First Congregational Church in Union, being convened at the house of Rev. Henry True, voted they are willing to confer with the brethren, Seth Luce, John Gleason, James Rice, David Robbins, and the sisters similarly situated, upon matters of agreement existing between them, and, if deemed expedient, join in calling a council for advice."

"October. Voted [by the other party] that Brother William Daggett sign letters missive, on our part, for a mutual council."

"Nov. 15, a committee was chosen to confer with Rev. Henry True relative to a union. Voted to dismiss Brother Samuel Hills from this church, agreeably to his offer to withdraw. . . . Dec. 19, after mutual confessions and forgiveness on both sides, it was simultaneously voted to be united in one body." The meeting was "closed with prayer by Rev. Mr. True."

Several persons now united, on condition that they might leave to join any other church within six months. The church-meetings held Dec. 26, 1821, and Jan. 10, 1822, were opened with prayer by Mr. True. But by the next church-meeting, Feb. 9, Mr. Hills had returned, claiming membership, and asserting that by his withdrawal he was to lose nothing but the privilege of voting. Accordingly, new dissatisfaction arose, and, at the church-meetings which followed, it would seem that Mr. True and Mr. Hills were absent; for the prayer was offered by Deacon Hawes.

After Mr. Hills's dismission, Nov. 15, there seems to have been a disposition to harmony and co-operation. At the next meeting, Dec. 19, Rev. Mr. True, Thomas Mitchell, and Daniel Walker, were chosen a committee to regulate and adjust past records. But the subsequent prevarication and evasion of Hills disgusted some. Many very severe remarks had been made against Mr. True. He had been falsely charged with want of piety, neglecting family worship, &c. June 13, Mr. True, in accordance with his request made June 8, and Mr. Jonathan Carriel, were dismissed from the church, and recommended to Mr. Huse's in Warren; and, Sept. 14, it was voted to dismiss Mary Barrett, Sibyl Carriel, Mary True, Harriet Harding, and George Wellington, to unite with any sister-church.

"June 12, 1824, voted, Whereas Brother Samuel Hills, on account of difficulties in the church of Christ of which he was a member, made a proposal to withdraw and unite with some sister-church, if said church would dismiss him and said proposals should be complied with, [and] the proposals were altered at the time the council were here and under the inspection of Brother Hills; [and] therefore we, the church, thought it our duty to dismiss Brother Hills, without the pledge specified in the first proposals, and we regret that any misunderstanding exists between Brother Hills and the church, — we ask forgiveness of Brother Hills and all concerned, wherein we have offended. We, therefore, the Congregational Church of Christ in Union, think[ing] it to be the duty of all Christians, especially of the same order, who live in the same town, to unite in worshipping God, move to invite Brother Samuel Hills to meet with us when he can make it convenient, that we may confess our faults one to another, and pray one for another that we may be healed. . . . July 9, voted and chose a committee to visit Brother Hills, to consult further with him respecting his being reconciled with the church, and the church with him. . . . Aug. 17, chose a committee to inquire and make report what personal objection existed in the church against Brother Samuel Hills being received to the fellowship of this church."

Accordingly, Sept. 11, the motion made June 12 was accepted, with the modifications that he was *persuaded* to make a motion to withdraw, and that it was *supposed* the alteration by the council was made with Mr. Hills's knowledge and consent. And, Oct. 13, 1825, it was "voted to invite Brother Samuel Hills to withdraw his relation from the church in Waldoborough, and unite with the church in this place." And, May 14, 1826, it was voted to receive Brother Samuel Hills into this church, agreeably to his dismission from the church in Waldoborough.

Thus, at last, the two churches were united. Nearly all the members of each of them have since died. Mr. Hills, on his death-bed, sent for Mr. True, and told him he should be glad " to talk with him half a day; but his strength was not equal to it." He did not experience the composure which he had supposed his doctrines would inspire. He complained of the darkness and clouds that hung around the valley of death. The asperity of feeling between different individuals has subsided. Several who left the church at the time of the union returned to it. Of the members now composing it, none are more cordial and kind to each other than the few who belonged to the two before they were united.

CHAPTER XXII.

ECCLESIASTICAL HISTORY, 1825—1850.

Preachers after the Union. — Freeman Parker. — George W. Fargo. — Ordination and Dismission of Oren Sikes. — Meeting-house. — Ordination and Dismission of Uriah Balkam. — Samuel Bowker's Ordination.

THOUGH the First and Second Congregational Churches and Societies were united, they were not able to support preaching constantly. Several persons officiated a few sabbaths, and some for a few months. Rev. Freeman Parker, of Dresden, preached two summers. After the lapse of ten years, the church, Nov. 13, 1830, gave an invitation to George W. Fargo to become the pastor, with a salary to be raised by taxation on property. Arrangements were made for an ordination; but he was not settled. May 11, 1831, Mr. Oren Sikes[1] was " called," with a salary of four hundred dollars a year.

[1] Mr. Sikes, son of Jonathan and Cyrena (Hoar) Sikes, was born at Ludlow, Mass., Aug. 26, 1805, and graduated at the Bangor Theological Seminary in 1830. He was installed at Mercer, Jan. 30, 1833, and dismissed May 2, 1846. He is now settled at Bedford, Mass., where he was installed June 3, 1846. His wife, Julia Knox, daughter of Hon. Ebenezer Thatcher, and granddaughter of Gen. Henry Knox, was born at Thomaston, Dec. 1805. Children, all born in Mercer : — 1. Oren Cornelius, Oct. 12, 1834; 2. Julia Cyrena, June 24, 1836; 3. Catharine Putnam, Dec. 14, 1838; 4. Henry Knox, May 8, 1841; 5. Caroline Holmes, Nov. 19, 1843, who died in Bedford, Sept. 9, 1846.

May 29, arrangements were made for the ordination. Invitations to form the council were sent to the Orthodox Congregational Churches and their ministers in Waldoborough, Newcastle, Warren, Thomaston, Camden, Belfast, Prospect, and Albion, and to the Rev. E. Gillett, D.D. and Rev. Amasa Smith. " Voted Rev. Henry True be invited to sit in the council." June 7, the "ecclesiastical council convened, organized, and examined Mr. Oren Sikes, the candidate, at Mr. John Little's; and, on Wednesday the eighth day of June, 1831, the public services of the ordination were performed in the Old Meeting-house." Sept. 29, 1832, Mr. Sikes "requested the connection between him and the church to be dissolved." A council was convened, Oct. 18, 1832, in which were represented the churches in Waldoborough, Camden, and Bristol; and his request was confirmed. No other clergyman was ordained till after the erection of the meeting-house.

The meeting-house, containing fifty-two pews, was built between the Common and Seven Brook, on the north side of the road, in 1839. It cost about three thousand three hundred or three thousand four hundred dollars. At its dedication, Jan. 22, 1840, two hymns, composed for the occasion by Mr. Hannibal Hamlin, then a trader in town, were sung by the choir, under the direction of Dr. Dakin, of Hope. On the first Lord's Day after the dedication, the Rev. Horatio Ilsley, from Portland, commenced preaching in it, and continued six months. Mr. Uriah Balkam, a graduate of the Bangor Theological Seminary, began on the last Sunday in October, 1840. Ere long, an agreement was made with him to preach one year for five hundred dollars; there being an understanding, that if, at the expiration of that time, it should be agreeable to both parties, he should be ordained. In April, 1841, when but about one half of the year was gone, he was asked to be settled. He was ordained June 15, 1841, on a salary of five hundred dollars, after an examination by a council consisting of pastors and delegates from the Hammond-street Church in Bangor, the First

Church in Prospect, the Congregational Churches in Belfast, Waldoborough, Washington, Camden, Warren, and the two in Thomaston. The introductory prayer and reading of the Scriptures were by J. G. Merrill, of Washington; prayer by Mr. Woodhull, of Thomaston; sermon by Prof. Shepard, of Bangor; ordaining prayer by S. McKeen, of Belfast; charge by N. Chapman, of Camden; right hand of fellowship by E. F. Cutter, of Warren; address by Mr. Thurston, of Prospect; concluding prayer by S. C. Fessenden, of East Thomaston; and benediction by the pastor. Mr. Balkam[1] continued, to the entire satisfaction of the parish, till he preached his last sermon, Sept. 20, 1844, when, to their great regret, he was obliged to leave them for want of adequate support.

Dec. 7, 1844, Rev. Samuel Bowker,[2] the present pastor, began to preach, under an engagement for six months. Oct. 21, 1845, the church voted to give Mr. Bowker a call to become their minister; and it was concurred in by the parish, Nov. 6. His letters of acceptance to the church and to the parish are dated Nov. 13, 1845. The ordination took place, Dec. 10, 1845. Churches in Waldoborough, Warren, Washington, Camden, Searsport, and the two churches in Thomaston, were represented. The services were, invocation and reading of the Scriptures by R. Woodhull; introductory prayer by J. G. Merrill; sermon by S. Thurston; consecrating prayer by N. Chapman; charge to the pastor by E. F. Cutter; right hand of

---

[1] Rev. Uriah Balkam, son of John and Abigail Balkam, was born at Robbinston, Washington County, Maine, March 27, 1812, and graduated at Amherst College, in 1837. He was installed, Jan. 21, 1845, over the First Parish, or Congregational Society, in Wiscasset. Aug. 23, 1841, he married Martha M., daughter of John M. and Eleanor Prince, of Guilford, in Piscataquis County. She was born at Portland, Maine, June 25, 1819, and died June, 1849.

[2] Samuel Bowker, son of Lazarus and Agnes (Lennan) Bowker, born at Phipsburg, Maine, Sept. 20, 1812, was a member of Bowdoin College one year, and graduated at the Bangor Theological Seminary in 1843. He married, March 21, 1848, Elizabeth, daughter of Joseph and Frances (Tyler) Eaton, born at Harpswell, June 3, 1821, and has one son, Charles Irwin.

fellowship by J. Dodge; address to the church and people by S. C. Fessenden; concluding prayer by R. Woodhull; benediction by the pastor.

CHAPTER XXIII.

ECCLESIASTICAL HISTORY.—METHODISTS AND BAPTISTS.

Methodist Church and Society.— First Methodist Preaching.— Circuits and Districts. — Organization. — Places of Worship. — Meetinghouse. — Camp Meetings. — Parsonage. — Preachers. — Baptist Church and Society. — Central Baptist Church.

METHODIST SOCIETY.

SOME incidents in the history of the Methodist Church and Society have been noticed in connection with the ecclesiastical proceedings of the town. The records of the society are incomplete and obscure; and from them but little can be gleaned. The first[1] sermon in town, by a Methodist, was preached by Jesse Lee. It was probably in 1793, during his first journey into Maine. It was delivered in the barn of Rufus Gillmor, a short distance north of the Lower Bridge. At this time, the whole of Massachusetts, New Hampshire, and Maine constituted one district, called "Boston District," of which Mr. Lee was presiding elder. "In 1796 it was found expedient to form a circuit, near the mouth of the Kennebec, called Bath Circuit, . . . extending as far east as Union. . . . At this time, the members in the several societies in Maine amounted to three hundred and fifty-seven, having among them six preachers regularly travelling. . . . . At the annual conference in 1797, it was found expedient to divide Boston District, and to constitute the several circuits in Maine into one dis-

[1] Mr. John Butler.

trict."[1] "February, 1804, Union Circuit, or a part of it at least, formerly belonged to what was called Bath and Union Circuit. But, at the annual conference held at Boston [in 1803], it was agreed, as the work of reformation had been great in different parts of the circuit, and the prospect was enlarged, it should be divided into two, of which Union Circuit is one, and Bristol the other."[2] In 1806, Maine was divided into the Portland and Kennebec Districts. In 1816, Union and Hampden were united; but were divided again in 1819. In July, 1828, Union became a station, retaining still a class in Liberty, and another partly in Hope and partly in Appleton.

ORGANIZATION AND PLACES OF WORSHIP. — The Methodist Society in Union was organized by Aaron Humphrey, in the house of Jason Ware, in 1797. The first preaching in the Old Meeting-house was by a Methodist. Methodist meetings for a considerable time were held there on the Lord's Days. Money was raised in town-meeting to support the preaching. When a strong movement was made to settle a Congregational minister, the Methodists withdrew, and held meetings at the dwelling-houses of Jason Ware and Matthias Hawes, till the Round Pond Schoolhouse was built; after which they assembled there.

THE MEETING-HOUSE was built by subscription about 1810. At first the seats were loose. The sexes sat on different sides of the broad aisle. Wall-pews[3] were built, probably in 1811; the seats being still continued in the part designed for the body-pews. Subsequently, pews were substituted for the seats; and, at a later period, pews were built in the gallery. March 18,

[1] Greenleaf's Sketches, p. 281.   [2] Methodist Church Records.
[3] The following note shows how one pew at least was to be paid for: "I, the subscriber, do promise to pay Matthias Hawes, Jason Ware, Cornelius Irish, and Nathan D. Rice, trustees for building a Methodist Meeting-house in Union, twenty-three dollars; it being for pew No. 27, in the proposed house, and which is to be paid as follows, viz.: Three quarters of said sum to be paid in corn, grain, neat-stock, merchantable lumber, materials for building said house, or any pay that will suit a carpenter which may be employed in building said house, on demand; and one quarter in cash in four months from this date. — Witness my hand, this 8th day of March, 1809. Edwd. Jones."

1830, the society was incorporated by the name of " The First Methodist Episcopal Society in Union."

CAMP-MEETINGS. — The first camp-meeting began June 29, 1826. It was on the hill in the woods, west by south of Round Pond. The only other camp-meeting was held June 28, 1827, west of the Methodist Meeting-house, on the knoll where now stands the house of Moses Luce.

PARSONAGE. — Aug. 30, 1834, a committee was chosen to raise subscriptions for a parsonage, for making a contract, &c. A building was erected a few rods west of the meeting-house. It is leased to the preacher for the time being.

PREACHERS. — There never has been any ordained local preacher in Union, except the Rev. Cornelius Irish.

The following list of all the ministers who have been stationed at Union, from the time of the organization of the church, has been furnished by Mr. Madison Hawes, now of California: —

1798. Robert Yellalee, Aaron Humphrey.
1799. John Finnegan, Comfort C. Smith.
1800. Timothy Merritt, Reuben Hubbard.
1801. Timothy Merritt, Comfort C. Smith.
1802. Joseph Baker, Daniel Ricker.
1803. Daniel Ricker. — 1804. David Stimson.
1805. Samuel Hillman, Pliny Brett.
1806. Samuel Hillman, Jonas Weston.
1807. Samuel Baker. — 1808. John Williamson.
1809. John Williamson, Benjamin Jones.
1810. David Stimson, George Gary.
1811. Nathan B. Ashcraft. — 1812. Amasa Taylor.
1813. John Jewett. — 1814. Jona. Cheney, Joseph B. White.
1815. Benjamin Jones.
1816. Benjamin Jones, Daniel Wentworth.
1817. William McGray, Jeremiah Marsh.
1818-19. Henry True. — 1820. John Briggs.
1821. John Lewis.
1822. John Lewis, Nathaniel Devereux.
1823-24. Sullivan Bray. — 1825-26. David Stimson.
1827. Ezra Kellogg, John Lewis.
1828. Ezra Kellogg. — 1829. Gorham Greeley.

1830. Ezra Kellogg. — 1831. Cyrus Warren.
1832. Peter Burgess. — 1833. Benjamin Jones.
1834. Charles L. Browning. — 1835. Joshua Higgins.
1836–37. Daniel Cox. — 1838–39. Moses P. Webster.
1840–41. Rushworth J. Ayer.
1842–43. Paschal P. Morrill.
1844–45. Mark R. Hopkins. — 1846. James Thwing.
1847. H. K. W. Perkins. — 1848–49. Benjamin Bryant.
1850. M. Mitchell.

BAPTIST SOCIETIES.

The early Baptists, as well as the Methodists, have already been alluded to. But little remains to be added, except what is contained in the few items which follow. In 1801, a church was organized by Elders Snow, Hall, and Fuller. It was called the Second Baptist Church in Hope. The members lived in that town and in the east part of Union. Their meeting-house, which was very small, was in Hope. They had no pastor, but were occasionally supplied with preaching by the neighboring ministers. In this condition they continued till the year 1808, when " a revival of religion took place in this town and the towns adjoining; and the church was revived, and a number joined, under the administration of Elder Andrew Fuller."[1] Daniel Pearson preached in 1809. " In July, 1809, the brethren in the town of Union and the Second Church in Hope met, and agreed to unite together, and alter the name, and call it Union Church. At this time, Elder James Steward was with us once a month, until 1813. . . . We had no regular preaching until 1815, when Elder S. A. Flagg preached once a month for upwards of a year." In January, 1816, a new interest was awakened. " Elder Lemuel Rich came amongst us, and preached the word with good success, so that about forty-seven were added to the church this year, which more than doubled our number. . . . In 1818, our church was well united; and, our places of worship [being] insufficient to commode the people,

---

[1] The extracts are from manuscript-notices by one of the church.

it was thought best to build a meeting-house. This was accomplished in 1819."[1] It was erected near Lermond's Mills. In 1820, the church numbered eighty-five members. Serious difficulties soon followed, and these continued for a long time. In August, 1821, Elder Rich left the society; having preached "almost five years, one quarter of the time." In 1821, Elder Abiathar Richardson and others preached. In 1822, Elder Rich returned. In "1824, the church had some of the most singular trials with some of our most esteemed members, which racked the church from centre to circumference.[2] ... In 1826, the connection between the church and Elder Rich, as pastor, was dissolved; [he] having preached about four years longer, one quarter of the time." In 1826, the church consisted of fifty-three members; sixteen of them belonging to Hope, and a few to other towns. "In a few months, obtained Elder A. Richardson to labor with us one fourth of the time. About five years, the church, generally, travelled comfortably along the most of the time. March 3, 1830, set apart Brother Simon Fuller, by ordination, to the work of an evangelist." In the winter of 1833, the church was so small and the members so scattered, that there were no meetings. In the spring, Elder S. Fuller moved into town, and began to preach. The attendance was small; "but a general union prevailed amongst them, and quite happy seasons were enjoyed.... A sabbath-school was set up, and continued two summers; but there was so little interest felt upon the subject, and so much opposition and bigotry, that it could not be sustained.... April,

[1] Probably an error for 1818.
[2] In the Congregational and Methodist Churches, as well as the Baptist, there were several cases of church-discipline. On inquiring into them, it was found that a transcript of the records would give accounts so brief that it would be unjust to the persons arraigned to publish them, without going into details impossible, in many of the cases, to be obtained. In the Congregational Church there was one excommunication for Universalism. In some cases, the parties arraigned, if their own statements had been recorded, would be considered by many persons as "more sinned against than sinning;" though there were other cases where, if ever, church-discipline was justifiable.

1837, a Quarterly Meeting of the easterly part of the Lincoln Association was held with the church, and protracted a few days, which proved a blessing." Elder Samuel Baker was here this year. " In May, 1838, Elder Rich again administered to the church two years, a quarter of the time." September, 1840, Elder Nathaniel Copeland commenced preaching half the time for one year. About December, 1842, " Elder Amariah Kelloch was here occasionally for a short time; then we had no other preaching till 1835, when Elder Rich began another term of service, preaching one fourth of the time for two years." After this there was " no regular preaching."

The Central Baptist Church was organized Feb. 28, 1844. For some time, meetings were held on alternate Sundays, in the hall of the tavern. Subsequently the worship has been in the town-house. There have been different preachers, and the meetings have generally been held once a fortnight.

CHAPTER XXIV.

ECCLESIASTICAL HISTORY. — UNIVERSALISTS.

First Universalist Preaching. — Organization. — Maine Association. — John Bovee Dods. — Constitution. — Preachers. — Meeting-house. — Bell.

FIRST PREACHING. — The first sermon by an Universalist was preached, probably, at a third service on the Lord's Day, about the year 1814 or 1815, at the house of George W. West, on the place since owned by Calvin Gleason, Esq., about two miles north-west of the Common. There are no records respecting the early movements of the denomination, and consequently no satisfactory account of them can be given. It was several years before a second sermon was delivered. About the year 1820, perhaps a little later, there was preaching occasionally.

ORGANIZATION. — April 11, 1825, the following statement was addressed —

"*To the Clerk of the First Congregational Society in the town of Union.*

"The following is a list of persons who have organized themselves into a religious society by themselves, and wish to withdraw themselves from said First Congregational Society : —

Nathaniel Bachelor	Elijah Gay
Herman Hawes	Nathan Hills
Samuel Stone	John Lermond
David Robbins, jun.	John Bachelder
Amariah Mero	Reuben Hills, jun.
Henry Fossett	Nathaniel Tobey
Henry Blunt	David Bullen
Ebenezer Cobb	Phillips C. Harding
John Drake	Joseph Gleason
Walter Adams	Nathan Bachelder
Elisha Harding	George Cummings
Jesse Drake	John Fogler
Abiel Gay	Ward Maxcy
Lewis Bachelder	Nathaniel Bachelder, jun.
Olney Titus	Charles Hichborn
Fisher Hart	David Cummings."
Richard Gay	

MAINE ASSOCIATION. — A letter, dated July 1, 1826, says: "On Wednesday and Thursday of the present week, we had the Universalists' Association for the State of Maine at our central meeting-house in Union; — seven ministers and as many delegates; a large concourse of people from different parts of the State; many ladies, who made a good appearance; excellent music; lectures more popular than any which have ever been delivered aforetime in this town. I did not see at meeting one Methodist or one Calvinist."

Another letter, dated June 21, 1829, says: "Yesterday, about 5 o'clock, P.M., all connection between J. B. Dods, *alias* J. D. Bovee, and the Universalist Society here, was dissolved by mutual consent. Bovee asked a dismission, and his society readily granted his request. We have had a remarkable excitement in Union and Thomaston for about ten or fifteen days,"[1] &c.

CONSTITUTION. — Sept. 9, 1840, the society was reorganized. Rev. Albion S. Dudley, Elisha Harding, and Nelson Cutler, were chosen a committee to draft a constitution; and Oct. 3, after some modifications, the following, drawn up by the chairman, was adopted: —

"Whereas it is the duty of every rational creature to pay his homage to the Supreme Creator and Governor of the universe; and whereas we are permitted in this land the unrestricted liberty of conscience and right of private judgment in matters of faith and duty, and are allowed to worship God in whatever manner it may seem good to ourselves,—we, the undersigned, believing in the existence of one living and true God, whose nature is love and whose perfections are infinite, and confiding in his gracious purpose, as revealed to us in the gospel of his Son and the Scriptures of truth, to bestow upon all his intelligent offspring a glorious and blessed immortality; and further believing that it is at once the duty and interest of all men to be careful to maintain good works, for these things are good and profitable unto men, — do hereby, for the better security of these objects, unite ourselves in an associate capacity, and agree to be governed by the following constitution:

"1. This society shall be called the First Universalist Society in Union.

"2. The officers of this society shall consist of a clerk; a prudential committee, who shall manage the affairs of the society; a treasurer, who shall collect all subscriptions and pay them out at the order of the prudential committee.

"3. This society shall hold their annual meeting on the third Monday in November, at such place as the standing committee may direct; at which meeting the officers of the

---

[1] There was great excitement during nearly the whole time of Mr. Dods's residence in Union. Very grave charges against him were published in the Bangor Register, March 23, 1820. These were reprinted, together with his reply, in the Thomaston Register, Jan. 9, 1827. Mr. Dods was subsequently at Taunton and at Provincetown, Mass. Afterward he was in various parts of the country, lecturing on animal magnetism.

society shall be elected, and such other business shall be transacted as shall appear for the good of said society.

"4. It shall be the duty of each member to contribute for the support of the ministry liberally as he can, without injury to himself and family.

"5. Any person may become a member of this society by signing the constitution.

"6. Any member may withdraw from this society by leaving a written notice of his intentions with the clerk of the society.

"7. No member shall be expelled from this society, except by a vote of two-thirds of its members, and not then unless the reasons of such expulsion are given in a public manner to the society.

"8. Ten members shall constitute a quorum for the transaction of business; but a less number may adjourn.

"9. This society is hereby declared independent of all other ecclesiastical associations, and will acknowledge no allegiance to any other power save the express will of a majority of its own members, in accordance with its own constitution and the laws of the land.

"10. This constitution may be altered or amended at any time, by a vote of the majority of the members present at any regular meeting, provided the amendment proposed is submitted in writing at a previous meeting and secured with its ministers.

"Obadiah Harris
Charles Miller
Christopher Young
Nathaniel Bachelor
Lyman Alden
Noah S. Rice
Cyrus G. Bachelder
Nelson Cutler
John P. Robbins
George Cummings
Fisher Hart
William Gleason
Stephen S. Hawes
Elisha Harding
Samuel Hills
John S. Bean
Milton Daniels

Asa Messer
Edward Alden
Jesse W. Payson
Gavinus Henderson
Rufus Gillmor
Lewis Bachelder
Ebenezer Cobb
Nathan Hills
John Payson
Wm. G. Hawes
Nathan Bachelder
James Rice
George W. Morse
Spencer Mero
Willard Robbins
A. S. Dudley."

PREACHERS. — Nov. 4, 1841, Rev. Mr. Dudley, who probably came here in the preceding spring, tendered his resignation; and it was resolved that "the connection, as pastor, between himself and the First Universalist Society, be amicably dissolved." He is now a physician and dentist in Boston. Mr. Whittier was the preacher in 1842. In 1843,[1] the preacher was F. W. Baxter.[2]

THE MEETING-HOUSE, containing sixty-two pews, and situated a little back of the first meeting-house built in town, was erected in 1839, and dedicated on Christmas Day.

THE BELL, weighing twelve hundred and thirty-nine pounds, was cast by Holbrook, of Boston; bought Oct. 22, 1839, and hung the day before Thanksgiving. It cost $322.14; and the wheel and yoke, $25. It was paid for by subscription, as follows: —

Nelson Cutler	$15	Spencer Walcott	$5
C. G. Bachelder	15	George Cummings	10
Jason Robbins	15	Leonard Barnard	5
Nathan Bachelder	15	Joshua Morse	10
John Payson	15	Samuel Hills	5
John Burns	10	James W. Brown	2
Ebenezer Cobb	10	William Libbey	3
Willard Robbins	10	William G. Hawes	5
Nathaniel Robbins, jun.	5	William Gleason	5
James Littlehale, jun.	6	Ebenezer Alden	15
Jesse Robbins, jun.	2	Augustus Alden	5
Rufus Gillmor	10	Nathaniel Bachelor	25
Nathaniel K. Burkett	2	Nathaniel Robbins	20

[1] Dec. 4, 1843, "voted that the Congregational Society in Union be allowed to have the use of the bell, when not occupied by the Universalist Society, provided they employ the same man to ring that is employed by said Universalist Society, and paying him for the same.

"N.B. The time of ringing to be arranged by the committees of the two societies, and notice given from the pulpit."

[2] During his ministry, the lamps in the Universalist Meeting-house were procured for $20.50, by subscriptions in sums of one dollar and of fifty cents each, with the addition of five dollars, given by the Female Sewing Circle, making the total amount raised $25.

Fisher Hart	$15	Jason Davis	$2
Levi Morse	10	Reuben Hagar	2
Lewis Bachelder	15	Philo Thurston	2
Spencer Mero	15	John P. Robbins	5
John Bachelder	15	Jesse Robbins, jun.	2
Elisha Harding	15	James Grinnell	2
James Rice	10	Charles Fogler	2
Thurston Whiting	2	Joseph Gleason	2
Jonathan Eastman	10	Reuben E. Lyon	5
P. C. Harding	10	Marlboro' Packard, jun.	5
John Lermond, jun.	5	Zuinglius Collins	5
Lyman Alden	5	D. F. Harding	5
John M. Thorndike	5	John W. Lindley	2
Stephen S. Hawes	5		

CHAPTER XXV.

DELUSIONS AND SUPERSTITIONS.

Signs and Omens. — Witchcraft. — Bewitched Horse.

SIGNS AND OMENS.

Not entirely unconnected with ecclesiastical history is that of popular delusions and superstitions. Many persons recollect the time when the breaking of a looking-glass was regarded as premonitory of a death in the family. If a cock crowed at the door, a stranger would come. "It was a bad sign" for a person to pick up a pin, if he found it with the point toward him. The acceptance of a knife, scissors, or other sharp instrument as a present, would certainly lead to a cutting of friendship between the receiver and the giver. A ringing in the left ear indicated slander from some one in that direction. Good news would follow a ringing in the right ear. If accidentally the new moon was first seen over the left shoulder, it was ominous of evil; but the reverse if it was over the right shoulder. When a corpse lay unburied over Sunday, there would certainly be another death in town before the end of the week. These and similar superstitions were considerably prevalent in the country at the beginning of this century; and there were some persons who, in their credulity or for mischief, took delight in inculcating them. Even now, kindred follies are perpetuated by the advocates of "clairvoyance" and "spiritual rappings."

WITCHCRAFT.

At the time of the persecutions in Salem in 1692, there were but few persons, either in Europe or America, who did not believe in witchcraft. Though the community in general is now too enlightened for such an absurdity, there may yet be a few individuals cherishing, amid many misgivings, the follies with which their minds were imbued in childhood. Some men and women have not forgotten the dreadful stories which the large school-girls, during the intermissions, mischievously repeated to the small children, till their eyes opened wide and cheeks turned pale. The superstition, however, never gained much credence among adults in this town; though there was one case which attracted considerable attention.

About the year 1813, a horse belonging to Henry Esensa was parted with to Samuel Daggett. Mrs. Esensa, who unfortunately had the reputation among a few ignorant people of being a witch, was dissatisfied with the trade. When the horse was taken away, she remarked that it had "always been a plague, and would never do the Daggetts any good." It was not not long before the horse was mysteriously untied in the stable. No vigilance could prevent it. John Tobey, an upright sea-captain, familiar with every kind of knot used on shipboard, warmed a new rope, "made a horse-knot, and put it round the horse's neck in proper style." He went to the barn, bored several holes through the planks, took half a dozen over-hand knots, and then carried the rope up to a brace and made it well fast, sailor-fashion, with two or three round-turns, and two or three half-hitches. After remaining a short time at the house, he started to go home; and, on stopping at the barn to see if all was right, he discovered that the horse and rope were gone. A light having been procured, the horse was found in a remote part of the barn, with the rope coiled securely around him. At another time, the horse was on the haymow, and the rope was stuck so far into the hay that it required two or three men to pull it out. At another time, the waxed ends, which were used about the seizings, were found lying uncut where the animal had been standing.

These circumstances could not be accounted for. The horse was tied, and the barn-doors nailed. Snow was sifted round so as to show tracks, if any person came. But the horse was nevertheless untied, and crawled out under the sill of the barn, leaving the marks of his shoes, where it was considered impossible for the animal to get through. If any person was present, the witches would not do any thing. Accordingly, after the horse was fastened, all the company would retire to the house, where Mr. Daggett would entertain them for an hour or so with the revolutionary and sailors' songs and stories. Then, going to the barn, they would find the horse untied. A great number of feats was performed. The community was excited. People thronged from all parts of the town. Even from Searsmont, persons came to see the bewitched horse. On some nights, fifty or one hundred and fifty, prompted by a variety of motives, were in attendance. Finally, to put an end to the witchcraft, the tips of the horse's ears were cut off, and to the bleeding ends was applied a red-hot shovel. This act drove off the witches. But Samuel Daggett told Captain Tobey that he broke the end of his awl in fixing the seizings to the rope to prevent it from ravelling, and left the point in the rope, and that afterward there was no more trouble. Shrewd people have latterly "guessed" that the Daggetts, and possibly one of Captain Tobey's sons, knew more about the matter than they ever had credit for.

CHAPTER XXVI.

POLITICAL HISTORY.

Voting. — Separation of Maine from Massachusetts. — Harmony and Diversity of Sentiment. — Embargo. — Petition to the President of the United States. — Reply. — Remonstrance. — Petition to the Legislature of Massachusetts. — Celebration, July 4, 1810. — Celebration in 1814. — Ode and Hymn.

VOTING.

THE votes of a town are not always an index of its political sentiments. Elections in Union, as well as as in other towns, have been affected by temperance,[1] sectarianism, private animosities, sectional

---

[1] The subject of temperance has at times excited much interest. The First Temperance Society, like all contemporary societies, did not exclude the use of wine. This was excluded in the Second Temperance Society, formed Nov. 24, 1835. At the town-meeting, April 5, 1830, it was voted to pass over an article "to see if the town will authorize the selectmen to grant licenses for mixing liquors." The subject was again brought forward Sept. 13, and it was distinctly "voted not to have licenses granted to sell mixed liquors." April 2, 1832, "voted that the selectmen be authorized to grant licenses to retailers to sell mixed liquors in their stores or shops." April 1, 1833, it was voted to drop the article on the subject. "Sept. 24, 1836, agreeable to notice, the selectmen, treasurer, and town-clerk met, and licensed Ebenezer Cobb, as an innholder, to sell strong liquors. Licensed Nelson Cutler as a retailer." April 17, 1843, it was voted to drop the article on licensing. Members of the Temperance Society commenced prosecutions. April, 1844, the town voted not to refund the amount of a fine imposed on Henry Fossett, jun., "at the last December term of the District Court, Middle District, on complaint of D. F. Harding." An unsuccessful application to the town was made in April, and again in May, 1846, "to see if the town will refund the fifty dollars fine-money paid by Nathan Hills, in consequence of retailing ardent spirits without license." April 5, 1847, the selectmen were instructed "to sue for penalties that may be due for selling spirituous liquors without license."

The first person ever licensed here was Philip Robbins. This was within one or two years after he came. Before temperance societies were popular, almost every man in the country drank ardent spirits. Rum was considered a necessary beverage. Washington, in detailing the distresses of his army, speaks of the want of rum much as he does of the want of provisions. Every workman thought it indispensable. Sling

feelings. Besides, in some instances, the records are not so explicit as they ought to be. Accordingly, the results, as recorded on the town-books, are sometimes to be taken with qualifications.

SEPARATION OF MAINE FROM MASSACHUSETTS.

One of the subjects early brought before the town was the separation of Maine from Massachusetts. May 7, 1792, at a town-meeting held in the barn of Moses Hawes, there were 27 votes to 2, in favor of a separation according to a resolve of the General Court, passed Feb. 13 in that year. Dec. 2, 1793, the town again voted in favor of a separation, and chose Samuel Hills, Edward Jones, and Moses Hawes, a committee " to write to Hon. Peleg Wadsworth, as chairman of a committee consisting of a number of gentlemen from various parts of the district, on the 18th of October last, holden at the court-house in Portland." April 6, 1795, it was voted, 21 to 12, " to have the three upper counties in the province of Maine set off for a separate State." May 10, 1797, there were 26 yeas and 12 nays for separation; April 6, 1807, yeas 53, nays 69; May 20, 1816, the yeas were 41, nays 61, and the number of legal voters 216. Sept. 2, 1816, yeas 56, nays 98; at which time Robert Foster, having 83 votes, was chosen a delegate to represent the town in a convention to be holden at Brunswick, Sept. 30; John Lermond having 62 votes, and Nathan Blake, 1. Aug. 26, 1819, there were for separation, 19; against it, 84. Sept. 20, 1819, Robert Foster was chosen delegate to the convention, to form

and flip, as well as rum, were common at stores and taverns. Spirit, in some form, as well as wine, was provided at balls and parties. Even funeral solemnities were sometimes disturbed by the rappings of toddy-sticks. There have been cases, though none are recollected in Union, in which the tumblers and the decanter stood on the coffin, and that, too, in worthy families. The present generation has no conception of the extent of drinking throughout the country at the close of the revolutionary war, and afterward. The practice of " treating," when friends meet, has died away; and the false notions of former days have of late been giving place to a sense of duty, of humanity, and of happiness.

a State Constitution. Dec. 6, 1819, of 53 votes, 49 were in favor of the constitution formed in convention at Portland, Oct. 29, 1819. Since that time, Maine has been an independent State.

HARMONY AND DIVERSITY OF SENTIMENT.

According to the records, the vote for Governor and Lieutenant-Governor, as recently as 1797, 1798, and 1799, was unanimous. After the extraordinary vote of 1800, in which the two candidates are voted for, both for Governor and Lieutenant-Governor, there was a change. In 1801, there was one dissentient vote; in 1802 and 1803, there were two. It is not improbable that great electioneering efforts were made in the following years, by persons who moved into town. The harmony which had existed was disturbed; and violent political feelings were shortly aroused.

EMBARGO.

After the embargo was laid, an article was introduced into the warrant for the town-meeting, Sept. 17, 1808, "to see if it be the mind of the town to petition the President to have the embargo taken off, or act or do any thing relative thereto." The vote passed in the affirmative. "Samuel Hills, Edmund Mallard, William Pope, Esquire [Nathaniel] Robbins, and Capt. [Peter] Adams, were chosen" the committee, and instructed to "withdraw and report as soon as possible." The town voted "to accept the . . . petition, with such alterations as the committee think proper to make with regard to punctuation and spelling only;" and that the committee should send it to the President. The document, however, is not to be found. President Jefferson replied in a printed circular dated Oct. 8, 1808, superscribed to "Nathaniel Robbins, Esq."

It is said that the government-party thought the other party took advantage of them, and had the petition brought forward and accepted when there were but few persons present. They made an application to the other party for a copy of the petition. It was unsuccessful. They then issued a remonstrance which was signed by all the party, and forwarded to the President. The other party, confident of their strength, brought forward the subject again; and the following extracts, penned by William White, are from the town-records: —

PETITION TO THE LEGISLATURE OF MASSACHUSETTS.

Feb. 6, 1809, upon an article "to see if the town will petition the Legislature of this State to use their influence in any constitutional method which they may devise, to effect a removal of the embargo-laws, or act or do any thing relative thereto. . . . Voted that a committee be chosen to draught a petition to the Legislature of this State. . . . Voted that Charles Pope, Ebenezer Alden, Samuel Hills, Calvin Chase, and Esquire Robbins, be this committee. . . . Voted that this meeting be adjourned to Monday next.

"Feb. 13, 1809, voted to petition the legislature of this State to intercede for us in a constitutional way to have repealed the embargo-laws. Voted to accept the following resolves: —

"To assemble at all times in an orderly and peaceable manner, consult upon the common good, and request of the Legislature, by way of addresses, petitions, or remonstrances, a redress of the wrongs we suffer, is a right guaranteed by the constitution of the United States and of this commonwealth; and at a time when our greatest and most essential rights are attacked, — the right to acquire, protect, and enjoy property, and even our liberties threatened with being wrested from us, — it not only becomes a right, but a duty of the first importance, to watch with a vigilant eye every encroachment, and, as a free and independent people, remonstrate against every innovation, in a firm, manly, and dignified manner.

"Resolved, as the sense of this town, that we view the several acts of Congress, laying an embargo and prohibiting all foreign commerce by sea and land, as arbitrary, oppressive, and unconstitutional.

"Resolved that the numerous restrictions and embarrassments laid upon our coasting-trade are calculated to reduce many thousands of our seafaring brethren, together with all those whose dependence is on commerce, to a state of abject penury and want.

"Resolved that the raising a standing army in a time of peace, and subjecting the civil power to the military control, is alarming to our apprehensions, and creates a trembling for the liberties of our country.

"Resolved that the power given to the collectors and their deputies places them entirely out of the reach of the law; affording them a strong temptation to oppress, and deprive the oppressed of the right of a trial by jury, with the almost certain consequence of being taxed with treble cost, without the collectors' being obliged to prove an intent to evade the law, or so much as a well-grounded suspicion; and the authority given them to array the naval and military force of the United States against the peaceable inhabitants in the prosecution of their lawful business, is a stretch of power never before witnessed in the annals of a free, independent people.

"Resolved that the patriotic though ineffectual struggle made by the minority in Congress to save the country from impending ruin, entitles them to our warmest gratitude.

"That a respectful address be transmitted to the Legislature of this State, stating our grievances, and praying that honorable body to use every constitutional measure which they in their wisdom shall deem expedient to put a speedy termination to our sufferings.

"Voted to accept the following petition: —

"*To the Honorable Senate and House of Representatives of the Commonwealth of Massachusetts.*

"We, the inhabitants of the town of Union, county of Lincoln, beg leave humbly to represent, that we have long endured the evils which press peculiarly hard on this portion of the Union, resulting from the strange system of policy pursued by the government of the United States; and, having petitioned the executive of that government without deriving the least consolation, but on the contrary the burthens having been unmercifully and unconstitutionally increased, we now turn our eyes and our hopes to the Legislature of this State. We look to you as our fathers, feeling an inward presentiment that when we ask bread you will not give us a stone, and when we ask a fish you will not give us a serpent. We are willing to eat our bread in the sweat of our faces; but we are not willing that our hard-earned morsel should be plucked from the mouth of labor by idle spies or greedy harpies.

"The spot we inhabit does not furnish the luxuries nor all the conveniences of life. Much of our living has been drawn from the proceeds of articles exported; and, if we are not suffered to barter our lumber for needful supplies, vast numbers will be reduced to a most forlorn and wretched condition.

"Many owe in part for lands, or are indebted for the necessaries of life, and no way is left to cancel the demands. A dreary prospect opens upon the eyes of the debtor. He knows not which way to turn himself. His former sources are dried up. Dejection is seated on his brow; we see no possible method of procuring a sufficiency of money even to pay our taxes. To demand them from us now would be like exacting brick without straw. We cannot compare the present with the past without a sigh; for we experimentally feel that our glory is departed. We turn back our eyes to the golden days of federal administration, and lament the folly that has reduced us to our present humiliating condition.

"The embargo-system appears void of all form and comeliness, the offspring of night and twin of chaos. The total occlusion of the port of Boston, effected by the aid and terror, of military force, is a wanton stretch of power, calculated not only to injure the capital, but to spread additional distress among the inhabitants of the district of Maine. The constitution of the United States plainly shows us, that the coasting trade within the State is not under the care of Congress even for regulation. This trade has been subject to regulations of Congress, only because no inconvenience resulted therefrom.

"But, as this Legislature must know our circumstances best, we pray you, gentlemen, to take this remaining branch of trade under your direction. We feel the honorable Legislature of this State will not philosophize on the word *regulate*, so as to make it mean *annihilate*.

"We pray you to take our case into serious consideration, and, as far as the constitution will authorize, do that for us which your wisdom and patriotism shall direct. We are willing to submit to any laws founded in good policy and directed to the good; but we esteem the constitution of the United States and the calls of nature paramount to any law of Congress. We pledge ourselves to support such measures as your wisdom shall direct for our relief. If we are by others considered the most worthless part of the community, and threatened with having our blood drawn from us, still we humbly trust that you will view us in a different light, and grant us a ray of hope to cheer our spirits.

"That the Guardian of empires may direct and protect you in this trying season is the prayer of your memorialists.

"Voted that the town-clerk[1] sign the petition to the General Court."

FOURTH-OF-JULY CELEBRATIONS IN 1810 & 1814.

There was probably no time when politics ran so high as in 1810. In that year, each party had its Fourth-of-July Celebration. In the night preceding the Fourth, a straight and graceful liberty-pole, about seventy feet high, erected by the democratic party, was cut down by a member of the other party, who, it has since been ascertained, was Samuel Bunting. The orations of Mr. Whiting, of Warren, and William White, Esq.,[2] were delivered in the meeting-house, the one in the forenoon and the other in the afternoon; and the occasions were known long afterward as "the morning and afternoon service." It was agreed that the old cannon "should speak" for both parties; who dined, the federalist at Rufus Gillmor's, and the democratic in a temporary booth in front of John Little's.

In the Boston Weekly Messenger, July 15, 1814, is the following account of the celebration in that year by the federal party: —

"The birthday of our nation was celebrated at Union with lively emotions of joy. The celebration was intended as

---

[1] This vote was probably passed because the town-clerk was a leading man in the opposite party.

[2] Mr. White's oration was printed. The following is the "DEDICATION: Neither through fear or affection, but of mere charity, — the author of these sheets bestows them upon that snarling, hungry horde of curs, called 'The Critics.'" On the preceding page, "the public are advertised not to read a single page of this pamphlet, unless they undertake it entirely at their own hazard; as the author has no concern in the thing, — being determined to receive no reward from such as may be gratified with the perusal, and to make no remuneration to those who may esteem their labor lost."

well in honor of the great events in Europe which have secured, as those which obtained, our independence. The Washington Benevolent Society in Union was joined by a great number of citizens of that town, Warren, Waldoborough, Thomaston, and the vicinity. The oration by George Kimball, Esq., would rank high among productions of this class. It exhibited an able and correct view of the origin and leading measures of the two great political parties which have divided our country, in a chaste style. Aiming principally at correctness and utility, it rose occasionally into brilliancy, and communicated an electric shock to the audience, which was evinced by loud and repeated testimonials of applause. Two hymns and an ode were prepared for the occasion. They do great honor to their author. The music has rarely been excelled on any similar occasion. A handsome and liberal dinner was provided under the direction of Captain Barrett and Major Gillmor. The escort duties were performed by the Union Light Infantry in a soldier-like manner. The honors of the table were, at the request of the company, conducted by the Washington Benevolent Society. Major Foster, their president, took the chair, assisted by Nathaniel Robbins, Esq., and the other officers of the society. Every part of the celebration evinced ' the feast of reason and the flow of soul.'

"ODE.—SUNG AT TABLE.

"Tune—'Adams and Liberty.'

" Our fathers, impelled by the zeal of reform,
   Sought a lodgment secure from the scourge of oppression ;
Ariel directed their bark through the storm
  To a land wild and drear from the hand of creation,
    Which destiny's page,
    From time's early age,
Had marked an asylum from ambition's rage;
Where altars to freedom in future should rise,
In majesty towering from earth to the skies.

Soon the labors of industry gladdened the hills,
   And the vales with the music of artists resounded ;
The commerce of Europe, restricted by ills,
  Cast a look on the empire ' the pilgrims ' had founded,
    Where liberty sate
    In majesty's state,
Securing to commerce a happier fate ;
At once she resolved again to be free,
And the snow of her robes whitened every sea.

Columbia the blest, with unparalleled stride,
  Ascended the steep of her national glory;
The blaze of her grandeur soon wounded the pride
  Of the mistress of ocean — the lion, in story;
      Her hero arose,
      All harm to oppose,
Maintained her rights in the face of her foes,
Till the angel of battles proclaimed the decree,
' Great Washington conquers — Columbia is free.'

Old Anarch, the author of man's greatest curse,
  Soon broke the sweet calm that her policy cherished;
Of spirits infernal the fostering nurse,
  The demon enlisted the imps he had nourished.
      From their caverns they poured,
      A poisonous horde,
More deadly than pestilence, famine, and sword;
But Justice eternal holds dominant sway,
And darkness is deepest at dawning of day.

The flames of the far-famed Moscow proclaimed,
  That yet to stern virtue remained probation;
And *the son of the Czars* has the trial sustained,
  And purchased redemption for every nation.
      Delusion must cease,
      Truth's empire increase,
Till the 'star of our peace' shall appear in the east;
Then altars to freedom again shall arise,
And their incense ascending envelop the skies.

Then virtue shall take her ascendance again,
  Political truth guide political reason;
No more shall that phantom, *philosophy*, reign,
  Adherence to principle ne'er be made treason;
      But philosophers keep
      Their '*eternal sleep,*'
And their vile host of demons be laid in the deep,
And ages successive their freedom defend,
Till darkness and day in eternity blend.

"HYMN. — SUNG IN THE MEETING-HOUSE.

"TUNE — '*Old Hundred.*'

" Creator God! the first, the last,
  The same in future as in past,
  Enthroned in majesty above,
  Eternal Source of life and love, —

When man, forgetful whence he came,
Contemns thy law, profanes thy name,
He's in thy hand, one awful breath
Blasts him in everlasting death.

> When nations lose respect to God,
> They make atonement with their blood;
> But when their sins no more abound,
> He breaks the sword and heals the wound.
>
> So Europe, while she fed her lust,
> Was with a tyrant's bondage curst;
> But when she looked in faith to God,
> He heard, and broke the scourging rod.
>
> Almighty God! thou art our trust,
> We kiss the rod, we feel it just;
> But spare us, that we may adore
> And praise and serve thee evermore."

The other hymn sung on the occasion was not printed.

CHAPTER XXVII.

POLITICAL HISTORY.

(Continued.)

Members of Congress.— Governors. — Lieutenant-Governors. — Town Representatives. — Justices of the Peace. — Coroners. — Post Offices and Postmasters.

MEMBERS OF CONGRESS.

A VOTE was passed Dec. 18, 1788, when the Federal Constitution was about to go into operation, not to ballot for a member to Congress, as the "General Court had not furnished the town with a resolve for it." Accordingly, the first voting for any officer, under the Constitution of the United States, was for a representative, Oct. 4, 1790, when William Lithgow had nine votes, and Daniel Cony two. There was no election. Jan. 25, 1791, " William Lithgow, jun., had every vote of the town present, which was thirteen." At a third trial, April 4, 1791, the record states, " The inhabitants met, and made choice of William Lithgow, jun.; twenty-four votes." At the meeting, Nov. 2, 1792, for choosing three representatives to Congress, Edward

Cutts for the county of York, Enoch Freeman for the county of Cumberland, and Waterman Thomas for the three lower counties, "had each twenty votes. Of the other candidates, Tristam Jordan for York had twenty-one, Peleg Wadsworth for Cumberland had nineteen, and Henry Dearborn for the three lower counties" had twenty. At a second trial, April 1, 1793, the delegate for Congress, Peleg Wadsworth, had thirty-five votes; Nov. 3, 1794, Henry Dearborn had nineteen, as representative for the Eastern District; Nov. 7, Isaac Parker, subsequently Chief Justice of the Supreme Court of Massachusetts, had sixteen votes, Feb. 6, 1797, twenty-nine votes, and May 10, thirty-seven votes; and, May 10, Henry Dearborn had one vote. Nov. 5, 1798, Silas Lee had thirty-two, and Nathaniel Dummer five votes. Nov. 3, 1800, Silas Lee had thirty-nine votes. Mr. Lee resigned; and, Sept. 20, 1801, Nathaniel Dummer had thirty votes.

After this time, the votes, according to the records, are as follows: —

1801, Dec. 7. Orchard Cook, 31.
1802, April 1. Orchard Cook, 64.
1802, June 7. Samuel Thatcher, 49.
1802, July 9. Samuel Thatcher, 36; Martin Kinsley, 2; Jonathan Sibley, 2.
1802, Nov. 1. Samuel Thatcher, 31.
1804, Nov. 5. Samuel Thatcher, 22; Orchard Cook, 45.
1806, Nov. 3. Orchard Cook, 50; Mark L. Hill, 26.
1808, Nov. 7. Orchard Cook, 66; Alden Bradford, 67.
1810, Nov. 5. Alden Bradford, 40; Peleg Tolman, 57.
1812, Nov. 2. Abiel Wood, 140; Erastus Foot, 2; Daniel Rose, 2.
1814, Nov. 7. Thomas Rice, 50; James Parker, 23.
1816, Nov. 4. Thomas Rice, 43; James Parker, 25.
1817, Jan. 9. Thomas Rice, 27; James Parker, 23.
1817, May 1. Peter Grant, 37; James Parker, 27.
1817, Sept. 29. Peter Grant, 23; Joshua Gage, 4.
1818, Nov. 2. Peter Grant;[1] Joshua Gage.[1]
1819, April 5. Thomas Bond, 56; James Parker, 24.

---
[1] Number of votes not recorded.

MEMBERS OF CONGRESS. 241

1820, Nov. 6. James Parker, 30; Ebenezer Herrick, 16.
1821, Jan. 8. Joshua Gage, 25; Ebenezer Herrick, 12; Peter Grant, 1.
1821, May 7. Ebenezer Herrick, 3.; Joshua Gage, 26; James Parker, 3.
1822, Nov. 4. (No record.)
1823, April 7. Jeremiah Bailey, 113; Mark L. Hill, 3; Daniel Rose, 11; Ebenezer Herrick, 1; Ebenezer Thatcher, 1; Edwin Smith, 1; Isaac Barnard, 1.
1823, June 30. Jeremiah Bailey, 48; Mark L. Hill, 8; Ebenezer Herrick, 4; Samuel Thatcher, 7; Oliver Pratt, 1; M. Hill, 1.
1823, Sept. 8. Ebenezer Herrick, 60; Mark L. Hill, 9.
1824, Sept.13. Ebenezer Thatcher, 52; Ebenezer Herrick, 8; Ebenezer Cobb, 1.
1825, Jan. 3. Ebenezer Thatcher, 47; Albert Smith, 2.
1825, April 4. Ebenezer Thatcher, 88; Ebenezer Herrick, 20; Albert Smith, 3; Henry True, 1.
1825, Sept.12. Ebenezer Herrick, 35; Daniel Rose, 25; Albert Smith, 2.
1826, Sept.11. Joseph F. Wingate, 43; Daniel Rose, 34.
1828, Sept. 8. Joseph F. Wingate, 73.
1830, Sept.13. Edward Kavanagh, 104; Moses Shaw, 93.
1830, Nov.22. Moses Shaw, 52; Edward Kavanagh, 54.
1833, ... Jeremiah Bailey, 128; Edward Kavanagh, 129; John McKown, 11.
1834, Sept. 8. Edward Kavanagh, 152; Jeremiah Bailey, 147; John McKown, 10.
1836, Sept.12. Jeremiah Bailey, 139; Jonathan Cilley, 112; Edwin Smith, 3; George Fish, 1.
1836, Nov. 7. Jeremiah Bailey, 101; Jonathan Cilley, 99.
1837, April 3. Jeremiah Bailey, 136; Jonathan Cilley, 92.
1838, April 2. Edward Robinson, 163; John D. McCrate, 137; William F. Farley, 18.
1838, Sept.10. Benj. Randall, 196; John D. McCrate, 160.
1840, Sept.14. Benjamin Randall, 210; Joseph Sewall, 146.
1843, Sept.11. Freeman H. Morse, 139; Charles Andrews, 127; Charles C. Cone, 12.
1843, Nov.13. Freeman H. Morse, 128; Charles Andrews, 116; Charles C. Cone, 7.
1844, Sept. 9. Freeman H. Morse, 198; John D. McCrate, 182; Charles C. Cone, 13.

1844, Nov. 11. Freeman H. Morse, 183; John D. McCrate, 171; Charles C. Cone, 14.
1846, ... John D. McCrate, 179; Freeman H. Morse, 171; Zury Robinson, 16.
1847, ... Freeman H. Morse, 135; Franklin Clark, 137; Charles C. Cone, 13.
1848, ... John D. McCrate, 161; Rufus K. Goodenow, 172; William H. Vinton, 14.
1849, ... Isaac Reed, 182; Charles Andrews, 172.

GOVERNOR AND LIEUTENANT-GOVERNOR.

There is no record of votes for Governor or Lieutenant-Governor before April 2, 1787. The warrant for the town-meeting on that day contains an article " to see whom the town will choose for Governor, Lieutenant-Governor, and senator for the year ensuing." The record of the meeting would convey the idea that the result depended entirely upon the inhabitants of Union; for it states, " By written ballot, made choice of John Hancock for Governor, and Major-General William Heath for Lieutenant-Governor." April 3, 1788, " Governor, His Excellency John Hancock; Lieutenant-Governor, Major-General Lincoln four, and eight for Hon. William Heath." In April, 1789, the statement is more explicit: " Chose the Hon. John Hancock, Esq., Governor by thirteen votes; and the Hon. Benjamin Lincoln, Esq., Lieutenant-Governor by thirteen votes." April 5, 1790, " John Hancock had all the votes for Governor, which were seven; and, for Lieutenant-Governor, William Heath had seven, and Benjamin Lincoln three." From this time, the votes, during the connection of Maine with Massachusetts, are as follows: —

GOVERNOR.		LIEUTENANT-GOVERNOR.	
1791.			
John Hancock . . .	22	Samuel Adams . . .	21
1792.			
John Hancock . . .	23	William Heath . .	27
Charles Jarvis . . .	2		
1793.			
John Hancock . . .	17	William Heath . .	21

GOVERNORS AND LIEUTENANT-GOVERNORS. 243

GOVERNOR.		LIEUTENANT-GOVERNOR.	
\multicolumn{4}{c}{1794.}			
Samuel Adams	20	William Heath	10
		Moses Gill	10
\multicolumn{4}{c}{1795.}			
Samuel Adams	22	Moses Gill	23
William Heath	6		
Elbridge Gerry	1		
\multicolumn{4}{c}{1796.}			
Samuel Adams	18	Moses Gill	20
Moses Gill	3	William Heath	1
\multicolumn{4}{c}{1797.}			
Increase Sumner	28	Moses Gill	21
\multicolumn{4}{c}{1798.}			
Increase Sumner	30	Moses Gill	30
\multicolumn{4}{c}{1799.}			
Increase Sumner	40	Moses Gill	37
\multicolumn{4}{c}{1800.}			
Caleb Strong	28	Moses Gill	28
Moses Gill	18	Caleb Strong	9
\multicolumn{4}{c}{1801.}			
Caleb Strong	54	Edward H. Robbins	57
Elbridge Gerry	1		
\multicolumn{4}{c}{1802.}			
Caleb Strong	64	Edward H. Robbins	60
Elbridge Gerry	2	William Heath	1
\multicolumn{4}{c}{1803.}			
Caleb Strong	45	Edward H. Robbins	43
Elbridge Gerry	2		
\multicolumn{4}{c}{1804.}			
Caleb Strong	50	Edward H. Robbins	51
James Sullivan	23	William Heath	8
\multicolumn{4}{c}{1805.}			
Caleb Strong	42	Edward H. Robbins	41
James Sullivan	52	William Heath	60
William Heath	1		
\multicolumn{4}{c}{1806.}			
Caleb Strong	51	Edward H. Robbins	49
James Sullivan	78	William Heath	83

POLITICAL HISTORY.

GOVERNOR.		LIEUTENANT-GOVERNOR.	
1807.			
Caleb Strong	62	Edward H. Robbins	51
James Sullivan	102	Levi Lincoln	102
		Jonathan Sibley	1
		James Sullivan	1
1808.			
Christopher Gore	57	David Cobb	56
James Sullivan	88	Levi Lincoln	88
Caleb Strong	2		
David Cobb	1		
1809.			
Christopher Gore	88	David Cobb	84
Levi Lincoln	93	Joseph B. Varnum	93
Joseph B. Varnum	2		
1810.			
Christopher Gore	84	David Cobb	81
Elbridge Gerry	91	William Gray	88
1811.			
Christopher Gore	58	William Phillips	57
Elbridge Gerry	80	William Gray	75
William Phillips	1	Joseph B. Varnum	1
		George Wellington	1
		John Lermond	1
1812.			
Caleb Strong	75	William King	92
Elbridge Gerry	95	William Phillips	69
William Phillips	1	Samuel Dana	1
		Jonathan Sibley	1
1813.			
Caleb Strong	94	William Phillips	92
Joseph B. Varnum	101	William King	98
		Caleb Strong	2
		William Eustis	1
		Joseph Varnum	1
		Nathaniel Robbins	1
1814.			
Caleb Strong	97	William Phillips	96
Samuel Dexter	103	William Gray	104
William Phillips	1		

GOVERNORS AND LIEUTENANT-GOVERNORS.

GOVERNOR.		LIEUTENANT-GOVERNOR.	
\multicolumn{4}{c}{1815.}			
Caleb Strong	98	William Phillips	99
Samuel Dexter	92	William Gray	90
		Samuel Dexter	1
		Nathaniel Robbins	1
		Mark L. Hill	1
		Martin Kinsley	1
		James Campbell	1
\multicolumn{4}{c}{1816.}			
John Brooks	88	William Phillips	88
Samuel Dexter	74	William King	72
\multicolumn{4}{c}{1817.}			
John Brooks	89	William Phillips	89
Henry Dearborn	66	William King	72
\multicolumn{4}{c}{1818.}			
John Brooks	58	William Phillips	58
Benj. W. Crowninshield	51	Thomas Kittredge	51
Thomas Kittredge	1		
\multicolumn{4}{c}{1819.}			
John Brooks	71	William Phillips	71
Benj. Crowninshield	33	Benjamin Austin	33

Of the preceding candidates for Governor, Hancock, Adams, Sumner, Strong, Gore, Brooks, belonged to the federal party; and each of them has been in the chair. Of the anti-federal or democratic party were Bowdoin, Gerry, Sullivan, Heath, Lincoln, Varnum, Dexter, Dearborn, Crowninshield; of whom the first three have been Governors.

The gubernatorial election in the spring of 1819 was the last in which Maine voted with Massachusetts. After the separation, there was no office of Lieutenant-Governor. The first election of State officers by Maine was April 3, 1820, when William King had fifty-seven votes for Governor, Stephen Longfellow twenty-nine, and Jeremiah Bailey one. The election since that time has been held in September, and the votes for Governor are recorded as follows: —

1821.
Ezekiel Whitman . . 68
Joshua Wingate, jun. 18
Albion K. Parris . . 3
William King . . . 1
1822.
Ezekiel Whitman . . 47
Albion K. Parris . . 41
Samuel Fessenden . 6
1823.
Albion K. Parris . . 37
Benjamin Whitman . 1
Joseph H. Becket . . 1
1824.
Albion K. Parris . . 57
1825.
Albion K. Parris . . 48
Avery Rawson . . . 1
1826.
Enoch Lincoln . . . 51
Noah Rice 2
1827.
Enoch Lincoln . . . 62
1828.
Enoch Lincoln . . . 72
1829.
Jonathan G. Huntoon 110
Samuel E. Smith . . 64
Daniel F. Harding . 1
James Rice 1
1830.
Jonathan G. Huntoon 145
Samuel E. Smith . . 114
1831.
Samuel E. Smith . . 130
Daniel Goodenow . . 111
1832.
Daniel Goodenow . . 154
Samuel E. Smith . . 147
1833.
Daniel Goodenow . . 127

Robert P. Dunlap . . 105
Samuel E. Smith . . 23
Thomas A. Hill . . 11
1834.
Robert P. Dunlap . . 152
Peleg Sprague . . . 156
Thomas A. Hill . . 10
Noah Rice, jun. . . 1
1835.
William King . . . 115
Robert P. Dunlap . . 112
Noah S. Rice . . . 9
Thomas A. Hill . . 2
Jonathan Sibley . . 1
Jack Downing . . . 1
1836.
Edward Kent . . . 139
Robert P. Dunlap . . 115
Jonathan Sibley . . 1
1837.
Edward Kent . . . 181
Gorham Parks . . . 117
1838.
Edward Kent . . . 196
John Fairfield . . . 160
1839.
Edward Kent . . . 179
John Fairfield . . . 123
1840.
Edward Kent . . . 210
John Fairfield . . . 146
1841.
Edward Kent . . . 174
John Fairfield . . . 168
Ezekiel Whitman . . 11
Jeremiah Curtis . . 3
1842.
Edward Robinson . . 175
John Fairfield . . . 155
James Appleton . . 4
Asa Redington . . . 1

REPRESENTATIVES.

1843.	
Edward Robinson	134
Hugh J. Anderson	116
Edward Kavanagh	18
James Appleton	12

1844.	
Edward Robinson	198
Hugh J. Anderson	183
James Appleton	13

1845.	
Hugh J. Anderson	153
Freeman H. Morse	150

1846.	
David Bronson	179
John W. Dana	180
Samuel Fessenden	16

1847.	
David Bronson	134
John W. Dana	137
Samuel Fessenden	14

1848.	
John W. Dana	161
Elijah L. Hamlin	172
Samuel Fessenden	14

1849.	
Elijah L. Hamlin	182
John Hubbard	161
George Talbot	10

1850.	
William G. Crosby	176
John Hubbard	173
George L. Talbot[1]	7

Of the Governors since the separation from Massachusetts, all, except Huntoon and Kent, have belonged to the democratic party.

TOWN REPRESENTATIVES.[2]

In 1807, " Edward Jones, by a majority of the voters present, he having seventy-five votes," was chosen the first representative from Union to the General Court of Massachusetts. In 1811, John Lermond was elected by seventy-eight out of one hundred and forty-five votes. The town was liable to a fine, if it voted not to send any; and the mode of evasion was by voting to " drop the article." Generally, in each party, there was a majority in favor of this. In 1812, John Lermond, of the democratic party, being chairman of the selectmen, presided at the meeting. The vote to pass over the article was adopted as usual. Spencer Walcott, of the democratic party, then went up to the

---

[1] Free-soil.

[2] In 1825, Nathaniel Robbins had twenty votes for State Senator. In 1849, Elbridge Lermond had one hundred and thirty-five votes; and in 1850, one hundred and sixty-nine votes; and in 1851, he was chosen senator by the Legislature. Dr. Harding was senator while he resided in Union.

moderator, and observed, " You have warned me here to vote for representative. Here is my vote, reject it if you dare." The meeting, or at least the federal party, was taken by surprise. His vote could not be rejected. After some discussion and an adjournment for an hour or two, during which runners were despatched to bring in voters, the ballots were called for. The poll was about being closed, when Warren Ware, sick and feeble, was passing by on a bed in a cart. He was solicited to vote; and, being supported on each side, he was walked up to the box, and put into it a federal vote. At the counting, it was found that his vote had elected the federal candidate; Nathaniel Robbins having seventy-seven votes, and John Lermond seventy-six.

In 1819, Nathaniel Bachelor had thirty-nine votes, and was chosen; Robert Foster having twenty, and Nathaniel Robbins seven. No other representatives were sent from Union to the Legislature of Massachusetts, during its connection with Maine.

In 1820, after Maine became a State, Nathaniel Bachelor had seventy-four votes, and was elected; John W. Lindley had fifty-five votes, Robert Foster one, and Micajah Gleason one. The State was districted March 23, 1821, and Union was united with Washington;[1] each of the towns furnishing the representative, according to its proportion of the population. From this date the following is the record; the representatives not taking their seats till the year after their election: —

1821, Sept. 10. Nathaniel Bachelor, 48; † John W. Lindley, 29; Robert Foster, 17.
1821, Oct. 1. Nathaniel Bachelor, 61; † John W. Lindley, 12; Robert Foster, 1.

[1] Union and Washington have not always made one district. Washington has elected a representative in some of the years when one was sent from Union. In 1831, it elected William Rust; in 1832, William Rust, jun.; in 1833, Isaac Heaton; in 1835, James McDowell; in 1836, William Newhall; in 1839, Joshua Linniken; and in 1840, Ichabod Irish.

† Elected.

1822, Sept. 9. Robert Foster, 45; Nathaniel Bachelor, 36; John W. Lindley, 2 ; John Lermond, 2.
1822, Sept.27. Samuel Doe,* 27 †; Robert Foster, 11.
1823, Sept. 8. John W. Lindley, 33 ; Nathaniel Bachelor, 22 ; Henry True, 11 ; John Lermond, 2 ; Joseph H. Becket, 1.
1823, Sept.22. Nathaniel Bachelor, 41 † ; Henry True, 12 ; John W. Lindley, 11.
1824, Sept.13. John W. Lindley, 34 ; Nathaniel Robbins, 33 ; Robert Foster, 4 ; John Lermond, 10.
1824, Nov. 1. John W. Lindley, 53 ; Nathaniel Robbins, 45 † ; Robert Foster, 2.
1825, Sept.12. Samuel Doe, ‡ 53 † ; Daniel McCurdy, 16 ; George Bailey, 4 ; John W. Lindley, 1.
1826, Sept.11. Nathaniel Robbins, 53 † ; John W. Lindley, 41 ; Henry True, 17.
1827, Sept.10. Nathl. Robbins, 59 † ; John W. Lindley, 56.
1828, Sept. 5. Daniel F. Harding, 76 ; Isaac Heaton, 11 ; Moses Pelton, 5 ; William Witt, 1 ; William Newhall, 8.
1828, Nov. 3. Daniel F. Harding, 72 ; William Witt, 9 ; William Newhall, 8 ; Isaac Heaton, 9 ; Moses Pelton, 2.
1828, Nov.22. Isaac Heaton, 17; William Witt, ‡ 3 † ; Ezra Kellog, 1.
1829, Sept. 5. Daniel F. Harding, 104 ; John Lermond, 22 ; John Butler, 21 ; Nathaniel Bachelor, 1 ; Walter Blake, 1.
1829, Oct. 10. Nathl. Bachelor, 56 ; John Lermond, 52 † ; Jno. W. Lindley, 8 ; Daniel F. Harding, 4.
1830, Sept.13. Ebenezer Alden, 118 ; John Lermond, 117 † ; John W. Lindley, 5 ; Joseph Morse, 1.
1831, Sept.11. John Lermond, 131 † ; Daniel F. Harding, 75 ; Herman Hawes, 6 ; Cornelius Irish, 5 ; Nathaniel Bachelor, 1 ; John W. Lindley, 1 ; Ebenezer Alden, 1.
1832, Sept.10. Nathaniel Bachelor, 154 † ; John Lermond, 139 ; Herman Hawes, 1.
1833. Sept. 9. Nathaniel Bachelor, 129 ; William Shepard, 111 ; Cornelius Irish, 10 ; Henry Blunt, 5 ; Jno. W. Lindley, 4 ; Thos. Mitchell, 1.

* Of Putnam, afterwards called Washington.   † Elected.
‡ Of Washington.

1833, Sept.16. Nathl. Bachelor, 124 †; Wm. Shepard, 80;
    Henry Blunt, 21; Cornelius Irish, 4.
1834, Sept. 8. John Lermond, 151; Nathaniel Bachelor,
    142; Thomas Mitchell, 12.
1834, Sept.15. John Lermond, 162 †; Nathaniel Bachelor,
    139; Thomas Mitchell, 16.
1835, ... John W. Lindley, 128 †; William Shepard,
    110; Cornelius Irish, 2; Phillips C. Hard-
    ing, 2; Calvin Gleason, 1; John Bachel-
    der, 1; Nathan Daniels, jun., 1; Joseph
    Shepard, 1.
1836, Sept.12. John W. Lindley, 135 †; Calvin Gleason,
    99; Phillips C. Harding, 6; Cornelius
    Irish, 3; Obadiah Harris, 3; William
    Shepard, 1; —— ——, 1.
1837, ... Peter Adams, 174 †; Cornelius Irish, 117;
    Samuel Stone, 1; John W. Lindley, 1.
1838, ... Peter Adams, 195 †; Amos Drake, 158.
1839, Sept. 9. No choice; adjourned to —
1839, Sept.16. No choice; adjourned to —
1839, Sept.23. Samuel Hills, 116 †; Cornelius Irish, 16;
    Nelson Cutler, 2; Joel Adams, 2; Wil-
    liam Libbey, 1; Augustus Alden, 1; Au-
    gustus C. Robbins, 1.
1840, Sept.14. No choice; adjourned to —
1840, Sept.21. No choice; adjourned to —
1840, Sept.28. Nelson Cutler, 174 †; Leonard Barnard,
    148; Peter Adams, 12; Hannibal Ham-
    lin, 5; John W. Lindley, 3.
1841, ... Phillips C. Harding, 145 †; Peter Adams, 5;
    Joel Adams, 2; Leonard Bump, 2; N.
    Bachelder, 1; John Gowen, 1.
1842, ... Wm. McDowell, 179; Phillips Clark Hard-
    ing, 153 †; Elijah Vose, 1.
1843, Sept.11. Wm. McDowell, 147; George Jones, 124;
    D. F. Harding, 3; Jonathan Sibley, 1.
1843, Oct. 2. Wm. McDowell,* 147 †; George Babb, 69;
    Wm. Young, 3; Joseph Irish, 1; Moses
    Pelton, 1; D. F. Harding, 1.
1844, Sept. 9. Otis Hawes, 200; Steph. Carriel, 181 †; D. F.
    Harding, 8; John Butler, 1; Stephen, 1.

* Of Washington.   † Elected.

1845, Sept. 8.   No choice.
1845, Sept.29.   Wm. Young,* 128 †; Otis Hawes, 114;
                 Moses Pelton, 4; Samuel Stone, 2.
1846, ... James Newhall, 183; Elbridge Lermond,
                 173†; Christopher Young, 1.
1847, ... Thomas Burns, 134; William Witt,* 137†;
                 Samuel Bowker, 9; Joshua S. Green, 1.
1848, ... Christopher Young, 124†; Stephen S. Hawes,
                 181; C. Young, 5; Silas Hawes, 1; C.
                 Y., 1.
1849, ... Elias Skidmore, 175; Timothy Cunning-
                 ham,* 143 †; Church Burton, 13; Ste-
                 phen S. Hawes, 1.
1850, ... James Burns, 176; Joseph Irish, 150†.

JUSTICES OF THE PEACE.

Oct. 6, 1781, "a commission was made out to Mason Wheaton, Esq., of Sterlington, to be a justice of the peace in the county of Lincoln." This was before there was any organization of the inhabitants. An early movement of the town toward procuring a commission for a justice of the peace was very democratic. The warrant calling a town-meeting, July 8, 1793, contains three articles on the subject: one "to see if the town will vote to have a person put in the commission of the peace;" another "to see if the town will vote for any particular person;" and a third "to see if the town will choose a committee to petition the Governor, or act or do any thing relative thereto." The votes in connection with these articles are recorded very distinctly and explicitly. The inhabitants "voted they will choose a man for justice of the peace. . . . Voted they will have Mr. Edward Jones for a justice of the peace," upon which the town-clerk makes the memorandum, — " He had thirteen votes; which were all but one that voted." " Voted that the town will choose a committee of three to petition the Governor for the peace. . . . Voted Messrs. Josiah Maxcy, Amariah Mero, and Samuel Hills, for this committee.

* Of Washington.   † Elected.

... Voted that the town-clerk give the committee an attested copy of the votes." This is the only record of any action by the town on the subject. Jones, however, was not nominated, notwithstanding the movements of the town in his favor. Ebenezer Jennison, though objected to, probably by Jones's friends, was commissioned. In the following lists, the dates of qualifications, which were on record in the offices of the Secretaries of the States of Massachusetts and Maine, in August, 1850, are subjoined. Whether the others were ever qualified or not, does not appear. The first list is from the records of Massachusetts: —

Names.	Dates of Commissions.	Of Qualification.
Ebenezer Jennison	Oct. 1795	
Edward Jones	Feb. 10, 1802	
Nathaniel Robbins	Feb. 14, 1806	
Stephen March *	Feb. 2, 1809	
Edward Jones	Feb. 21, 1809	
Nathan Blake	May 13, 1811	
Jonathan Sibley	June 28, 1811	
Nathaniel Robbins *	Jan. 28, 1813	Feb. 4, 1813.
Timothy Stewart	Feb. 11, 1813	April 26, 1813.
Stephen March *	Jan. 19, 1816	
William Brown	Jan. 24, 1816	June 21, 1816.
Nathan Blake	Feb. 16, 1818	
Jonathan Sibley	Aug. 19, 1818	April 24, 1819.
Nathaniel Robbins *	Jan. 29, 1820	Feb. 8, 1820.

The commissions in the office of the Secretary of the State of Maine are recorded as follows: —

Names.	Dates of Commissions.	Of Qualification.
Nathan Blake	Feb. 16, 1818	
John Bulfinch	Jan. 24, 1821	
Nathaniel Robbins *	Jan. 29, 1820	
Jonathan Sibley	Aug. 19, 1818	
William Brown	Jan. 24, 1818	
Nathaniel Robbins	Feb. 23, 1821	
Nathaniel Bachelor	Feb. 23, 1821	

* Justices of the peace and quorum.

JUSTICES OF THE PEACE.

Names.	Dates of Commissions.	Of Qualification.
Jonathan Sibley	Feb. 23, 1821	
Joseph H. Beckett	March 13, 1821	
Daniel F. Harding	May 10, 1821	
Timothy Stewart	Feb. 8, 1822	
Walter Blake	Feb. 14, 1824	March 27, 1824.
Joseph H. Beckett*	Feb. 5, 1825	
[Re-appointed	April 8, 1825]	
Henry True*	Feb. 21, 1825	March 28, 1825.
Nathaniel Robbins*	Feb. 22, 1825	March 19, 1825.
Nathan D. Rice	June 22, 1827	Jan. 15, 1828.
John W. Lindley	Oct. 19, 1827	Jan. 19, 1828.
Nathaniel Robbins*	Feb. 7, 1828	Appointed before.
Nathaniel Bachelor	Feb. 7, 1828	
Jona. Libby [Sibley]	Feb. 7, 1828	
Daniel F. Harding	March 1, 1828	
Timothy Stewart	Feb. 13, 1829	
Elisha Harding	Nov. 1, 1830	
John Little	Jan. 31, 1831	
Walter Blake	March 12, 1831	April 4, 1831.
Joseph H. Beckett*	Feb. 3, 1832	Feb. 10, 1832.
Thomas Mitchell	Feb. 10, 1832	
Nathaniel Robbins*	Feb. 17, 1832	Feb. 29, 1832.
Daniel F. Harding*	Feb. 17, 1832	
John S. Abbot	March 2, 1832	March 14, 1832.
Calvin Gleason	Dec. 24, 1832	Jan. 30, 1833.
William Shepard	Oct. 22, 1834	
William Shepard*	Dec. 31, 1834	Feb. 20, 1835.
John W. Lindley*	Dec. 31, 1834	Jan. 26, 1835.
Benjamin Gallop	March 19, 1835	
William Gleason	Jan. 21, 1836	Feb. 6, 1836.
Nelson Cutler*	March 30, 1837	April 7, 1837.
Augustus C. Robbins	March 13, 1838	April 14, 1838.
Walter Blake*	March 24, 1838	April 7, 1838.
Joseph H. Beckett*	Feb. 7, 1839	Feb. 26, 1839.
Nathaniel Robbins*	March 7, 1839	April 24, 1839.
John Whiting	April 24, 1839	
George Cummings	Dec. 31, 1839	
Calvin Gleason*	Jan. 23, 1840	Jan. 28, 1840.
Thomas Mitchell	Feb. 13, 1840	
Ebenezer Cobb*	March 18, 1840	

* Justices of the peace and quorum.

Names.	Dates of Commissions.	Of Qualification.
Elijah Vose	Oct. 8, 1840	
Ebenezer W. Adams*	Feb. 18, 1841	April 5, 1841.
John Gowen	March 12, 1841	April 5, 1841.
Nathan D. Rice*	June 25, 1841	
John W. Lindley*	Jan. 22, 1842	Feb. 7, 1842.
Phillips C. Harding	Feb. 24, 1842	
Nathan B. Robbins	March 3, 1842	April 9, 1842.
Nathan Bachelder*	June 21, 1843	
William Gleason	Feb. 2, 1843	
Elisha E. Rice*	June 21, 1843	Oct. 6, 1843.
Daniel F. Harding	Feb. 22, 1844	
Asa Master†	Feb. 22, 1844	
Willard Robbins	Feb. 22, 1844	
Edward Hills	Feb. 22, 1844	
William Gleason	March 14, 1844	April 18, 1844.
Asa Messer*	March 15, 1844	April 3, 1844.
Hiram Dorman*	Jan. 15, 1845	
Nelson Cutler*	Jan. 15, 1845	Feb. 6, 1845.
M. R. Hopkins*	May 2, 1846	May 15, 1846.
Elijah Vose*	Nov. 2, 1847	Nov. 11, 1847.
John Gowen	May 1, 1848	June 10, 1848.
John Goodwin*	May 26, 1848	

Jan. 28, 1825, Nathaniel Robbins was commissioned to qualify civil officers.

CORONER.

Dec. 18, 1809. Ebenezer Alden.
May 5, 1810. Ebenezer Alden.
Feb. 1, 1827. Ebenezer Alden.

POST-OFFICES AND POSTMASTERS.

The first post-office was established in 1810, through the influence of the Hon. Mark Langdon Hill, on condition that it should be without expense to the government. Accordingly, for many years, the postmasters, though they made quarterly returns to the General Post Office, were entitled to all the money received by them. At their own expense, they sent for the mail

---

* Justices of the peace and quorum.
† Error for Asa Messer.

to Waldoborough or Warren. It was generally brought in saddle-bags on horseback, once or twice a week. William White was the first postmaster, and held the office till he removed to Belfast. He was succeeded by Ebenezer Alden, whose commission was dated Jan. 19, 1813. During the greater part of Mr. Alden's administration, the business was transacted by deputies, residing on the Common. He held the office for the long period of thirty-two years. When the rates of postage were reduced in 1845, he resigned, and was succeeded, Aug. 12, by Jesse Wentworth Payson. Mr. Payson was removed, and succeeded by Edward Hills, Esq., May 11, 1849.

QUARTERLY STATEMENTS OF POSTAGE,

From which must be deducted Dead Letters, Papers, Pamphlets, &c., which average perhaps four per cent.

Year.	First Quarter.	Second Quarter.	Third Quarter.	Fourth Quarter.
1821.	—	$25.20	$17.93½	$21.74½
1822.	$19.04½	17.94	20.20	20.62
1823.	23.85½	20.11½	17.62	15.99½
1824.	24.63	19.59	21.96	21.87
1825.	23.70	30.34	27.67	26.63
1826.	28.58	28.50	27.85	33.01
1827.	25.83	25.93	25.95	25.91
1828.	28.82	25.71	21.46	25.99
1829.	25.83	30.42	25.59	23.08
1830.	23.30	24.74	31.22	23.86
1831.	28.84½	35.08	36.56¾	30.17¾
1832.	29.75	37.09¾	46.55½	36.80
1833.	39.90	43.33½	29.07¼	31.60½
1834.	39.06¾	38.52	33.20¾	29.89¾
1835.	39.94¾	42.65	39.59¼	37.77
1836.	40.05¾	42.66½	45.54	46.10½
1837.	41.42¼	46.62	47.25	42.55½
1838.	52.14¾	56.25½	51.44	50.74
1839.	56.68¼	50.13¾	62.20¼	56.33
1840.	72.14½	48.19	53.66¼	65.61¾
1841.	76.52¾	63.82	66.83¾	74.62
1842.	89.98	76.33¾	62.26½	60.63
1843.	70.73	73.52¼	66.03	68.45
1844.	73.82½	74.15	75.34	51.32
1845.	81.07	73.41	31.54	28.15
1846.	62.59	70.80	70.50	70.25
1847.	82.13	73.18	93.40	82.73
1848.	85.53	85.94	85.18	85.00
1849.	91.47	—	—	—

A post-office was established at East Union, Feb. 28, 1849, and Joshua S. Greene appointed postmaster, He resigned Nov. 1, 1849, when he was succeeded by E. G. D. Beveridge, Esq.

Feb. 12, 1851, Capt. Samuel Stone was appointed postmaster of the North Union Post Office, which was opened March 3, 1851, near Fossetts' Mills.

CHAPTER XXVIII.

FINANCIAL HISTORY.

Taxes. — Early Apportionment of Taxes. — Controversy with Warren. — Petition to the Legislature in 1780. — Petition to the Legislature in 1783. — Plantation Taxes. — Taxes since the Incorporation. — Taxes paid in Produce. — Exemption of Philip Robbins, jun. — Table. — Adams's Petition to the Legislature in 1794. — State of the Finances in 1795. — Dollars and Cents. — Taking the Valuation. — Payment of Taxes.

TAXES.

EARLY APPORTIONMENT. — There is a tradition, that, soon after the settlement of the plantation, it was thought advisable to levy a tax. The population was very small. The assessor of the taxes, who it seems was also collector, not being expert in figures or penmanship, verbally informed the tax-payers of the amount which he apportioned to each; and they readily paid him, without even the formality of taking receipts. If this be true, the golden age of tax-paying without grumbling has long since passed away. But it is to be feared that such a happy state of things never existed.

CONTROVERSY WITH WARREN. — The earliest authentic information which has been found is contained in a copied volume of the records of Warren. Capt. McIntyre was constable of Warren in 1779. Nov. 9, 1780, the inhabitants of that town voted, that " Capt.

McIntyre proceed according to law in collecting the taxes committed to him to collect." Nov. 30, 1780, Moses Copeland, William Lermond, and Robert Montgomery, were chosen a committee " to treat and agree with Mr. Philip Robbins of Union respecting the collecting of taxes;" and they " were empowered to sign arbitration-bonds with him in behalf of the town."

PETITION TO THE LEGISLATURE IN 1780. — The next information is from a document found in the office of the Secretary of the Commonwealth of Massachusetts. As it contains incidental information of interest, it is printed entire: —

"To the Honorable the Senate and House of Representatives of the Commonwealth of Massachusetts, Dec. 1780.

"The petition of the subscribers, inhabitants of a plantation called Sterlingtown, in the county of Lincoln, humbly showeth, — That the said Sterlingtown is an entire new settlement, consisting of nine families and a few single men.

"That three[1] of the said families have been settled about four years, two[2] about three years, and none of the others more than one year; and several of them obliged as yet to depend on their friends at the Westward for support.

"That Sterlingtown, and the settlements therein, are situate at a great distance from any other settlement.

"That we have no other way of passing to said plantation from other settlements only through the woods, or up St. George's River, part of the way by water and part by land; but the passing that way is prevented nearly six weeks every spring and fall by reason of the ice.

"That we have waited on the inhabitants of the town of Warren (by our committee chosen for that purpose), requesting them to lay out a road through the woods from the settlements in their town to the line between said Warren and Sterlingtown; but they utterly refused to have any thing to do about said road, but only would consent that we might clear out a road (without the same being laid out), the length whereof would be about six miles, as it must run,

[1] Philip Robbins, David Robbins, and Richard Cummings, in 1776.
[2] Probably, Ezra Bowen and John Butler, in 1777.

crossing St. George's River twice in its way, which would require two large bridges.

"That, in December, A.D. 1778, a large barn belonging to Mr. Robbins, in which was stored almost all the grain raised that year by the [then] inhabitants of the place, was consumed by fire, with twenty tons of hay; which brought the inhabitants into great want, and occasioned the loss of ten head of cattle that winter.

"That we lie exposed, as a frontier settlement, to the scouting parties of the enemy from Majorbagaduce, who, often passing this way, keep us in continued alarm; and, by order of Gen. Wadsworth, we have the summer past, and yet do keep up a watch and scouting party to discover and detect them.

"And lastly, notwithstanding all these our difficult circumstances and sufferings, we were taxed by the assessors of Warren in the year 1779; and they seem further determined to assess us in all the taxes.

"Wherefore your petitioners humbly pray your Excellency and Honors to take our case under your wise, just, and paternal consideration, and grant that we may be exempted from paying taxes until we are in circumstances to bear the burden thereof. And, as in duty bound, shall ever pray, &c.

" RICHARD COMINGS.	DAVID ROBBINS.
MOSES HAWES.	EBENEZER ROBBINS.
EZRA BOWEN.	JESSE ROBBINS.
JOHN BUTLER.	MASON WHEATON.
PHINEHAS BUTLER.	PHILIP ROBBINS."
JOEL ADAMS.	

[Consequently], "On the petition of the inhabitants of the town of Sterlington, in the county of Lincoln, Resolved [May 11, 1781] that the town of Warren, in the county of Lincoln, be directed to pay to the inhabitants of Sterlington such taxes as they have taxed and received of said town; and the said town of Warren is further directed not to tax the inhabitants of Sterlington until the further order of the General Court, any law to the contrary notwithstanding."

PETITION TO THE LEGISLATURE IN 1783.

"To the Honorable the Senate and House of Representatives of the Commonwealth of Massachusetts, Sept. 1783.

"The petition of the inhabitants of the plantation called Sterlingtown, in the county of Lincoln, showeth, — That your petitioners feel themselves insupportably burdened by being heavily taxed, and exposed to execution, considering the smallness of our number now, being only seventeen ratable polls, though we have had twenty-seven; the newness of our settlements, and being in the wilderness at a great distance from other inhabitants (though bordering on other incorporated towns, through the uninhabited parts whereof we have not as yet been able to procure any roads), our sufferings by fire and from the war, and our having been taxed as adjacent inhabitants to another town; all which we have largely set forth in former petitions to the Honorable Court. Add to these, that we have no power or authority amongst ourselves to assess and collect a tax, though it has been requested of the Court of General Sessions of the Peace in this county.

"Wherefore your petitioners humbly pray, that our taxes may be abated until we are in circumstances of ability equal to our other brethren in the commonwealth, and then we will gladly pay our proportion; and that we then may be invested with proper authority to assess and collect the same. And your petitioners, as in duty bound, shall ever pray, &c.

"PHILIP ROBBINS.
EBENEZER ROBBINS.
EZRA BOWEN.
JOHN BUTLER.
JOEL ADAMS.
MOSES HAWES.
RICHARD COMINGS.

DAVID ROBBINS.
JESSA ROBBINS.
ABIJAH HAWES.
MATTHIAS HAWSE.
JASON WARE.
PHINEHAS BUTLER."

"Resolve on the petition of the inhabitants of the plantation called Sterlington, directing the treasurer to stay his execution, March 20, 1784: —

"On the petition of the inhabitants of the plantation called Sterlington, in the county of Lincoln, setting forth that they have been taxed in two continental taxes, and the last [State] tax, the sum of twenty-five pounds each, and representing their inability to pay the same, —

"Therefore resolved, that the prayer of the petitioners be so far granted that the treasurer of this commonwealth be, and he hereby is, directed to stay his execution upon the said inhabitants until the expiration of twelve months from the date hereof."

FINANCIAL HISTORY.

PLANTATION TAXES. — In accordance with an Act of the Legislature of Massachusetts, passed July 9, 1784, for apportioning and assessing a tax of £140,000, for the sole purpose of redeeming the army notes, issued pursuant to an Act, passed July 5, 1781, payable in the years 1784 and 1785; and for raising the further sum of £11,035. 6s. 6d. for the purpose of replacing the same sum, which had been paid out of the treasury to the representatives for their attendance on the five last sessions of the General Court; viz. from November, 1782, to March, 1784, — the plantation of Sterlington was taxed £17. 10s.

The next attempt at taxation seems to have been made in consequence of the tax-act of the Legislature, passed March 23, 1786. The object of this was to raise £300,439. 1s. 3d.: viz., £145,655 to meet the requisition of Congress, made Sept. 27, 1785; for £25,781. 1s. 3d. for the support of government; £29,000 for the payment of interest on the consolidated notes of the State; and £100,000 for redeeming the remainder of the army notes, so called, which became payable in 1784 and 1785; and £1,786 not provided for; and also £11,001. 18s. to replace the same sum drawn out of the treasury, to pay the members of the House of Representatives for their attendance the five last sessions of the General Court. The apportionment for Stirlington was £65;[1] and the warrant issued May 3, 1786, by Mason Wheaton, Esq., of Thomaston, gives an additional memorandum of £2. 11s. for the county tax, and £1. 12s. 4¾d. for soldiers' bounty.

These appear to be all the recorded notices respecting taxes, before the incorporation of the town. The

---

[1] By way of comparison, it may be observed, that the apportionment to Pittston was £285. 12s. 6d.; to Medumcook, £175. 18s. 9d.; to Belfast, £78. 8s. 9d.; to Camden, £98. 2s. 6d.; to Hallowell, £473. 2s. 6d.; these towns and plantations not being assessed for the payment of representatives. The apportionment to Bristol was £715, also £67. 4s. for payment of representatives; to Warren, £223. 2s. 6d., also £25. 4s.; to Thomaston, £204. 7s. 6d., also £57. 15s.; and to Bath, £498. 2s. 6d., also £39. 11s. for the payment of representatives.

TAXES SINCE INCORPORATION.

£65 levied by the last Act led the inhabitants to make an application to the Legislature, which resulted in the Act of Incorporation.

TAXES SINCE THE INCORPORATION. — Since the town has been incorporated, the taxes, so far as can be ascertained from obscure and imperfect records, are as follows; probably including school-money, except in the years 1787—1803, 1805, 1808, 1809, and 1814:—

1787, £10	1803, $250	1819, $1200	1835, $1300
1788, £10	1804, $550	1820, $1200	1836, $1300
1789, £15	1805, $350	1821, $1100	1837, $2500
1790, £15	1806, $800	1822, $1100	1838, $2000
1791, £15	1807, $800	1823, $1100	1839, $2000
1792, £15	1808, $400	1824, $1500	1840, $2500
1793, £15	1809, $250	1825, $1200	1841, $1500
1794, £10	1810, $1100	1826, $1300	1842, $1800
1795, —	1811, $1000	1827, $1000	1843, $2500
1796, $150	1812, $750	1828, $1000	1844, $2000
1797, $50	1813, $600	1829, $1100	1845, $1600
1798, $100	1814, $250	1830, $1000	1846, $1500
1799, $100	1815, $775	1831, $1250	1847, $1600
1800, $120	1816, $900	1832, $1000	1848, $1500
1801, $200	1817, $900	1833, $1000	1849, $1500
1802, $150	1818, $1050	1834, $1200	1850, $1500

TAXES PAID IN PRODUCE. — The pecuniary distress of the country, and the poverty and hardships of the early settlers, compelled them to resort to all practicable means for relief. As for specie, it may be said, that, during many years, it was hardly seen. When it was required for taxes, the only way to get it was to trap and hunt, and send the furs to Boston for sale. The tax for 1787 was only £10. But it had not been paid July 14, 1788; for then the vote of April, 1787, was reconsidered; and it was voted that the town should have the privilege of paying "town-charges and schooling at the following prices in produce, in lieu of specie: Rye at 4s. 6d. per bushel, flax at 8d. per pound, butter at 8d. per pound, and wool at 2s." This plan, it seems, did not work well; for it was reconsidered Sept. 13, and the town voted " to have it paid in specie."

When the grant for town-charges was made April 6, 1789, a vote was also passed that it might be " paid in produce at the following prices, if paid by the 15th of November; if not, must be paid in specie: Rye, 4s. 6d. per bushel; sheep's wool, 2s. per pound; flax, 8d. per pound; butter, 8d. per pound; and boards, staves, and shingles, at market-prices." It was also voted that ten pounds should be paid in the same way " to procure schooling; to be laid out at the discretion of the selectmen." April 4, 1791, it was again voted that the taxes might be paid in produce, at the prices affixed in 1789, " the produce to be merchantable." Oct. 26, an unsuccessful effort was made to reconsider the vote of April 4, with a view to have a part of the amount paid in specie.

EXEMPTION OF PHILIP ROBBINS, JUN. — " March 7, 1791, agreeable to the request of Mr. Philip Robbins, jun., voted that Mr. Philip Robbins, jun., shall have his taxes for the year 1790, and not be assessed for the year 1791,[1] as a bounty for having two children at a birth."

TABLE.

NUMBER.	1793.	1794.	1795.	1796.	1797.	1798.	1799.	1800.	1840.	1843.
Polls	50	48½	58	79	96	160½	131½	129	346	348
Houses	13	16	20	26	32	36	42	62	250	241
Barns	14	17	19	22	28	34	36	42	262	228
Saw-mills	3	3	4	4	4	1	3	3	8	8
Grist-mills	1	1	1	1	1	1	1	1	5*	4†
Horses and colts	12	14	19	22	25	33	37	53	255	228
Oxen	54	56	66	71	84	85	104	100		
Cows	—	110	119	140	147	165	208	236	1459	1443
Two-year-olds	—	42	51	43	38	76	72	62		
Yearlings	—	37	52	47	83	66	57	47		
Swine	79	73	76	84	107	114	123	109	363	195

ADAMS'S PETITION.

" To the Honorable Senate and House of Representatives in General Court assembled.

" The petition of Joel Adams, of Union, in the county of Lincoln, humbly shows, — That he was appointed collector

---

[1] The earliest tax-bill preserved is for the year 1791. The one for 1792 is probably destroyed.

* With twelve pairs of stones.

† With ten pairs of stones.

of State-tax, No. 5, in said town of Union, which was committed to him in the year 1786. That, at that time, the inhabitants of the town were few in number, and very poor. Remote from navigation, they are destitute of the common means of procuring money on the eastern shore. That sundry persons were assessed in said tax who paid the same in the towns they respectively came from; and that sundry others left the town before the petitioner had opportunity of collecting their respective rates. That, owing to these and other unfortunate circumstances, he has been able to collect but a small part of said tax, though he has been at great pains and expense in attempting it; and that he has sustained considerable loss on what he has collected, as he was obliged to take it of the inhabitants in articles other than money; and that, as to a great part of the residue, he utterly despairs of ever being able to collect it of the persons assessed.

"Further shows that the sheriff of the county now holds an execution against your petitioner for the sum he is deficient on said tax, being about forty-five pounds, which, if extended, will reduce him and his family to great inconvenience and want.

"Your petitioner, therefore, prays your Honors to take his case into your wise and good consideration, and order such relief as your Honors in your wisdom shall think fit.

"And your petitioner, as in duty bound, shall ever pray.
"JOEL ADAMS.

"Union, June 3, 1794."

The preceding application led to a —

"Resolve on the petition of Joel Adams, collector for the town of Union.

"On the petition of Joel Adams, a collector of the tax No. 5, in the town of Union, for the year 1786, praying for relief respecting said tax, which amounted to the sum of sixty-five pounds, one-third part of which he has paid into the treasury, and execution is now in the hands of the sheriff of the county of Lincoln for the remainder: —

"Resolved, for reasons set forth in said petition, that the prayer thereof be so far granted that the sum of twenty pounds, part of the balance now due from the said Joel Adams to this Commonwealth, be laid out in repairing the public roads and bridges in said town of Union; and, upon a certificate of the selectmen of the said town of Union being returned into the treasury office of this Commonwealth, within nine months from the passing of this resolve, that the said sum has been so expended, the treasurer thereof is hereby ordered and directed to pass to the credit of the said town of Union the balance due from the said Joel Adams, as collector for the said town of Union; and the sheriff of the said county of Lincoln is hereby ordered and directed not to levy the said execution on the said Joel Adams, for the balance aforesaid, until the expiration of twelve months from the date hereof."

STATE OF THE FINANCES.[1] — April 6, 1795, Jason Ware, Joseph Maxcy, and Amariah Mero, were chosen a committee to examine into the state of the town-finances. They reported, May 6, 1795, that "there was due from the several collectors to the town, £146. 12s. 6d.; and that there was due from the town to several of the inhabitants, £29. 6s." It was immediately "voted not to grant any money for town-charges, as there appears to be enough due the town." It was also "voted not to grant any money for the meeting-house."

DOLLARS AND CENTS. — At this time, it is observable that the taxes are reckoned by dollars instead of pounds. This was in conformity with an Act of the Legislature of Massachusetts, passed Feb. 25, 1795, ordering that, after the first day of the following September, "the money of account of this commonwealth shall be the dollar, cent, and mille; and all accounts in the public offices, &c., shall be kept and had in conformity to this regulation."

---

[1] April 4, 1791, it was voted that "the assessors may put all town-taxes in one tax-bill, except the highway-tax."

In 1812, a statement in behalf of the town was made to the Legislature by William White and Nathan Blake, that thirty polls had been added to the number which had been returned for the State valuation.

Nov. 28, 1814, Nathaniel Robbins, Simeon Butters, and Joseph Morse, were chosen to consult the principal assessor of the Direct Tax for the Third Collection District, for the purpose of having the tax better proportioned among the different towns in the district.

VALUATION. — PAYMENT OF TAXES.

TAKING THE VALUATION. — April 3, 1815, an unsuccessful effort was made to "order the assessors to take the valuation under oath;" but, in April, 1835, it was voted that it should be done. A list of suspected persons was made out; but it was too much trouble to test all the inhabitants. April 6, 1846, upon an article "to see if the town will instruct the assessors to go all together, and take the valuation," it was "voted that they do not go together to take the valuation."

PAYMENT OF TAXES. — In 1834, "Voted that the treasurer be collector of taxes, and that all those who pay in their taxes to said collector within thirty days from the time he receives the bills from the assessors, shall have ten per cent discount on said taxes; and all those who pay their taxes in sixty days, as aforesaid, shall have five per cent discount; and all those who pay their taxes in one hundred and twenty-five days, as aforesaid, shall have two and a half per cent discount on said taxes." In 1839, probably to promote the promptness of payment by the collector, as well as the tax-payers, it was ordered that the taxes should "be collected within the year from the time the" collector received the tax-bills.

April, 1841, voted "that the money be paid into the treasurer the ensuing year; and that he give notice to the town immediately on receiving the bill, by posting notices at the places for notifying town-meetings. And all moneys paid in within sixty days from the date of said notice shall receive six per cent discount; one hundred and twenty days, four per cent; one hundred and eighty days, two per cent; and, after that time, the treasurer proceed to collect the remainder according to law, and within one year from receiving the bills, if possible."

CHAPTER XXIX.

FINANCIAL HISTORY.

(Concluded.)

Reed's Case. — Surplus Revenue. — Paupers. — Warning out of Town. — Maintenance of the Poor.

REED'S CASE.

IN the early settlement of the town, there was considerable difficulty respecting the taxes on wild land and the property of non-residents. A warrant issued for a meeting, Jan. 4, 1790, contains three articles on this subject: —

1. "To know in what manner the collectors shall proceed with regard to the taxes now in their hands unsettled, against Josiah Reed,[1] non-resident proprietor of wild land in this town. 2. To see if the town will indemnify the collectors, if they proceed to distrain the goods or chattels, lands or tenements of the said Josiah Reed, according to their different tax-bills. 3. To see if the town think it necessary for some person to advise with some gentleman, respecting the taxes, to know whether they will stand in law as they are now made, before the collector shall proceed to distrain for them." "Voted to accept of all the taxes as they are now assessed by the assessors chosen in Union, since the town was incorporated." "Voted that the assessors petition the General Court to establish the taxes as they are now assessed."

June 25, 1790, "Voted that Mr. Josiah Reed shall have liberty, if he will find all the plank necessary for the bridge across the main river, and twenty days' work on said bridge, then he shall have liberty to work the remaining part of his highway-taxes elsewhere, as he shall think proper, on roads

---

[1] Josiah Reed was Dr. Taylor's son-in-law; and his daughter married Henry, son of Major-General Henry Knox. In 1798 and 1799, he was representative from Thomaston to the Massachusetts Legislature.

to the northward of said bridge, that are now laid out, or may be in the course of this season, provided he shall work them this season."

Oct. 4, 1790, an article was introduced into town-meeting, " to see if the town will choose three men to examine the taxes, as was proposed by Mr. Reed and others." Samuel Hills, Philip Robbins, and Josiah Robbins, were appointed a committee for that purpose. They were " empowered to agree with Mr. Reed without choosing a committee of indifferent men, if they could upon any terms they should think reasonable. If they could not agree, then they were to proceed and choose a committee with him to settle said taxes." Nov. 8, 1790, " after hearing the report of the committee, the town voted they would have a new committee (by the old ones dismissing themselves), namely, Samuel Hills, Joseph Guild, and Samuel Daggett." The meeting was adjourned to the next Friday, when the report signed by Guild and Hills was read as follows: —

" They found the real value of the wild land, as was taxed in 1788, £6,627. 14s.; that the third part of the value [was] £2,209. 5s.; that the sum total for taxation in 1788 was £3,158. 16s. The value of Mr. Reed's land for taxation stood at two per cent, or one third the value was $998.18s.

" Mowing and tillage we have doubled from what it was in the valuation of 1788. The town, we find, granted for highways, in 1788, £110; after deducting out the polls, there remains to be laid on property £96. 4s. We find that Mr. Reed was taxed according to the valuation £31. 4s. 4d.; and, by doubling the mowing and tillage, he has to pay of the above tax £30. 2s. 5¼d. We have gone by the valuation of 1788, and done as nearly as we can as was recommended by Thomaston committee, and find, when the abatement is made in all his taxes, he is only abated £5. 5s. ½d. We would be understood it is only on wild land "

[The town voted they were satisfied with the report.] " A debate arose between Mr. Reed and the town. Mr Reed supposed the town did not rightly understand the mind of

Thomaston committee, and made the following motion, viz.
That the town would choose one or more men, to go down
to Thomaston with him to the committee to get their opinion in writing." "Voted that Mr. Moses Hawes go down
with Mr. Reed to Thomaston to the committee; and the
committee are desired to say how much of his taxes are
abated. For which we pledge our honors to abide their
judgment. Mr. Reed pledges his honor also. The committee are desired to give their opinion in, in writing."

Dec. 25, "The report of Thomaston committee was read.
Voted to adjourn to Jan. 10.

"Jan. 10, 1791. The inhabitants met on the adjournment,
and gave the report of Thomaston committee the second
reading, and voted they would accept of the report, if they
would rectify two mistakes, viz. To cross out of their verdict one tax which the town never had, or rather they have
put one in twice, and put in No. 8 State-tax and a tax of
nine pound granted by the town. Then, if they will rectify
these mistakes, they will be in full accepted." "Voted,
that, if Mr. Josiah Reed does pay to the several collectors
the sums that [have been adjudged by] the committee mutually chosen by the town and said Reed, then the collectors shall give him a receipt in full of the tax he shall pay."

May 23, 1791, the town passed a vote, giving "orders to
the collectors, that, if Mr. Reed pays them what the committee ordered within one month after they have demanded or
shown him his taxes, they shall give him a receipt in full for
the whole, as they were before they were abated; otherwise,
upon his neglecting or refusing, to distrain for the whole, as
they were on the rate-strikes before the committee abated
them."[1]

Mr. Reed still declined paying his taxes. His land
was put up at auction, and bid off by Samuel Hills
for Mr. Ichabod Irish, who sold it to Dr. Webb.
Finally, the land being sold irregularly, the town had

---

[1] At the same meeting it was "voted that thirty pounds be raised,
as soon as may be, to pay back-taxes." This sum may have been to
meet the deficiency caused by the reduction of Reed's taxes. There
is no record to show whether it was ever collected or not.

Nov. 3, 1794, there was an article before the town to see if it would
abate one-half of Josiah Reed's meeting-house tax in Mr. Edward
Jones's bills." "Voted not to abate Mr. Josiah Reed's tax."

to settle with Mr. Irish, and lost the case, though there was no lawsuit.

SURPLUS REVENUE.

A surplus of public money having accumulated in the treasury of the United States, Congress voted, June 23, 1836, that it should be apportioned among the several States of the Union, on deposit, until repayment thereof should be required by the secretary of the treasury. The Legislature of Maine, Jan. 26, 1837, passed an Act, providing for the acceptance of that portion of it to which the State was entitled. March 9, 1837, the Governor approved a bill, authorizing it to be deposited with the several towns, in proportion to their population, on condition that, whenever it should be called for by Congress, it should be refunded within sixty days after notice. Selectmen were authorized to cause a new census to be taken, distinguishing all persons under the age of four years; those of four and under twenty-one; and those of twenty-one and upwards, belonging to each town on the first day of March, 1837.

Accordingly, April 3, 1837, the inhabitants of Union voted to receive their proportion of the money, and chose John Lermond agent to procure it of the State treasurer, and "to loan it to the best advantage, upon such security as the selectmen might approve, he giving bonds to the town for the faithful discharge of his duty." No person was to have more than five hundred dollars, provided there were "other good applications sufficient to take the sum. Interest annually. The above subject to be called for in sixty days." A verbal report made by the agent, July 1, 1837, was accepted; and he was "directed to give notice to the subscribers of the several notes holden by him, sixty days previous to the next April meeting, that they may be paid then, unless sooner called for by the General Government." He was also instructed to get what was still due from the Government, and to keep it till the town should dispose of it at the September meeting. In September the agent made his report, and the vote was that "the money remain in the bank, where he has deposited it; and, should the fourth instalment be received, it be put in the bank also." But the fourth instalment never came. The sum received was $3,500, from which $21.74 were deducted for expenses.

April 2, 1838, John Lermond, Peter Adams, and Phillips C. Harding, were chosen to divide the money, between the first and the tenth of May; paying two dollars apiece to all persons whose residence was in town on the first day of March, 1837, whether neglected through mistake, or absent at the time the census was taken; "the remainder (if any) to be appropriated for schooling." Three persons, who had borrowed probably with the expectation that the money would not be called for, made an unsuccessful request to have an extension for a year, more or less. And the special agent was directed to "obtain, upon the faith of the town, so much of the surplus money as should be deficient on notes given for said money on the seventeenth day of April instant." Neither the town nor individuals were benefited.

PAUPERS.

WARNING OUT OF TOWN. — Union has never been burdened with paupers. There was a custom of warning "new comers" out of town, in order to prevent them from gaining a residence, and consequently a claim for support. In a town in Massachusetts, a selectman, in his official capacity as selectman, is said to have signed an order to the constable, warning himself out of town. The inhabitants of Union, willing to be on the safe side, availed themselves of the privilege. Accordingly, in a warrant calling a town-meeting, May 20, 1787, there is an article "to see what the town will do about warning out all persons that appear likely to be a town-charge hereafter. Voted the selectmen should warn out all they think necessary." Hence we find the following records: —

"To the constable of the town of Union, in the county of Lincoln.—You are hereby forthwith to warn Silvester Prince, and Rhoda Prince his wife, and Naaman, and Sarah, Olive, and Susa, and Silvester, their children, late of Waldoborough, in the county of Lincoln, as they say, immediately to depart out of the bounds of this town, as they are here now residing, and like to be a town-charge. Hereof fail not, and make due return of this warrant, with your doings thereon, to one or more of the selectmen, or to the town-clerk, as soon as may be.

"Given under our hands, at Union, this seventeenth day of December, in the year of our Lord one thousand [seven] hundred and eighty-seven.

"PHILIP ROBBINS, } Selectmen
"JASON WARE.   } of Union.

"Union, Dec. 21, 1787."

"By virtue of this warrant to me directed, I have notified and warned the within-named Silvester Prince, and Rhoda Prince his wife, Naaman, Sarah, Olive, Susa, and Silvester, their children, of the contents thereof, by reading the same to them, and warned them immediately to depart out of the bounds of said Union, as I am directed.

"ABIJAH HAWES, Constable."

At the same date, Molly Robbins, late of Fox Island, was warned out, and so were Phinehas Butler, and Elizabeth Butler his wife, late of Thomaston. The only other notice of the kind on record occurred in 1789, and stands thus:—

"I have warned Philip Robbins, jun., an inhabitant of Senabec, and also Jonathan Newhall, of Warren, to depart the bounds of this town, by order of the selectmen.

"MOSES HAWES, Town-clerk."

MAINTENANCE OF THE POOR.— March 7, 1803, David Robbins, Samuel Hills, and Joel Adams, were chosen overseers of the poor. None have been chosen at any other time; unless we except the selectmen, who were particularly appointed to the office in 1819, 1822, and 1826. When any aid has been wanted, the selectmen or the town have been appealed to. Very few towns have been taxed so little as this, for the support of the poor. The earliest mention of payments is in March, 1804, of $25.23, for Susannah Olney,—a squaw,—and of $13.50, in March, 1805, "for her black child." In 1806, some assistance was rendered to one man and his family. There seems not to have been any further aid afforded to any one till 1818, when the family of a man, in consequence of his inability to work at his trade of shoemaking, became a charge. From that time to the present, there have always been a few to be aided. Those requiring considerable assistance have generally been put up at auction, and taken by the lowest bidder. Notwithstanding this practice, which is commonly regarded as very inhuman, there is generally a disposition to make the situation of the unfortunate as comfortable as circumstances will admit. The overseers or selectmen have frequently been instructed by the town to provide for them; and thus, without being put up at auction, they have often found comfortable homes, or been taken care of by persons who felt a friendly interest in them, but upon whom it was too much of a tax to give them a support for years. If the number should increase, it would occur to the inhabitants that the most economical as well as humane disposition which could be made of them would be to provide an almshouse, where they could feel that they had a permanent home. For several years, this course has been adopted with great success in many of the towns in Massachusetts, and been found less expensive than the other, even when the inmates were few and the majority of them infirm.

CHAPTER XXX.

HIGHWAYS.

Early Difficulties in Travelling. — Moss. — Paths. — Spotted Trees. — Exposure of Matthias Hawes. — First Roads. — First Highway Districts. — Character of the Roads. — Corduroy Roads. — Boating and Visiting. — Ox Sleds. — First Teaming to Neighboring Towns.

EARLY DIFFICULTIES IN TRAVELLING.

It is not easy to imagine the difficulty of the travelling, when there was no way of coming to this place but through the woods or up St. George's River. Philip Robbins came in 1776; and then there was not a footpath between this and either of the neighboring towns. In the woods, particularly if the weather was cloudy, the inhabitants were often saved from being lost, and sometimes even from perishing, by the information obtained of the Indians, that moss grows on the north side of trees situated on low ground. Meadow-roads and hunters' paths for hand-sleds were bushed out for winter, when the settlers could not be better accommodated on the ice. Footpaths were early marked out, by spotting trees and removing the underbrush. The chips were taken from two sides of the trees, so that the white spots were visible to travellers going in either direction. The incision was only through the bark; for a wound in the wood soon healed. But such paths were of little or no use, except in the daytime, when the spots could be seen.

It was probably in the fall of 1782 that Matthias Hawes went down the river, to borrow a yoke of oxen to harrow in rye. The only guide was the spotted trees. On his way home, a violent storm arose; and dense darkness came on so suddenly, that he chained the oxen to a tree not far below the place afterward settled by Samuel Hills, and spent the long, tedious night in walking and exercising, to keep himself warm.

In the memorial to the Legislature in December, 1780, it is stated that there was no way of getting to Stirlington but through the woods and up the St. George's, part of the way by land and part by water; and that even this was obstructed nearly six weeks every spring and fall by the ice. No roads had been laid out in 1786, when the petition was made for an Act of Incorporation.

FIRST ROADS.

March 5, 1787, the town voted that the selectmen should lay out two roads, and that all the roads should be three rods wide. Accordingly, in relation to the first road laid out in the town, the report of the selectmen states:—

"They have spotted and looked it out as followeth:— May 7, we looked and spotted: Beginning at Warren line, at a hemlock, which we spotted; then running northwardly through the land of Ezra Bowen by stakes and spotted trees; thence across the land of Abijah Hawes is northwardly by stakes and spotted trees, till it comes to the corner of David Robbins's field; thence through said Robbins's field by stakes, till it comes to Richard Cummings's barn and house; thence running northwardly, as it is staked out; thence through Moses Hawes's, as the road now runs, to the west end of said Robbins's house; thence running by stakes north-east, in said Robbins's pasture, till it comes to the bridge at the head of Seven-tree Pond over St. George's River; thence north-east by spotted trees, to Josiah Robbins's field of rye; thence through said field by stakes, till it strikes the road leading to Senebec."

The road, as it now runs, does not agree with the selectmen's report. Josiah Robbins had cleared the land from the pond to the present road by the Old Burying Ground. Not willing to appropriate for the public good a field on which he had expended so much labor, he fenced it. The neighbors, with an accommodating spirit, passed along in the woods near to the fence on the west side of his rye, and a path finally became the road, leading over the hill instead of winding round it, as was intended by the selectmen.

The preceding report was followed by the one pertaining to the second road, which will be readily recognized as on the south and west sides of Round Pond.

"May 10. Then Mr. Philip Robbins, Mr. Ezra Bowen, and Mr. Jason Ware, met and laid out a road, beginning between Mr. Moses Hawes and Mr. Richard Cummings, on said Hawes's land, west-north-west, to Mr. Jessa Robbins; through his lot and a lot known by Dunbar's land, and through by Mr. Adams; through his land, and through the land of Mr. Ware, to Mr. Matthias Hawes; and through his land, and the land of Mr. Woodward, until it comes to the land of Mason Wheaton, Esq. (cleared ground), nearly as it is now cleared; then running straight to the east end of his house; thence to the north-east corner of his chopped land; thence nearly a north-east course, by spotted trees, till it comes to John Taylor, Esquire's, north line, by Senebec."

May 30, the day on which the two roads were confirmed, it was voted that another should be laid out east of Seven-tree Pond, and another through Ebenezer Robbins's land to Waldoborough. At the same town-meeting, the first movement was made in relation to highway-districts. The town gave " the selectmen orders to divide the highways for the surveyors, and proportion the inhabitants to do the work in each of their divisions."

"July 9, 1787, Mr. Philip Robbins, Mr. Ezra Bowen, and Mr. Jason Ware, met and laid out" [the third road, which was from Mr. Matthias Hawes's to Dr. William Jennison's] " as follows, viz.: Beginning a little south-east of Mr. Matthias Hawes's hovel, running northwardly across his pasture to a spotted oak, then by spotted trees till we come to the old road that Dr. William Jennison cleared, and then on the road, with small variations, just enough to straighten the road, by spotted trees, to the clear land of Dr. William Jennison."

"Nov. 19, 1787, voted that the road to Barretts Town shall stand as the selectmen laid [it] out, the twenty-second of September; Mr. Philip Robbins and Mr. Jason Ware, selectmen; and Mr. Jessa Robbins, pilot. Beginning at the brook north-east of Mr. Josiah Robbins, then running east-north-east until we come nearly to the end of the second tier of lots, then running north-east half a mile, then running north-east and by east, then north-east with small variations to Barretts Town."

"Oct. 6, 1787, Mr. Ezra Bowen and Mr. Jason Ware, two of the selectmen of Union, met, looked and laid out the road through to Waldoborough, as follows, viz.: Beginning at Round Pond Road on Mr. Joel Adams's land, at a white birch-tree spotted; then running south-west until it comes to the land of Mr. Dunbar, then running west by spotted trees till [it] comes to the old road from said Adams to said E. Robbins, then running nearly south-west by spotted trees and stake through the improvements of said Robbins, and on nearly the same course to Waldoborough."

The last three roads and the following, which was on the east and north sides of Seven-tree Pond, were confirmed or accepted Nov. 19, 1787, when it was—

"Voted that the road laid out from Warren, at the east end of Mr. Samuel Hills's land, through the farm improved by Mr. Royal Grinnell to the head of Seven-tree Pond, shall stand, and is confirmed as was laid by the selectmen, Nov. 5, A.D. 1787. The road begins as follows, viz.: At a white birch-tree spotted, by Warren line, then running nearly north, by spotted trees, until we come to Mr. Amory's grist-mill, then over the flume of said mill, then just east of the house and barn, then on or near a north course across to the woods, then nearly a north course to Oliver Lailand's [Leland's], then turning north-west to west till we come to the brook running into Seven-tree Pond, then on nearly the same course until we come to the road laid out by Mr. Josiah Robbins in the old Senebec Road."

These roads opened communication not only between all the inhabitants of Union, but with Barretts

Town, as Hope was then called; with Waldoborough; and with Warren, both on the east and the west sides of Seven-tree Pond. They were all laid out during the year after the incorporation of the town.

CONDITION OF THE ROADS.

For several years, the roads, though laid out, could have been of but little value. In 1789, and even later, there were in reality none but winter roads. When William Hart and wife moved here in October, 1793, the summer roads were almost impassable with ox-carts. On one side might be a stump in the track, on the other side a hole two or three feet deep, and possibly between them a large stone. There was but little travel. The only sleigh seen by Mrs. Hart during the winter after her arrival was owned by David Robbins.

CORDUROY ROADS. — Small logs were laid across wet and muddy places; and sometimes earth — if it could be conveniently procured, which at first was seldom the case — was thrown on to fill the interstices. These, from their resemblance to the thick-ribbed cotton-fabric, corduroy, were often called corduroy roads. Sometimes the logs were crooked, and would not fit compactly. Parts would rot, and then there would be dangerous holes. Travelling over such roads was not altogether agreeable, particularly in wagons without springs, the only kind then used by the very few persons who had any. Sometimes these roads extended a mile or two. As the wagon-wheels rolled over each log, from eight to fifteen or twenty inches in diameter, they struck with force upon the next, and so onward through the whole distance; affording more exercise than was coveted by men whose fortune it was to fell the trees of the forest before they could have room to raise bread for subsistence.

BOATING AND VISITING. — Among the early settlers, the travel and transportation were mainly by water; and, in the management of boats, several of the women became quite as dexterous as the men. If a person wished to cross Seven-tree Pond, Mrs. Mero could paddle him over with the skill of a ferryman. Perhaps Mrs. Matthias Hawes wanted to visit her neighbors; and, in those days, all were neighbors, though two or three miles distant. Immediately after dinner, which was as early as noon, she took one or two of her youngest children, perhaps asked Mrs. Ware or Mrs. Adams to go with her, got into a boat, paddled it through Round Pond, passed the rocks and shoals near the Lower Bridge, and landed on the shore of Seven-tree Pond, near the place of her destination. After spending the afternoon in knitting or sewing, and beguiling some of the solitary hours, of which there were many in the new settlement, she partook of an early supper, and returned with her company in season to get supper for her husband and his hired men, if he had any, and to "do the milking and other chores before dark." In this way, social intercourse was, for a time, maintained; and it was customary, till the population became considerably large, for every family to visit every other family in town, at least once a year.

Ox Sleds. — As the roads became better, intercourse was generally kept up in winter by means of sleds, drawn by oxen. For some time, Amariah Mero's horse was the only one in town. Matthias Hawes had a steer, which he trained from a calf to move quickly. With a yoke and a light sled made for the purpose, the steer travelled at a pretty brisk trot, a little to the envy of some of the neighbors, whose heavy sleds were drawn by sluggish oxen. Sleds were used in summer as well as in winter. It was long before carts were substituted. When they became common, the mode of carrying boards to Warren was to bind them on the axletree of the cart, and let the rear-end drag in the dirt. But few farmers could then purchase wagons, because they cost so much.

Teaming to Neighboring Towns. — Mr. Olney Titus thinks that Amariah Mero, in 1793, drove the first team which went to Warren with wheels. David

Robbins was the first person who went to Waldoborough with wheels. The household effects of the Rev. Mr. Humphrey were moved by him to Union in an ox-wagon. Nathaniel Robbins, Esq., was the first to drive an ox-cart into Washington. The team went to the Medomac River, and Robbins camped there over night, under a large yellow birch. The second day, by working hard and cutting and laying alders for the oxen to walk on, he got through the bog-swamp to what was called the Lakin Farm.

For a long time, the travel between Union and Warren came up on the east side of the river, but went down on the west side and crossed at Libbey's Bridge.

CHAPTER XXXI.

HIGHWAYS.

(*Concluded.*)

Surveyors and Commissioners. — Taxes. — Compensation. — Time for doing the Work. — Breaking Roads in Winter. — Comparative Value of Money and Labor.

SURVEYORS AND COMMISSIONERS.

THE work on roads is generally done under the superintendence of surveyors, chosen annually in the spring. Each surveyor notifies the inhabitants in his district of the time to begin work, designates the places where the roads are to be repaired, the kind and amount of work to be laid out at the different places, keeps the accounts with the workmen, and withholds pay in cases of negligence and idleness. The management of these officers, however, has not always been satisfactory. Sometimes they have been accused of expending too much of the labor in the vicinity of their own houses and farms, and of permitting the remote parts of the districts to suffer. With a view to obviate the evil, the town voted, April 1, 1833, "that the selectmen appoint surveyors of the highways the present year;" but the vote was reconsidered at an adjourned meeting, April 15, and surveyors were chosen as before. The excitement on the subject increased; and at the town-meeting, April 6, 1835, it led to serious and animated discussion. The meeting was adjourned to April 8, and again to April 15. It was agreed to choose commissioners, and to raise $2,500, and put the whole money at their disposal. The commissioners chosen were John Payson, Elisha Harding, Nathan Hills, and Nathan Bachelder. In 1836, they were John Payson, Nathan Bachelder, Cyrus Robbins, Herman Hawes, and John Gowen. In 1837, they were John Lermond, Herman Hawes, Aaron Bryant, Nathaniel Bachelor, and Noah Rice. The subject was again brought up the next year; but the town chose surveyors in 1838 and 1839. After the vote for choosing surveyors had passed in 1840, it was reconsidered, and the inhabitants chose five commissioners, viz. John Payson, Marlboro' Packard, Samuel Stone, Nathan Bachelder, and Stephen Carriel. Their pay was "$12\frac{1}{2}$ cents per hour for their labor and services." In 1841, the commissioners were E. Lermond, Marlboro' Packard, jun., Elias Skidmore, Mace Shepard, and Willard Robbins. Commissioners were not again chosen till 1844, when the town elected Samuel Stone, Leonard Barnard, Jason Davis, Nelson Cutler, and Joseph M. Gleason. In 1846, they were Joseph M. Gleason, John Lindley, Jason Davis, Lewis Bachelder, and Jeruel Butler. In 1845, it was "voted that the selectmen be highway-surveyors for the ensuing year, and that they appoint one man in each highway-district to keep a correct account of the labor done in said district."

HIGHWAY TAXES.

The following statement is the best which it has been practicable to make, after a careful examination of records, sometimes obscure and confused: —

HIGHWAY TAXES.

1787, £80	1803, $1000	1819, $1500	1835, $2500
1788, £110	1804, $1075‡	1820, $1500	1836, $2000
1789, £100	1805, $1500	1821, $1200	1837, $2500
1790, £80	1806, $1500	1822, $1500	1838, $2000¶
1791, £60	1807, $1500	1823, $1800	1839, $2500
1792, £80	1808, $2000	1824, $2000	1840, $2500¶
1793, £80	1809, $1500	1825, $1800	1841, $2000
1794, — *	1810, $1500	1826, $2000	1842, $2000
1795, £50	1811, $1000	1827, $1700	1843, $2500
1796, $300	1812, $1000	1828, $2000	1844, $3000
1797, $400	1813, $1200	1829, $2800	1845, $2500
1798, $400†	1814, $1500	1830, $2150§	1846, $3000
1799, $600	1815, $1500	1831, $2400	1847, $2000
1800, $700	1816, $1500	1832, $2100	1848, $2500
1801, $800	1817, $1500	1833, $2550	1849, $2500
1802, $800	1818, $1600	1834, $2000‖	1850, $2500

* "April 7, £80 to be worked out on the ways for 1795.... Sept. 1, 1794, £20 additional, so as to use £20 cash granted by the General Court to finish the meeting-house.... April 6, 1795, voted to reconsider the vote passed last April respecting highway-taxes." See also pages 148 and 263. How much was raised this year?

† Also "voted to consider Capt. John Tobey, 'in the loss of an ox at work on the highway,' six dollars and fifty cents, which is to be allowed him out of the first taxes to be made against him." In the same year, May 30, upon an article to see what the town will do respecting an action commenced by David Fales, Esq., against Moses Hawes and Amariah Mero, for surveying the county-roads from Warren to Senebec, it was voted "that Amariah Mero go and get advice respecting the suit;" and "that he be directed to act according to his best judgment in the business, as he thinks shall be most for the interest of the town." Sept. 10, "voted to choose a man to go to Waldoborough, to see Silas Lee, Esq., attorney-at-law, on the business of the suit.... Chose Mr. Amariah Mero, with instructions to do the best he can in behalf of the town."

‡ Also one hundred and twenty-five dollars to repair highways, and build a bridge over Capt. Maxcy's mill-stream. Part of the appropriations for highway-taxes in other years went to build bridges. For other remarks on appropriations, see next chapter.

§ The selectmen's report in April, 1830, has the item "Fines for repairing roads, one hundred and fourteen dollars eighty cents."

‖ Also voted to raise three hundred dollars in money, to be laid out under the direction of the selectmen. Also July 5, voted to raise one thousand dollars in money, "to be expended in building and repairing highways the present season, and to pay damages on new roads and pay costs of county-commissioners, &c." Also voted, July 5, to raise two hundred dollars, in addition to the one thousand "to be expended in the same way under the selectmen." Also July 13, 1835, voted to raise seven hundred dollars, "to be expended in labor on the roads."

¶ "In labor and materials."

HIGHWAYS.

Respecting the preceding sums, it may be observed, that, in some years, a part of the highway-taxes was expended under the direction of the selectmen; the object being to provide for injuries from freshets and other causes. It was thus with two hundred dollars of the highway-tax of 1821, with three hundred dollars of that of 1822, with two hundred dollars of that of 1824, and with three hundred dollars of that of 1825.

Sometimes part of the highway-tax was in money, and laid out according to the directions of the selectmen. This was the case with two hundred dollars of the tax of 1829, one hundred and fifty dollars in 1830, with two hundred or four hundred dollars in 1831, five hundred dollars in 1832, five hundred and fifty dollars in 1833, &c.

Sometimes a specified sum has been voted for a particular purpose. To the four hundred dollars in 1797, a hundred dollars was added "for the benefit of new roads, to be apportioned by the assessors." In April, 1817, in addition to the one thousand five hundred dollars, fifty dollars was raised, "to be expended on the highway near Thomas Hemenway's;" and, in 1818, in addition to the one thousand six hundred dollars, sixty dollars were raised "to be laid out on the road from Quiggle's Mill to Camden Line." In 1848, one thousand dollars was raised to meet a road from Waldoborough, and some other expenses, besides the two thousand five hundred dollars raised in the spring of the same year.

COMPENSATION.

This has been reckoned by the day or by the hour. In April, 1798, it was voted "that eight hours should be considered a day." The town-records are not always explicit; but, with the exceptions elsewhere mentioned, the compensation was probably as follows: —

MAN'S WORK. — From 1787 to 1789 inclusive, and in 1796, five shillings; and from 1790 to 1793, and probably in 1794 and 1795, four shillings a day. In 1815, one shilling, or 16⅔ cents an hour. In all the other years, one dollar for a day of eight hours, or in that proportion. " Men, when carried out of their districts, to be paid for going and returning," according to a vote passed in 1825.

YOKE OF OXEN. — In 1787 and 1790, 2s. 6d.; in 1791, 1792, 1793, and probably in 1794 and 1795, 2s. 8d; in 1788 and 1799, three shillings; and, in 1796, fifty-eight cents a day. From 1797 to 1814, and from 1816 to 1821, and in 1829, it was one-twelfth of a dollar an hour; and from 1822 to 1828, and from 1830 to 1836, it appears to have been ten cents an hour. In 1815, also in 1837 and since, twelve and a half cents an hour.

PLOUGHS. — In 1788, and subsequently, two shillings a day. In 1796 and 1797, two-thirds of a dollar; from 1798 to 1822, in 1829, from 1831 to 1836, and from 1838 to 1840, one dollar a day, or twelve and a half cents an hour, for large, and proportionally for small ploughs. From 1824 to 1830, and in 1837, 1841, and 1846, the compensation was left to the decision of the surveyors or road-commissioners.

Nov. 15, 1837, it was voted that Elias Skidmore and E. Lermond should be paid for ploughs purchased for the use of the town. April 20, 1844, the road-commissioners were authorized to purchase ploughs, to be kept in their possession during the year. June 7, 1846, it was voted to accept of three ploughs, bought by the commissioners.

CARTS. — In 1787, one shilling a day; in 1790, 1s. 6d.; in all other years, two shillings, or one-third of a dollar, except from 1824 to 1828, and in 1837, when the compensation depended on the decision of the surveyors or commissioners.

SCRAPERS. — There is no early mention of scrapers, though they were used. In 1837, the road-commissioners were to allow "for ploughs, carts, scrapers, and other materials, what they see fit." In 1841 and in 1846, the allowance was fifty cents a day.

TIME FOR DOING THE WORK.

The usual time for working on the roads is in June, after the farmers " have done planting," and in September, after they have harvested their grain. Occasionally, the town designates the time. May 30, 1787, the record, after assigning to the selectmen the business of dividing the highways for the surveyors, and proportioning the inhabitants, adds, " as the inhabitants think it highly necessary there should be work in the ways immediately." In 1796, it was " voted that the highway-work be done before the first of October." May 27, 1801, to meet the case of delinquents, the surveyors were " empowered to collect the taxes the same as other collectors." April 4, 1803, and April 2, 1804, the assessors were " directed to issue warrants to the surveyors to collect the highway-taxes when they are not worked out." To hold out further inducements for seasonable labor, it was ordered in 1815, that, before July 10, man's labor should be one shilling, and oxen's twelve and a half cents, per hour; but, after that time, the pay for men should be twelve and a half cents, and for oxen as in previous years. In 1816, it was twelve cents for a man before July 1 ; but, between that time and Oct. 1, ten cents. It was the same in 1819, excepting the substitution of Oct. 1 for July 1. In 1820 and 1821, it was ninepence before July 10, and sevenpence afterward.

BREAKING ROADS IN WINTER.

For many years, the roads, after drifting storms, were broken out by voluntary labor. The inhabitants of a highway-district turned out, with oxen, sleds, shovels, as soon as the storm ceased. Each man began at his own door, drove his team, shovelled through the deep drifts, and worked his way towa ' his neighbor. Ere long, neighbors would thus meet, and small gangs be at work in different parts of the district. As the gangs met, they would unite and work onward together.

The interest felt in this mode of breaking the roads gradually subsided.

March 1, 1813, "Voted the highway-surveyors' warrants shall be drawn in such a manner as to authorize them to keep the roads passable in the winter, as well as the other seasons. . . . April 1, 1822, voted that the highway-surveyors shall cause the snow to be trod down or removed from the roads in their several districts, so that the same shall be passable; and they to present their accounts to the selectmen for allowance, and the amount to go towards next year's tax. Men and oxen are to have eight cents per hour. . . . Nov. 1, 1824, voted that the surveyors of highways allow ten cents per hour for men and for oxen [to break roads the ensuing winter]. . . . May 11, 1833, voted that the overwork on the highway, and the expense of breaking roads in the winter, be returned to the assessors by the surveyors before the highway-taxes are made the present year, and that they who have done this work have the same credited to their highway-taxes for the present year. . . . Sept. 9, voted that the highway-surveyors be authorized to employ men and oxen to keep the roads open in the several districts, on the best terms that they can for the town, and present their bills with sufficient vouchers to the selectmen before the next April meeting. . . . April, 1836, voted that all those who are deficient in working their highway-tax on the last year's bills have credit for the last winter's work on said bills.[1] . . . Voted[2] to pay for the breaking the roads the last winter in money. . . . Nov. 29, 1838, voted that the selectmen appoint in each highway-district, as they may see fit, a suitable person to keep the roads open the ensuing winter; and such person shall keep a perfect list of the work, and return it to the selectmen; and that each sum shall be paid in cash, allowing men ten cents, and oxen twelve and a half cents, per hour. . . . Nov. 2, 1840, voted that the roads be kept open as usual, and that men be allowed ten cents per hour, and oxen twelve and a half cents per hour, and be allowed on

---

[1] According to the record, the compensation seems to have been twelve and a half cents an hour for oxen, and ten cents for men.

[2] This vote probably had reference to the cases which were not delinquent in the tax of 1835. When the two thousand five hundred dollars was raised, April 15, 1837, it was to be appropriated for the highways the present year, and breaking roads the past winter.

their money-tax 1841. . . . April 17, 1843, voted that the highway-surveyors procure such men to break out the roads the ensuing winter as are willing to have it allowed on their next year's highway-tax, and be allowed the same per hour as in the summer season." [The same principle was again adopted April 1, 1844, and in 1845 and 1846, and at the same price, viz.] "twelve and a half cents an hour for men and for oxen."

The sums annually expended in breaking roads have been very unequal, depending on the depth of the snows and the extent of the drifting. In one winter, the cost of keeping the roads open was perhaps one thousand dollars; while in others it has been comparatively nothing. From the details given, it is evident that there have been many difficulties, and that almost every year a new method has been tried.

COMPARATIVE VALUE OF MONEY AND LABOR.

In regard to the comparative value of the money and the labor, it may be remarked that it is different in different seasons of the year. The sums raised, and the pay for labor, have always been greater than if the same had been in specie. In 1836, it was voted that "twenty-five per cent from the highway-tax should be allowed, if the tax was paid in money by the 20th of June." In 1836, in addition to the two thousand dollars, there was raised in money five hundred and fifty dollars, to defray the expense of breaking out the roads during the preceding winter; and it was "voted that those who receive the money make twenty-five per cent discount on their accounts." In 1837, it was voted to allow on the two thousand five hundred dollars, "twenty-five cents on a dollar to those who pay the money on demand." Nov. 29 of the same year, it was "voted to pay in cash ten cents an hour for a man, and twelve cents an hour for oxen, for breaking out roads." In 1843, it was "voted to pay four shillings on a dollar on such bills as have been or shall be handed in by the surveyors [for breaking roads the preceding winter]. The persons in whose favor the bills are, shall make oath of the truth of the bill." In 1844, there was a substitute of "two-thirds in cash for all those who chose to pay money in lieu of highway-work." For specie, persons can always be found to work out a highway-tax for one-half or two-thirds of the nominal amount.

CHAPTER XXXII.

BRIDGES.

Log Bridges. — Lower, or True's Bridge. — Middle Bridge, at Bachelor's Mills. — South Union Bridge. — Upper Bridge, at Hills' Mills. — Report on Bridges in 1805. — Appropriations.

LOG BRIDGES.

In Union, as in other new towns, it was common to build bridges, particularly short bridges, by laying small logs in close proximity across large logs, which were extended over the streams. This practice continues in some degree to the present day.

LOWER, OR TRUE'S BRIDGE.

It may be remembered, that the petition for an Act of Incorporation, dated Sept. 12, 1786, contains the request that the State-tax which had been apportioned to Stirlington might be laid out "in defraying charges of a bridge, now a building, of one hundred and ten feet long, and in opening and making roads and building another bridge of one hundred and seventy feet long; which bridge must be built before there will be any passing by land or water to or from this place." Some progress, it seems, had been made. April 2, 1787, the question was brought forward " to see if the town means to purchase the bridge now building at the head of Seven-tree Pond, or allow what has been done by individuals on said bridge towards their work on the ways the year ensuing;" and the latter alternative was adopted.

This was the first bridge built by the town. It was probably rebuilt in 1801; for, April 6, it was " voted to build a bridge across the river near Rufus Gillmor's;" and Nathaniel Robbins, Amariah Mero, and Rufus Gillmor, were chosen the committee to superintend it. At the same time, it was "voted that fifty dollars be granted, to be paid in cash for said bridge, and that two hundred dollars be deducted from the highway-tax by the assessors." Dec. 2, 1811, at auction, the furnishing of two thousand five hundred feet of pine plank, four inches thick and eighteen feet long, was bid off by Reuben Hills, to be delivered at this bridge for $15.75 per thousand. The bridge was repaired in 1819 or 1820, and again in 1831 and in 1841. " The first mud-sills were of green oak, cut on Josiah Robbins's farm just below the burying-ground. They were hewed on two sides, and put in with the bark on; and a few years ago, when the bridge was rebuilt, these same mud-sills were found perfectly sound and green, having always been kept underwater."[1]

MIDDLE BRIDGE, AT BACHELOR'S MILLS.

May 28, 1788, it was voted to build two bridges; one across the main river by Mr. John Butler's, the other across Crawford's River at South Union. From the records it appears that the Middle Bridge was rebuilt in 1800, when it is described as " the bridge near Capt. George West's." At that time, Amariah Mero was " chosen as a suitable person to superintend the building." Nov. 3, 1800, " Voted that Mr. Amariah Mero have an order for enough to pay his taxes in Mr. Mitchell's bill toward his superintending the bridge." A freshet carried away the bridge in less than ten years. May 7, 1810, an article was introduced into the town-meeting —

[1] MS. communications of A. C. Robbins, Esq.

MIDDLE BRIDGE.   289

"To see if the town will provide materials for rebuilding the bridge over St. George's River at the Lower Mills, in Union, and order the two districts adjoining to do the labor. . . . Voted that sixty dollars be drawn in labor from such highway-district, and in such proportion as the assessors may think proper." [A temporary bridge was erected.] Nov. 19, " Voted to build a bridge over the river near Nathaniel Bachelor's, and that it should be built in the following way and manner, viz. that there should be two king-posts with four braces in each, with a beam across the top with two braces, and a timber across the underside of the string-pieces and strapped to the foot of the king-posts with bars of iron and bolts of the same; and that there should be five string-pieces fifty-two feet long, and planked with pine plank twenty feet long and four inches thick, and be railed; and that the highway-district on the west side of the river should build a good and sufficient butment to receive the end of the bridge; and the district on the east side of the river should do the work of putting on the bridge, and finish the same in a workmanlike manner; and the town voted to procure the materials for building the said bridge and deliver them on the premises by the first of March next. Voted to set up the different articles to the lowest bidder, as follows, viz.: —

"Five string-pieces, fifty-two feet long, fourteen inches thick, — bid off by John Butler for five dollars each. Two hundred feet of square timber of the following size, — bid off by Reuben Hills for six dollars. Two posts 12 by 14, twenty-five feet long; four braces 10 by 10, thirty feet long; four braces 10 by 10, twenty feet long; one beam 10 by 10, twenty-two feet long; one sill 12 by 12, twenty-two feet long; two hundred feet of joist for railing, four inches one way, and five the other, — bid off by Samuel Hills for $1.75. A thousand and forty feet of planks, twenty feet long and four inches thick, — bid off by Jonathan Eastman for $17.75. All the timber and planks for the above bridge to be prime and of a good quality."

Nathaniel Robbins, Nathaniel Bachelor, and Joseph Vaughan, were chosen a committee to receive the above materials and procure the irons.

In April, 1840, the selectmen were made a committee to survey the road, and examine the state of the bridge. When their report was made, Nov. 2, John W. Lindley, Nathan Bachelder, and Ebenezer Alden, were chosen a committee to make a plan and estimate the expense, and were also instructed to build the western end of it as far north as the laying out of the road would admit. They were further "authorized to remove all obstructions that were in the way, before the builders commenced building the same." The building of the bridge was to be put up at auction to the lowest bidder, and to be completed by the first day of the following October. In April, 1841, there was a reconsideration "so far as to build said bridge across the stream, without interfering with the buildings on either side of the road." The job was taken by Nathan Hills. In April, 1842, when the question of acceptance was brought up, the selectmen were made a "committee to examine the plan and ascertain whether said bridge was built according thereto." They made their report Aug. 27, and it was accepted "on condition that Nathan Hills shall pay all damages that may arise in consequence of the old stringer being put in on the upper side, and give bonds to that effect."

SOUTH UNION BRIDGE.

The other bridge ordered, May 28, 1788, to be built at South Union, continued in use about sixteen years. It was supported in the middle by one pier, and built nearly east and west upon the ledge below the present bridge, or a little below the position now occupied by the mill-dam. April 2, 1804, it was "not safe;" and Josiah Robbins, David Robbins, Matthias Hawes, Amariah Mero, and Nathan Blake, were chosen a committee to view the ground, and consider whether it will be best to rebuild or repair the old bridge. Twelve hundred dollars were raised for highways and the bridge.

"May 14, voted to build a hundred and twenty feet bridge, by the last day of September, 1805, provided the district build the abutments; and to accept the written motion for building the bridge, expressed in manner following, viz.:

Posts twelve inches square, if made of pine; cap-pieces the same; three posts to each pier; five tier of string-pieces twelve inches square, to be covered with pine plank 18 feet long and three inches thick; braces five by six inches square, and two to each pier, five piers; mud sills, 12 inches or more, and railed in a workmanlike manner and braced upon each pier, and one between each pier upon each side. The undertaker to be entitled to his pay in the month of September, 1805, if the bridge is then completed to the acceptance of the selectmen."

It was put up at auction, and bid off by Christopher Butler, at ninety-seven dollars. This was the first time that the bridge was built nearly north and south. It was again rebuilt in 1823 by Capt. Noah Rice. Oct. 25, 1841, there was a vote to rebuild the bridge, by Joseph Vaughan's, twenty-four feet wide. The selectmen were chosen the committee to superintend it, and it was "voted that the building of said bridge be left discretionary with" them.

UPPER BRIDGE, AT HILLS' MILLS.

There was a log-bridge at Hills' Mills, above the present bridge, before any other was built. The first movement by the town was probably June 7, 1802, when it was proposed "to build a bridge across George's River, near the foot of Sennebec Pond." The selectmen were instructed "to view the place, estimate the length," &c. When they made their report, Aug. 28, it was voted to build "across the river near the proposed mills, between Mr. Nathan Blake's and Mr. Reuben Hills's, as the selectmen report," in the course of the next summer. Nathaniel Robbins took the job, to complete it in fifteen months, for $200. The selectmen for the time being were to see that it was "built in due order, and similar to the [Lower] Bridge near John Mero's and Joseph Vaughan's."

In December, 1811, Reuben Hills agreed for $16 per thousand to furnish 1,500 pine plank, four inches thick and eighteen feet long, to be used on the bridge near his mills. This bridge was carried away by a freshet; and, June 19, 1813, it was voted to build another. Henry Blunt, John Lermond, and Micajah Gleason, were chosen a committee to "examine the different places and the conditions on which they can procure the land," &c. Upon their making a report, Sept. 6, 1813, it was voted to build one on the spot where the old one stood, but to postpone the further consideration of the article until the next town-meeting. March 7, 1814, Amariah Mero, John Tobey, Daniel Shepard, Joseph Morse, and Herman Hawes, were chosen a committee to examine the situation, "and to make report to the town as soon as may be." The bridge was built several rods below the old one. This occasioned the circuitous route now travelled in order to cross the river.

July 4, 1820, the town was called on "to hear the report of the committee on the bridge near Walter Blake's... Voted to build a bridge across St. George's river, at or near the north line of Reuben Hills's land, and on the south line of Lewis Robbins's land, unless the selectmen can make an agreement with Reuben Hills and others more to the advantage of the town." This would have been to place a bridge where the one stood originally. But it seems that a favorable agreement was made; for the bridge was built where the one was erected in 1814. This was carried away by a freshet; and, May 21, 1831, another was voted. June 11, 1832, the selectmen were authorized to contract for it at a sum not exceeding two hundred dollars. It was built by Nathan Hills for $150. In 1848 it was broken down and again rebuilt.

REPORT ON BRIDGES.

April 1, 1805, the selectmen were directed to view the bridges, and see what proportion of them ought to be considered as town-bridges. Their report, made May 15, assigns to the town the bridge by Mr. Blake's, or the Upper Bridge, two hundred and twenty-three feet, and thirty-eight feet abutments; by John Lermond's saw-mill twenty-five feet, and thirty-five feet abutments and causeway; by Sterling Davis's saw-mill twenty feet, forty feet abutment and causeway; by Capt. Barrett's saw-mill, or the Middle Bridge, forty-five feet, and forty-five feet abutment; by Medomac River fifty feet, and abutment and causeway fifty feet; by Joseph Vaughan's [he then lived near the Lower Bridge] two hundred feet, abutment and causeway eighty feet; by Jason Ware forty feet, abutment and causeway eighty feet; by the meeting-house, on the brook east of the Common, twelve feet, abutment and causeway one hundred feet; by Mr. Quiggle's, in the easterly part of the town and northwardly of Lermond's, twelve feet, abutment and causeway one hundred and eighty feet; by Samuel Hills, near Warren, on the east side of the pond, one hundred and fifty feet, abutment and causeway one hundred and thirty feet; by Capt. Maxcy's one hundred feet, abutment forty feet; by Mr. Rogers's [Bowker Brook] twenty feet, abutment and causeway one hundred feet."

APPROPRIATIONS.

Some appropriations for bridges previously to this time were not recorded. Probably the accounts were burnt in 1837. The records do not always give explicit information how bridges were paid for. The inference is that sometimes it was in money, at other times in labor; that sometimes the town, at other times the highway-districts to which a bridge belonged, paid for it either entirely or in part. Still, from what has been stated, enough may be learned as to the nature of the work, and the materials which have been used.

CHAPTER XXXIII.

EDUCATIONAL HISTORY.

Earliest Schools and Teachers. — Schools at a later Period. — School-children in Summer. — Drink. — Recess. — Josiah. — Complaints and Punishments. — Girls' Work in School. — Reading. — Spelling. — Noontime and Dinners. — Winter Schools. — Severer Punishments. — Intermissions in Winter. — Studies. — Evening Schools.

SCHOOLS.

Soon after the first marriage of Jessa Robbins, his wife taught the first school in town. It was kept in his log-house, about ten feet back of the present house. Her compensation was two shillings a week; she boarding herself, and providing a room for the school. There was an agreement with the parents that the scholars should assist her in doing house-work, and render any other services she might require. The school was very small. It was kept about the years 1785 and 1786. Not far from the same time, probably the next summer, Eunice Adams, from Franklin, Mass., began a private school in the log-house of David Robbins. The school was moved from house to house, that it might be continued longer, and that the several scholars might be accommodated. In the year 1788, or thereabouts, Ebenezer Jennison taught school in Moses Hawes's log-house, which had two rooms. This probably was the first "man's school" in town; unless, as some think, one may have been previously taught by Dr. Bernard. A school was taught in the barns of Philip Robbins and David Robbins, about the year 1788. There was a "school-ma'am," as the female teacher was called, from Warren. These were the earliest educational movements. They were made while the inhabitants were few and poor. The literary standard must have been low; for it was low throughout the land. There were no books suitable for common schools; and those in use were scarce and dear. Teachers did not understand the science of education. But these humble movements of the fathers of the town were highly praiseworthy.

It was several years before the common schools were in successful operation. Pass over their history for the succeeding quarter of a century. Imagine a bright summer morning, say thirty-five or forty years ago. The prospect is that the day will be very warm. The children, all barefoot, the boys wearing nothing but chip-hats, shirts, and pantaloons supported by knit suspenders, go from home about eight o'clock. They carry in one hand a basket or glittering tin-pail; and in the other, a rose, a piony, a marigold, white lilies, or a bunch of flowers strongly scented with tansy. Part of the flowers are for the schoolmistress. They proceed leisurely, looking at objects which interest them. They make bows or courtesies to every man and woman they meet. Perhaps they are an hour in going a mile. Near the junction of two or more roads stands the old school-house. It is a square building, one story high; the roof from the four sides meeting in a common centre, and sloping barely enough to carry off the rain. No part of it has ever been touched with paint, except a patch about as large as a hat, which was daubed red one day by a painter's rude boy when passing. The board-shutters are thrown back; and against some of them are placed long poles, or rails taken out of the fence. The lower part of the windows and the doors are wide open. At a distance the high-pitched voice of some one reading is heard, and the teacher is prompting and correcting him. The school is begun. They enter, " making their manners " as they go in, hasten to the closet to put away their chip-hats and cape-bonnets, and then take their places; while the whole school, except the very small children, are reading two verses apiece in the Bible. This being over, they go to their seats. Perhaps some take Webster's Spelling Book or Third Part, or the Art of Reading, or the Columbian Orator, and try to learn their lessons. A murmuring sound pervades the room; and the mistress, while hearing a class recite, tells the school "not to study so loud." The grave monotony is soon broken by a boy, who rises and calls to the mistress across the room, " Please, ma'am, m'I g'out?" If leave is granted, he hurries down the hill to the spring, and drinks at the half-hogshead. Schoolboys are always "dry." At half-past ten, the scholars have read " once round " in their respective classes, and it is time for the recess.

" The boys may go out." They go out as fast as they dare; each one, as he gets near the door, tossing off a bow over his shoulder. All make a rush for the spring. There is no tin-cup. As many as can, kneel around the half-hogshead, and, applying their mouths, drink; while others attempt to pacify their thirst by scooping up the water in the hollow of the hand, or stopping it with the hand, and drinking from the spout. When they have done drinking, some plunge their heads into the water, even to their necks; and, in a few minutes, the flowing spring is as clear as if it had not been disturbed. Then up the hill, on the run, all go to the school-house; and, by the time they arrive, they are about as thirsty as when they went down to drink. In seven or eight minutes, the mistress raps with her rule on the window. It is the signal for them to go in. One boy near the door enters first. Shortly comes a second, and then a third. And now they pour in, bobbing or jerking their heads, instead of making graceful bows. " The girls may go out," says the teacher. They too drink, perhaps comb their hair into fanciful forms, and in a few minutes return. A busy hum succeeds.

Occasionally there is an interruption. James rises in his seat, and says, " Please, ma'am, Josiah keeps pinching and pricking me." Josiah, a mischievous but not malevolent boy, eight or nine years old, very composed when called out for a misdemeanor, has already received several *marks*, not very heavy, however, of the teacher's displeasure. " Josiah, come out here," says the teacher. The boy advances to the open floor. "Josiah, I have a great deal of trouble with you: I do not know what I shall do with you." The lad looks up, a little anxious, but still quite calm and composed. "I must ferule you, Josiah. It makes my heart ache to do it. But I see no other way to make you mind. How many blows do you think I ought to give you?" Josiah, becoming a little more anxious, and wishing to make as favorable a trade as he can with the teacher,— unwilling to set the number either too high lest he should receive too many, or too low lest no attention would be given to his words,— waits a few moments, while the mistress is endeavoring to humble him by an awful suspense. At length he looks up a little sheepishly, and says to her, " I guess about three."

Sometimes a long stick, with the leaves left on the end that they may rustle, is extended, and shaken towards an offender. Perhaps he is not allowed to go out at the next recess. The top of a quill is cut off, the feathers stripped, and his ears or forehead are snapped with it. Sometimes it is split, and put astride the nose. A long string is tied around his ear, and he is required to wear it " all noontime." The thimbled finger is snapped on the forehead. One offender must stand in the middle of the floor, or take his seat there on a stone. Another is tortured by being required to press his back against the side of the house and squat down, thus " sitting on nothing," or by keeping his forefinger on a nail in the floor, and thus becoming almost crazy through the rush of blood into the head. Perhaps the mistress stows away a little offender under her desk; and, ere long, the other scholars espy him peeping out to see what is going on. And then, perhaps, he is ordered into the dark closet; the door being kindly left open a very little, so that he may not be in total darkness.

In the meantime, the school-exercises are conducted as well as can be expected. The mistress helps the girls to fit their patchwork, and take up the stitches in their knitting, and renders important aid in that necessary feat of every girl, — the working of a sampler. Notwithstanding these interruptions to the studies, the girls, by some peculiar tact, learn as fast as the boys, who give their whole time to them, and as often as otherwise are above them in the class.

A class is called out to read. Boys and girls come out and take their places promiscuously. There you see two girls, cronies, who happen to stand side by side. They have hold of each other's hands, and are swinging them backwards and forwards. The teacher says to the class, "Stand in a straight line." Each pupil looks at his toes, and puts the ends of them just at the edge of the long crack in the floor. "Attend." All hands are dropped, the forefinger being retained at the place in the book where the lesson commences. "Begin." Bows and courtesies are simultaneously made along the whole line, and the books are raised and opened. The child at the head of the class reads a short paragraph, and then the word "next" from the teacher is a signal for the next in order to commence. "Speak up loud." A hale little fellow thereupon squeaks up his voice to the highest pitch, and ekes out, drawlingly and at long intervals, one word after another, till his portion is ended. Thus the work goes on till the reading is done.

"Shut up your books and spell." No sooner said than five or six at the head of the class spell the first five or six words in the column, before the teacher has time "to put them out." The teacher is not displeased with the incident, the children are consequently gratified, and afterward this mode of beginning is frequently repeated.

A hard word comes. A little ambitious, anxious, nervous girl fails to spell it. She tries again, and again fails. As she can try only twice, she begins, hurriedly and stammeringly, to recall her last attempt; but her teacher stops her, because "it would not be fair to let her try again," and calls on the next. The little girl, with eyes opened wide and a throbbing bosom, stretches forward her head to see if any one will spell it. As it passes along down the class, others also stretch out their necks. Finally, some one, a little more fortunate or who has studied the lesson a little better, spells it correctly. "Take your place." The speller, in a kind of childlike triumph, walks up above the one who first failed, and there places herself. The anxious girl feels mortified and humbled. A tear glistens in her eye; perhaps tears flow fast and freely. But no matter, she will "try harder" next time. The spelling goes on. After this is over, come questions in the abbreviations, or the punctuation, or the numerals, at the end of the book. Perhaps part of them are assigned as the closing exercise in the afternoon. But in all there is an eagerness to climb towards the head of the class.

It is "noontime." What a noise and tumult! The baskets and tin-pails are brought forward. And such a variety of contents! Doughnuts, cold sausages, bread and butter and cheese, pieces of pie, Indian bannocks, fried cakes, and a multitude of other eatables. Look there! one tin-pail contains bread and milk for dinner. The school-children swallow their food greedily, that they may have time to play.

Not altogether unlike these are the scenes in winter. And yet they differ. The older children, who are kept at home in summer to assist their fathers on the farm, or their mothers in making butter and cheese and in spinning, now come to the schoolmaster. Harder blows and heavier punishments are generally inflicted than in summer. And, in some cases, the punishments are inhuman. Possibly the ears are pulled till they are nearly started from the head, or they are cuffed; and thus sometimes is laid a foundation for deafness. A savage master throws a rule across the room, and hits a boy on the head. One of the older boys dislikes the master, and, on the way home, tells his playmates he is an old fool. A mischievous boy repeats the words to the master, who becomes enraged. The offender is marched out into the floor, and the ferule or the rod applied till the room rings with his screams, and then he is flogged again to be made to stop screaming; or he is told to step on a seat or chair, or on the steps to the teacher's desk, and for twenty minutes to hold a book at arm's length. It is a punishment which only a semi-barbarian would inflict. But few minutes elapse before he is unable to keep his arm extended. It flags, and a blow is struck on the elbow to straighten it. It soon flags again, in spite of all the boy can do to prevent it, and the savage master repeats his blows upon his writhing and crying pupil. It flags more and more. The master flies at him in a passion, and applies his broad, flat ferule furiously to the calves of his legs. Before the twenty minutes elapse, the boy is so exhausted that the master relents and sends him to his seat. The effects are felt for a long time. The boy's arm is so lame that he cannot raise it to his head. With his left hand he is obliged to pass his food to his mouth. Thus is wasted, and worse than wasted, a portion of the six hours which should have been given to instruction. The girls, too, have to share in the discipline; and those that are large are punished by being made to sit on the ends of the boys' seats, and expose their crimsoned faces to the whole school.

It is intermission, and there is snow. Of course there is snowballing in abundance. There are hand-sleds, and the boys slide down hill, carrying the little children in their laps. Boys and girls are dry. They make hard snowballs, bring them into the school-house, and, standing on tiptoe before the rousing fire, melt them against the high mantel-piece, letting the dropping water trickle down to their elbows. The school-room becomes wet in consequence of the running in and out, and the floor is dirty.

It is school-time, and no punishment is going on. Some are studying their parsing lessons in Pope's Essay on Man, the book almost universally used for learning grammar. Adams's, Walsh's, Welch's, and, for a very extraordinary "cipherer," Pike's Arithmetics, are recommended. A "smart scholar," after a few seasons, gets as far as the Single Rule of Three; and, if he gets through the Double Rule of Three, he is "something extra." There was in town one boy so "smart," that, before he was fifteen years old, he ciphered through Pike's large volume.

There were sometimes ciphering-schools in the evening, when the master met only those who wanted to cipher more than they could in school-hours; and there were also evening grammar-schools and evening spelling-schools. The lessons were announced previously. The pupils came together. Two prominent scholars were chosen captains, and they cast lots for first choice. This being settled, they chose alternately the different scholars, till all were taken up. A word was put out by the master. If it was missed, it was put to the other side. If the answer was then given correctly, the person whose answer was incorrect went over to the other party. After an hour or so, the captain, or the party which had the most scholars, was considered victorious. Sometimes the victory was decided by merely noting the number of errors made on either side. There were two or three such trials in an evening.

Such were some of the features of common schools, thirty-five or forty years ago. In summer they were continued perhaps ten weeks, and in the winter eight. Considering the improvements now made, how few persons will ever know the school-boy's or the school-girl's experience at the commencement of the nineteenth century!

CHAPTER XXXIV.

EDUCATIONAL HISTORY.

(*Concluded.*)

School Districts. — School-houses. — School Committees. — School Agents. — School Children. — School Money. — High Schools. — Lyceum. — Libraries.

SCHOOL DISTRICTS.

THERE was probably no division into school-districts before May 26, 1790, when "the town voted to be divided into squadrons or divisions for the benefit of schooling, and that David Woodcock, Joel Adams, and Moses Hawes, be a committee to divide said inhabitants." April 7, 1800, there was a favorable vote on an article, "to see if the town will order the selectmen to divide the school-squadron about Round Pond, &c., into two squadrons, agreeable to the request of a number of the inhabitants." Feb. 8, 1802, there was an unsuccessful attempt to "incorporate the squadron north of ... the Round Pond squadron to and with the said Round Pond squadron, and define the said district as is hereby requested of both squadrons," &c. Joseph Maxcy, Nathaniel Robbins, Matthias Hawes, Jonathan Newhall, Jonathan Carriel, Bela Robbins, and Nathan Blake, were chosen a committee, "one man out of each squadron, ... to fix the bounds of all the rest of the squadrons for schooling." Their report was made and accepted April 5; "only individuals who are aggrieved may apply for redress to a future meeting." The boundaries are on record. Various modifications were subsequently made or proposed, till Sept. 22, 1823; when a new division of the town was made, and the limits of the several districts again recorded. April 15, 1833, a committee was chosen to re-district the town, and report at the next annual meeting. The report has not been found, nor is there evidence on the town-records that any was made. There have been some changes; but, if the records are correct and full, there has been no general districting of the town since 1823.

SCHOOL-HOUSES.

The first school-house was built near the dwelling-house of Moses Hawes. This was probably in 1791, as a town-meeting was held in it Aug. 29 of that year. The next school-house was probably put up in 1791 or 1792; for, May 7, 1792, it was mentioned in a vote "to accept the road from Mr. Irish's to the school-house near Mr. Thomas Daggett's."

The records do not show how the expenses of building were met, except in one case. June 10, 1843, the warrant contained an article "to see if the town will order a sufficient sum of money to be raised by School District No. 4, in said town of Union, for the purpose of building a school-house in said town; and also to hear the opinion of the town upon the subject of a disagreement of the voters of said district. . . . Voted to raise two hundred dollars for the purpose of building a school-house in District No. 4." Generally, when a school-house is to be built, the district votes the amount required: it is assessed by the town-assessors on the inhabitants of the district, and the town-collector collects it.

SCHOOL COMMITTEES.

1795. Samuel Hills, Matthias Hawes, Moses Hawes.
1796. Moses Hawes, Josiah Maxcy, Matthias Hawes.
1797. Matthias Hawes, Joel Adams, Samuel Hills.
1798. Joel Adams, Samuel Daggett, Levi Morse.
1799. Joel Adams, Edward Jones, Waldron Stone, Moses Hawes, Amos Barrett.
1800. Stephen March, Esq., Dr. Jonathan Sibley, Capt. Joseph Maxcy, Edward Jones, Capt. Amos Barrett.
1801. Jonathan Sibley, Ebenezer Jennison, Stephen March, Moses Hawes, Daniel McCurdy.
1802. Jonathan Sibley, Ebenezer Jennison, Stephen March, Amos Barrett, Nathan Blake.
1803. Nathan Blake, Stephen March, Moses Hawes.

1804. Samuel Quiggle, Samuel Hills, Jonathan Sibley, Marlboro' Packard, Joel Adams, Jeremiah Mitchell, Jonathan Carriel, Nathan Blake.
1805 and 1806. (No record.)
1807. Josiah Maxcy, Robert Bunting, J. Warren Lindley, Nathan Blake, Joel Adams, Edward Jones, Henry Blunt, John Lermond, Henry Starrett.
1808. Josiah Maxcy, Robert Bunting, Noah Rice, Nathan Blake, Jason Ware, Jere. Mitchell, Pente Walcott, John Lermond, Wm. Starrett, Nathaniel Robbins.
1809. Edmund Mallard, John Little, Robert Bunting.
1810. William White, John Little, Charles Pope.
1811. William White, Henry True, Charles Pope, John Little, Jonathan Sibley. After this election, which was in March, a change was made ; and, in April, a committee-man for each district was chosen. — These were Micajah Gleason, Nathaniel Robbins, Noah Rice, Jonathan Sibley, Nathaniel Bachelor, Thomas Mitchell, jun., Jonathan Carriel, John Lermond, William Starrett.
1812—1814. (No record.)
1815. Major Robert Foster, John Little, Jonathan Sibley.
1816. Robert Foster, John Little, Jonathan Sibley.
1817. Henry True, Robert Foster, John Little.
1818. Henry True, Daniel F. Harding, John Bulfinch.
1819. Daniel F. Harding, John Bulfinch.
1820. Henry True, D. F. Harding, John Bulfinch.
1821. Henry True, D. F. Harding, Jonathan Sibley.
1822. Henry True, D. F. Harding, John Bulfinch, Elisha Harding, Jonathan Sibley.
1823. Daniel F. Harding, Elisha Harding, Henry True.
1824. Henry True, Daniel F. Harding, Jonathan Sibley.
1825. Henry True, Noyes P. Hawes, Elisha Harding.
1826. Henry True, Elisha Harding, Daniel F. Harding.
1827. Henry True, Elisha Harding, Daniel F. Harding.
1828. Henry True, Daniel F. Harding, John Bovee Dods.
1829. John B. Dods, Elisha Harding, Noah Bartlett.
1830. Elisha Harding, Daniel F. Harding, Josiah F. Day.
1831. Elisha Harding, Daniel F. Harding, Noah Bartlett.
1832. Daniel F. Harding, Thomas Gore, Oren Sikes.
1833. Elisha Harding, Daniel F. Harding, John S. Abbot.
1834. Elisha Harding, Daniel F. Harding, Josiah F. Day.
1835. Henry True, Amos Drake, Joel Adams.

SCHOOL AGENTS.

1836. Elisha Harding, Josiah F. Day, Peter Adams.
1837. Elisha Harding, Josiah F. Day, Peter Adams.
1838. Elisha Harding, Isaac Flitner, Nelson Cutler.
1839. Isaac Flitner, Elisha Harding, Joel Adams.
1840. Moses P. Webster, A. S. Dudley, Horatio Ilsley.
1841. Asa Messer, Robert Thompson, jun., Edward Hills.
1842. Robert Thompson, jun., Edward Hills, Asa Messer.
1843. Joshua S. Green, Amos Drake, Asa Messer.
1844. Joseph Irish, John Adams, Andrew Libbey.
1845. Elijah Vose, Joseph Irish, John Adams.
1846. Rev. F. W. Baxter, Rev. Samuel Bowker, Rev. M. R. Hopkins.
1847. Samuel Bowker, Joseph Irish, Perez B. Sayward.
1848. Joseph Irish, Albert Thurston, Robert Thompson, jr.
1849. Joseph Irish, John Adams, Seth M. Cushman.
1850. The Selectmen and Treasurer.

Since the separation of Maine from Massachusetts, there have been superintending school-committees and school-agents. The duties of superintending school-committees are to fill vacancies happening in their Board during the term of their office, to examine candidates for teaching, to direct the general course of instruction and designate the books to be used, to visit the schools, to dismiss unsuitable teachers, to expel refractory scholars, and to make to the selectmen, within fourteen days preceding the annual town-meeting, a return of the state of the schools.

SCHOOL AGENTS.

1820. Spencer Walcott, Herman Hawes, Marlboro' Packard, Walter Blake, Nathaniel Bachelor, John Walker, Henry Blunt, John Lermond, Fisher Hart, Samuel Hagar.
1821. Spencer Walcott, David Robbins, jun., Benjamin Litchfield, William Libbey, Matthias Hawes, Nathan D. Rice, Joseph Morse, Henry Fossett, Joseph Miller, Moses Morse.
1822. Joseph Vaughan,[1] David Robbins, jun., Benjamin Litchfield, Oliver Pratt, Ebenezer W. Adams, Thomas Mitchell, Jonathan Carriel, jun., Robert Foster, Obadiah Gardner.

[1] Some members of the family spell the word Vaughn without the *a*.

1823. Amos Walker, David Robbins, jun., John W. Lindley, Nathan Hills, Nathan D. Rice, Calvin Gleason, William Bryant, Abel Walker, Micajah Gleason, Samuel Hagar.

1824. Ebenezer Alden, David Robbins,[1] jun., Leonard Wade, Isaac Hills, Nathan D. Rice, Joseph Morse, Samuel Stone, Simon Fuller, Fisher Hart, Samuel Hagar.

1825. Abiel Gay, Herman Hawes, Spencer Mero, Phinehas Butler, Nathaniel Bachelor, Thomas Mitchell, Robert Thompson, John Hemenway, Sanford Hills, Leonard Bump, John C. Robbins.

1826. Jesse Drake, John C. Robbins, Spencer Mero, Phinehas Butler, Galen Hawes, John Gowen, John Walker, Obadiah Gardner, Leonard Follansbee, Leonard Bump.

1827. Zaccheus Litchfield, John P. Robbins, Ebenezer Cobb, John Bachelder, Isaac Upham, Lewis Bachelder, Joseph Miller, John Hart, Martin Sidelinger, David Cummings.

1828. Josiah F. Day, Moses Simmons, William Libbey, Galen Hawes, John Gowen, John Walker, John Lermond, William Gleason, Martin Sidelinger, Herman Hawes.

1829. John Butler, Jason Robbins, Noah Rice, Ebenezer Cobb, Philo Thurston, Daniel Law, Ebenezer Blunt, Hermon Mero, Phillips C. Harding, Benjamin L. Law, Nathan Bachelder.

1830. Daniel F. Harding, Noah Bartlett, Ebenezer Robbins, Ebenezer Cobb, Ebenezer Adams, Jonathan Morse, Henry Fossett, Jason Davis, Leonard Follansbee, Sewell Hagar, Nathan Bachelder.

1831. Ebenezer Alden, John L. Robinson, Marlborough Packard, jun., Isaac Hills, Nathan D. Rice, Thaddeus Luce, Jacob Sibley, Gilbert Blackington, Daniel Sidelinger, Elias Skidmore, Nathan Daniels, jun.

1832. John Payson, John L. Robinson, Ziba Simmons, Isaac Hills, John Bachelder, Nathaniel Tobey, Ebenezer Blunt, Christopher Young, Sewell Hagar, Elias Skidmore, Sanford Hills.

---

[1] May 3, Charles Whiting Hawes was chosen in place of David Robbins, jun., resigned.

1833. Nathan Daniels, Josiah F. Day, Waldron S. Butler, Daniel Sidelinger, Joseph Vaughan, William Libbey, Leonard Barnard, Stephen Carriel, Joseph Miller, William S. Luce, Walter Adams, Jonathan Eastman.

1834. Elisha Harding, Nahum Thurston, John K. Post, Isaac Hills, Marlboro' Packard, jun., Cyrus Robbins, Christopher Young, Charles Hibbard, Daniel Sidelinger, Jason Robbins, Charles Hall.

1835. Elisha Harding, Josiah F. Day, Joseph Vaughan, jun., Vinal Hills, Spencer Mero, Nathaniel Tobey, Sterling Davis, jun., Elias Skidmore, Benjamin L. Law, George Cummings, Peter Adams.

1836. Spencer Walcott, Josiah F. Day, Ambrose Leach, Joshua Morse, Benjamin Litchfield, William Daggett, Stephen Carriel, John Burns, Elbridge Lermond, Elias Skidmore, Sewell Hagar, Stephen S. Hawes, Ebenezer Cobb.

1837. " Voted that the several school-districts choose their own agents."

1838. J. W. Lermond, Nathaniel Robbins, jun., Daniel Sidelinger, Judson Caswell, Elisha Harding, John Stevens, Amos Drake, Jason Robbins, Suell Cummings, Nathan Hills, James Grinnell, Samuel Daggett, William Coggan.

1839. Amos Drake, William G. Hawes, Noah Rice, Joshua Morse, Nathan Bachelder, E. H. Small, Milton Daniels, William Gleason, Samuel Sidelinger, Robert Thompson, C. G. Bachelder, David Grafton, Samuel Stone.

1840. Voted that the school-districts choose their own agents, and make returns of those chosen to the town-clerk in April next.

1841. Amos Walker, David Robbins, Marlboro' Packard, Walter Blake, Otis Hawes, John Walker, jun., Benjamin Gowen, Lewis Andrews, Charles Fogler, Sewell Hagar, Elias Skidmore, Ebenezer Cobb, Daniel D. Law.

1842. Spencer Walcott, Willard Robbins, Suell Cummings, James Thompson, Vinal Ware, Daniel Walker, jun., Joseph Bryant, Wilbur Davis, Fisher Hart, Samuel Hagar, William Caswell, Nelson Cutler, Joel Adams.

1843. Joseph Daniels, Isaac Fuller, Isley Martin, Joshua Morse, Joseph Irish, Samuel C. Fuller, William Coggan, John Lermond, Joseph Gleason, John Hagar, Elijah Lermond, C. Young, Thaddeus Luce. There is an obscurity in the records; for afterward were chosen Peter Adams, Benjamin Achorn, J. M. Gleason, Israel Barker.
1844. F. A. Daniels, Jason Robbins, Asa Morse, Josiah Sterling, Joseph Cole, Calvin Gleason, jun., Samuel Stone, Jason Davis, Robert McGuier, Ebenezer Sidelinger, Walter W. Clark, John Jones, S. Carriel, Phinehas Butler.
1845. J. F. Hart, Leonard Barnard, Nathan Hills, Nathan Bachelder, Asa Walker, Calvin Boggs, Lyman Alden, Ebenezer Sidelinger, Samuel Cummings, John Stevens, Pond Davis, Elias Skidmore, and, subsequently, John H. Gowen, David Robbins.
1846, 1847, 1848, and probably since, the town has "voted that the several districts choose their own agents."

The duties of school-agents are to employ teachers, to provide fuel and utensils and make repairs, to notify superintending school-committees of the commencement of the schools, and to make annual returns of the number of scholars.

SCHOOL CHILDREN.

Relating to the number of school-children, there is no record earlier than March 5, 1804, when it was —

"Voted to accept the following motion: That, in future, each school-district shall appoint a committee to make and return to the selectmen annually, in the month of May, a list of the names by families of the children who have their actual home in the district, and have a legal right to draw school-money, viz.: All such as have arrived to the age of four years on the first day of the same month, and those who are no more than sixteen [on] said day, and all who are of the age between the two described; and, if such returns shall be neglected, it shall be the duty of the selectmen to proportion the school-money in the manner following, viz.: To take the list of the preceding year, and deduct therefrom one-half the number, and proportion the money accordingly.

SCHOOL CHILDREN.

[May 14, 1806], "Voted to return the number of school-children in the same manner as they were returned last year."

[April 1, 1811], "Voted to accept the following motion as made by Nathan Blake, viz. : That a committee be chosen in each school-district, and the people of each district be allowed the privilege of nominating their committee; and it shall be the duty of said committee to make a list of all the school-children in their district, between the age of four and sixteen years, as they are on the first day of May, with the Christian and surname, and the family to which they belong; likewise to procure teachers of the school, agreeable to instructions they may receive from their district; and, after the close of a school-term, said committee shall certify to the selectmen how much money has been expended in schooling, and to whom they wish to have the money ordered. And, if a list of any district shall not be presented to the selectmen on or before the first of June, it shall be the duty of the selectmen to ascertain the number of scholars in each district, by deducting for the list of the preceding year one-eighth part."

[April 5, 1817], "Voted that the number of scholars in each school-district be numbered, and that number be turned in to the selectmen in the month of June; and, if any district fail to do it, such district shall lose twenty per cent of their money."

The next year it was voted that the return should be made on or before the first of June, under a penalty of ten per cent deduction; but July 1 was subsequently substituted for June 1.

The number of scholars has not generally been entered on the town-records. An approximation may be made when there is a specification of the sum of money raised for each scholar.

Between four and sixteen years of age, there were in—

Years.	Scholars.	Years.	Scholars.	Years.	Scholars.
1803	261	1807	347	1816	427
1804	287	1809	306	1817	427
1805	327	1810	323	1819	461

In 1826,[1] "there were 715 scholars between the ages of four and twenty-one."

[1] Mr. N. P. Hawes. — At this time, "the books recommended by the superintending school-committee to be used in the schools were the United States Spelling-book by N. P. Hawes, Testament, Murray's Eng-

The following is the number of scholars between the ages of four and twenty-one on the first day of May, as returned at different times by the school-committee, under oath, to the State-treasurer's office. Upon this is based the proportion of school-money which has been received by the town from the State.

Years.	Scholars.	Years.	Scholars.	Years.	Scholars.
1833	... 358	1839	... 773	1844	... 812
1834	... 714	1840	... 757	1845	... 851
1835	... 713	1841	... 810	1846	... 841
1836	... 706	1842	... 798	1847–8	.. 870
1837	... 701	1843	... 784	1848–9	.. 873
1838	... 738				

SCHOOL-MONEY.

It has been stated, that, July 14, 1788, the vote of April, 1787, was modified, so that the inhabitants could have the "privilege of paying town-charges and schooling" in produce.[1] Hence it may be inferred, that an appropriation for schooling was made as early as 1787. There is, however, no record of any before April 7, 1788; and the £10 voted for town-charges in 1787 was no more than was voted for the same purpose in 1788, when there was an additional £10, expressly for schooling. Sometimes the total amount of school-money has been recorded; at other times, only the amount for each scholar;[2] and, when both sums are mentioned, they do not always agree. Sometimes, when the amount for each scholar is given, there is no record of the number of scholars. At other times, the number of scholars is not given, and the amount for each is not unequivocally stated. Accordingly, the following is but an approximation to the annual expenditure:

lish Reader, Introduction to Murray's English Reader, all of the pronouncing kind; Kinne's Arithmetic, Ingersoll's Grammar, large and small; Woodbridge's Geography, large and small; and Walker's Dictionary."

[1] In 1791, the tax was paid in produce.

[2] In 1803, the appropriation for each scholar was $1.15; in 1804, either $1.25 or $1.50; in 1805 and many other years, $1.25; in 1820, $1.12½. The law now requires, that each town shall raise for schooling an amount equal at least to forty cents for each inhabitant.

SCHOOL MONEY.

Years.	Sums.	Years.	Sums.	Years.	Sums.	Years.	Sums.
1788,	£10	1796,	$100.00	1804,	$351.75	1811,	$385.00
1789,	£10	1797,	$125.00	or	$654.00	1812,	$408.00
1790,	£19	1798,	$150.00	1805,	$654.00	1813,	$412.00
1791,	£20	1799,	$180.00	1806,	$644.00	1814,	$452.00
1792,	£20	1800,	$200.00	1807,	$694.00	1815,	$575.00
1793,	£20	1801,	$200.00	1808,	$341.00	1816,	$533.75
1794,	—	1802,	$250.00	1809,	$385.00	1817,	$533.75
1795,	£10	1803,	$300.15	1810,	$496.00		

After the year 1817, the records contain the apportionment for each district.

By an Act of the Legislature of Maine, passed in 1828, all money derived from the sales of public land was to constitute a permanent fund, the annual income to be distributed for the purposes of education among the towns, according to the number of persons therein, between the ages of four and twenty-one. By another Act, passed March 31, 1831, every bank was taxed one per cent annually. March 4, 1833, a law was made that the whole of this tax should be regularly distributed, like the income of the permanent fund. Accordingly, at different times, the town has received its proportion, as follows: —

Years.	Sums.	When Paid.
1833	$29.54	
1834	$95.67	
1835	$102.54	
1836	$135.53	Feb. 27, 1837.
1837	$179.34	April 17, 1838.
1838	$176.29	June 30, 1840.
1839	$169.47	Nov. 18, 1840.
1840	$151.11	March 22, 1841.
1841	$129.93	April 21, 1842.
1842	$111.65	April 27, 1843.
1843	$101.77	April 6, 1844.
1844	$97.44	March 27, 1845.
1845	$100.51	June 30, 1846.
1846	$98.98	July 21, 1847.
1847–48	$96.73	Sept. 9, 1848.
1848–49	$98.31	July 7, 1849.
1849–50	$116.10	1850.

EDUCATIONAL HISTORY.

In the following Table, when there are more lines than one for a year, the second line contains the apportionment of the money received from the State.

NOS. OF THE DISTRICTS.

Year.	1. $ cts	2. $ cts	3. $ cts	4. $ cts	5. $ cts	6. $ cts	7. $ cts	8. $ cts	9. $ cts	10. $ cts	11. $ cts	12. $ cts	13. $ cts	14.	Total. $ cts
1818	78 75	37 50	65 00	71 25	53 75	105 00	88 75	76 25	51 25	17 50					645 00
1819	88 75	36 25	60 00	87 50	48 75	93 75	96 25	90 00	45 00	20 00					666 25
1820	77 62	31 50	54 00	82 12½	31 50	83 25	78 75	75 37	41 63	7 87½					563 62
1821	72 24	32 68	48 16	72 24	35 26	78 26	80 84	75 26	37 41	7 74					543 52
1822	67 86	37 21	45 24	69 60	40 89	76 56	87 87	78 26	37 41	7 83					551 57
1823	77 43	42 63	50 46	70 47	44 37	79 17	66 99	80 90	34 80	9 57					555 93
1824	78 85	33 18	49 80	73 87	39 84	80 51	69 76	80 04	34 40	14 11					558 73
1825	79 20	38 40	46 40	80 30	34 40	78 40	70 40	83 00	29 98	16 80					558 70
1826	74 88	34 32	51 48	83 12	44 46	76 44	67 08	80 00	34 40	13 26					557 86
1827	78 78	38 22	49 92	86 48	43 68	71 76	74 68	79 56	35 26	18 72					554 48
1828	70 84	32 34	53 90	91 63	44 66	67 76	64 74	68 64	33 54	21 56	7 70				554 71
1829	93 46	33 11	52 36	84 47	40 81	62 37	59 29	73 92	31 11	19 44	8 47				555 83
1830	89 91	35 64	51 84	84 24	41 31	67 23	56 95	65 45	36 79	21 56	7 26				558 87
1831	103 79	35 89	67 90	97 97	58 20	80 51	94 96	63 18	38 88	27 16	12 61				651 90
1832	101 20	43 24	61 64	97 52	45 08	75 44	71 76	53 08	46 56	25 76	17 48				652 28
1833	93 60	33 60	63 90	102 60	55 80	71 76	72 00	68 40	45 90	26 10	18 00				654 60
1834	111 32	34 96	54 28	106 72	55 20	76 36	65 32	59 80	53 36	26 68	17 48				656 88
1835	107 64	35 88	60 72	89 24	52 44	71 76	70 84	79 12	41 40	26 68	20 24				655 96
1836	52 44	35 88	59 80	96 76	60 72	43 24	69 00	58 88	40 48	32 20	14 72	57 04	30 36		651 52
1837	47 49	45 63	67 05	90 31	51 22	37 25	76 36	58 67	36 32	27 94	27 94	57 74	28 87		652 79

SCHOOL MONEY.

Year.	1.	2.	3.	4.	5.	6.	7.	8.	9.	10.	11.	12.	13.	14.	Total.
	$ cts.	$ cts.	$ cts.	$ cts.	$ cts.	$ cts.	$ cts.	$ cts.	$ cts.	$ cts.	$ cts.	$ cts.	$ cts.	$ cts.	$ cts.
1838	47 50	41 50	54 00	97 20	53 10	34 20	81 90	55 80	39 60	26 10	35 10	56 70	29 70		652 30
1839	15 73	13 65	17 81	32 06	17 51	11 28	27 01	18 40	12 23	8 61	11 57	18 70	9 79		214 35
1840	56 18	49 82	67 84	136 74	77 38	48 76	96 46	62 54	55 12	24 38	37 10	68 90	38 16	56 44	819 38
1841	11 66	10 34	14 08	28 38	16 06	10 12	20 02	11 98	11 44	5 50	7 70	14 30	7 92	8 83	169 06
1842	38 25	39 95	59 50	94 35	54 40	42 50	71 40	66 30	36 55	25 50	33 15	51 00	30 60	58 88	643 45
1843	10 05	10 05	15 63	24 69	14 29	11 77	19 08	17 42	9 60	6 70	8 71	13 40	8 04	8 39	169 28
1844	56 38	44 00	56 38	76 88	63 43	38 77	76 63	74 89	47 58	03 00	37 00	58 14	36 12	63 00	632 28
1845	11 52	9 09	11 52	20 88	12 96	7 92	17 66	15 30	9 72	4 50	7 56	11 88	7 38	8 58	147 28
1846	53 36	44 04	53 36	102 69	50 90	39 29	76 79	86 62	41 07	22 32	42 04	62 51	36 61	63 00	709 60
1847	10 10	10 07	10 10	18 74	9 29	7 17	14 01	15 81	7 49	4 07	7 66	11 41	6 52	6 58	130 03
1848	55 52	42 29	48 24	58 25	51 87	37 32	78 28	91 00	40 95	16 39	39 16	60 00	37 32	62 48	713 64
1849	8 69	43 10	7 55	9 11	8 12	5 83	12 25	14 24	6 41	2 56	6 12	9 40	5 84	6 90	130 60
1849	49 22	6 14	48 68	46 64	50 88	42 21	72 94	81 52	58 83	26 31	36 93	61 52	37 75	8 74	713 60
1850	7 02	43 68	7 64	6 64	27 96	6 01	14 40	11 65	8 39	3 76	5 26	77 77	4 38	62 99	101 72
1846	49 56	6 95	55 44	39 48	57 90	36 12	74 76	82 32	59 64	47 98	80 15	7 33	32 76	8 00	714 75
1847	6 75	43 27	7 56	5 38	7 61	4 93	10 19	11 22	8 13	3 98	5 15	50 91	6 47	62 58	97 52
1848	50 91	9 09	45 82	40 73	61 90	35 64	83 15	81 45	53 46	25 45	41 58	54 62	32 64	63 48	713 58
1849	7 17	6 72	6 45	5 74	8 60	5 02	11 71	11 47	7 43	3 58	5 85	7 59	35 02	8 90	99 45
1850	46 35	39 52	44 69	40 56	46 44	47 18	85 24	88 56	57 10	28 98	30 64	57 17	40 56	62 74	713 45
	6 44	42 92	6 21	5 64	6 44	6 56	11 84	12 30	7 94	4 03	4 26	7 51	5 63	8 99	99 14
	49 91	42 85	39 69	39 69	46 98	43 74	74 52	87 47	89 61	34 02	34 85	57 57	39 69	63 00	710 88
	6 73	43 83	5 40	6 40	6 40	4 96	10 15	11 91	7 61	4 63	4 74	7 51	5 40	8 72	96 73
	42 18	6 14	35 68	31 65	49 60	37 95	81 67	91 58	52 80	40 63	36 37	67 65	39 60	62 81	713 89
	6 02	4 97	4 97	4 39	6 96	5 33	11 52	12 91	7 42	5 67	5 09	9 52	5 55	8 13	100 30
	55 65	37 22	36 22	30 72	42 20	37 98	66 24	97 16	56 53	36 22	37 98	72 43	38 89	67 13	813 54
	9 05	6 18	5 89	5 03	6 90	6 18	10 78	15 80	9 20	5 89	6 18	11 78	6 32	10 92	116 10

27*

It is very common, after the school of a district is finished for the season, to continue the teacher several weeks longer; each parent paying a specified sum each week for every child that he sends, so that the amount considerably exceeds what is stated in the preceding tables.

April 6, 1801, two articles relating to school-money were "dropped." The first was to see if the town would "grant a sum of money to purchase books for the use of schools in the several districts;" the second, to see if the town would "allow the collector to pay in their part or proportion of schooling-money to the treasurer of each district."

April, 1816, "Voted that the selectmen should not give an [order] to draw any money from the treasury, unless the instructors first produce a certificate from the school-committee that they are duly qualified to teach said school." This vote was repeated in substance the succeeding year. And May 1, 1817, when an article was brought forward to see if the town would "vote to have the selectmen grant orders to the school-districts, where their teachers have not obtained a recommendation, viz. District No. 7 and No. 10, it was voted to drop the article."

April, 1817, voted to pass over an article to see if the town would "allow Jonathan Sibley to have his proportion of the school-money, and apply it to schooling his own children in his own way." July 4, 1820, upon a proposition to "let Leonard Bump receive his proportion of money that his scholars drawed in 1819, and what they will draw in 1820 from School-district No. 7," the money was granted, "provided he satisfied the selectmen that it had been expended in schooling his children." In 1822, it was again granted; but "he was first to produce a certificate from the master or mistress that the same had been expended in schooling his children, they being duly qualified as the law requires for school-instructors."

It appears from the preceding votes, that there were brought forward, in advance of the times, some considerations which have since been reduced to laws; and that, whatever may have been the motive or the result, there was vigilance that the money should be spent for the general good. There are, however, some evils yet to be remedied. One of these is the subdivision of districts, and the consequent shortness of the schools; another is too great lenity in examining into the qualifications of teachers. Thorough teachers are the cheapest; and long schools, though considerably large, are much better for a town than short schools with but few pupils. Two neighboring districts might unite, and let the scholars in each attend both the schools, which might be taught in different months. By the union of several, there might be grades and one high school in town, without additional expense.

HIGH SCHOOLS.

The liberally educated men in town have always been ready to aid any person who wished to pursue studies not ordinarily taught in the common schools. There have sometimes been private schools for teaching the higher branches of education. During the latter part of each of the years 1824, 1825, and 1826, Noyes P. Hawes kept a private school on the common. The first strictly classical school was probably taught by J. B. Pitkin.

"He came to Union on foot, with his earthly effects, real and personal, in a bundle under his arm, in the fall of 1828. He was poorly clad, and had the appearance of one far gone in consumption. He announced himself as a writing-master, and soon opened a writing-school. He did not take the pupil's writing-book and reverse it when he wrote, but penned the copy across the desk, not only inverted but backward. His writing, though done in this way, was pre-eminently beautiful. The proceeds of his school supplied his wants, and he continued to live among us. There was about him an air of great reserve; and no one knew his acquirements, his history, whence he came, or whither he was destined. After teaching a writing-school for some time, in the fall of 1829 he opened a school for the higher branches, such as Latin, Greek, grammar, geography, &c., in the Round Pond School-house. And there for the first time we learned that he was a good classical scholar, who had received an education at the seminary in Quebec. After teaching several months, he commenced preaching, and connected himself with the Universalist denomination. He remained at Union the next year preaching. Early in the year 1830, Mr. Pitkin left Union for the south. His health was much improved, though the seeds of consumption were too deeply rooted in his constitution to be eradicated. He went to Richmond, Va., became connected with the Unitarian denomination, and a fine church was erected for him in the city, where he preached for several years, and died some years ago, universally lamented and beloved by all who knew him. Mr. Pitkin was distinguished for his reserve, for his quiet, unassuming demeanor, and his gentle, unoffending manners." [1]

With the exception of the summer months, a high school has been taught for the most part of the time, during several years, by Joshua S. Greene, who for about two years was a member of Bowdoin College. Here studies are pursued which are required for admission to College.

During five or six months in the year 1832, a high school for young ladies was taught by Susan B. Owen, a native of Brunswick. She afterwards married Rev. James B. Britton, of Dayton, Ohio, who in 1849 declined the bishopric of Illinois.

LYCEUM.

In the winters of 1830–31 and of 1831–32, there was a Lyceum. Dr. Jonathan Sibley was the president. Of the lectures one was by Dr. Harding on quackery; one by Dr. H. A. True on a library, and its beneficial influence; and two were given by the president on historical incidents and events connected with the town of Union, and the early settlement of the country.

[1] MS. Journal of A. C. Robbins, Esq., of Brunswick. Mr. Pitkin died early in 1835, probably at St. Augustine, Fa., where he went for his health. See Christian Register, March 28, 1835.

LIBRARIES.

At the close of the last century, there was a library, which contained several valuable books. March 3, 1800, an article was brought forward " to see if the town would choose a committee to meet a committee of the 'Federal Society' on the subject of turning the Union Library to the town." The article was dropped. The volumes were kept together many years afterward; but no additions of consequence were made to them. Finally, the proprietors in town severally took what they considered their share of the volumes, and the library was broken up.

In 1814, the young men made a movement to form another library. It was carried on with considerable spirit for some time. Their constitution was signed by Noyes P. Hawes, Walter Morse, Joel Hills, Otis Hawes, John Bowes, Whiting Hawes, Reuben Hills, jun., Ebenezer Barrett, Robert N. Foster. To these were subsequently added Jonathan Eastman, Ezra Bowen, Isaac Hills, Barnard Morse, Galen Hawes, Thomas A. Mitchell, and Russell Sargent. Several of the young men moved from the town in two or three years, and the interest subsided.

The Union Library Society was organized in 1825, with about forty members. In the course of a year or two, the library contained nearly two hundred volumes. At the present time, there are, including large and small, several hundred volumes, belonging to the Sunday-schools of the different religious societies.

CHAPTER XXXV.

PROFESSIONAL HISTORY.

College Graduates. — Lawyers. — Physicians. — Indian Doctor. — Urine Doctor. — Singing Masters and Singing Schools. — Brass Band.

COLLEGE GRADUATES.[1]

ISAAC BOWEN, Brown University, 1816.
JOHN LANGDON SIBLEY, Harvard University, 1825.
HENRY AYER TRUE, Bowdoin College, 1832.
AUGUSTUS COGGSWELL ROBBINS, Bowdoin College, 1835.
HENRY FISKE HARDING, Bowdoin College, 1850.

LAWYERS.

ROBERT MCCLINTOCK, an educated Englishman or Scotchman, having a wife and two or three children, was in town, according to the tax-bill, as early as 1791. He lived near Hills' Mills, and occasionally "did law-business." Not being able to adapt himself to the Yankee mode of getting a living in a new country, he became poor, and, it is said, lived for some time in a barn, in the McGuier neighborhood in Waldoborough, and finally died in it.

WILLIAM WHITE, of Chester, N.H., a graduate of Dartmouth College in 1806; commenced practice in August, 1809; and in September, 1812, moved to Belfast, where he died.

LITHGOW HUNTER, a graduate of Bowdoin College in 1809; in town from November, 1812, to March 13, 1813; now lives in Topsham or Brunswick.

---

[1] The first four graduates were born in one school-district. The second, third, and fourth were born on the Robbins Neck; the first two of them in the True House, so called, now owned by Mr. Fogler; and the other, sixty or eighty rods north of it. Another native of Maine, Freeman Luce Daggett, son of Edmund Daggett, for many years resident at Hope, is an undergraduate of Bowdoin College. In comparison with the neighboring towns, the number is large. In the vicinity are some towns which have not furnished any college graduates.

LAWYERS.

GEORGE KIMBALL, probably of Harvard, Mass., a graduate of Dartmouth College in 1809; began to practise March 12, 1813; went to the Bermuda Isles in the early part of 1815, where he taught a singing-school, and was married. He returned and settled in Canaan, N. H., became distinguished in the anti-slavery movement, and went to Alton, Ill.

DANIEL FISKE HARDING, a graduate of Brown University in 1809, commenced practice in November, 1815, and still resides in town.

JOHN BULFINCH, of Lynn, born in Boston, a graduate of Harvard University in 1812; read law in the office of the Hon. Samuel Thatcher, of Warren, and with B. P. Field, Esq., of Belfast; opened an office here in January, 1816. He remained till November, 1823; then removed to Waldoborough, where he now lives. In 1825 he married Sophronia, daughter of Thomas Pike, of Camden, and has six children, the oldest son a graduate of Bowdoin College in 1850.

JOHN S. ABBOT, a graduate of Bowdoin College in 1827, began practice in 1831, moved to Thomaston in 1833, and now lives in Norridgewock.

AUGUSTUS C. ROBBINS, after graduating, studied law six months with Jonathan Thayer, of Camden, and subsequently with John S. Abbot, of Thomaston; and was admitted to the bar, at Topsham, in August, 1838. He immediately commenced business in Union, and continued till late in the fall of 1839, since which he has practised in Brunswick. From November, 1841, to Dec. 31, 1850, he was cashier of the Brunswick Bank. Jan. 1, 1851, he entered on his duties as cashier of the Union Bank at Brunswick. He has for many years been an unwearied and successful advocate of thorough, extensive, and elevated common school education.

ELIJAH VOSE has been in business since 1842.

ELISHA ESTY RICE, now Governor's aid, commenced practice in May, 1843, and was deputy-sheriff. He left town in 1845, and is now engaged in manufactures at Hallowell.

PROFESSIONAL HISTORY.

RICHARD DRURY RICE was by profession a printer, edited an anti-masonic paper at Hallowell, after which he kept a bookstore several years in Augusta. He then studied law with the Hon. J. W. Bradbury, United States senator, afterward was in partnership with him, and in 1848 was appointed Judge of the Middle District Court of Maine. He resides at Augusta.[1]

NELSON CUTLER,[2] a farmer till twenty-one years of age, then lime-cask-maker two years, trader from 1827 to 1837, also at the present time; began to practise at the bar about May, 1843, and still continues in the profession.

PHYSICIANS.

It was many years before any physician was permanently settled in the town. Dr. Dodge, of Thom-

[1] James Rice, born June 24, 1758; died April 3, 1829. He came from Framingham, Mass. He was the son of Richard Rice, born Oct. 21, 1730; died June 24, 1793. Nathan Drury Rice, son of the before-named James Rice, was born Aug. 29, 1784; and married, Feb. 10, 1806, Deborah Banister, born June 9, 1786, died Nov. 1, 1843. He married second, in 1851, the widow Emery, of Augusta. The children are — I. Harriet, born Nov. 19, 1806; married Amos Barrett. II. Albert Perry, born June 14, 1808; died March 27, 1834. III. Richard Drury, born April 11, 1810; married Anne R. Smith, of Hallowell, April 12, 1836. She died June 15, 1838, leaving Albert Smith, born April 4, 1837. He married, Nov. 8, 1840, Almira E. Robinson, by whom he has Abby Emery, born May 18, 1842. IV. Nathan Foster, born March 25, 1812; baker in New Orleans, La. V. James Banister, born June 14, 1814; died Sept. 15, 1835. VI. Sarah, born June 25, 1816; married, Sept. 4, 1847, James Hodges, of Washington. VII. Cyrus Cushman, born June 14, 1818; married, Oct. 17, 1839, Emily S. Wade; lives in Bangor. Children : Abby Celestia, born Aug. 13, 1840; Deborah Caroline, born Sept. 9, 1843; Emma Eveline, born Dec. 26, 1846. VIII. Elisha Esty, born May 7, 1820; married, Jan. 2, 1842, Almira W. Sampson, of Winthrop. IX. Lyman Lyon, born July 21, 1822; died at the Marine Hospital, Liverpool, England, Feb. 23, 1842. X. Eveline, born July 3, 1824; married Simeon Savage, and resides at Lowell. Mass. XI. Ann Maria, born April 6, 1828; married, December, 1847, James French; residence Lewiston.

[2] N. C. born at Lewiston, April 25, 1805; married, in Warren, March 8, 1827, Love Thompson, born in Hope, April 3, 1810. The children, all born in Union, are — I. Ethelbert Nelson, born Feb. 19, 1828. II. Malinda Ann, born June 16, 1829; died May 30, 1848. III. John Emery, born Nov. 1, 1831. IV. Mary Celeste, born April 23, 1834. V. Caroline Matilda, born June 21, 1836. VI. Charles Henry, born Oct. 19, 1839. VII. Frank Melvin, born June 22, 1842. VIII. Clara Augusta, born March 27, 1846. IX. Coraella, born 1849.

aston, and subsequently Dr. Buxton, of Warren, were occasionally sent for in difficult cases. At an early period, probably about the year 1787 or 1788, Dr. Isaac Bernard was in town a short time. He settled in Thomaston, and married a widow Hanson. He was captain of a company of light-horse, frequently moderator of the town-meetings, and was chosen representative to the Massachusetts General Court, at least in 1806, 1807, 1809-13, 1815-17, and 1819.

Mrs. James, of Warren, was sent for occasionally. But the wife of Philip Robbins, better known as "Aunt Mima," did more business than all of them. In the autumn of 1786, Mr. Samuel Hills agreed to announce to "Aunt Mima" the expected arrival of a little stranger, by going to the pond and blowing a conch. When the time came, Aunt Mima responded to the call. The ice was thin. Amariah Mero, holding a long pole by the middle, so as to recover himself if he broke through, drew his mother-in-law on a hand-sled to the place appointed. The little stranger, Jabez F. Hills, was the first person born in Union after it was incorporated. Aunt Mima acquired considerable skill as a doctress. If a person was wounded, commonly he was carried to Aunt Mima, who had medicines and lancets, and prescribed and bled, as the case required.

JONATHAN SIBLEY was the first physician who established himself here permanently. After studying his profession with Dr. Carrigain, of Concord, N. H., he was examined and admitted to the New Hampshire Medical Society, Jan. 9, 1799; receiving, it is said, the first diploma ever given by the society. Subsequently he became a member of the Massachusetts Medical Society. It is supposed that he is not only the oldest man, but the oldest physician, who practises any in this part of the country, and possibly in the State. Many years since, he published several articles in the medical journal printed in Boston.

WILLIAM DOUGHERTY, of Framingham, settled here about the year 1807, and continued several years.

Dr. PELATIAH METCALF came from Massachusetts in 1809, remained one or two years, and went into a factory at Pawtucket, R. I. He now lives at Smithfield, R. I.

Afterward came Dr. BRACKETT, from Vassalborough. He continued but a short time, moved to Thomaston, and afterward to Virginia.

ELISHA HARDING, M. D. at Brown University in 1819, was here from the spring of 1819 till 1842, when he moved to Thomaston, where he died in 1850.

ISAAC FLITNER, M. D. at Bowdoin College in 1837, came in 1837, and is still in practice.

GAVINUS HENDERSON came in 1842, and moved away in two or three years.

Dr. THOMAS GORE was here a short time, moved to Cushing, and was representative from that town in 1844, and senator in 1846 and 1847. He now lives at East Boston, Mass.

EDWARD ALDEN attended one course of medical lectures at Bowdoin College in 1844. Afterward he attended two courses at Cincinnati, Ohio, and received a medical degree from the Botanico-medical College of Ohio, Feb. 21, 1845. After practising two years at Providence, R. I., he came here in April, 1848.

The following physicians went from Union, and settled in other places : —

ISAAC BOWEN, son of Ezra and Experience (Tolman) Bowen, after graduating at Brown University in 1816, taught an academy at Providence, R. I., and afterward at Taunton, Mass. He went to the South in October, 1818, to teach ; settled in Applington, Ga., and subsequently in Augusta, where, having attended medical lectures in Philadelphia, he practised medicine. His wife kept a boarding-school, in which he took an active part when his practice permitted. He died in Augusta, in 1839, of the yellow fever, after five days' sickness.

CYRUS HILLS, son of the late Reuben Hills, is a practitioner in Friendship, Cushing, and on the islands.

HENRY AYER TRUE, son of the Rev. Henry True, studied medicine with Drs. Estabrook, of Camden, and McKeen, of Topsham or Brunswick; attended one course of medical lectures in Boston, and two in Brunswick; and received his medical degree at the latter place. He was then appointed assistant superintending physician at the McLean Asylum, Somerville, Mass. Afterwards he was in a dispensary, and subsequently was a druggist, in New York city. He moved to Marion, Marion county, Ohio, where ill health obliged him to abandon an extensive medical practice, and where he is now a merchant.

JOHN HAWES, born Dec. 31, 1810, died at Grenada, Miss.

BENJAMIN HIRAM BACHELDER, son of Capt. Nathaniel Bachelor, was born Sept. 18, 1811; graduated at the Bowdoin Medical School in 1836; and in December, 1836, settled in Montville, where, in October, 1837, he married Betsey White Ayer, daughter of Perley and Polly (White) Ayer. In 1848 he adopted the homœopathic system of practice.

JOHN BAYLEY WALKER, son of Amos Walker, received a medical degree at Bowdoin College in 1847. April 21, 1849, he married Bertha E. Rust, of Washington, where he is settled.

INDIAN DOCTOR. — During the summer and autumn of 1805 or 1806, an Indian doctor, named Cook, was here. On the east side of White Oak Pond, called by the Indians Ponoke or Pawnoke, the Indians once had a garden, in which they cultivated many medicinal plants. From this deserted garden, Dr. Cook obtained most of his medicines. He had a pipe made from a maple-sprout. The bulb where it adhered to the stump was hollowed out for the bowl, and the sprout pierced for the passage of the smoke. He was sent for to visit a patient; and, it never being convenient for him to pass the tavern without making a call, he stopped there on his way. After " taking a little refreshment," and lighting his pipe, he attempted to mount a horse from the *off* side. Not able to keep his balance, he pitched over the animal, and thrust the pipe-stem through his neck. It was extracted, and he visited his patient; but, in consequence of the injury, he died about a week afterward, and was buried not far from the Methodist Meeting-house, in a north-westerly or westerly direction, on the pitch of the hill near the road which runs west, and in the vicinity of his wigwam.

URINE DOCTOR. — As the inhabitants have sometimes consulted physicians in the neighboring towns, it may perhaps be excusable to insert two extracts from letters respecting a doctor who in his day probably was as much celebrated as any man ever was in the vicinity. The first extract is dated Nov. 18, 1819:

"A German urine-doctor has lately come from Virginia to Warren. The people flock to him by hundreds; his house has been so thronged that some days he could not attend to half the applicants. It has been reported, that he had an hundred people under his care at the same time. Samuel Bennet died at his house. The body was brought to this town, and opened by Drs. Sibley and Harding, to find a great worm which the learned doctor said was in him; but none was to be found. The fellow says Micajah Gleason has a worm as many feet long as Gleason is years old, and that the worm adds one foot to its length every year. He says Gleason has not got the asthma. He says he shall certainly cure Mr. Gleason, if he can obtain the aid of a seventh son."

The second extract is from a letter dated March 12, 1820: —

"Dr. Lambricht, of Warren, has buried his wife and both his children. Some of the people think he poisoned them. A jury of inquest was had on one of the bodies; but no discoveries were made. His house is continually thronged with people, some with bottles of urine, some with lame legs, and others with diseased livers, rotten lungs, and crazy brains. His practice extends more than fifty miles, and I think I might say more than an hundred. Many of his patients have died, and several at his own house. He is so much engaged in business that many people have to call several times before they can have their urine inspected. I hear he has a box or barrel, in which he keeps salts and brimstone pounded together, and feeds all his patients from the same mess. Some are directed to take it in brandy, and some in rum, and others in different ways; but those who have diseased livers must swallow it dry, so that it may adhere to the liver and heal it. He calls Dr. Brown [of Waldoborough] a fool, and says the physicians in this country ought to be hung for their ignorance. He says in Germany there were several hundred men appointed to translate the Bible; and, after they had finished the work, they submitted it to him to see if it had been correctly done. Public opinion seems to be divided concerning him: while some call him a great physician, others say he kills a great many and cures none."

SINGING-MASTERS AND SINGING-SCHOOLS.

The first singing-school was taught by Ebenezer Jennison, in Moses Hawes's log-house. Candlesticks were scarce, and potatoes, with holes in them, were substituted. Afterward, in cases of emergency, candles were tipped till the melted tallow dropped on the long board which served as a table, and then the bottoms of the candles were held in the tallow till it cooled, — a practice not uncommon in new settlements at the present day. The Rev. Mr. Starr, a carpenter and Calvinistic Baptist preacher, and John Fairbanks, taught singing in the latter part of the eighteenth century.

In the early part of the nineteenth century, funds were raised by subscription, and the schools were free for all. About the years 1814 and 1816, Benjamin Franklin Waters, from Ashby, Mass., was the teacher. His compensation was one dollar for an afternoon and evening. He was employed in three towns; and he so arranged his schools as to teach in Union on two days in each week, from two to nine, P.M., with a recess from five to six o'clock. The school was kept in the hall of the "Mallard House," which stood on the spot now occupied by the house of Elijah Vose, Esq. In the evenings, sixty or seventy persons were commonly present. Some of them lived four or five miles distant. They were dismissed at nine o'clock, then considered a late hour, to go home in the searching cold, through snow-drifts and along dreary roads.

Two evenings thus spent in each week relieved the winters of the monotony which frequently prevails in country-towns. There was no satisfactory substitute for the enjoyment. Sometimes there was rudeness at the meetings; but it was more than counterbalanced by frankness and kind feelings. After the school was ended, if it was in winter, the singers commonly met on Sunday evenings, at different private houses within a mile or two of the Common. Before Sunday-schools were established, there was singing in the meeting-house, between the morning and afternoon services, on the Lord's days, in summer. Two or three persons would make a beginning. Occasionally there would be a "break-down;" but, as other singers came in and joined them, the music became better. Marcus Gillmor was commonly present with the bass-viol, bought by the Rev. Mr. True for the use of the society, and occasionally there were other instruments; but the want of skill in the performers was often the occasion of sundry discords. Gillmor always could be relied on to sustain his part. In summer there was generally a singing-meeting at five o'clock, at the old hall. A maiden lady, who afterwards became dependent on the town for support, lived in the house part of the time, and, for an occasional gratuity of a dollar or two, kept the hall well swept and sanded. Some persons may possibly recollect the elastic step and perpendicularity with which she was regularly expected to go out and come in, two or three times at each meeting.

Singing-schools have been kept in later years; but they have been, for the most part, confined to the particular religious societies. They have not been got up and sustained on the broad and free principle on which they were conducted thirty-five years ago.

BRASS BAND

Very early in the present century, a school for instrumental music was taught, and some steps were taken towards forming a band. Subsequently, teaching was given by Mr. Whittemore. About the time the war of 1812 closed, a fifing-school was taught by Edmund Daggett. But nothing of importance was effected till 1845 or 1846, when several young men — *amateurs* — took hold of the subject in earnest, employed a very skilful teacher, and were organized Aug. 8, 1846, as the " Union Brass Band." It has had a high reputation; though, of late, it has lost some of its members by their removal from town.

Members.	Instruments.
William Adams	Cornopeon.
John M. Bachelder	Drum.
Nathaniel Q. Bachelder	Tuber.
Nathaniel K. Burkett	Trumpet.
Lyman Chapman	Bass Drum.
Frederic Daggett	Post Horn.
Freeman L. Daggett	Tenor Trombone.
Willard Hart	Ophicleide.
Isaac C. Hovey	Cornopeon.
Benjamin L. Jones	Drum and Cymbals.
William B. Morse	Tenor Trombone.
George W. Payson	Bugle.
Jesse W. Payson	E flat Bugle.
Madan K. Payson	B flat Bugle.
Nathan D. Payson	Trombone.

CHAPTER XXXVI.

MILITARY HISTORY.

Revolutionary Soldiers. — Loyalist. — Incidents in the Revolutionary War. — French War. — Military Appropriations. — Powder House. — Military Spirit.

REVOLUTIONARY SOLDIERS.

MANY of the early settlers were connected with the army of the American Revolution. Ezekiel Hagar, who said he was at the execution of André; Abijah

Hawes; Matthias Hawes; Moses Hawes; Ichabod Maddocks, who was in the movement against Penobscot, born June 7, 1764, and died Jan. 4, 1823, aged sixty-five; Titus Metcalf, who died at the age of ninety-two years; and Jason Ware, were revolutionary soldiers. To these should probably be added David Gillmor and Reuben Hills.

Capt. JOEL ADAMS was in the service between three and four years; and, when he left it, he was at least one hundred dollars poorer than when he entered it. After nine and a half months' campaign, he was finally discharged from the United States Army, with sixty dollars of continental money. With this, in coming through Hartford, he bought a pair of buckskin breeches; and the three remaining dollars he paid for a dinner, or something equivalent to it.

NATHAN BARNARD, born at Waltham, Mass., died July 21, 1830, in his seventy-ninth year. He married Sarah Wellington, who was born in Waltham, Mass., April, 1760, and moved from Jaffrey, N. H., to Union in April, 1802. He was out twice in the war. At Bunker Hill he did not take part in the battle, but was a sentry at a short distance. The balls cut to pieces a barberry bush within two rods of him. Afterward he was at West Point. He "tended one end" of the chain put across the North River to obstruct the upward passage of the British vessels. The chain was made of square bars, about one foot long and one inch thick, secured upon logs to prevent it from sinking. He was also in a skirmish near Ticonderoga.

Capt. AMOS BARRETT was at the North Bridge in Concord, Mass., April 19, 1775. According to him, the orders to the Americans were not to fire first. The British moved to the bridge, and began to tear it up. Capt. Davis, of the Acton Company, said they should not do it, and marched down with warlike deportment. The British fired. Davis leaped from the ground, brandished his sword, shouted " Fire, for God's sake, fire!" sprang to one side of the road to avoid the shot, was struck by a ball and fell. Capt.

Barrett followed the British when they retreated. He said he found men dead, wounded, dying, and undergoing indescribable suffering. One man was trying to drown himself in a mud-puddle. Another, who was wounded, hung himself in a barn with a harness. Capt. Barrett was also at the capture of Burgoyne.

PHINEHAS BUTLER served three years. He went to Ticonderoga, and was in the retreat. Having got ammunition, arms, and re-enforcements, the party went back to meet Burgoyne. He was also at Valley Forge, where he had the small-pox. Afterward he went to West Point, and had a sergeant's command of horse-guard in that vicinity; and there he got a discharge.

SAMUEL DAGGETT was captured on board a privateer, and confined four months in the Jersey prison-ship at New York. Of ninety who went on board with him, all died but himself and eight more.

Col. JOHN GLEASON was in the service, and in the Shays Rebellion. By a resolve of the General Court, passed Feb. 19, 1781, he was appointed a muster-master, to muster into the continental army the men raised in the county of Middlesex, Mass.

RICHARD GRINNELL was privateering, and also in the regular land-service. He died at or near Springfield, Mass.

ROYAL GRINNELL was in service in Rhode Island.

AMARIAH MERO was in the service about six years, chiefly in short enlistments. He went to Sorel, Trois Rivières, Montreal, Ticonderoga, and was subsequently at West Point. He was for some time at Boston or vicinity, guarding the Burgoyne troops. He never was in any engagement. His last enlistment was for three years, and he was discharged at Fort Stanwix. He sold his rations of rum to the Indians for beaver-skins. He sold the skins for five dollars, which paid his expenses to Northampton, where he procured five dollars more of a friend to pay his expenses home.

LEVI MORSE went in a privateer to France. He served six weeks in Rhode Island at the time of Gen.

Sullivan's expedition, under the command of Capt. Perry, of Sherburne, in Col. Hawes's regiment. A memorandum found among his papers, dated July 24, 1832, says: " In 1788, was engaged several days and nights in constructing redoubts, and exposed to cannon shot and shells several days. We were overtaken with a severe storm, whilst on the island, without tents to cover us. In 1779 and '80, I served in Sherburne fifteen months; enlisted under Reuben Partridge, commanding officer, in the State of Massachusetts, for the term of three months at each engagement. In 1781, I served three months in the State of New York, at West Point, Peekskill, and vicinity." Another paper, dated August, 1783, labelled " List of towns from Sherburne to West Point," contains " Messmates, Sergt. Joseph Dows, Daniel Brick, Abraham Coolidge, Joseph Fairbanks, Jesse Phips, Levi Morse."

BELA ROBBINS, under the name of William Robbins, enlisted for three years just at the close of the war; went to West Point, and was dismissed in about nine months. There was difficulty about his procuring a pension, because the application was by Bela Robbins. There was no such name on the roll; but there was William Robbins. The difficulty may be explained by the fact that Billy is a familiar abbreviation for William; and hence the transition to Bille and Bela was easy. He finally received three hundred silver dollars, and obtained a pension.

EBENEZER ROBBINS, son of Philip Robbins, privateered in boats with Perry and Thompson, making it also an object to guard the shore. The party went on to the land to eat some victuals. The tories saw them and fired on them, probably to frighten them off and plunder them. One of the balls wounded Robbins in the calf of the leg. Mortification followed. He died and was buried on Cranberry Island. This was probably near the end of the war.[1]

JOSIAH ROBBINS served nine months. He was at West Point at the time of the deep snow.

---

[1] Mrs. Mero and Mrs. Dunton.

PHILIP ROBBINS, at the commencement of the revolutionary war, resided at Walpole, Mass., and was lieutenant of a company. Within a week before the battle of Lexington, he was in Boston, and, in conversation with some boasting British officers, said to them : " You have as good officers and men as any in the world; but the Americans will fight as well without officers as your men will with officers, and will take them one to two, and cut them all off for one breakfast, if they go out into the country in a riotous way." The officers, highly incensed, put him under arrest, and kept him several hours.[1] Very early on the morning of the day of the Lexington Battle, he and the captain and the ensign of the company were in Boston with their teams. On learning that the British had "gone out," each, leaving his team to be driven home by others, took off his horse and mounted it without a saddle, and drove to Walpole as fast as he could go, changing horses twice on the way. The military company was mustered, and hurried to Cambridge, where it arrived in the evening, after the battle was over, and had only the satisfaction of eating some of the provisions which had been taken from the British.

When Robbins was first coming to Union, he was obliged to go to Salem and take passage in an eastward-bound vessel; it being immediately after the evacuation of Boston; while the British were probably lying off Boston harbor. The captain of a privateer said he would convoy the eastward-bound vessel, as he " should like to try his legs," never having been out.

[1] This account of Jessa Robbins differs somewhat from the one by Jacob Robbins. According to the best of his recollection, which was rather indistinct, his father went to Boston from Walpole with a load of timber, one or two days before the battle of Lexington, and called at the bar-room of a tavern where British officers were drinking punch. He also called for some ; and, as he was drinking, " he heard the officers chatting how easy it would be to march through the country to New York. He interrupted them, and said, 'Friends, you are much mistaken: I should not be afraid to undertake, with five hundred such men as we have in the town I came from, to cut you off before you got forty miles.' They immediately put him under guard, kept him three or four hours, and let him go again."

At about eleven o'clock, A. M., after one or two hours' sail, all on board were surprised to see the privateer suddenly put off from them. Before long, the captain discovered she had gone in pursuit of a prize. It was subsequently ascertained that the privateer took it the same day, and that it contained provisions, clothing, &c., for the British army; it probably not being known to those on board that the British had left Boston in the possession of their enemies.

GEORGE WELLINGTON was at the Lexington Battle. He said, when the British came in sight, the captain of the Lexington Company asked all who were willing to stand their ground "to poise their fire-locks.'' Every man did it. When Pitcairn ordered the rebels to disperse, none moved; but, when the British fired, all ran. At one time, a British officer came upon a Yankee with a gun, and asked him what he meant to do with it. The man hesitatingly replied, " Not much." The officer presented his pistol; the man, taken by surprise, gave up his gun, went off, and in great mortification told his companions of his ill-fortune. As the British advanced to Concord, the Americans kept gathering and hanging about them. Wellington followed them on their advance, and on their return. A noble horse trotted by him, with portmanteau, saddle, bridle, pistols, &c., but without a rider; the officer probably having been killed. At another time, three or four British grenadiers entered a house, and were followed by Americans for the purpose of surrounding it and making them prisoners. One of the Americans went round the house to the back-door. A grenadier opened it. They " drew upon each other " instantly. The American shot the grenadier through the heart, and he fell dead. The grenadier, firing at the same moment, shot the American through the abdomen. Wellington conversed with the latter, who said he should die, and he did. Wellington took up the grenadier's cap, made of leather and brass, carried it a mile or two, found it very heavy, and threw it over the fence. A person who spent an evening with him and Capt. Barrett said they could not agree whether the first resistance to the British was made at Lexington or Concord; but Wellington observed that one of his relatives remarked after the battle, " D—n them! I gave them the guts of my gun " at Lexington when they fired. Wellington was also engaged at the time of the Shays Rebellion. He moved to Appleton, and afterward to Albion, where he died.

LEMUEL WENTWORTH's gravestone is in the abandoned burying-ground at East Union. It states that he was at the battle of Bunker Hill. This is a mistake. From a memorandum made in 1820, it appears that " he served the United States, a whole year at one time, in what was then called the Year's Service; that he marched from Winter Hill to New York, and then to Albany, Ticonderoga, Montreal, and subsequently back to Mount Independence; and then he went to Trenton, and helped to capture the Hessians."

Besides the persons mentioned, there may have been some other revolutionary soldiers, who have not been noticed because not known to be such.

WILLIAM COGGAN was in the battle of Bunker Hill, on the British side. He passed over from Boston after the commencement of action.

LOYALIST.

About the year 1814 came Edward Foster from Halifax. He was the father of Major Robert Foster. He had left Massachusetts when the loyalists, or tories as they were called, were obliged to go off. There seem to have been two men of the name, a father and a son. Edes's Gazette, July 29, 1776, states, " We hear that yesterday a prize was sent into Salem, with Ben. Davis and son, Edward Foster, and about a dozen other tories, on board. She was bound to New York, with stolen dry goods." It is said that Edward Foster was a blacksmith; and, when Boston was besieged by the American army, he assisted in making horse-shoes, to which were commonly affixed three prongs, one or two inches long; and that these were buried on Boston Neck for the purpose of laming the American cavalry, in case they should attempt to enter the city in that direction. Mr. Foster appeared to be a very worthy, quiet man, and resided with his son till he died July 17, 1822, aged seventy-two.

INCIDENTS IN THE REVOLUTIONARY WAR.

When Castine, then called Biguyduce or Penobscot, was taken by the British troops in the year 1779, Philip Robbins, as commissary, and his son Jacob Robbins, as his waiter, joined the expedition [1] against them. These were the only persons who went from Stirlington. When the Americans were obliged to abandon their movements against Biguyduce, a company on the retreat encamped one night on Crawford's Meadow. [2] The few inhabitants here always kept their guns loaded by their beds, and had dogs. They often went out as scouts, but in the disguise of hunters. In Waldoborough and Warren were many tories; "the old country people were almost all for the king." [3] A road was beaten down from Waldoborough through the upper part of Union, by the driving of cattle to Biguyduce. Two British officers named McGregor and Roakes, deserters from Castine, piloted by Oliver Miller, of Lincolnville, passed through the settlement. They could not be prevailed on to

---

[1] It was in this expedition that Christopher Newbit, who settled on the point of land at the north end of Sunnybee Pond, had his right arm taken off, July 28, 1779, by a cannon-ball, which glanced round a tree. By a resolve of the Legislature, passed Feb. 28, 1781, his father John Newbit was paid " £13, in bills of the new emission, in full for all surgeons' bills and other expenses incurred by the loss of his son's arm in the battle aforesaid." C. Newbit lost his right eye, and afterward fractured his right leg so badly that it scarcely escaped amputation. Notwithstanding these infirmities, it is almost incredible with what skill he would drive his team, load stones, and do other work, with his left arm. A pension was settled on him; and it appears, from the Report of the Secretary of the United States, that, when he died in September, 1826, forty-seven years afterward, he had received $2,790.27.

[2] C. Eaton, Esq.   [3] Mrs. Mero.

lodge in the house of Philip Robbins, but spent the night in the top of his barn.[1]

Occasionally some of the inhabitants were alarmed. Two famishing deserters from the British called at the house at South Union, and asked for ham, a leg of which they saw in the cellar-way. "Mrs. Butler cut off and cooked a generous quantity, and set it with brown bread before them. She was so frightened that she would have given them any thing they had asked for in the house."

When General Wadsworth and Colonel Benjamin Burton were prisoners of war at Castine, Philip Robbins and others visited them, with a flag of truce.[1] Some sharp words then passed between some of the British and Robbins. This was probably towards the end of April, 1781. Shortly afterward, Philip Robbins was sent express from Camden to Boston, to guard Capt. John Long, a tory prisoner. His bill, bearing date May 1 to May 5, 1781, so great was the depreciation of the continental paper, amounted to £1,128. 2s., including the charge to meet the expenses on his return. Long afterward escaped. Robbins took him again and carried him back. Long swore vengeance. He afterwards persuaded the enemy at Biguyduce that it would be a good plan to come and burn Union. Just at that time, the British officer in command at Biguyduce was changed; and a friend of Robbins succeeded in informing the new commander, that the whole affair was a spiteful movement originating with Long, that there was nothing at Stirlington worth going for; and he accordingly put a stop to it.[1]

When General Wadsworth and Col. Benjamin Burton made their wonderful escape from the British fort at Castine, of which there is a minute account in the second volume of Dwight's Travels, they came on to Mount Pleasant, June 21, 1781, and down by Crawford's Pond, to Warren and Thomaston.

[1] Mrs. Mero.

FRENCH WAR.

In the latter part of the last century, when a war with France was anticipated, orders came for an ensign and eleven men. Accordingly, eleven men enlisted under William Hart. They frequently met for drill, and held themselves in readiness to march. But they were never ordered from Union. The ensign, however, seemed determined to make something out of it. Accordingly, he once told his soldiers, when he was about to have a training, "to fetch their girls" and any friends whom they wished to invite, and have a ball at his house. The consequence was a merry time to all, except one of the eleven, who, on account of the unpopularity of his wife, was not invited. The guests "paid for the fiddle and the liquor," and Hart furnished the entertainment and provided for the horses.[1] This appears to have been all the part which the inhabitants took in the expected French war.

MILITARY APPROPRIATIONS.

Sept. 1, 1794, upon an article "to see what sum of money the town will grant for raising minute-men," — that is, men to be ready to march against the enemy at a minute's warning, — it was voted to give "three dollars' bounty, and to make their wages ten dollars per month with what Congress gives." Another war with Great Britain was anticipated, because the British government would not give up, according to treaty, the posts at Detroit and in the West.

Aug. 28, 1797, the sum of fifty-five dollars was granted " to purchase military stores, viz., 60 lbs. powder, 100 lbs. ball, 100 flints, &c., agreeable to law; said money to be assessed and collected as soon as convenient." Edward Jones was to purchase the stores as soon as the money was collected. Amariah Mero was "chosen to go to Waldoborough Court, to represent to said court that we are in preparation to get

---

[1] Mrs. Wm. Hart.

stores, and to get the town cleared of the fine, if he can."

Jan. 31, 1804, the town paid " Rufus Gillmor, one of the selectmen, $51.33, to purchase ammunition for the town's use." There is another charge, without date, of one dollar and twenty-five cents, by Jessa Robbins, " for flints for the town."

The selectmen's records contain the following notices: Sept. 2, 1806, " Took from the town stock of powder 23 lbs., for the use of the two companies in this town." June, 1807, " Put into the town stock of powder one hundred weight, which cost $38.25." Oct. 14, 1808, " Took from the town stock 26 lbs. for the use of the two companies in this town." In 1810, " The selectmen supplied the two companies with 28 lbs. of powder."

POWDER-HOUSE.

The town's powder was stored in the garret of the Old Meeting-house. An unsuccessful attempt was made, May 8, 1815, to provide a powder-house. April 7, 1816, " Voted to build one, the expense not to exceed fifty dollars." Accordingly, not long afterward, the villagers were surprised one morning at seeing a little wooden building about six feet square and ten feet high, with a peaked roof, perched on the highest part of the hill, north of the Common; where, having been made to order, it had been hauled in the night. It still stands there, though somewhat the worse for the storms and the boys' knives. An effort was made, April 7, 1845, to have the town dispose of it and of the " utensils therein."

MILITARY SPIRIT.

In different parts of the town, when the day's work was over, almost every evening's breeze bore with it the sounds of the drum and fife, before and after the war of 1812. The swivel was placed near the powder-house. For several months after the war, it was generally fired once each day, between sunset and dark.

May 6, 1816, it was "voted that the militia should have the privilege of the meeting-house for inspection." A military spirit pervaded the town. Those were the "glorious days," when soldiers would volunteer, and meet for the purpose of drill.

July 4, 1820, a good day for appeals to patriotism, the town " voted that Capt. Noah Rice draw from the town-treasury fifteen dollars, to be applied towards the purchasing a stand of colors." The rifle-company made a similar application, April 1, 1822; but it was " voted to drop the article." A standard, however, was afterward presented by the ladies through Miss Foster, who made an appropriate address, which was replied to by Capt. Lewis Bachelder, who received it.

CHAPTER XXXVII.

MILITARY HISTORY.

(*Continued.*)

Infantry Officers. — L'ght Infantry. — Its Organization and Dress. — Its Officers. — Rifle Company. — Its Organization and Dress. — Rifles. — Its Officers. — Disbandment.

INFANTRY.

OFFICERS. — Joel Adams, elected captain, Oct. 19, 1791; discharged May 14, 1798. He was the first captain, and for some time used a moose-wood cane, instead of a sword. Previously to this, there was no military training in Union.

Joseph Maxcy, the first lieutenant, Oct. 18, 1791; captain, June 25, 1798; major, Sept. 5, 1805.

William Hart, first ensign, Oct. 18, 1791.

David Gillmor is said to have been the second lieutenant.

INFANTRY.

John Blanchard, lieutenant, Aug. 30, 1802.
Rufus Gillmor, captain, May 2, 1805; major, June 26, 1810; discharged Feb. 2, 1814.
Joseph Pitman, ensign, June 16, 1806.
Joseph Vaughan, lieutenant, June 6, 1808; discharged June 21, 1813.
Peter Adams, captain, Jan. 7, 1811; discharged Aug. 21, 1813.
David Grafton, ensign, Jan. 7, 1811; lieutenant, Oct. 2, 1813; captain, Jan. 8, 1814; moved from town; discharged March 24, 1817.
Rufus Gillmor, jun., ensign, Oct. 2, 1813; lieutenant, Jan. 8, 1814; moved to Searsmont; discharged March 9, 1816.
Bailey More, ensign, Jan. 8, 1814; lieutenant, May 22, 1816; moved to Searsmont; discharged March 20, 1817.
Noah Rice, ensign, May 22, 1816; captain, April 30, 1817; re-elected captain, Sept. 24, 1825; removed.
Millard Gillmor, lieutenant, April 30, 1817; moved from town; discharged July 6, 1819.
Nathaniel Tobey, ensign, April 30, 1817; lieutenant; discharged 1823.
Cyrus Robbins, ensign, Aug. 30, 1819; discharged May 27, 1820.
John Pearse Robbins, captain, May 24, 1823; removed 1825.
Philo Thurston, ensign, July 5, 1825; discharged March 17, 1834.
Ebenezer Ward Adams, captain, Sept. 18, 1832; cashiered Sept. 8, 1835.
John Fuller, lieutenant, Sept. 18, 1832; discharged March 5, 1840.
George Robbins, captain, May 10, 1834; discharged by limitation, Jan. 3, 1842.
Alexander Skinner, lieutenant, May 10, 1834; discharged by limitation, Jan. 3, 1842.
Life W. Boggs, ensign, May 10, 1834; discharged by limitation, Jan. 3, 1842.

LIGHT INFANTRY.

GENERAL ORDERS. — "Head Quarters, Feb. 26, 1806. The Commander-in-chief, having been authorized by a resolve of the General Court, on the petition of Micajah Gleason and others, and having the advice of Council, thereupon orders that a company of light-infantry be raised in the Fourth Regiment, First Brigade and Eighth Division of the Militia, to be annexed to said regiment, and subject to all the regulations established by law; provided, nevertheless, that no standing company of foot be reduced thereby to a less number than sixty-four effective privates.

"By order of the Commander-in-chief,
"WM. DONNISON, Adjutant-General."

ORGANIZATION AND DRESS. — The light-infantry was accordingly organized in 1806. The dress consisted of blue short coats with buff facings, blue pantaloons, half-gaiters bound with buff, oval black leather caps, with a red painted stripe two or three inches wide around them, and a strip of bear-skin about three inches wide, extending from the brow over the top of the head to the back of the neck. On the right side of the caps was a cockade, from behind which rose a perpendicular red plume. The musicians substituted red or buff coats and white pantaloons.

OFFICERS. — Nathan Williams, captain, May 22, 1806.

Joseph Morse, lieutenant, May 22, 1806; discharged Feb. 20, 1812.

Micajah Gleason, ensign, May 22, 1806; resigned Feb. 28, 1809.

Edmund Mallard, ensign, Aug. 24, 1809.

Herman Hawes, the second person born in Union who did military duty, was elected captain, April 23, 1811; major, May 7, 1814; breveted lieutenant-colonel, July 1, 1816, according to an Act of the Legislature, passed June 20, 1816; discharged April 9, 1818.

John W. Lindley, lieutenant, May 11, 1812; captain, Aug. 25, 1813; discharged April 9, 1818.

Hervey Maxcy, ensign, May 11, 1812; lieutenant, Aug. 25, 1814; discharged April 9, 1818.

Samuel Stone, ensign, Aug. 25, 1814; captain, May 19, 1818; discharged and company disbanded, June 14, 1819.

Eben Stone, lieutenant, May 19, 1818; discharged and company disbanded, June 14, 1819.

RIFLE COMPANY.

ORGANIZATION. — Nathan Bachelder and forty-one others petitioned the Governor and Council that the light-infantry, commanded by Capt. Samuel Stone, might be disbanded, and that they might be formed into a rifle-company. The measure was approved by the officers commanding the regiment, brigade, and division, and by Capt. Stone, most of whose men were among the petitioners. It was alleged, that the light-infantry was small in number, and not fully officered and not easily recruited. The committee of the council reported favorably June 12, 1819, and the report was accepted by the Governor on the same day. June 14, the adjutant-general issued his orders accordingly. They passed down from the major-general, June 21; from the brigadier-general, July 6; and from Col. Isaac G. Reed, Aug. 9. The meeting for election of officers and organization was held Aug. 23. The company was recruited by voluntary enlistment within the regiment.

DRESS. — The dress consisted of short, blue round-jackets, single-breasted, trimmed with yellow ferret and ball-buttons; of pantaloons with a row of ball-buttons down each leg on the outside seam, with three rows at the bottom, six buttons high; and of thin half-boots, and of white neck-handkerchiefs and white vests. The leather caps had a yellow strap painted round them, and a strip of bear-skin, about three inches wide, running from the brow, over the head, to the back of the neck.

The rifles, about forty in number, were purchased in 1820, for fifteen dollars each, with merchantable boards at nine dollars per thousand. Upon each of them were stamped the words, " Union Rifle Company."

OFFICERS. — John Bachelder, captain, Aug. 23, 1819; lieutenant-colonel, March 3, 1823; discharged Aug. 27, 1825. Lewis Bachelder, lieutenant, Aug. 23, 1819; captain, May 24, 1823; removed. Spencer Mero, ensign, Aug. 23, 1819; resigned. Ebenezer Cobb, lieutenant, May 24, 1823; resigned Feb. 3, 1829. William Shepherd (or Shepard), lieutenant, Dec. 27, 1823; discharged Dec. 6, 1825. Marcus Gillmor, ensign, May 24, 1823; discharged. Nathan Bachelder, captain, Sept. 24, 1825; discharged and company disbanded, July 2, 1831. Lemuel S. Rice, lieutenant, Aug. 19, 1830; discharged and company disbanded, July 2, 1831. Cyrus Gale Bachelder, ensign, Aug. 19, 1830; discharged and company disbanded, July 2, 1831.

DISBANDMENT. — June 28, 1831, the Standing Committee on Military Affairs reported to the Governor's Council that there was no evidence in the office of the adjutant-general to show that the company had done any duty since 1824; and that the last inspection-return was handed in by the officers, " without a non-commissioned officer, musician, or private; and that the company ought to be disbanded." A vote for disbanding it was passed the same day. The general order to carry it into effect was dated July 2; the division-order, July 5; brigade-order, July 25; and regimental order, Aug. 5, 1831. The officers were discharged; and the members of the company, liable to do military duty, were ordered to be enrolled in the standing companies of infantry within whose bounds they respectively resided.

CHAPTER XXXVIII.

MILITARY HISTORY.

(*Continued.*)

War of 1812. — Pay voted by the Town. — Drafts. — Alarm. — Companies ordered out. — Parade on Sunday. — March to Camden. — Peace. — Soldiers from Union in the Army. — Texan War. — Mexican War.

WAR OF 1812.

AFTER the declaration of war in 1812, the first movement of the town on military affairs was, July 16 of the same year, upon an article " to see if the town will consider the state of the militia who are detached, and hold themselves in readiness to march at a moment's warning, and act or do any thing relative thereto." It was " voted that the militia of the town drafted for the service of the United States shall, in addition to the pay they receive from the United States and individual States, be entitled to so much money, to be paid out of the treasury of this town, as shall make the whole sum of their pay received from all the above sources to amount to ten dollars for each month which they shall serve as aforesaid; provided, nevertheless, that no soldier shall be entitled to any pay from the town, unless he shall be honorably discharged."

There were occasionally drafts of a few persons during the first two years; but, in Sept. 1814, the apprehension of an attack on Camden was so strong that orders came for every man to turn out. British armed vessels were occasionally seen along the coast. " A body of men, despatched in barges from two armed ships lying at the mouth of St. George's River, entered in the night-time, without opposition, the fort below Thomaston, spiked the guns, destroyed the munitions of war and buildings, set fire to one vessel, and towed away two others. It is said the barges ventured within a mile of Knox's Wharf, near the Old Fort, and were only hastened back by the appearance of day-light. So bold was this adventure that it excited a general and extensive alarm. Col. Foote, of Camden, ordered out a great part of his regiment to guard and defend the neighboring coast and country."[1]

To Union orders came on Saturday to be ready to march on Sunday morning. At the appointed time, the members of the military companies assembled on the Common; though the light-infantry did not march till Monday. To many the call occasioned great inconvenience. Farmers were summoned away, not knowing how long they might be absent, and with the expectation that what of harvesting remained must be done by the women and the children, or not done at all. Besides, — let people say what they may, — the prospect of facing bullets backed with gunpowder is not agreeable. There was a general sadness. Women and children assembled to witness the military movements. In thoughtlessness or with anticipations of various evils, boys of all ages were running about among the men. A lad, nine or ten years old, was greatly distressed about a favorite fife, which he had lent to one of the musicians, whose intention evidently was to carry it with him. "It would be taken by the enemy." The answer to his reluctant application for it was insufficient to quiet him.

With the uncomfortable feelings of the occasion were mingled those of regret at the profanation of the Lord's Day, for which in many minds there was a deep reverence. When the hour for worship came, several of the soldiers wished to attend the service. As the arrangements for marching were not completed, permission was given, on condition that the men would come together again at the beat of the drum. They went to the meeting-house in their military accoutrements. Before Mr. True had finished the sermon, the summoning sound was heard. The

[1] Williamson's Hist. of Maine, ii. 641-2.

men simultaneously rose, and went out of the meeting-house. The novel movement, at such a solemn time, awakened deep emotion; and many of the remaining members of the congregation could not refrain from tears.

The soldiers immediately repaired to their posts, and marched away, to the solemn music, either of Roslin Castle or Boyne Water, in the playing of which the boy had the melancholy satisfaction of hearing his fife. Upon arriving at South Union, they paraded before the store of Major Robert Foster, partook of refreshments, and were met by the selectmen, who provided fresh cartridges. They marched through Warren and Thomaston to Camden, there not being any road then between Camden and Union. Sadness, ere long, gave place to merriment. Fun and frolic and wit abounded. Long faces were not tolerated. The only drawback on the enjoyment was that the selectmen were not very good quarter-masters. Each person was ordered to carry three days' provisions; but, after that, there was not the variety of food which might have been expected, if the military had had more experience as cooks, or the selectmen as providers.

When the few days of service were over, the companies moved homeward. The sound of the martial music gave notice of their approach, before it was generally known that they were coming. The women and children were delighted. To the little boy, it seemed as if his fife had never before sounded so loud or so well. The soldiers were welcomed to the houses and fields, which were deserted and almost desolate during the absence of nearly every able-bodied man in the town. When the boy went for his fife, he found that it had not been "taken by the enemy," and that the welcome sounds, which fell so delightfully on his ear, came not from his instrument, but from a D fife, one having been furnished by the government to each company of the regiment.[1]

[1] Two or three years afterward, the boy was provided with a suit of the uniform worn by the light-infantry; and, at the head of the

346   MILITARY HISTORY.

In November, the companies were again ordered out, and went through Warren and Thomaston to Camden, and were absent about as long as before. A sloop, containing a cargo of bale-goods, invoiced at forty thousand dollars, bound from Halifax to Castine, was captured by Major Noah Miller, deputy-collector, and an armed crew from Lincolnville. The deputy-collector was to retain ten thousand dollars of it as his portion. The cargo was carried to Warren for the purpose of having it immediately sent to Boston. The vessel was in the St. George's. Capt. Mountjoy, in the " Furieuse," of thirty-eight guns, sailed from Castine to Camden, and, supposing the vessel and cargo to be there, demanded them, and threatened, in case of non-compliance, to lay Camden and Lincolnville in ashes. Two of the selectmen went off with a flag of truce. They were detained, and threatened with imprisonment till the vessel and cargo should be given up; though they were subsequently released.[1]

Nov. 28, 1814, after the last turn-out of the companies, the town " voted that the selectmen, with the assistance of Major Gillmor, should procure twenty barrels of good beef, on a credit of six months, for the use of the militia when marched out of town." The news of peace came in February, 1815. For two days a long white streamer, upon which were sewed an eagle

company, he marched and played his fife at trainings. These were his happiest days. At the age of thirteen, he ended his military career, by going to Waldoborough, "playing the fife all day on the muster-field," and exhibiting his red coat and military cap before Governor Brooks, when he made his eastern tour in the year 1818.

On training-days, the small boys were generally attracted to the light-infantry, on account of its showy uniform. A very few of them marched behind it. The officers were always pleasant to them. Ere long, they put themselves at the head of the company; and, taking hold of each other's hands, and stretching their little legs, in order "to keep step with the music," they preceded the captain. Then, if they could get two or three little red feathers which had dropped from some one's plume, and stick them under their hatbands, they were in the *ne plus ultra* of happiness. On such occasions, the large boys always amused themselves in playing ball on the west side of the ledge on the Common.

[1] Williamson's Hist. of Maine, ii. 643 ; C. Eaton, Esq., of Warren.

and stars of red cloth, ingeniously cut by Sarah Bunting, floated from a flag-staff, temporarily erected near Major Gillmor's door. During the first of the two days, the swivel,[1] which had been substituted for the old cannon, was made to speak as loud and as often as practicable. The beef was not wanted; and, by a vote of the town, April 3, 1815, the selectmen were instructed to dispose of it "to the best advantage which they can find." There is also a memorandum, dated April 15, 1815, which shows, that, however imperfectly supplied with food, the soldiers were provided with another article, which, in those days as well as in the days of the Revolution, was considered quite as important: "Received of the inhabitants of Union $14.24, in full for spirits furnished Capts. J. W. Lindley and David Grafton, in November last, for use of troops from Union. JNO. NICHOLSON."

Jonathan Brown was in the military movement down the St. Lawrence River, and in a severe fight in the regiment of Col. Eleazar W. Ripley. Ebenezer Robbins and Richard Cummings, jun., entered the army. The latter was wounded at the battle of Bridgewater, and draws a pension. Daniel Jacobs and James Gay also went into the army, and never returned. Jeremiah Stubbs enlisted, and deserted three times, the penalty for which was to be shot; then went to the British Provinces, where he remained till the war was over. Jonas Stone was with Commodore Perry in the action on Lake Erie, and helped to row the boat

---

[1] The cannon was unearthed in digging the cellar to the house of Mrs. Hastings, near Green's Wharf, in Thomaston, where it may have been brought in the Old French War, or in the time of General Wadsworth. It was purchased by Mallard and Chase, about 1809 or 1810, brought to Union, and kept in the middle of the Common, on the ledge which has since been removed. It went into the possession of Major Gillmor, who exchanged it for the swivel; and it was used for privateering in the war of 1812. The swivel was also sold and carried to Thomaston. Subsequently, another swivel was obtained by subscription. It was carried in 1847 to the summit of the hill, about midnight, filled with powder, plugged, fired, and burst; and one piece, weighing several pounds, was thrown to within a few rods of Seven Brook.

which bore him in the heat of the battle to the vessel, of which, after his own was crippled, he took command. Perry stood up in the boat, exposed to the enemy's fire; and Stone pulled his coat to haul him down.

TEXAN WAR.

MILTON IRISH was in several slight skirmishes; also in a sharp one, Nov. 26, in the vicinity of San Antonio de Bexar. He took part in the siege which terminated in the capitulation of that place, Nov. 11, 1835, and was slightly wounded in the neck by a musket-ball. He was one of the party which, in March, 1836, capitulated to the enemy about twenty miles from Victoria, on the Warlope [Guadaloupe], and was conducted to Labadea. April 2, they were marched out into an enclosure to be shot. They had no intimation of the purpose till they were on the ground, and conjectured it from the manœuvres. After the discharge of the musketry, and amid the death-shrieks which, in his letter,[1] he says still ring in his ears, hastily glancing his eyes around, he discovered on his "left about a dozen men, who had made their way over the brush-fence," near to which they had been drawn up. He "sprang for the fence as springing for his life," and "was soon on the other side." He was pursued by an officer with a drawn sword, and then by a horseman; but he changed his route, and attention was diverted from him to some of the others who were going in a different direction. He succeeded in reaching some bushes; "bent his course for the river, which he crossed; and proceeded some distance on the bank." He again swam the river, and concealed himself till dark, and then proceeded towards the American settlements. After ten days, he reached the Colorado. May 18, after six weeks' concealment, he learned that Santa Anna was a prisoner; and, in two days afterward, upon the arrival of the Texan army, he joined it, and

---

[1] Long extracts from this letter to his father were published in the Lincoln Telegraph, at Waldoborough, Feb. 10, 1837.

went to Labadea, where he " witnessed the funeral services of his former companions, whose remains after the massacre had been partly burned." He continues: " This was the most trying scene through which I ever passed. I continued in the army till June 2, when I procured my discharge, and reached San Augustine the 25th of the same month."

ANDREW BENNER, of Waldoborough, now resident in Union, entered the Texan army in 1838. When Texas, under Lamar's administration, declared war against the Indians, he was brought into several skirmishes. Nov. 1, 1839, he was wounded in the hand, in a skirmish with the Camanche Indians, about sixty miles east of Austin.

MEXICAN WAR.

ABNER BILLS was a private, and afterwards a warrant-officer and clerk under Capt. Bodfish, in the Ninth or New England Regiment. Aug. 12, 1847, he joined the army of Gen. Scott at Puebla. He was in the battles of Contreras and Churubusco, and, with the army, entered the city of Mexico. After being there about three months, the regiment went to Pachuca, near the head-quarters of the English silver mining company of Rio del Monte. May 4, 1848, after remaining here about five months, the regiment took up the line of march for home by the way of Vera Cruz.

OREN ROBBINS enlisted in the army against Mexico, and died in that country, Nov. 20, 1847.

CHAPTER XXXIX.

MILITARY HISTORY.

(*Continued.*)

Difficulty with the Waldonian Officers. — The Dinner. — Waldonian Influence in the Field. — Election of Lieut.-Col. Bachelder. — Precedence of Rank on the Field. — Remoteness of Musters. — Pecuniary Considerations. — Indignation at a Military Election. — Acts of the Legislature. — Excitement.

SOON after the conclusion of the war of 1812, there commenced between some of the inhabitants of Union and of Waldoborough a state of unfriendly feeling, which led to one of the most important events in the history of the town. It ended in the entire overthrow of all military organization. At first the incidents were trifling. It was not long, however, before the difficulty began to assume a serious aspect. The first open expression of the state of feeling was at a military muster. The officers were in the habit, such as chose, of going to a tavern and dining together; each one paying his own bill. On the present occasion, one of the Waldoborough officers invited the others to dine in his *marquee*. They supposed the entertainment was meant as an act of courtesy, and would be gratuitous. The surprise may be imagined, when the officer, just before they dispersed, observed to them, in a manner not to be misunderstood, that he trusted no one would go away without leaving a dollar. Rumor said that the compensation was enough to provide the dinner, and purchase the table-furniture; and that the officer took what remained, carried home the knives, forks, and dishes, and made a speculation. The story was probably exaggerated; but there was enough truth in it to make the Union officers think that an imposition had been practised on them. The next year they manifested their indignation by not presenting themselves at the *marquee*.

About the time when the Union Rifle Company was formed, the Waldonians were divided into one independent and three infantry-companies. This arrangement gave a great portion of the officers to the Waldonians, and nearly enabled them to control the elections. In addition to this, it was conjectured that the commissions of officers who had been elected were kept back till after a succeeding election, so that the Waldonians carried the day in the choice of officers.

March 3, 1823, Capt. John Bachelder, of Union, was elected lieutenant-colonel over Major Gorham Parks, then of Waldoborough. There was a violent snow-storm on that day, and the roads were almost impassable. Several of the captains and subalterns remonstrated against the result. They stated that the major, on "whose courage and conduct they could rely," and whose rank and date of commission would have pointed him out for promotion, was superseded. They addressed the commander-in-chief, stating that they should have voted for the major; and requested him "to set aside the proceedings of the third of March, and issue orders for a new choice of lieutenant-colonel; which request they conceived themselves in honor bound to" make. This movement of the Waldonians did nothing toward a reconciliation of the Unionites, who naturally said that these remonstrants might have attended the election as well as themselves.

On one occasion, a dispute arose between the Union and the Waldoborough officers respecting precedence in rank. According to military rule, companies, when formed into line on parade, take places according to the date of the captains' commissions, the oldest on the right. At one of the musters, a field-officer being sick, the senior captain, who belonged to Waldoborough, was called to do duty on horseback. His company, commanded by a lieutenant, was placed on the right. Thus, a Waldoborough lieutenant had, to all appearance, command over the captains; and the Union officers could not take their proper place in the line.

For many years, the complaints of the Union people had been on the increase, because they were always required to go to Waldoborough, or to a part of Warren near to Waldoborough, to attend the annual muster. The inhabitants living near Mount Pleasant were obliged to parade beyond Waldoborough Bridge, and not far from the Nobleborough line, a distance of nearly eighteen miles; whereas, on the other side of the muster-field, there was not probably half of one company belonging to the regiment. Previously, the regiment had occasionally mustered in Warren, not very far from the village. The inhabitants of Union naturally said, " Let us sometimes have the muster here." And it is a remarkable fact that there never was a general muster in Union.[1]

Pecuniary considerations also may have had some weight. The money which is spent by the crowd of people on a day of military parade is not unimportant to a small town. The Waldoborough officers may not have been indifferent to this; and the Unionites may have thought it would not be amiss occasionally to reap the benefit of it. Generally some person was sent each year to the vicinity of the muster-field, a short time before the day of parade, to make arrangements for entertainment. The charges for refreshments became very high. Most of the Union people accordingly concluded to take the matter into their hands, and provide for themselves. And when, at the time of the explosion, some of the militia carried hay and provender, and tied their horses by the fences, instead of pasturing and stabling them, there was said to be at least one of the officers whose notice it did not escape; and he exclaimed with an oath, that the people of Union would not leave money enough in town to pay for their horse-keeping.

Feb. 23, 1824, there was an election of officers. According to the best information which has been ob-

---

[1] There was once, and once only, a sham-fight. It was on the Philip Robbins Place, south or south-east of the present residence of Mr. S. C. Hawes, and west or south-west of the island.

tained, parties were for a time equally divided. The Union and Warren officers united, and chose William Ludwig colonel. He declined. They were called on to bring in their votes again. The Union officers had gone from the hall. One of the Waldoborough officers mentioned the fact that they had not voted. His observation elicited from some one the remark, " D—n the Union officers! who cares for them ? " The votes were counted, and Avery Rawson was declared colonel. He accepted the appointment, thanked his friends for the honor which they had conferred on him, and assured others that they should not want a colonel so long as he could ride a horse. At that time or subsequently, it is said he observed, referring to the Union people, that he should " hold their faces to the grindstone."

Within two years after Colonel Bachelder's election, probably through the Waldoborough influence, the Legislature passed a law that " no election for the choice of brigadier-general or field-officer should be valid, unless a majority of all the electors qualified to vote in such choice (including all existing vacancies in the offices of such electors) should be present at such election." This was one of the legislative acts, passed from time to time, particularly to meet the emergencies in Union, and commonly known in Union and the vicinity by the name of " The Union Laws." Of course the Unionites were provoked, and were inclined either to show their defiance of such acts, or to exercise their ingenuity in evading them.[1]

These events may not have occurred in the order of the narration. But so much dissatisfaction had arisen, that this course of affairs could not be continued. The excitement in Union had been growing till it was very great. There was hardly any one who did not enter into it with some spirit. Persons who were

---

[1] A few years afterward, when the penalty for neglecting to warn a training was a fine, the captain issued his order to some private, who he knew would not warn the men, and who still had no property which could be taken to pay the fine. Irresponsible persons were chosen to do every thing.

exempted from military duty, officers who had resigned, and influential citizens not connected with the companies, were willing to aid in evading what they considered imposition and abuse.

CHAPTER XL.

MILITARY HISTORY.

(Continued.)

Violent Rain-storm. — The Companies at Waldoborough Meetinghouse. — Uncomfortable Feelings. — Burial of the Colonel under Arms. — Uneasiness. — Anecdotes. — Line formed. — Irregular March to the Muster-field. — Rogue's March. — Unsuccessful Attempt to stop the Music. — Orders misunderstood. — Confusion. — Desertion. — Hurrah.

As the story goes, orders came, either in 1823 or 1824, to muster in battalions. The colonel requested the general to countermand the orders. The general replied that he could not, unless the officers of the regiment were in favor of it. If the colonel found they were, he might write to him to that effect, and he would accommodate them. The colonel, it is said, after a few days wrote to him that they would like the change. The Union officers, when they heard what was going on, went to Waldoborough. According to their account, they could not find an officer, whom the colonel had consulted; nor would the colonel do any thing about making another representation, or having the muster nearer Union.

The companies were ordered to be at Waldoborough at eight o'clock on the morning of Sept. 8, 1824. They arrived at the time appointed. The weather was stormy. The distance from Union Common was about twelve miles. A considerable part of the night had been spent by them on the road. Some persons lived sixteen or eighteen miles distant. They were cold and wet and cross. There seemed to be a determination not to be imposed on any longer. Almost every man — for it was then a universal custom at military trainings and musters — drank a glass of grog to prevent his taking cold, and to enable him the better to do his duty.

The Union Infantry Company was commanded by Capt. John P. Robbins. They assembled at the hour appointed, near the meeting-house. After a while, the adjutant came to the captain, and said, if it continued "wetting," the men would probably be inspected under cover. The captain remarked that he had as good a shelter as he wanted, in the lee of the meeting-house, and told the adjutant, if he wanted a better, he might provide it. Capt. Robbins then marched his men down to the village, and dismissed them till beat of drum.

The Union Rifle Company, commanded by Capt. Lewis Bachelder, was ordered to assemble at the corner opposite to the colonel's residence. Respecting what passed immediately afterward, there is diversity of opinion. One statement is, that the company was before the colonel's door. The rain fell in torrents. The colonel observed to the officers who were in the room with him, "They mean to act the soldier," and sent out and invited the company to come in and take some refreshment. Capt. Bachelder asked the messenger if the colonel had said any thing about quarters. The answer was in the negative. They declined going in. A consultation was then held among the officers in Rawson's house; and a person was sent out to repeat the invitation. But the company still declined. The only reply was, "We are neither sugar nor salt; but, if you have any military duty to do, we are ready to do it." Such is one view of the case.

The other statement is, that no such invitation was extended to the rifle-company. Capt. Bachelder asserts positively that he never received any official notice to go into the house. The colonel sent the adjutant to the captain, with a request that he would put his company into quarters. The captain took no notice of it. The adjutant then brought to the captain positive orders to do it forthwith. The captain's reply was, that he had not seen a quarter-master that day, and that he should not provide quarters at his own expense : when suitable quarters were provided, he would occupy them. The adjutant observed that there were barns and sheds. The captain said he should not put his company into a *barn* or *shed* in *Waldoborough;* and, as to hiring quarters, he should not do it. This was the last which the captain heard from the colonel or the adjutant on the subject. He took care, however, to remain on the ground a sufficient time for the quarter-master to appear, or to receive information from the colonel respecting quarters, if any were provided. The company then proceeded to the lee of the meeting-house from which Capt. Robbins had marched.

In the mean time, after having dismissed his company, Capt. Robbins, with the other officers of the infantry, went back to the meeting-house, where the rifle-company was formed. The captain of the rifle-company remarked, that, as they were all from Union, they had better come together, and have something to drink, — a practice, in those days, indicating cordiality and a reciprocation of friendly feelings. Upon this, Capt. Robbins returned, ordered the beat of the drum, and took up the line of march toward the meeting-house. Before Robbins arrived there, the rifle-company was on the march. Ex-Capt. Rice and Dr. Harding came to the company, and gave Capt. Robbins a hint to stop his music, fall in the rear of the rifle-company, and reverse arms.

The captain and the privates of the rifle-company understood each other. They commenced their march in open columns of platoons. The captain gave no orders. He went forward, and the company followed him. As they wheeled into the street, the music struck up a funeral dirge. It was Pleyel's German

Hymn, meant probably, in part, as an intentional disrespect to the Waldonians, who were chiefly of German origin. Arms were reversed. The infantry fell in the rear with reversed arms also, and marched to the music of the rifle-company. The colonel, on seeing them from his window, said to his by-standers, "Now, we will let them know that *we* are neither sugar nor salt: we will give them enough of it." The adjutant was dispatched with orders to the Union companies to form a line in thirty minutes. As there was ample time, they continued their march. There was a *marquee*, where, in a military point of view, were the colonel's quarters. This, to evade any charge of military disrespect, they carefully avoided. Various reports respecting the purpose of the Union companies were circulated. Some persons said they were going off; others, that they were burying the colonel under arms. Some of the Unionites said that the colonel did not want to come out in the rain, and get his new uniform wet. Others, while standing in the rain at the meeting-house, had said they supposed he must be dead. They had previously heard that he was in ill health; and they persisted in saying, that, if he were alive and well, he would not permit soldiers to stand in the rain, without letting them do their duty. He must be dead.

The houses, stores, streets, and corners of the streets, were occupied by wondering spectators. The companies marched to the music of muffled drums and the dirge, with as great solemnity as at a military funeral, up the hill by the colonel's house, in which he then was. They then wheeled, and, striking up quick time, marched the whole length of the village. Some say they even went to the gate at the head of the lane leading to the burying-ground. The adjutant, very soon after giving his first order, probably for the purpose of stopping these proceedings, ordered the line to be formed in fifteen, instead of thirty minutes. The order was obeyed. The line was formed near the meeting-house.

The major soon commanded the regiment to take the position of " open order." This brought the officers about six paces in front. The infantry were impatient and uneasy. The major came to the captain, and asked him if he did not mean to obey orders. " Certainly I do," said Capt. Robbins. " Then keep your company in order," was the reply. The captain spoke to his men; but, as soon as his back was turned, they again showed a spirit of restlessness. The major renewed his rebuke. The captain told the major it was " wrong for an officer to come there with his head under an umbrella, like a partridge with her head under a leaf, and keep the soldiers exposed to the cold storm."

The officers were ordered to form the line about twelve o'clock. They waited some time. The colonel did not make his appearance. John Chapman Robbins came forward, and announced to the companies that the colonel was dead, and that they had just buried him under arms. There was no colonel. He begged them to be as patient as possible; for Mr. Penty Walcott had gone with his ox-team to the cedar-swamp, — some twenty miles distant, — to get a colonel, and he would be along with one shortly.

Colonel Rawson appeared as soon as notified that the line was formed, and assumed the command. They began the march in battalions toward the muster-field. The first battalion advanced with regularity. Capt. Robbins's company, being on the right of the second battalion, was, of course, at the head of it as they marched, and was immediately preceded by the major of the battalion, who was a Waldonian. This battalion kept losing ground, and the major was constantly requesting Captain Robbins to order the company to lengthen step. The captain was ready to make excuses. It was " clayey and slippery and uphill," &c. The first battalion was several rods in advance. The major was repeating his orders to lengthen step, and the captain repeating his reasons for not moving faster. At last, the infantry-captain said, "You go along, major! We will fetch up, by and by." In this spirit the Unionites went on to the ground.

It may be proper to make a distinction between what passed before the men were formed into regimental line, and what transpired afterward. In the former case, they did not consider themselves under the colonel's orders; in the latter case, they were. The rifle was an independent company. Probably there was not in the State one company superior to it. The men prided themselves on their excellent discipline and military appearance. For the present occasion they had procured the best music which could be obtained. One of the Warren men procured a fife, and took his station outside the muster-field, near the gate. When the colonel was marching through the gate, he played the "Rogue's March." The colonel, after arriving on the field, received the ordinary salute. The musicians of the rifle-company had halted. They, too, immediately struck up the "Rogue's March." Of course, it was played with great spirit and effect. This was done without orders from the captain. The colonel immediately sent orders to stop playing that tune. It was stopped, and the officer withdrew. Afterwards the musicians would occasionally play a few notes of it. Orders then came from the colonel for the music of the rifle-company to repair to the right of the regiment. Capt. Bachelder said, that his music — consisting of bugle, clarionets, C fifes, &c., and differing from that of the regiment — would be of no use there, and endeavored to plead off. Then came positive orders for the musicians. The captain told the officer that he could not be accommodated. He refused to let them go, as his was an independent company, and asserted that the colonel had no authority to detach the music from the company. Various orders were given by the sergeant-major; but the sergeants were very ignorant: they could not possibly comprehend the orders. Though one of the Union orderly-sergeants had served four months in the war of 1812, they pretended not to understand the sergeant-major. They were continually making mistakes. In wheeling, the men would scatter. When in line, some would fall in the rear, and others advance. In " ordering arms," some guns would be put on the ground, and others raised. In " carrying arms," they were in all positions, from the erect to the horizontal. When the sergeant-major commanded a captain to keep his men in order, the men would obey the captain; but, in a few minutes, disorder would again reign triumphant. Immediately before inspection, the colonel urged upon the troops the importance of military deportment. He particularly charged them not to look round when the inspectors were in the rear. Accordingly, when the inspectors were passing behind, several of the men clubbed their muskets and faced right about.

Three or four Unionites who were not required to do military duty, among whom were Ex-Capt. Rice and Dr. Harding, came to different places along the rear of the line, and entered into familiar conversation with the members of the Union companies. The time approached for firing. At the order " Make ready," one of these men shouted " Fire." All in his vicinity fired. At the words " Take aim," the word " Fire " was again given in another quarter, and there was another discharge of fire-arms. Before the command " Fire " was officially given, nearly all the muskets were discharged. The commanding officer then rode down and administered reproof. The men replied that they distinctly heard the word " Fire," and obeyed it; and as he was so far off, on the right, they had probably confounded his order with that of some other officer; but they certainly heard the word " Fire," and they obeyed the order as they heard it. This manœuvre was repeated. Then followed a loud hurrah. There could be no longer any military precision. Each man loaded and fired as often as he pleased. There was an incessant, irregular, scattering fire along the line. Shortly the officers ceased to give orders; and, if they had not, the orders would have been unheeded. The colonel, during the day, did not venture to ride in front of the regiment. The Union troops stole off in the rear, two or three together; and, before the time for dismission came, every member of the infantry, except the captain and one private, was gone. The regiment at last left in confusion. The soldiers and spectators swung their hats, and sent up loud shouts and hurrahs; and thus, amid uproar, storm, and drenching rain, ended the day.

CHAPTER XLI.

MILITARY HISTORY.

(Continued.)

Col. Avery Rawson: Charges against him stopped. — Charges against Officers in Union. — Trial of Lieut.-Col. John Bachelder. — Trial of Capt. Lewis Bachelder.

AVERY RAWSON was commissioned major, Aug. 13, 1822; and colonel, Feb. 25, 1824. His death, Feb. 22, 1827, it is said, was hastened by his military troubles. He was highly esteemed by his townsmen; and it is not known that the people in Union entertained towards him, personally, any unfriendliness, except what originated in his military relations to them. It is supposed that he was considerably influenced by his predecessors in office. When the storm came, he had to bear not only the consequences of his imprudence, but also the ill-will which had been increasing against the Waldoborough officers, till the inhabitants of Union were wrought up to such a pitch that they were determined not to serve under one of them.

It is stated by some, that, notwithstanding what passed on the muster-field, Sept. 8, 1824, the colonel was willing to let the whole affair subside. Capt. Bachelder says, that, after the parade was over, the colonel expressed satisfaction with his movements through the day, and invited him to call at his house and take refreshments; but it was declined. The Union officers, however, very soon preferred charges against the colonel for unmilitary conduct, for threats, and for oppression in ordering the Union companies to muster at a remote part of the regiment. These charges were passed up; and it was suspected that they were suppressed by the brigadier-general. Without hearing from them, the Union officers had charges brought in turn against themselves.

The first officer to be noticed is Lieut.-Col. John Bachelder. From the date of the charges against him, it is probable that they were made previous to those by the Union officers against Col. Rawson. Before his election, March 3, 1823, he had repeatedly made application to be discharged from his captaincy, on the ground of ill health. At his election as lieutenant-colonel, he pleaded off on the same ground, and said he would not serve if there was any other one to take the commission. As the Union officers were able to secure a field-officer, in consequence of the absence of several of the Waldonians, he was elected; but it was with the determination, on his part, not to serve on the field under Rawson, nor to be at the expense and trouble of providing himself with dress and equipments. It was probably with a view to put him to the test, that the colonel, about one year after, ordered him to Friendship, when the mud was so deep that the roads were almost impassable, to preside at an election. He had an interview with the colonel, represented the impropriety of sending him to a remote part of the regiment in such travelling, when the Waldoborough and other officers were nearer, and urged, moreover, the state of his health. The colonel was immovable. The lieutenant-colonel obeyed the orders.

Though one of the specifications against Col. Bachelder had been of long standing, it was not till Sept. 24, 1824, about a fortnight after the muster, that the colonel, Avery Rawson, made complaint of him to

Albion K. Parris, governor and commander-in-chief, for unmilitary conduct, neglect of duty, and disobedience of orders. The specifications were, that he unnecessarily, and without justifiable cause, disobeyed a regimental order to attend the parade at Waldoborough, Sept. 10, 1823, and another to attend parade, Sept. 8, 1824; and further that from March 3, 1823, to Sept. 24, 1824, he had neglected to provide himself with the dress, arms, and equipments required by law and the orders of his superior officers. Lieut.-Col. Bachelder was immediately put under arrest. A court-martial was held at Waldoborough, March 8, 1825. Maj.-Gen. John McDonald was president. The plea of ill health was put in for non-attendance at both the parades, with the additional plea of inclemency of weather for not attending the latter. As Lieut.-Col. Bachelder had never appeared in his capacity as lieutenant-colonel on the field, there was no violation of any order as to dress and equipments. He was acquitted on every charge, and released from arrest by orders from the commander-in-chief, signed by Daniel Cony, adjutant-general, and dated Head Quarters, Portland, March 26, 1825.

As Col. Bachelder belonged to Union, the proceedings did nothing towards allaying the hostile feelings between the two military parties. He had been put under arrest some months before any thing was brought against the other Union officers in relation to the muster; but, before his trial came on, charges were brought against his brother Capt. Lewis Bachelder, and against Capt. John P. Robbins. Thus the excitement was continually increasing. All the people in town were becoming united as one man. It seemed as if they were ready to do and dare any thing. What would have been applauded as a proper military spirit, on going to a field of battle, was beginning to show itself in a manner very far from agreeable to the field-officers.

The time for the trials of Capts. Bachelder and Robbins approached. The results, though not foreseen, have probably produced a greater effect on the State, in a military point of view, than any thing else which has ever occurred.

TRIAL OF CAPT. BACHELDER.

Officers for the court-martial appeared at the house of Rufus Gillmor, June 21, 1825; but it was deemed advisable for convenience, and on account of the crowd, to adjourn to the Old Meeting-house. There the trial was held. After ineffectual attempts to proceed on the 21st and 22d of June, "there not appearing the number of members required by law, and no supernumerary member being present, the court decided to adjourn" till Aug. 16.

At the adjourned meeting, Aug. 16, the court consisted of "the president, Col. Alexander Drummond, jun.; members, Lieut.-Col. George Jewett, Major Alfred I. S. I. G. Lithgow, Capt. James Ayer, jun., Capt. Rufus Campbell; supernumeraries, Capt. William D. Gould, Capt. Hugh Patten; marshal, Lieut. John G. Brown; judge-advocate, Major Joseph Sewall."

Hon. John Ruggles, of Thomaston, counsel for the respondent, raised objections "to the sitting of Major Lithgow as a member of the court;" but they were overruled. He also maintained that the present court consisted, in part, of different officers from the one convened June 25; that they were illegally detailed, and that it was not the same court-martial before which he was ordered and ready to be tried; and that he could not be holden to answer to this. This objection was also overruled. The charges were then read.

"To Dwelly Turner, Esq., Major-General of the Fourth Division of the Militia of the State of Maine.

"Avery Rawson, colonel of the third regiment in the second brigade of said division, complains against Capt. Lewis Bachelder of said regiment for disobedience of orders, for unmilitary and unofficer-like conduct in the following particulars, to wit:—

"1. That the said Capt. Lewis Bachelder, having been

duly ordered by said colonel to parade the company under his command at Waldoborough, on the eighth day of September, A.D. 1824, for review and inspection of arms, then and there marched his said company past the quarters of said colonel, with reversed arms, and the music thereof playing a funeral dirge, with intent to insult said colonel and other field-officers then present.

"2. That the said Capt. Bachelder, then and there being in regimental line with his said company in obedience to the regimental order for the purpose of review and inspection of arms, refused to send the music belonging to his company to the head of the column, when ordered by the colonel of the regiment so to do.

"3. That the said Capt. Bachelder, ... being ordered by said colonel, through the adjutant of said regiment, to detach from his said company a rear-guard of one section to cover the rear of said regiment while making in column from the place of formation of the regiment to the place of review and inspection, refused to obey said order, and neglected and refused to detail a guard accordingly.

"4. That the said Capt. Bachelder . . . . permitted his musicians to play the Rogue's March while the colonel and other field-officers of said regiment were about entering the field, with intent to insult and abuse said colonel and other field-officers.

"5. That the said Capt. Bachelder . . . . permitted his musicians to play the Rogue's March while the Waldoborough Light Infantry Company, commanded by Capt. Ralph Cole, were passing, with intent to insult said company and its officers.

"6. That the said Capt. Bachelder, well knowing the disorderly and unmilitary conduct of his musicians belonging to his said company, mentioned in the preceding specifications of charge, did not cause reprimand or impose fines upon them therefor; thereby justifying and encouraging disobedience of orders, disorderly behavior, and unmilitary conduct.

"Wherefore your complainant requests, that said Capt. Bachelder may be held to answer to the foregoing charges, and be further dealt with relative to the same, as law, justice, and military usages, may direct.

"AVERY RAWSON, { Col. of the 3d Reg., 2d Brig., 4th Div.

"Waldoborough, March 1, 1825."

The trial proceeded; Capt. Bachelder pleaded not guilty; witnesses were examined. The record of the proceedings of each session of the court was read at the opening of the next adjourned meeting. The defence of the respondent by his counsel was heard, and "the judge-advocate then stated to the court the evidence both for and against the accused. The doors were then closed; and the judge-advocate then put to the members of the court the following question, beginning with the youngest in grade: 'From the evidence that has been adduced both for and against Capt. Lewis Bachelder, and from what has been urged in his defence, are you of opinion that he is guilty or not guilty of the first specification of charge contained in the complaint of Col. Avery Rawson against him as aforesaid?' Upon which the court decided, that, of said first specification of charge, the said Capt. Lewis Bachelder is guilty. The question being put in the same form as relating to " [each of the other specifications, the court decided him to be guilty also on the second, third, and sixth, but not on the fourth and fifth]. "The court then took into consideration the several offences of which it had adjudged the said Capt. Lewis Bachelder to be guilty, and, after deliberation thereon, sentenced the said Capt. Lewis Bachelder to be removed from office, and did adjudge him to be disqualified for and incapable of holding any military office under the State for the term of three months."

CHAPTER XLII.

MILITARY HISTORY.

(*Continued.*)

Trial of Capt. John P. Robbins. — Objections and Protest. — Charges and Specifications. — Result.

THE court for the trial of Capt. John P. Robbins was organized Aug. 17, 1825. The judge-advocate, as in the case of Capt. Bachelder, then administered to each of the members singly, and to the marshal, and to the supernumeraries, and then the president administered to the judge-advocate, the oath required by the " Act to organize, govern, and discipline the militia of the State of Maine." The court was opened in due form by the marshal. Capt. Robbins gave reasons for challenging Capt. James Ayer and for objecting to Major Lithgow, and moreover denied, as Capt. Bachelder had done, the authority of the court. These points were overruled. The charges were then adduced as follows: —

"To Dwelly Turner, Esq., Major-General of the Fourth Division of the Militia of the State of Maine.

"Avery Rawson .... complains against Capt. John P. Robbins .... for disobedience of orders, for unmilitary and unofficer-like conduct, and for exciting, encouraging, and permitting, in the company under his command, mutiny, disorder, and insubordination in the following particulars, to wit: —

"1. That said Capt. John P. Robbins, having been duly ordered by said colonel to parade the company under his command at Waldoborough, on the eighth day of September, A.D. 1824, for review and inspection of arms, then and there marched his said company past the quarters of said colonel, with reversed arms, and the music thereof playing a funeral dirge, with the intent to insult said colonel and other field-officers there present.

"2. That the said captain .... then and there, being in regimental line with his said company in obedience to a regimental order for the purpose of review and inspection of arms, neglected and refused to call his company to order and attention, when required so to do by the adjutant of said regiment at the command of said colonel.

"3. That the said captain, ... under the command of Major Cole, acting as lieutenant-colonel in the absence of Lieut.-Col. Bachelder, disobeyed the orders of said Major Cole, then and there commanding said regiment, and behaved in an insulting, disrespectful, and disorderly manner to his said commanding officer, and then and there permitted and encouraged his said company to behave in an indecorous and contemptuous manner toward said Major Cole, and then and there permitted his said company to club their arms, with intent to insult and abuse the said Major Cole and other his superior officers.

"4. That the said captain, ... while marching from the place of parade to the place of review and inspection, marched his company in a disorderly and irregular manner, in disobedience of the orders of said colonel and in violation of the rules of discipline.

"5. That the said captain .... permitted his men to fire or discharge their muskets without orders from his superior officers, to conduct in an unsoldier-like and disorderly manner, and to leave their ranks and to retire from duty without the consent of the said colonel or of the officer commanding the battalion in which they were formed.

"6. That the said captain .... withdrew and discharged his musicians from the command of the fife-major and drum-major, under whose order they had been placed by said colonel, without the consent of said colonel.

"7. That the said captain, ... while in regiment with his said company, treated his superior officers with insolence and contempt, and uttered abusive and insulting language to said colonel and others his superior officers, while on parade and under command.

"8. That the said captain, ... well knowing the disorderly and unmilitary conduct of the men composing his said company, mentioned in the preceding specifications of charge, did not censure, reprimand, or impose fines upon them therefor; thereby justifying and encouraging disobedience of orders, disorderly behavior, and unmilitary conduct.

"9. That the said captain, ... from the first day of January, in the year of our Lord 1824, to the first day of March, in the year of our Lord 1825, has neglected to appoint non-commisioned officers in his said company; though, during all said time, his said company has been, and still is, destitute of non-commissioned officers.

"10. That the said captain, ... on said eighth day of September, A.D. 1824, at said Waldoborough, having been duly ordered by regimental orders of Aug. 2, A.D. 1824, to appear then and there with the company under his command for review and inspection of arms, did, previous to and during said parade, endeavor to excite and encourage in the company under his command, and in other officers and soldiers of said regiment, and did participate and join in a spirit of mutiny, insubordination, and disrespect against said colonel and other officers then in lawful command of and in said regiment.

"All which is utterly subversive of the good order, destructive of the discipline, and repugnant to the subordination, which ought to distinguish the militia, and without which it can be neither a defence nor an honor to the State.

"Wherefore your complainant requests, that the said Capt. John P. Robbins may be held to answer to the foregoing charges, and be further dealt with relative to the same, as law, justice, and military usages, require.

"AVERY RAWSON, { Colonel of 3d Reg.
{ 2d Brig., 4th Div.
"Waldoborough, March 1, 1825."

After evidence in support of the complainant and of the respondent, the respondent moved the court for leave to prove "that the complainant in this case conducted, prior to the day of muster, in such an unbecoming and oppressive manner toward the soldiers under the command of the said J. P. Robbins as to excite in them, or some of them, a spirit of insubordination, which may possibly, in two or three instances, have manifested itself, and altogether without the approbation, consent, or previous knowledge of the said Robbins, against his will, and not by him to be foreseen or prevented." "The court directed that the evidence offered therein is improper and irrelevant." The evidence being all in, the respondent was heard in his defence by his counsel, John Ruggles, Esq. After a statement of the evidence by the judge-advocate, the court ordered the house to be cleared of spectators, and the respondent was found guilty of specifications 1, 2, 5, 7, 8; but not guilty of the others. He was sentenced to be removed from office, and adjudged "to be disqualified for, and incapable of, holding any military office under the State for the term of one year."

Thus terminated the trials by court-martial; that of the lieutenant-colonel having cost the State $431.96, and that of the captains $409.47.

CHAPTER XLIII.

MILITARY HISTORY.

(Continued.)

Evasion of the Laws.— John Chapman Robbins becomes Clerk.— Loss of the Company Roll. — Muster near Trowbridge's, in Warren. — Lieut. Ebenezer Cobb. — " A good time." — Horsemen ride about the Muster-field. — Robbins gives Orders. — Unsuccessful Attempts to arrest him. — Notes for Fines burnt as Wadding.

FROM this time the Unionites evaded or set at defiance every military order which was sent to them. The Legislature either could not pass or could not enforce any Act which would bring them into subjection. In the infantry no man could be found to serve as clerk. Probably with the understanding that it would not be taken, a public offer of the clerkship was made; but nobody came forward to accept it. After a while, it was taken by John Chapman Robbins, who was exempted by law from doing military duty. At the training, a few days before the annual parade in 1825, the question was agitated whether there should be a baggage-wagon for the muster. Robbins, the new clerk, discouraged it; said there was " no necessity for it: let every man carry his own baggage, and he will fare better." The question was put, and decided in the negative. After the companies were dismissed, it was whispered about that the roll probably would not be called, and that it would be well for all to go on horseback without equipments, and "have a good time." On the day before the muster, Robbins's company-roll was missing. He could not possibly account for its loss, unless his children had got it and dropped it into the well. It was exceedingly unfortunate; muster the next day; no list of the company; and no means to collect any fines for absences. Accordingly, on muster-day there was no roll to be called. Robbins, more than twenty years afterward, said that, on his way home from the training, he hid the roll in a kingfisher's nest in the bank by the Old Burying Ground.

The rifle-company's officers met on the field; and, as the captain was removed from office, the command devolved on Lieut. Cobb. Ward Maxcy called the roll of the company; but not one private was there to answer to his name. Lieut. Cobb sent word to the field-officers, that he was ready for duty; and, if they had none for him, he wished to be discharged for the day. He was requested by them to ride as major; but "the exercises were so different from what he was accustomed to, that he declined;" and he was accordingly released.

Almost every person who could get a horse went to the muster-field on horseback, as had been suggested. Perhaps the number from Union was one hundred or one hundred and fifty; John Chapman Robbins procuring the fleetest horse he could hire. The field-officers, when they saw them, anticipated mischief, and ordered the guard not to let them pass. Accordingly, they were vigorously opposed; but, while the sentries were keeping out two or three at one point, the whole troop rushed in at another, following Hudson of Union, who played the Kent bugle, and thus became a leader. Among the most active was Robbins. The horsemen rode wherever they chose, within the guard or without it. At a signal, all would start off and gallop round the regiment. Then they would stop, and parade in front of it. The Kent bugle gave signals; and this and the clarionet, both carried by Hudson, were played alternately, according to circumstances.

In due time came the colonel to assume the command. Robbins, on his fleet horse, rides up near to him, and shouts "Shoulder arms." The words are uttered with a stentorian voice, and are distinctly heard along the whole line. The order is instantly obeyed by the whole regiment. An officer is immediately despatched to arrest Robbins, and put him under guard; but his horse is too fleet to be overtaken, and the officer, after an unsuccessful chase, returns. Robbins also returns. The commanding officer is about giving the order, "Attention the regiment," when Robbins, interrupting him, shouts "Attention all creation." The officer is again ordered "to arrest that fellow, and put him under guard." Robbins is a skilful horseman. The ground is moist and muddy. He suffers the officer to come within a rod or two; then he wheels his horse, and dashes off so dexterously and furiously, that the face and vest of his pursuer are covered with the mud tossed up by the horse's feet. Robbins comes and gives orders a third time. "Attention the whole world! Wheel by kingdoms." He is again pursued, but it is to no purpose: his horse is the fleetest on the field.

Robbins calls to the officers, and tells them he will dine with them that day in their *marquee*. During the hours that intervene, he mingles wit and impudence and drollery in such proportions and comical combinations, that he gets them in good humor; and, at the dinner-hour, he is one of the first to enter the *marquee*, where he dines with as much impunity as if he had not done any thing to which they could object. Before night, he succeeds in pulling up, one by one, all the sentry flag-staffs, and rides round the field with them under his arm. Thus ends the day. From that time to the present, the Unionites have not taken part in any of the regular musters. The muster of 1824 was, in reality, the last in which they participated.

After the affair was over, Lieutenant Cobb warned the rifle-company to meet, and answer for non-appearance on the muster-field. Their answer "went by default." Accordingly, he demanded a fine. As the company had no immediate use for money, the clerk was ordered to take notes. What became of the notes, the commander never was officially informed. The fact, however, is that, at a voluntary training some time afterward, Ward Maxcy gave back to each man his note; and the notes were all used as wadding, and burnt in the vicinity of the powder-house.

CHAPTER XLIV.

MILITARY HISTORY.

(*Continued.*)

Orders to elect Officers. — Movements to re-elect Capts. Bachelder and Robbins. — Nathan Bachelder chosen Captain. — Pardon Robbins and the Cabbage. — Re-election of Capt. Noah Rice. — He is cashiered. — Voluntary Trainings and Muster. — Aroostook War. — Rifle Company disbanded. — Philo Thurston. — Ebenezer Ward Adams chosen Captain. — His Trial and Imprisonment.

IMMEDIATELY after the removal of the captains, and probably a few days after the parade at Trowbridge's in 1825, orders came for an election of officers to fill their places. The men were ready to re-elect Capts. Bachelder and Robbins. But such a movement was discouraged. "If you re-elect me," said Robbins, "my election will be declared null and void; and, if but one vote should be thrown for any other person than myself, he would be declared elected, on the ground that I am ineligible." He advised them to vote for an officer who had resigned and been honorably discharged.

There had been but two captains of the rifle-company, viz. John Bachelder and Lewis Bachelder. The former was in poor health, and the latter was in the same condition as the captain of the infantry. Nathan Bachelder, brother of the two preceding of the same name, was elected captain, Sept. 24, 1825.

The officer detailed to preside on this occasion was from Waldoborough. For many years before the military difficulty, there had been good-natured sparring between the two towns; the Waldonians teasing the Unionites about beans, and the Unionites in turn teasing them about sour kraut. On this occasion, Pardon Robbins dressed himself very neatly, and placed on his head a paper-cap having a peaked top, from which rose a cockerel's long tail-feather. He was humpbacked, and in his ordinary walk naturally swaggered. Having procured a large neat wash-bowl, he placed in it an excellent head of cabbage, about the size of a peck-measure, gashed it neatly with a knife, and sprinkled salt over it. Thus prepared, he deliberately strutted up the broad aisle of the Old Meeting-house to the deacon's seat, where the officer was discharging his duty in a dignified and gentlemanly manner, and addressed him with the greatest gravity and courtesy: "As you must be somewhat fatigued, colonel, and this is a favorite dish among the Waldoborough people, please to refresh yourself, while the men are preparing to vote, with some sour kraut." With a gracious bow, he placed the bowl of cabbage on the table before him, and retired. It was an act too gross, however, not to elicit general condemnation, excited even as the Unionites were.

Probably on the same day that Nathan Bachelder was elected captain of the rifle-company, — for the commissions bear the same date, — Capt. Noah Rice was re-elected captain of the infantry. He was a worthy farmer, and had been a good officer. From the first, he was a sturdy opponent of the Waldonians. At the muster in 1824, he was one of the most active of the three or four men who, from time to time, gave hints to the privates of the Union companies, and raised the confusion in which they dispersed. And so elated was he, that in the enthusiasm of the moment, and amid the uproar and shouts that rent the skies, he huzzaed and swung his market-bag around his head till the cheese in it was pommelled to pieces. After his re-election, his commission was sent to him. It is said that he would neither be qualified, nor call out the company; that he would not return the commission; and that it could not be got away from him, but by a court-martial. Accordingly the following notice is taken of him :—

"To Samuel E. Smith, Esq., Governor and Commander-in-Chief, in the State of Maine.

" Charges and specifications preferred against Noah Rice, Captain of a Company of Infantry, in the 3d Regiment, 2d Brigade, and 4th Division, by George Jewett, division-advocate of said division, on the complaint of Henry Kennedy, colonel and commanding officer of said regiment.

" CHARGE I. — Neglect of duty.

" *Specification.* The said Noah Rice, on the 13th day of September, A.D. 1831, was captain as aforesaid ; and, being so in office, it was his duty, on the Tuesday following the second Monday of September aforesaid, it being the 13th day of said month, to parade his said company at some convenient place, within the limits thereof, at one of the clock in the afternoon, for inspection and drill. Yet the said Noah Rice, regardless of his duty aforesaid, neglected so to parade his company, or to give the proper orders for said purpose ; and, in consequence thereof, the said company lost entirely the benefit of the annual inspection and drill contemplated by law.

" CHARGE II. — Disobedience of orders.

" *Specification* 1. That the said Noah Rice, . . . having been duly ordered . . . to notify and summon his said company to meet at Warren . . . on the 29th day of September, A.D. 1831, for military inspection and review, . . . in disobedience of his said orders, neglected and refused to notify and summon his said company, or to give the proper orders therefor ; whereby, and by reason of said Rice's neglect and disobedience of orders, the said company did not appear at said Warren on said day for military inspection and review.

" *Specification* 2. That the regiment . . . paraded . . . for review, and the said Rice . . . was duly ordered . . . to notify his said company to assemble . . . on said day, for review ; but the said Rice neglected and refused to assemble . . . and to appear with his said company.

" CHARGE III. — Unmilitary conduct.

" *Specification* 1. That the said Noah Rice, from the date of his commission as captain aforesaid to the 1st day of October, A.D. 1831, . . . has wholly neglected his duty as

captain aforesaid, and repeatedly and often neglected to
obey the proper and legal orders to him directed. . . .

"*Specification* 2. That the said Rice, from the date of
his commission as captain of said company, as aforesaid,
to the 1st day of October, A.D. 1831, . . . has frequently
and often excited, encouraged, and advised other officers
belonging to said regiment to disobey and not perform the
express orders and commands of their superior officers.

"*Specification* 3. That, on the day the order directing the
regimental review of September, 1831, was served upon
said Rice, he then and there did use and utter insulting and
contemptuous language respecting said order and the commanding officer of said regiment.

"*Specification* 4. That the said Rice was formerly captain
and commanding officer of the same company whereof he
is now commanding officer, and did receive his discharge
therefrom some years since; and the said Rice has repeatedly and often stated that he accepted the commission
as captain aforesaid for the purpose of furnishing him
opportunities of insulting the officers of said regiment, and,
by his disobedience of orders and total neglect of duty in
his said office, to bring contempt and ridicule and disgrace
upon the officers of said regiment.

"The above charges and specifications are respectfully
submitted for your consideration.

"GEORGE JEWETT,
"Division-Advocate of the 4th Division.
"Jan. 24, 1832."

The court held at Waldoborough, June 12, 1832, found
him guilty of every charge and specification, except the last
three specifications of the last charge. They sentenced him
to be removed from office, and adjudged "the said Rice to
be disqualified for and incapable of holding any military
office under this State for life.

"JOHN C. HUMPHREYS, President.
"JOHN A. DUNNING, Member.
"Waldoborough, June 12, 1832.
Attest: GEORGE JEWETT, Division-Advocate."

Although, after the difficulty on the field at Waldoborough and the arrest of the captains, neither
company would perform military duty under field-

officers, there were voluntary trainings for a few years. Once they met, with the Hope and the Appleton companies, near McLean's Mills, and had a voluntary muster, which passed off with great order and decorum. A love for military affairs still continued. When the Aroostook war, in relation to the north-eastern boundary, broke out, as all military organization had gone down, notice for drafts was served on the selectmen. There was made a list of all the persons in town who were required by the laws of the State to do military duty. At the time for drafting, the Common was thronged. A draft of all the men required was made without any difficulty. Before this was done, a voluntary company was organized. Nelson Cutler, Esq., was chosen captain; Lewis Andrews, lieutenant; and John Adams, ensign. The officers never applied for nor received commissions. The company was several times called out for inspection and drill, and always readily responded to the call. The drill was kept up till after the arrival of the news of peace, and then the organization was allowed to subside. The drafts from this section of the State were not called for; but the spirit with which the requisition for them was received, showed the manner in which the Unionites were inclined to act, when what they considered the honor of their country was involved, and its territory invaded.

The rifle-company was disbanded, and the officers were discharged, July 2, 1831. The members were ordered to be enrolled with the infantry. Philo Thurston had been chosen ensign of the infantry, July 6, 1825. Although, in a quiet way, he had done his part at the muster-farce, he was the only officer in town with whom the field-officers had not had difficulty. The field-officers not only did not aid him in getting a discharge, but kept urging him to act. He was the only officer, and maintained that it was unreasonable to require him alone to attempt to organize the three or four hundred men in Union, in the state of things which then existed, and he would not move in the matter.

Finally, after the disbanding of the rifle-company and the removal of Capt. Rice, orders came for another election of officers. The meeting was held in the Old Meeting-house, Sept. 18, 1832. The presiding officer made a few remarks on the "iron grip of the law," which, instead of alarming or awing the men, only excited contempt and a spirit of defiance. Ebenezer Ward Adams was chosen captain; and John Fuller, lieutenant. After leaving the meeting-house, Capt. Adams uttered a remark, from which the inference was plain that he should never order them out after that afternoon. They paraded and marched and drilled an hour or two. The storekeepers and others contributed the treat, which was always furnished, from some source or other, at trainings and musters. Capt. Adams received his commission, but would not get qualified. Efforts were made to hire him to do it; but he was immovable. He never called on the company to turn out after the day of his election. July 5, 1835, Nathaniel Groton, division-advocate, brought against him the following charges:—

1. That he neglected to call out his company, May 1, 1834, for an annual inspection and examination.
2. That he did not, as the law required, parade his company on one other day between the first Tuesday in May, and the annual review of the troops in September.
3. Disobedience of orders in not appearing at Warren, Sept. 25, 1834, for annual review and inspection.
4. Not turning out on the first Tuesday in May, 1835.

The court-martial held at Thomaston, Nov. 4, 1835, found him guilty, and adjudged him to be removed, and to be disqualified from holding any military office under this State for the term of fifty years. They further sentenced him to pay a fine of twenty-one dollars. The captain would not pay the fine, nor allow his military friends to do it. He was carried to jail at Wiscasset, and imprisoned; his prosecutors refusing to take bail. He consulted Judge Smith, who notified the jail-keeper that his case was bailable; and that, if he continued him in close confinement, it would be at his peril. He was, accordingly, released. Thus ended the fifth court-martial of Union officers.

CHAPTER XLV.

MILITARY HISTORY.

(*Continued.*)

Two Companies of Infantry. — Election of Officers at Amos Walker's. — March to the Common.

SUBSEQUENTLY to the disbanding and incorporating of the rifle with the infantry-company, the latter was divided into two companies, the river being the dividing line. According to one report, several persons, deeming a military organization important, presented to the governor and council a petition for this division; and it was favored by many of the residents on the east side of the river, who afterwards fell back, in consequence of a resuscitation of the hostility to the Waldonians. Another statement is, that the division into two companies was in answer to the petition of a few individuals of the old company.

The lieutenant-colonel, it is said, went to one in whom, it was supposed, he could confide, and prevailed on him to summon such men, on the east side of the river, as were favorable to the measure, to meet for the election of officers at the residence of Amos Walker, who lived in a retired place, near the first brook east of Seven Brook. Information of the movement was speedily circulated throughout the town. May 10, 1834, Amos Walker's barn was thronged. Almost every man in town, whether old or young, sick or well, on both sides of the river, turned out. Several persons came from neighboring towns. The lieutenant-colonel began to read the order for election. The boys blew wooden whistles. They annoyed him with paper-pellets. The object apparently was to irritate and disturb him. But a good degree of quiet was obtained, and he continued to read the order with the coolness and composure of an old soldier, till he finished it. Votes for a captain were called for. George Robbins was elected. He was immediately furnished by Dr. Harding and others with words for a speech. With an old wing stuck in the top of a hat which had no rim, he stepped forward, and remarked that he felt greatly flattered by the honor which had been conferred on him, and that, though he was conscious he had hitherto been somewhat neglected and overlooked, he should accept the appointment. The speech was followed by an outbreak of applause.

When the presiding officer found that every thing was intended to be farcical, he declined proceeding with the election. Then it was argued, with much gravity, that there was great unanimity in the election thus far, that every thing promised a harmonious re-organization of the military system in town, and that it was certainly advisable to proceed. "You ought to go on" was the remark of some of the persons present. "You must proceed with the election" was the remark of others. "You shall go on, or we will have you court-martialled, if it be possible to do it. You were detailed to preside at the election of officers, not of one officer of the company." Alexander Skinner was then elected lieutenant; and Life W. Boggs, ensign.

At Mr. Walker's were small wheels used in making ropes, and a log used in shortening them. The men placed the log on the wheels and began to march, styling themselves the *Independent* Artillery Company. A few turned in the sides of their hats, so as to make them somewhat pointed before and behind. Part were in single file, some in platoons three, and others four deep, and some were on horseback. For muskets they carried hoop-poles, staves, sticks of wood, clubs, sunflower stalks, — fastening to their hips sunflower-heads for cartouch-boxes; in short, taking, for equipments, any thing upon which they could lay their hands, provided it would tend to make the whole affair as ridiculous and unmilitary as possible. The new lieutenant brought up the rear of the company, carrying a feather in his hat and a rum-bottle in each hand. On each side of him was some one, acting in the capacity of an aid. In this manner they proceeded toward the Common. It could hardly have been possible to make a company appear more ridiculous. The new officers, according to universal custom at military elections, gave a treat. The other officers good-naturedly partook, though they are said afterwards to have expressed some doubt, judging from the appearance of the new officers, whether they paid for the rum themselves.

This was the last attempt ever made in town to elect military officers. It was the last training, if we except the voluntary movements in the time of the Aroostock war. The Unionites became completely triumphant. The presiding officer seems not to have been altogether satisfied with the result; for, in his return to the adjutant-general, he stated that neither of the officers "had any property;" that they were "the refuse of society; that the lieutenant" had "frequently been a town-charge;" that the "inhabitants of Union" had "not done military duty for nearly ten years; and that there seemed a disposition to evade the law, if possible." The three commissions were issued Aug. 9, 1834, bearing date May 10, 1834. The officers never called out the company, and, it is said, did not get qualified after receiving their commissions. They were discharged by limitation, Jan. 3, 1842.

CHAPTER XLVI.

MILITARY HISTORY.

(Concluded.)

Qualifying Remarks. — Extension of the Unmilitary Spirit. — Change of Public Sentiment. — Military Musters.

THE preceding military narrative may not be satisfactory to all readers. Considering the gleanings to be made, the conflicting statements to be reconciled, the chasms to be filled, the scattered incidents to be arranged in their proper places, and woven into a narrative, and that most of these unrecorded events occurred more than twenty-five years ago, it is obvious that the account must necessarily be somewhat incomplete and inaccurate, though great care has been taken to make it as correct as the nature of the case would admit.

It is to be observed, too, that the narrative has not been confined to what the companies did. Some of the conduct could not have received the sanction either of the town or of the military companies themselves. The same is undoubtedly true of Waldoborough. The Waldonians were naturally glad to have the annual military musters near their own doors. But it is not to be supposed that the citizens at large wished to have them there, unless they were fairly entitled to them; or that, as a body, they would sustain oppression or injustice in their officers. Let the blame fall where it belongs. In as great and general excitement as prevailed, there are always some eccentric men ready to shoot off from the orbits in which the body of the people move, and do acts which are disreputable. Such are some of the transactions which have been mentioned. Individuals have been guilty of them; the better part of the inhabitants have been ashamed of them; the good sense of the towns has been against them. And yet the reproach, instead of being cast where it ought, upon the eccentric or reckless few who were guilty, has been unjustly brought upon the towns.

It is not expedient to occupy the room that might be given to a justification or reprehension of the several acts which resulted in the overthrow of the military system. It may be remarked, however, that the people of Union considered they were oppressed. They were repeatedly irritated; they were threatened; they could get no redress. The power of the Legislature was brought to bear on them in stringent laws to meet their special case. The officers said that they were ready to do military duty, but that it must be done fairly and honorably; and, feeling that such was not the case, the men took the matter into their own hands. And when they acted, it was not with violence and bloodshed, but with ridicule. If still it be said that all this was in opposition to the law of the land, they argue—*parvis componere magna*—" So were the proceedings of the whigs in the revolutionary war. And if you justify them," say they, "for rebelling and fighting eight years, when they had petitioned and remonstrated, and could not even be heard, surely there is but little to be said against the Unionites for taking redress into their own hands, when they used no weapons but neglect and ridicule to effect relief from what they considered oppression and insult."

One thing is certain: the consequences of this movement were important; it was the beginning of a change of the military laws and feelings of the State. People in the neighboring towns continued for a few years to do military duty, as an evil to which they were doomed by the law; while the inhabitants of Union evaded or disregarded all laws of the State and all commands of all military officers in Maine, and pursued their avocations, undisturbed through the year. It was not long before men declined going from McLean's Mills, through Union and Warren, to muster at Thomaston, twenty miles distant, when they saw the inhabitants of Union neglecting with impunity a journey to Waldoborough for the same purpose. How far the spirit has since extended is not known; but the movements in this town have probably, in their remote consequences, done more than any thing else to turn into ridicule and abolish, so far as it is abolished, the military pageantry, which belongs to the Dark Ages, when brute-force triumphed over right, rather than to civilized society, which professes to be governed by reason and principle. The law said, TRAIN: the Unionites said, No. There is something novel in the fact, that an institution which has existed from the infancy of the human race, which all nations have considered indispensable, — an institution to which mankind has always yielded as implicitly as to fate, should be entirely disregarded, and in fact overthrown, here. So quiet and orderly is every thing now, that, but for past recollections, it would not be known that there had ever been a training or military movement of any kind in the place.

MILITARY MUSTERS.

Although much has already been said respecting military musters, it may be well to add a few particulars, as they were occasions of great interest, and the time is coming when they will be entirely unknown, except in history. The days on which they took place were among the few holidays of New England. They were anticipated with satisfaction by adults and with delight by boys. As the time approached, the intervening days were carefully counted by the young. There were two or three military trainings within a week or two before the appointed day, for the purpose of drill. The men who were not required to do duty, and the boys, were busy in getting choice apples, plums, and other fruit, to retail. Four-pences and cents were in great demand, as every boy wanted something to spend on the occasion. Eagerness was manifested in securing modes of conveyance to the muster-field. Persons who had relatives or intimate acquaintances in the vicinity went the day before. Others travelled in the night. Sometimes several members of a company made an arrangement to meet at the captain's, or at some central place, at one or two o'clock in the morning, to go together; and the first sound at the captain's door, to wake him, might be the jarring occasioned by a heavy discharge of a field-piece under his bedroom window. From break of day, vehicles of various kinds were moving towards the place. In some were merchandise. In others rode men wearing their military uniforms, and carrying guns and equipments, — with their wives, daughters, or young children, dressed in their gayest holiday attire, by their sides. Along the roads were men and women and boys, on foot, hastening forward with as much ardor as if the existence of the nation depended on their being there at the earliest practicable moment. Upon their coming together from various places, the pulse was quickened, and more energy aroused by the rapid driving, the loud talking, the trooping of the boys, the beating of drums, and the marching and countermarching of companies, before going upon the field. Then there were the officers' loud tones of command, the crowding of people, the occasional crying of children and barking and yelping of dogs, the glittering of guns and bayonets, the nodding of plumes, and the indescribable feeling experienced on seeing the machine-like movements of a large mass of living beings when marching and drilling. From towns far and near was poured in a great tide of life. Temporary tents, wheelbarrows, stands, handcarts, and horsewagons, with produce, lined the muster-field and places of congregating. Rum and brandy and gin; gingerbread, cake, and molasses; honey, new cider, and apples; ham and bread and sausages; cheese and oysters and crackers; doughnuts and pies and peppermints; clothes, hats, and tin-ware;— in short, almost all things which could be bought or be sold were brought together and exposed in great profusion. "Walk up," "walk up, gentlemen," — and sometimes "Walk up, ladies," — greeted the ears from various quarters. Fiddlers played, the lads and lasses danced; and, on planks and slabs temporarily laid down, clowns exercised themselves with the double shuffle. Old topers got drunk and swore, and others became tipplers. The irritable would become angry, and strip off their coats; and then a cry would be raised, "A fight, a fight;" and a crowd, unless the constables interfered, would run and gather round in a ring, to give the combatants room and see that they had fair play. Everybody seemed to be trying to be happy in his own way; and, amid the vast variety of character, habits, and tastes which were brought together, there were, of course, many queer manifestations of enjoyment. So great has been the change within thirty years, particularly where the temperance-movement has had control, that the young have no adequate idea of the old musters of New England, which were substantially the same on Boston Common and in the town of Waldoborough.

CHAPTER XLVII.

ZOOLOGICAL HISTORY.

Early Hunting and Hunters. — Boggs. — Anderson. — Davis and the Tortoise. — Dické. — The dogs Tuner and Lion. — Laws about Deer and Moose and Deer-reeves. — Deers. — Moose. — Their Haunts.— Time and Manner of hunting them. — Their Yards. — Transportation of Moose Beef. — Dressing and cooking it. — Moose in Summer. — One killed in Seven-tree Pond.

EARLY HUNTING AND HUNTERS.

BEFORE there were any permanent settlements, this place was probably much resorted to by hunters. Samuel Boggs, of Warren, at a later period, ranged along the rivers and ponds. Each week or fortnight, a boat with provisions was despatched from his home to Seven-tree Pond; places having been previously designated, where he left signs to enable the boatman to find him. Archibald Anderson, of Warren, and a man named Davis, hunted here in the fall and spring for many years. After an unsuccessful search during four days, Davis, almost famishing, once returned to his old camp, near Crawford's River, and kindled a fire. With great astonishment he soon saw the sand and ashes, on which it was built, begin to move. He was not disturbed by their surging and sinking; but knelt down, and dealt heavy random-blows among them with his hatchet. In a short time, he was luxuriating on a roasted tortoise, which had unceremoniously imbedded himself in the ashes.

David Dické, of Warren, says that in his boyhood the great hunting-ground was the meadows at the head of Round Pond. When he was in pursuit of moose, he commonly passed the night on the little island at the outlet of the pond. The early settlers were naturally interested in hunting and trapping. Furs were valuable. The flesh of some of the game was at times almost indispensable to their existence. Beef was scarce. When grain failed, fish, fowl, and wild game were their only substantial food. So that all the early settlers were hunters, and had traps, guns, and hunting-dogs.

David Robbins had a very large dog, named Tuner. Tuner accompanied his master in his excursions for game. When night came, Robbins trod a hole into the snow, threw hemlock-boughs into it, and called Tuner to share his comfort. If his feet were cold, Tuner was required to lie on them to keep them warm. As soon as these were made comfortable, Tuner was ordered to abandon his warm nest and take lodgings at his master's back. Thus Tuner was imposed upon; being obliged, during the whole night, to move from place to place at his master's bidding.

Once Tuner was missing. Men hallooed and guns were fired to entice him home. He came in a state of great excitement, and used all his canine eloquence of crying and whining to prevail on some of his master's family to follow him. After they had run about a mile, the dog, far in advance, began to bark. He had returned to the carcass of a yearling moose, which had been pursued and killed by him.

Richard Cummings had a dog named Lion. Lion and Tuner were great friends. Lion's favorite employment was bear-hunting. The two dogs followed a moose to Warren, where Lion probably found a bear's den, and was seriously injured. They returned on the east side of the pond, as far as the Hills Point. Lion could go no further. Tuner swam to the David Robbins Point, and set up a mournful howling. He could not be prevailed on to enter the house, but continued to look across the pond and whine. Accordingly, to the great joy of Tuner, a float was sent across the pond, and Lion brought over, so wounded, probably by the "bear's hug," that he never entirely recovered.

LAWS ABOUT DEER AND MOOSE AND DEER-REEVES.

The office of deer-reeve included the duties of moose-reeve. An Act of the Legislature of Massachusetts was published, Feb. 4, 1764, for the preservation and increase of moose and deer. The penalty for killing any moose or deer between Dec. 21 and Aug. 11 in any year, or for having in one's possession the flesh or raw skin of any moose or deer killed within that time, was £6 and the cost for prosecution for each and every offence. Suspected persons were to be examined before justices of the peace, sheriffs to search for flesh and skins, and justices to require security of suspected persons and to bind over persons to give evidence. Towns which neglected to choose deer-reeves annually, at the March meeting, incurred a penalty of £30. Every person chosen deer-reeve was required "forthwith to declare his acceptance or refusal thereof." If he refused to accept the trust, or to be sworn to the faithful discharge of it, he was fined £5. If he refused to pay the fine, he was to "be convened before the court of sessions;" and, if he could show no just cause for his refusal, the court was empowered to commit him to jail, "there to remain till he had paid the said fine and the costs of prosecution." The "more especial business" of deer-reeves was "to inquire into and inform of all offences against this Act, and to prosecute the offenders." It was further enacted that the grand juries should from time to time "diligently inquire after and prosecute all breaches of this Act." It was probably in consequence of this Act that the town chose Bela Robbins deer-reeve in the years 1787, 1788, and 1789. There is no record of any other action of the town in relation to the subject.

DEERS.

There were never so many deers in the New England as in the other States. In the fall, a few years after the incorporation of Union, five or six made many tracks on a point of land, perhaps one mile south of the outlet of Crawford's Pond. The ground was muddy and soft, and they were evidently trying to get across to the east side. In the following winter, they were found by hunters from Warren, and every one was killed. About twenty years ago, two fawn were seen drinking at a fountain by the side of the road, in the Cedar Swamp in Appleton. One of them was shot near Quantabacook Pond. Stragglers, probably from the wilderness, are occasionally seen in Union at the present day. In December, 1845, a deer was discovered between Hills' Mills and Sunnybec Pond, pursued and finally killed near John Payson's, in the easterly part of the town. Another, probably the mate, was seen a few days afterward. It is supposed they had strayed from the Penobscot country.

MOOSE.

The early settlers of New England had singular ideas respecting moose. In a manuscript of President Dunster, of Harvard University, now in possession of John Belknap, Esq., of Boston, is this notice: "Moose, a beast as big as an oxe; it is thought they will be brought to be very useful for labour, when their yonge are brought up tame."

Probably, there was no part of the United States in which moose were so numerous as in Maine. It is said, that, as recently as 1849, more than fourteen hundred were killed in one year by the Indians, chiefly for the value of their skins. In Union, a favorite place for them was the meadows north of Seven-tree Pond. Before the town was settled, there were many paths running in various directions from the clear, unfailing, and never-freezing spring near the head of it. They were probably made by moose, who in summer commonly go to one place for drink. Another and better ground was the meadows at Round Pond. It was here that, on a Thanksgiving-day, Jessa Robbins killed his first moose. It weighed 840 pounds. The horns had thirteen prongs; and not one of the three men who came to look at him could, with outstretched arms, touch the extremities of both the horns at once. Here, too, it was that Archibald Anderson and Samuel Boggs often climbed into the crotch of a large sloping maple, which stood on the east side of the river near the pond, to watch. When either of them espied one, if he could not kill him from the tree, — and it was too far to fire across the river into the meadow on the north-west, — he came down cautiously, and approached him in the best way he could. He commonly took a float, as thus he could get comparatively near without alarming him.

After the settlers came, the favorite place of resort for moose was the vicinity of the Medomac River. There were found most of those which were killed. Generally they were shy. Their hearing and smelling were so acute that it was very difficult to come within gun-shot, except from the windward of them. Hunters took advantage of the circumstance that they always fed with their heads to the wind, and thus they sometimes came upon them unawares. They were killed at all seasons of the year; but the best time to hunt them was in March. Then these heavy animals were impeded and their legs lacerated by breaking through the crust, which was strong enough to sustain their pursuers; or they were worried down by the deep snow, over which hunters on snow-shoes successfully followed them. This month was generally the time for an onslaught. A party procured high, narrow, and light hand-sleds, which had runners four or six inches wide to prevent their sinking into the snow. They took gimlets, shaves, hatchets, an axe to mend their sleds, and a little salt to make their moose-meat palatable. With guns, ammunition, and dogs, they started off for their favorite ranges and hunting-grounds, dragging their sleds on ponds and rivers and over carrying-places.[1] On arriving at the proposed hunting-ground, they "struck up a camp," kindled a fire by means of their gun-flints and powder, and then were ready for action.

One old hunter says the moose were generally found in the vicinity of springs or places where they could drink, and between the highland and what is called the "black land," or the ground where spruces and hemlocks grow. When the snow was deep, their ranges became limited. They browsed upon the hemlocks, maples, white birches, moose-wood, and the saplings and bushes within their reach, and thus trod down the snow about them and made yards. These yards, which in winter were commonly on "black land," varied in size with the number of animals in the herd, the time of their being there, and the depth of the snow. Sometimes, though seldom, they extended over forty or fifty acres. They were enlarged as the animals, impelled by hunger, stepped into the snow to reach more browse. When undisturbed, a few moose would remain a month on an acre or two.

When attacked by dogs, moose would turn and

[1] One of these carrying-places, from the head of Seven-tree Pond, across the Robbins Neck, nearly in the direction of the canal, struck St. George's River, a few rods below Bachelor's Mills. Another began at the Pettengill Brook, crossed Appleton Ridge, and terminated at the St. George's, about half a mile above the head of Sunnybec Pond. It was travelled by nearly all the hunters on the Medomac River.

fight them, not by kicking, but by striking at them with their feet. Sometimes they would become so intent that the hunter could get near enough to shoot them. If, however, a moose was started from the yard by dogs, he commonly made but few plunges into the deep and hard snow, before he turned upon them. As he was annoyed, on the one side or the other, he kept changing his position in order to meet the attacks, and thus trod down the snow and made a small yard around him. The dogs continued to vex him, and, by their incessant and violent barking, brought up the gunners. If, when the men approached, the moose made another effort to escape, the dogs, set on and encouraged by their masters, attacked him the more furiously. They seized him by the nose,[1] bit his legs, gnawed the hair from his flanks and ribs, and harrassed him till the hunters approached and despatched him with balls. But, when there was only a little snow, the moose, with the dogs on the full leap after him, would distance his pursuers and escape, or draw them into a race, which sometimes continued a hundred miles or more.

When moose were routed, their course was almost invariably toward the South, and calculations were made accordingly to intercept them. The old hunters said that they took this direction, because the farther they went, the softer became the snow and crust. The settlers in Union, and the towns below, considered the circumstance fortunate; for, if the course had been toward the North, the pursuit of them would have drawn them from their homes. In the winter of 1785-6, several moose were started in the vicinity of Quantabacook. One or more was killed; and one fled to the Robbins Neck, where he yarded,

[1] William Thompson spoke particularly of three dogs. One would seize a moose by the ribs, and take out a mouthful of hair at every bite. Another small dog would seize him by the nose, and, curling up his legs, hold on so firmly that the moose would swing him from side to side. A third large dog " would fly up close to him" on the crust, and " bark and roar terribly," without venturing to touch him. They seemed to have a common understanding how each should annoy him

near the sloping maple, till the spring opened. Then he was again started, and ran to Friendship, where he was killed.

When the hunters killed a moose, they skinned it, and split the carcass into halves or sides. A small tree was then bent down, and the ends of the limbs lopped off. The sides were hung upon the stubs of the limbs, and then the tree was allowed to spring back to its natural position. Thus the meat was protected from wild animals. A little bird called the whetsaw, because its notes resembled the filing of a saw, would light upon it and pick it; but it did no harm worth noticing. To keep off the crows, which were troublesome, long white splinters were stuck into the meat before it was suspended. Having thus disposed of a moose, and left the offal on the snow, or used it to bait traps for sable or other game, the men proceeded to hunt again.

When the time drew near for returning home, measures were devised for carrying the meat. Hunters always took advantage of the ponds and rivers. When there was a thaw, they went forward on snow-shoes, and trod down the snow in the paths and carrying-places. When the paths were frozen by the cold weather which succeeded, they sometimes transported their meat on packhorses. Commonly, however, they drew it on their light hand-sleds, — one side of moose-beef being considered load enough for one man to drag. The hunters at the Medomac,[1] having arrived at the end of their carrying-place, followed down Sunnybec Pond and St. George's River, and discharged their loads on Seven-tree Pond. Sixteen carcasses have been brought on to this pond at one time. Some were eaten by the inhabitants, and others hauled off by teams to Warren and the lower towns. Sometimes more moose were killed than were wanted, or could be given away. There was one winter in which one of the Robbins family, it is said, owned shares in

---

[1] The Waldonians had a place farther west, and hunted by themselves.

forty-seven moose and seventeen bears. The meat was an important article of food. The large bones were removed; and the flesh, put loosely together in tubs or barrels, was dried and smoked. When broiled and buttered like beef-steaks, the meat was considered much better than when boiled. The bones were roasted and broken; and the marrow, which was taken out, was salted, and eaten by the white people as a substitute for butter.

In summer, moose frequented meadows and swamps in the daytime, and ponds and coves in the night. A young one was caught — some say in Round Pond, others by being driven into a river in Warren — by Archibald Anderson, and tamed. He was owned in Warren. In the daytime, he would lie about the house in the shade; and, at night, go to feed on lily-leaves and aquatic plants in the brooks and bogs, from which he would return early in the morning.

Within three or four years after Philip Robbins moved here, as he was coming from Warren in his float with his dog and gun, he saw a moose enter the pond on the east side, to cross over. It was summer. The moose's horns were short, and appeared as if covered with velvet. With his foot, Robbins kept his dog down on the bottom of the boat till he was near enough to fire. As soon as he fired, the dog sprang so furiously out of the boat as almost to upset it, and seized the moose by the nose. The dog of Richard Cummings came to his aid, and got upon the moose's head. Before he could reach the shore, the dogs drowned him. The few inhabitants soon got together, and took from the carcass thirty pounds of tallow.

CHAPTER XLVIII.

ZOOLOGICAL HISTORY.

(Continued.)

Bears. — Bear Traps. — Setting Guns. — Bears caught by David Robbins and Jessa Robbins. — Baited and killed by Ezekiel Hagar. — Love Rum. — Taken to Boston and shot. — Encounters on Seventree Pond: on Hart's Hill: on Hills Point: on Simmons's Hill: on the Robbins Neck. — Adam Martin. — Jason Ware and his Dog Sambo. — Fate of Sambo. — Mrs. Hart and the Bear Trap.

BEARS.

BEARS were numerous, and troublesome to the early settlers. They broke into their corn-fields, and destroyed their corn. They carried off sheep and hogs, much against the wishes and intentions of the owners. Bruin's hide, too, was good for caps, mittens, moccasons, and even great-coats. When killed in the fall or spring,[1] he was very fat. If the spare-rib was cut through in the manner of pork, it was necessary to slice off three-quarters of the thickness, because it was so fat it could not be eaten. The flesh, not altogether unlike pork in taste, was a rich morsel to persons pinched with hunger. Consequently, Bruin and the early settlers were always at war. Sometimes he was caught in large steel-traps, baited with mutton; at other times in log-traps so constructed, that, when he seized the bait, the stick to which it was tied released a heavy log that fell on his back and crushed him.

The practice of setting guns in corn-fields to kill bears was very common and dangerous. People were frequently wounded or killed by their accidental dis-

---

[1] Old hunters have said, that, on retiring in the fall to hibernate, bears are taught by instinct to eat balsam or something else, which entirely obstructs the alimentary canal. When spring opens, the same instinct teaches them what to take to remove the obstruction. It is said they are about as fat when they come from their dens as when they enter them.

charge, though there does not appear to have been any fatal case in Union. A long line was fastened at one end. It was then extended between two rows of corn; and, in order that its weight might not cause the discharging of the gun, it was supported at short distances by crotched sticks stuck in the ground. Near the unfastened end of the line were driven down two short stakes, split at the top. Into these splits, and pointing so as to range with the line, and at a proper elevation to take effect, was crowded a loaded gun, which was covered with a long piece of bark to conceal it, and to protect it from dew and rain. Very near the lock was another stake. The unfastened end of the line was then tied to one end of a short stick, the other end of which was placed behind the stake and before the trigger. The gun was cocked and primed, and left for the night. Bruin, intent on getting corn and regardless of the line, pressed against it. As the line was always left a little slack, on account of its liability to be shrunk by the weather, the bear generally brought his trunk in range with the gun before it was discharged. Then, as the charge commonly consisted of two balls and a slug, the consequences were not trifling. A man who saw two bears, which were killed in this way, says that one of them was shot with two balls through the lungs, and the other through the neck.

The number killed was large. Almost every man who settled in town before the year 1800 had something to do with them. Jessa Robbins, about a week after he had killed a moose on Gillmor's Meadow, was going toward the spot, and, perceiving something there, he made a noise. The animal raised its head till its ears appeared just above the tall grass. Robbins fired, and "shot a bear through the lights." He went up to him, and "affectionately" took hold of his paw; but Bruin resented the treatment, and it was necessary to give him another shot. The same man caught seven bears in five weeks, eighty or a hundred rods south of his house, in one log-trap baited with the entrails of fish. David Robbins caught five more in the same five weeks, within a few rods of the same spot. At a much later date, Ezekiel Hagar, from Concord, Mass., after living in the west part of the town about twenty-five years, said that he had killed forty. Some he caught in a large steel trap; others he shot in cornfields; and, with the assistance of a faithful dog, he took others in dens. He would set in different places small sap-troughs, into which he would pour New England rum, of which the bears were as fond as topers. To make the rum more palatable, he would even sweeten it. Two small cubs were taken by him and sold to Rufus Gillmor, who kept them till the following autumn. They were commonly confined in a pen. When occasionally let out, they would climb the willows east of his house. Once, when N. Robbins, Esq., being highway-surveyor, was carrying a keg of rum to the men at work, they came down from the trees, hugged the keg, and licked it; and he was obliged to call for help to take them off and shut them up. A traveller took them to Boston. A shooting-match was made; they were taken to Dorchester Heights; a fee was exacted for each shot; they were placed at a great distance; — and there they were killed.

Jessa Robbins says, that, on a Sunday morning, John Butler, then a young man, living at the Mill Farm, called to him across the pond to bring him some fire, as he had none, and no gunpowder to enable him to get any. After he had gone over, and had begun to assist Butler in kindling it, an object was discovered swimming from Hills Point towards the other shore. Taking an axe, they hastened to the boat, threw into it a few stones, and plied the paddles. At first it was thought it might be a loon; but, as they approached it, they discovered it to be a bear swimming towards Philip Robbins's cow-pasture, which was on the south side of the river, where it enters the pond. Hogs were in the pasture; and a gentle, steady breeze, blowing from that quarter, had probably been snuffed by the bear, and led him to make a movement for a dinner of pork. Jessa Robbins and John Butler shouted, and thus aroused Philip Robbins's family. The bear was alarmed, and put forth all his strength to reach the land. Robbins and Butler redoubled their exertions, and it became a race between them and Bruin. The bear, however, was intercepted about five or six rods from the shore. Robbins sprang to the bow of the boat, and, with the axe raised, was about to strike him; but he was dissuaded from it by Butler, who was afraid, if the blow should not be fatal, that Bruin would attack the boat, and their lives be endangered. Bruin was terribly enraged. He growled, and ground his teeth; but, finding he could not be permitted to land, he turned towards the island. He crossed it from the north end to the south, and again entered the water to swim to the shore. Here he was intercepted by Philip Robbins's boat, and obliged to return to the island. No alternative now remained for him but to climb one of the seven trees. He went to the foot of a large dead pine; and, after deliberately seating himself, and looking towards the top, he made a leap up the tree. He hugged it, holding on to the sides with his paws and claws, and climbed; using sometimes his legs, at other times taking hold of the limbs with his teeth, till he went up nearly to the top. After seven or eight discharges of a gun, the bear fell dead at the bottom of the tree.[1]

John Butler was a fleet runner, and often said that he could outrun any bear. An opportunity occurred to put him to the test. He treed three cubs on a tall pine which stood on the hill-side back of Hart's house. The barking of his dog, and his hallooing "A bear! a bear!" were heard by Jessa Robbins and others on the other side of the pond. They, with their dogs,

---

[1] Mrs. Mero says the occurrence was within three, or at most four, years after her father moved into Stirlington; and that he, being at Warren the day before, did not come home till that morning. When he heard the firing, he hurried as fast as possible, expecting the enemy had come. She also differs as to some of the details.

hastened to the spot. The cubs were very high. The balls, which were too small for the bores of the guns, did not seem to produce any effect. After firing several times, Robbins proceeded to climb the tree. As he was going up, he found that one of the young bears had been seriously wounded. On climbing nearer, the three ran out on one limb. He went out on the limb next below, till he came to a bend in the upper limb, which then struck off in a different direction from the one on which he was standing. Being thus prevented from getting any nearer, he took a large jackknife, and, resting his chest against the upper limb, reached his hand as far as he could, to cut it off. The limb being borne down by the weight of the cubs, he had cut but partly through it, when it suddenly cracked and broke. As the bears jumped, the stub part of it sprang back against Robbins, and "knocked the breath out of his body." One of the bears was killed by clubs, as soon as it reached the ground. Another was treed, about half a mile off, by the dogs, and shot. The third one, which had been seriously wounded, fell into the top of a leaning tree, and, what was very uncommon, ran head foremost to the ground. He started off over the hill, and Butler after him. "Each did his best." For a few minutes, they went as fast as their legs would carry them. But, as neither of the dogs happened to follow with Butler, the young bear escaped. Butler's companions laughed at him and teased him a good deal, because he had so often bragged that he could outrun any bear; and yet, when it came to the test, he had been beaten in the race by a lame or wounded young cub. Jessa Robbins says, in justice to Butler, however, it ought to be added, that on level ground he was probably as fleet as Bruin; and, if he had not been obliged to climb a hill in the race, he would have been the victor.

John Butler's dog treed a bear very near the pond, on land now owned by Lyman Alden. Butler heard the barking, and hastened to the tree. Philip Robbins and his son Jessa Robbins, on the other side of the pond, heard Butler halloo as was usual, "A bear! a bear! bring a gun." Accordingly, they took their guns and dog, and put off in their boat to go to his aid. The dog, knowing what was at stake, stood at the bow of the boat, and, the moment it was near enough, jumped on shore, and thus shoved the boat back. On coming to the shore again, Jessa Robbins jumped, and the boat was again pushed back. Philip Robbins called to his son, and told him not to fire till he came. The son hastened to find Butler. Shortly, on looking round, he saw his father raising his gun and seeking a good opportunity to aim and fire. Jessa Robbins, being six or eight rods nearer, raised his gun and shot Bruin through the vitals. The bear fell dead to the ground. Although he was killed, the father was a little vexed that he should have been so adroitly deprived of the satisfaction of doing it. "Jess! Jess!" he exclaimed, "did I not tell you not to fire till I came?" "Oh, yes!" coolly replied the son; "but, father, I was afraid you would not hit him."

Not long after the town was incorporated, there was a field of corn on Simmons's hill. The bears made such havoc that it was feared they would destroy it all. Guns were borrowed in all parts of the town, and set round the field. Among them was a long kings-arm, owned by Samuel Hills, which was loaded for the occasion with two iron slugs, one about an inch and a half, and the other about three inches, in length. In the evening, the people, listening attentively, as was usual when guns were set, heard a heavy discharge. On going to the field, it was found that it was from Hills's piece, and that the bear was gone. The next movement was to get dogs and follow him. Jason Robbins had taken part in setting the guns; and immediately, though it was before midnight, he went to Mero's and Josiah Robbins's for assistance. Richard Cummings and Nathaniel Robbins turned out; and from the place where John P. Robbins now lives, they "struck west" into the woods, intending to keep the dogs with them and be quiet till morning.

They had gone but a short distance when the dogs "set up a terrible yelling." They had found the bear; and it was a huge one. Neither of the men had a gun; for all the guns in town were around the cornfield. Accordingly, with their jackknives they cut cudgels; and remained, and kept their dogs, near the bear. When daylight came, Jason Robbins, who could go to the guns without hazard, took one from the field and despatched him. Both slugs were in his body. He could not travel well, though he would fight the dogs furiously. When shot, he was in a gulley. It was necessary to drag him out, so as to manage him to advantage. All present took hold of him. The dogs inserted their teeth into Bruin's hide, pulled with great strength and with as much zeal as their masters. He was then carried on poles to the cleared land, and "dressed."

When Capt. George West, about the year 1795, lived on the hill afterward owned by Capt. Bachelor, his cattle frequently swam the river to browse and feed on the Robbins Neck. One evening, just before dark, all except a very fat beef-cow came home in a great fright. It seems that a bear had killed the cow on the brink of the river, exactly opposite to West's house, and the other creatures had escaped. It was obvious that the bear was then on the Neck. The alarm was given, and the Philistines prepared to come down upon him. Men assembled the next morning; and several of them stationed themselves at short distances from each other on the west side of the river, to intercept him where he would be likely to cross it. A party was sent on to the Neck to stir him up. Samuel Martin, maintaining that the bear would go as far as he could on the land before he "took to the water," stationed himself near the outlet of Bowker Brook. After a time, he saw Bruin on the Neck across the river. The distance was immense for a shot to take effect; but, thinking it his last chance, he fired. The bear, however, "made off," and crossed the river within a rod or two of Capt. Tobey, who, being more of a sailor than a hunter, did not think to fire at him. Thus Bruin got safe into the meadow, where several persons were making hay. All started after him upon the run; "Old Uncle Sam Hills," then a comparatively young man, chasing him with a rake. Bruin, however, escaped. The party came back to West's tavern "to get something to drink," provoked with Martin for firing, and with Tobey for not firing; and "poking fun" at them both. Martin, however, insisted that when he fired he saw the bear plunge forward. Many words passed, and many jokes were cracked at the expense of Martin and Tobey, till it was finally agreed to go to the spot where the bear was when Martin fired. It appeared that Martin was correct in his statement. One of the bear's large teeth, which the ball had knocked out, was picked up, and his course to the river was tracked by the blood. Some days afterward, Bruin was scented by his carcass, and found dead in the vicinity of Muddy Pond; the ball having passed through the mouth, and cut off the tongue.

At a later period, Adam Martin, of German origin, who lived in Union, near Waldoborough line, was in the woods at work with an axe early in the spring. Hearing the bellowing of a creature, he ran and found a bear killing it. The bear saw him, and stopped. Martin and Bruin stood, and looked at each other ferociously. But, as neither succeeded in looking the other out of countenance, Martin struck his axe upon a hollow log to intimidate his enemy. Bruin resented it; and, in a state of great exasperation, hastened toward him. Martin ran; but, finding the bear gain on him, he sprang up into a tree so small that the bear could not climb it. When Bruin put his paws up against it, he could almost touch him. There Martin had to cling, with his legs drawn up to keep out of his reach. The bear went round the tree and snuffed. He was evidently very hungry. Twice he went away and returned. Martin became almost exhausted; and when, at the third departure, the bear went a little further, and the view was intercepted,

Martin let go his hold, dropped to the ground, and ran. The same night, he set a trap and caught him. Martin said he was never frightened before.[1]

Jason Ware had a small white dog, named Sambo, who entered into the spirit of his profession with even more zeal than his master, and who acquired great reputation among the people and hunters in this section of the country for his skill and success. In one season, Sambo assisted in killing thirteen bears. There was no dog in town quite equal to Sambo. He would follow any person carrying a gun. If he was wanted, it was only necessary for him to hear his name, and he would go, however far it might be. He has been known to obey a call, and run from his kennel to the Old Burying Ground hill, whether his master went or not.

His method of pursuit was to keep near Bruin's heels, and bite him. The bear, not pleased with such strong attachments on the part of Sambo, would tumble over backwards, or turn about to attack him. As he was large and clumsy, Sambo was always able to retreat a few steps, and then he would stand in security and watch the bear's motions. "As soon as the bear picked himself up, and began to go ahead again," Sambo renewed his attacks. The bear would again turn, and Sambo again retreat. Though Sambo seemed to take much satisfaction in this mode of travelling, his bearship evidently was not well pleased. He could not get along so fast as he desired. And, more than this, he was frequently delayed by Sambo's remarkable attention, till the gunners came near

---

[1] "I have heard this story told in one of our grog-shops, by one of our ancient fathers, in native eloquence equal to that of Logan. This patriarch [David Robbins] was a large man, and had been a great bear-hunter. He wore a black overcoat and bearskin socks; his hair and complexion peculiarly favoring the occasion. After speaking his prologue, this orator walked round the floor in a bear's gait, as he supposed the bear went round the tree; and then, in imitation of the bear, he turned up his eyes and nose, and, after exhibiting a ghastly grin and making a frightful growl, he snuffed like the bear to smell the German." — *MS. Letter.*

enough to shoot him; or was so overcome by it that he would be obliged to take leave of Sambo and climb a tree.

Elisha Partridge was paddling his boat up the river above Round Pond one evening, and, by the bright moonlight, saw an old bear munching acorns on the point of land on the east side. He whistled for Sambo, whose kennel was not far distant. Sambo sprang out, ran furiously down to the river, and at the first bound went half-way across the channel. He was immediately at the bear's heels, drove him up the river, and treed him on a pine which stood on the Robbins Neck, not far from the barn now owned by Hugh S. Gordon. He was watched till morning, when he was found to be very large, and to have climbed only about twenty feet from the ground. He was fired at. The ball struck him in the breast, but too low to wound the heart. Bruin then went up the tree about sixty feet. He was fired at and wounded several times. Finally, a ball was shot through his heart. He fell dead to the ground, breaking and clearing every limb in his way.

But, alas! poor Sambo! His end was tragical. In March, he went, with Joseph Meservey and others, into the Medomac country to hunt. The men, having ousted a bear from his den, thought it best, availing themselves of Sambo's assistance, to drive him toward home, instead of killing him at once and carrying or hauling him. When they had gone some distance, and were crossing Appleton Ridge, the dog, in attempting to leap back after biting the bear's legs, as the snow was deep and soft, came in contact with a tree. Bruin struck him with his paw, knocking him up into the air; and, as he came down, hit him again. Meservey wrapped him in his blanket, and brought him home; but he was about dead. Thus fell poor Sambo, a martyr to the cause of bear-hunting. No record remains of his obsequies; no marble monument points out his resting-place; no epitaph records his valorous deeds. He was probably buried like a dog.

MRS. HART AND THE BEAR-TRAP.

Sometimes the alarms from bears led to ludicrous, and at other times to painful, results. In 1794, when the men had gone to a military training, and the only persons at South Union, except little children and Hervey Maxcy, who was about ten years old, were Mrs. William Hart, Mrs. Josiah Maxcy, and Mrs. Joseph Maxcy, they were disturbed by the squealing of hogs. As the noise was loud and continued long, the women came to the conclusion that the hogs must be attacked by a bear, and resolutely went out against him. They found the old porker and her two young ones dangling in the air, and squealing so loud that they might be heard one or two miles. The swine had been caught in a bear-trap, which had teeth or spikes as long as one's finger. It had been so fastened to a bent tree, that, when it was sprung, the tree, with the suspended trap, would return to its natural position. The women bent down the tree, two of them with their feet pressed upon the springs; and the two pigs jumped out and ran off. But the old porker could not get away so easily. The teeth of the trap had penetrated under the cords. Mrs. Hart undertook, when the other women were pressing down the springs, to open the jaws of the trap, and release the animal. She succeeded; but, just at that moment, the jaws were sprung together, and caught her by both hands. The long teeth or spikes penetrated them, and the scars of the wounds are visible to this day.

CHAPTER XLIX.

ZOOLOGICAL HISTORY.

(*Continued.*)

Wolves. — Wolf Hunt. — Cat-vaughan. — Foxes. — Personal Experience. — Fox seized by Asa Messer. — Beavers. — Raccoons. — Musquash. — Minks, Sables, and Loup-cervier. — Weasel.

WOLVES.

The wolves in this part of the country seem to have had their principal head-quarters in the dense, gloomy, and almost impenetrable forest along the seashore between the St. George's and the Muscongus Rivers. There they suckled and reared their whelps in low ledges and dens. Thence they went forth on their "long gallop" to a great distance, ranging and prowling through the wilderness and the new settlements, and making night hideous with their howlings. In early times they were numerous and saucy; bold when famishing, but generally sneaking from danger; and howling piteously and imploringly when caught alive. They were carnivorous, but would eat vegetables, and in winter have been known to feed on sumach-berries. They were very fond of the sheep of the early settlers; but they would on an emergency accept poultry. Young colts and calves were not exempts, and they have sometimes attacked swine. Seldom were any seen in Union on the east side of the river. Farmers surrounded their barn-yards with fences of long poles placed perpendicularly and contiguously, and pinned or spiked on transverse poles or joists, to keep these thieves from their herds and flocks. In summer, light fences were made in the woods, with gaps at the wolves' paths. A log was laid across each of these openings, and a trap set so that when the wolf stepped over the stick he would put his foot upon the trencher. These animals were also shot, and baited and caught in steel-traps and wood-traps. The reputation gained by killing a wolf; the bounty of four pounds for every grown wolf, and one pound for every wolf's whelp; sweet revenge for losses of sheep, swine, and poultry; and the excitement of hunting, — kept up a perpetual and implacable warfare, and thinned their number. Large parties, from time to time, scoured the woods to kill them.

WOLF HUNT.

About the year 1820, late in the fall, a general wolf-hunt was announced through several towns in the vicinity. At the appointed time, there was as large a gathering as at a military muster. With guns, dogs, and ammunition, the men from several towns met at Trowbridge's Tavern, on the Warren and Waldoborough post-road. Joseph Farley, Esq., of Waldoborough, was chosen headman. As his health was poor, instead of going on foot, he rode and gave directions, and he entered with great zeal upon the expedition. Nathaniel Robbins, Esq., of Union, took a position about half-way between the St. George's and the Medomac Rivers. The men stretched out on his right and left, each one in sight of his right-hand and left-hand man, till the cordon extended from river to river. Robbins had a surveyor with him. The orders to him were to run a south course till he struck the salt water. As it was afternoon, it was agreed to camp on the road between the Narrows at Thomaston and Broad-bay on the Medomac. There, along the whole route, — a distance of probably eight miles, — fires were built so near to each other that a wolf could not pass between them without being seen; and, what would frighten the wolves back, a tumultuous noise of firing and hooting was kept up all night. The next day the party went through to the salt water, and even down to the clam-beds. Not a wolf was seen by any of them. If any secreted themselves, they were exterminated by a terrific fire, which swept through the forest, in a very dry season, not many years afterward.

CAT-VAUGHAN, OR CATAMOUNT [?].

In 1777 or 1778, Richard Cummings and Jessa Robbins went beyond Crawford's Pond, near to Miller's present residence, to hunt. Their three dogs set up a violent barking, and treed a wild-cat, or "cat-vaughan;" an animal, however, which seemed to differ somewhat from a wild-cat. It was about as large as a middle-sized dog, and had very sharp claws and very heavy teeth. Cummings and Robbins were short of ammunition; for "powder was one dollar a pound, and hard to be got at that." Robbins said he believed he would go up and get her. Accordingly, he swung his club on his back, and began to climb. As he approached the animal, she growled and "spit" at him, and, from time to time, gave indications of an inclination to attack him. Robbins took his club, and kept up a noise by pounding on the tree as he ascended. She receded from him, and went out on a limb so far that he could not quite reach her with his club. He then began to shake the limb violently, and she jumped. The moment she touched the ground, Cummings, with his club and the three dogs, pounced upon and killed her. The scientific name of the animal is not known. Old hunters told Robbins that his was a very hazardous undertaking.

FOXES.

Formerly, foxes were very numerous. About the years 1816 and 1817, their tracks were so thick on Capt. Barrett's land, on the east side of Seven Brook opposite to Hills' Mills, that, sometimes after a light snow, the fields appeared as if they had been raced over by sheep. Then a good skin was sold for one dollar. Men and boys hunted, and set traps. They enjoyed the excitement, and did not object, when they had skins, to take the money for them. Everybody was talking about foxes, boasting of the number he had shot and denned and trapped; and describing, sometimes in too strong language to bear rigid criticism, his various expedients to outwit Reynard.

Entering into the spirit which then prevailed among the boys, the writer, just at night when a snow-storm was coming on, set his trap a little beyond the brow of the hill, east of Seven Brook, on his father's land. On going as near to the trap as was expedient, in the morning of the two or three following days, it seemed not to have been disturbed. Finally, as the settling snow would spring it, and thus alarm any foxes which might be prowling about, a stick was punched into the fox-bed. The trap was gone. The excitement became intense. A movement was made toward the woods. Sir Reynard heard the noise, and was soon discovered springing and making great exertions to get through or over a brush-fence which the hooks on the end of the trap's chain had prevented him from passing. He was speedily pounced upon and made prisoner. In trying to release himself, he had gnawed through the skin and flesh, and broken every bone in the leg by which he was caught. He was held by nothing but a single cord, and with a few bites he might have severed this and set himself at liberty.

When taken, he feigned sleep, and in this condition was carried a quarter of a mile or more to the kitchen. Here he opened his eyes upon such a scene as he had never beheld. Before him were the culinary implements pertaining to civilized life. Whether his foxship would have preferred a luxurious mode of living to the irregular course to which he had been accustomed, or a chicken "with fixens" to one without them, is left to conjecture, as he was not consulted. His head, up to his ears, was plunged into a pail of water. The skin was taken off and stuffed with hay. A peculiar sensation was experienced when a few months afterward it was removed from the nail on the rough stud by the garret-window, and parted with to a tin-peddler for one bright silver dollar. Such is the history of the only fox which the writer ever had any part in trapping or killing. Hundreds of miles has he travelled, and hundreds of hours has he spent, with his gun and traps; though, with the exception just mentioned, his nearest approach to success was that he once had a "glorious" snap at a fox; but the gun would not go off.

Now for another fox-story; which, though it may seem improbable, is satisfactorily authenticated. On a Sunday morning, about the year 1821 or 1822, Asa Messer was going to a ten-acre cornfield which he had planted on burnt land. Exactly at the corner of the roads leading to Washington and to Skidmore's Mills, within five or six rods of the house afterward built by Robert Pease, and within twenty-five rods of the cornfield, he saw and heard a red squirrel. It was on a spruce, had a piece of an ear of corn, and, for so small an animal, was making a great outcry. As Messer drew nearer, he saw a large fox on a small knoll, lying flat on his belly, and watching the squirrel with intense interest. The squirrel kept descending toward him, and chippering and running back. A large white birch stood three or four feet from the fox, and nearly in a range with Messer. Messer stealthily crept up to the birch. The attention of the fox, with his back toward Messer, was entirely engaged in watching the squirrel, whose repeated attempts to come down had been for some time tantalizing him. After looking round once or twice from behind the tree, Messer concluded to make an attempt to jump on him and seize him. He sprang. Reynard, taken completely by surprise while licking his chops and watching the squirrel, did not attempt to run, but squalled and rolled over upon his back. Messer's feet and hands struck the ground exactly where the fox lay; but, in rolling over, the fox had moved a foot or two. In an instant he seized him by the neck. Reynard, however, soon came to his senses. Messer picked up a stick, one end of which had become rotten, and attempted to strike him. Twice Reynard seized the stick with his jaws, and broke it off. With the remaining part, which was short but harder, Messer pommelled him to death, and carried the carcass to Ichabod Irish, who helped him to skin it.

During the last twenty or thirty years, John F.

Hart's dogs and the zeal of hunters have been thinning the foxes and driving them away. Now they are very scarce.

BEAVERS.

It is said that there must have been many beavers in Union when it was a wilderness, and that to them the inhabitants are mainly indebted for the meadows. As their dams, one after another, have decayed and been destroyed, meadow-grass has grown where there was none when the ground was flowed. Be this as it may, there is no doubt that there were beaver-settlements on the meadow at the north end of Seven-tree Pond and in other places. Within the recollection of the early inhabitants, a very few beavers have been killed at Muddy Pond. The barrier, more than forty rods long and from two to six feet high, which extends from Vinal Ware's land on the north side of Round Pond to St. George's River, is the work of beavers; the bottom probably having been made of logs, and fastened by them, till the dam, which made the meadows on the north of it, was completed. Samuel Boggs, of Warren, availing himself of the circumstance that these animals always hasten to repair their dams when broken, made a breach in it, set his trap there, and caught one. The river at that time, down which logs were rafted, entered the pond twenty or thirty rods east of the place where it now does; and hay is carted over the old channel, while the little opening made by Boggs has become the main outlet. The singular circumstance may be added, that, as late as the time of the incorporation of the town, the water of Round Pond extended to the beaver-dam; and it was not till the present century that hay was cut south of it.

RACCOONS.

Raccoons were plenty. Phinehas Butler shot one on the top of the old camp at South Union. In cutting a road to the Medomac Meadows, forty were taken or killed in the course of a few days. One man

caught forty in one season. He took nine in one
hollow log or in dens in three different years, and
seven at another time. The flesh was palatable; and
their skins, about the year 1815, were sold for about
one dollar each.

MUSQUASH.

Musquash abounded in the streams and meadows.
Amariah Mero took sixteen out of one hole. When Dr.
Sibley resided on the farm south of the Old Burying
Ground, he shot and caught in traps fifty-one in one
season. When they were drowned out of their nests
by a freshet, William Hart would take some man with
him, row along the rivers and meadows, and bring
home a back-load of them. Their flesh was not eaten,
except in cases of oppressive want; but their skins
commanded a fair price, at a time when hats were
manufactured of fur.

MINKS, SABLES, AND LOUP-CERVIER.

Minks and sables were hunted, the former with
success. Some twenty-five or thirty years ago, Story
Thompson killed a loup-cervier near Mr. Stewart's.

WEASEL.

Thirty or thirty-five years ago, a weasel was in the
habit of coming to the premises of Dr. Sibley, immediately after he assumed his white winter dress, and
remaining till the color of it was changing the next
spring. He became quite tame, but would never allow himself to be touched with the hand. During his
sojourn at the house, he was an exterminator of the
rats and of all the mice which came in his way. He
became mischievous at last among fresh-meat, eggs,
and the like, and finally disappeared, after having
spent four, five, or six winters on the premises.

CHAPTER L.

ZOOLOGICAL HISTORY.

(*Continued.*)

Ducks. — Wild Pigeons. — Loons. — Crows and Blackbirds. — Hunting Matches.

DUCKS.

In early times, ducks were very plenty. They were not much hunted, as there were but few inhabitants, and they had but little time to go after them. Ammunition, too, was scarce and dear. Wood-ducks came in flocks of thirty or forty. Towards night, they would go to the land to get acorns and other food. At low water, there was a sandy beach two or three rods wide on the margin of Seven-tree Pond, at the line dividing Josiah Robbins's farm from the one on the south. Robbins baited them there with green corn, and caught them in a pigeon-net. It was necessary to set the net very near to the water, so as to intercept them; for, when alarmed by its springing, they always hurried in that direction. Here Robbins, having set his net the evening before, entered his bough-house before daybreak, which was the time of their coming. During one summer, when flax was rotting in Seven Brook, at the stone bridge east of Dr. Sibley's, several wood-ducks came to feed on the seeds. Some were killed. Two or three were wounded and caught; but all attempts to tame them were useless.

WILD PIGEONS.

Many years ago, when the country was new and rye-fields were numerous, wild pigeons came in countless multitudes. It seemed as if they were sent, like the quails of old, to relieve the wants of the people. Early in spring, when they flew high, flocks have been seen so large and long that the two ends were not in sight at the same time. Great numbers were caught by all the early settlers. Sometimes they were salted, and kept till winter. Many were taken on the Old Burying Ground hill. Nathaniel Robbins, Esq., repeatedly caught twenty-five dozen at once. He sold many to General Knox, who kept them alive till winter, and fatted them. Jessa Robbins caught thirty dozen and ten at one haul. He sold them at Thomaston, mostly for eightpence a dozen, which was considered a good price. Some he sold to General Knox, when he was examining the river, before he moved to Thomaston. Mrs. Dunton says her father, David Robbins, caught so many that he was called Pigeon Robbins. She has known him to take twenty dozen before breakfast, twenty dozen after dinner, and twenty dozen more before dark, — making sixty dozen in a day.

In order to take pigeons by baiting them, the stubble in a rye-field was entirely removed; and a spot ten or twelve feet wide, and fifteen or eighteen feet long, was levelled, and made like a carrot-bed. When there were no leafless small trees near, some were cut, and stuck down as stands for the pigeons to light on. The grain, of which there must always be enough on the pigeon-bed, was laid along in rows. As, in rising from the bed, pigeons always fly in the direction of the stands, the net is set so as to intercept them. A bough-house was built, into which was extended one end of the rope of the net. The catcher commonly secreted himself in the bough-house before daylight, so as to be in season. The pigeons came early, and lighted on the stands. Sometimes they would sit an hour before going down to the bed. At first one would go down, then two or three more. Immediately afterward, nearly the whole flock would pour down. The net was then sprung by pulling the rope. Sometimes, when the flock was very large, it was necessary, in order to prevent the pigeons from raising the net and escaping, to confine it with stones or crotched sticks, placed there for the purpose. The skulls were then broken by nipping the heads between the thumb and finger.

Many were caught by hoverers. A wild pigeon was tamed, which was easily done. A bed was made. The hoverer was tied down in the middle of it, with string enough to let him act freely. When a flock passed over, wishing to join them he would flutter, and call them. Although there was no bait, they would be thus decoyed. As they would not light unless there was bait, the catcher was ready to spring the net upon the flock the moment it struck down where the hoverer was.

LOONS.

Loons have always been numerous, particularly in Seven-tree Pond. Their legs are placed far back on the body, and stick out behind like paddles. Of course they cannot walk on the land. A favorite place of resort for them in breeding-time was the north end of the island. On to this they shoved themselves. There they laid their eggs and hatched their young. They require considerable surface of water to rise on the wing, and can never rise in a calm, nor in any direction except against the wind; and sometimes they have been known to scoot along on the top of the water for half a mile, and yet not succeed.

About the year 1826, Nathaniel Robbins, jun., saw two loons fighting. One would attack the other, which appeared to be the weaker, and the weaker would immediately retreat toward the shore. At last the weaker darted up to the land. Robbins ran about knee-deep into the water, caught it, and carried it to his father's. It was kept a day in the front yard, not being able to rise from the ground, or even walk; and then it was returned to the pond.

Loons often passed between Seven-tree Pond and Round Pond, in the river. They have the power of letting themselves down so low in the water that nothing but the head will appear above the surface.

They often do this in small places. When Nathaniel Robbins, Esq., was fishing for salmon with a seine, these birds would sometimes enter the river to go to Round Pond; and, in consequence of letting themselves down, they would stick their heads into the net-work below the rope. Their feathers being stiff, they could not draw them back; and, being very muscular, they would flap their small but very strong wings, till they wound up a great part of the seine into a snarl. Commonly, they do not go in flocks, but in pairs; though in Crawford's Pond several have been seen together. If they halloo loudly, it is always regarded as a sign of a storm.

John Jones, with a rifle, on the shore opposite the house of Willard Robbins, fired at a loon which he saw at a great distance. The loon was not wounded, and it dived. Upon rising, it hallooed, as if in defiance. Jones stood still, and fired a second time. Again the loon went down, and after a few minutes re-appeared. With each dive he made great advances towards the shore. He uttered another loud scream. As his body was sunk into the water, Jones fired, the third time, at his head. The ball struck very near the eye, and killed him instantly.

CROWS AND BLACKBIRDS.

May 28, 1788, the town voted to " allow as a bounty on crows eightpence per head, and one penny for blackbirds, for all killed in town by town-inhabitants for the year ensuing. ... June 20, 1803, voted that twenty cents be given for crows and five cents for blackbirds. Voted that the town-treasurer be empowered to receive crows and blackbirds, and pay for the same; and that he cut off their heads." May 14, 1804, an article " to see if the town will allow a bounty for crows and blackbirds, striped and red squirrels," was dropped. No bounties have been voted since.

Crows continue to be numerous. Half a century after the settlement of the town, flocks containing several hundreds would light on the hills and pastures in summer, and early in autumn, to feed on grasshoppers. They have never been quite so saucy in Union as they have occasionally been in other places. A few years ago, in Hopkinton, N. H., they killed seventeen turkeys in one flock, not taking one daily, as a hawk does, but destroying an entire brood at once. One farmer in that town discovered, on one of his lambs, a crow, which had picked out one eye, and was thwacking the lamb over so as to pick out the other. A neighbor lost eight lambs in one spring, which were undoubtedly killed by them. Of some of the lambs the tongues as well as the eyes were picked out. The crows in the neighborhood had become very bold. But in Union probably nothing of the kind has occurred. The most which is apprehended from them is the injury they may do in the cornfields; and to these it is believed they do no harm in spring, by pulling up the corn, unless they have young. When it is considered that it is very easy to scare them away at the seasons of the year when they do mischief, the policy of killing them may be questionable. They are scavengers and carrion-eaters, and destroy an immense number of insects and worms, which, without their co-operation, would in time bring desolation on many a rich field.

HUNTING MATCHES.

When the town was first settled, game was plenty; and for a long time there was one hunting-match or more yearly. Men who proposed to take part met and agreed on a day to which the hunt should be restricted, and determined the comparative value of different animals, according to their scarcity. A bear, perhaps, would count 100, a fox 20, a racoon 15, a partridge 6, a crow 5, a grey squirrel 3, a red squirrel 2, a blackbird 1, and so on. The party then chose two captains, and they cast lots for the first choice. After the successful captain had selected a man, they proceeded alternately till all present were enrolled in the one or the other company. On the day appointed, every man went to hunt. In the evening, all came together. The game killed by each one was counted, according to the principles before laid down. The company which was victorious sat down with the other to a supper, the expense of which was paid by the vanquished. Sometimes, instead of joining in companies, the hunters paired off against each other, and the man who came at night with the least game paid for his rival's supper.[1] Game, however, is now scarce, and the old hunters are nearly all gone.

CHAPTER LI.

ZOOLOGICAL HISTORY.

(*Concluded.*)

Fish Laws. — Salmon. — Alewives. — Fish-hawks and Eagles. — Eels. — Smelts. — Trout and Pickerel. — Other Fish.

FISH LAWS.

JULY 7, 1786, after the inhabitants here had made a movement to obtain an Act of Incorporation, and about three months before the Act was passed, the Legislature made a law "to prevent the destruction, and to regulate the catching, of the fish called salmon, shad, and alewives, in the Kennebec," and several other rivers, including the St. George's. No obstructions were to be built, or to be continued, which would prevent the fish from going up to the lakes and ponds

---

[1] This kind of enjoyment suggests another, which sometimes was had sixty or seventy years ago, though it was not common. A man had wood to be sledded, or corn to be gathered or to be husked. He procured as much liquor as he thought would be necessary, prepared a supper, and invited his neighbors to the Bee. They came and assisted him in the afternoon. After the supper, the more genteel and the better dressed would go into the room, and dance with the young women; while those who were somewhat ragged, or wanted courage to enter, would at the same time be dancing the double-shuffle in the entry or around the door, to the same music which was sung to the dancers within the house.

to cast their spawn, between April 20 and June 10, annually. The owners of all dams were required to open sufficient sluice-ways and passages, at their own expense, for the fish to go through. During the same period, no persons were allowed to catch them "at any other time than between sunrise on Monday and sunset on Thursday in each week," or at any time to "set any seine, pot, or other machine, for the purpose of taking any ... within two rods of any sluice or passageway;" and no seine or net was to extend at any time more than one-third across the stream. It was ordered that the Act be read in town-meetings, in the month of March or April, annually. Every town and plantation was required to choose a committee to see it enforced, and to prosecute offenders. "Any person so chosen," who should "refuse to serve," unless he were elected to some other office, incurred a penalty of forty shillings. It was in accordance with this Act that fish-wardens were first chosen, at the first regular meeting after the town-organization. They were then denominated "a committee to take care that the fish should not be stopped contrary to law, the year ensuing."

FISH.

SALMON[1] remained in ponds and deep places in the river during the summer. In the fall, when the autumnal rains came, they went up the river, and cast their spawn in large holes, which they made in the sand at the bottom of the stream. From the upper and the lower end of the little island at the bottom of the eddy below the Middle Bridge, John Butler extended to the western shore two wears, the lower one having in it an eel-pot for the fish to pass through. From the water between the wears he would not unfrequently, in the morning, take out two or three large salmon[2] with a pitchfork. Between the years 1790 and

---

[1] Salmo salar. — *Lin.* The scientific names have been furnished by the eminent ichthyologist, Horatio Robinson Storer, of Boston.

[2] Nathaniel Robbins, Esq.

1800, Royal Grinnell, with pitchforks, took from half a barrel to a barrel of them in a hole in the river opposite to his house in the summer;[1] but they were not so good as if the weather had been cool. About the year 1790, Josiah Robbins, with Philip Robbins, Amariah Mero, and Rufus Gillmor, made a salmon-net, and set it off Gillmor's land below the bridge, and in one year took more than two thousand pounds of salmon, which were salted for winter. About the years 1803 or 1804, when mills were first erected at the Middle Bridge, the workmen killed these fish with axes and carpenters' tools. They were plenty, and furnished an important and luxurious means of subsistence to the early settlers. They disappeared many years ago.

ALEWIVES[2] are numerous. Formerly the best places for them were near Taylor's Mills and Hills' Mills. The object in choosing fish-wardens in 1823, after neglecting it for some time, was to prevent the boys from taking the fish, as they had done for several years, at Crawford's River. In the morning, the alewives would pass up to the falls; and, being prevented from going further, they would all return in the course of the afternoon. By putting a rack across the river, ten or twelve rods from its mouth, the boys were enabled before night to take all that had gone up. William Gleason, Esq., observed that, if the fish were allowed to go down, a little time intervened before others came. The conclusion was, that they went off in search of another stream, and were followed by one or two of the shoals near them. In one, two, or three days, would be seen a few stragglers or pioneers, apparently part of a shoal. If these were caught, others would come, and finally the whole shoal, and the shoal be followed by others.

Soon after casting their spawn, multitudes of alewives, seeking a passage to the ocean, may be seen above the dam at Warren. Those which are nearest eddy round, a few each time dropping over, till finally

---

[1] Lyceum Lecture. [2] Alosa tyrannus. — *Dekay.*

the whole shoal, with a rush, goes over, tail first. The young go down later; and, when they arrive at Warren, being about three and a half inches long, and of a suitable size for bait, they are vexed and driven in all directions by eels. The eels are also seen to lie quietly in the grass at the bottom of the water, and dart their heads up from time to time, and take as many as they want from the millions with which the river is crowded. Many years ago, when the only way of carrying boards down the St. George's was by rafting, so many would be killed by getting between them, that the boards would be slippery. When the old canal was used, the posts at the locking would be made greasy by the grinding of them.

FISH-HAWKS AND EAGLES. — With the return of alewives in the spring was that of fish-hawks and eagles. Col. Herman Hawes says he has seen the white-headed eagle, more than fifty times, sitting on a dry tree on Seven-tree Island, watching the fish-hawks to rob them. A fish-hawk would come sailing along, stop in the air, suspend himself with easy flappings at a moderate height, select his prey, then plunge into the water, and, if successful, bring up a fish, shake himself, and think to bear away the prize to his nest. The white-headed eagle, improperly called the bald eagle, in the mean time being on the watch, would start and swiftly pursue him. After many trials, finding he could not escape, he would drop the fish. In an instant the eagle would close his wings, follow it down, and commonly seize it before it struck the ground, or he would pick it up, and, pirate-like, bear it off. Once a fish-hawk in Union dived into the water, brought up a fish, flapped his wings, and attempted to fly, but failed and was carried down. He rose again, and made another attempt, but was again drawn beneath the water, and seen no more.

EELS[1] are not popular; and, as the streams and ponds are favorable to their multiplication, they are

---

[1] Anguilla Bostoniensis. — *Dekay.*

numerous. Thirty or forty years ago, one or two bushels might sometimes be caught in an eel-pot placed over-night at an opening in Bachelor's dam. More recently, for about two months, beginning with the early part of August when they are passing down the river, the wash-box of the factory at South Union is found to contain from a peck to a bushel every morning. When the water is so high that the waste-gate is opened, none are caught. The fish pass into the flume, and are carried into the wash-box by the water, which rushes so furiously into it through a four-inch aperture, that they cannot re-ascend. This is their only passage down; as, during this season, but little if any water runs over the dam.

The question naturally arises, How do these fish go up? Every year when the water is low, in July, it is found that the dam needs gravelling in several places. Did the eels work their way up by removing the gravel? Small eels have been seen two feet out of water on the side of a wet flume, apparently endeavoring to ascend St. George's River. It has been intimated that there appeared to be something like a glutinous property on the fish, and that it aided them somewhat in adhering to a wet board or timber, when not immersed in water. When the boys were in the practice of catching alewives in wooden racks at South Union, experience taught them to remove the alewives at night; for eels would frequently reach up and eat them in the box, though it was at least five inches above the surface of the water.

When the young go down the river, they sometimes collect in large numbers at the dams; and so bent are they on effecting a passage to the ocean, that they are not unfrequently found with their tails inextricably wedged into the cracks between the planks.

SMELTS. — William Gleason, Esq., says that, in the fall of 1823, part of the wing-dam of the paper-mill, where the factory at South Union now stands, together with a quantity of stove-wood, was carried off by a freshet. After the snow-water had gone, in the spring of 1824, the proprietors of the paper-mill went down the stream to pick it up. There had been a heavy north-west wind the preceding evening; and, while collecting their wood, they found among it, near and at the mouth of Crawford's River, a few dead smelts. Although there were known to be smelts in the lake in Hope, it had not occurred to any one that they were also in Union. Mr. Gleason, inferring from their being found on the bank of the river that there must be some in the river and in Crawford's Pond, immediately made a small net, and was the first person who caught any in town.

When these fish appear in Seven-tree Pond, which is immediately after the snow-water is gone, they are dipped up in nets just at dusk, at the "height of flowage;" that is, where the level and comparatively calm water of the pond makes a small breaker with Crawford's River as they meet. These fish, it is said, are long and slim, and differ from the salt-water smelts. Many are caught in the wash-box of the factory, when the snow-water ceases to run; and this seems to prove, that at that time they go down instead of going up. In September, for the last four or five years, bushels of smelts, lying in windrows, have been found dead along the south-east side of the long island in Crawford's Pond, and on the south-west shore of the pond. As a south-east wind wafts them into Crawford's River, it is a natural inference, that the mortality prevails in the southerly part of the pond.

TROUT[1] AND PICKEREL.[2] — There was formerly a tolerably good supply of trout, and in Crawford's Pond they were plenty; but there was not a pickerel in St. George's River or its tributaries. During the five or six years when the boys caught alewives at Crawford's River, they took with them so many trout that they were nearly exterminated from that river and the pond above. A contribution was raised afterward; and, in March 1827 or 1828, John F. Hart and Marcus

---

[1] Salmo fontinalis. — *Mitchill.*   [2] Esox reticulatus. — *Le Sueur.*

Gillmor made two journeys to Whitefield to obtain pickerel.[1] Having prepared a box with holes in the top to admit air, they succeeded, by changing the water two or three times on the journeys, in bringing alive and slipping into the water under the ice, just below the Lower Bridge, eleven of them. Nine, at the same time, were put into Sunnybec Pond, and nine into Crawford's Pond. The expectation of a favorable result was not very sanguine. There was, however, an understanding that there should not be any fishing for pickerel before the expiration of four or five years. In the fifth year, it was found that they had so multiplied as to be caught in large numbers in the ponds. In a few years, they were found in every pond on St. George's River, and in the tributary streams, and in the ponds in Waldoborough. The small fish on which they feed were so plenty, never having been disturbed by them, that they rioted in unwonted luxury. Some of them weighed five or six pounds, though their average weight at the present time is from eight ounces to one pound. They have nearly exterminated the trout.

Besides the fish mentioned are others, which are common in Maine. Among them are the white perch,[2] yellow perch,[3] roach or cousin-trout,[4] bream or flatside,[5] pout,[6] sucker,[7] &c., the number of some of which has been greatly diminished in consequence of the voracity of their unwelcome intruders, the pickerel.

[1] In 1797 there were pickerel in all the eastern tributaries of Kennebec River, but none in the western. Between the years 1810 and 1820, the Hon. Robert H. Gardiner employed a man to procure some from Nahumkeag. Seven were put into the Cobbesseeontee above his mills, and now pickerel are abundant in the streams and ponds which make that river.

[2] Labrax mucronatus. — *Cuvier.*
[3] Perca flavescens. — *Cuvier.*
[4] Leuciscus pulchellus. — *Storer.*
[5] Pomotis vulgaris. — *Cuvier.*
[6] Pimelodus catus. — *Lin.*
[7] Catostomus Bostonienses. — *Le Sueur.*

CHAPTER LII.

CONCLUSION.

Design. — Sources of Information. — Changes since the Settlement. — Possibilities and Responsibilities.

THE narrative and statistical portion of this history is now concluded. The preparation of it has required much more time and labor than was anticipated. As historical facts cannot be "manufactured to order," and Union is far behind many other towns in the number and variety of topics of general interest, it was at first thought impossible to eke out any thing more than a pamphlet. But materials, such as they were, accumulated; and the result is a volume, designed rather for the inhabitants and the descendants of the early settlers, and for a few friends, than for the public or "the snarling, hungry horde of curs called 'The Critics.'"[1] Accordingly, to some persons it will seem open to the objections of too great minuteness of detail, and of occasional violations of good taste.

Though accuracy and completeness have been particularly attended to, it is obvious that there must be errors and omissions. The writing and printing have been done where the town-records and the inhabitants of Union could not be easily consulted. The information has been taken from a very great variety of sources. Much reliance has been placed on the statements of Messrs. Phinehas Butler and Jessa Robbins, in relation to what occurred among the earliest settlers. Constant use has been made of contributions by Nathaniel Robbins, Esq., and his son Augustus C. Robbins, Esq.; and to the former of them, for verification, nearly all the manuscript was read, in the winter before his decease. It is hardly necessary to state, that the

---

[1] Page 236, note.

letters, lyceum-lectures, and oral communications of Dr. Jonathan Sibley have been of great value in relation to events of the nineteenth century, and have furnished many of the incidents of an earlier date. The most important source of information, however, is the town-records. The loan of these was voted to the writer, "on condition that he give to the clerk, for the benefit of the town, a receipt for the same to be returned in one year, or pay the sum of forty dollars as a forfeiture on failure to return the same in one year or sooner, if wanted." After a few months, they were needed for consultation, and it was necessary to restore them. More information probably would have been obtained from the clerk's office, but for a barbarous act, about the year 1837, by which "all the useless papers," so called, were destroyed. In addition to the sources mentioned are many others, for which credit is often given in the narrative.

A town-history ought to be just and truthful. The bad as well as the good should be told. Though some undesirable occurrences have been recorded, it may be said with truth, that Union contains an industrious, thriving population, and will not suffer in comparison with a majority of other country-towns. Extreme want is not known. Abject degradation and beggary do not, as in cities, dwell side by side with luxury and extravagance. Though there are not probably six persons worth ten thousand dollars each, there is hardly a man who is not in comfortable circumstances. There are but few towns in the county, or even in the State, where the property is so equally divided. A consequence is, that there is no aristocracy of wealth or of family. Every man is a monarch, and independent. At the same time every man is a subject, and amenable to his equals. Upon all a kind Providence has showered down gifts with a lavish hand. The hills and the valleys, the woods, the streams, the soil, the water-privileges, the treasures yet unearthed, the health of the people, show that here are elements of thrift, contentment, and happiness.

The age of the nation and the age of the town are nearly the same. The first family moved here in 1776, the year of the declaration of the Independence of the United States. Four of the oldest settlers are yet living. Mrs. Mero, now of Cape Elizabeth, and Mrs. Dunton, of Hope, were then children. Messrs. Phinehas Butler, of Thomaston, now ninety-three years of age, and Jessa Robbins, the oldest person in Union, being ninety-two, were among the first to wield the axe, and break in upon the wilderness and solitude which reigned where rich fields and beautiful landscapes now meet the eye at every turn. Their lives cover more than the entire period of the existence of the town and the nation. When they came here, thirteen little colonies, containing three millions of inhabitants, were beginning an almost hopeless, but, as it proved, a successful struggle against the oppression and the military and naval force of one of the most powerful nations of the Old World. Since that time, the Federal Constitution has been formed and adopted; the French Revolutions, the career of Bonaparte, the war of 1812, and the Mexican War, have become historical facts. Empires have risen and fallen, thrones have been overturned, science and art have drawn from nature her concealed treasures, steam has been applied to ships and harnessed to cars, and made to do man's bidding, and the telegraph with winged words to outstrip the lightning. The thirteen little colonies have become thirty-one states, containing twenty-three millions of souls, extending from the Atlantic to the Pacific; and their intellectual and moral power is so formidable, that the monarchs of Europe, with their hundreds of thousands of troops always armed and on duty in all their cities and villages, are in awe of a people which has not a military police in a single city in the Union.

The little colony which was begun here three quarters of a century since with one family has become one of the little republics which constitute the great republic of the United States. It is continually sending abroad influences, which, though almost imperceptible, are nevertheless affecting in some degree the destinies of the nation. No individual lives here or elsewhere, however humble, virtuous, or vicious, whose influence is not far more extensive than he imagines. The eloquence and power which waken into life the energies of a people, perhaps are first discovered when opposing iniquity and misrule, or pleading in behalf of justice, virtue, humanity, in a quiet country-town. Men are often surprised at the discovery of talents, of which they were utterly unconscious, till a dire necessity or pressing emergency drew them out. Possibly from the colony planted on the shores of Seven-tree Pond may spring up for mankind a reformer, whose good deeds shall create a reverence for the spot where he was born. The time has been when people would smile, if directed for benefactors of their race to such unpromising youths as Christopher Columbus and Martin Luther begging bread, George Washington surveying land in the wilderness, Andrew Jackson a servant-boy, Benjamin Franklin assisting his father in making candles for a living, or Noah Worcester in humble but honorable poverty pounding on his lapstone. A casual remark overheard by a boy has sometimes awakened ambition and talent which have changed his destiny, and made him a blessing to mankind. So it may be here under genial influences. No man can foresee the important consequences which may result from his one vote at town-meeting, or even from an apparently insignificant word or act in his intercourse with his child, his neighbor, or society. If you wish the town to present attractions for intelligent strangers to settle among you, and your children to become *men* and *women*, and to do something for the improvement of the world, you must liberally and zealously encourage public worship, common-school education, temperance, integrity, piety.

FAMILY REGISTER.

THE following notices pertain to residents before the year 1800, and to their families and descendants. Before deciding hastily that dates are incorrect, it should be considered that a gravestone, a family Bible, and a town-record, may contain three different dates of the same birth or death, and that a private memorandum made at the time is generally preferable to either. A common and almost unaccountable error on records and gravestones is the confounding of the years a person lived with the year of his age when he died; it being stated, for instance, that a man died in his forty-second year, when it is meant he was forty-two years old, and was in his forty-third year.

EXPLANATIONS. — The names of parents are printed in small capitals. The names of the children or second generation are distinguished by the Roman numerals I. II. III. &c. and the common Roman letters; of the grandchildren or third generation, by the Arabic numerals 1, 2, 3, &c. and italics; and of the great-grandchildren or fourth generation, by the Arabic letters (1), (2), (3), &c. enclosed in parentheses, followed by names having spaced letters. The names of children are placed immediately after those of their parents. The descendants of females are placed under the husband, when he is a descendant of an early settler; otherwise they follow their mother.

ABBREVIATIONS. — b. *born;* br. *brother;* c. *childless;* ch. *children;* d. *died;* dr. *daughter;* f. *father;* h. *husband;* m. *married;* p. *parents;* r. *residence;* s. *son;* u. *unmarried;* w. *wife.* A date preceded by the letter t. indicates the year when a man's name first appears on a tax-bill, and may be of value in determining the time of his coming to reside. The earliest tax-bill is for 1791; the next, for 1793.

ADAMS, JOEL, Captain, son of Peter Adams, was born at Franklin, Mass., July 21, 1753; and died, according to the family records, Oct. 22, but gravestone Oct. 23, 1830. In the Christian Advocate, vol. v., No. 18, it is stated that he came in the twenty-sixth year of his age, when there were but three families in Stirlington. In 1781 he married Jemima, or Mima, who died Jan. 1, 1844, dr. of Philip Robbins; had — I. Polly, b. Feb. 28, 1782; m. Rev. Cornelius Irish, Dec. 5, 1804. — II. Peter, b. Jan. 19, 1784; d. Dec. 21, 1793. — III. Jacob Smith, b. Jan. 14, 1786; m. Abigail Heald, who d.; residence, Lincolnville. — IV. Emma, b. Aug. 12, 1787; m. Jeremiah Stubbs, Sept. 16, 1808; ch. 1. *Peter Adams*, b. April 4, 1809; m. Rachel Collins; r. Appleton. 2. *Mercy Ann*, b. Nov. 19, 1811. 3. *Alfred Adams*, b. April 29, 1815; d. about 1824. 4. *Olive Daggett*, b. Aug. 2, 1817; m. a Hart, of Appleton. 5. *Jemima Jane*, m. William Lincoln, of Appleton. 6. *Joel Adams*, d. 7. *Sarah Maria*, m. a Collins, of Appleton. — V. Alford, b. Aug. 9, 1789. — VI. Mima, b. June 22, 1791; m. her cousin Ebenezer Ward Adams; b. at Franklin, Mass., July 23, 1787, son of Ward Adams, of Franklin, and Olivia Daggett, of Wrentham; had 1. *Ward*, tailor, b. July 4, 1812; m. Martha O. Gordon, of Augusta, and has (1). M a r t h a M. S.; (2). W e s l e y F.; (3), O l i v i a C.; (4). E l v e r t o n W. 2. *Calvin Metcalf*, b. Dec. 21, 1813; d. Oct. 5, 1839. 3. *John Martial*, b. April 22, 1815; d. Aug. 1, 1815. 4. *James Orson*, b. Oct. 24, 1816. 5. *Olivia Daggett*, b. June 8, 1818. 6. *Aldres Addison*, b. Feb. 9, 1820; m. Eveline Kilgore, of Waterford; r. Norway. 7. *True Page*, b. Dec. 26, 1821, a Methodist preacher. 8. *Alfred Smith*, b. Dec. 5, 1823, a Methodist preacher, tailor; m. Aroline Davis, of Unity. 9. *Esther Ann*, b. June 18, 1826. 10. *Maryan Day*, b. April 25, 1828. 11. *A son*, b. June 3, 1829; d. June 3, 1829. — VII. James, b. Jan. 15, 1794; m. Caroline Eddy, of Exeter. — VIII. Esther, b. June 25, 1796; m., 1822, Rev. True Page, Methodist minister, who d. in Union, Sept. 4, 1838. — IX. Joel, b. Jan. 30, 1800, a Methodist preacher; m. Jane Hunt, of Readfield; r. Friendship. — X. Ruth, b. Jan. 9, 1804.

ALDEN, EBENEZER, son of Job A., b. at Middleborough, Mass., Sept. 20, 1774; came to Union in the spring of 1795, settled on the hill east of Seven Brook; m. at Franklin, Mass., March 4, 1799, Patience (b. at Franklin, Mass.), dr. of

D. Gillmor; had — I. Horatio, b. Feb. 4, 1800; r. Camden; m., first, in 1822, Sally (b. Readfield, Sept. 12, 1802; d. Feb. 7, 1835), dr. of Capt. Nathaniel Bachelor; and, second, in 1835, Polly, b. June 19, 1807, sister of his first wife; has children. — II. Louisa, b. Jan. 30, 1802; d. in Thomaston, Sept. 29, 1827; m. 1823, Phineas Tyler; and had 1. *William Parker*, b. March 30, 1824. 2. *Edwin*, b. Oct. 25, 1825. — III. Silas, b. June 23, 1804; r. Bangor; m. Jan. 27, 1828, Sarah, dr. of Capt. John W. Lindley. — IV. Selina, b. Dec. 26, 1806; d. Nov. 15, 1807. — V. Lyman, b. Dec. 1, 1808; r. South Union; m., Sept. 17, 1835, Sarah Elizabeth Williams, of Orono, Stillwater; ch. are 1. *Helen Louisa*, b. Aug. 25, 1836. 2. *Eugene Beauharnois*, b. Jan. 1, 1839. 3. *Lyman Martell*, b. Sept. 29, 1842. 4. *Henry Eben*, b. April 4, 1847. — VI. Melina, b. June 16, 1811; r. Thomaston; m., May 25, 1837, George Abbot, Esq. of Temple, who d. 1850; ch. 1. *Lucy Ellen*, b. June, 1839. 2. *George Roscoe*, b. Feb. 1842. — VII. Augustus, b. July 3, 1814; r. homestead; m., Dec. 10, 1840, Margaret Wiley, b. Jan. 24, 1815, dr. of Ebenezer Bancroft Williams, of Gardiner. 1. *Patience Gillmor*, b. March 2, 1844. 2. *Sarah Williams*, b. April 17, 1846; d. March 1, 1847. 3. *George Adelbert*, b. May 25, 1848. — VIII. Ebenezer, b. Dec. 14, 1816; r. East Thomaston; m., June 29, 1845, Caroline Snow, of Thomaston; and has 1. *Francis Marion*, b. May 23, 1848. — IX. James Gillmor, b. March 1, 1819; r. Janesville, Wisconsin; m. Oct. 24, 1842, Alvitia C. Miller, of Bangor; has 1. *James Francis*. 2. *Louisa;* both b. Bangor. — X. Edward, physician, b. 1821, Dec. 13 [family records], or 21 [himself]. — XI. Henry, b. Aug. 5, 1824; d. Oct. 16, 1847. — XII. George Adelbert, b. July 29, 1828; d. May 9, 1829.

BARRETT, AMOS, Captain, b. April 23, 1752, Concord, Mass.; d. Jan. 25, 1829; son of Deacon Thomas Barrett, who m. Mary Jones. Deacon Thomas was the son of Benjamin and Lydia (Minott) Barrett. Benjamin Barrett, who d. Oct. 25, 1728, was son of Humphrey B., who d. Jan. 3, 1716; whose first wife was Elizabeth Payne, and whose second was Mary Potter. This Humphrey was the son of Humphrey B., who came from England to Concord about the year 1640. Mr. Amory, wishing to dispose of his real estate here, agreed with Capt. Amos Barrett to lay out his part in lots, for which he received about four hundred acres

of land, joining Levi Morse's on the north. Part of it is
now owned by Gorham Butler. Capt. Barrett came in 1795.
Mary Hubbard, of Concord, Mass. (whom he m. March 31,
1779), b. Aug. 12, 1755; d. Aug. 4, 1839; had — I. Amos,
b. Jan. 6, 1780; m., first, Feb. 15, 1804, Susanna, or
Sukey, who d. Feb. 17, 1834, aged fifty, dr. of Nathan
Blake; and, second, in 1836, Harriet, dr. of Nathan D.
Rice; f. of 1. *Charles*, b. March 19, 1806; m. Margaret
Giraldman, of New York city; r. Mansfield city, Richland
county, Ohio. 2. *Sarah*, b. Oct. 8, 1810. 3. *Amos*, b.
Aug. 6, 1818; d. March 16 [or 18, according to gravestone],
1834. 4. *Henry*, b. Dec. 12, 1821. 5. *Susan*, b. Nov. 3,
1826; d. Nov. 13, 1829. — II. Silas, b. Aug. 11, 1781;
drowned April 25, 1803, in the mill-pond at the Middle
Bridge, while getting logs into the saw-mill. — III. Mary,
b. June 8, 1784; m., Aug. 2, 1810, Rev. Henry True; ch.
1. *Henry Ayer*, physician, b. Aug. 10, 1812; r. Marion,
Marion county, Ohio; m. Elizabeth Pierce, of Pittsfield,
Mass. (b. Deerfield, Mass.; dr. of James Reed), and has
(1). H e n r y, b. Jan. 26, 1848. 2. *Mary Barrett*, b.
Aug. 28, 1820; m., May 16, 1843, Elijah Vose, Esq., b. at
Warren, March 19, 1807, son of David and Alice (Eastman)
Vose; and has (1). H e l e n A y e r, b. March 5, 1844;
(2). M a r y T r u e, b. Dec. 17, 1849. 3. *Amos Barrett*,
b. July 22, and d. Aug. 6, 1825. — IV. Abigail, b. April 15,
1786; m. Rufus Gillmor, and d. Sept. 30, 1821. — V.
Sarah, b. Nov. 16, 1788; d., of consumption, Sept. 19,
1808. — VI. Harriot, b. April 13, 1791; m. July 29, 1822,
Daniel Fiske Harding, Esq., who was b. Nov. 30, 1784, at
Southbridge, Mass., son of Joshua (b. Medway), and of his
w. Jemima Fiske, b. Watertown, Mass.; ch. 1. *Amos Barrett*, b. March 13, 1825. 2. *Henry Fiske*, b. March 28,
1827. 3. *Daniel*, b. April 10, 1829. 4. *Harriet*, b. May
24, 1832. — VII. Ebenezer Hubbard, b. Jan. 19, 1797; r.
Hampden; m. Joanna E. Vose, May 3, 1825; c.

BLAKE, NATHAN, b. January, 1745, at Wrentham, Mass.;
d. March, 1819, at Albion; m. Mary Day, who was b.
March, 1755, at Wrentham, Mass., and d. January, 1834,
at Albion. He came in 1799, bought the farm of William
Lewis, west of the old Upper Bridge; had — I. Walter, seaman, surveyor, b. May 2, 1782, at Wrentham;
d. Aug. 23, 1846; m., Jan. 15, 1809, Jane, b. July 3,
1784, dr. of Daniel and Emily (Pease) Reed, of Edgar-

ton, Mass.; and had 1. *Emily Reed*, b. Nov. 9, 1809; m., March 25, 1845, Hiram Dorman, who d. in Sanford, August, 1849. 2. *George*, b. June 8, 1811; d. Sept. 18, 1812. 3. *Julia Gillmor*, b. March 31, 1813; d. March 16, 1831. 4. *Charles Frederick*, b. Oct. 24, 1814; r. homestead. 5. *Eliza Tobey*, b. July 27, 1816; d. Feb. 14, 1842. 6. *Augusta Livermore*, b. July 23, 1818. 7. *Clarissa*, b. Oct. 7, 1820; m., June 16, 1848, Samuel Ezra Kellogg; r. Battle Creek, Mich. 8. *Theron*, b. Aug. 12, 1822. 9. *Edward*, b. Dec. 31, 1824; d. Jan. 1, 1825. — II. Polly, or Mary, m., Jan. 10, 1804, Joshua Hemenway; r. Searsmont; and had 1. *George*, b. Nov. 2, 1804; m. Hannah Ferguson; r. Belfast; c. 2. *Mary*, b. Aug. 15, 1806; m. Darius Daggett. 3. *Harriot*, b. Aug. 22, 1809. 4. *Louisa*, b. Dec. 29, 1811. 5. *Anson Blake*, d. 6. *Joshua*. [Thomas, f. of Joshua Hemenway, d. Feb. 6, 1847, aged ninety-four; and Sally Hemenway, Aug. 1, 1820, aged sixty-three.] — III. Sukey, or Susan, m. Amos Barrett, jun. — IV. Clarissa, m., Jan. 22, 1811, Hon. Joel Wellington, of Fairfax, now Albion; r. Houlton. — V. Nancy, d. Sept. 3, 1812, æt. twenty-two. — VI. Eunice Day, m., Jan. 9, 1817, Bailey More, of Searsmont; both d. Nathan Blake had also a son George, who d. Nov. 12, 1802.

BLANCHARD, JOHN; m. Huldah Carriel; came with Capt. Stone; t. 1796; returned to the West, perhaps went to New York; f. of — I. Lydia, b. Nov. 28, 1798. — II. Jonas, b. Nov. 1, 1801; d. Jan. 15, 1802. — III. Nancy, b. June 7, 1803.

BLUNT, HENRY, b. at Bristol, March 28, 1771; paid his first poll-tax here in 1794; lived near the summit of the hill, about two miles north-west of Sunnybec Pond, and d. Aug. 29, 1838. He m. Miss Betsey Clark, b. at Bristol, Jan. 23, 1775; d. May 2, 1839; had — I. Ebenezer, b. June 1, 1796, r. on a part of the homestead; m. Susannah Fuller, of Warren, b. Sept. 29, 1798; had 1. *Henry*, b. Sept. 14, 1821; m. 1846, Emily Andrews, of Wallingford, Conn. 2. *Eliza*, b. Nov. 5, 1822; d. May 21, 1823. 3. *Thomas Johnson*, b. Oct. 22, 1824, lives where his grandfather did; m. Nancy Stone, in 1847, and had (1). E l i z a F r a n c e s, b. Oct. 25, 1847; (2). M a r t h a A n n, b. Feb. 2, 1849. 4. *Isaac*, b. June 19, 1826; d. March 8, 1849. 5. *Arthur*, b. April 4, 1828; d. March 23, 1850.

6. *Mary Ann*, b. Sept. 7, 1830. 7. *Martha*, b. Aug. 13, 1832. 8. *Betsey*, b. April 20, 1834. 9. *Sarah Frances*, b. April 15, 1838; d. June 1, 1842. 10. *Oscar*, b. Aug. 25, 1842.

BOWEN, EZRA, b. Rhode Island, in consequence of a cataract, was nearly blind for many years before he d. Feb. 14, 1832. He m., first, Experience Tolman, of Thomaston, who d. Nov. 8, 1803; and, second, in 1805, the widow Elizabeth (Jones) Erskine (or Aikin, according to the record of the publishment), who d. in Bristol, among her children by her first husband. E. B. had — I. Polly, b. May 26, 1776; d. very young. — II. Sally, or Sarah, b. May 17, 1778; m. John Walker. — III. Susa, or Susan, b. Aug. 15, 1780; d. about two years old. — IV. Polly, or Mary, b. Dec. 8, 1783; m. Daniel Patch; r. Knox. — V. Susan, or Susannah, b. July 9, 1785; m., first, March 29, 1807, Daniel Gibbs, of Thomaston; second, Levi Spaulding, of Searsmont; third, Aaron C. Hadley, of Waldo, where she d. — VI. Ezra, b. Feb. 9, 1788; r. Knox; u. — VII. Isaac, b. July 19, 1790, physician; m. Sarah Martha Andrews, a southern lady, and d. in Augusta in 1839; f. of 1. *Tolman Andrews*, d. 1838, aged seven years; 2. *Eliza Andrews*. — VIII. Amos, b. Feb. 22, 1793; m. Athelinda Gough, in Burnham, and was killed by a tree. — IX. Esther, b. July 22, 1795; m., May 29, 1823, Rev. Peter Burgess, a Methodist minister; r. Palmyra. — X. Oliver, b. Sept. 26, 1799; m., first, July 29, 1824, Eliza Fisher, of Warren; and, second, July 29, 1827, Margaret Roakes, of Warren, and had *James Fisher*, b. May 22, 1825. — XI. Tolman, b. Nov. 8, 1803; m. Charlotte Woodman; r. Belmont.

BOYDEN, JUSTUS, from Stoughtonham (?), t. 1791; took up the Obadiah Morse lot of land, tarried a short time, and returned to Massachusetts.

BROWN, JONATHAN, t. 1795, son of Jonathan Brown, from Thomaston; m. Sally, sister of Edward Jones. His father bought for him the land, with the standing crop of rye, belonging to John Fairbanks. He lived on that and other places; was a Methodist, and also, it is believed, a Free-will Baptist, preacher, and moved to Bowdoinham. — I. Ruth, b. Dec. 25, 1794. — II. Polly, b. Nov. 15, 1797; d. Jan. 17, 1798. — III. Edward, b. Jan. 9, 1799; m. Mary Clark, of Appleton, Oct. 21, 1824; r. Liberty; had *James Gardner*, b. Aug. 25, 1825; *Calvin S.*, b. Feb. 6, 1829;

Edward, b. Feb. 12, 1834; *William*, b. Oct. 11, 1836; *Jacob*, b. Nov. 30, 1839; and probably others. — IV. Phebe, b. Dec. 20, 1800. — V. Reliance, b. Feb. 18, 1803. — VI. Joel, b. Aug. 10, 1804. — VII. Jonathan, b. July 9, 1806. — VIII. Sally, b. Oct. 25, 1808; and probably others.

BUTLER, CHRISTOPHER, son of John, was b. Sept. 18, 1750, at Edgarton, Mass.; d. Jan. 26, 1821, of lung-fever. Early in life he "went whaling" to Davis's Straits. His fondness for society led him often to visit the inhabitants in different parts of the town and to go out of town. He seldom, perhaps never, rode, but walked. Instead of wearing a hat, which affected his head painfully, he always wore a green baize cap. His voyages in early life made him familiar with the signs of the weather, and his prognostications were regarded by many people as almost oracular. Jan. 2, 1772, he m. Lydia, dr. of Joseph Luce, of Chilmark, Mass., who was b. Nov. 10, 1750, and d. Jan. 28, 1843; had — I. Jane, b. Nov. 2, 1772; m., first, Jason Robbins; and, second, Sterling Davis. — II. Nabby, b. July 14, 1774; m. Joseph Robbins, and d. of dropsy, Oct. 7, 1818. — III. Polly, b. Oct. 2, 1796; m., Oct. 28, 1799, Adam Kelloch, of Warren, and moved to China. — IV. Betsey, b. Oct. 20, 1778; d. Sept. 12, 1793. — V. John, b. June 16, 1780; m. Feb. 11, 1803, Hannah Harthhorn, of Cushing, who was b. Oct. 8, 1779, dr. of Samuel and Elizabeth (Tewksbury) Harthhorn, of Marblehead, Mass.; and had 1. *William*, b. Sept. 9, 1804; m., Nov. 18, 1827, Lois Newbit, and had (1). L y d i a S e l i n a, b. Sept. 28, 1828; (2). E l m i r a I r a v i l l a, b. May, 1831; (3). J a c o b W a r d, b. Feb. 1835. 2. *Lydia*, b. April 18, 1806; m., May 2, 1833, Andrus Dwinell, of Orono, Old Town. 3. *Selina*, b. Feb. 11, 1808; m., first, William Bartlett, of Thomaston, Sept. 20, 1832; and, second, John O'Neil, of Thomaston. 4. *Gorham*, b. Nov. 20, 1809; m., Nov. 1845, Catherine Gallop, of Thomaston, and has (1). J o h n, b. Sept. 1846. 5. *Ward*, b. Aug. 18, 1811; r. Thomaston; u. 6. *Elbridge*, b. Oct. 18, 1816; d. Aug. 7, 1826. 7. *Christopher*, b. May 18, 1820; r. homestead; m. Sally Healey, of Thomaston, and has (1). L y d i a A m e l i a, b. Aug. 14, 1846; (2). W i l l i a m O s c a r, b. Aug. 29, 1848. — VI. Rebecca, b. Oct. 5, 1782; m. Joel Robbins. — VII. Gorham, b. May 9, 1785; m., Sept. 25, 1808, Sally, dr. of Seth Luce; and fell down dead in his cow-yard, Sept. 17, 1836; f.

of 1. *Elmira*, b. Oct. 23, 1809; m., first, Prince, son of Thaddeus Luce; and, second, in 1849, William Bishop; r. Belfast or vicinity. 2. *John*, b. Feb. 6, 1813; m. Ann Maria, dr. of Simeon Noyes, of Hope; and had (1). G o r h a m, b. Jan. 6, 1838; (2). S i m e o n N o y e s, b. April, 1840. 3. *Wesley*, b. Sept. 3, 1817; r. homestead.

BUTLER, JOHN, brother of Phinehas, b. Feb. 10, 1756, at Framingham, Mass.; d. Thomaston, Feb. 6, 1840; m. 1777, Lucy, dr. of Oliver Robbins, of Thomaston, and she d. Jan. 29, 1840. He was in the service of Dr. Taylor till twenty-one years old; ch. — I. James, b. Nov. 8, 1778; m. Mary Gray; r. Rockland; had three sons and four drs. The second son, *Calvin*, d. July, 1848, leaving three drs. — II. Lucy, b. March 15, 1780; m. David Gay; r. Rockland; had nine sons and three drs.; lost three sons. — III. John, b. May 18, 1781; m. and d. at Smithfield, R. I.; had three sons. — IV. Betsey, b. Aug. 22, 1783; d.; m. Rd. Smith; r. Rockland; had two sons and one dr., having lost one son and one dr. — V. Hannah, b. June 17, 1785; m. John Spear; r. Rockland; three sons and two drs.; one of the sons d. — VI. Briggs, b. March 3, 1787; m., Feb. 3, 1817, Ruth Rowell; r. S. Thomaston; has six sons. — VII. Alden, b. Dec. 7, 1788; d. Oct. 15, 1792. — VIII. Otis, b. March 9, and d. April 29, 1791. — IX. Brackett, b. Thomaston, Jan. 28, 1793; r. S. Thomaston; m., first, Dec. 25, 1816, Nancy Matthews, who d. Aug. 21, 1827, and had five drs.; and, second, Jan. 1, 1834, Eliza Kelloch, of Warren; had five drs. and two sons. — X. Brinton, b. April 18, 1795; r. S. Thomaston; m., Harriet Perry, Jan. 1822, and had eight sons and two drs. — XI. Charles, b. Feb. 12, 1798; m. Jane Houston Russ, of Camden, Feb. 1, 1825; had 1, *Lucy Jane*, b. April 14, 1826. 2. *Charles Edwin*, b. April 20, 1828. 3. *William Henry*, b. April 8, 1831; d. June 7, 1831. 4. *William Thomas*, b. May 19, 1832. 5. *Sarah Elizabeth*, b. March 12, 1835. 6. *Roswell*, b. Jan. 6, 1837; d. Jan. 11, 1838. 7. *Isabella Cecilia*, b. Aug. 7, 1839. 8. *Albert Xavier*, b. Dec. 19, 1841. — XII. Sukey, or Susan, b. Aug. 29, and d. Sept. 15, 1800.

BUTLER, JOSEPH, br. of Phinehas, b. at Framingham, April, 1764; was, like John and Phinehas Butler, but later, bound to Dr. Taylor till twenty-one years of age. He m. Margaret Martin, of Bristol; went with his son Martin to the western part of Pennsylvania, where he spent a few of the last years of his life in the practice of medicine, for which he was never regularly educated. He had — I. Nancy, b. Feb. 18, 1790; m., 1809, Pelatiah Pease, of Appleton Ridge. — II. John, b. Jan. 28, 1792; d. Sept. 16, 1831; m., 1814, Sally Ulmer, of Thomaston; f. of 1. *Elizabeth*, b. Sept. 28, 1814. 2. *Margaret*, b. Sept. 22, 1817. 3. *Harriet*, b. Dec. 18, 1820. 4. *Jane*, b. April 13, 1822. 5. *Matthias*, b. Aug. 7, 1824. 6. *Nancy*, b. April 21, 1827. 7. *Ephraim*, b. Oct. 17, 1829. — III. Martin, b. March 12, 1794. — IV. Susannah, b. June 25, 1796. — V. Peggy, b. Dec. 9, 1798; m. Daniel Roakes, of Appleton, in 1819. — VI. Mary, b. Feb. 25, 1802; m. a Sprague. — VII. William, b. Nov. 15, 1805; d. Dec. 5, 1803; and probably others.

BUTLER, PHINEHAS,[1] son of Phinehas and Bathsheba (Graves) Butler, was b. at Framingham, Mass., April 8, 1758; m., Oct. 18, 1781, Milea, dr of Oliver Robbins, of East Thomaston or Rockland, where he and his wife are now living. Descendants — I. William, b. April 11, 1782; r. Thomaston; m., first, Judith Loring, of Thomaston; and, second, Jane Singer, of Thomaston; had ten ch. all b. in Thomaston. — II. Sarah, b. April 20, 1784; d. Nov. 26, 1792. — III. Shepard, b. March 21, 1786; d. Dec. 17, 1795. — IV. Phinehas, b. April 13, 1788; r. Union; m., first, Catherine Ulmer, of Thomaston, and had twelve ch.; and, second, Hannah Demerritt, of Liberty, in 1833; had two ch.; and, third, Silence Jameson, of Warren; ch. 1. *George Washington*, b. June 10, 1809; m. Eleanor Collins, and had (1). R a c h e l C o l l i n s, b. Aug. 8, 1829; (2). C a t h a- r i n e U l m e r, b. June 11, 1831; (3). S u s a n n a h R o- b i n s o n, b. May 28, 1833; (4). M a r y A n n D o d g e, b. March 16, 1835; (5). H o s e a C o l l i n s, b. Jan. 14, 1837; (6). J o h n S p e a r, b. March 28, 1839; (7). A l- b e r t C o l l i n s, b. Aug. 8, 1841; (8). Clara Ellen, b.

[1] The Lime Rock Gazette, published at East Thomaston, Nov. 8, 1849, says, "Our correspondent at Union furnishes us with the following remarkable and almost unparalleled piece of family history. 'On Sept. 7, 1849, a child was born in Searsmont, who has five great-great-grandparents still surviving, viz.: Mr. and Mrs. Phinehas Butler, of Thomaston; Mr. and Mrs. Thomas Robinson, of Liberty; and Mrs. Elizabeth Ulmer, of Thomaston. The ages of these great-great-grandparents are 92, 85, 88, 88, 85, respectively. The little one is also blessed with three great-grandparents and four grandparents, together with a host of other relatives.'"

FAMILY REGISTER.

Sept. 21, 1843; d. Oct. 23, 1835. 2. *Elioenai Crocket*, b. Sept. 11, 1810. 3. *Thomas Jefferson*, b. July 18, 1812; m., in 1834, Harriet Kinney, of Liberty; r. South Thomaston; had (1). A n d r e w J a c k s o n, b. April 15, 1835; (2). E u n i c e A r o l i n e, b. Sept. 5, 1836. 4. *Sally Ulmer*, b. Aug. 8, 1814. 5. *Eunice Gallop*, b. April 16, 1816. 6. *Catharine Sarepta*, b. May 1, 1818. 7. *Joanna Dean*, b. July 17, 1820. 8. *Mima Robbins*, b. Sept. 11, 1822; d. July 17, 1850; u. 9. *Lucy Tolman*, b. Jan. 20, 1825. 10. *Hannah Richardson*, b. Nov. 15, 1826. 11. *Phinehas Shephard*, b. March 9, 1828; d. Jan. 7, 1832. 12. *Maria Jane*, b. April 23, 1830. 13. *Phinehas Walker*, b. Jan. 6, 1834. 14. *Melea E.*, b. Jan. 4, 1835; d. Sept. 26, 1849. — V. Melea, b. Feb. 23, 1790; d. Sept. 9, 1792. — VI. George, b. Aug. 27, 1792; r. Thomaston; m., Feb. 24, 1820, Mima, dr. of Jessa Robbins, of Union; and had 1. *Ruth Pearce*, b. Sept. 7, 1821; m., Sept. 1, 1844, Albert Sleeper, of South Thomaston; and is f. of (1). M a r y A r o b i n e, b. June 21, 1845. 2. *Catharine Ulmer*, b. April 21, 1824; m., Sept. 5, 1844, William Glidden Colby, of Patricktown; and had (1). W i l l i a m F r a n k l i n, b. June 15, 1846; (2). A l b i o n C e p h a s, b. April 28, 1848; (3). *a son*, b. 1850. 3. *George Washington*, b. Feb. 22, 1826. 4. *Walter Amandar*, b. June 12, 1829. 5. *Caroline Augusta*, b. March 22, 1832. 6. *Jason Robbins*, b. Jan. 17, 1835. 7. *Laura Angeline*, b. June 16, 1837. 8. *Lucinda Arobine*, b. Nov. 21, 1839. 9. *Shepard F.*, b. Oct. 23, 1845. — VII. Levi, b. Jan. 22, 1795; r. Appleton; m., first, Lucy Tolman, of Thomaston; and, second, January, 1848, Mary, dr. of John Walker. — VIII. Melea, b. Oct. 18, 1797; m., Dec. 24, 1829, Samuel Dean; r. South Thomaston. — IX. Joanna, b. Oct. 20, 1800; m. Israel Dean, of South Thomaston; had ten ch. — X. Walter, b. Nov. 22, 1802; m. Joanna Packard, of Nobleborough; r. Rockland.

BUTLER, THOMAS, b. July 15, 1769, at Tisbury, was son of Thomas Butler, whose w. was a Mayhew. He came to Union in May, 1791; m. widow Katharine Toothaker, dr. of Benjamin and Elizabeth (Hathaway) Daggett, who was b. at Dartmouth, Nov. 25, 1772, and d. Aug. 21, 1849. — I. Waldron Stone, b. Jan. 6, 1801; m., July 5, 1838, Harriet, dr. of Otis Bills; and has 1. *Otis Nelson*, b. Oct. 24, 1839. 2. *Eben Edward*, b. Sept. 4, 1841. — II. Jeruel, b. Feb. 14, 1802; r. homestead; u.

CARRIEL, or CARROLL, DAVID, of Groton or Sutton, Mass.; unsuccessful as a merchant in Charlestown, Mass., where he m. Patty Leathers; t. 1797; purchased the farm about one-third of a mile north of the Common; sold it to Dr. Sibley; and d. Sept. 20, 1837, æt. seventy-two. His wife lived in Charlestown when it was burnt by the British, and it is said was with her father in the last boat that, before the battle, crossed Mystic River with any of the citizens. She d. March 4, 1829, aged fifty-eight. They had — I. David, b. Jan. 21, 1792. — II. Nathan, b. March 17, 1793; carpenter; m. twice (once to Betsey Bartlett, of Springfield, Mass.), and d. at Springfield, June 20, 1849. — III. Benjamin, b. Sept. 17, 1794; a mason; went to Manchester [?], Ohio, where he m. twice. — IV. George, b. June 21, 1796; paper-maker; m. in Taunton, Mass.; r. Conn. — V. William, b. March 5, 1798; d. at Gardiner, June 4, 1815. — VI. John, b. Jan. 7, 1801; paper-maker; r. Suffield, Conn., many years, now at New Marlborough, Conn.; w. Ann. — VII. Patty, or Martha, b. Feb. 1, 1803; m., first, April 8, 1824, Cyrus Nye; and had 1. *Edward Thomas*, b. Aug. 9, 1825. She m., second, Dec. 12, 1833, Charles Fogler; and had 2. *Cyrus Nye*, b. Nov. 9, 1834. 3. *Mary Frances*, b. Oct. 20, 1836. 4. *John Fairfield*, b. May 24, 1839. 5. *Martha Ann*, b. April 19, 1841. — VIII. Phebe, b. Jan. 23, 1805; m., first, July 3, 1823, Obadiah Morse; and, second, April 14, 1847, James Adams Ulmer, of Thomaston, by whom she had her fifth child, *Matilda Morse*, b. Oct. 8, 1848. — IX. Hannah, b. Feb. 22, 1807; m. Jesse Robbins, jun., and d. August, 1843. — X. Charles, b. Feb. 5, 1809; started for Ohio; never heard from; supposed lost in a steamboat, which exploded about the time. — XI. Isaac, b. Feb. 7, 1811; d. March 6, 1830. — XII. Lydia, b. Dec. 6, 1812; m., first, Ralph Rising, of Suffield, Conn.; and had 1. *Ralph Wesley*, b. March 3, 1839. She m., second, Thurston Whiting, of Union; and had 2. *Frederick Parker*, b. March 22, 1844. 3. *Mary Buxton*, b. Feb. 6, 1846. — XIII. Amos, b. in 1814.

CARRIEL, JONATHAN, br. of David, was b. at Sutton, Mass.; d. Sept. 5, 1827, aged seventy; came June, 1796, from Groton, Mass. His wife, Sibyl, d. March 31, 1842, aged eighty; had ch., the first eight not b. in Union. — I. Jonathan, b. May 29, 1782; m., May, 1808, Rachel Ripley, who d. Feb. 3, 1814, aged twenty-nine; had 1. *Danford*,

b. Jan. 4, 1810; m., 1841, Harriet Norwood; ch. (1).
M a r c e l l u s, b. June 23, 1842; d. Sept. 13, 1848; (2).
S y l v a n u s R o s c o e, b. Jan. 17, 1844; d. Sept. 19,
1848; (3). A u r e l i u s, b. Sept. 11, 1845; d. Sept. 2,
1848; (4). R a c h e l H e l e n, b. May 28, 1847; (5).
F l o r a R., b. April 6, 1849. 2. *Mahala*, b. July 20,
1812; d. March 5, 1817. — II. Betsey, b. March 22, 1784;
m., October, 1806, Abram Ripley, of Appleton, and d. —
III. Sibyl, b. Jan. 11, 1786; u. — IV. Nathaniel, b. Jan.
29, 1788; m. Rebecca Goodspeed, and d. — V. Polly, b.
April 29, 1790; m., October, 1810, Archelaus Ripley; and
d. July, 1850. — VI. Sally, b. April 3, 1792; d. March 11,
1820; m., 1814, Samuel Norwood, from St. George, who d.
Aug. 31, 1828, æt. thirty-eight; had 1. *Harriet*, b. Sept.
18, 1815. 2. *Samuel*, b. April 12, 1817; m. Sibyl Carriel;
and had (1). L y s a n d e r, b. Aug. 7, 1840; (2). S a r a h,
b. Dec. 25, 1841; (3). S a l l y, b. June 9, 1819. — VII.
Patty, b. Feb. 13, 1794; u. — VIII. Joseph, b. April 27,
1796; d., of consumption, June 2, 1817. — IX. Lucy, b.
Jan. 8, 1798; m., Oct. 17, 1822, James Bryant; and d. —
X. Greenard, b. Nov. 1, 1800; m. Eliza Clark, of Stratham,
N. H.; and d. April 11, 1850. — XI. Stephen, b. Sept.
18, 1802; m., 1827, Jane West Tobey; and had 1. *Sylvester Brown*, b. March 2, 1828. 2. *Leander Tobey*, b.
Feb. 12, 1831. *Adelia West*, b. July 13, 1833. 4. *Charles*,
d. 5. *Augustus Greenwood*. 6. *Albion Dudley*, b. Aug.
19, 1843. — XII. Olive, b. July 31, 1804; u. — XIII.
Silas, b. Feb. 25, 1809; m. Sally, dr. of John Ripley.

CASE, BARNARD, came from Martha's Vineyard in 1787,
and did much in laying out the town. He lived first on the
east side of Sunnybec Pond (where Alpheus Collamore
afterward settled); and, secondly, on the farm of Thomas
Butler. He was considered an excellent scholar for the
place and the time, taught school, worked some as a blacksmith, and was very much respected. In consequence of his
recommendation, the purpose of making a Common of the
Old Burying Ground hill was abandoned. It is said that
he recommended the spot near where the canal crosses the
road; also the present Common. Before many of the roads
were laid out, he surveyed and recommended one from the
neighborhood of the Reuben Hills farm, to run south-east,
along west of Levi Morse's, and perhaps forty rods east of
the falls at South Union, in a direct line to Warren. His

wife d. at Tisbury before he came. He d. of consumption at George West's.

CLARK, ASA (w. Mary); a blacksmith; t. 1799; from Boston; r. near Calvin Gleason's; moved to Newburgh; ch., the first three b. Boston, — I. Allen, b. April 2, 1791. — II. Sally, b. April 4, 1794. — III. Peter M., b. Nov. 23, 1796. — IV. Mary, b. July 14, 1799. — V. John, b. Oct. 27, 1800. — VI. Willard, b. April 1, 1803.

COFFIN, URIAH, in some way connected with the Daggetts in coming to town; t. 1791, and several years afterward; had a w.; c.; believed to have gone back to Martha's Vineyard.

CUMMINGS, or COMINGS, RICHARD (ninth child of Samuel and Susanna Comings), b. Sharon, Feb. 19, 1750, O.S ; m., March 8, 1774, Elizabeth, dr. of Philip Robbins. They had — I. David, b. Nov. 2, 1775; m., March 12, 1799, Rosanna Kelloch, commonly pronounced Kellar, of Warren, and d. March 24 (not 17), 1842; ch. 1. *George*, b. Dec. 3, 1799; m., first, Freelove Dedman, Sept. 2, 1827, who d. Feb. 22, 1839, æt. 31 ; and, second, May 3, 1839, Avis, widow of Sanford Hills ; and had (1). L o a n a, b. June 24, 1828 ; d. Sept. 11, 1828; (2). L o a m m i D e d m a n, b. Sept. 2, 1829; (3). G e o r g e E t h e l, b. Jan. 29, 1832; (4). P l y m p t o n, b. June 9, 1837. 2. *John*, b. Aug. 8, 1801 ; m. and r. Belmont; killed in a skirmish with Indians in Texas, sometime before the Mexican war. 3. *Milton Robbins*, b. Aug. 26, 1803 ; m. Susan Copp, of Merimachi ; r. Appleton. 4. *Avis*, b. Oct. 31, 1805 ; m. Isaac Fuller, and d. 5. *Samuel*, b. Nov. 20, 1807 ; m., first, March 21, 1838, Elvira Jane Litchfield, who d. Aug. 25, 1842 ; and, second, 1843, Paulina Pottle Robertson ; and had (1). V i l e t t a A d e l a i d e, b. March 4, 1839 ; (2). A u r e l i a A n n, b. June, 1844, d. Nov. 1847; (3). G e o r g e W a t s o n, b. Dec. 1845, d. July, 1849 ; (4). E l z o r a, b. June, 1847 ; d. Oct. 1848; (5). E l v i r a P a u l i n a, b. April 23, 1850. 6. *Esther*, b. Nov. 29, 1809 ; m., Sept. 15, 1836, Caleb O. Billings, of Northport; r. Belfast. 7. *Eleanor*, b. July 1, 1812 ; m., 1841, Brice Jameson, of Warren. 8. *Joseph Gilman*, b. March 9, 1815 ; m. Margaret Kelloch, from Warren, and has A m o s ; A v i s M.; S a m u e l L., b. March 1, 1847 ; Susannah E., b. Aug. 18, 1849. 9. *Otis*, b. Feb. 27, 1819 ; m. Abby Pendleton, of

Northport, and lives there. — II. Esther, b. Oct. 9, 1777; d. May 11, 1793 [see page 69]. — III. Polly, b. Feb. 17, 1780; d. Dec. 18, 1781. — IV. Elizabeth, or Betsey, b. Oct. 25, 1781; m. Samuel Perham, March 6, 1800, who was drowned in St. George's River, in Warren; had 1. *Otis*, who d. 2. *William*, m. Cecilia Tobey, of Jefferson, and d. at sea. 3. *Mary*, m. George Tobey; r. Jefferson, a widow. — V. Susanna, b. April 30, 1783; m., July 11, 1798, John Mahoney; r. Lincolnville. — VI. Sally, b. Feb. 18, 1785; m., first, John Robinson, of Hope, Feb. 6, 1831; and, second, Franc. Fletcher, of Lincolnville. — VII. Philip, b. May 6, 1787; m. Hannah Grafton; r. Waldoborough; had 1. *Ambrose*, b. Sept. 16, 1812; m. Mary Ann Nash, of Waldoborough. 2. *Polly Grafton*, b. Dec. 10, 1814; m. Wallace Cunningham; r. Belfast. 3. *Sarah*, b. Dec. 27, 1816; m. Silas Law. 4. *Hannah*, m. Saul Benner, of Waldoborough; r. there. 5. *Philip*, m. Clarissa Burns, of Waldoborough; r. there. 6. *Eliza*, m. William Kelloch; r. Waldoborough. 7. *Pierce*. 8. *Ignatius Sherman*. — VIII. Suell, b. Jan. 2, 1789; m., Feb. 4, 1818, Sophia Barnard; had 1. *Philena*, b. Sept. 24, 1819; d. Oct. 3, 1843. 2. *Jason Robbins*, b. May 31, 1821; m. Abby Maria S. Stoddard, of Boston, July 18, 1847. 3. *Leonard Barnard*, b. June 28, 1823. 4. *Lydia Maxcy*, b. June 28, 1825. 5. *Josiah*, b. July 30, 1827. 6. *Maria*, b. Nov. 5, 1829. 7. *Delana*, b. Oct. 9, 1831. 8. *Nancy*, b. Feb. 8, 1834. 9. *Suell*, b. April 22, 1837. 10. *William Augustus*, b. March 24, 1842. — IX. Melinda, b. Jan. 2, 1791; m., first, James Fuller, Jan. 22, 1817; and, second, his brother Givens. — X. Chloe, b. May 2, 1792; m., Jan. 1, 1813, Alpheus Collamore (whose first wife was Deborah Grinnell), and had 1. *Deborah Grinnell*, b. Jan. 10, 1814; m., 1837, Benjamin Brown, jun., of Appleton. 2. *Elbridge Gerry*, b. July 10, 1815. 3. *Melenda C.*, b. Oct. 29, 1816. 4. *Elison*, b. Sept. 5, 1818. 5. *Jane*, b. March, 1820. 6. *Susan*, b. Sept. 26, 1822. 7. *Nancy*, b. Dec. 8, 1823. 8. *Richard*, b. Jan. 20, 1826. 9. *Polly*, b. July 4, 1829. 10. *Andrew Jackson*, b. Dec. 11, 1831. — XI. Richard, b. July 27, 1794; m., March 1, 1821, Elsie Robinson, of Hope.

CUSHMAN, MATTHEW SMITH, carpenter; t. 1797; bought the place now owned by N. D. Rice; returned to Bellingham, Mass., and moved to Providence, R. I. By w. Cynthia had — I. Sabin, b. Aug. 5, 1796; m.; r. Bellingham.

— II. Asa, b. Oct. 27, 1798 ; shoemaker ; r. Providence. — III. Smith, b. Nov. 15, 1800.

DAGGETT, AARON, fourth child of Thomas ; m. Rebecca, dr. of Stephen Peabody, of Warren ; went to sea, and was probably lost. He had — I. Ruth, b. Jan. 1, 1792 ; m. Jacob Kuhn, of Waldoborough, in 1816 ; had 1. *William Harriman*, m. Julia Augusta Groton ; and had (1). A n g e- l i n a, b. 1845 ; (2). W i l l i a m F r a n k l i n, b. July, 1847. 2. *Peter*, lost at sea. 3 and 4. Twins, *Albert*, who d., and *Gilbert*. 5. *Almond Orlando*. — II. Olive, b. Feb. 2, 1794 ; m., Jan. 8, 1818, George Clouse, of Waldo- borough, who d. Nov. 22, 1825 ; leaving 1. *Horatio Nel- son*, b. April 22, 1822 ; seaman, farmer ; r. Union. 2. *Angelica Frances*, b. Sept. 2, 1824 ; m., April 13, 1846, Gardner Light, of Waldoborough ; r. Worcester, Mass. ; and has (1). M a r y F r a n c e s, b. Sept. 10, 1848. — III. Peggy, or Margaret, b. July 17, 1796 ; m. Peleg Wiley, in 1819 ; and had 1. *Almira*, m. Oliver Simmons, of Hope. 2. *Aaron Daggett*. 3. *Ephraim*. 4. *William Hovey*. 5. *Jacob Kuhn*. 6. *Peleg*. 7. *Rebecca ;* d. 8. *Charles ;* d. 9. *Ruth Kuhn*. — IV. Polly, b. Feb. 23, 1798 ; d. 1802. — V. Aaron, b. April 7, 1800 ; d. 1801. — VI. Lucy, b. Nov. 10, 1802 ; m. Abraham Gushee, of Hope ; had *Frederic Augustus*, b. August, 1825 ; *Louisa*, d. young ; *Rebecca*, m. Elijah Ripley, of Hope (who has (1) F r e d e r i c k, b. July 5, 1847) ; *Almond ; Ambrose ; Elijah Daggett*. — VII. Elijah A., b. March 2, 1806 ; M.D. at Bowdoin College, 1833 ; physician in Waldoborough ; m. Ruth Ann Waters, of Jefferson ; and had 1. *Ann*, b. May 28, 1847. 2. *Athearn*. — VIII. Aaron Athearn, b. Dec. 17, 1808 ; m. Bethiah, dr. of William Thompson ; had 1. *Simon Elijah*, b. in Jefferson. 2. *A dr.*, d. in Appleton. 3. *Emeline Ore- ville*, d. 1849. 4. *Morrill Stanford*, b. 1845 ; d. 1849. 5. *Augusta*, d. 1849. Mrs. Aaron Daggett, m., second, John Newbit, of Waldoborough, in 1815 ; and had Jonathan Newhall, who d. in 1848.

DAGGETT, MATTHEW, a sea-captain, who followed the sea from boyhood, was nephew of Thomas, senior ; lived a while in Union, and settled in Warren. N. Robbins, Esq., said the first national vessel was built for a present to France. On going out, she anchored off Holmes's Hole. It being Christmas, the officers and some others went on shore to enjoy themselves. A violent storm came on. The officers could not get on board, nor the seamen from the ship to the shore. Many on board died. Matthew Daggett was thawed off from a gun to which he had been frozen.

DAGGETT, SAMUEL, b. at Tisbury, May 19 (?); d. Oct. 2, 1835, æt. eighty-two; son of Thomas and Rebecca (Athearn) Daggett. He m. Jedidah, sister of Christopher Butler; and she d. Feb. 21, 1830. They had — I. Brotherton, b. at Tisbury, Mass., Jan. 4, 1778; m., first, Sarah, or Sally, Kimball, of Bristol, in the winter of 1802–3; and, second, Mrs. Emily (Chadwick) Marshall, of Thomaston, December, 1838, who d. Oct. 14, 1844; and had 1. *Eleanor Martin*, b. Jan. 7 or 30, 1804; m., Dec. 29, 1834, John Oakes. 2. *William*, b. Aug. 27, 1805; r. Michigan. 3. *Mary*, b. May 18, 1808; d. June 4, 1830. 4. *Sophronia*, b. March 4, 1810; m., March 5, 1833, Jonathan D. Breck; r. Brighton, Mass. 5. *Orinda*, b. Dec. 26, 1811; m. Reuben Sherror; r. Thomaston. 6. *Arunah Weston*, b. Feb. 16, 1814; m. a Whitney; r. Bangor. 7. *Timothy Kimball*, engineer of a steamboat, b. Feb. 26, 1816; r. Mobile, Ala. 8. *Eliza Mitchell*, b. Aug. 8, 1818. 9. *Elvira*, b. Nov. 17, 1820; m. George Hatch, of Thomaston; r. Boston. 10. *Brotherton*, b. Nov. 25, 1822; r. Boston. 11. *George Bartlett*, b. Aug. 23, 1824; m. Mary Jane, dr. of John Burns; r. homestead; had R e u b e n S h e r r o d, b. Feb. 1, 1849, who d. Feb. 16, 1850. 12. *Elisha Harding*, b. Sept. 6, 1827; r. Thomaston. — II. James, b. Sept. 9, 1779, at Tisbury; m., in Waldoborough, Aug. 31, 1800, Deborah Upham, from Bristol; r. Hodgdon; had 1. *James*, b. Jan. 22, 1802. 2. *Isaac*, b. Nov. 2, 1803; drowned in the Penobscot; and others. — III. Polly, b. May 12, 1781; m. Thomas Mitchell. — IV. Jonathan, b. May 20, 1783; m., first, in 1804, Betsey Martin, of St. George; and, second, Mary Robinson, of Belmont. They had issue, 1. *Athearn*, b. Sept. 1, 1805; d. July 5, 1806. 2. *John*, b. Aug. 29, 1806; m. in Waldoborough; killed by a fall in the night from the haymow; left a widow and two children. 3. *Wilbert*, b. Oct. 30, 1807; m. Susan Lair, or Lehr; r. Waldoborough. 4. *Julia Ann*, b. March 17, 1809; d. Aug. 21, 1814. 5. *Richard Martin*, b. Jan. 15, 1811. 6. *Sarah*, b. Feb. 13, and d. Nov. 7, 1813. 7. *Silvia Weston*, b. Aug. 6, 1814, m. a Wing; r. Belmont. He also had other ch., all by the first wife. — V. William, b. April 9, 1785; m., in 1813,

Silvia Church Weston; and had 1. *Amelia*, b. Feb. 26, 1814. 2. *Sarah Ann*, b. Aug. 23, 1815. 3. *Jane Tobey*, b. Oct. 9, 1818; m. a Crawford, in Searsmont. 4. *Joshua*, b. Sept. 16, 1820; r. Bristol. 5. *Nancy Alford*, b. Oct. 25, 1822. 6. *Lucy Weston*, b. Jan. 11, 1825. 7. *Margery*, b. June 22, 1827; d. Jan. 8, 1828; also others. — VI. Samuel, b. Oct. 15, 1792; d. Oct. 11, 1846; m., first, in 1817, Priscilla Coggan; and, second, Mrs. Sarah, dr. of Jacob Wade, and widow of Jacob Stetson. He had 1. *Augusta Bachelder*, b. Aug. 24, 1818; m., 1840, George Barter, of Thomaston. 2. *Martha*, b. Aug. 7, 1822; d. Sept. 16, 1823. 3. *Hancey*, b. Nov. 6, 1825; d. Sept. 21, 1842. 4. *Cyrenus Chapin*, b. Dec. 13, 1830; also two ch. by the last w.; one of them d. — VII. Ebenezer, b. Aug. 2, 1797; m., first, in 1819, Margaret Miller, of Waldoborough, who d. May 31, 1830; and, second, June 9, 1831, her sister Salome; had 1. *Cyrus*, b. Oct. 22, 1819; r. in Camden. 2. *Thurston*, b. Nov. 28, 1820; m. Rachel, dr. of Andros Mitchell. 3. *Elzina*, b. March 31, 1822; m. Reuben Ghentner, of Waldoborough; lives there. 4. *Barbara D.*, b. Nov. 30, 1823; d. Sept. 5, 1825. 5. *Mary Miller*, b. June 4, 1825; m. George, s. of Ebenezer Robbins. 6. *Erastus*, b. April 23, 1827; m., June 11, 1846, Pamela Ripley, of Appleton. 7. *An infant child*, d. May 31, 1830. 8. *Lysander*, b. Jan. 10, 1832; seaman; d. June 10, 1850. 9. *Charles Miller*, b. March 8, 1834. 10. *Clementine C.*, b. Oct. 26, 1835. 11. *Darius*, b. March 18, 1838. 12. *Harriet D.* 13. *A dr.*, who d. 14. *Lucius C.* 15. *Angelia*. — VIII. Daniel Weston, b. May 19, 1800; d. April 4, 1833; m., Dec. 3, 1827, Lydia Jameson, of Warren; had issue, 1. *Ozias*, b. Sept. 29, 1828; d. Feb. 2, 1830. 2. *Daniel O.*, b. Jan. 18, 1831. The widow m. Caswell, who committed suicide.

DAGGETT, THOMAS, senior, d. May 15, 1806; and his w., Rebecca Athearn, d. Aug. 3, 1805. They had Samuel; Thomas; Hannah, who m. a Norton on Martha's Vineyard; Aaron; Rebecca, who m. her cousin, Matthew Daggett, of Warren, and d. October, 1848. With Thomas Daggett, senior, probably came Ebenezer, a blind brother, whom he maintained, and who d. April 29, 1816, æt. seventy-eight; and Andrew, a foolish son, who also d. in town.

DAGGETT, THOMAS, son of Thomas and Rebecca (Athearn) Daggett, d. Jan. 13, 1822, sixty-seven; m. Rebecca Luce,

who d. Feb. 6, 1832; sister of Mrs. C. Butler. They had —
I. Hannah, b. April 14, 1783; d., of consumption, April 23,
1826; u. — II. Berintha, b. Sept. 11, 1786; m., April 23,
1809, John Chapman Robbins; and d. July 5, 1839. — III.
Thomas, Captain, b. June 4, 1788; farmer in Searsmont;
went to sea as mate of a vessel; became acquainted, on his
voyage from England, with an English lady, Martha Maidman, whom he m. in New York city, and returned with her
to his farm. She spent the last weeks of her life at his
father's, in Union, where she d., of consumption, Aug. 23,
1818, aged twenty-two, having had one child, which died
young in Union. Afterward he went to his wife's kindred
in New York, engaged in business, and d. — IV. Sally, b.
May 6, 1790; d.; m., Sept. 20, 1818, Samuel Goodwin, of
Searsmont; had ch. — V. Edmund, b. Aug. 23, 1792; m.,
1818, Deborah, dr. of Josiah Keene, of Camden; r. some
years on the homestead, but now near Hope Corner; ch. 1.
Frederic, valise and trunk-maker, b. Aug. 13, 1819;
m., Oct. 3, 1815, in New York, Helen Lauretta, dr. of
Captain Lewis and Hannah (Morse) Bachelder; and had
(1). Frederic La Forrest, b. Jan. 12, 1847, d.
April 5, 1849; (2). a son, b. November, 1850. 2. *Martha*,
b. March 7, 1821; d. March 16, 1823. 3. *Thomas*, a grocer, b. May 4, 1822; d. Philadelphia; u. 4. *Ephraim
Gay*, b. July 31, 1824; afflicted with epilepsy and mental
and religious depression and derangement; took the life of
a child and his own life, in Roxbury, Mass., June 7, 1851.
5. *Freeman Luce*, valise and trunk-maker, b. Feb. 8, 1827;
r. Boston. 6. *Lucinda*, b. March 26, 1828; d. Oct. 1, 1831.
7. *John Sibley*, b. Feb. 7, 1830; r. Bowdoin College. 8.
Sarah Gay, b. Jan. 25, 1832; m., 1849, John Rich; r.
Hope. 9. *Patience Hewett*, b. June 1, 1834; d. young.
10. *Esther*. 11. *Mary*. 12. *Helen*. 13. *Caroline*. — VI.
Henry, b. Aug. 3, 1794; m., Sept. 26, 1816, Meribah Jackson; settled in Belmont, and moved to Wisconsin. — VII.
Matthew, b. Oct. 1, 1798; d. Dec. 10, 1798.

DANIELS, NATHAN, Deacon, son of Henry and Lois
(Pond) Daniels, b. at Franklin, Mass., Sept. 7, 1771; took
up land where he settled, in the easterly part of the town,
probably in 1797; m., 1797, Lois Ellis, of Franklin, who
d. March 7, 1844, aged sixty-seven years eleven months.
They had — I. Lois, b. Oct. 10, 1797; m. John Payson, May
1, 1823; ch. 1. *Nathan Daniels*, b. Jan. 6, 1825. 2. *John*

Ellis, b. Aug. 8, 1826. 3. *George Washington*, b. Feb. 12, 1828. 4. *Eliza Ann*, b. Jan. 30, 1831. 5. *James Madison*, b. Oct. 28, 1836. — II. Ellis, b. Oct. 15, 1799; m. Freelove Wentworth; r. Hope. They, beside others, had *Sylvia A.*; d. Dec. 12, 1846, aged twenty-one years, ten months, twenty-nine days. — III. Nathan, b. March 15, 1801, m., June 2, 1825, Mehitable, dr. of Amos Walker; had 1. *Mary Elizabeth*, b. May 13, 1826. 2. *Harriet Newell*, b. Feb. 7, 1829; m., Oct. 1849, a Hartford. 3. *Sarah Eliza*, b. Sept. 18, 1831; d. Sept. 24, 1832. 4. *Joel*, b. Dec. 10, 1833. 5. *Levi*, b. March 18, 1838. — IV. Milton, b. April 12, 1803; m., first, in 1829, Lucy, dr. of Lewis Robbins; second, in 1835, Nancy Miller; had 1. *Lewis Robbins*, b. March 3, 1831. 2. *Lucy Ann*, b. May 17, 1837. 3. *Laura Maria*, b. May 15, 1842. — V. Eliza, b. Nov. 29, 1804; m. Levi Morse. — VI. Joseph Hawes, b. Aug. 8, 1807; m., Oct. 30, 1830, Sarah, dr. of Amos Walker; and had 1. *Edwin Roscoe*, b. March 8, 1831. 2. *Lucy Robbins*, b. Nov. 3, 1833. 3. *Sarah Eliza*, b. March 14, 1836. 4. *Zilpah Ellis*, b. Oct. 12, 1838. 5. *Joseph Henry*, b. Aug. 8, 1841; d. Jan. 9, 1844. 6. *Lois Ann*, b. June 24, 1844. 7. *Frances E.*, b. Oct. 8, 1848. — VII. Fisher Ames, b. Sept. 6, 1808; m., Sept. 2, 1832, Julia Ann Gardner; and had *Obadiah G.*, b. Aug. 26, 1833; also *Lois*, d. June 24, 1842, aged six months; and probably others. — VIII. Mary, b. Feb. 17, 1811; m, Jan. 1, 1838, Edward Taylor, of Hope; and d. April 18, 1850. — IX. Julia, b. March 13, 1813; d. Feb. 26, 1841; c.; m., Nov. 28, 1839, Zuinglius, b. June 10, 1812, son of William Collins. Z. C.'s second w. was Julia Ann Bachelder. — X. Rhoda Cordelia, b. Aug. 22, 1815; d. Oct. 23, 1840; m., Oct. 29, 1839, George L. Folger, of Hope. — XI. Cynthia Abigail, b. July 31, 1818; m. Nathan Robbins.

DAVIS, MARK, from Friendship; t. 1797; m., in 1799, Betsey Pickering, of Fox Islands, who is said to have originated from or near Portsmouth, N. H. He lived, when it was burnt, in Capt. Barrett's old house, many rods north-west of the one recently burnt on the spot now occupied by Gorham Butler's.

DAVIS, STERLING, t. 1799; d. Jan. 29, 1849; m. Jane, widow of Jason Robbins; had — I. Jason, b. March 13, 1801; m. Chloe, dr. of Josiah Maxcy; had 1. *Elizabeth*, or

Betsey, b. Aug. 1, 1824; m., Jan. 20, 1848, Calvin Robinson, of Hope. 2. *Hervey Marcy*, b. Sept. 8, 1826. 3. *Statira*, b. January, 1828; m., Jan. 15, 1848, Josiah Howard Shepard; has (1). Susan Caroline, b. April 10, 1850. 4. *Jane*, b. November, 1831. 5. *William Tilson*, b. January, 1834 (?). 6. *Roxana*, b. July, 1835. 7. *Chloe Alvina*, b. 1838 (?). 8. *Elvira Robbins*, b. May 31, 1843. — II. Sterling, b. June 20, 1803; m., 1828, Betsey Miller; had 1. *Lucena Keller,* b. Aug. 15, 1829. 2. *Joseph Miller*, b. Dec. 16, 1833. — III. Wilber, b. Dec. 11, 1808; m. Rosanna Noyes, of Hope; had 1. *Oscar*. 2. *Benjamin Bussey*. 3 and 4. Twins; *Elisha Harding* and *Dexter Hovey*. 5. *A daughter*, d. few months old. 6. *Edwin*. 7. *Sarah Allen*. 8. *Emily Jane*. 9. *Alice*. 10. *Marshall*, b. July 16, 1848. — IV. Jane, b. April 27, 1810; m., 1829, William Tilson, jun., of Thomaston; and d.; leaving *Davis*, a cadet, at West Point.

DUNHAM, SAMUEL, r. on the Simmons Farm. The town records say, "Moved into town from Warren, sometime in June, 1790, Samuel Dunham and Kate Dunham his wife; Joseph Dunham, James Dunham and Sarah Dunham, the children of Samuel and Kate Dunham." He brought into town, "June 22, 1792, from Warren, Mary Sumner, wife of Ezra Sumner, Mary Davis, Liddia Sumner and Charles Sumner." It is said that he was not faithful to his wife. About the year 1794, she, becoming a little deranged, went to visit her little boy, who was living with Capt. William Starrett, of Warren, with whom she resided when m. On her way back, she was seen fording the river near Hart's Falls, and afterward near Crawford's Pond. She took a hay-road, went into the woods, and was lost. About that time there was at Warren a town-meeting. The people adjourned to the next day for the purpose of exploring the woods. The search was unsuccessful. About two years after this, William Hart, having been out on a trapping excursion, found her bones and a piece of her gown in the very easterly part of Union, near Grassy Pond. Her bones were taken up, and buried in the graveyard." He moved to Friendship, it is believed, and there died. Probably his dr. Abigail m., June 13, 1796, James Pease, of Barrets Town.

DYER, RUFUS, carpenter, from Bridgewater, Mass.; t.

1795; r. Appleton; m., March 5, 1797, Abigail. b. 1768, dr. of Jacob and Hannah (Jones) Booth, of Gloucester, R. I. — I. John, b. Sept. 7, 1800; r. Appleton; m., first, May 1823, Anna Walker; and, second, Lydia McCurdy, in 1835; had 1. *Anna W.*, b Jan. 1825, or Feb. 21, 1826; 2. *Fanny W.*, b. March 28, 1827, or March 28, 1828; m., first, Samuel Leach and had (1). W i l l i a m. S. L. went off, and she m., second, George Cox, in 1848, and had (2). a s o n, d. young. 3. *Infant dr.*; d. 4. *Rufus*, b. April 4, 1831. — II. Betsey, b. Sept. 14, 1802; d. July 11, 1805. — III. Abigail, b. Aug. 7, 1804; m. True Door, of Harmony; and d. — IV. Cecilia, b. July 10, 1806; m. Shadrach Snell.

ESENSA,[1] HENRY, b. Brunswick, in Hanover, Germany;

[1] Mr. Esensa belonged to the cavalry in Germany, came to Quebec under Col. Baum, and was captured by Gen. Stark at Bennington, where "the balls flew so thick he did not think one soul could escape alive. The Hessian cavalry," he said, "had been promised horses, and been told that they should get enough from the rebels; but they never got any." He described Col. Baum as a man of "remarkable appearance, and having a remarkably brilliant eye." Esensa was introduced into Waldoborough by Capt. Schenck; and not long after the battle, while yet u., he came to Union, and labored in company with Suchfort. As Suchfort joined the British army in England, and Esensa was one of the Hessians despatched from Germany to aid the British, it is not probable that they ever met till in Stirlington. They often worked together; and so similar were their movements in felling trees and in taking hold and lifting logs, that one of them remarked, from this alone he should have known the other to be a Hessian. He afterward lived several years in Hope. Before the year 1800, he returned to Union, and bought the farm now owned by Philo Thurston, about one-third of a mile above the Middle Bridge, on the west side of the river. After he had been from Germany about thirty years, he was threshing grain for Mr. Samuel Hills, and the conversation turned on Germany. Hills asked him why he did not write to his relatives and friends there. E. asked Hills to write. The flails were thrown down, and a letter immediately written, superscribed to several persons, and mailed, without much probability, in those days, of his receiving a reply. An answer came from friends whom he had left thirty years before, and who had supposed him to be dead. The joy of the old Hessian, who had not heard from his relatives in Germany since he came away, could hardly be restrained. In consequence of this movement, he received about three hundred dollars, which had been reserved for him from his father's estate, and was a great relief to him in his somewhat straitened circumstances. Towards the close of life, he moved to a place in Appleton beyond Fossetts' Mills, where he d. not far from the year 1831. The graves of him and his friend Suchfort are within a mile and a half of each other.

In the burying-ground of West Springfield, Mass., is a gravestone

m. Susannah Rolfe, of Bristol (?), and had children, the first four b. in Hope. — I. Peggy, b. Aug. 26, 1790.; m. John Stanley. — II. Nancy, b. Dec. 7, 1792; m. — III. Charles, b. Oct. 22, 1794; m. Sally Overlock; r. Appleton. — IV. Susannah, b. Nov. 22, 1796; m. Peleg House; r. Liberty. — V. Sally, b. Feb. 15, 1798; m. Daniel Briggs Grinnell. — VI. David, b. Nov. 23, 1799; m. thrice; r. near Fredericton, N. B. — VII. Reuben, b. Sept. 21, 1801; r. Canada. — VIII. Elizabeth, b. May 18, 1803. — IX. Henry, b. Aug. 29, 1804; r. Appleton. — X. Eunice, b. June 22, 1807; m. John Lermond; r. Appleton.

EVERTON, ZEPH., came with William Lewis from Thomaston; t. 1791 and 1793; worked at the mills by the Upper Bridge, and boarded himself. Mischievous wags, to tease him, accused him of frying doughnuts in a tin lantern. He appears to have been a "likely, respectable" man, and, it is said, afterward was toll-gatherer at the bridge in Thomaston, where he d.

FAIRBANKS, JOHN, from Sherburne, Mass.; b. May 18, 1760; probably came about the same time with William Hart and Levi Morse. He was taxed in the tax-bill of 1791, but did not reside constantly in town. He m. Eunice, b. April 20, 1769, dr. of Samuel and Sarah Payson. — I. Abner Hills, b. Nov. 15, 1789; m. Nancy Mac——, of Parkman, Ohio; and d., Feb. 10, 1826 or 1827; and had *Maria*, who m. Rev. Daniel H. Mansfield, a Methodist minister. — II. Eunice Payson, b. March 6, 1792; m. Lewis Robinson, of Hope; and d. — III. John Noyes, b. March 10, 1794; m., June 16, 1822, Martha Preble; ch. 1. *Eunice Payson*, b. Aug. 4, 1823; m. John Dean; had (1). a son, d. one week old; (2). J a m e s G r e g o r y, b. Sept. 1847; (3). J o h n B a r t h o l o m e w, b. April,

"In memory of John Andrew Isense, born in Little Biwene; was a Dragoon in the Prince of Brunswick's Regiment; who was killed by lightning, Aug. 16, 1780, in the 28th year of his age. 'Ich weiss das mein Erloeser lebt, und er wird mich wieder aus der Erden auferwecken.' — Job xix. 25. The *British Dragoon Isense* was some twenty feet from the tree, when he was killed, having taken shelter from the storm under a cock of hay." See Bridgman's Inscriptions. The German pronunciation of Isense is the same as the English of Esensa; and it is not improbable, both being Germans and engaged on the British side in the revolutionary war, that they may have belonged to the same family.

1850. 2. *Nancy McMellen*, b. April 1 ; d. March 18, 1826 (?). 3. *Martha Elizabeth*, b. Feb. 16, 1837 ; m. William Boynton ; r. Bath ; and has ch. 4. *John Noyes*, b. Jan. 31, 1829. 5. *Henry Norris*, b. June 12, 1831. 6. *Caroline Olive*, b. March 15, 1833 ; d. Sept. 4, 1833. 7. *William Franklin*, b. July 11, 1834. 8. *George Hollis*, b. Nov. 1, 1836. 9. *Clotilda Ann*, b. Dec. 2, 1838 ; d. Dec. 2, 1838. — IV. Sarah, or Sally, b. Aug. 2, 1796 ; m. Lewis Wentworth, previously h. of her sister. — V. Hills, b. Nov. 8, 1798. — VI. Caroline, b. Dec. 10, 1802 ; m. Joseph Gleason, Nov. 25, 1827. — VII. Eliza, b. Dec. 12, 1804 ; m. Lewis Wentworth ; and d. March 1834. — VIII. Olive C., m. John Homes Stewart.

FALES, PETER, blacksmith, m. Chloe Shepard, came from Attleboro', Mass., about 1799 ; settled first at the head of Seven-tree Pond, and afterward on the farm now owned by Moses Morse, and returned to Mass. ; had — I. Samuel Turner, b. Dec. 8, 1797. — II. Sabry Turner, b. Jan. 16, 1800. — III. Willard, b. Feb. 14, 1802. — IV. Lewis, b. March 29, 1804. — V. John, b. Sept. 2, 1806. One of his children d. 1809.

GAY, JONAH, t. 1794 ; and his w., Mary Thomas, of Meduncook. At the raising of a saw-mill on the west side of the river, at the Middle Bridge, Nov. 19, 1802, the broadside began to sway before it was secured. Gay, seeing it was about to come over, sprang and seized a post with a view to prevent it. The broadside came down. The end of the post struck him, crushed his chin and chest together, and he died instantly. His w. d. March 13, 1843 ; eighty-one ; ch. — I. Abiel, b. July 22, 1791 ; r. Waldo ; m. Judith Sayward, of Thomaston ; had 1. *Mary*, b. Sept. 19, 1816 ; d. Oct. 18, 1822. 2. *Judith*, b. Dec. 4, 1818. 3. *Clarinda*, b. June 1, 1821 ; d. Oct. 17, 1821. 4. *Mary*, b. Feb. 13, 1823. 5. *Abiel*, b. Jan. 31, 1825. 6. *Sarah*, b. July 14, 1827 ; d. Aug. 29, 1832. 7. *Richard*, b. May 13, 1829 ; d. Aug. 24, 1832. — II. James, b. May 2, 1793 ; d. in the army, in the war of 1812. — III. Polly, b. Feb. 15, 1795 ; d. March 2, 1795. — IV. Rachel, b. April 2, 1796 ; m., 1814, David Gay ; r. Waldo ; had 1. *Edward*, b. Nov. 25, 1816. 2. *Nancy*, b. Jan. 4, 1818. 3. *James*, b. March 13, 1822. 4. *Sally*, b. April 18, 1824. — V. Elijah, b. Feb. 8, 1798 ; d. Feb. 10, or 11, 1837 ; m. Joanna Curtis; had 1. *a child*, d. Aug. 22, 1826. 2. *John Curtis*, b. Oct. 2, 1827. 3. *Eliza Ann C.*, b. Sept. 28, 1830. 4. *James*, b. Dec. 17, 1832. 5. *Sarah W.*, b. April 2, 1834. 6. *Mary Fales*, b. Sept. 7, 1835. His widow m., Jan. 6, 1839, John S. Dunton. — VI. Richard, b. May 10, 1800; m., first, 1827, Nancy Boggs; and, second, Nancy Robbins. — VII. Jonah, b. March 9, 1802; d. June 21, 1805.

GILLMOR,[1] GILLMORE, or GILMORE, DAVID, son of David and Joanna (Miller) Gillmor, came in the spring of 1795; became an extensive landholder, owning, it is said, one-twelfth of the town. His land was on the east side of the river. He m., 1784, Mary, b. Nov. 1, 1769, who d. at Newburgh, Jan. 12, 1834, second child of Josiah Robbins. He d. Jan. 28, 1849, at Newburgh. They had — I. Sarah, b. May 18, 1785; m. Hervey Whiting; r. Wrentham, Mass. — II. Rufus, b. Oct. 26, 1787; m. Julietta Fairbanks, of Franklin; r. Newburgh. — III. Mary, b. Feb. 24, 1790; m. Dr. Charles Ulmer, of Hampden; r. Newburgh. — IV. David, b. Aug. 30, 1794; m. Lydia Croxford, of Newburgh; r. Monroe. — V. Patience Melinda, b. April 6, 1796; m., Jan. 18, 1818, Ebenezer Cobb, of Union, who was b. Oct. 9. 1793, at Carver, Mass., son of Capt. Barnabas Cobb (who m. Jerusha Cobb, b. at Kingston, Mass., granddaughter of Ebenezer Cobb, of Kingston, who d. Dec. 8, 1801, aged one hundred and seven years, eight months, and six days). They had 1. *Mary Jerusha*, b. Jan. 12, 1819; m. Jesse Arnold, of Hope. 2. *Sarah Whiting*, b. June 19, 1821; m., June 13, 1839, Nathaniel Miller, s. of Elisha Harding, M.D. 3. *William Ebenezer*, b. May 15, 1824; m., November, 1849, Elvira Weston Snow, dr. of Edward and Mary (Twining) Snow, of Frankfort. 4. *Joseph Orlando*, b. Jan. 28, 1827. 5. *Minerva Clementine*, b. May 29, 1829; d. March 9 [according to gravestone, 8], 1832. 6. *Sylvanus Gillmor*, b. Nov. 2, 1831. 7. *David Barna-*

---

[1] His father, David Gillmor, b. Raynham, Mass., March 27, 1732; r. Franklin, Mass.; and d. there, Oct. 21, 1831. He m., April 20, 1762, Joanna Miller, b. in Rehoboth, Sept. 9, 1740; d. June 3, 1816. They had — I. John, b. March 27, 1763. — II. David, b. May 3, 1765. — III. Joseph, b. April 17, 1768. — IV. Rufus, b. April 26, 1770. — V. Rhobe, b. Dec. 4, 1772; d. March 10, 1816. — VI. Abigail, b. April 15, 1775; m. Olney Titus. — VII. James, b. Dec. 10, 1777. — VIII. Patience, b. Jan. 16, 1782; m. E. Alden. Of these, David, Rufus, Abigail, and Patience settled in Union.

bas, b. Jan. 15, 1834. 8. *Marcellus Lewellin*, b. July 6, 1836. — VI. Apollos Robbins, b. April 2, 1798; m. Hannah Newcomb; r. Hampden.

GILLMOR, NATHAN, son of William, of Franklin; t. 1799; a mason; m. Nancy Fisher, of Franklin; settled and built a house on the farm now owned by Dr. Sibley, and returned to Franklin.

GILLMOR, RUFUS, b. April 26, 1770, at Franklin, Mass.; m., at Union, June 19, 1788, Sally, dr. of Josiah Robbins. He was in the expedition against Shays; came here in 1787; r. south of the Old Burying Ground, and afterward on the north side of the Common. Having sold this place to Ebenezer Cobb, he now lives nearly opposite. Descendants, — I. Polly, b. April 2, 1789; m., 1805, Jesse Drake; had 1. *Amos*, b. March 28, 1806; m., 1828, Melancey Gushee; ch. (1). Oramel Luolphus, b. Jan. 24, 1830; (2). Mary Oscarine, b. Oct. 5, 1833; (3). Statira Maria, b. Sept. 5, 1835; (4). Amos Leroy. 2. *Jesse*, b. Nov. 30, 1807; d. July 19, 1842; m. Maria, dr. of Lewis Robbins. 3. *Lusena*, b. April 7, 1809; m., 1828, Silas Kelloch, or Kellar; and d. 4. *Elvira*, b. Feb. 8, 1812; m., 1833, Almond Gushee, jun., of Hope. 5. *Julina*, b. Nov. 12, 1813; m., 1831, Josiah Thwing, of Vassalborough; r. Gardiner. 6. *Luther*, b. Nov. 10, 1815; m., June 10, 1838, Abigail P. Davis, of Warren; ch. (1). Lucena Augusta, b. May 27, 1839; (2). Melvina Oraville, b. Oct. 9, 1841; (3). Louisa Jameson, b. Aug. 9, 1843; and others. 7. *Olive*, b. Aug. 27, 1817; m., first, in 1840, Hiram Arnold, of Appleton; and had (1). Almeda; m., second, David Gushee, by whom she has (2). Armena. 8. *Millard Gillmor*, b. Sept. 9, 1821. 9. *Almena*, m., Nov. 17, 1844, Edward Hills; ch. (1). Julia Almeda, b. Dec. 17, 1845; d. Oct. 1, 1848; (2). Hiram Arnold, b. Aug. 5, 1847; (3). Helen Maria, b. Oct. 12, 1849. — II. Rufus, b. Dec. 25, 1790; r. Searsmont; m., first, Abigail, dr. of Capt. Amos Barrett, Jan. 18, 1816; and had 1. *Anson Blake*, b. November, 1817. 2. *Amos Barrett*, b. August, 1819. He m., second, Polly, dr. of Ezekiel Hagar, Dec. 28, 1823; and had *Abigail*, who d. ; and *Rufus;* and perhaps others. — III. Lusena, b. Aug. 11, 1792; m., October, 1808, Michael Crowell, b. Kingston, Mass.; had 1.

Statira, b. March 7, 1809; m. Stevens Davis; r. Wisconsin. 2. *Rufus Gillmor*, b. May 22, 1811; d. Utica, N.Y., April, 1839. 3. *Mary*, b. May 15, 1813; m. Samuel White; r. Orono. 4. *Caroline Elizabeth*, b. Aug. 6, 1815; m. Hugh Reed; r. Orono. 5. *James Parker*, b. Dec. 26, 1817; r. Wisconsin. 6. *Sarah Gillmor*, b. May, 1820; m. Jeremiah Page, of Dexter. 7. *Hannah Parker*, b. Dec. 26, 1822; m. Charles Thayer; r. Cleavland, Ohio. 8. *Lusena Elizabeth*, b. Aug. 6, 1825; m. Paul Webster; r Orono. 9. *Polly*, b. April 22, 1828. 10. *Charles Gillmor*, b. Jan. 4, 1831; d. July 27, 1841. 11. *Michael*, b. May 24, 1834; d. August, 1834. 12. *Samuel White*, b. June 15, 1836.— IV. Millard, b. Sept. 28, 1794; widower, sea-captain. — V. Julia Metcalf, b. April 3, 1797; m., 1818, Lieut.-col. John M. Bachelder, b. Aug. 8, 1792, at East Kingston, N. H., son of Captain Nathaniel Bachelor; had 1. *Almeda Adaline*, b. May 16, 1819; d. Dec. 23, 1839. 2. *John Morrill*, b. Aug. 11, 1820; drowned Aug. 21, 1825. 3. *Julia Ann*, b. March 8, 1822; m. Zuinglius Collins; and had (1). Leroy Zuinglius; (2). Azelia Matilda, b. Dec. 8, 1847. 4. *Sarah Gillmor*, b. May 28, 1823; m. Aurelius, s. of Christopher Young. 5. *Harriet Loana*, b. Jan. 12, 1826. 6. *John Morrill*, b. Jan. 4, 1829. 7. *Frances Viana*, b. Aug. 22, 1831; m., 1850, Ziba Simmons. 8. *Charles Gillmor*, b. June 3, 1833. 9. *Eliza Matilda*, b. June 2, 1835. 10. *Mary Celesta*, b. July 18, 1837.— VI. Marcus, b. Oct. 21, 1799; d., of delirium tremens, May 13, 1832; m. Elsie, dr. of John Lermond; had 1. *Ann*, b. Sept. 16, 1823; m. Robert Thompson Bowley. 2. *Millard*, b. Dec. 15, 1824; d. Aug. 18, 1826. 3. *Martha*, b. March 7, 1826; m. Ezekiel G. D. Boveridge. 4. *Louisa Alden*, b. April 6, 1828; m. William H. Gowen. 5. *Gustavus*, b. Dec. 28, 1830.— VII. Sarah Robbins, b. Sept. 10, 1803; m., 1827, Abijah P. Judd; r. Bethany, Conn. — VIII. Charles Pope, b. Sept. 21, 1808; drowned at Orono, May 22, 1833. — IX. Nancy, b. Jan. 29, 1815; m., 1829, Robert Thompson, jun.; and had 1. *Adelia Marilla*, b. Jan. 5, 1830. 2. *Sarah Amanda*, b. Nov. 3, 1831. 3. *Marcus Albury*, b. Dec. 4, 1833. 4. *Oseola Adelphus*, b. June 5, 1836. 5. *Hollis*, b. Jan. 20, and d. March 29, 1839. 6 and 7. Twins; *Eli Moor* and *Ali Mehemet*, b. June 19, 1840. 8. *Flora Maria*, b. Dec. 25, 1844. 9. *Richard Edwin*, b. Jan. 18, 1848.

GLEASON,[1] MICAJAH, b. Framingham, Jan. 27, 1777,

[1] "GLEASON, or GLEISON, or GLEZEN, and (as sometimes written and pronounced) LEESEN." Thomas Gleason early took the oath of fidelity, and is named, in 1657, on Cambridge town-records. He was of Charlestown, in March, 1662, in the occupation of the "tract of land reserved to Squa Sachem." He d. in Cambridge, probably about 1684. By his w. Susanna, he had, in Cambridge, Mary, b. Oct. 31, 1657. His other ch., b. before, were Thomas, Joseph, John. Of these, Thomas, the oldest, belonged to Sudbury in 1665, bought of Benjamin Rice, in the south part of Framingham, was received to Sherburne, Oct. 5, 1678, and d. in Framingham, July 25, 1705. By his w. Sarah, who d. July 8, 1703, he had 1. Sarah, b. Feb. 6, 1665; m. Jeremiah Morse. 2. Anne, m. John Gibbs, 1688. 3. Thomas. 4. Isaac. 5. Patience. 6. Mary, b. June 19, 1680. 7. John. The seventh of these children, viz. John, was constable in Framingham in 1710, three years a selectman, and d. there, May 9, 1740. By his w. Abigail he had 1. Ebenezer, b. probably in Sherburne, Sept. 1, 1708; and in Framingham. 2. John, b. Feb. 27, 1710-11. 3. Anne, b. May 3, 1713; m., Nov. 22, 1733, John Drury. 4. Samuel, b. Dec. 13, 1715. 5. Abigail, b. Nov. 23, 1717; m., James Cloyes, May 28, 1740. 6. Martha, b. May 1, 1720; m., Nov. 11, 1742. Jonathan Maynard. 7. Sarah, b. Feb. 6, 1723-4; m., Jan. 4, 1749, John Crooks, of Hopkinton. 8. Patience, b. July 7, 1729; m., Aug. 25, 1748, Daniel Ball; moved to Athol.

Samuel, the fourth of the children, m., first, Elizabeth How, Jan. 6, 1735, who d. soon after the birth of the child Elizabeth, who d. æt. eighteen. Samuel, m , second, Dorothy Faux, March 14, 1740, who d. 1751; and, third, Abigail Livermore, April 3, 1755. By his second wife he had 2. William, b. June 6, 1740; d. July 10, 1741. 3. Samuel, b. Oct. 9, 1742. 4. John, b. July 22, 1746. 5 and 6. Twins, b. Oct. 18, 1748; viz. Dolly, m. Asa Drury, of Natick, and Martha, m. Asaph Bigelow, of Framingham, and d. 1830. 7. Mary, b. February, 1751; m. James Morse.

The fourth of these, Col. JOHN GLEASON, b. July 22, 1746; m. Anna Eames, of Holliston, who d. of fever, aged about seventy-five, Jan. 24, 1824. He was selectman in Framingham; moved to Union with his son Calvin, in May, 1805; settled about one mile and a half west of the south part of Sunnybee Pond; and d. Sept. 20, 1827; had — I. John b. March 31, 1771; r. Thomaston; d. 1832. — II. Molly, b. July 27, 1773; m., Sept. 21, 1801, Capt. Nathan Miles, of Barretts Town. — III. Lydia, b. March 11, 1775; m. Joseph Morse, and d. at Union; c. — IV. Micajah, b. Jan. 27, 1777. — V. Calvin, b. at Framingham, March 13, 1779; d. 1850; m., Oct. 18, 1801, Sally, dr. of James and Sarah (Perry) Rice, and b. at Natick, April 17, 1781; had issue, 1. *James*, b. July 14, 1802; d. Jan. 18, 1824. 2. *Nathan Miles*, b. May 17, 1807; m., Nov. 17, 1831. Mary Morton, of Bristol. 3. *Joseph Morse*, b. Dec. 8, 1808; m., Nov. 1839, Frances Martin, of Bremen. 4. *Sally Perry*, b. Aug. 22, 1811; m., Feb. 24, 1831, Cyrus Morton, of Bristol. 5. *Calvin*, b. Sept. 23, 1813; m., Dec. 24, 1840. Abigail S. Simmons, of Union. 6. *Charles*, b. Feb. 28, 1818; d. March 31, 1824 — VI. Anna, or Nancy, b. Jan. 25, 1781; m. Joshua Underwood, of Holliston. — VII. Rebeckah, b. Oct. 18, 1782;

fourth child of Col. John; was t. 1799. He erected a fulling-mill on Crawford's River. He m., March 22, 1801, Polly, dr. of Onesimus and Jemima (Leland) Cole, of Sherburne, who d. Sept. 22, 1836. He was greatly afflicted with asthma, often going to Boston and back in a vessel for the relief it gave him; and d. in Union, June 19, 1823. He had children — I. Joseph, b. March 22, 1802; m., first, Caroline, dr. of John Fairbanks, Nov. 25, 1827, who d. Aug. 17, 1847; c.; and, second, Ann, dr. of Thaddeus Luce, Jan. 9, 1848, who d. Feb. 17, 1850, leaving 1. *Ann Caroline*, b. Feb. 17, 1850. He m., third, Betsey, dr. of William Collins, of Appleton, Sept. 15, 1850. — II. Eliza, b. Oct. 2, 1803; m., 1821, David Norris Piper, of Thomaston; had 1. *Aaron G.*, b. Feb. 27, 1822. 2. *Sarah Jane*, b. Dec. 3, 1823; m. a Fales, of St. George. 3. *Mary E.*, b. Jan. 1825; m. Barnabas Webb, of Thomaston. 4. *Martha Frances*, b. March 20, 1828; m., George W. Beveridge, of Hope. 5. *David Norris*, b. Jan. 1831. — III. William, b. Aug. 18, 1805; m., April 12, 1827, Lydia Le Doit, b. in North Yarmouth; whose father, from France, d. May 24, 1814, and was buried in Union. Their ch. 1. *Infant dr.*, b. Feb. 20, 1828; d. Feb. 21, 1828. 2. *Eliza*, b. Feb. 14, 1829; d. Oct. 21, 1832. 3. *Abigail Childs*, b. Dec. 15, 1830. 4. *Mary Cole*, b. Dec. 14, 1832; d. April 7, 1842. 5. *Micajah*, b. Feb. 16, 1835. 6. *Hannah Irish*, b. June 17, 1838. 7. *Hellen Elizabeth*, b. July 23, 1841. 8. *Edward*, b. Sept. 18, 1843. 9. *Edgar*, b. Feb. 18, 1846; d. March 2, 1848. — IV. Mary, b. July 17, 1807; m., Nov. 14, 1850, Samuel Beals, of Abington, Mass. — V. Harriet, b. Jan. 21, 1810; m. Nathaniel Robbins, jun. — VI. Olive, b. Oct. 4, 1812; m., 1837, Stetson Vaughan, of Warren, Me.; r. Abington, Mass.; had 1. *George D.*, b. June 18, 1838. 2. *Louisa E.*, b. Nov. 29, 1839. 3. *Orianna A.*, b. Oct. 15, 1841. 4. *Francis L.*, b. Jan. 18, 1844. — VII. Sarah, b. March 13, 1817; m. John Williams,

m. Jonathan Morse, and d. in Union, 1831. — VIII. Olive, b. July 20, 1784; m., Oct. 7, 1804, Micah Stone, of Warren, and d. 1812. — IX. Hitty, b. Sept. 30, 1786; m., Feb. 8, 1805, John Hemenway, of Royalston, and moved to Union. — X. Aaron, b. Feb. 17, 1791; m. Rachel Metcalf; d. Thomaston, 1829. Of the sons, Micajah and Calvin settled here. For fuller details of the early genealogy, see Barry's "History of Framingham," from which much of this account of the early generations is derived.

of Warren; r. Union; ch. 1. *George F.*, b. May 15, 1844.
2. *Augustus E.*, b. June 24, 1848.

GRINNELL, BAILEY, b. Little Compton, R. I.; came probably soon after his br. Royal; t. 1791; r. north side of Muddy Pond; moved to Exeter, where he d. in the fall of 1834. His w., Reliance Spooner, b. Rhode Island; d. in Union, May 20, 1834. They had — I. Richard, cast away and drowned at sea, Nov. 19, 1807 — II. Samuel Spooner, m. Catherine Morse, of Friendship; r. Appleton. — III. Mace Shepard, b. Little Compton, R. I., Aug., 15, 1786; m., in Union, Jan. 19, 1812, Rachel Butters, b. Feb. 4, 1789, at Jaffrey, N. H.; moved to Exeter, in March, 1814; ch. 1. *Jane*, b. and d. 1812, a few days old. 2. *William Spooner*, b. Union, Sept. 20, 1813; m., Dec. 31, 1838, Mahala, dr. of Rev. Cornelius Irish, and had (1). Esther Arvilla, b. Oct. 14, 1839; (2). Cornelius Irish, b. July, 1841; (3). Jane Mabry, b. Jan. 1843; (4). Albert; d.; (5). Mary A.; (6). Ada A. 3. *Sarah*, b. Exeter, June 17, 1815; m., Jan. 26, 1843, Isaac Worth, of Exeter; c. 4. *Albert*, b. Jan. 7, 1817; m., June 15, 1843, Angela Hayden, of Bangor, from Castine; had (1). Ellen Maria, b. Boston, April 10, 1844; (2). Charles Edwin, b. Boston, Aug. 20, 1847. 5. *Charles B.*, b. Aug. 17, 1818; m., Sept. 27, 1844, Mary Thomas, b. May 16, 1818; dr. of Asa and Mary (Hill) Shaw, of Exeter; c. 6. *Elvira*, b. May 17, 1820; m., April 22, 1841, Nathaniel, s. of Nathaniel Barker, of Exeter; and had (1). Mary Esther; (2). Charles F.; (3). Frederick; (4). Frank. 7. *Susan*, b. May 3, 1822; d. July 25, 1824. 8. *Diana R.*, b. Feb. 4, 1824; d. Sept. 1826. 9. *Arvilla*, b. Nov. 13, 1826; d. June, 1827. — IV. Philip, b. Nov. 1, 1789; m., first, a Cunningham, Aug. 7, 1823; and, second, Mary K. Jameson; all d. — V. Susanna, b. March 9, 1792; m., Oct. 1815, Joshua Spear, of Warren; and d. of consumption. — VI. Rebecca, b. June 30, 1794; u. — VII. Bailey, b. Jan. 25, 1797; drowned, Nov. 21, 1807, below the mill on Muddy Brook. — VIII. Cornelius, b. —— 25, 1799; d. March 19, 1833, of consumption; u. — IX. Reliance, b. Feb. 9, 1802; m., 1822, Joshua Morse, from Friendship, in 1822; and had 1. *Elijah*, b. July 20, 1823. 2. *Lucinda*, b. Nov. 6, 1824; d. Sept. 5, 1825. 3. *Lucinda*, b. Dec. 15, 1825. 4. *Clarinda*, b. Jan. 18, 1827. 5. *Louisa*, b. Oct. 16, 1828. 6. *Reliance*, b. Aug. 14, 1830.

7. *Delena*, b. Aug. 15, 1832.   8. *Susanna*, b. Aug. 16, 1834.   9. *Harriet*, b. July 1, 1836.   10. *Olive Celeste*, b. June 1, 1839.   11. *Anthony Adelbert*, b. Jan. 5, 1841.   12. *Charles Leroy*, b. May 19, 1843.

GRINNELL, ROYAL, b. at Little Compton, R. I., June 1, 1755; d. in Union, Nov. 1, 1837; m., Oct. 18, 1781, in Dartmouth, Mass., Hannah Briggs, b. there April 13, 1760; ch. — I. *Betsey*, b. Sept. 18, 1782; d. Oct. 6, 1782. — II. *Deborah*, b. Oct. 1, 1783; d. of consumption, Feb. 23, 1812; m., Nov. 13, or 14, 1806, Alpheus Collamore; had 1. *Royal*, b. Oct. 16, 1807; d. Jan. 1823.   2. *Peter*, b. May 14, 1809.   3. *William A.*, b. March 5, 1811.   A. C., m., second, Chloe Cummings; [A. Collamore's father, Joshua, d. June 18, 1821, 81.] — III. *Hannah*, b. Jan. 20, 1786; m., Aug. 2, 1804, Asaph Lucas; and had 1. *Willard*, b. Aug. 17, 1805; m., 1829, Anna Fossett.   2. *Edwin*, b. May 2, 1807.   3. *Mary*, b. May 3, 1810; m. George Washington Messer.   4. *Abram*, b. May 31, 1820; d. June 4, 1820.   5. *Martha*, b. April 20, 1823; d. Oct. 15, 1826. — IV. *Charity*, b. Jan. 20, 1788; d. April 13, 1809, "disorder in the head." — V. *Mercy*, b. Jan. 3, 1791; m. John Allen, Sept. 5, 1812 (?); r. Buffalo, N.Y. — VI. *Daniel Briggs*, b. April 22, 1793; m., April 15, 1819, Sally Esensa; r. Appleton; had 1. *Elijah*, b. Jan. 1820; m. Susan Fish, who d. 1847.   2. *Nancy*, m. Bailey Grinnell.   3. *Eunice*, m. William Lehr.   4. *Sarah*, m. Joseph Light.   5. *Lavinia*, b. April, 1836. — VII. *Mary*, b. April 30, 1795; m., Dec. 6, 1812, Isaac Booth; moved to Exeter, and d. April 12, 1836; had 1. *Albert*, b. Dec. 15, 1813.   2. *Orlando*, b. Sept. 12, 1815.   3. *Ira*, b. July 29, 1817.   4. *Mary Elizabeth*, b. July 30, 1819.   5. *Jacob*, b. June 1, 1821.   6. *Isaac*, b. March 25, 1823.   7. *Hannah Briggs*, b. March 25, 1825.   8. *Martha*, b. March 30, 1827.   9. *Royal Grinnell*, b. June 23, 1829. — VIII. *James*, b. Dec. 1, 1797; m. Sally Lothrop, of Union, 1819; and had 1. *Olive*, b. June 14, 1820.   2. *Sarah Ann*, b. March 16, 1822; m., Jan. 1, 1846, Edward Cleaveland, of Camden. 3. *John*, b. Feb. 17, 1824.   4. *William*, b. March 26, 1826. 5. *Martha*, b. Feb. 11, 1828; d. Feb. 23 (gravestone 24), 1828.   6. and 7. *Julia Maria*, and *Arthusa Kellogg*, twins, b April 12, 1829.   8. *Royal*, b. Aug. 22, 1831.   9. *James Adelbert*, b. April 22, 1835. — IX. *Lavina*, b. March 16, 1800; m., first, Stephen Huse, Sept. 12, 1819, who d. Feb.

15, 1834; and, second, Thomas Kellerin, of Cushing; had *Margaret McCall*, b. Feb. 3, 1821. *John Stoyell*, b. March 27, 1832; and probably others. — X. Eliza, b. May 12, 1803; m. William Boggs, Aug. 24, 1826; r. Illinois.

GUILD, JOSEPH, several times Moderator of town-meetings, came from Attleborough, Mass., with Joseph Maxcy, in 1788. They bought together, and afterwards divided the land. He took the lot now owned by Amos Walker, and finally, in Sept. 1793, went back to Attleborough.

HART, WILLIAM, particularly skilful in fishing and hunting, b. in Dedham, Mass., s. of William and Mary (Fisher) Hart; d. Dec. 14, 1831, æt. sixty-seven; m., April 22, 1792, Miriam, b. Aug. 24, 1767, dr. of John and Mary (Hill) Brick, of Sherburne, Mass. They had — I. Betsey, b. Sherburne, June 1, 1793; m., Aug. 20, 1812, John McThorndike; r. on the Gay Farm; ch. 1. *Miriam Hart*, b. July 13, 1813; m., July 15, 1835, Horace Miller; and had (1). Martha S.; (2). Dudley; (3). Mary Olive. 2. *William Hart*, b. Oct. 25, 1815. 3. *Eliza*, b. May 3, 1818; m. Lory Kelloch, of Warren; has a son. 4. *Abigail Crane*, b. Feb. 28, 1821. 5. *George*, b. July 13, 1823; d. Aug. 21, 1826. 6. *Mary*, b. Jan. 5, 1826. 7. *George Washington*, b. Aug. 28, 1828. 8. *John Emery*, b. July 21, 1831. 9. *Sarah Barrett*, b. Dec. 11, 1834. 10. *Lucy Eells*, b. March, 1840. — II. John Fisher, b. Dec. 23, 1795; r. homestead; m., June 8, 1817, Polly, or Mary, Flint, b. Reading, Mass., and very early left an orphan. Their ch. are 1. *Willard*, b. July 1, 1818. 2. *Joseph Fisher*, b. Dec. 21, 1820; d. in Union, of ship-fever, June 15, 1848; u. 3. *Lucy Ann*, b. Dec. 7, 1824; m., November, 1850, Charles, s. of Amasa Russell, of Warren. 4. *Avery Sanger*, b. Jan. 24, 1827. 5. *Abigail Sanger*, b. Sept. 8, 1829. 6. *William*, b. Aug. 1, 1833. 7. *John Amory*, b. Feb. 26, 1836. 8. *Edwin*, b. May 27, 1839.

HAWES,[1] ABIJAH, b. (new style), Sept. 11, 1752, at

---

[1] From a manuscript-genealogy of Madison Hawes, of California, it appears that Edward Hawes, of Dedham, Mass., d. June 28, 1686; m., April 15, 1648, Eliony Lumber. He had Lydia, b. Jan. 26, 1649; m. a Gay; Mary, b. Nov. 4, 1650; Daniel, b. Feb. 10, 1652; d. March 15, 1737; Hannah, b. Feb. 1. 1654-5; m., Jan. 5, 1676, John Mason; John, b. Dec. 17, 1656; d. Feb. 21, 1731-2; Nathaniel, b. Aug. 14, 1660; d. Oct. 16, 1714; Abigail, b. Oct. 2, 1662; m. Fales; Joseph,

Wrentham, now Franklin; d. Jan. 10, 1839; m., December (?), 1782, his second cousin, Margaret Hawes, who was b. May 9, 1756; and d. March 24, 1833. They had — I. Abial (altered to Nancy), b. Jan. 17, 1784. — II. Pliny, b. July 22, 1787; d. Dec. 4, 1794. — III. Sanford, b. July 1, 1789; d. Dec. 9, 1794. — IV. Whiting, b. Sept. 13, 1792; m., 1842, Julia, dr. of David Fales, of Thomaston; r. homestead. — V. Abijah, b. Feb. 28, 1795; r. China.

HAWES, MATTHIAS, six months a revolutionary soldier; b. at Wrentham, now Franklin, Mass., Oct. 6, 1754; d. Nov. 4, 1828; m., Jan. 1, 1783, in Warren, Maine, Sarah, b. Feb. 18, 1765, in Sharon, Mass., dr. of Capt. Samuel Payson, of revolutionary memory, who subsequently moved from Warren to Hope, and there died. Descendants, — I. Sarah, or Sally, as the name was more commonly called by people half a century ago, b. April 5, 1784; d. Dec. 10, 1850; m., Dec. 24, 1809, William (s. of James and Ruth Brown), who was b. Feb. 24, 1786; and d. Aug. 16, 1822. They had 1. *John*, b. Dec. 31, 1810; physician; d. Jan. 25, 1841, at Grenada, Mississippi. 2. *James Weed*, b. Aug. 10, 1812; m., Oct. 8, 1837, Rowena Melinda Peabody; r. Saccarappa; and has (1). V i e n n a A u g u s t a, b. March 9, 1839; (2). J a m e s M i l f o r d, b. Nov. 13, 1840; (3).

b. Aug. 9, 1664; Deborah, b. Sept. 1, 1666; m. a Pond. Daniel, b. Feb. 10, 1652; m., Feb. 11, 1677. Abial Gay; and had Mary, b. Sept. 17, 1679; Abigail, b. Nov. 15, 1681; Daniel, b. March 30, 1684. d. Jan. 15, 1763; Josiah, b. April 6, 1683; Hezekiah, b. Nov. 22, 1688; Ruth, b. July 9, 1691; Benjamin, b. March 14, 1696. Daniel, of Wrentham, b. March 30, 1684; m., Dec. 20, 1710, Beriah Mann; and had Daniel, b. Oct. 24, 1711; Samuel, b. Jan. 7, 1713; Pelatiah, b. Oct. 8, 1714; Moses, b. Aug. 28, 1716; Aaron, b. April 13, 1718; Ichabod, b. Sept. 18, 1720; Timothy, b. June 21, 1722; twins, b. March 20, 1724, viz. Beriah and Josiah; Mary, b. Feb. 11, 1725-6; Joseph, b. March 21, 1727-8.

JOSIAH HAWES, of Franklin, born March 20, 1724; died Feb. 28, 1804; m., Dec. 18, 1751, Maria Lyon, who d. Aug. 28, 1779; and had — I. Abijah, b. Aug. 31, 1752. — II. Mary, b. Oct. 27, 1753; d. Aug. 8, 1755. — III. Matthias, b. Oct. 6, 1754. — IV. Jemima, b. Jan. 28, 1761; d. April 23, 1835; m., Nov. 23, 1782, Eliab Wright; d. — V. Beriah, b. April 17, 1763; d. Oct. 20, 1818. — VI. Levi, b. May 22, 1765; d. May 9, 1839; m., Jan. 1, 1793, Permela Clark, who d. Sept. 4, 1839.

Briefly, Abijah Hawes and Matthias Hawes were sons of Josiah, b. March 20, 1724; the son of Daniel, b. March 30, 1684; the son of Daniel, b. Feb. 10, 1652; the son of Edward, of Dedham, Mass., who m., April 15, 1648, Eliony Lumber.

Stillborn, Dec. 6, 1842; (4). Arthur Lindall,
b. Dec. 5, 1843; (5). Francelia Ann, b. May 4,
1846; (6). Azelia Melinda, b. July 29, 1848. 3.
Noyes Payson Hawes, b. April 5, 1815. 4. *William Hawes*,
b. Sept. 23, 1817. 5. *Sarah Noyes*, b. Jan. 7, 1820; m.,
in Boston, March 9, 1842, William L. Wight, b. May 26,
1815, at Otisfield, where he d. Jan. 3, 1851; ch. (1.)
Charlotte D., b. Dec. 1, 1842, in Boston, and d. Aug.
14, 1843, in Roxbury; (2). Sarah Noyes, b. March 24,
1844; d. Otisfield, Oct. 15, 1849; (3). Mary Susan, b.
July 20, and d. Oct. 21, 1845, at South Boston; (4).
Mary, b. Sept. 23, 1846, at South Boston; (5). William
L., b. Dec. 30, 1847; d. Aug. 1, 1848; (6). Martha, b.
Jan. 4, 1849; d. April 24, 1850. — II. James, b. Nov. 11,
1785, d. Nov. 23 or 24, 1793, of throat-distemper. — III.
Mary, b. June 17, 1787; m., Aug. 14, 1808, Simon Barrett, b. Concord, Mass., Sept. 24, 1765; r. Hope. He d.
April 20, 1845, at the insane hospital at Augusta; ch. 1.
Simon Hawes, b. Aug. 24, 1809; m., June 1, 1849, Mary
Esther Jane Fox, who was b. Jan. 3, 1825, in England. 2.
Mary Hunt, b. June 18, 1811; d. Oct. 26, 1837. 3. *Noyes
Payson Hawes*, b. June 15, 1813; m., Oct. 7, 1836, Jeanette
Kingsley Frary, who was b. Dec. 11, 1817, at Riga, N.Y.;
and she d. April 1, 1850; had (1). Amos William, b.
Nov. 29, 1838; (2). Charles Spencer, b. Aug. 1,
1841, d. Dec. 26, 1842; (3). Franklin Noyes, b.
Aug. 15, 1844; (4). Horace Frary, b. Oct. 18, 1846.
4. *Maria Lyon*, b. March 20, 1818; d. Aug. 20, 1843; m.,
Dec. 12, 1838, Joseph Muzzey, who was b. March 14, 1807;
r. Searsmont; had Mary Maria, b. Aug. 22, 1841. 5
and 6. Twins, b. March 25, 1820; viz. *Charles;* d. May,
1847, Elizabethtown, N. J.; and *Amos;* r. Elizabethtown,
N. J. 7. *Fidelia H.*, b. Sept. 26, 1823; m., May 22, 1845,
Horace Muzzey, who was b. May 29, 1814; r. Searsmont;
and has (1). Fidelia, b. April, 1850. 8. *Matthias*, b.
April 6, 1825; r. California. — IV. Sukey, twin with Mary,
b. June 17, 1787; d., of throat-distemper, Dec. 20, 1793. —
V. Oliver, b. March 8, 1789; d. March 11, 1789. — VI.
and VII. Twins, *Hermon* and *Pliny*, both b. Jan. 16, and
d. Jan. 17, 1790. — VIII. Melatiah, b. April 21, 1791; m.,
June 2, 1825, David Crabtree, who was b. Feb. 26, 1781;
r. Hope; had 1. *Emeline*, b. April 26, 1826. 2. *Caroline*,
b. Sept. 15, 1827; d. Jan. 17, 1839. 3. *Maria*, b. Oct. 3,

1829. 4. *Sophia*, b. May 18, 1832. 5. *Amelia*, b. Oct. 8, 1837. — IX. Otis, b. Jan. 21 or 31, 1793; m., Sept. 20, 1818, Elsie, b. March 25, 1797, dr. of John Davis, of Appleton; and had 1. *Sarah*, b. April 9, 1820; d. Sept. 23, 1838. 2. *Silas*, b. Dec. 26, 1821; m., Sept. 10, 1848, Margaret, dr. of Samuel Hills; and has (1). Emma F., b. 1850. 3. *Roxana Nott*, b. Dec. 18, 1823; m., 1843, Isaac C. Hovey; and has (1). Harriet Luella; (2). Sarah; (3). George. 4. *Lavinia*, b. July 20, 1825. 5. *Philander*, b. Sept. 22, 1827. 6. *Julia*, b. Dec. 17, 1829. 7. *Cyrene*, b. Feb. 9, 1833. 8. *Laurinda*, b. July 19, 1835. 9. *Edwin*, b. Nov. 3, 1839. 10. *Charles Barrett*, b. Nov. 26, 1841. — X. Austin, b. Sept. 22, 1794; d., April 5, 1795, of influenza. — XI. Noyes Payson, r. Boston and California, b. Feb. 4, 1796; m., Oct. 25, 1827, Abigail, b. Sept. 21, 1797, dr. of John Wilkes Richardson, of Franklin, Mass.; had 1. *Harriet*, b. b. Aug. 22, 1828; teaching in Tuscaloosa, Ala. 2. *Abigail*, b. Oct. 2, 1830. 3. *William*, b. Sept. 19, 1832. 4. *Edward*, b. July 31, 1834; d. Aug. 11, 1835. 5. *Silas*, b. Aug. 3, and d. Aug. 4, 1836. 6. *Caroline*, b. July 15, 1838. — XII. Julia, b. Nov. 17, 1797. — XIII. Silas, b. June, and d. Aug. 1, 1799. — XIV. Lavinia Anthony, b. Sept. 28, 1800; m. Vinal Ware. — XV. Galen, b. April 13, 1802; r. homestead; d. Aug. 4, 1834; m., Jan. 6, 1831, Harriet, dr. of Capt. John W. Lindley; and had 1. *Mary Barrett*, b. Jan. 16, 1832; m. Prentiss M. Blake. 2 and 3. Twins, b. March 9, 1833, viz. *Horace*, d. Aug. 14, 1833, and *Levi Lindley*. [Galen's widow m. Elias Blake, of Bangor.] — XVI. Levi, b. Dec. 24, 1804; d. Aug. 12, 1805, of canker-rash. — XVII. Stillborn, July, 1806. — XVIII. Stillborn, August, 1807. — XIX. Madison, b. March 24, 1809; printer; r. California; m., May 1, 1834, Nancy Nelson Dam; had 1. *Sarah Maria*, b. Aug. 30, 1836; d. Nov. 13, 1837. 2. *Edward Payson*, b. Jan. 29, 1839; d. July 15, 1844. 3. *William Wirt*, b. Feb. 17, 1841; d. April 14, 1842. 4. *Nancy Cornelia*, b. July 24, 1842.

HAWES, MOSES, town-clerk, schoolmaster; s. of Joseph and Hannah; was b. at Franklin, Mass.; m. Mary, dr. of Alexander Kelloch (commonly pronounced Kellar), of Warren; in the spring of 1806, returned to Franklin, where he d. Descendants, — I. Hannah, b. April 27, 1781 (the first female b. in Stirlington who grew to be an adult); m., March 6, 1801, Nathan Allen; became a widow, and her father took her to his home in Franklin, Mass., where she d.; had 1. *Sabin,* b. Aug. 25, 1801; m.; r. Pawtucket, Central Falls, R. I. 2. *Amos,* b. Feb. 14, 1804; m. thrice; r. Franklin. 3. *Clarinda,* b. July 22, 1806; m. Sumner Pond, of Franklin; and d. — II. Herman, b. Sept. 23, 1783; settled on the homestead; m. Abigail Simmons, of Waldoborough, Feb. 22, 1804, who d. May 2, 1851. They had 1. *Matilda,* b. Feb. 2, 1805; m., first, 1826, Noah Bartlett, grandson of David Robbins; and had (1). O s c a r A l o n z o, b. April 16, 1827; (2). F o s t i n a M a r i l l a, b. Dec. 28, 1829; (3). A d o l p h u s L e w e l l y n, b. Sept. 13, 1832. After Mr. Bartlett's death, his w. became second w. of Fisher Hart. 2. *Martha Maria,* b. Jan. 27, 1808; d. Oct. 10, 1808. 3. *Stephen Simmons,* b. Aug. 28, 1809; r. the Philip Robbins Place; m., 1830, Alzina, dr. of Spencer Walcott; had (1) and (2). Twins, A r a v e s t a M a t i l d a, and A r a v i l l a A v i s, b. Feb. 1, 1831; (3). N o a h B a r t l e t t, b. March 28, 1839; d. March 10, 1840; (4). M a r i e t t a B a r t l e t t, b. Sept. 20, 1841; (5). A b i g a i l S i m m o n s, b. Feb. 14, 1849. 4. *William Groton,* b. July 18, 1811; m., May, 1834, Roxana Robbins; r. homestead; ch. (1). H e r b e r t A l o n z o, b. April 28, 1839; (2). H e n r y A u g u s t u s, b. Nov. 23, 1840; (3). E d w i n R u t h v e n, b. Feb. 10, 1843; (4). E m e r y R o s c o e, b. July 7, 1845; d. June 22, 1850; (5). P h e b e R o b b i n s, b. Oct. 9, 1848. 5. *Hannah Allen,* b. July 4, 1813; m., March 13, 1843, Asa Messer. 6 and 7. Twins, b. Aug. 24, 1816, viz: *Moses,* m. Lucinda C. Libbey; and *Mary,* m. Manning Walcott. 8. *Charles A.,* b. Nov. 3, 1818; m., 1837, Sarah Angelina, dr. of B. R. Mowrey; had (1). L l e w e l l y n, b. Nov. 15, 1837; (2). E l l e n A d e l i a, b. March 16, 1840; (3). E l i z a M a t i l d a, b. July 29, 1842; (4). M a r t h a M a r i a, b. Sept. 20, 1844; (5). H a r r i e t R h o b e, b. Feb. 17, 1847; (6). C o l i n, b. March 3, 1849. 9. *Abigail,* b. Oct. 28, 1822; m. Jesse Wentworth, writing-master; r. Boston; b. in Hope, Nov. 15, 1815, s. of Asa and Hannah (Hewitt) Payson; and has (1). M a t i l d a H a w e s, b. Dec. 14, 1844. — III. Abigail, b. Jan. 26, 1786; m. Dr. Pelatiah Metcalf, from Wrentham. — IV. Mary, m. Peter Fisher, of Franklin; and d. — V. Eleanor, m. Alfred Knapp, of Franklin. — VI. Amelia, b. 1798; m Elisha Harding, M. D.; had 1. *Harriet Augusta,* b. June 7, 1820; d. Aug. 2, 1826. 2. *Nathaniel Miller,* b.

Feb. 9, 1822; m., June 13, 1839, Sarah Whiting, dr. of E. Cobb; r. Rockland; and had (1). Amelia Alwilder, b. Nov. 3, 1841; d. May 13, 1842; (2). a son, b. 1849.

HILLS, JOHN, br. of Samuel; t. 1797; with Sylvanus Prince bought land joining Stewart's on the north, sold it to N. Robbins, Esq., and returned to the West.

HILLS,[1] SAMUEL, b. Feb. 14, 1760, at Pawtucket, R. I.; spent a large part of his minority at Wrentham, Mass.; was the first blacksmith in Union; very deaf; d. of consumption, Aug. 5, 1829. March 2, 1786, he m., in Upton, Mass., Abigail Child, who d. Feb. 7, 1837. They had — I. Jabez Fisher, b. Nov. 27, 1786; d. Sept. 13, 1802. — II. Peggy, or Margaret, b. Aug. 19, 1790; d. Oct. 15, 1794. — III. Elizabeth, b. March 31, and d. March 31, 1794. — IV. Joel, b. April 20, 1795; m., Sept. 1, 1825, Abigail, dr. of Levi and Pamelia Hawes, of Franklin. He was a storekeeper in partnership with Walter Morse in Belmont; afterward lived many years at Bangor, and went to Boston a year or two before he d. at South Boston, Sept. 25, 1849. His ch. are 1. *William Sanford*, b. July 5, 1826. 2. *Joel Hawes*, b. Nov. 28, 1828. 3. *Edward Hawes*, b. Aug. 20, and d. Nov. 1, 1832. 4. *Sarah Smith*, b. July 28, 1835. 5. *Abigail Pamelia*, b. Oct. 8, 1837. 6. *Mary Maria*, b. April 26, 1840. 7. *Caroline*, b. Feb. 6, 1842. — V. Sanford, b. May 3, 1797; m., May 3, 1821, Avis, dr. of Spencer Walcott; r. homestead; and d. Aug. 10, 1832; had 1. *Abigail Ann*, b. April 5, 1822, m. Madan King Payson; r. Natick, Mass., and had (1). Lauriston, d. 1851; (2). Lisette. 2. *Joel Fisher*, b. Oct. 1, 1823. 3. *Spencer Walcott*, b. March 24, 1825. 4. *Hannah Walcott*, b. Feb. 3, 1827. 5. *Samuel George*, b. Nov. 5, 1829. 6. *Sanford Manning*, b. Jan. 15, 1832.

HOLMES, ELIJAH, b. in Stoughton, now Sharon, Mass., Sept. 29, 1764; m., Aug 25, 1785, Dorcas (dr. of Elisha Partridge, by his first wife), b. March 31, 1767, in Frank-

---

[1] This family must be distinguished from that of Reuben Hills, who came in 1803 or 1804 from Hawke, now Danville, N. H., and who was b. at Chester, N. H., and d. here Sept. 28, 1828, aged seventy-six. His w., Sarah Currier, d. Nov. 1, 1835. They had Samuel; Sarah, m., Jan. 20, 1803, John Dickey, r. Searsmont; Nathan; Reuben; Josiah; Isaac; Nancy, m., Jan. 16, 1817, Jonathan Eastman; Cyrus; Betsey, d. young; Alden, drowned; Charlotte, d. young; Louisa, m., Feb. 14, 1822, George Silloway, and d. 1850.

lin, Mass., where she d. in 1813 (?). A short time before the war of 1812, he went to the British Provinces; m. a second time; and settled at Moose River, near Lubec, Maine. From about 1829, when he returned to Rockland, he lived with his son Charles, and d. there Feb. 10, 1839. His ch. — I. Dorcas, b. May 26, 1786. — II. Bernard, b. Jan. 1, 1788; d. Dec. 25, 1825. — III. Elijah, b. Dec. 11, 1789. — IV. Willoughby, b. May 17, 1791 [town-record], 1792 [family-record]; d. July 19, 1791 [town-record], 1792 [family-record]. — V. Charles, b. Aug. 20, 1793; r. Rockland. — VI. Susanna, b. Dec. 28, 1794, or Dec. 29, 1796; d. Feb. 8, 1795, or February, 1797. — VII. and VIII. Twins, b. March 20, 1798; Mary, d. May 26, 1835; Hannah, d. Oct. 24, 1800. — IX. Anna, b. March 31, 1800; d. Oct. 22, 1800. — X. Amos, b. Feb. 14, 1802; d. — XI. Oliver, b. May 12, 1803. — XII. George, b. Aug. 24, 1805. — XIII. Robert, b. May 4, 1808.

IRISH, ICHABOD, b. Jan. 6, 1740, O. S., at Little Compton, R. I; d. Aug. 5, 1815. His first wife, Polly, d. before he came here. His second wife, Hannah Grinnell, b. Aug. 31, 1745, O. S., d. July 30, 1794. Early in 1795, he m. his third w., the widow Jane (Story) Thompson, of Barretts Town, who d. June 16, 1810, æt. sixty-three. In his seventy-first year he was m., Oct. 23, 1811, at Vassalborough Friends' Meeting, to his fourth wife, Deborah Conklin, then in her fifty-first year. His ch. were — I. Betsey, m. Ebenezer Whitcomb, of Barretts Town, and d.; had ch. 1. *Ebenezer.* 2. *Ira,* d. young. 3. *John,* d. a young man. 4. *Ira.* 5. *Thirsa,* m. Abel Blood. 6. *Betsey,* m. a Dillingham. 7. *Mahala,* m. William Fletcher. 8. *Henry.* 9. *Nancy,* m. Kingman Gurney. 10. *Sally,* m. John Whitcomb. 11. *Benjamin,* twin with Sally. 12. *Ruth,* m. Charles Elliott. 13. *Eleazar.* — II. Ruth, m. Jonathan Fletcher, of Lincolnville, and d. Her dr. *Sally,* m. Robert Moody. — III. Mary, or Polly, d. March, 1792. — IV. Permelia, b. July 22, 1773; d. May 30, 1797. — V. Comfort, b. Jan. 18, 1775; d. May 1, 1796. — VI. Thankful, b. April 8, 1778; d. Jan. 20, 1798; m. Walter Philbrook; and had 1. *James.* — VII. and VIII. Twins, b. Aug. 13, 1780, viz. Mahala, d. Dec. 20 or 25, 1799; and Thirsa, d. Aug. 6, 1797. — IX. Cornelius Bailey, b. March 10, 1782, at Westport Point, sixteen miles in a southerly direction from New Bedford, Mass., near Seconnet Point, lives on the Capt. Joel Adams Place. He was ordained deacon at the New England Methodist Conference at Providence, R. I., by Bishop Enoch George, June 15, 1823; and elder by Bishop Elijah Hedding at the conference at Gardner, July 12, 1829. He m., Dec. 5, 1804, Polly, dr. of Capt. Joel Adams; had 1. *A son*, b. and d. March 24, 1806. 2. *Mahala*, b. July 22, 1807; m., Dec. 31, 1838, William S. Grinnell. 3. *Milton*, b. May 7, 1812; m. Emily Eves, of San Augustine, Texas, where they live; ch. (1). Benjamin Milam, b. September, 1845; (2). A daughter, b. September, 1848. 4. *Lewis*, b. May 25, 1814; w. Sophronia; ch. (1). Mary Jane, b. March 2, 1843; (2). Cordelia, b. Sept. 27, 1844; (3). Wilder, b. Sept. 3, 1846; (4). Judson Greeley, b. June 6, 1849. 5. *Joseph*, b. July 19, 1816; m., Oct. 14, 1839, Cordelia Clary, of Jefferson, who d. Nov. 18, 1850; had (1.) Milton, b. Oct. 5, 1840; (2). Austin, b. Jan. 4, 1843; d. July 18, 1849; (3). Mary Ella, b. Oct. 5, 1846; (4). George A., b. Aug. 22, 1849. J. I. m., second, June 17, 1851, Nancy, dr. of Jonathan and Nancy (Hills) Eastman. 6. *Melia*, b. Aug. 31, 1818; r. Salisbury, Mass.; m. Joseph Homer Walton; and had ch. (1). Luella; (2). Edward Morse; (3). Henry Adams, who d. 7. *Mary*, or *Polly*, b. Sept. 13, 1822. 8. *Esther*, b. Oct. 31, 1824; d. Sept. 23 or 24, 1826. — X. Hannah, b. May 10, 1784; m., first, Abiel Le Doit; and, second, David Haskell; r. Foxcroft. — XI. Levi, b. May 19, 1786; m., Oct. 4, 1810, Anna, widow of Banham Pease, of Appleton, and d. May 1, 1820. — XII. Ichabod, b. May 31, 1790; m., first, in July, 1812, Lucy, dr. of Jeremiah Mitchell; and, second, a Curtis, of Newcastle. He had *Charles West*, b. Dec. 28, 1812.

JENNISON, EBENEZER, son of Dr. J., schoolmaster, surveyor, &c., was here till after the beginning of the nineteenth century; moved to Dixmont, and there d.

JONES, EDWARD, Esq.; probably from Bridgewater, Mass.; t. 1791; d. of paralysis, June 3, 1815; and his w. Phebe, "of decline," June 5, 1815, both aged fifty-five; c. Their funerals were at the same time, and both were buried in one grave.

KIEFF, JOHN, from Thomaston or vicinity; carpenter; r. Belmont; m. Mary, or Betsey, Peabody; had — I. Alexander, b. Feb. 21, 1798. — II. Jane, b. Aug. 29, 1799. —

III. Polly, b. Barretts Town, May 4, 1801. — IV. Greenleaf, b. May 13, 1803.

LERMOND, JOHN, from Warren; probably belonged to one of the Scotch families which came from Ireland to Londonderry, N.H. While a boy, it is said he was in the fort at Thomaston when the French and Indians besieged and attempted to burn it. He m., July 8, 1771, Elizabeth Lamb, b. at Cushing. Though t. 1794, he probably did not move here till 1797. He d. Feb. 20, 1805. His son John, b. Oct. 1, 1772; m., Dec. 1, 1796, Nancy (though baptized Agnes) Bird; came about 1799; d. June 5, 1840; had — I. George, b. Sept. 2, 1797, at Warren; m., 1824, his cousin, Lois Lermond, of Warren; r. Hope. — II. Betsey, b. Jan. 8, 1799, at Warren; m., Nov. 25, 1821, Abijah Miller, of Whitefield. — III. Sally, b. March 3, 1801; m., Dec. 13, 1825, Theodore Scott; r. Belfast. — IV. Elsie, b. Oct. 31, 1803; d. July 20, 1834; m. Marcus Gillmor. — V. Nancy, b. July 2, 1805; m. William Hilt; and d. — VI. Lucinda, b. April 27, 1808; m., 1829, Jones Taylor, of Hope; and d. March 15, 1844. — VII. John, b. Feb. 1, 1810; m. Hannah Hastings; and has 1. *Adelbert*, b. Jan. 9, 1838. 2. *John Francis*, b. Jan. 30, 1840. 3. *Eliza Emily*, b. April 22, 1842. 4. *Frederic*, b. July 29, 1845. — VIII. Elbridge, b. Aug. 24, 1812; m., 1833, Huldah, dr. of Ephraim Bowley, of Hope; and had 1. *Ephraim*, b. March 16, 1834. 2. *Julia*, b. Feb. 4, 1839. 3. *Albert Smith*, b. March 24, 1840. 4. *Elbridge G.*, b. Aug. 23, 1841. 5. *Huldah Elizabeth*, b. Jan. 31, 1845. 6. *Frank Justin*, b. April 13, 1846.

LEWIS, WILLIAM, t. 1793; probably came to reside in 1793. After working a while in town, he m , at his house in Thomaston, Prudence Merry, who came here to live in the family of Capt. George West. N. Robbins, Esq., with the lady whom he afterward m., accompanied them to the wedding. Each of them, as the roads were bad and vehicles scarce, went on horseback, with his betrothed behind him on a pillion. He lived on the hill west of the Middle Bridge, and there dug lime-rock, built a lime-kiln, and made the first lime burnt in the town. Afterward he moved to the place on the west side of the Upper Bridge. He sold this farm to Nathan Blake in 1799, moved to Sandy River, and subsequently to the sea-shore or to the islands at Thomaston or vicinity. In the war of 1812, he enlisted, went to Sackett's Harbor, N.Y., and vicinity (?), where he was shot by an Indian, when he, with three others, went with his canteen to a spring to get water.

LINDLEY, JOAB, br. of John W.; bought a lot of land; and d. of consumption, Nov. 22, 1793, in his twenty-fourth year.

LINDLEY, JOHN W., Capt. (s. of Levi, of Rehoboth, by his w., Polly Smith), b. at Walpole, Mass., Sept. 3, 1782; came in the spring of 1794; r. in the south-west part of the town; m., Sept. 30, 1803, Lucy Williams, b. Feb. 27, 1785, at Concord, N.H., dr. of Thomas Jones, an Englishman. They had — I. Sally, or Sarah, b. Nov. 29, 1804; m. Silas Alden. — II. Levi, b. Nov. 12, 1806; d. Sept. 29 [or 25, according to gravestone], 1831; u. — III. Harriet, b. Sept. 29, 1808; m., first, Galen Hawes; and, second, Elias Blake, of Bangor, who d. 1849, by whom she has one *dr.*, and perhaps others. — IV. Chloe, b. Jan. 21, 1811; d. March 22, 1811. — V. John, b. April 28, 1812; m., 1835, Margaret Libbey; and had 1. *Katharine Josephine*, b. Aug. 21, 1836. 2. *Rienzi Melvil*, b. Aug. 7, 1838. 3. *Ada A.*, b. June 1, 1841. 4. *William L.*, b. Sept. 13, 1843. 5. *John W.*, b. Sept. 5, 1847. 6. *Eliza*, b. April 21, 1850. — VI. Warren, b. Nov. 21, 1823. — VII. Amanda, b. Aug. 10, 1825.

LUCE, SETH, b. Martha's Vineyard; d., March 5, 1833, about eighty years old; m. his cousin, Sarah Luce, who died Sept. 8 or 9, 1825, sixty-eight. The first five children b. at Martha's Vineyard. — I. Freeman, r. Newburgh; m. Eliza Clark; had 1. *Seth*, b. Nov. 17, 1798; m., 1819-20, Olive Sweetser, of Newburgh, who d. at Dixmont. He then m. again; and d. 2. *Freeman*, b. March 9, 1801. 3. *Eliza*, b. Feb. 7, 1803. 4. *Deborah Allen*, b. April 9, 1805. Also *George* and *William*, and probably others. — II. Jeremiah, m., 1806, Susannah Hathorne; r. Appleton; had 1. *Mary*, b. March 19, 1807; m. a Lermond; r. Appleton. 2. *James Claghorn*, b. Nov. 19, 1808. 3. *William*, b. Nov. 30, 1810. 4. *Eliza*, b. Oct. 20, 1812. 5. *Rhoda*. 6. *Edward*; and others. — III. Thaddeus, b. July 13, 1782; m., Nov. 18 or Dec. 18, 1806, Lavina, dr. of Prince Pease, of Appleton; had 1. *Ann*, b. Jan. 27, 1808; m. Joseph Gleason. 2. *Prince*, b. Feb. 16, 1809; m. Almira Butler, and d. Dec. 4, 1846; u. 3. *George*, b. Oct. 16, 1810; m.

Patience Copeland, of Warren; had (1). F r a n c e s; (2).
C h a r l e s. 4. *Nancy*, b. April 18, 1814; m. Reuben
Hagar; and had (1). C h e s t e r; (2). W e s t f o r d; (3).
N o r r i s; (4). L a u r a, d. 5. *Sally*, b. Nov. 14, 1816;
m. Isaac Burns; had (1). L e o n o r a; (2). V i l i n d a.
5. *Mariah*, b. July 29, 1819. 6. *Huldah*, b. March 8,
1821; m. William Burns; c. 7. *Miles*, b. March 25, 1823.
8. *Rosilla*, b. Oct. 11, 1825. 9. *Sullivan Bray*, b. Jan. 11,
1829. — IV. Obadiah, m., 1804, Marcy Chaffin; had 1.
Hepsy, b. May 24, 1805. 2. *Freeman*, b. Dec. 29, 1806.
3. *Whitman*, b. June 13, 1809; and probably others since
they moved to Ohio. — V. Sally, b. Sept. 10, 1786; m.
Gorham Butler. — VI. Remembrance, b. Oct. 22, 1789. —
VII. Thankful, b. Feb. 22, 1793; m. Ebenezer Robbins.
— VIII. Betsey, b. May 31, 1795; m., 1839, Caleb Howard. — IX. Maria, b. Aug. 4, 1800; d. of fever, Sept. 8,
1819.

McCurdy, Daniel; t. 1797; b. Bristol; d. Calais; r.
Fossetts' Mills, built the first saw-mill there; had nineteen
ch.; m. thrice, the first time a widow Grafton, and the last
time, at Calais, Elizabeth Dresser (?).

Maxcy, Benjamin, Lieut., b. Attleborough, Mass., May
11, 1740; d. July 26, 1791; s. of Josiah; m., first, Sarah
Fuller; had three ch.; and, second, Amy, dr. of Nathaniel
Ide, of Attleborough; she was drowned at Union, May,
1793. Descendants, — I. Joseph, Major, b. March 12,
1764; d. Dec. 14, 1810, from taking cold in a wound cut
in his knee with an axe; m. Hannah Page, of Attleborough,
who d. suddenly of colic, April 8, 1811, in her forty-third
year. He settled at the Mill Farm, at South Union, where
Mr. Vaughan now lives; ch. 1. *Nancy*, b. July 4 or 14,
1788; m., Dec. 25, 1808, Dr. William Dougherty; and d.
June, 1832; had (1). N a n c y, b. July 4, 1808; (2).
W i l l i a m, b. April 28, 1811; (3). A l a n s o n, b. May 4,
1813. 2. *Sally*, b. Feb. 24, 1791; m., March 21, 1817,
Cyrus Kendrick; r. Gardner. 3. *Lydia*, b. June 4, 1794;
d. Jan. 31, 1849; m., March 18, 1813, David Robbins. 4.
Waterman, b. Jan. 22, 1796; m., 1816, Olive, dr. of
Nath'l Robbins, and d. Searsmont, May 11, 1827; had (1).
N a t h a n i e l R o b b i n s, b. Jan. 9, 1817; r. California; u.; (2). E l i z a b e t h R o b b i n s, b. April 5, 1818;
m. a Shorey; r. Augusta; (3). J o s e p h, b. Feb. 16,

1820; d. Oct. 6, 1821; (4). Mary, b. April 15, 1822; m. Ansel Lennan; r. Belfast; (5). William W., b. Jan. 4, 1824; d. Dec. 29, 1824; (6). Lydia, b. Nov. 5, 1825; m. a Whittier; r. Augusta. 5. *Leonard*, b. Oct. 29, 1797; m. a Fuller, and d. 1832, in Bangor. 6. *Hannah*, b. March 6, 1800; m. Jonas Hamlin, of China; r. Winslow. 7. (?) *Lucinda*, d. Aug. 4, 1804. 8. *Almira*, b. April 26, 1806; m., March, 1830, John Baxter Priest, of Vassalborough; r. China. 9. *Caroline*, b. July 4, 1808; m., May 12, 1831, Robert McGuier, of Waldoborough; r. South Union; had ch. (1). Mary Angela, b. April 10, 1832; (2). Orison, b. Oct. 23, 1834; (3). Caroline Augusta, b. Jan. 23, 1836; (4). Edwin Constantine, b. May 7, 1843. — II. Josiah, b. July 25, 1766; m., first, Chloe, who was b. April 15, 1769, and drowned May, 1793, dr. of Mayhew Daggett, of Attleborough. He m., second, 1794, Sally Pickering, who originated from Portsmouth, N.H., or vicinity; had 1. *Smith*, b. Feb. 3, 1795; m., first, June 14, 1819, Clarissa Boggs; and, second, a dr. of Moses Crane, of Warren, who d. 1849; r. Gardiner. 2. *Chloe*, b. June 6, 1797; m., Oct. 10, 1822, Jason Davis; had (1). Elizabeth B., b. Aug. 31, 1823; (2). Maxcy H., b. Sept. 8, 1825; (3). Statira, b. Jan. 4, 1827; (4). Jane, b. Nov. 1, 1830; (5). William T., b. Feb. 22, 1834; (6). Roxana, b. July 16, 1835. 3. *Ward*, b. May 16, 1799; m. July 14, 1825, Mary S., widow of Peter Robbins; had children, and d. in Searsmont. 4. *Hervey*, b. March 8, 1801; m. an Andrews, of Camden. 5. *Polly*, b. June 8, 1803; m. an Andrews; r. Camden. 6. *Ama*, b. Aug. 15, 1805; m.; r. Camden. 7. *Daniel*, b. 1807; m. a Blood; r. Warren. 8. *Micajah G.*; r. Camden; b. 1809 (?); m., first, Betsey Blood; and had by her (1). Julina, b. Nov. 1, 1838; (2). Josiah A., b. June 6, 1841. He m., second, a dr. of Abel Walker; and, third, Sarah M., dr. of Thomas Taylor, of Hope, and widow of Waterman Leach, of Warren; and had Sarah M., b. Camden, Oct. 4, 1848. — III. Benjamin, b. July 16, 1772, in Connecticut, as was his brother Josiah during a temporary residence; m. Esther Fuller of Attleborough; had *Barnard*; d.; *Joseph*; *Eaton Whiting*; *Esther*; d. — IV. Sally, or Sarah, b. Nov. 20, 1778; rescued from drowning, May, 1793; returned to Attleborough in the fall of 1793; m., Sept. 3, 1797, Ebenezer Daggett, of Attleborough, who was b. April 16, 1763; was selectman, town-clerk, representative, and d. at Boston, March 4, 1832, while member of the Senate; ch. 1. *Lydia Maxcy*, m. Capron Peck, of Attleborough. 2. *John*, author of the History of Attleborough; graduate of Brown University in 1826; lawyer; representative, 1837–41; senator in 1849; m., June 18, 1840, Nancy M., dr. of Rev. J. B. Boomer, of Sutton, Mass. 3. *Ebenezer*, d. Nov. 17, 1831. 4. *Hervey Maxcy*, m., first, Susan S. Daggett; and, second, Nancy Bates. 5. *Amy Ide*, m. John McClellan, of Sutton, Mass. 6. *Mercy Shepard*, m. Erastus D. Everett, Boston, and d. leaving three ch. 7 and 8. Twins, viz. *Handel N.*, m., first, Eunice W. Shepard, of Wrentham; and, second, Jane Amelia Adams, of Livonia, N.Y.; and *Homer M.*, m. Angelina Daggett, of Surry, N.H. — V. Lydia, b. March 26, 1780; drowned, May, 1793. — VI. Hervey, b. April 30, 1782 or 1783; m., 1805, Sally, dr. of John and Hannah (French) Eastman, b. Kingston, N.H. (?), Feb. 15, 1785; lived on the northerly part of the Mill Farm; now r. Thomaston; ch. 1. *John Eastman*, b. Aug. 7, 1806; m. Ann, widow of John Henry Adams, and dr. of Benjamin Boody, of Westbrook; r. Cushing. 2. *Hannah*, b. Jan. 4, 1808; m. Reuben Hills; r. Lincolnville. 3. *Joseph*, b. Oct. 29, 1809; d. Jan. 1811. 4. *Joseph*, b. Jan. 29, 1811; r. Thomaston. 5. *Nancy E.*, b. Jan. 18, or June, 1812; m. Charles Hook; r. Danville, N.H. 6. *Hervey*, b. July 28, 1814; m. Mariah Staples; r. Swanville. 7. *Josiah*, b. Jan. 22, 1816; d. Feb. 9, 1849, in Thomaston. 8. *Henry*, b. March 10, 1821; r. Thomaston. 9 and 10. Twins, b. July 1, 1823, viz. *Cyrus* and *Sarah*. — VII. Amy, b. Oct. 26, 1784; m. Joel Reed, Princeton, Mass.; r. Hermon.

MERO, AMARIAH, b. May 14, 1757, at Stoughton, Mass., son of Hezekiah (whose father and mother came from Ireland, and lived in Dorchester) and Mary Mero (the latter d. Aug. 26, 1827, aged ninety-four); introduced to Stirlington by Philip Robbins, whose dr. Susan he m.; moved to Starks in advanced age, afterward to Mercer, and lately to Cape Elizabeth, to live with a son. They had — I. Avis, b. June 19, 1787; d. Dec. 8, 1792. — II. Vyna, b. June 16, 1789; d. Nov. 28, 1792. — III. Milla, b. June 1, 1791; d. Nov. 29, 1792 [three deaths in ten days; the last two buried in one coffin]. — IV. Spencer, b. Oct. 21, 1793; m., Sept. 6, 1818, Esther Winslow, dr. of David Robbins's second

w. by a former husband; ch. 1. *Hermon*, b. Feb. 17, 1821; m., 1846, Electa Aroline Litchfield; has (1). A r t h u r L e r o y, b. Jan. 3, 1847. 2. *Eli Sprague*, b. Dec. 10, 1822; m., Jan. 22, 1847, Elizabeth Libbey Kelloch; r. Warren; has (1). E l d o n H e r b e r t, b. May, 1849. 3. *Laura*, b. April 24, 1825; d. Nov. 2 [or 4, gravestone], 1849. 4. *Elisha Harding*, b. April 1, 1827. 5. *Spencer*, b. Nov. 4, 1829. 6. *Sarah Frances*, b. Sept. 16, 1832. 7. *Anson*, b. June 2, 1835. 8. *Chester*, b. March 25, 1841. — V. Avis, b. Aug. 5, 1795; d. May 6, 1797. — VI. Hermon, b. Feb. 11, 1798; r. Waldoborough; m., March, 1827, Lovey West, dr. of Nathaniel Robbins; had 1. *Martha Melvina*, b. Jan. 14, 1828; d. Oct. 2, 1849; m. Anthony Kastner, of Waldoborough; left (1). M a r t h a, nine days old. 2. *Harriet Augusta*, b. Nov. 30, 1829; d. Feb. 23, 1830. 3. *Helen Aurelia*, b. March 17, 1831. 4. *Augustus*. 5. *Sarah Simmons*, b. June, 1835. 6. *Roderick Lionel*, b. 1841. 7. *Albert Curtis*. 8. *Charles Hermon*. — VII. Charles, b. Jan. 27, 1800; m., March 1, 1828, Louisa, b. Jan. 4, 1809, dr. of Capt. Nathaniel Bachelor; r. Cape Elizabeth; ch. 1. *Euphrasia Louisa*, b. Jan. 25, 1831. 2. *Ruphelia Bachelor*, b. March 16, 1834. — VIII. Susan, b. March 9, 1802; m. Samuel Craft; r. Jay; had 1. *Helen Wallace*, d. three and a half years old. 2. *Helen*, b. March, 1841. 3. *Samuel Henry*, b. June, 1843. 4. *Charles*, b. Dec. 1844. — IX. Luther, b. Sept. 17, 1804; d. Jan. 1, 1832; u. — X. Austin. b. Oct. 14, 1806; m. Sally, dr. of James Simmons, of Nobleborough; had seven drs., viz. 1. *Barzana*. 2. *Maranda*. 3. *Alwilda*. 4. *Rachel*. 5. *Susan*. 6. *Mary*. 7. *Electa Allen*. — XI. Julia, b. June 21, 1808; m., 1830, John Williamson, of Starks; had 1. *Luther Austin*, b. Feb. 25, 1831. 2. *Susan Melvina*, b. February, 1833. 3. *Albert Wallace*, b. March 27, 1843. 4. *Fostina Melinda*, b. March, 1845. — XII. Melinda, b. Oct. 15, 1810; m., first, William Richardson, of Newton, Mass.; and had 1. *William Wallace*, d. eleven months old. 2. *Georgia Ann*. She m., second, Timothy Hunting; r. Taunton. — XIII. Chloe Lindley, b. Nov. 2, 1813; m., in the winter of 1828–9, Henry Jameson, of Waldoborough; d. July 13, 1835; having had 1. *Julia Melvina*. 2. *Arvesta Delia*. Both d.

MESSER, ASA, t. 1796; m. Hannah Davis; and d. Jan. 16, 1835. His father, Jonathan, m. Abigail Parker, of

Groton, Mass., who d. in Union, Sept. 13, 1828, aged ninety-nine. Jonathan's ancestors were from Methuen, Mass. Asa had ch. — I. *Sally Commit*, b. March 12, 1803; m. Benjamin Gowen; r. Montville. — II. *Almond*, b. Feb. 18, 1805; m., 1828, Melinda Reed Titus; r. Montville. — III. *Asa*, b. March 2, 1807; d. — IV. *George Washington*; r. Montville; b. March 2, 1807; m., Oct. 18, 1827, Mary Lucas; and had 1. *Willard Lucas*, b. July 20, 1828. 2. *Martha*, b. Jan. 11, 1830; m. William Penny; r. Montville. 3. *Edwin*, d. 4. *Mary Anna*, b. March 17, 1833. 5. *Sarah*, b. Dec. 5, 1835. 6. *Aldana*. 7. *George Riley*, b. July, 1841. 8. *Charles*, d. 9. *Melinda*. 10. *Loantha*, b. June, 1845; d. Aug. 16, 1847. 11. *Flora Ellen*. 12. *A dr.* b. April, 1850. — V. Hannah, b. Feb. 28, 1809. — VI. Eunice, b. May 14, 1811; m., 1831, William Caswell; ch. 1. *Elmira L.*, b. Feb. 14, 1832. 2. *William E.*, b. Jan. 17, 1834. 3. *Ethelbert*, b. June 27, 1836. 4. *Charles Augustus*, b. June 26, 1838. 5. *Amos Roscoe*, b. March 26, 1841. 6. *Sarah Melinda*, b. March 8, 1843. 7. *Hannah Mary*, b. Sept. 18, 1845. 8. *Nathaniel Harden*, b. Aug. 21, 1847. — VII. Ebenezer Stone, b. Feb. 23, 1813; m., Feb. 25, 1834, Nancy S. Adams; ch. 1. *Augustus*, b. Jan. 9, 1835. 2. *Louisa Maria*, b. Jan. 12, 1836; and others. — VIII. Asa, b. Oct. 8, 1815; m., first, May 8, 1836, Caroline C. Littlehale, who d. May 10, 1840; and, second, March 13, 1843, Hannah Allen, dr. of Moses Hawes; and has 1. *Caroline Medora*, b. Oct. 25, 1844. — IX. Parker, b. June 24, 1800, adopted child of Asa Messer; m., 1828, Eliza, dr. of Pente Walcott; ch. 1. *Robert Mathews*, b. March 17, 1829. 2. *Charles Hibbard*, b. March 13, 1833. 3. *Ambrose*, b. March 31, 1835. 4. *Eliza E.*

MESSER, THOMAS, br. of Asa; t. 1796, and again in 1799; b. Lunenburg, Mass.; m., 1802, Phebe Vinal, b. Scituate, Mass.; had — I. Vinal, b. Dec. 17, 1803; d. 1837. By a fall, his spine was injured, so that for twelve years he was without sensation in his lower limbs. — II. Minot, b. April 20, 1805; m., 1826, Lydia Bowman, of Washington; had 1. *John Bowman*, b. Oct. 8, 1826. 2. *Caroline Hills*, b. Feb. 23, 1809. 3. *Samuel Loring*, b. June 6, 1831. 4. *Thomas Guilford*, b. Aug. 25, 1833. 5. *Vinal*, b. Aug. 27, 1835. 6 and 7. Twins, b. July 18, 1837; viz. *Lydia Ann* and *Hannah Maria*. 8. *Eliza*, b. Jan. 6, 1840. 9. *Margaret Miller*, b. July, 1842. 10. *Emelina*, b. January,

1845. 11. *Aravilla Bryant*, b. Oct. 29, 1848. — III. Emeline, b. Oct. 4, 1807; m., Dec. 23, 1830, Aaron Bryant; ch. 1. *Elizabeth*. 2. *William Henry*. 3. *Mary Elizabeth*. 4. *Delphina*. 5. *Sarah*. 6. *Phebe Jane*. 7. *Martha*. 8. *Augustus;* d. 9. *Julia*. 10. *James*. 11. *A daughter*.

MITCHELL, ANDROS, or ANDREWS, cousin to Jeremiah; t. 1798; d. April 6, 1819; m. 1802, Rachel Pearson, of Cushing, who d. June 23, 1830, aged sixty; ch. — I. Elizabeth, b. June 16, 1804. — II. Richard P., b. June 27, 1806; w. Sally; had 1. *Andrews*, b. March 26, 1832. 2. *Levi*, b. Sept. 8, 1837. — III. Enos, b. April 23, 1809; m., 1838, Mary J. Butler.

MITCHELL, THOMAS, from North Yarmouth; t. 1796; w., probably, Dinah, who d. March or May 10, 1821, aged seventy-nine; ch. — I. Jeremiah, m. Mercy Fairbanks, sister of Mrs. West; had 1. *Lucy*, b. Aug. 4, 1793; m., 1812, Ichabod Irish. 2. *Thomas Andrews*, b. Aug. 19, 1795; m., March 25, 1819, Deborah Jameson, of Waldoborough. 3. *Mary*, b. Oct. 23, 1797; m. Rev. Solomon Bray. 4. *Ebenezer Allen*, b. Aug. 15, 1800; m. Keziah Furbush; and had T h o m a s A., b. Sept. 21, 1834. 5. *Hannah*, b. Sept. 10, 1803, and d. Oct. 13, 1829; m. Judson Caswell, Nov. 7, 1824; had (1). H a n n a h, b. Nov. 9, 1831; (2). J o h n C h a n d l e r, b. Feb. 1, 1834; (3). L e n d a l l, b. Jan. 23, 1836. 6. *Henry True*, b. Aug. 8, 1806; m., 1829, Dolly Raizor. 7. *Olive*, b. March 26, 1809; m. Jacob Pevee. 8. *Mercy Dyer*, b. Nov. 18, 1811; after her sister Hannah's decease, m., Jan. 13, 1831, Judson Caswell; and had (1). L o z e a h, b. Oct. 18, 1838; (2). M a r y O., Feb. 18, 1842; (3). C h r i s t i a n a A., b. Dec. 14, 1843; (4). C a r o l i n e, b. May 20, 1847. 9. *Jeremiah Ward*, b. Nov. 6, 1814; m. Emily Lehr. 10. *Asa Lyman*, b. April 15, 1818. 11. *Jeruel Butler*, b. Dec. 1, 1821. — II. Jabez Norton; t. 1798; m., March 29, 1800, Hepzibah Ripley; had 1. *Abraham*, b. March 6, 1801. 2. *Dinah*, b. March 8, 1803. 3. *Enos*, b. Sept. 21, 1805. 4. *Jabez*, b. Aug. 15, 1807. 5. *Silas*, b. March 7, 1810. — IV. Thomas; t. 1796; d. Oct. 14, 1843; m., Sept. 5, 1799, Polly, dr. of Samuel Daggett; and had 1. *Elizabeth*, b. June 30, 1800; m., Dec. 10, 1818, Samuel Stone. 2. *Jedidah Cutter*, b. Jan. 18, 1802; d. of consumption, April 8,

1828. 3. *Rebecca Athearn*, b. April 25, 1807; d. Jan. 26, 1836; m., 1835, Elias Breck, of Springfield, Mass. 4. *Brotherton Daggett*, b. June 7, 1810; d. July 10, 1811. 5. *Thomas Harrison*, b. Aug. 30, 1812; d. July 9, 1839. — V. A dr.; m. Edward Oakes. — VI. Mary, m., Dec. 25, 1800, Calvin Morse. — VII. Dinah, m., Oct. 10, 1801, John Murray; and had *Thomas*, b. July 29, 1802.

MOORE, AUGUSTUS, from Massachusetts, t. 1796.

MORSE, CALVIN, b. Nov. 22, 1773, according to Barry's Framingham; was fourth child and third son of Jonathan, of Framingham, who m. Mehetabel Nurse, and d. young. Jonathan's father Jonathan, who was son of Joseph, m., May 16, 1734, Mary Cloyce. The family early belonged to Watertown. CALVIN, t. 1799; m., 1800, Mary, dr. of Thomas Mitchell; and d. Aug. 6, 1846, in Washington. They had — I. Josiah, b. Oct. 2, 1801. — II. Dinah, b. June 1, 1803. — III. Jonathan, b. Sept. 21 or 24, 1805; m., Jan. 26, 1834, Catherine Sherman; and had 1. *John Q.*, b. Oct. 25, 1834. 2. *Achsah*, b. Oct. 24, 1835. 3. *Joseph*, b. Aug. 9, 1837. 4. *Charles*, b. March 20, 1839. 5. *Calvin*, b. March 25, 1842. 6. *Mary*, b. Nov. 21, 1845. 7. *Lydia A.*, b. April 29, 1848. — IV. Eliza, b. Nov. 13, 1807. — V. Joseph, b. March 25, 1810. — VI. Calvin, b. April 11, 1812. — VII. Mary Ann, b. Aug. 27, 1814; m. James Hodge, 1834; and had *Elizabeth*, b. April 8, 1835. VIII. Orson Adams, b. Aug. 8, 1817; r. Washington; m., 1846, Jane W. Mitchell, and had *Zoar A. C.*, b. Feb. 9, 1847. — IX. Thomas Andrews, twin with Orson Adams. — X. William H., b. June 22, 1821. — XI. Jabez M., b. Oct. 21, 1824; r. Washington.

MORSE, JONATHAN, b. March 24, 1776; d. Nov. 19, 1850; t. 1799; probably came to Union with his brother Calvin; m., May, 1808, Rebeckah, who was b. Oct. 18, 1782, and d. Aug. 11, 1831, dr. of Col. John Gleason. They had — I. Anna, b. Sept. 6, 1809; d. Oct. 14, 1843. — II. Lydia Gleason, b. Dec. 13, 1811; d. June 10, 1835. — III. Aaron Gleason, b. Dec. 13, 1814; d. Aug. 21, 1834. — IV. Micajah Gleason, b. Jan. 8, 1819; m., Dec. 16, 1841, Elizabeth U. Demuth; ch. 1. *Susan A.*, b. May 2, 1843; d. March 28, 1847. 2. *Helen L.*, b. Feb. 14, 1845. 3. *Ann E.*, b. March 29, 1850.

FAMILY REGISTER.

MORSE, JOSEPH, br. of Calvin and Jonathan; t. 1799; b. March 27, 1771; m., first, Oct. 11, 1795, Lydia, dr. of Col. John Gleason, who d.; and, second, widow Prior, of Waldoborough; c.

MORSE,[1] LEVI, b. at Sherburne, Mass., Jan. 5, 1762; d.

[1] Samuel Morse, probably from Sherborn, England, or the vicinity, husbandman, at the age of fifty, and his wife, Elizabeth, at the age of forty-eight, and his son, Joseph, at the age of twenty, in consequence of the persecutions by Bishop Laud, in April, 1635, embarked for New England in the Increase, Robert Lea, master, and came to Watertown, Mass. In 1636, land was assigned to him in Dedham. He was collector, treasurer, and selectman. A few years afterward, he settled at Medfield, and, it is supposed, built the house which was first set on fire by the Indians, at the destruction of the town and the killing of eighteen inhabitants, Feb. 21, 1675. He died at Medfield, April 5, 1654, and his w. June 20, 1654.

His second son, Daniel, b. 1613, and whose w., Lydia, d. Jan. 29, 1690, aged seventy, moved from Dedham to Medfield in 1651. About 1656, he bought eight hundred acres of land, which, May 22, 1650, had been granted by the General Court to Simon Bradstreet, afterwards Governor, and since called "The Farm," situated in the east part of what is now Sherburne. He moved to Sherburne probably in 1657, where he appears to have been the leading man of the place, and d. June 5, 1688.

Daniel Morse's second child, Daniel; r. Sherburne; b. 31 : 11 : 1640; d. Sept. 29, 1702; m. Elizabeth Barbour, of Medfield, who d. 1714. This Daniel Morse's son, Daniel, b. July 10, 1672; d. April 4, 1719; m., 1696, Susanna Holbrook, who d. 1717. He inherited the place of his uncle, Deacon Obadiah, whose only son d. in infancy.

OBADIAH MORSE, fourth child of this Daniel, b. Aug. 15, 1704; d. 1753; m. Mercy Walker, of Sherburne. This Obadiah's third child, Obadiah, b. March 20, 1732-3; d. in Sherburne, Jan. 7, 1800, in consequence of a fall from a scaffold; m., first, July 10, 1755, Grace Fairbanks, who was b. June 16, 1734, and who d. May 30, 1772; and, second, in 1776, Abigail, dr. of Caleb and Abigail Death, of Framingham. His children were 1. *Mercy*, b. May 7, 1756; d. July 31, 1845; m., 1777, Asaph Merrifield; r. Holden. 2. *Hannah*, b. Feb. 7, 1758; m. Josiah Ward, of Southborough; r. and d. at Bradford, N. H. 3. *Adam*, b. Dec. 9, 1759; d. about 1779, from an injury of the knee received in the army. 4. *Levi*, b. Jan. 5, 1762, settled in Union, Me. 5. *Grace*, b. March 16, 1764; m., first, Reuben Esty; and, second, Samuel Whitney; now r. Charlestown, Mass. 6. *Obadiah*, b. Dec. 11, 1765; settled in Union. 7. *Mary*, b. Jan. 18, 1768; m. Phares Sawin, of South Natick. 8. *Samuel*, b. Jan. 3, 1770; d. January, 1826; merchant and hotel-keeper in Boston; m., first, March 25, 1794, Sally Dix, at Newton; and, second, May 11, 1800, Elizabeth Barnard, at Cambridge. 9. *Persis*, b. April 20, 1772; d. Feb. 5, 1847; m. Dr. J. Sibley, of Union, Maine. 10. *Daniel*, b. Nov. 26, 1776; went West about 1792, in the service of Pomeroy; never heard from. 11. *Judith*, b. July 3, 1778; d. 1779. 12. *Ezra*, b. Sept. 1, 1779; d. June 24,

Feb. 3, 1844; was s. of Obadiah; was in the revolutionary army, and in the expedition for the suppression of the Shays Rebellion, in 1786, — a rebellion for which he said he could not blame the Shays party so much as many did; "the country being poor, no money, taxes high, people could not pay them." He was at Annapolis, Nova Scotia, in 1785; and perhaps from one to two years there in all. In 1789, he taught school in Meduncook, now Friendship, and boarded in the family of the father of Polly Gay Bradford, who was b. at Annapolis, now Onslow, Nova Scotia, Nov. 8, 1772; and whom he m., March 8, 1792. "May 22, set out from Meduncook to move my wife to Union; arrived there May 23." She d. Oct. 25, 1845.[1] Descendants, — I. Persis, b.

1842; m., first, Betsey Stratton; and, second, widow Morse, of Boylston, or West Boylston. 13. *Moses*, b. June 8, 1784; m., 1814, Hannah Prentice, of Sherburne, b. Sept. 15, 1789; r. Union; ch. (1). Feroline Pierce, b. Sept. 8, 1815; r. Boston; (2). Edward Phillips, b. May 1, 1817; m. his half-cousin, Martha Alice, dr. of Obadiah Morse; (3). Dexter Perry, b. Jan. 2, 1824; (4). Hannah Prentice, b. Jan. 1, 1828. 14. *Asa*, b. June 14, 1787; m. Susanna McFarland; had a leg amputated in consequence of a tree falling on it, while on a visit at Union, Maine; r. South Bridgewater. 15. *Pede*, b. Sept. 15, 1790; r. Sherburne; u. Of these, Levi, Obadiah, Persis, and Moses settled in Union. The information in the first part of this note is abridged from a work of great labor and research, entitled Memorial of the Morses, by Rev. Abner Morse.

[1] The name Bradford is derived from the Saxon, Bradenford, or Broad-ford. According to Dugdale, "Bradford, situated near the Avon, ... owes its name to the broad ford of the river." Mrs. Morse's father, Carpenter Bradford, b. at Kingston, Mass., Feb. 7, 1739, was "put out" to a shoemaker, ran away, enlisted in the Old French War, was captured when about sixteen years old, detained as a prisoner in Canada one year, during which he was waiter to a Catholic priest; returned, and m. in Stoughton, Mass., June 18, 1761, Mary, b. Sept. 17, 1736, dr. of David and Hannah Gay. When the Neutral French, or Acadians, were barbarously exiled from Nova Scotia, and their lands, with the improvements, were offered gratuitously to settlers, he went to Annapolis, N. S., where he was at the commencement of the American revolution. Then the British authorities summoned the inhabitants to take the oath of allegiance. He held up his hand; and, being a staunch whig, when the following words, or words to the same effect, were uttered, "You solemnly swear to be true to King George," he substituted the words George Washington for King George, and thus really swore allegiance to the rebels. "Tut, tut," said the officer, "that will not do." Conscious that it was time for him to flee, he, in company with another whig, left the place the same night, and proceeded by land toward Halifax. Just before arriving there, they came to a small river, across which a boatman, either timid or loyal, refused to take them. They threatened

Nov. 11, 1792; d. Oct. 4, 1839, of paralysis; u. — II. Walter, Captain, b. July 16, 1794; m. Miss Betsey Poor, of
to shoot him; but the difficulty was compromised by their being allowed to row themselves over, and leave the boat on the other side. Mr. B. proceeded by land to Castine, where he enlisted, and remained some time. After other services in the revolutionary war, he sent for his family, which was landed at Camden. He ended his days in Meduncook. For his services, more than nine hundred acres of Ohio land, it is said, were granted to him, from which he probably did not realize any thing.

The New England Historical and Genealogical Register, vol. iv., contains two articles evincing great research, from which are gathered the following items respecting his ancestors. His father, Elisha, who m., first, Hannah Cole, and, second, Sept. 7, 1718, Bathsheba Le Brocke, had many children. Carpenter was the eleventh child by this second wife. His parents moved to Meduncook (now Friendship), where, May 27, 1756, they were both killed by Indians, who carried some of the children to Canada, whence they did not return to Meduncook till after the capture of Quebec by Wolfe. "Deb. Sampson," who, disguised as a man, under the assumed name of Robert Shurtleff, served three years in the revolutionary army, and afterward married Benjamin Gannett, of Sharon, and drew a pension, was cousin of Mrs. Morse.

Carpenter's father, Elisha, was the oldest child of Joseph Bradford, b. 1630, who m., May 25, 1664, Jael, dr. of Rev. Peter Hobart, the first minister of Hingham; and d. July 10, 1715. She d. 1730, æt. eighty-eight. He resided in Kingston (then Plymouth), Mass., on Jones's River, half a mile from its mouth at Flat House Dock; so called, perhaps, because he lived in a house with a flat roof.

Elisha's father, Joseph, was son of the Governor of Plymouth Colony, Wm. Bradford, who was b. at Austerfield, in Yorkshire, England, in March, 1588-9, and was left fatherless when about two years old. He went to Holland, probably in 1608, whence he came to Plymouth in the May Flower, while yet a young man, and d. May 9, 1657. He was chosen Governor in 1621, and re-elected every year till 1657, except the five years 1633, 1634, 1636, 1638, 1644. The first of the accompanying *facsimiles* represents his handwriting in 1631-2; the other, in 1645. Governor Bradford's first w. was Dorothy May. She was drowned, Dec. 7, 1620, in Cape Cod Harbor. She was the first female who d. at the Plymouth Colony, and the first whose death is recorded in New England. Aug. 14, 1623, he m. the widow Alice Southworth, whose maiden name is supposed to have been Carpenter. She d. March 26, 1670, aged about eighty. Governor Bradford had by his second w. three children, William, Mercy, and Joseph.

Gov. Bradford's father, William, m. Alice Hanson, and was buried July 15, 1591, a short time before his father William, who lived at

Belmont; and d., April 20, 1825, of consumption; ch. 1.
John Poor, a sea-captain; m. Abby Y. Cotterell, of Belfast.
2. *Mary;* m. a Cotterell, of Belfast. — III. Hannah; b.
April 24, 1796; m., 1819, Capt. Lewis, b. at East Kingston, N.H., June 21, 1794 or 1795, s. of Capt. Nathaniel
and Ruth (Morrill) Bachelor; had 1. *Augusta Diana*, b.
June 29, 1820, who m., Sept. 3, 1838, Noah Shattuck, b.
April 3, 1813, s. of Capt. Noah and Sally or Sarah (Shattuck) Rice; and had (1). C a r o l i n e L o u i s a, b. Aug. 2,
1840; (2). H e n r y C l a y, b. Nov. 22, 1843. 2. *Caroline
Louisa*, b. April 23, 1822; d. Feb. 14, 1829. 3. *Helen
Lauretta*, b. May 16, 1826; who m. Frederic, s. of Edmund
and Deborah (Keene) Daggett. 4. *Nathaniel Quincy*, b.
Aug. 11, 1828; r. Boston. 5. *Edwin Aurelius*, b. March
11, 1834. 6. *William George*, b. Oct. 11, 1838; d. Oct.
19, 1840. — IV. Sally, b. May 13, 1798; m., March 17,
1817, Jacob Hahn,[1] of Waldoborough, subsequently of Monmouth, and now of East Boston, Mass., s. of Frederick and
Hannah (Burns) Hahn; had 1. *Levi Morse*, b., Waldoborough, Feb. 3, 1819; d. March 6, 1845; m. Betsey
Tinkham, of Winthrop, who m., second, a widower, Oakes
Howard, of Winthrop; ch. (1). S a r a h E l i z a b e t h, b.
June 2, 1843. 2. *Silas Briggs*, b. Dec. 7, 1820; graduated
at Bowdoin College; lawyer; r. East Boston; u. 3. *Dexter
Ward*, b. Dec. 30, 1823; d. April 26, 1851; u. 4. *Rodolphus
Franklin*, b. April 1, 1826; r. California. 5. *Nelson
Washington*, b. July 4, 1828. 6. *Sidney Bradford*, b. Sept.
8, 1831; r. California. 7. *Edwin Lafayette*, b. Sept. 9,
1833, in Monmouth; d. Oct. 5, 1837. 8. *Ammi Ruhamah*,
b. Oct. 19, 1841. — V. Barnard, b. June 11, 1802; farmer
in Belmont; m., 1824, Mary Ann Fales, of Hope; had 1.
Lewis B., b. June 18, 1825, at Belmont; m.; r. Vinalhaven.
2. *Leander*, b. Aug. 20, 1826. 3. *William Bradford*, b.
Dec. 8, 1828; m. widow Abigail Hart, dr. of Edmund Luce;

Austerfield in or about 1575, and was buried Jan. 10, 1595. Further
than this the family has not been traced. But, from what has been
said, it appears that Mrs. Morse's ancestors were first, Carpenter, who
m. Mary Gay; second, Elisha and his w. Bathsheba Le Brocke; third,
Joseph and his w., Jael Hobart; fourth, Governor William and widow
Alice Southworth; fifth, William and his w., Alice Hanson, of
Austerfield; sixth, William, of Austerfield.

[1] Jacob Hahn's father, Frederick Hahn, came from Germany when
about eleven years old. At the same time came Frederick's brother
George, who settled in North Carolina.

r. Camden. 4. *Mary Ann*, b. Feb. 14, 1832. 5. *Samuel*, b. Nov. 11, 1833. 6. *George W.*, b. Jan. 14, 1839, at Lincolnville. 7. *Abby J.*, b. Nov. 9, 1840, at Belmont; d. Aug. 3, 1843. 8. *Lucius C.*, b. May 14, 1845. — VI. Mary, b. June 11, 1802; Feb. 4, 1824, became second w. of Capt. Daniel Lunt, of Eastport; subsequently moved to Lincolnville, where she d. of consumption, Dec. 19, 1833. She had 1. *Edwin;* r. Galena, Ill.; now in California. 2. *Daniel;* shot in the Mexican War. 3. *Martha*, m., 1849, James Henry Upham, of Readfield; r. California. — VII. Levi, b. Oct. 18, 1804; r. homestead; m., Feb. 13, 1834, Eliza Daniels; and had 1. *Caroline Elizabeth*, b. Dec. 14, 1835. 2. *Edwin Lafayette*, b. Aug. 5, 1837. 3. *Levi Roscoe*, b. Aug. 12, 1842. 4. *John Adelbert*, b. Jan. 21, 1845. 5. *Nathan Daniels*, b. March 4, 1847; d. Sept. 4, 1848. — VIII. Nancy, b. Jan. 6, 1807; m., Dec. 29, 1841, Aaron Starrett, of Warren; and d. of consumption, July 11, 1844; leaving 1. *Ellen*. — IX. Samuel, b. March 18, 1809; d. of consumption. March 7, 1831; u. — X. Chloe Bradford, b. April 6, 1811; became the third w. of Capt. Daniel Lunt; and d. of consumption in Lincolnville, Jan. 5, 1841; leaving 1. *Mary Grace*. 2. *Chloe*. — XI. George Washington, b. Aug. 24, 1813; settled on part of the homestead; m., 1840, Mary Harding, b. July 19, 1815, dr. of Capt. Noah and Sally (Shattuck) Rice: ch. 1. *Edward Franklin*, b. Feb. 28, 1841; d. Feb. 19, 1848. 2. *Leslie Melvyn*, b. July 16, 1842. 3. *Orville Dana*, b. April 6, 1844; d. March 23, 1845. 4. *Sarah Alfaretta*, b. Oct. 28, 1846. 5. *Harriet Estella*, b. June 7, 1848. — XII. William Bradford, twin brother of George Washington, b. Aug. 24, 1813; limeburner; r. Rockland; m., Oct. 12, 1837, widow Emma Gould (Parsons) Ross, of Stillwater; ch. 1. *Penelope Colburn*, b. Aug. 29, 1838. 2. *William Henry*, b. Jan. 1, 1841. 3. *Charles Bradford*, b. Dec. 24, 1847. — XIII. Harriet Newell, b. May 14, 1816; m., Oct. 11, 1843, Benjamin, br. of Aaron Starrett, of Warren; c.

MORSE, OBADIAH, son of Obadiah, b. at Sherburne, Mass., Dec. 11, 1776; came to Union as early as 1798, having previously lived one or two years in Malden, Massachusetts, and in Chester, N. H. He settled west by south of Round Pond, about half-way to the summit of the hill, on the north side of the road; m., first, Sally Palmer, of Newton, Mass., who d. of consumption, Sept. 15, 1821, aged forty-two; and, second, July 3, 1823, Phebe, dr. of David and Martha Carriel; and d. Aug. 8, 1837. His widow m. James Adams Ulmer, of Thomaston. He had — I. Alice, b. Jan. 12, 1804; d. March 18, 1804. — II. Eliza, b. Feb. 22, 1805; m., July 3, 1831, Isley Martin, who was b. in Union, Feb. 23, 1806, son of Adam (who was b. in Waldoborough), and Mary (Lamson) Martin, who was b. in Thomaston; ch. 1. *William*, b. Feb. 17, 1833; d. Sept. 24, 1841. 2. *George Young*, b. Nov. 10, 1836. 3. *Sarah*, b. May 29, 1839. — III. Palmer, b. May 2, 1807; d. Sept. 24, 1808. — IV. Asa, b. Jan. 27, 1809; m., in Union, Eliza Jane, b. at Cushing, Sept. 30, 1810, dr. of Benjamin and Nancy (McLellan) Litchfield; settled on the Bela Robbins Farm, but now lives in Rockland; has 1. *Edwin Palmer*, b. July 20, 1836. 2. *Fostena*, b. March 7, 1838. 3. *Argyl Dudley*, b. March 23, 1841. 4. *William Spofford*, b. Nov. 29, 1843; all b. at Union. 5. *A son*, b. June, 1851, in Rockland. — V. Margaret Palmer, b. March 10, 1811; m., Oct. 1839, James Libbey, of Warren; c. — VI. Obadiah, b. May 18, 1813; m., 1836, Chloe, dr. of Charles and Rebecca (Cobb) Copeland, of Warren, and settled in Thomaston, where he d. July 14, 1847, in consequence of the caving in of clay at a brickyard, July 11. Children, 1. *Lucius Kendall*, b. May 19, 1837. 2. *Newell Austin*. 3. *Charles Copeland*. 4. *Benjamin Wentworth*. 5. *Obadiah*, b. April, 1847. — VII. Jedidiah, b. Sept. 19, 1815; m., 1840, Rebecca Barnes, dr. of Moses and Mary (Jones) Simmons; and has *Alenzer Forrest*, b. Nov. 13, 1846. — VIII. Sarah Ann, b. June 27, 1818; m., Dec. 25, 1836, David Seavey, the 2d, from Cushing; c. — IX. Martha Alice, b. May 31, 1824; m., June 8, 1846, her half-cousin, Edward Phillips, s. of Moses and Hannah (Prentice) Morse, of Union; and has 1. *Quincy Adams*, b. May 15, 1848. — X. Matilda, b. Oct. 19, 1826; d. May 9, 1844. — XI. Mary Frances, b. June 9, 1829; m., 1851, a son of James A. Ulmer. — XII. Melina Amelia, b. Oct. 10, 1835.

MORTON, ZENAS, t. 1797; bought Guild's farm; returned to Friendship.

NEWHALL, JONATHAN, from Lynn, Mass.; t. 1791; m. Hannah Peabody, sister of Mrs. Ware, from Warren; moved to Washington, and d. there; ch. — I. Amos, b. Oct. 11, 1791; m. Elizabeth Conklin, b. at Camden; both

Friends. — II. Lois, b. Feb. 2, 1793; m., May, 1814, Rev. Roland Collier, of Washington, but b. Northport. — III. Lucy, b. July 2, 1795; d.; u. — IV. Stephen, b. Feb. 6, 1797; m., 1822, Louisa Daggett. — V. Jonathan, b. Aug. 12, 1799; m. a Boyd, of Washington, who d.; and he m. again. — VI. William, b. June 6, 1802; m. Abigail, dr. of Deacon McDowell, of Washington. — VII. James, b. March 2, 1804; m. a Wetherbee, of Northport; r. Washington. — VIII. Joseph, b. Dec. 9, 1807; m., first, a Newbit; and, second, Priscilla Jameson. Jonathan Newell made the first horse-wagon ever built in Union. William Newhall, a younger brother, was taxed in 1791.

NYE, THOMAS, t. 1798; a carpenter, who had worked on the State House, in Boston, Mass., when it was building; b. at Barnstable, Mass., Jan. 20, 1773; m., in Warren, 1796, Anna Dunbar, b. in Bridgewater, Mass., Jan. 27, 1776. He settled on the west side of George's River, at the corner of the road about half-way between Hills' Mills and Sunnybec Pond, and d. of consumption, Oct. 22, 1827. Descendants, — I. Stillman, b. Jan. 18, 1797; d. of consumption, April 4, 1822; m., 1820, Mary Sargus,[1] b. Feb.

---

[1] The name of Thomas Harris (br. of William Harris, an associate with Roger Williams, who was one of the founders of Providence, R. I.), first appears on the records of Providence, in August, 1637. His son, Thomas, treasurer of Providence, surveyor, d. Feb. 22, 1710-11; m. Elethan Tew; had ten ch., the third of whom, Nicholas, b. April 1, 1671, r. Cranston, had six children. Nicholas, the second of these ch., b. 1691, at Johnston, R.I., then called Providence Woods, moved to Wrentham, Mass., and m. Hannah, dr. of an English gentleman named Blake, and d. April, 1775; had a large family, all sons, but the one dr., who m. an Ellis, of Nantucket. The sons suffered greatly in the war before the treaty of 1763. Two went to the siege of Havana, and, it is said, never returned. Sylvanus was killed at Falmouth, Me., by the Indians. Obadiah, deacon, supposed to be the youngest of Nicholas's children, b. Wrentham, July 7, 1736, in 1785 moved to Hallowell, Me., where he d. July, 1800; m., June 27, 1759, Lois Ellis, who was b. June 1, 1736, at Wrentham. He was at the battle near Ticonderoga, July 6, 1758, when Lord Howe was killed; and at Fort William Henry, soon after the massacre there. Charles, deacon, soldier in the revolutionary war, oldest child of Obadiah and Lois Harris, was b. June 3, 1760, at Wrentham, and d. at Winthrop, Me., July 1, 1832. May 12, 1784, he m. Meletiah, b. Wrentham, Dec. 30, 1763; d. in Mercer, Sept. 3, 1834; dr. of Timothy and Mary Hawes. Obadiah Harris, fifth s. of Charles and Meletiah, b. at Winthrop, Nov. 18, 1795; m., June 22, 1826, the widow of Stillman Nye; and had 1. Herman, b. May 9, 1828. 2.

4, 1796, at Waldoborough, dr. of emigrants from Germany; and had 1. *Anson Blake*, carpenter, b. Oct. 9, 1820; r. Boston. 2. *Stillman*, b. April 30, 1822; m., 1848, Emily, who d. June 17, 1850, dr. of Caleb Maddocks; and, second, 1850, Caroline, dr. of Nahum Thurston. — II. Cyrus Crocker, b. Dec. 23, 1799; d. of consumption, May 27, 1828; m., April 8, 1824, Patty, or Martha, dr. of David Carriel. She m., second, Charles Fogler; ch. 1. *Edward Thomas*, a seaman, b. Aug. 25; m., 1850, Belinda, dr. of Jesse and Miranda (Fogler) Dunbar, of Warren. — III. Darius, b. April 18, 1802, for many years clock-peddler, now storekeeper at Milo; m., first, Oct. 4, 1827, Eleanor Ayres, of Newton, Mass.; and, second, Eliza, dr. of John Burton, of Warren; had 1. *Helen Ann*, who d. 2. *Darius;* also others, including at least two by last wife. — IV. Caroline, b. Sept. 22, 1804; d. of consumption, March 6, 1834; m. 1828, Israel Barker (who afterward m. Mary Severance); and had 1. *James*, cabinet-maker, b. Oct. 10, 1828. 2. *Eliza Ann*, b. Aug. 1, 1831; r. Warren. — V. Charles Austin, b. May 26, 1807; d. of consumption, April 27, 1832; m., March, 1831, Caroline, dr. of David Gillmor, of Newburgh; had 1. *David*, b. January, 1832. — VI. Eliza, b. June 22, 1809; d. of consumption, June 7, 1830; u. — VII. Harriet, b. Oct. 11, 1811; m., April 17, 1831, Joseph Barker; r. Searsmont; ch. 1. *Harriet Lavinia*, b. Sept. 29, 1831; m. a Swan; r. Saccarappa. 2. *Caroline.* 3. *Elizabeth;* also several others. — VIII. Thomas, b. Jan. 16, 1814; m., 1840, Jane, dr. of Daniel Stetson, of Warren; ch. 1. *Emeline*, b. Aug. 1841. 2. *Laura Ann*, b. Aug. 17, 1844; d. July 11, 1846. — IX. Maria, b. Aug. 12, 1816; m., Dec. 7, 1840, at Marlborough, Mass., Thomas, a widower, b. Feb. 28, 1808, at Kingston, Devonshire, Eng., son of Thomas and Grace Harris, of Boston; r. Charlestown, Mass.; ch. 1. *Catharine Loring*, b. Sept. 7, 1841, at Marlborough, Mass. 2. *Caroline Maria*, b. Feb. 20, 1849, in Boston. 3. *Charles Thomas*, b. Jan. 20, 1851.

OAKES, EDWARD, shoemaker; t. 1797; from North Yarmouth; came with the Mitchells; m. a Mitchell, and moved away.

William Shepherd, b. Sept. 19, 1829. 3. Mary Frances, b. May 2, 1831. 4. Charles Henry, b. October 26, 1832. 5. Edwin, b. January 9, 1835. 6. Isaac Sargus, b. June 15, 1836.

OLNEY,[1] EDWARD, from Providence, R. I.; a mulatto; brought into town by David Gillmor, jun.; m. Susanna, a Penobscot squaw, who lived in the family of David Robbins; moved to Newburgh, having had — I. Edward, b. July 26, 1799. — II. Sally, b. May 22, 1802. — III. Ebenezer, b. Jan. 22, 1804.

PARTRIDGE, ELISHA, s. of Edward and Sarah; b. at Medfield, according to Medfield records, July 8; but, according to family records, Aug. 8, 1734. He was moderator, June 12, 1786, of the only plantation-meeting on record before the one for town-organization. In 1786 he r. on Colonel Mason Wheaton's Place, now owned by Nahum Thurston. He left the house of Philip Robbins on horseback, Jan. 1, 1787, for his residence; but, as the horse returned without him, search was immediately made, and he was found, before noon, dead on the Western Meadows, so called, near Round Pond. This was the route commonly taken by him, as there were no roads. By some it was supposed he fell from his horse in an apoplectic fit; by others, that there were indications of his having dismounted and walked by his horse's side a few rods before he died. He m., first, March 16, 1756, Dorcas Pond, who was b. June 22, 1740, and d. Feb. 2, 1778; and, second, Jan. 28, 1779, Sarah Fales (of Franklin, Mass.?), who was b. March 18, 1755, and d. Nov. 15, 1834. Issue, the first seven b. in Franklin; the others in Union. — I. Simeon, b. May 19, 1758. — II. Zibiah, b. June 18, 1760; m. David Fales, Esq., of Thomaston. — III. Judith, b. March 17, 1762. — IV. Miriam, b. Aug. 25, 1764. — V. Dorcas, b. March 30, 1767; m. Elijah Holmes. — VI. Elisha, b. Jan. 1, 1770. — VII. Alibeus, b. Nov. 14, 1779; m., Nov. 13, 1808, Prudence Brown; and d. Dec. 12, 1840. — VIII. James, b. Sept. 10, 1782; r. Rockland; m., first, Oct. 11, 1804, Betsey Brown, of Thomaston, who was b. May 19, 1784, and d. Dec. 9, 1837; and, second, Aug. 8, 1838, Sarah Vose. — IX. Sarah, b. July 4, 1786.

PEABODY, SAMUEL, t. 1791; from Warren; had a family, lived west of Sunnybec Pond, where afterwards lived Ichabod Maddocks; then near to the school-house in the

---

[1] The almost entire absence of colored people since the town was settled is remarkable. — See PRINCE, MELVIN.

Daggett neighborhood; moved to Penobscot County; probably m. Betsey Martin, of Bristol, in 1794.

PEABODY, WILLIAM, t. 1793; m. Lynda, dr. of David and Abigail (Holmes) Woodcock, about 1794; moved to Penobscot County, and d. there; had — I. Jason, b. Dec. 17, 1795. — II. Esther C., b. Aug. 29, 1797. — III. Almond, b. Dec. 1, 1800. — IV. Hannah, b. Jan. 22, 1804.

PRATT, OLIVER, t. 1799, lived on the place now owned by John Burns, and was one of the early emigrants to Ohio.

PRINCE, MELVIN and SYLVANUS, mulattoes, or rather half Indian, quarter French and quarter English, sons of Sylvester Prince, from the South Shore, Mass.; worked considerably for Philip Robbins. Melvin Prince was taken, when a small boy, by Amariah Mero, and brought up. He was here perhaps twelve years, and his father three or four. These, with Olney and his wife, are the only colored people who ever resided in town.

QUIGGLE, SAMUEL, t. 1797; b. Dedham, Mass., Nov. 19, 1771; came from Franklin about the same time with N. Daniels; m., first, at David Robbins's, Nov. 30, 1797, Dimmis Hammond, b. Oct. 9, 1775, at Needham, who had taught school in the Round Pond district. She d. March 11, 1838; and he m., second, at Mansfield, Mass., May 6, 1840, Eunice (widow of Amasa Pratt), b. Mansfield, July 29, 1778, dr. of Elijah and Elizabeth Williams. He had — I. Dimmis, b. Feb. 14, 1800; d. at Waldo, February, 1842; m., Oct. 26, 1817, Daniel Linniken; ch. 1. *Thomas*, b. in Union, Nov. 5, 1818; m. 2. *John*, b. Dec. 15, 1820; m. 3. *Hannah*, b. Jan. 14, 1823; m., March 28, 1848, Nathaniel Bartlett; r. Lynn, Mass.; and has (1). E u g e n e H e n r y. 4. *Mary*, b. May 27, 1825; m. a Doty; r. Warren. 5. *Jane*, b. Waldo, July 7, 1827. 6. *Harriet*, b. May 17, 1830. 7. *Maria*, b. 1832. 8. *William*, b. January, 1835. 9. *Daniel*, b. 1837. 10. *Rufus*, b. 1840. — II. Sally, b. June 7, 1801; m., first, 1818, Thomas Staples Perkins, of Hope, who settled in Belmont, and d. Sept. 9, 1824; and, second, John Shepherd Bean, and lives in Searsmont. She had ch. (three of them by her first husband); 1. *Tamson*, b. in Union, April 21, 1819; m., May 8, 1840, Kiah Bailey Somes; r. North Chelsea, Mass.; and had (1). A d e l a i d e E l i z a b e t h, b. Jan. 8, 1842; (2). G e o r g e F r e d e r i c,

b. Aug. 31, 1845; d. Oct. 7, 1845; (3). Abby Arabella, b. Aug. 31, 1847; (4). Thomas Perkins, b. Sept. 18, 1849.   2. *Abijah*, d. young.   3. *Betsey*, or *Elizabeth*, b. in Union, Sept. 8, 1822; m., April 29, 1847, John Smith Nichols, of Malden, Mass.; and has (1). Nathan, b. Jan. 18, 1848; (2). John Smith, b. Jan. 5, 1850. 4. *Joseph Shepherd*, b. Nov. 3, 1827, at Belmont; d. at sea, April 1, 1850.   5. *John Lewis*, b. Jan. 3, 1830, in Union.   6. *Olive Holmes*, b. Nov. 15, 1831; m., April 29, 1851, Joseph M. Somes, of North Chelsea, Mass.   7. *Harriet Louisa*, b. Sept. 26, 1833.   8. *Sarah Dimmis*, b. April, 1835.   9. *Helen Josephine*, b. Feb. 15, 1837.   10. *Elisha Lorenzo*, b. Feb. 1, 1842.   11. *Samuel Smith*, b. 1844. — III. Hannah H., b. Sept. 25, 1803; d. May 23, 1824. — IV. Phanne, Fanny, or Frances, b. June 24, 1805; m., June 29, 1826, William Bennet, of Searsmont; ch. 1. *Martin Paul;* and others. — V. Hammond, b. Aug. 5, 1807; killed himself in jail in Belfast. — VI. Harriet, b. Nov. 21, 1809; m., Sept. 26, 1837, Daniel Wood, b. at Prospect, Me., s. of Daniel Tibbetts; and he d. March 23, 1844, at Edgefield Court-house District, S.C.   She r. Boston; ch. b. at Edgefield, 1. *A son*, b. Feb. 17, 1839; d. June 4, 1839.   2. *Otis Nelson*, b. June 23, 1841.   3. *Abby Louisa*, b. July 14, 1844, at Ashland, Mass. — VII. Samuel, b. Dec. 15, 1811; m., 1838, Clementine Blood, of Warren; ch. 1. *Llewellyn Augustus*, b. March 11, 1839; drowned June 10, 1841.   2. *Guilford Williams*, b. Jan. 10, 1841.   3. *Sarah Ann*, b. Jan. 8, 1843.   4. *Margaret Adelia*, b. July 23, 1845.   4. *A son.* — VIII. Nathaniel Emmons, born Feb. 20, 1816; d. July 24, 1838. — IX. Mary Louisa, b. Sept. 23, 1818; m. William Bacon; r. Ashland, Mass.; ch. 1. *Charles William.*   2. *Louisa*, d. young.   3. *Mary Dimmis*, b. October, 1845.   4. *Andrew Jackson.*   5. *A child*, b. February, 1851.

ROBBINS, BELA, b. May 2, 1761; d. April 19, 1831. He was son of Ebenezer;[1] came with his father from the

---

[1] All the persons named Robbins, who live in Union and vicinity, are said to be descended from WILLIAM and PRISCILLA ROBBINS. If so, the former, probably, is the person of the same name who d. at Walpole, Aug. 18, 1725; and the latter the one who d. March 5, 1744–5. Their son Ebenezer, b. May 19, 1691; d. July 3 [family-record] or 6 [Walpole record], 1762; all his ch. probably b. in Walpole, Mass.; the first four by his first wife, Mary; the others by his second

Fox Islands, and soon after "went out in the war," where, it is said, he served three years. He m. Margaret Meservey, 1785. "He would take a log and make one of the best and handsomest of canoes, and canoes were of great consequence at the time. He had not a chair or bedstead in the house for many years after marriage. The furniture consisted of benches for seats, and shingle blocks with boards on them for benches." The ch. were — I. Lewis, b. Dec. 22, 1786; m., 1811, Nancy Fales, of Thomaston. — II. Sabra, b. May 4, 1788; m., May 16, 1805, Leonard Bump; and had 1. *Leonard*, b. Aug. 13, 1806; d. July 30, 1829. 2. *Lewis*, b. Oct. 16, 1807. 3. *Josephus*, b. June 3, 1810. 4. *Maria*, b. Feb. 17, 1813. 5. *Almond*, b. Sept. 18, 1816; d. Oct. 8, 1831. 6. *Matilda*, b. Sept. 18, 1819. 7. *Lovey*, b. March 17, 1821. 8. *Sabra*, b. Feb. 14, 1823. 9. *Darius W.*, b. April 10, 1829. — III. Becca, b. March 15, 1790. — IV. Harvey, b. Sept. 17, 1794; m. Susan Brazier, Feb. 2, 1812; r. Appleton. — V. Chloe, b. May 25, 1795; m. Benjamin Simmons, June 23, 1811; r. Hope. VI. Ebenezer, b. April 29, 1797; m. Polly Weaver in 1816; r. Winsor; had 1. *Polly*, b. Feb. 27, 1817. 2. *Lucinda*, b. Jan. 28, 1819. 3. *Philinda*, b. Feb. 25, 1821. 4. *Juliann*, b. March 6, 1823. 5. *Spencer*, b. Aug. 15, 1825. 6. *Lavina*, b. Dec. 29, 1827. — VII. Cyrus, b. May 12, 1799; m., 1819, Olivia Ransom; ch. 1. *Wilbert*, b. May 20, 1820. 2. *Cyrus*, b. Aug. 29, 1822; m. Margaret Burns, and had (1). Wilmot C.; d. Dec. 29, 1849; (2). Eldred, b. Jan. 3, 1850. 3. *Alvin N.*, b. March 20, 1824; m. 4. *Eber A.*, b. Sept. 29, 1826. 5. *Diantha Atelia*, b. Oct. 3, 1829. 6. *Olivia Verdilla*, b. June 1, 1830. 7. *Lorrilia Arvilia*, b. Sept. 14, 1831. 8. *Almatia*

wife, Experience Holmes, who was b. June 7, 1706; viz. 1. *Mary*, b. Nov. 12, 1720; d. July 18, 1746. 2. *Sarah*, b. Oct. 23, 1722. 3. *Ebenezer*, b. Sept. 11, 1724; settled in Union; d. March 1, 1798. He lived in Attleborough a while, came to Fox Islands before the Revolution broke out, and came off, as many others did at the time, to get away from the British. [See page 47.] 4. *Oliver*, b. Oct. 1, 1727; settled in Thomaston; d. March 27, 1792. 5. *Philip*, b. Aug. 20, 1730; settled in Union. 6. *Margaret*, b. May 29, 1732. 7. *Benoni*, b. June 21 [family-record], or 22 [Walpole record], 1733. 8. *Experience*, b. June 2, 1735. 9. *Josiah*, b. July 23, 1737; settled in Union. 10. *Margaret*, b. Jan. 16, 1739-40. 11. *Tabitha*, b. April 9, 1742; d. Sept. 25, 1775. 12. *Isaac*, b. July 3, 1744; d. Nov. 12, 1762. 13. *Nathaniel*, b. Feb. 6, 1746-7; d. July 8, 1747. 14. *Nathaniel*, b. Nov. 21, 1748; d. Oct. 1, 1770.

Welthania, b. Nov. 29, 1832. — VIII. *Clarissa,* b. Sept. 23, 1801; m., 1822, Osmyn Davis, of Warren; r. Waldoborough. — IX. *Sophronia,* b. April 24, 1804; m., Dec. 31, 1822, Philip Newbit. — X. *Harriet,* b. July 26, 1806; m., Dec. 28, 1820, John Robinson; ch. 1. *Elmira,* b. in Waldoborough, May 18, 1822; d. 2. *Warren,* b. July 12, 1823. 3. *Roxana R.,* b. April 21, 1825, in Jefferson; d. 4. *Lenora,* b. July 15, 1827. 5. *Clarinda,* b. Oct. 5, 1829. 6. *Darius,* b. Sept. 20, 1831. 7. *Stillman,* b. Aug. 20, 1833. 8. *Horatio,* b. Jan. 8, 1836, in Union. 9. *Alvira,* b. Dec. 23, 1837. 10. *Avilla,* b. Dec. 28, 1840; d. April 20, 1841. 11. *Delano,* b. April 5, 1841.

ROBBINS, DAVID, b. at Walpole, Mass., March 21, 1752; d. Aug. 12, 1831; owned the first horse in town, the first chaise, the first sleigh, the first hack; and his was the first w. or woman who moved into town to reside. He m., first, Elizabeth, Feb. 11, 1772, who d. June 18, 1801 (dr. of John Chapman, a Scotchman, and his w., Betsey Jellard, at the time of marriage the widow Quiggle); and, second, widow Marcy (Hunt) Winslow, b. in Waldoborough, and who d. in Waldoborough, December, 1848, aged eighty-one. Issue, — I. *Jason,* b. March 13, 1772, at Walpole, Mass.; d. July 10, 1794; m. Jane, dr. of C. Butler, and had 1. *Betsey,* b. March 7, 1794, who m. Benjamin Buzzell in 1813. Mrs. R. m., second, in 1800, Sterling Davis. — II. *Chloe,* b. Walpole, Mass., Sept. 11, 1773; m., first, Samuel Bartlett, a widower, of Barretts Town, now Hope (who was b. at Newton, Mass., July 18, 1763, and whose w., Abigail Knight, d. April 15, 1784); and, second, Sept. 1, 1806, Abner Dunton, b. Lincolnville, April 26, 1781. She had, by her first husband, 1. *Jason,* b. Aug. 15, 1795; d. in New York city, u., March, 1833. 2. *Sophronia,* b. Dec. 12, 1796; m. Abram Nason. 3. *Isaac,* b. March 7, 1798; w. Clarissa. 4. *Noah,* b. Feb. 26, 1800; d. Nov. 19, 1834; m. Matilda, dr. of Herman Hawes. 5. *Samuel,* b. March 3, 1802; m. Mary Jane, dr. of Jacob Sibley. 6. *Joel,* b. April 24, 1803; m. Mary Dunton, of Westfield. 7. *Joseph,* b. June 3, 1805; d. March 22, 1825. By her second h. she had 8. *Abner,* b. Aug. 1, 1807; m. Susanna W. Harwood. 9. *Seldom,* writing-master, b. Feb. 14, 1809. 10. *Chloe,* b. Nov. 30, 1810; d. Aug. 11, 1817. 11. *Alvin,* writing-master, b. April 13, 1812; m. Elizabeth Harris, of Liberty, who d. 1850. 12. *Washington,* b. Sept. 14, 1813. 13.

Nancy Gushee, b. April 9, 1815; d. March 30, 1848; m. Joseph Wiley. 14. *John B.*, b. May 18, 1817; m., first, DeHora Bartlett; and, second, Caroline, dr. of David Robbins. — III. Joseph, b. Thomaston, July 7, 1775; d. February, 1850; r. near Mount Pleasant; m., first, April 5, 1798, Abigail, dr. of C. Butler; and, second, in March, 1820, Hannah Sterling, of Appleton, from St. George; had 1. *Lucy*, b. July 30, 1801; d. 2. *Christopher Butler*, b. June 11, 1803; m., 1829, Mary Noyes, of Warren. 3. *Samuel H.*, b. May 1, 1805; m., 1829, in Searsmont, a Bennet; r. Hope. 4. *Eliza*, b. July 9, 1807; m. John Briggs. 5. *Nancy Gushee*, b. May 8, 1809; m. a Jones; r. Goose River in Camden; and d. 1851. 6. *Mercy W.*, b. June 22, 1811; m. 7. *Chloe M.*, b. Jan. 17, 1816; d. Nov. 25, 1834; m. Oliver Matthews, of Warren. — IV. Silence, b. Feb. 22, 1777; d. Feb. 22, 1777; the first white child b. in town. — V. Lucy, b. Feb. 19, 1778; d. March 1, 1778; the second white child b. in the town. — VI. Joel, b. June 3, 1780; the first male child born in town, and the first person born here who was required to do military duty; settled at the east part of the town; m., Oct. 16, 1799, Rebecca, dr. of Christopher Butler. — VII. Nancy, b. April 22, 1782; m., Nov. 14, 1799, Almond Gushee, of Hope. — VIII. Ebenezer, b. Oct. 4, 1783; m. Thankful, dr. of Seth Luce; r. Appleton. — IX. Pardon, b. June 18, 1785; was left in a store on the Common, the night of April 2, 1838, where he was found dead the next morning; u. — X. David, b. Feb. 20, 1788; settled on the homestead; became blind; in a state of depression, after several unsuccessful attempts, succeeded, July, 1850, in killing himself, " by taking a twist in his neckhandkerchief with a stick." He m., March 18, 1813, Lydia, dr. of Joseph Maxcy; had 1. *Gilbert*, b. Jan. 3, 1814; d. Aug. 29, 1834. 2. *Oren*, b. Feb. 1, 1815; enlisted; d. in Mexico, Nov. 20, 1847. 3. *Elvira*, b. Oct. 6, 1816; m., July 4, 1843, Asa Crockett, of Thomaston. 4. *Olive*, b. Feb. 14, 1819; m., Jan. 11, 1844, Philo Thurston, jr.; and has a son. 5. *Hannah Elizabeth*, b. Dec. 29, 1821. 6. *Waterman Maxcy*, b. Feb. 4, 1823. 7. *Mary Weeks*, b. Nov. 12, 1824; m., Nov. 1848, Samuel Winslow; r. Newton, Mass. 8. *Nancy Maxcy*, b. Nov. 18, 1826; d. Jan. 1851. 9. *Caroline Marcy*, b. Sept. 16, 1828; m. John B. Dunton. 10. *Maxcy*, b. July 13, 1830. 11. *Ermina Gushee*, b. Aug. 22, 1832. 12. *Lydia*

Amanda, b. Jan. 24, 1836. 13. *Mandalene Victoria*, b. Oct. 29, 1837; d. May 21, 1850. — XI. John Chapman, b. April 17, 1791; m. Berintha, dr. of Thomas Daggett; ch. 1. *Spencer*, b. Aug. 6, 1809; d. June 27, 1834. 2. *Cordelia*, b. March 17, 1811; m., Sept. 8, 1833, Vinal, s. of Nathan Hills; r. Northport; had (1). Spencer R., b. Dec. 25, 1833; (2). Adilate, b. Oct. 30, 1835, d. April 16, 1836; and probably others. 3. *Hannah*, b. Nov. 27, 1812; r. Saccarappa; m., May 30, 1830, Otis Hunnewell, from Newton, Mass.; and had Edwin Emery, b. Sept. 13, 1830, d. June 27, 1831; Charles Edwin, d. June 27, 1840, aged nine months; also Henry and Elias. 4. *Irene*, b. Feb. 9, 1815; m., Jan. 11, 1835, Paul Lincoln, of Appleton; and d. 5. *Laurinda*, b. May 10, 1817; m. Orson Cromett, who was killed by the bursting of a grindstone, at South Union. 6. *Elias*, b. April 2, 1819; travels, as musician, with a caravan of animals. 7. *Aldina*, b. April 22, 1821; d. June 12, 1841. 8. *John Chapman*, sea-captain, b. March 5, 1823; r. Northport. 9. *Martha M.*, b. May 31, 1825; r. Saccarappa. 10. *Almond Gushee*, b. Oct. 30, 1828; d. March 17, 1830.—XII. Maxcy, b. June 23, 1793; clothier, musician, accompanied a circus or caravan of animals; and d., 1832, of cholera, in Upper Canada; m., 1818, in Stratham, N.H., Mary W., b. Stratham, N.H., Nov. 21, 1797, d. Manchester, N.H., Dec. 4, 1849, dr. of Walter and Nancy (Jewett) Weeks; and had 1. *Ann Elizabeth*, b. Sept. 24, 1818, Exeter, N.H.; d. Aug. 1819. 2. *Hannah*, b. Sept. 23, 1820, Epping, N.H.; d. Oct. 18, 1844, Manchester, N.H.; c.; m., June 9, 1840, Daniel Clark, lawyer, Manchester, N.H. — XIII. Eliza, b. Aug. 14, 1802; d. March 18, 1805. — XIV. Sally Simmons, b. Sept. 25, 1807; d. Oct. 7, 1807. — XV. Sarah Simmons, b. Dec. 2, 1808; m., first, James Woodcock; had *a son*, d. young; *Leonora Levenseller*, b. Feb. 17, 1830, m. Isaac Kahler, 1848; *Esther Mero*, b. Jan. 16, 1832; also *a son;* having lost *Harriet*. Mrs. W. m., second, Nathaniel Hunt, of Waldoborough; and has *Octavia, Seldom Dunton, Statira, Oren Robbins, &c.*

ROBBINS, JESSA, s. of Philip, b. Walpole, Mass., April 16, 1759; m., first, in the fall of 1783, Jemima, sister of Capt. Joel Adams, who was b. at Franklin, Mass., and d. Oct. 20, 1790; by whom he had — I. Submit, d. Aug. 7, 1790. He m., second, in the spring of 1792, Ruth Pearce; b. Rehoboth, Mass., Oct. 16, 1760; who d. April 9,

1838; and had — II. John Pearce, b. Sept. 2, 1793; m., April 2, 1815, Polly, b. Nov. 26, 1790, dr. of John and Elizabeth Mero; and had 1. *Caroline*, b. Jan. 15, 1816. 2. *John*, b. Feb. 20, 1818; m. Hannah Douglass; r. Gardiner. 3. *Mary Ann*, b. Sept. 23, 1819; m. Oren Oxford Stewart. 4. *Jesse*, b. June 21, 1823; m., Feb. 22, 1849, Harriet Newell Young, of Jefferson. 5. *Catharine*, b. March 3, 1826 (?). — III. Milton, b. Jan. 8, 1796; d. Oct. 23, 1802. — IV. Jason, b. July 2, 1799; r. homestead; m., March 28, 1824, Lucy Thorndike, of Searsmont; and had 1. *Adaline*, b. March 23, 1825; m., May, 1849, Emery Franklin Joy. 2. *Clementine Thorndike*, b. Nov. 25, 1832. 3. *Alphonso*, b. July 29, 1835. 4. *Jason*, b. June 25, 1838. 5. *Lycurgus*, b. May 17, 1844. — V. Mima, b. Aug. 14, 1801; m. George Butler, of Thomaston. — VI. Jesse, b. May 28, 1806; m., first, May 9, 1830, Hannah, dr. of David Carriel; and had 1. *Ann Augusta*, b. March 28, 1831. 2. *Charles C.*, b. Dec. 4, 1832. 3. *Dexter*, b. Sept. 9, 1834. 4. *Mary Ellen*, b. Aug. 14, 1836. 5 and 6. Twins, *Emery* and *Emerson*, b. 1837. 7. *Levi*, b. 1840. He m., second, in 1845, widow Louisa (Smith) Dutton; c.

ROBBINS, JOSIAH, b. Walpole, Mass., July 23, 1737; d. Union, Jan. 5, 1811; m., in Franklin, Sarah, b. April 24, 1746; d. of dropsy, Feb. 27, 1825; dr. of Matthew Smith, of Bellingham; had — I. Olive, b. Feb. 23, 1766; m., first, Robert Gillmor, of Franklin, Nov. 15, 1785; and, second, Deacon James Metcalf, of Franklin, and had ch. by the first husband only. — II. Molly, or Mary, b. Nov. 1, 1767; m. David Gillmor. — III. Sarah, b. Feb. 19, 1770; m. Rufus Gillmor. — IV. Nathaniel, b. Stoughtonham, Oct. 2, 1773; m., 1793, Lovey, b. Holmes's Hole, Mass., April 1, 1775, dr. of Capt. George West. She d. of lung-fever, Nov. 9 [10, gravestone], 1812. He m., June 15, 1814, Elizabeth, whose maiden name was Lummus, b. Feb. 4, 1776, in Hamilton, Mass., widow of David Coggswell, of Ipswich, Mass. N. R. lived in Union till the fall of 1840, when he moved to Brunswick, where he d. of dropsy, July 4, 1850. His remains, in a massive, black walnut, silver-mounted coffin, were taken by railroad to Portland, thence by steamboat to Rockland, and brought to Union, agreeably to his desire; and, before the religious services on Sunday, July 7, were buried by the side of his family, in the town where he had lived and labored during the greater part of his life. Appropriate services were then held in the Universalist Meeting-house, by the Rev. Dr. Adams, of Brunswick, who officiated in accordance with his request. His ch. were 1. *Peter West*, captain, b. Nov. 14, 1794; r. Searsmont; m., July 16, 1815, Mary S. Jones, dr. of the wife of Susman Abrams by her first husband. He d. Nov. 9 [or 10, gravestone], 1821, and was buried under arms; having had (1). L o v e y W e s t, b. June 16, 1816, now Mrs. Thorndike, r. Searsmont; (2). H e n r y, b. Oct. 29, 1818, r. Union, u.; (3). P e t e r W e s t, b. Dec. 26, 1820; m.; r. Searsmont. Peter's widow m., second, Ward Maxcy, who d. She now r. Augusta. 2. *Olive*, b. March 26, 1797; m., 1816, Waterman Maxcy, and June 20, 1830, Silas Kellar; r. South Thomaston; by whom she had [see p. 469] (7). O s c a r, b. May 7, 1831; (8). S i l a s, b. Dec. 14, 1833; (9). O l i v e, b. May 11, 1837; (10). M o r t i m e r, b. March 18, 1840; d. Sept. 4, 1849. 3. *Willard*, b. Dec. 14, 1799; m., at Lincolnville, April 5, 1821, Deborah W. Moody, b. Lincolnville, Oct. 1, 1799, dr. of Wm. Moody (b. York, March 30, 1766, d. Feb. 27, 1840) and Patience Thorndike, b. Camden, Dec. 15, 1768, d. April 22, 1846; and settled in Searsmont, where six of the children were born. They now live on his homestead in Union. Had (1). P a-t i e n c e M., b. March 21, 1822, m. Franklin, s. of Noah Rice; (2). N a n c y E., b. Feb. 18, 1824; m., 1850, John Little, from New York State; (3). N a t h a n i e l A., b. July 4, 1826; d. Oct. 15, 1828; (4). D e b o r a h M., b. July 19, 1828; (5). W i l l i a m M o o d y, b. Sept. 13, 1830; (6). W i l l a r d, b. July 19, 1832; (7). N a t h a n i e l A., b. Aug. 24, 1834; (8). A d e l b e r t P., b. Nov. 14, 1837; (9). A u g u s t a A., b. Nov. 9, 1840; (10). E d w i n L., b. Oct. 12, 1843. 4. *Mary Chase*, b. Aug. 30 [31, town-rec.], 1802; m. Moses Walcott; and d. of consumption, Dec. 7, 1849. 5. *Nathaniel*, b. Jan. 20, 1805; m., April 7, 1831, Harriet Gleason; and had (1). F r a n c e s A u g u s t a, b. Feb. 19, 1832; (2). A n n E l i z a b e t h, b. Aug. 10, 1833; (3). L o v e y W e s t, b. Oct. 20, 1834; (4). E d w a r d K e n t, b. April 9, 1839. 6. *Lovey West*, b. Oct. 4, 1807; m. Hermon Mero. 7. *Charles*, b. April 28, 1810; d. May 1, 1810. 8. *Sarah Smith*, b. June 2, 1811; m., Dec. 5, 1833, James, b. July 29, 1808; d. July 23, 1847, s. of John McDowell, of Washington, from Scotland; had (1). M a r y W a l c o t t, b. Dec 2, 1834; (2). R o s c o e, b. March 21, 1837; (3). S a r a h M a r i a, b. Nov. 2, 1838; d. Jan. 13, 1845; (4). J a m e s, b. Nov. 19, 1841;

(5). Flotealia, b. Jan. 26, 1843; (6). Sarah Theresa, b. Feb. 18, 1845; (7). William Augustus, b. Feb. 25, 1848. 9. *Augustus Coggswell*, b. June 3, 1816; m., April 9, 1838, Maria Theresa, b. Brunswick, Nov. 15, 1814, dr. of Capt. William and Priscilla (Merritt) Curtis; and had, b. at Brunswick, (1). Harriett Maria, b. April 13, 1841; (2). Charles Augustus, b. July 2, 1843. — V. Lewis, b. Franklin, Sept. 11, 1782; m., Feb. 7, 1805, Phebe, b. Feb. 8, 1787, dr. of Nathan and Sarah (Wellington) Barnard; had 1. *Josiah*, b. Nov. 7, 1805; r. Stephensport, Ky.; a farmer; m. Mahala, b. Nelson County, Ky., dr. of Thomas and Mary (Martin) York; and had (1). Roxana, d. young; (2). Lewis; (3). Charles Warren; (4). Willard; (5). Ann, b. March 13, 1840; (6). Nathan Barnard; (7). Thomas; (8). William Jesse. 2. *Lucy*, b. Nov. 10, 1807; m. Milton Daniels; and d. Oct. 29, 1833. 3. *Maria*, b. June 7, 1809; m., first, Jesse Drake, who d. July 19, 1842, and, second, Dec. 30, 1848, Horace Blood; and had (1). Josiah, b. Dec. 4, 1830; (2). Jesse, b. Feb. 22, 1843; (3). Meriam Hooper, b. Sept. 28, 1849. 4. *Roxana*, b. June 27, 1812, m. William G. Hawes. 5. *Nathan Barnard*, b. July 22, 1815; m., March 17, 1842, Cynthia Abigail Daniels; and had (1). Levi Morse, b. July 30, 1843; (2). Edgar Milton, b. July 30, 1845; (3). Nathan D. b. April 30, 1849. 6. *Lewis*, b. May 12, 1817; m., Dec. 4, 1845, Matilda, b. in Hope, Nov. 28, 1826, dr. of Benjamin and Lydia (Fletcher) McAllister; and had (1). Roscoe Benjamin, b. Jan. 30, 1846; (2). Charles Augustin, b. Nov. 15, 1848. 7. *Phebe Ann*, b. June 25, 1821; d. Aug. 22, 1826. 8. *Charles*, b. March 20, 1823; d. June 10, 1848, seventy miles above New Orleans, and was buried in the Methodist Burying-ground on the plantation of John Preston, on the east side of the Mississippi River, and five miles below Donaldsonville.

ROBBINS, PHILIP, b. in Walpole, Mass., Aug. 20, 1730, old style; d. March 9, 1816; m., Nov. 1, 1750, O.S., Jemima, commonly called "Aunt Mima," b. March 3, 1731, O.S., and d. Nov. 9, 1815; dr. of Joseph Smith, of Walpole. A correspondent, who was young at the time of the death of Philip Robbins and his wife, writes, "They came often to our house, were most simple-hearted and honest people. Old Philip used to wear a round-top hat, just large enough for his head, with a broad brim; also breeches with knee-buckles and shoe-buckles. They sleep side by side in the graveyard, having attained great age." Many a middle-aged person retains a distinct recollection of his appearance, as he rode his black horse (on each side of which were panniers, lashed over the horse's back with straps) from house to house, collecting calves and lambs, which he killed, and was in the habit of carrying to market, at Thomaston, till within a few years of his death. He left six children, fifty-one grandchildren, eighty-five great-grandchildren, and five great-great-grandchildren; having lost three children and fifteen grandchildren. His ch. all b. in Walpole, Mass. — I. David, b. March 21, 1752. — II. Elizabeth, b. July 8, 1754; m. Richard Cummings. — III. Jemimah, or Mima, as she was commonly called, b. Jan. 10, 1757; m. Capt. Joel Adams. — IV. Jess, b. April 18 or 16, 1759. — V. Ebenezer, b. April 30, 1761; buried on Cranberry Island. — VI. Jacob, b. Nov. 14, 1762; m. Susan Meservey; r. Appleton, and, in 1848 or 1849, found dead in his bed. — VII. Joseph, b. Aug. 7, 1765; d. Jan. 7, 1769. — VIII. Susanna, b. Sept. 22 [Walpole rec.], Oct. 22 [herself], 1768; m. Amariah Mero. — IX. Philip, b. Aug. 27, 1771.

ROGERS, JESSE, from Stoughtonham; t. 1795; w. Salome Bosworth; built a house near Bowker Brook; moved to Penobscot; ch. — I. Nancy, b. Nov. 27, 1787. — II. Shepherd, b. April 24, 1789. — III. Abigail, b. June 23, 1791. — IV. Salome, b. May 6, 1793; d. March 20, 1794. — V. Sally, b. July 11, 1796 — VI. Jesse, b. June 2, 1798. — VII. Wm., b. April 27, 1800. — VIII. Hannah, b. Aug. 18, 1802.

SHEPARD, or SHEPHERD, DANIEL, from Acton, Mass.; d. July 3, 1829. "The Shepherd and Law families were among the first," according to Shattuck's Concord, who, about the year 1656, commenced a settlement in Acton. His wife was Mary Adams, of Acton. They came to Union in June, 1795, and settled about one and a half or two miles north-west of Round Pond. Jane Shepherd died Nov. 27, 1807, aged ninety-one. — I. Daniel, b. Nov. 2, 1775; m., April 23, 1802, Alice, sister of Asa Messer, and had 1. *Nancy*, b. Oct. 16, 1803; d. Aug. 23, 1841. 2. *John Adams*, b. Nov. 26, 1805. 3. *Eliza*, b. May 28, 1807. 4. *William*, b. April 7, 1809. 5. *Daniel*, b. March 28, 1811; d. Aug. 10, 1811. 6. *Elsie*, b. July 23, 1812. 7. *Daniel*, b. Sept. 15, 1815. 8. *Amanda*, b. April 30, 1819. — II. Artemas, b. July 1, 1777; m. Martha Dole, of Waterville.

— III. Thaddeus, b. May 13, 1779; m. Susan, dr. of Caleb Howard, of Waldoborough, and had 1. *Mace*, b. Oct. 16, 1809; m. Jane Chapman, of Nobleborough; c. 2. *James Sanford*, b. June 5, 1811; m. Nancy Stone, dr. of Jonas C. Davis, of Appleton; had (1). J a m e s I r v i n g, b. Jan. 9, 1836 or 1835; (2). S u s a n C a r o l i n e, b. April 19, 1837 or 1836; (3). G e o r g e A p p l e t o n; (4). M a r y C a t h a r i n e. 3. *Thaddeus S.*, b. April 15, 1813; m. Sally Sayward; c. 4. *Sarah Catherine*, b. Sept. 17, 1817; m. March 7, 1839, George Fossett, and has (1). J a m e s; (2). G e o r g e E m e r s o n. 5. *Josiah Howard*, b. Sept. 16, 1819; u. 6. *Noah Emerson*, b. March 13, 1822. — IV. Sarah, m. Michael Jones; r. Jefferson. — V. Lucy, m. Samuel Hagar, 1804, and had 1. *Sarah*, b. April 11, 1805. 2. *Samuel*, b. Sept. 13, 1807; d. July 2, 1842. 3. *Reuben*, b. March 27, 1810. 4. *Lucy*, b. Dec. 1, 1812. 5. *John*, b. July 26, 1816. 6. *Thomas*, b. Aug. 26, 1820. 7. *Ezekiel*, b. Nov. 26, 1825; d. Aug. 2, 1826. 8. *Esther Ann*, b. June 16, 1827. — VI. Nathan; u. — VII. Mercy, m., Nov 3, 1814, Daniel Jones, of Washington. — VIII. Nancy, m. John Ames, of Jefferson.

SIBLEY,[1] JONATHAN, b. at Hopkinton, N. H., Jan. 4,

[1] The word *Sibley* may be compounded of the words *sib* and *lea*. The former means *relationship* or *alliance*; or, in earlier times, *peace*; and the latter, a *field*. Hence the words combined may mean *kinsmen's land*. Perhaps several kinsmen lived together in the same place, or on the same *lea*. If the earlier meaning of the word *sib* be adopted, the meaning may be *peace-lea*, or *land of peace*; perhaps because of the harmony of the people, or because the place was exempt from war. This explanation of the origin of the word, however, is merely conjectural.

The description of the Sybly arms, in Burke's General Armory, is " Per pale azure and gules a griffin passant between three crescents argent." In heraldry, the griffin, which is an imaginary animal, half eagle and half lion; denotes strength and swiftness. The close agreement of the armorial bearings of the families of *Sileby* and of *Sybly* seems to show that one of the names is a variation of the other, — the latter probably being a corruption of the former. But it is certain that *Sibley* is of considerable antiquity, as it is found in the Rotuli Hundredorum of the reign of Edward I. (1272—1307), in the counties of Huntington, Kent, Oxford, and Suffolk, where it is spelt *Sybeli, Sibeli, Sibely, Sibili, Sibilie, Sibli;* and where the name *Sileby* does not seem to occur. The Public Records published by the Record Commission spell it *Sibille*, in the reign of Richard II. (1377—1399); and *Sibyle* in that of Henry V. (1413—1422); and in that of Elizabeth (1558—1603), it is *Sybley, Sibley,* and *Sibly;* and once (with an *alias*) *Sybery*. A very similar name of about the same antiquity is *filius*

1773; came to Union, Sept. 17, 1799; m., Nov. 1, 1803, Persis, b. at Sherburne, Mass., April 20, 1772; d. of para-

Sibillæ, or *Fitz-Sibyl*, which may have been the original of the name in some cases; in other cases, it may have been derived from the parish of *Hingham Sibyl*, or *Sible*, or *Sibleys*, in Essex.

From Felt's Annals of Salem, i. 172, it seems that the first of the Sibleys in this country came to Salem in the fleet of 1629. It is said that they were from the north part of England or south part of Scotland, or that they came from Northamptonshire. In Willis's Cathedrals, ii. 172, it is stated that "John Sibeley collated 1459," succeeded Roger Mersham as prebendary of Lincoln. In Rymer's Fœdera, xix. 348, is recorded "Pro Johanne Sibley. Rex, vicesimo sexto die Maii [1631 or 1632] concessit Johanni Sibley et aliis Officium Clerici et Clericorum omnium et singulorum brevium et processuum in Curia Camere Stellate, durante vita. P[rivato] S[igillo];" meaning Clerk of the Court of the Starre Chamber for life. In Dugdale's Warwickshire, Knightlow Hundred, Marton, i. 327, under the patronage of "Rob. Fysher miles & Bar.," is found "Thom. Sybley Cler. in Art. Magr. xvii. Oct. 1623 [v. p. m. Ric. Seale ult. Incumb.]" In the same volume, Birdingbury, p. 325, is "[Tho. Sibley Cler. ii Julii 1633]." In Besse's Sufferings of the Quakers, i. 638-644, Thomas Sibley, a blacksmith, is "sent to gaol" and fined — though he was afterward released and the fine remitted — "for being at an unlawful Meeting or Conventicle, in the parish of Crewkherne," in Somersetshire, on the fourth of June, 1684. In the same volume, page 345, William Sibley is named as a prisoner in 1685, in Leicester, — the town where Higginson was settled before he came to Massachusetts in 1629. Possibly some of these Sibleys were related to the early settlers in New England. A comparison of the situation of the places mentioned, and of places from which came some individuals in the fleet of 1629, may be of value in making further investigations in the mother-country.

"John Sybley with Sarah his wife" was admitted to the church in Charlestown, Mass., on the 21st day of the 12th month, 1634-5, old style. He took the freeman's oath, May 6, 1635. It is not certain that there is any other information respecting him or his family, except —

"A true Inventory of the Lands: Goods: Cattell, and Chattells of John Sybley Inhabitant of Charlestowne lately deseased the 30th of 9th mo: 1649

Imprimis A House and Barne and 6 Akers of Arrable Land Broken up and meadow ground and cows commons, valued at	50	00	00
more 4 cows 2 caves, A mare wth foale, 3 swine at	36	00	00
more Puter and Brasse and Iron Kettell and frying pan with iron pot hangers pot hooks gridiron and other iron	05	10	00
more Armes As A corslet headpeece sword and pike	02	00	00
His Cloaths As A cloath coat, and cloath suight made and a carse suight unmade a Buther suight [butcher suit] and hats and other cloathing wth bands and shirts at	08	00	00
more Bedding and Lynnen at	16	00	00
more Barke, Indian, Pease and Rye at	08	00	00
A cart and furniture And tooles tubs and other Lumber	05	00	00
A Table, chest, chaire, And Bookes at	02	10	00
Summa	133	00	00

This was valewed the 27th of the 1st moneth i6

JOHN GREENE
RAPH MOUSELL."

lysis, Feb. 5, 1847 ; dr. of Obadiah Morse ; had — I. John Langdon, b. Dec. 29, 1804 ; fitted for college at Phillips's

The inventory is preserved, on a small piece of loose paper, in the Probate Office at East Cambridge. In the record of its acceptance, " at a County Court held at Cambridge the 2th of the 2th mo. 1650," the name is spelt " Siblie."

JOHN SIBLY, who took the freeman's oath, Sept. 3, 1634, is the sixteenth on the list of members of the First Church in Salem. In 1636 he was selectman of Salem. The same year, 20th 10th month, he had half an acre of land granted to him at Winter Island Harbor, " for the fishing trade and to build upon." He also had a grant of fifty acres at Manchester, 20 : 12 : 1636, O.S. Hanson, in the History of Danvers, page 31, says he had land near Salem village, now Danvers, in 1638, and settled. Probably these Salem references are to but one John Sibley, — the same man who settled at Manchester in 1636, was selectman there, an extensive land-owner, and died there in 1661. In the inventory, mention is made of nine children, four boys and five girls. His widow, Rachel, brought the inventory into court, and " yᵉ Court doe order that yᵉ estate be left in yᵉ widoe's hands to bring up yᵉ children till yᵉ Court take further order." They had Sarah, baptized at Salem Church, 18 : 7 : 1642. Mary, bapt. 8 : 7 : 1644 ; m., 26 : 11 : 1664, Jonathan Walcott ; had *John*, b. Dec. 7, 1766 ; *Hanna*, b. 6 : 10 : 1667 ; *Jonathan*, b. 1 : 7 : 1670 ; and many others. Rachael, bapt. 3 : 3 : 1646 ; m. a Bishop. John, Capt. bapt. 14 : 3 : 1648 ; admitted to the church in Beverly. April 5, 1696 ; m. Rachel (admitted to Beverly Church, 5 : 5 : 1685), dr. of Ama. Pickworth. Capt. John was selectman of Manchester many years, representative to the General Court, leading man in town-affairs, and d. as early as the spring of 1710. Hannah. bapt. 22 : 4 : 1651 ; m., 25 : 12 : 1676, Steeven Small ; had *Mary*, b. March 21, 1677 ; *Elizabeth*, b. March 4, 1678-9 ; *John*, b. 7 : 7 : 1680 ; *Hannah*, b. 18 . 12 : 1681. William, bapt. 8 : 7 : 1653 ; yeoman and butcher ; d. of consumption at Salem Village, April 28, 1691 ; m. 1 : 9 : 1676, Ruth, dr. of William Canterbury, and widow of William Small ; and had 1. *Ruth*, b. August, 1677 ; m., Aug. 6, 1706, Thomas Needham. 2. *John*. 3. *Joseph*, probably the Joseph of Lynn in 1717 ; d. 1718 (?). 4. *Nathaniel*, husbandman, b. about 1686 ; d. about 1733. 5. *Rachel*, b. about 1688 ; m., Nov. 16, 1710, Joseph Flint. Samuel, b. 12 : 2 : 1657 ; m. Mary, of witch-memory, whose confession is in the Collections of the Massachusetts Historical Society, vol. iii. of the third series. Abigail, bapt. 3 : 5 : 1659. There was Joseph, probably between William and Samuel. In 1693, he and others, according to Felt's Annals of Salem, ii. 214, on their homeward passage from a fishing-voyage to Cape Sable, were impressed on board a British frigate. After seven weeks' service in the vessel, the captain forced him to go on board another ship. He m., Feb. 4, 1683, Susanna Follet ; and had 1. *Joseph*, b. Nov. 9, 1684. whose w. was Mary. 2. *John*, b. Sept. 18, 1687 ; m., May 22, 1718. Zeruia Gould. 3. *Jonathan*. b. May 1, 1690. 4. *Hannah*, bapt. May, 1695. 5. *Samuel*, bapt. 1697 ; m. Martha Dike, said to be of Ipswich. 6. *William*, bapt. April 7, 1700 ; d. about the age of fifty,

Exeter Academy; graduated at Harvard University in 1825; Assistant Librarian at Harvard University in 1825-6; having a cancer on his tongue; m. Sarah Dike. 7. *Benjamin,* bapt. Sept. 19, 1703; had a w., Priscilla. Of these sons, the first two and last three settled in Sutton, Mass., and vicinity, in the first part of the eighteenth century. Benjamin, after living in Sutton a few years, went to Union, Conn., and d. at Ashford. From them have descended the Sibleys in New York, and in the South and West. The late Dr. John Sibley, of Natchitoches, La., s. of Timothy, was b. at Sutton. There are, however, some of the name in Florida, who are not of this stock. There was another, of whom nothing is known, except that, among Washington's Papers, now in the Capitol at the city of Washington, is "A return of Captain Joshua Lewis Compa. August 17th, 1756, on the South Branch.... Rank and File — 8 on Command, at Sibley's Mill."

RICHARD SIBLEY, "traie-maker," from whom the families in Union are descended, d. 1676. His widow was living in 1700. In the inventory of his effects, 30 : 4 : 1676, mention is made of drawing-knives and shaves. What relation he sustained to John, of Salem, is not known; perhaps both were sons of John, of Charlestown. He and his w., Hannah, were in Salem in 1656, as appears from charges against them in an old account-book of Curwen. They had — I. Samuel, b. 10 : 1 : 1658. — II. Hannah, b. 20 : 7 : 1661. — III. Sarah, b. 20 : 10 : 1663. — IV. Damaris, b. 26 : 6 : 1666. — V. John, b. first week in April, 1669; supposed to be the John who m., July 4, 1695, Elizabeth Peale; and had 1. *Elizabeth,* b. Oct. 3, 1696; d. twenty months old. 2. *Elizabeth,* b. April 13, 1699. 3 and 4. *Mary* and *Hannah,* twins, b. March 14, 1701; both d. within a week. 5. *Mary,* b. April 25, 1702. 6. *John,* b. Dec. 1, 1704. — VI. Mary, b. Jan. 25, 1671. — VII. Elizabeth, is mentioned in the inventory.

SAMUEL, b. 10 : 1 : 1658, named in Rd. Sibley's will, being the oldest son, had a double share of the property. He m., in Salem, Sept. 13, 1695, Sarah Wells, from whom the settlers in Union are descended. There is a tradition that he was killed at Haverhill, Mass., while throwing water upon the meeting-house which had been set on fire by the Indians, Aug. 29, 1708. He belonged to Salem, and was probably under Major Turner, upon the arrival of whose men, according to Mirick's History of Haverhill, the whole body of the enemy commenced a rapid retreat. Many persons from Salem were then killed. He had no children after that time. The inventory of his estate is dated Dec. 8, 1710. July 7, 1712, letters of administration were "granted unto John Sawyer and Sarah Sawyer, alias Sibley, former widow." The children named are Jonathan, Samuel, Hannah, and Sarah. The widow, before this time, had m. John Sawyer, of Newbury, blacksmith, to whom she was published, Nov. 25, 1710, perhaps the John Sawyer who d. in Newbury, March 27, 1756. She spent her last days with her son Jonathan Sibley, at Stratham, N.H. The children as recorded are — I. Hannah, b. May 17, 1696; d. Nov. 8, 1729; m., Oct. 4, 1712, Batt Moulton, of Newbury, and afterward of Salisbury and Amesbury; and had *Jonathan,* b. Nov. 19, 1720, and *Jonathan,* b. May 17, 1722, and perhaps others. Moulton's next wife was Jemima.

studied Divinity at the Cambridge Divinity School; ordained a Congregationalist at Stow, Mass., May 14, 1829; left

— II. Richard, b. January, 1698; d. young. — III. Sarah, b. March 27, 1699; m., Dec. 19, 1719, Edward Emery, carpenter; both at that time of Newbury. — IV. Jonathan, b. Nov. 25, 1701, ancestor of the Union Sibleys (of whom more will be said after the notices of the descendants of the Samuel b. May 5, 1705). — V. Samuel, b. July, 1704, d. young. — VI. Samuel, b. May 5, 1705, of Salem in 1723, and of Newbury in 1726; published, March 2, 1727-8, then of Newbury, to Meribah Bartlett, then of Exeter, N. H.; r. Salem; d. 1749; butcher and cordwainer. His will, dated May 9, and proved July 14, 1749, makes his brother-in-law, John Ropes, his executor. The Sibleys, in the several branches, have generally been remarkable for their integrity. It is not known that any one of the name, in this country, however much he may have deserved it, was ever hung, or punished by the civil authority for any offence. The butcher carried about his meat in panniers on horseback. There is a saying to this day in Salem respecting him, "Like Sibley's beef, never so fat, never so lean, see for yourself," which he was accustomed to utter in commendation of his provisions, and which is considered as indicative of his honesty. There is also another saying, which shows that at times he was not without wit: "Like Sibley's beef, all fat but the bones, and they are full of marrow." It is not improbable that some force was given to his expressions by the manner of his uttering them.

The SAMUEL b. May 5, 1705, had — I. Samuel. — II. John. — III. Nathaniel. The last three, though living in the spring of 1749, probably d. young. — IV. William, moved from Salem to Exeter, N. H., some years before the Revolution; m., first, July 8, 1762, Sarah, dr. of Elijah Shaw, of Kensington, N. H.; moved to Gilmanton, N. H., where he d. 1790, and his wife of consumption in 1786. He m., second, widow Lydia Hopkinson, dr. of Richard Smith, of Exeter; ch. 1. *Samuel*, b. Nov. 7, 1762; d. Nov. 1, 1788. 2. *Abigail*, b. July 22, 1766; m., John Swain; had a dr. 3. *William*, b. July 16, 1768; d. June 22, 1828; m. Nancy Thing, of Brentwood, N. H.; and had one child, S a l l y, who m. John Elkins. 4. *Sarah*, b. Dec. 8, 1770; d. young. 5. *Eunice*, b. Feb. 12, 1773; d. young. 6. *John*, b. Feb. 8, 1775; d. May 28, 1795; u. 7. *Caleb*, b. Feb. 14, 1777, moved to New York about 1804; left many ch.; d. Sept. 13, 1828, not far from Hudson River. 8. *Nathaniel*, b. Sept. 14, 1778; d. July 23, 1794. 9. *Hannah*, b. July 16, 1780; d. Sept. 7, 1832; u. 10. *Polly*, b. May 16, 1782; d. Dec. 21, 1841; m. John Crosby. 11. *Joseph*, grocer, b. Dec. 13, 1783; r. Salem, Mass.; m., first, Oct. 14, 1810, widow Dorcas Valpey, b. March 26, 1782, dr. of Jonathan and Mehitabel Abbot, of Andover. She d. April 18, 1841; and he m., second, Nov. 14, 1841, widow Sarah Patterson Ward, dr. of John and Hannah (Webb) Patterson, of Salem, and had (1). J o s e p h   A b b o t, a tailor; b. June 21, 1812; d. March 4, 1836; (2). G e o r g e   V a l p e y, b. July 17, 1813; r. Salem; m. Phebe Phillips, b. March 22, 1813, dr. of Stephen Abbot, of Andover (and had Martha G., b. April 21, 1837; George, b. Nov. 6, 1839; Phebe Ellen, b. April 2, 1846); (3).

Stow, March 31, 1833, precisely four years from his acceptance of the invitation to settle there. During part of the

John Shaw, b. June 15, 1815; r. Salem, Mass.; m., June 24, 1838, Tamma Hanson (and had Sarah Ann, b. May 31, 1840; Joseph Abbot, b. Oct. 11, 1841; Emma Bosson, b. Jan. 1, 1845; John Henry, b. April 26, 1848; d. Sept. 10, 1848); (4). Moses Howe, b. Sept. 15, 1816; m., Feb. 1842, Lucy Ann Knights (and had Caroline, b. Nov. 21, 1842; Moses Henry, b. Aug. 22, 1846; Mary Harrington, b. April 6, 1849); (5.) William Henry, b. Oct. 29, 1818; m. Mary Clark, of Rowley (and had Charles Augustus, b. May 24, 1846); (6). Sarah Ann, b. May 24, 1820; d. Sept. 12, 1826; (7). Charles Augustus, b. Dec. 19, 1823; d. Sept. 21, 1824. — 12. *Littlefield*, probably of the second marriage, b. September, 1787; name changed to George Littlefield, in 1816; r. Meredith Bridge, N.H.; through the Rev. Isaac D. Stewart, furnished much of the information respecting his father's family. He m. Harriet, b. May 27, 1790; dr. of Daniel Kimball, of Exeter; and has (1). Harrison, b. Feb. 27, 1814; m. Hannah Leavitt (and has Flora, b. Nov. 27, 1839); (2). Harriet Kimball, b. Aug. 17, 1816; m., Jan. 14, 1837, Dr. Charles C. Tibbets (and has George Harrison, b. Aug. 19, 1844); (3). Eliza Jane, b. Oct. 6, 1824. 13. *Nancy*, d., three months old. (Of these thirteen children, ot — IV. William, all but three d. of consumption, or of feebleness in infancy.) — V. Littlefield, bapt. May 6, 1739; master of a privateer, lost in the revolutionary war; m., Aug. 19, 1765 (possibly for a second w.), Sarah Lambert, a worthy woman, who d. in Salem about 1828; had sons and drs., among them *Hannah, Sally, Samuel*, and *Nathaniel.* — VI. Sarah. — VII. Hannah, b. April 12, 1740; d. March 20, 1801; m., Oct. 3, 1764, Joshua, b. Jan. 27, 1742, s. of Nathaniel and Seeth (Hardy) Phippen; r. Salem, Mass. He d. April, 1811. They had 1. *Nathaniel*, b. Jan. 28, 1765; d. March 9, 1809; m., Sept. 4. 1786, Anna Picket, of Beverly, who d. Dec. 22, 1834. 2 and 3. Twins, b. July 30, 1767; viz. *Joshua*, d. Oct. 8, 1767, and *Samuel*, d. Jan. 1, 1768. 4. *Hannah*, b. Dec. 26, 1768; d. June 15, 1837; m., March 25, 1798, George Hodges, who d. 1827. 5. *Mary*, b. Oct. 12, 1770; d. 1811; m., 1790, Benjamin Babbidge. 6. *Sarah*, b. Dec. 8, 1772; d July 25, 1801; m., July 26, 1791, George Dean. 7. *Joshua*, b. July 2, 1774; d. April 28, 1805; m., March 18, 1799, Nancy, dr. of Ebenezer Trask, of Beverly. 8 and 9. Twins, b. Dec. 22, 1775; viz. *Eunice*, d. Oct. 30, 1776, and *Margaret*, lived a few days. 10. *Hardy*, b. July 6, 1778; m., March 18, 1804, Ursula Knapp, dr. of Jonathan and Ursula Symonds; and had (1). Joseph Hardy, b. June 10, 1807, m., March 26, 1840, Susan Harris Lord. (2). Ursula Symonds, b. Sept. 21, 1809, m., March 10, 1840, Isaac Needham Chapman (and has Francis Needham, b. Oct. 21, 1844; Hardy Phippen, b. Aug. 20, 1846; and twins, a boy and girl, b. Feb. 3, 1850). (3). Joshua, b. Dec. 17, 1812, m., April 22, 1841, Betsey Barr Holman (and has Mary Elizabeth, b. May 20, 1842). (4). George Dean, b. April 13, 1815, m., April 13, 1840, Margaret, b. July 23, 1815, dr. of John and Mary (Webb) Barton (and had George Barton, b. Feb. 12, 1841; Samuel Webb, b. Oct. 13, 1846, d. June 22, 1847; Arthur Henry, b. Sept. 7, 1848). 11. *Eunice*, b. March 22, 1780; d. Dec. 18, 1799. 12. *Joseph*,

year 1837, he was editor, and became proprietor, of the American Magazine of Useful and Entertaining Knowledge,

b. March 14, 1783; lost at sea, Aug. 31, 1818; m., March 1, 1807, Lois Fairfield. — VIII. Susanna, bapt. March 13, 1743. — IX. and X. Twins, bapt. Oct. 7, 1744; viz. Eunice, m. a Dean of Exeter, N.H.; and Priscilla, d. as early as 1749. — XI. Mary, bapt. Sept. 6, 1747; m. Elisha Odlin, of Exeter, or Gilmanton, N.H. One of the drs. of Samuel and Meribah m. a Taylor, of Gilmanton; and another, Capt. Somerby Gilman, of Gilmanton.

To resume the notice of Jonathan, b. Nov. 25, 1701, fourth child of Samuel and Sarah (Wells) Sibley. It is not improbable that his mother, after she m. John Sawyer, took him and other ch. with her to Newbury. He was a resident in Amesbury in 1723; in Newbury in 1726; and when, Nov. 27, 1730, he m. Hannah, b. Feb. 1, 1712-13, dr. of Samuel and Hannah (Frazer) Goodridge, of Newbury. [Joshua Coffin, Esq. says, Hannah Frazer, b. Aug 31, 1692, who m., June 30, 1710, Samuel Goodridge, was third child of Colin Frazer, who m. Anna Stuart, Nov. 10, 1685. Samuel Goodridge, b. Aug. 15, 1681, was s. of Benjamin, who m., second, Nov. 16, 1678, Sarah Croad; and Benjamin was s. of William Goodridge.] Jonathan afterward settled in Stratham, N.H.; was farmer, and maker of chairs and wooden heels. The hill where he lived is yet called Sibley Hill, and the inhabitants to this day gather pond-lilies from roots which he planted in a running brook in the vicinity. Many amusing and some ridiculous stories are told about him. It is even asserted that he whipped his beer-barrel because it *worked* on Sunday; and his cat, because she caught a mouse when he was at prayers. Becoming embarrassed, and indebted to a physician and Baptist preacher, named Shepherd, he exchanged with him his farm for one in Poplin, where he d., Dec. 18, 1779, about one year afterward, in the seventy-eighth year of his age. He is said to have been quite petulant, and his w. to have been a very worthy, pious woman. There is a tradition, that, a short time before his w. died, the question was put to her whether she thought her husband was a Christian. She replied, "If he marries after I am gone, and his w. pays all my debts, he will probably die a Christian." Not long before his decease, he m. an execrable woman, b. Nov. 15, 1719, named Patience Thurrell, probably from Newbury. Her extravagant professions of Christian conversion and reformation prevailed more with him, as he had become somewhat childish, than the advice and opposition of all his friends and neighbors. She d. Nov. 16, 1820, nearly one hundred and one years old, at Poplin, where she had been a pauper twenty-seven years. If tradition is true, before her husband d. she paid all the first wife's debts, with compound interest.

JONATHAN SIBLEY'S descendants, all by his first wife. — I. Abigail, b. Oct. 6, 1731; m. a widower, Rogers, and d., c., at Meredith, N.H., where she lived the last ten years of her life with Mrs. Robinson, the dr. of her brother Samuel. — II. Hannah, b. April 2, 1734; taken sick, March 5; d. March 7, 1736; probably of the throat-distemper. — III. Jonathan, b. March 8, 1736; lived six years seven months and three days, and d. Oct. 11. — IV. Hannah, b. Feb.

commenced by the Bewick Company in Boston. He has been assistant-librarian and editor of the Triennial Cata-

4, 1738; lived four years seven months and twenty-three days, and d. Sept. 27. — Daniel, b. March 16, 1740; lived two years six months and twenty (?) days, and d. Oct. 15. The last three within a few days of each other, and probably of the "throat-distemper." — VI. Anna, or Nancy, b. May 3, 1742; d. Sept. 14, 1792; buried by the side of her first husband; m., first, William Stevens, who d. of consumption, February, 1775, in Hopkinton, N.H., and was buried on his farm, on Sugar Hill. He had one child, *Abigail*, b. March 26, 1773, who m. James Seaton, of Bradford, N.H. They went into the northern part of New York, whence they returned about 1808 to Hopkinton, and afterward lived at Goffstown; c. Mrs. Stevens m., second, June 18, 1778, Samuel Hoyt, a widower; and had 2. *Lydia*, b. April 9, 1779; m. Jonathan Bean, a schoolmaster, of Salisbury; moved away; had several ch., among whom were t w i n s, one of them S o p h i a. 3. *Nancy*, or *Anna*, b. Sept. 26, 1781; m. Dr. Paul Tenney, of Hopkinton, who graduated at Dartmouth College in 1803; lived in Wilmot, had several ch., and died near Mechanicsburg, Ohio, in 1844. 4. *William*, b. July 24, 1783; m. Polly French, of Weare; lived on Sugar Hill; had F r e e m a n, S e w e l l, M a r y, F r e n c h, and d. of consumption, brought on by hard work. 5. *Sally*, or *Sarah*, b. Feb. 13, 1786; sickly; moved to Wilmot; d. at Grafton; m. John Hoyt, of Concord. — VII. Molly, or Mary, b. July 2, 1744; d. in Boscawen, Jan. 9, 1828; m. Daniel Murray, of Newmarket, N.H., b. Nov. 1, 1742; r. Hopkinton, N.H.; d. there, July 15, 1823. They were buried side by side in Weare; had four sons and ten daughters. — VIII. Jacob, b. May $\frac{18}{29}$, 1746, ancestor of the families in Union (of whom more will be said after the following notices of his brother Samuel's family). — IX. Samuel, b. Feb. 23, 1751; m., Oct. 30, 1775, Sarah Dow, of Kensington, N.H., b. Dec. 17, 1747; had land given to him at Meredith by his father; was one of its earliest settlers; d. there Sept. 16, 1838. He was short, and his w. tall. At the wedding, a young woman, not fancying this inequality, in a moment of delay while they were on the floor, seized a wooden oven-lid about two inches thick, and pushed it against his heels. He stepped upon it, and thus the pair stood at equal height while the ceremony was performed. The Rev. Isaac Dalton Stewart writes, that, when Mr. Sibley moved to Meredith, there was but one log-house at Meredith Bridge. "His nearest neighbors were three miles on one side, and four on the other. Carried his corn ten miles on his back to mill. Brought his salt from Exeter on horseback, after he was able to hire or keep a horse. In 1789, he went to Exeter for salt. Neighbors were then nearer; and he got Benjamin Perkins, who lived within half a mile, to assist his wife, if need be, in keeping off the bears, which made dreadful havoc among his corn. It was a beauti-ful, still, moonlight evening in the month of October. She heard a destructive crashing in the cornfield. Leaving her four children in bed, Mrs. Sibley called to her aid Mr. Perkins. With his loaded gun, he went into the field, found the bear, and discharged its contents." The bear, badly wounded, moved off as fast as he could. Mrs. Sibley

logues of Harvard University since the year 1841; u. — II.
William Cullen, b. March 1, 1807; r. on the homestead; u.

pursued him, caught him by the leg as he was climbing over a log, and held on till Perkins came up and despatched him by cutting his throat with a jack-knife. Descendants, — 1. *Josiah Dow*, b. 1779; d. fifteen months old. 2. *Hannah*, b. Feb. 7, 1780; m. Jeremiah Gove, of Hampton Falls. He d. 1843; having J o·h n, b. June 13, 1824. 3. *Richard*, b. 1782; m., 1808, Polly French, of Newmarket; was a rafter from Exeter to Portsmouth; and drowned in a squall, while picking up drift-wood on the Piscataqua River; had (1). J o s i a h, d. four months old; (2). N a n c y; (3). M a r k; (4). S o p h i a. 4. *Mary*, b. March 1, 1784; m., 1815, Paul H. Stanton, of Bartlett; had (1). R i c h a r d, b. 1816; (2). S a r a h, b. 1818, d. April, 1844; (3). N e w- h a l l, b. 1820; (4). R e b e c c a, b. 1823. 5. *Sarah*, b. Sept. 16, 1786; m., July 3, 1806, Wm. Robinson, of Sanbornton, who d. Nov. 18, 1813; had (1). B e n j a m i n D., b. April 9, 1807, m., Jan. 19, 1847, Lois Hall, of Sandwich. The widow Robinson went to her father's, and maintained both her parents during their last days. 6. *Benjamin*, b. March 7, 1790; in 1817, went to Woodstock [Mechanicsburg?], Champaign County, Ohio; and it was twenty-three years before he was heard from. He m. a Hilliard; had four children. 7. *Nancy*, b. Feb. 1792; d. seventeen months old.

To resume the notice of — VIII. JACOB SIBLEY, b. May $\frac{1\,8}{2\,9}$, 1746, father of Jonathan and Jacob, of Union. When eighteen years old, he was sent by his father, one of the proprietors of Meredith, to assist in building the first bridge across the Winnipiseogee River, near the outlet of the lake. In 1768, he went to Hopkinton, N. H., boarded with his sister Stevens, when the place was almost a wilderness, and the remotest settlement from the seaboard, except the valley of the Connecticut and of its tributaries; and d. at Hopkinton, June 25, 1831. Oct. 11, 1771, he m. Anna, dr. of Gideon George, a shoemaker and farmer of East Haverhill, Mass., whose wife, a Jewett, came to this country when fourteen days old. She was b. Sept. 11, 1749, and d. Sept. 20, 1828. After their wedding, they rode on one horse from Haverhill to his sister Stevens's, on Sugar Hill, in Hopkinton; whence, there being no road, they walked two miles in a narrow path, through the woods, to their humble dwelling, driving before them a little spotted pig. Her "fitting out" consisted of three white cups and three saucers, three knives, three forks, one coverlet made of hair and tow, and one of wool. In 1774, they took a journey, on horseback, to Haverhill and Stratham, and back; the mother seated behind the father, who carried his only child in his arms before him. In 1776, Jacob Sibley was in the military service at Portsmouth, and worked on Fort Constitution. While there, his wife, besides attending to her domestic duties and taking care of her two children, hoed three acres of corn upon burnt land. This was a few months before the birth of her third child. In the latter part of her life, her physical strength gradually failed, till she lost entirely the power of locomotion. Decendants : —

I. Jonathan, b. Jan. 4, 1773; r. Union, Me.
II. Hannah, b. Jan. 22, 1775; r. on the homestead till her parents'

— III. Moses, b. May 5, 1813; before three years old, was attacked with epileptic fits, which continued as long as he

and her brother Amos's decease, and now with her sister Eastman, at Warner, N. H.

III. Jacob, b. Dec. 1, 1776; went to Union in March, 1800. There he m., Feb. 25, 1802, Abigail, born at Scituate, Mass., March 14, 1779, dr. of Barnabas and Lydia (Wade) Simmons, and settled on the hill in the north-west part of the town. Descendants, 1. *Nancy*, b. Jan. 2, 1803; m., March 9, 1826, Joseph Bryant, of Union; and he d. Nov. 23, 1847; having had (1). S a m u e l S t o n e, b. June 4 or 5, 1827, m., March 7, 1850, Sarah Catherine Miller, in New York; (2). J a c o b S i b l e y, b. April 12, 1829; (3). J o s e p h, b. Oct, 6, 1831; (4). N a n-c y J a n e, b. June 5, 1833; (5). A b i g a i l, b. Jan. 4, 1836, d. Aug. 22, 1838; (6). A b b y M a r i l l a, b. April 6, 1839; (7). J o h n F a i r-f i e l d, b. May 7, 1841. 2. *Lydia*, b. Dec. 13, 1804; d. June 11, 1837; m., Oct. 20, 1829, John Hunt Gowen, who m., second, Dec. 2, 1840, Betsey, dr. of John and Sarah Linscott, of Nobleborough; had (1). R e b e c c a, b. July 6, 1830; (2). M a r y O l i v i a, b. Oct. 28, 1832; (3.) S y l v a n u s B a c h e l d e r, b. May 11, 1834; (4). May 11, 1835; (4). Z u i n g l i u s C o l l i n s, b. May 14, 1837. 3. *George*, b. July 30, 1806; r. Appleton; m., May 26, 1833, Lucy Huse Philbrook, of Hope, b. in Islesborough, Sept. 1, 1807; (1). B o i c e C r a n e, b. April 29, 1834; d. Dec. 30, 1834; (2). W i l l i a m A l b e r t o, b. Dec. 1, 1835; (3). G e o r g e F r a n k l i n, b. Aug. 25, 1837; (4) and (5). Twins, L y d i a A m e l i a and L o u i s a A d e l i a, b. April 14, 1839; (6). J o h n L a n g d o n, b. Feb. 19, 1841; (7). S t e p h e n B o a r d m a n, b. Oct. 6, 1842; (8) and (9). Twins, A l m i r a F r a n-c e n a, b. Oct. 1, 1846, and a s t i l l b o r n son. 4. *Betsey Ann*, b. June 25, 1808; m., May 16, 1832, Nathaniel Clark, b. Nov. 25, 1805, at Haverhill, Mass.; had (1). H a r r i e t A n n, b. March 11, 1833; (2) and (3). Twins, b. Sept. 17, 1834, viz. M a r y E l e c t a, d. Oct. 6, 1834, and S a r a h P e r s i s; (4). M a r t h a E l l e n, b. June 24, 1836; (5). O c t a v u s L e o n a r d, b. Jan. 18, 1840; (6). J u l i a F r a n c e s, b. March 9, 1842; (7). N a t h a n i e l S i b l e y, b. 1847. 5. *Louisa*, b. March 12, 1810; r. Appleton; m., Oct. 8, 1837, Gusta-vus Myrick, s. of Moses Kenniston, b. in Thomaston, Oct. 6, 1812; had (1) and (2). Twins, s o n s, b. June 3, 1838; d. a few hours old; (3). L e a n d e r M y r i c k, b. June 25, 1839, in Appleton; (4). L y d i a A m a n d a, b. in Union, May 10, 1842; (5). A b b y L o u i s a, b. Jan. 23, 1844; (6). L u c y A n n, b. May 29, 1848. 6. *Han-nah*, b. Jan. 5, 1812; m. Oct. 6, 1834, Asa, b. in Union, Sept. 17, 1810, s. of John and Rebecca (Hunt) Gowen; (1). H a r r i e t E l l e n, b. April 28, 1836; (2). A b b y E l e c t a, b. Oct. 6, 1840; (3). H a n n a h A u g u s t a, b. Dec. 15, 1845. 7. *Mary Jane*, b. Oct. 10, 1813; m., May 1, 1834, Samuel Bartlett (descendant of Philip Robbins), b. at Hope, March 3, 1802; r. Washington; ch. (1). L o u i s a S i b l e y, b. Nov. 2, 1835; (2). S o p h r o n i a N a s o n, b. Oct. 20, 1837; (3). S t e p h e n G e o r g e, b. Sept. 23, 1839; (4). J o h n E l d e n, b. Feb. 14, 1844; (5). E m i l y R i d e r, b. Aug. 23, 1847; d. Sept. 19, 1849; (6). M a r y E l l a, b. June 28, 1849. 8. *Jacob*, b. Oct. 27, 1815; r. Appleton; m., Oct. 4, 1847, Julia Ann,

lived, and entirely deprived him of reason several years before he d. of dysentery, Aug. 16, 1826.

b. Sept. 19, 1819, dr. of Alexander and Sarah (Barker) Pease, of Appleton, who d. Nov. 19, 1848; had (1). J u l i a A n n, b. Nov. 12, 1848. He m. second, Nov. 5, 1849, Charlotte, b. Feb. 6, 1826, dr. of Boice Crane, of Hope. 9. *Ebenezer Blunt*, b. Oct. 24, 1817; m., April 2 or 22, 1844, Melea Robbins, b. Jan. 6, 1826, dr. of Levi Butler, of Appleton, descendant of Phinehas B., of Thomaston; and had (1). L u c y A t l a n t a, b. Nov. 29, 1845; (2). F r a n k l i n E d s o n, b. May 2, 1847; (3). E l i z a b e t h F l o r i n a, b. Oct. 5, 1849. 10. *Abigail*, b. Jan. 18, 1820; r. South Boston, Mass.; m., Oct. 20, 1849, at Danielsonville, Conn., John Barclay Fanning, b. Aug. 13, 1820, in Boston, son of Edward and Caroline (Fanning) Barnard; has (1). C a r o l i n e M a t i l d a, b. May 20, 1851.

IV. William, b. Feb. 16, 1779; r. Freedom, Me.; m., March 4, 1805, Charlotte, of N. Yarmouth, now Cumberland, Me., b. July 13, 1783, dr. of Benjamin Buxton (b. in Falmouth, Feb. 28, 1748; d. March, 1810; originated from Danvers, Mass.); and his wife, Elizabeth Grant, b. at York, Me., June, 1749; d. Sept. 1841. They have 1. *Ann*, b. Jan. 20, 1806; m., Jan. 20, 1829, Edmund, b. Albion, Me., Oct. 3, 1804, son of Jonathan Fuller, b. at Newton, Mass., 1767, and his wife Hannah Bradstreet, b. at Rowley, Mass., Oct. 1, 1777; r. Freedom. They have (1). C h r i s t o p h e r C o l u m b u s, b. Nov. 28, 1829; (2). W i l l i a m S i b l e y, b. Dec. 17, 1832; (3). J u d i t h, b. April 28, 1837; (4). E d m u n d A l l e n, b. Nov. 21, 1839; (5). S e l d e n K i m b a l l, b. Jan. 14, 1842. 2. *Reuben*, b. Sept. 15, 1807, at Beaver Hill Plantation, now Freedom, Me.; merchant, Belfast, Me.; m., first, at Orono, Me., April 30, 1834, Margaret Sampson, dr. of John and Mary (Heywood) Read, b. at Fairfax, now Albion, Me., Oct. 12, 1812, d. Jan. 15, 1838. He m., second, at Portland, July 2, 1839, Hannah Cushing, dr. of Ammi and Hannah Cushing (Greeley) Cutter, b. at North Yarmouth, now Yarmouth, Me., Nov. 2, 1808; ch. b. in Belfast, (1). W i l l i a m, b. Aug. 24, 1835, d. Jan. 28, 1842; (2). J o h n R e a d, b. Aug. 21, 1837, d. July 28, 1850; (3). M a r g a r e t C u t t e r, b. June 8, 1840, d. Feb. 6, 1842; (4). H a n n a h E l i z a b e t h, b. March 10, 1842, d. Sept. 20, 1843; (5). E d w a r d, b. Sept. 5, 1843; (6). C h a r l o t t e, b. Aug. 15, 1845; (7). A m m i C u t t e r, b. Sept. 16, 1847; (8). E l i p h a l e t G r e e l e y, b. Nov. 14, 1849. 3. *Persis*, b. May 10, 1813; m., June 5, 1842, Charles, s. of Edward and Elizabeth (Nevans) Andrews, of Turner, afterwards of Dixfield, now of Paris, Me., b. at Paris, Me., Feb. 11, 1814, attorney at law, speaker of the Maine House of Representatives, clerk of the Courts of Oxford County, representative elect to Congress; and has (1). C h a r l o t t e B u x t o n, b. at Dixfield, July 15, 1843; (2). P e r s i s N e v a n s, b. April 13, 1847, at Paris, Me. 4. *William George*, b. May 25, 1815; m., Dec. 5, 1843, Nancy T., b. at Freedom, Me., May 9, 1823, dr. of Joseph and Sally (Davis) Russell; ch. (1). A l i c e T r u e, b. Aug. 30, 1844; (2) W i l l i a m, b. March 5, 1847; (3). J o h n L a n g d o n, b. March 31, 1849.

V. Stephen, trader, farmer, wool-grower, representative to the Legislature; b. Dec. 29, 1780; r. Hopkinton, N. H.; m., Dec. 31, 1809, Sarah, b. Nov. 26, 1780, dr. of Abraham Brown, b. at Salisbury,

SNELL, DAVID; wife's name Molly; came from Mass.; t. 1791; moved to Ohio, and d. Four of their children were

Mass., Oct. 28, 1747, and his wife, Sarah, dr. of Daniel French, of South Hampton, N. H.; ch. 1. *Abram Brown*, b. Feb. 22, 1811, d. of consumption, Dec. 21, 1834, at his father's; u. 2. *Nancy George*, b. April 25, 1813; m., Aug. 29, 1837, Charles Pinkney Gage, M.D., of Concord, N.H., son of John and Sally (Bickford) Gage, of Hopkinton, N.H., b. Sept. 1780; has (1). Charles Sibley, b. Dec. 30, 1843, at Concord; (2). Mary, b. at Hopkinton, N.H., April 18, 1847. 3. *John*, b. July 10, 1816; d. Aug. 23, 1824; palpitation and enlargement of the heart. 4. *Jacob*, b. Jan. 13, 1819; d. July 3, 1822. 5. *Philip Brown*, b. March 31, 1822; d. Aug. 11, 1825.

VI. Samuel, b. Dec. 12, 1782; r. Albion, Me.; m., Dec. 31, 1812, Charlotte, of Albion, b. Nov. 15, 1788, in Holden, Mass., dr. of Josiah Broad, b. in Holden, December, 1745, and his w. Lydia Wilder, b. in Lancaster, Mass.; and has 1. *Sarah Brown*, b. Nov. 24, 1813. 2. *Eliza*, b. Jan. 18, 1816; r. Manchester, N.H. 3. *Charlotte*, b. Sept. 22, 1817; m., Nov. 30, 1845, Francis, b. Albion, s. of Phinehas and Betsey Shorey; ch. (1). Catharine Almira, b. Sept. 23, 1846; (2). Charles Frank, b. Sept. 13, 1849. 4. *Catharine*, b. May 27, 1820; m., Jan. 19, 1845, Thomas Sprague, s. of William and Jane Stratton; r. Lawrence, Mass.; and has (1). Alton Marshall, b. Albion, Nov. 20, 1845; (2). Emma Jane, b. Lawrence, Oct. 31, 1848, d. Oct. 1, 1849. 5. *Margaret*, b. March 26, 1822; m., Sept. 27, 1846, John, s. of John and Susan Stinson, b. Nov. 16, 1820, at Clinton; ch. (1). Maria Bradstreet, b. April 2, 1849. 6. *Mary*, b. April 5, 1824; scalded, and d. Feb. 22, 1826. 7. *Kneeland*, b. March 31, 1826; r. Dedham, Mass. 8. *Manley*, b. Aug. 29, 1828; r. Albion. 9. *George*, b. Oct. 11, 1831; d. of measles, July 22, 1832.

VII. Amos, b. Jan. 31, 1785; settled on the homestead, and d. Aug. 20, 1839. It is a remarkable fact, that his is the only death among ten brothers and sisters during a period of more than sixty-four years. Dec. 26, 1814, he m. Dolley, b. Sept. 13, 1788, dr. of Obadiah Hadley, whose parents were Samuel Hadley, of Goffstown, and his w., Fanny, dr. of Winthrop Getchell, of Peterborough, N.H. They had 1. *Clerrinda Jewett*, b. Sept. 29, 1815; r. on the Old Sibley Place, in Hopkinton, N. H.; m., April 3, 1836, James, b. Nov. 12, at Henniker, N. H., s. of James and Hannah (Gould) Hoyt. 2. *Nancy Bean*, b. Jan. 16, 1826; m., Feb. 19, 1843, Franklin, r. Franklin, N. H., trunk and harness maker, s. of March Barber, of Canaan; ch. (1). Charles Frank, b. May 21, 1844, at Thetford, Vt., d. Feb. 17, 1845, at Franklin, N.H.; (2). Frank March, b. Franklin, July 10, 1846; (3). Ella Clerrinda, b. Sept. 22, 1849. 3. *Sarah Brown*, b. May 3, 1830; m., Oct. 1, 1848, George Washington Beard; r. Athol, Mass.

VIII. Moses, b. March 29, 1787; d. of nervous headache, Feb. 24, 1788.

IX. Betsey, or Elizabeth, b. Feb. 11, 1789; m., Oct. 3, 1815, Isaac, b. July 20, 1784, s. of Elijah and Peggy (Patterson) Rice, of Henniker, N. H.; has 1. *Hiram*, b. Nov. 9, 1816; r. on the homestead; u. 2. *Elizabeth George*, b. June 7, 1819; m., Feb. 8, 1843, Rev. Isaac Dalton Stewart, of Meredith Bridge, N. H., who was b. at Warner,

deaf and dumb. — I. *David*, b. April 26, 1784; m. Peggy Cook, of Friendship; and had 1. *Mary Ann*, b. Feb. 4, 1810. 2. *William*, b. Oct. 20, 1815; and probably others. — II. *Molly*, b. Jan. 27, 1787. — III. *Shadrach*, b. March 2, 1789; m., first, Cecilia, commonly called Celia, Dyer, March 30, 1823; and, second, Hannah Walker, 1835; r. Washington; ch. by last marriage, perhaps as follows: 1. *Shadrach*, b. May 5, 1836. 2. *Hannah Booth*, b. July 17, 1838. 3. *Daniel Walker*, b. Nov. 19, 1840; d. Jan. 7,

Dec. 23, 1817, s. of Capt. John Stewart; has (1). M a r i n d a F r a n c e s, b. July 6, 1845.

X. *Anne*, or *Nancy*, b. April 7, 1791; m., Oct. 26, 1819, Daniel, of Warner, N. H., a widower, b. Feb. 10, 1774, s. of Nathaniel Bean, of Exeter, N. H.; has 1. *Stephen Sibley*, b. Oct. 26, 1820; m., Aug. 31, 1845, Nancy Elizabeth, b. July 14, 1824, dr. of Philip and Sarah (Colby) Colby; r. Warner; c. 2. *Dolphus Skinner*, r. Warner; b. Feb. 26, 1824; m., Aug. 27, 1846, Mahala Cordelia, b. May 4, 1829, dr. of Waterman and Molly (Sargent) Flanders. She d. Dec. 2, 1847; c. He m., Nov. 7, 1850, Annie Robinson, b. Aug. 2, 1829, dr. of Thomas and Anna (Cressey) Eaton, of Hopkinton, N. H. 3. *Nancy Ann*, b. Oct. 25, 1829; m., Nov. 1, 1849, Nehemiah George, b. Warner, Nov. 10, 1828, s. of Nehemiah and Mary (Flanders) Ordway.

XI. *Polly*, b. July 30, 1794; m., March 26, 1820, Timothy, r. Warner, b. Jan. 29, 1790, Hopkinton, N. H. (s. of Simeon, s. of Enoch Eastman, proprietors' clerk, of Hopkinton, N.H.). They have 1. *Laura*, b. Hopkinton, March 20, 1821. 2. *George Sibley*, b. April 16, 1823, Warner, N.H.; r. Stoneham, Mass.; m., June 6, 1850, Mary Jane Buttman, of Stoneham. 3. *Mary*, b. June 3, 1827. 4. *Walter Scott*, b. Sept. 2, 1829. 5. *Timothy Brewster*, b. Jan. 17, 1832. 6. *Elisabeth Ann*, b. May 25, 1833. 7. *Eleanor*, b. Dec. 24, 1839.

Thus it appears that Jonathan and Jacob, who settled in Union, were sons of Jacob, b. May $\frac{18}{29}$, 1746, the son of Jonathan, b. Nov. 25, 1701, the son of Samuel, b. in Salem, Mass., 10 : 1 : 1658, the son of Richard. Richard probably was born in England, and may have been the son of John, of Charlestown, Mass., and have come with him in the Winthrop fleet.

It may be added that there is a remarkable similarity of appearance in the different branches of the family, though separated by several generations. Some years since, George Littlefield, of Meredith Bridge, N. H., whose features and movements were as like those of the late Amos, of Hopkinton, as if they were brothers, was followed a long distance in Washington-street, Boston, by a gentleman who mistook him for Jonas, of Sutton, Mass., the late U. S. marshal. These three individuals belonged to three branches which had been diverging from each other one hundred and fifty years or more.

In relation to the Sibleys who lived in Salem and the vicinity, most of the information and the arrangement have been furnished by George Dean Phippen, Esq., an enthusiastic and laborious genealogist and antiquarian, whose grandmother was one of the family.

1842. 4. *Frances Ann*, b. Feb. 20, 1845. 5. *Lydia.* 6. *Adeline.* — IV. Sally, b. June 30, 1791. — V. Amos, b. Dec. 14, 1793; deaf and dumb; d. on his way to Ohio. — VI. Appleton, b. Feb. 19, 1796. — VII. and VIII. Isaiah and Isaac, twins, b. April 22, 1798; one deaf and dumb. — IX. Lucy, b. Feb. 24, 1801. — X. Lydia, b. Jan. 15, 1804, deaf and dumb. — XI. John Broadhead, b. Nov. 3, 1805. — XII. Sena, b. March 25, 1808, deaf and dumb.

STEWART, HOLMES, seaman; settled adjoining to his brother Timothy; t. 1791; came with his brother; was lost at sea from a bowsprit in the winter of 1798-9; u.

STEWART, TIMOTHY, surveyor, b. Aug. 27, 1770, at Edgarton; d. March 29 [gravestone], 30 [town-record], 1844; t. 1791, and probably came earlier. He m., first, Jan. 26, 1792, Jedidah Pease, of Chappequiddick, who was b. June 3, 1768, and d. of consumption, May 12 [or, according to graveston, 19], 1815. He m., second, Oct. 1, 1818, Abigail Daggett, who was b. at Vinalhaven, Oct. 24, 1785. — I. Levina, b. Feb. 16 or 8, 1793; m., Dec. 31, 1815, John Coffin Ripley, of Appleton. — II. Anna, b. April 23, 1795; m. Timothy Weymouth, of Appleton. — III. Leonard, b. Aug. 2, 1797; d. a prisoner of war, on Melville's Island, August, 1814 (?). — IV. Hannah, b. Aug. 19, 1799; m., July 10, 1818, Ansel Snow. — V. Lovey, b. Feb. 22, 1802; m. Richard Harwood, of Hope. — VI. John Homes, b. Oct. 10 or 8, 1804; m., Oct. 28, 1830, Olive C. Fairbanks. — VII. William Dougherty, b. June 5 or 4, 1807; m., April 4, 1833, Maria Bills; ch. 1. *Harriet*, b. Aug. 24, 1834. 2. *Sarah*, b. Aug. 24, 1837. 3. *Cyrus Gail*, b. April 30, 1840. 4. *William Marrill*, b. May 30, 1843. — VIII. Thomas Martin, b. Oct. 10, 1810; m. a Butler, of Edgarton; r. Milwaukie, Wisc. — IX. Oren Oxford, b. Sept. 9, 1819; m., April 11, 1847, Mary Ann, dr. of John P. Robbins.

STONE, ALLEN, pump-maker; wife's name Hannah; t. 1797; d. several years ago, and his w. Nov. 8, 1821; had I. Millicent, b. May 13, 1798. — II. Sally, b. Oct. 28, 1800; and probably others.

STONE, WALDRON (s. of Eben), whose w. was Rachel Campbell, of Townsend, Mass.; came from Townsend, a surveyor and blacksmith, and settled in the north-west part of the town, on the farm now owned by John Adams; t. 1794, though probably not a resident before 1796; and d. 1799.

His ch., all born in Ashby and Townsend, — I. Sally, m. Oliver Wetherbee; r. Bath, N. H. — II. Polly, m. William Parks; r. Union, and now Skowhegan; had 1. *William H.*, b. at Townsend, Sept. 7, 1796; d. May 6, 1803. 2. *Waldron Stone*, b. Oct. 14, 1802; m. and r. Skowhegan. 3. *Matilda*, b. Nov. 1, 1806; m. John Plummer; r. Skowhegan. 4. *George*, b. Jan. 11, 1809; m. Ann Lamb; r. Skowhegan. 5. *John*, while a minor, d. of brain-fever. 6. *Charles*, m. Rachel Glass; r. Monmouth. There is an obscurity; perhaps *William*, b. after the death of William H., m. Betsey Harriman; r. on the Penobscot. — III. Daniel, m., and r. Syracuse, N.Y. — IV. Jonas; m., and r. Milwaukie. — V. Eben; went to Virginia with Capt. David Grafton, became unwell, and d. in Boston on his way home. — VI. John; lost at sea; u. — VII. Samuel, b. Dec. 14, 1787; m., 1818, Elizabeth, or Eliza, dr. of Thomas Mitchell; had 1. *Abigail*, b. July 12, 1819; d. July 26, 1819. 2. *Rachel Carriel*, b. Sept. 17, 1820; m., Nov. 1, 1840, John, son of Peter Adams, who was b. Jan. 22, 1819; and had (1). T h o m a s M i t c h e l l, b. Sept. 25, 1841; (2). F r a n c i s M a r i o n, b. Aug. 26, 1844; (3). S a m u e l, b. November, 1847. 3. *Mary Mitchell*, b. Feb. 12, 1823; m., 1846, Nathan Knowlton; and had (1). L e o n o r a, b. Sept. 27, 1848. 4. *Rufus*, b. Feb. 10, 1826; r. homestead. 5. *Nancy A.*, b. Oct. 11, 1828; m., 1847, Thomas Johnson Blunt. 6. *Elmira Adams*, b. Aug. 21, 1832. 7. *Samuel*, b. April 28, 1836. 8. *Roscoe*, b. Nov. 4, 1838. 9. *Augusta*, b. June 10, 1841. 10. *James Henry*, b. Aug. 23, 1844; d. Feb. 23, 1850. — VIII. Betsey, m., June, 1809, Peter Adams, and d. in Gardiner. — IX. Nancy, m., first, Feb. 12, 1824, Joseph Greeley; and, second, Sept. 20, 1827, Peter Adams; r. Skowhegan.

THOMPSON, JAMES, t. 1797, but not a poll-tax till 1798; m., 1804, Lucretia Brown, and d. March 22, 1825; ch. — I. Hannah Walker, b. Aug. 31, 1805. — II. James B., b. March 7, 1807. — III. Marlborough M., b. Aug. 1, 1808. — IV. Isaac, b. April 22, 1810; d. August, 1811. — V. Charles, b. Nov. 23, 1811. — VI. Milton, b. Oct. 3, 1813; m. Amanda, and had *Elmira*, b. Oct. 9, 1836. — VII. Isaac, b. Feb. 23, 1815. — VIII. Seldom, b. June 29, 1816; d. Sept. 3, 1816. — IX. Anna Booth, b. July 29, 1817. — X. Fanny Walker, b. Nov. 26, 1819; and others.

THOMPSON, STORY, b. in Bristol; t. 1795; m. Deborah, dr. of Erastus and Betsey (Doty) Sherman, who d. 1837, æt. sixty-five; ch. — I. *John*, b. in Bristol, Oct. 8, 1792; m. widow Martha, or Patty, Newbit, b. June 2, 1787, dr. of Ichabod and Mary Maddocks; and had 1. *Sarah*, b. May 25, 1815; m. Moses Luce. 2. *Story*, b. Jan. 24, 1817; m. Hannah, dr. of Nathaniel Maddocks, of Appleton. 3. *Huldah*, b. Sept. 21, 1819; m. Aurelius P. Lawrence. 4. *A son*, b. Feb. 22, 1822; d. March 2, 1822. - 5. *John*, b. July 20, 1823. 6. *Almond*, b. Aug. 31, 1825. 7. *Harriet*, b. March 22, 1828; d. Jan. 2, 1832. 8. *Ambrose*. — II. Story, b. in Bristol, Oct. 11, 1794; d. April 7, 1834. — III. Robert, b. Nov. 3, 1799; m. Elizabeth, dr. of John B. and Betsey (Richards) Coggan; and had 1. *Jedidah Mitchell*, b. March 26, 1829. 2. *Marius*, b. July 13, 1830; d. 3. *Marcellus*, b. Nov. 27, 1831. 4. *Ellen Augusta*, b. Feb. 15, 1833. 5. *Laura Elizabeth*, b. April 1, 1834. 6. *Harriet*, b. June 22, 1840. — IV. James, b. Nov. 6, 1802; m., 1829, Harriet, dr. of James Maxfield; and had 1. *Solomon*, b. March 10, 1830. 2. *Erastus Carter*, b. Feb. 9, 1832; d. Oct. 29, 1832. 3. *Erastus*, b. Sept. 5, 1834. 4. *Augustin*, b. Nov. 25, 1835. 5. *Lucy Ellen*, b. Feb. 15, 1839. 6. *Martha Jane*, b. Feb. 2, 1841. 7. *Lewis*, b. Sept. 30, 1842. — V. Lucy, b. Feb. 28, 1805; d. Dec. 1848. — VI. William, b. Dec. 7, 1807. — VII. Polly, or Mary, b. Oct. 17, 1810; m. William Coggan, 1828; and had 1. *Ethelda*, b. June 29, 1829. 2. *Emily Blake*, b. Dec. 15, 1833. 3. *Deborah Maria*, b. Aug. 19, 1836. 4. *Esther Francina*, b. Sept. 26, 1838. 5. *Alanson Marius*, b. Dec. 4, 1840.

TITUS, OLNEY, b. at Mansfield, Mass., June 11, 1772; m., Feb. 5, 1795, Abigail Gillmor, of Franklin, Mass.; came to Union, April, 1794; settled on the west side of the river, below Hills' Mills, and near Royal Grinnell's, on the farm on which some chopping had been previously done by the Daggetts. Descendants, — I. Joanna Gillmor, b. March 17, 1796; d. July 16, 1823; m., Sept. 4, 1813, Oliver Pratt, from Pittston, who d. May 27, 1825; ch. 1. *Abigail Titus*, b. Sept. 11, 1814; m. James Linniken; r. Boothbay. 2. *James*, b. Oct. 21, 1816; m. Martha Linniken; r. Rockland. 3. *Patience Alden*, b. May 18, 1819; m. Patrick Nolen; r. New Castle. 4. *Rebecca Eveline*, b. May 3, 1821; m. Alvan

Litchfield; r. Manchester, N. H. 5. *Luther*, b. June 12, 1823; d. March 4, 1824. Oliver Pratt, m., second, Nancy Robinson, Feb. 15, 1824; and had 6. *William L.*, b. Jan. 30, 1825; d. July 9, 1825. — II. Charles, b. April 8, 1798; m., first, Parmela, dr. of Simeon Butters, and, second, Oct. 18, 1840, Eleanor, dr. of John Newbit; r. Appleton; had 1. *A child*, d. Sept. 1818. 2. *Levi Cheever*, b. Oct. 22, 1820; m. 3. *Sophronia Caroline*, b. Aug. 8, 1822; m. George Shaw; r. Exeter. 4. *Joanna Pratt*, b. June 19, 1824; m. a Dodge. 5 and 6. Twins, b. Jan. 29, 1826, viz. *Julia Ann* and *Mary Ann*. 7. *Daniel Butters*, b. Jan. 1828; r. Exeter. 8. *Sarah Ethera*, b. Dec. 6, 1829. 9 and 10. Twins, b. March 31, 1832, viz. *Rhobe Melinda* and *Chloe Matilda*. 11. *Andrew J.*, b. April 6, 1834; and others by his second wife. — III. Rhobe, or Roby, Gillmor, b. April 21, 1801; m. Bradley R. Mowry, Jan. 24, 1819; and had 1. *Sarah Angeline*, b. Sept. 16, 1820; m. Charles A. Hawes, 1837. 2 and 3. Twins, b. Jan. 11, 1822, viz. *Laura Amelia*, m. Chauncy Himes; and *Chloe Matilda*, d. Oct. 31, 1843, m., June 15, 1842, Isaac Flitner, M.D., who was b. Sept. 28, 1809, at Pittston, and had (1). G e o r g i-a n a, b. April 1, 1843. [Dr. F. m., June 10, 1846, Clementine, dr. of Deacon Isaac Stanwood, of Ipswich, Mass.; and had (2). G e o r g e F r e d e r i c k, b. May 11, 1847.] 4. *Hansi Emeline*, b. April 28, 1824. 5. *Harriet Rhobe*, b. April 6, 1826. 6. *Ann Maria*, b. May 3, 1829. 7. *Augustus*, b. Sept. 8, 1831. 8 and 9. Twins, viz. *Irene* and *Oscarene*, b. Feb. 11, 1834. 10. *Mortimer H.*, b. July 11, 1836. 11. *Josephine*, b. July 9, 1841. — IV. Chloe, b. Aug. 27, 1803; m. Jabez Ware. — V. Weston, b. Feb. 8, 1808; m. Sarah Emerton; r. Waldoborough; ch. 1. *Anson Lorenzo*, b. Nov. 9, 1833; d. April 17, 1837. 2. *Charlotte Louisa*, b. Dec. 21, 1834; d. Feb. 1848. 3. *Laura Eveline*, b. March 28, 1835. 4. *Olney Weston*, b. Oct. 3, 1836. 5 and 6. Twins, viz. *Frances Helen* and *Lucy Ellen*. 7. *Lorenzo Miller*, b. Aug. 1840. 8. *Sarah Isabel*. 9. *A son*, d. two weeks old. 10. *Albert*. 11. *Caroline Augusta*, b. June, 1846; d. 1849. 12. *Zeruah Ferroline*. — VI. Melinda Reed, b. Aug. 17, 1810; m. Almond Messer; r. Montville. — VII. Horace, b., according to his own record, Sept. 8; his father's records, Sept. 9, and town-records, Sept. 10, 1812; m., Jan. 1, 1837, Ertheny Avery, of Topsham, Vt.; who was b. April 3, 1813; r. homestead; and has 1. *Horace Newell*, b. Oct. 27, 1838. 2. *Lura Ellen*, b. Aug. 25, 1840. 3. *Mary Matilda*, b. Aug. 15, 1848. — VIII. Lorenzo Miller, b. May 30, 1816; m.; r. Illinois.

TOBEY, JOHN, son of Samuel and Rebecca (Hatch) Tobey, b. at Falmouth, Mass., Nov. 5, 1768; came to Union in 1791; m., June 13, 1791, Mary, dr. of George and Mary (Chase) West, who was b. at Tisbury, Martha's Vineyard, Dec. 11, 1772, and d. Aug. 27, 1832. He m., July 5, 1835, the widow Melicent Wingate, b. at Hancock, N. H., Aug. 17, 1796, dr. of Thomas Jones, an Englishman. He has been a sea-captain more than sixty years, but for some time has lived on his farm, full of activity and hilarity, though afflicted with very great deafness. He had — I. Rebecca, b. Jan. 17, 1793; m., Nov. 1810, Calvin Chase, from Warwick, Mass., a storekeeper in Union; and had 1. *Mary*, b. Sept 27, 1811; m. a Martin; r. Hallowell. 2. *William Witt*, b. Aug. 22, 1813. 3. *Almeda*, d. at Mirimachi, where they moved and where C. C. also died. She m., second, Thomas, brother of her first husband; r. Warwick, Mass.; by whom are *Emily*, *Elvira*, *Almira G.*, *Edward*, and *Martha*. — II. Polly, alias Mary, b. Jan. 16, 1795; d. at Gardiner, Nov. 5, 1831; m. John Palmer, and had 1. *Gilman*, m. Mary Brown, of Salisbury, N. H.; r. Lancaster, Mass. 2. *John*, d. young. 3. *Nathaniel Tobey*, M.D., b. Feb. 27, 1817; r. Brunswick; m., Nov. 27, 1844, Mary Merritt, second dr. of Capt. William Curtis, of Brunswick, b. May 8, 1812. 4. *Mary*, m. Rd. Webster, of New Vineyard, Me.; r. Hampton, Ill. 5. *Eliza Jane*, m. a Webster; r. Hampton, Ill. 6. *Augustus*, m. Mary Sanford; r. Bath. 7. *Dudley*. 8. *Harriet*; r. Thomaston. — III. Nathaniel, b. July 21, 1796; m. Hannah Miller, March 5, 1820; r. Jefferson. — IV. Love, b. July 26, 1798; m., April 24, 1831, Seth Miller; and d. Nov. 28, 1838; c. — V. Eliza, b. May 3, 1800; m., Nov. 13, 1818, John Stevens; and d. June 5, 1837. — VI. Jane West, b. May 25, 1802; m. Stephen Carriel, in 1827. — VII. Lydia, b. April 26, 1804; d. Feb. 12, 1835; u. — VIII. John, b. March 8, 1806; d. of consumption, April 8, 1828. — IX. Edward, b. Feb. 19, 1808; m. Eliza Gilchrist; r. Montville. — X. Caroline, b. June 30, 1810; d. July 3, 1810. — XI. Harriet, b. July 8, 1811; m. Dec. 22, 1833, William C. Jackson. — XII. Caroline, b. July 10, 1813; m., 1835, Leander Martin; r. Jefferson. — XIII. Leander, b. Sept. 17, 1815; m. Harriet Bagley; r. Montville; c.

WALCOTT, PENTY, PENTE, or PENTECOST; t. 1797; from Attleborough; died March 4, 1844 (son of Pentecost); m., first, 1801, Elizabeth Matthews, from Warren; and, second, 1840, Eliza Standish, who afterwards m. Benjamin Clark, and d. in Union, August, 1850; ch. — I. Elizabeth, b. May 3, 1805; m. Parker Messer. — II. Hannah, b. Jan. 27, 1802; m. Elijah House, of Washington, in 1832 (?). — III. Katherine, b. Sept. 21, 1809; m., 1830, Cornelius Spear, of Warren; r. Searsmont. — IV. Robert, b. April 9, 1813; d. June 11, 1814. — V. Lydia, b. Sept. 21, 1809; m., Dec. 5, 1830, Charles Hibbard. — VI. Mary, b. March 21, 1815.

WALCOTT, SPENCER, nephew of Penty, and son of Moses and Mary (?) (Blackington) Walcott; t. 1791; settled north of William Hart; b. at Attleborough, Mass., May, 1767; d. Sept. 22, 1826; m. Hannah, b. at Attleborough, Aug. 15, 1774, dr. of David Woodcock. She m., second, Dec. 2, 1830, widower Deacon Robert Thompson, who d. in Hope, 1849. Descendants, — I. Sarah, b. June 30, 1792; d. Oct. 7, 1836, in Searsmont; m., March 18, 1813, Sylvanus Hemenway; and left *Cyrus Thomas, Bickford Nelson, Alzina Walcott, Avis Walcott, Gustavus Adolphus, Rebecca Matthews, Anson Bartlett, Gardner Ludwig.* — II. Fanny, b. Aug. 6, 1795; m., March 16, 1818, John, s. of George Bowes, of Washington, a farmer and weaver from England, or perhaps from the Isle of Man; and had *Spencer George*, whose w. was Louisa; *Norris Piper*, d.; *Joseph Henry; John; Hannah; Elizabeth*, d. Feb. 1847; *Mary Ann; Moses Walcott; Avis Hills.* — III. Rebecca, b. March 23, 1797; m., 1819, Morrill Matthews, of Searsmont; and had *Albert Dillingham, Noah Morrill, Daniel, Spencer Walcott, Sanford Hills, Adolphus, Avis Hills, James Bowdoin.* — IV. Avis, b. Sept. 3, 1799; m., first, Sanford Hills, and, second, Geo. Cummings. — V. Vyna, b. July 19, 1801; m., July 9, 1823, Bickford C. Matthews, of Searsmont; and had *Jane Bishop, Hannah Mary, Lois Manning, Anastasia Rebecca, Noah Morrill, Sarah Frances.* — VI. Moses, b. Oct. 21 [or, according to town-record, Oct. 9], 1804; m., first, June 3, 1828, Mary Chase, dr. of Nathaniel Robbins; c.; r. Washington; and, second, m., early in 1850, Mary,

widow of Andrew Suchfort, and dr. of Isaac Witham. — VII.
Spencer, b. March 11, 1807; r. homestead; m., May 6, 1830,
Esther, b. in Littleton, Mass., April 18, 1807, dr. of Joseph
and Betsey (Pike) Dedman; and has 1. *Hannah*, b. Jan. 30,
1831. 2. *Loana Maria*, b. June 10, 1835. 3. *Mary Adams*,
b. May 6, 1837. 4. *Sanford Hills*, b. April 7, 1839. 5.
Joseph Dedman, b. April 20, 1841. 6. *Martha Clotilda*, b.
July 23, 1849. — VIII. Alzina, b. Nov. 15, 1808; m. Stephen S. Hawes. — IX. Manning, b. April 18, 1813; m., Sept.
12, 1837, Mary, dr. of Herman Hawes; and had 1. *Herman
Hawes*, b. Aug. 3, 1838. 2. *Edgar Hartley*, b. May 6, 1842.

WALKER, DANIEL, son of Asa and Sarah (Burbank)
Walker, b. at Ashby, March 18, 1774; came to Union in
1797; m., June 2 or 10, 1799, Fanny, dr. of Jacob and
Hannah (Jones) Booth, of Gloucester, R. I., b. Nov. 16,
1778, in Uxbridge, Mass; settled in the north-west part of
the town; ch. — I. Hannah, b. June 2, 1800; d. July 23,
1805. — II. Anna, b. Nov. 14, 1802; m. John Dyer. —
III. Fanny, b. Aug. 16, 1806; m. Sept. 4, 1828, Benjamin
Achorn; had ch. — IV. Hannah, b. Sept. 30, 1808; m.,
Nov. 15, 1835, Shadrach Snell. — V. Asa, b. Oct. 6, 1810;
m., 1832, Ruth Lermond, of Bremen; has ch. — VI. Daniel,
b. March 28, 1813; m. Lydia Prior, of Bremen; had ch.

JOHN WALKER, br. of Daniel, b. at Ashby, Mass., March
23, 1776; came to Union in 1798; m., Jan. 1, 1802, Sarah,
or Sally, Bowen; ch. — I. Nathan, b. Oct. 22, 1802; m.,
Nov. 13, 1841, Emeline Amanda Mills, of Natick, b. Sept.
19, 1807; r. Woodburn, Ill.; and has 1. *John Oscar*, b.
March 6, 1845; 2. *Charles Emmett*, b. Dec. 22, 1847. — II.
Julia, or Juliana, b. March 3, 1805; m. Godfrey Miller, Dec.
26, 1830, b. at Waldoborough, March 10, 1799; r. Washington; and had 1. *Nathan Walker*, b. Dec. 24, 1831. 2. *Everson Rider*, b. April 29, 1833. 3. *Helen Arethusa*, b. April
23, 1836. 4. *John Walker*, b. Oct. 4, 1838. 5. *Sarah Elizabeth*, b. May 20, 1841. 6. *Moses Donnel*, b. March 7, 1844.
7. *A child*, b. Nov. 29, 1846. — III. Mary, or Polly, b. Dec.
11, 1807; m., Jan. 30, 1848, Levi Butler. — IV. Esther
Bowen, b. June 5, 1810; d. Nov. 17, 1837; m., Sept. 11,
1834, Josiah Eley, in Nansemond County, Va., b. at Isle
of Wight County, Va., Oct. 22, 1798; and had *Sarah E. C.*,
b. Sept. 13, 1835. — V. Sarah, or Sally, Bowen, b. Sept.
27, 1813; m., Sept. 11, 1839, her sister Esther's husband;

c. — VI. John, b. April 29, 1817; u. — VII. Elizabeth, b. May 15, 1823.

WARE, JASON, b. at Franklin, Mass., March 10, 1756; d. May 11, 1843; m., first, Sept. 16, 1782, Polly, dr. of Stephen Peabody, from Saccarappa, then living in Warren, b. April 11, 1756, d. March 5, 1815; and, second, April 16, 1817, Sally Severance, b. April 21, 1770, d. April 3, 1849. His ch. were — I. Greenleaf, b. Aug. 22, 1783; d. Sept. 29, 1802. — II. Peggy, b. Dec. 9, 1784; m. Alford Butters, July 18, 1804, who moved to Ohio, and d.; ch. 1. *Rachel*, b. May, 1805; d. 1811. 2. *Alford*, b. May 11, 1807; r. Ohio. — III. Polly, b. July 8, 1787; m. Nathan, s. of Reuben Hills, July 9, 1807; and had 1. *Vinal*, b. July 27, 1808; m. Cordelia, dr. of John C. and Berintha Robbins; r. Northport. 2. *Isaac*, b. April 23, 1811; m. Eliza Hall, of Cushing; and had (1). L y s a n d e r, b. July 4, 1834; (2). S y l v a n u s, b. Nov. 26, 1836. 3. *Mary*, b. Oct. 3, 1813; d. March 10, 1814. 4. *Polly*, b. March 2, 1815; m., 1836, Nathaniel K. Burkett; and had (1). I s a a c H., b. Aug. 24, 1835; (2). O s c a r A., b. May 15, 1837; (3). M a r y A., b. March 27, 1840; (4). E l l e n M a t i l d a, b. April 5, 1842; and others. 5. *Nancy*, b. April 30, 1817; m. a Clary, of Jefferson. 6. *Nathan*, b. Sept. 26, 1820; m. Mary Severing, of Knox; and had (1). E s t e l l e, b. Nov. 23, 1844; (2). M a r j e t t, b. Dec. 31, 1846. 7. *Caroline*, b. July 11, 1823. 8. *Silas*, b. March 29, 1826. 9. *Lavinia*, b. April 21, 1828. 10. *Matilda*, b. April 18, 1831. — IV. Vinal, b. July 9, 1789; m., Nov. 3, 1825, Lavinia Anthony, dr. of Matthias Hawes; ch. 1. *Harriet Miranda*, b. April 1, 1833; 2. *Erastus*, b. Sept. 27, 1834. — V. Mela, b. Dec. 1, 1791; d. Dec. 3, 1791. — VI. Chloe, b. Nov. 5, 1793; m., Jan. 19, 1817, Isaac, s. of Reuben Hills; ch. 1. *Jason*, b. Dec. 12, 1817. 2. *Harriet*, b. Aug. 22, 1819. 3. *Cyrus*, b. June 7, 1823; d. Sept. 18 [or gravestone, 19], 1824. 4. *Rufus Philander*, b. July 21, 1825. 5. *Miranda*, b. June 22, 1828; d. Sept. 28, 1828. — VII. Susa, or Susanna, b. June 19, 1795; d. Jan. 2, 1796. — VIII. Jabez, b. July 3, 1798; m., April 24, 1823, Chloe Titus; r. Northport; and had 1. *Sarah Melinda*, b. Sept. 26, 1824; d. Oct. 19, 1848. 2. *Rhobe Ann*, b. May 26, 1826. 3. *Chloe Elvira*, b. June 26, 1828. 4. *Mary Miranda*, b. Aug. 26, 1830. 5. *Eliza Mansfield*, b. Feb. 9, 1833. 6. *Catharine Hatch*, b. Feb. 11, 1835. 7. *Jason*, b. Jan. 27, 1837. 8. *Eunice Augusta*, b. June 3, 1839; d.

June 11, 1839. 9. *Harriet Amelia*, b. June 23, 1840. 10. *Horace Lorenzo*, b. May 31, 1842. 11. *Jabez Gilbert*, b. July 10, 1844.

WEST, GEORGE, sea-captain, b. March 17, 1744; d. Sept. 4, 1800, from voluntary starvation;[1] m. Mary Chase, of Martha's Vineyard, b. June 11, 1749, d. May 17, 1802. During several of the last days of his life, he retained his senses, but was too feeble to speak, and conveyed his ideas by making signs. — I. Peter, sea-captain; m. Sarah Daggett; r. and d. Martha's Vineyard. — II. Peggy, m. Lot Luce, a sea-captain; r. and d. Martha's Vineyard. — III. Mary, b. Dec. 11, 1772; d. Aug. 27, 1832; m. John Tobey. — IV. Lovey, m. Nathaniel Robbins. — V. George Washington, m., Oct. 21, 1798, Hannah Fairbanks; moved to Ohio, and subsequently still further; had 1. *Charles*, b. May 9, 1801. 2. *Mary*, b. Sept. 9, 1803. 3. *Lovey*, b. July 22, 1806. 4. *Elvira*, b. April 5, 1809. 5. *Sarah*, b. May 7, 1812. 8. *George Washington*, b. Jan. 9, 1815. — VI. Thomas, m. Sally Spalding; r. Martha's Vineyard, and lately moved West. — VII. Jane, m. David Grafton, Dec. 31, 1804; and d. June 4, 1814, aged twenty-nine years four months; had 1. *George*, b. March 18, 1806. 2. *John*, b. June 29, 1807; m. Webb; r. Warren. 3. *David*, b. Oct. 2, 1808. 4. *Thomas West*, b. Sept. 3, 1810. 5. *Lydia*, b. Dec. 4, 1811. 6. *Peter West*, b. Jan. 2, 1813. 7. *Jane West*, b. Feb. 18, 1814.

WIGHT, JOHN M., b. Wrentham, now Foxborough, Mass.; m. Lavinia Morse, Jan. 20, 1793; was here in 1787. He was in the army, where it is said he was whipped. He taught school near the head of Tolman Pond, and it seems eloped with the wife of his landlord. The Thomaston town-records say, "Daniel, b. April 18, 1793. James Ware, b. Oct. 29, 1795. Henry M., b. March 15, 1798. And, on the sixth day of December, 1799, the above-named John M. Wight went away, and left his wife, his family, and this part of the country; and, after his departure, his wife bare twins, viz. Charles and Ormond, b. March 9, 1800."

WOODCOCK, DAVID, b. at Attleborough, Mass.; moved from Medway to Union; d. Dec. 9, 1790, in his forty-ninth year; lived on the mill-farm; m., Sept. 17, 1765, Abigail

---

[1] Widow Moody, aged sixty-two, died in the same way, April 11, 1809.

Holmes, who d. Sept. 25, 1823, aged eighty-four; and had — I. Benjamin, b. Oct. 16, 1766; d. Feb. 9, 1768. — II. David, b. Oct. 23, 1771; m. in the winter of 1794-5, Affa Peabody; and had 1. *Dexter Hatch*, b. Sept. 11, 1795. 2. *Nancy*, b. Oct. 29, 1796. 3. *David*, b. Aug. 26, 1798. 4. *Rufus*, b. Sept. 26, 1800. 5. *John*, b. Nov. 25, 1801; m., 1824, Lucy H. Tyler, of Leominster, Mass.; and had Jane Sophia, b. June 27, 1825; r. at the Eastward. 6. *Polly*, b. May 16, 1803; m. Benjamin Gowen. — III. Hannah, b. Aug. 15, 1774; m. Spencer Walcott. — IV. Lynday, b. Jan. 27, 1777; m., 1794-5, William Peabody; r. Eastward. — V. Nancy, b. March 23, 1779; m., Oct. 13, 1796, Samuel Tifft, of Thomaston, and moved to Attleborough. — VI. Theodore, b. Jan. 12, 1786; r. and d. Searsmont; m. Rebecca Packard.

WYMAN, JOHN, t. 1796; fiddler, carpenter; lived at the west part of the town; worked with Charles Barrett on locks and canals; moved East; fiddled for a company; complained of being unwell, lay down, and d. immediately.

GENERAL INDEX.

A.

Abbot, pages 253, 304, 319, 431, 499.
Abrams, Susman, a Jew, 74, 110, 127, 154, 492.
Achorn, 83, 85, 91, 308, 514.
Adams, 75, 76, 83, 90, 196, 223, 305, 307, 327, 490, 492.
Adams, Ebenezer Ward, 75, 202. Family of, 75, 88, 201, 430. In office, 122, 123, 127, 129, 254, 305, 306. Military notices of, 339, 378.
Adams, Eunice, teacher, 294.
Adams, Joel, Capt., 42, 51, 57, 69, 114, 152, 258, 259, 304, 338, 490. An early settler, 46. His marriage and family, 49, 64, 67, 75, 430. On committees, 60, 143-145, 164, 192, 195, 302-304. In office, 117-120, 123, 127. Methodist, 194-196. His petition to the legislature, 262. In the army, 328.
Adams, John and Peter, and others, 94, 118, 232, 250, 270, 305, 307, 308, 339, 377, 471, 473, 494, 508, 509.
Adams, Ward, and family, 83, 430.
Agassiz, Louis, Prof., 56.
Aglar, Nathaniel K., 78.
Aikin, 434.
Alden, Ebenezer, 74, 109, 111, 112, 114, 134, 154, 201, 226, 249. His family, 74, 82, 430. In office, 120, 128, 306. On committees, 195, 199, 233, 290. Coroner, 254. Postmaster, 255.
Alden, Ed., Dr., 82, 225, 322, 431.
Alden Lyman, 29, 225, 227, 308, 399. His family, 85, 431.
Alewives, 55, 420.

Alexander, Timothy, 96.
Alford, 76, 194, 195, 197.
Allen, 75, 177, 458, 462.
Ames, John, 495.
Amory, landowners, 42, 65, 143-145, 276, 431.
Anderson, and Anderson party, 27-31, 59, 105, 387, 390, 394.
André, John, 327.
Andrews, 81, 85, 307, 377, 433, 434, 470, 505.
Annapolis, Nova Scotia, 477.
Apples, 107.
Arnold, 92, 452, 453.
Aroostook War, 377.
Articles of Faith, 173.
Ashcraft, Nathan B., Rev., 219.
Assessors, 119.
Athearn, Rebecca, 444, 445.
Attleborough, Mass., 68, 69, 71, 451, 469, 516.
Audubon, J. J., 99.
Avery, 33, 511.
Ayer and Ayers, 220, 323, 364, 367, 483.

B.

Babb, George, 250.
Babbidge, Benjamin, 500.
Bachelder, Benjamin, and others, 92, 223, 323, 472.
Bachelder, Cyrus G., 117, 225, 226, 307, 342.
Bachelder, John, 75, 116, 223, 227, 306. Family of, 75, 92, 327, 447, 454. Town-clerk, 117. Military officer, 342, 351, 353. Court-martialled, 362.
Bachelder, Lewis, and family, 76, 96, 223, 225, 227, 280, 306, 479. Military officer, 338, 342. At the muster, 355, 361. Court-

GENERAL INDEX.

martialled, 364. Proposition to re-elect him, 373.
Bachelder, Nathan, 76, 223, 225, 226, 280, 290, 306-308, 341. Family of, 92. Selectman, 118. Justice, 254. Captain, 342, 374.
Bachelder, Nathaniel Q., 96, 327, 479.
Bachelor, Nathaniel, Capt., 43, 201, 223, 225, 226, 305, 306, His family, 75, 431, 479. Offices held by, 118, 280. On committees, 170, 198, 289, 304. Representative, 248, 249. Justice, 252.
Bachelor's Mills, 2, 11, 28, 288, 391, 467.
Bacon, William, 486.
Bagley, Harriet, 513.
Bailey, George, 249.
Baker, Joseph and Samuel, Rev., 219.
Balkam, Uriah, Rev., and family, 32, 215.
Ball, Daniel, 455.
Band, 326.
Banister, 320.
Bank-tax for schools, 311.
Baptists and societies, 194, 195, 197, 220.
Barber, 506.
Barbour, Elizabeth, 476.
Barker, 84, 86, 308, 457, 483, 505.
Barley, 105.
Barnard, 75, 88, 120, 197, 226, 280, 307, 308, 328, 442, 476, 493, 505.
Barns, built, 39, 41. Burnt, 43.
Barrett, 74, 92, 113, 317, 320, 461, 517.
Barrett, Amos, Capt., 19, 129, 154, 201, 237, 303. On committees, 150, 163, 164, 166, 167, 169, 170, 195, 303. In Concord battle, 328. Family of, 431. His houses burnt, 447.
Barrett's Pond, 3.
Barrett's Town, 68, 113, 276, 488.
Barter, George, 445.
Bartlett, 74, 120, 304, 306, 435, 439, 463, 485, 488, 489, 499, 504.

Barton, 500.
Bates, Nancy, 471.
Baum, Col., 449.
Baxter, F. W., Rev., 226, 305.
Bayley, Kiah, Rev., 172, 178, 182, 191.
Beals, Samuel, 456.
Bean, 225, 485, 502, 507.
Beard, 506.
Bears hunted and killed, 36, 395, 502.
Beauchamp, John, 22.
Beavers, 411.
Becket, 110, 249, 253.
Bees, 418.
Belden, Jonathan, Rev., 189, 208.
Belknap, John, 389.
Bell, the, 135, 226.
Bemis, 74, 96.
Benner, 349, 442.
Bennet, 154, 201, 324, 486, 489.
Bernard, Isaac, Dr., 294, 321.
Beveridge, 81, 256, 454, 456.
Bewitched horse, 228.
Bickford, Sally, 506.
Bigelow, Asaph, 455.
Biguyduce, 47, 71, 258, 334.
Billings, Caleb O., 441.
Bills, 75, 96, 127, 349, 438, 508.
Bird, Nancy, or Agnes, 467.
Bishop, 436, 497.
Blackbirds, 416.
Black land, 98, 391.
Blackington, 79, 122, 306, 513.
Blacksmithing, early, 43, 56, 58, 464.
Blake, 462, 468, 482.
Blake, Nathan, 113, 467. Offices held by, 118, 252. Motions made by, 165, 166, 169. On committees, 167-170, 192, 195, 290, 302-304. His complaint against Hills, 181. His family, 432.
Blake, Walter, and family, 75, 86, 127, 128, 249, 292, 305, 307. On committees, 132, 156, 164, 198. Justice, 253.
Blanchard, 192, 339, 433.
Blood, 95, 465, 470, 486, 493.
Blunt, Ebenezer, in office, 63, 119, 121, 122, 124, 306. His family, 76, 87, 133, 433.

GENERAL INDEX.

Blunt, Henry, and family, 76, 223, 249, 250, 305, 433. Assessor, 120, 121. On committees, 133, 198, 292, 304.
Boating, 277.
Boggs, 14, 35, 452, 459, 470.
Boggs, Calvin, and family, 80, 128, 308.
Boggs, Life W., 76, 339, 380.
Boggs, Samuel, 25, 386, 390, 411. Escapes from Indians, 26.
Boggs, William, 76, 120, 127, 140, 195.
Boggs's Landing, 30.
Boody, Benjamin and Ann, 471.
Books used in schools, 295, 309.
Boomer, J. B., Rev., and Nancy M., 471.
Booth, 76, 196, 449, 458.
Bosworth, 146, 494.
Boundaries, 1, 62. French and English, 22.
Bowen, Ezra, and others, 42, 64, 75, 117, 130, 143, 194, 195, 197, 258, 259, 317, 434.
Bowen, Isaac, Dr., and family, 318, 322, 434.
Bowes, 127, 317, 513.
Bowker, S., Rev., and family, 82, 128, 216, 251, 305.
Bowker Brook, 3, 37, 401.
Bowley, 134, 454, 467.
Bowman, Lydia, 473.
Boyd, 482.
Boyden, Justus, 434.
Boynton, William, 451.
Brackett, 94, 322.
Bradbury, J. W., Hon., 320.
Bradford genealogy, 477.
Bradstreet, 476, 505.
Brass band, 326.
Bray, S., Rev., 219, 474.
Brazier, Susan, 487.
Breck, 76, 444, 475.
Brett, Pliny, Rev., 219.
Brick, 330, 459.
Bride's dowry, 53, 503.
Bridges, 40, 61, 287.
Briggs, 79, 177, 219, 458, 489.
Bristol, 58, 433, 434, 469.
Britton, James B., Rev., 316.
Broad, 506.
Brown, 75, 76, 83, 90, 94, 95, 127, 196, 226, 252, 325, 364, 442, 460, 484, 505, 509.
Brown, John, Dr., 323, 460.
Brown, John Carter, library of, 2.
Brown, Jonathan, and family, 347, 434.
Browning, Charles L., Rev., 220.
Bruce, Abigail, 94.
Bryant, 76, 94, 133, 280, 306, 440, 474.
Bryant, Benjamin, Rev., and family, 96, 220.
Bryant, Joseph, and family, 76, 91, 307, 504.
Bulfinch, John, 252, 304, 319.
Bullen, 74, 223.
Bump, 77, 196, 250, 306, 314, 487.
Bunker Hill battle, 33, 328, 333.
Bunting, 140, 236, 304, 347.
Burbank, Sarah, 514.
Burgess, Peter, Rev., 220. Family of, 434.
Burgoyne's surrender, 42, 43, 329.
Burials, 135.
Burkett, 75, 83, 84, 112, 226, 327, 515.
Burns, 76, 90, 91, 94, 226, 251, 307, 442, 444, 469, 479, 487.
Burroughs, 82.
Burton, 85, 251, 483.
Burton, Benjamin, Col., 38, 41, 335.
Burying-grounds, 18, 19, 130.
Butler, 75, 79, 80, 86, 90, 127, 474, 508.
Butler, Christopher, 67, 145, 146, 148, 151, 152, 164, 291. In office, 119, 126, 127, 129. Methodist, 194, 196. His family, 435.
Butler, E. N., family of, 90.
Butler, George W., and family, 86, 127, 437.
Butler, Gorham, and family, 74, 79, 194, 196, 435.
Butler, Gorham, and family, 78, 432, 435, 447.
Butler, Jedidah, 444.
Butler, Jeruel, 87, 280, 438.
Butler, John, 30, 144, 258, 259, 288, 289, 419. With Dr. Taylor, 30, 32, 34. His marriage and family, 43, 64, 436. In

GENERAL INDEX.

office, 125, 126, 129. Hunter, 397.
Butler, John, 74, 194, 196, 217, 306. His family, 74, 79, 435.
Butler, John, 75, 437.
Butler, John, family of, 78, 436.
Butler, Joseph, 126, 194, 196. Family of, 436.
Butler, Matthias, family of, 86.
Butler, Phinehas, 25, 39, 258, 259, 411, 425, 427. With Dr. Taylor, 30, 32, 34, 35. Kills a bear, 36. In the army, 41, 50, 329. Settles in town, 50. His wife and family, 50, 437.
Butler, Phinehas, and family, 75, 86, 127, 129, 306, 308, 437, 505.
Butler, Thomas, and family, 76, 87, 152, 194, 196, 438, 440.
Butler, Waldron S., and family, 87, 307, 438.
Butters, 120, 127, 192, 194, 196, 457, 511, 514.
Buttman, Mary Jane, 507.
Buxton, 321, 505.
Buzzell, 197, 488.

C.

Camden, 1, 20, 21, 55, 343.
Camp at South Union, 28, 31, 35, 387, 411.
Campbell, 364, 508.
Camp-meetings, 219.
Canals, 112.
Cannon, 347.
Canterbury, Wm. and Ruth, 497.
Carkin, Isaac, 194, 196.
Carriel, or Carroll, 90, 91, 94, 308, 433.
Carriel, Danford, family of, 91, 439.
Carriel, David, and family, 75, 201, 439.
Carriel, Jonathan, and family, 76, 127, 133, 169, 177, 201, 212, 302, 304, 439.
Carriel, Jonathan, 76, 91, 118, 201, 305, 439.
Carriel, Stephen, and family, 90, 280, 307, 440. Representative, 250.
Carrigain, Philip, Dr., 321.

Carrying-places, 391, 393.
Carting goods to Boston, 112.
Carver, Nathan, 194, 195, 197.
Case, 119, 162, 440.
Cashman, 3, 42, 164.
Castine, 334, 346. See Biguyduce.
Caswell, 445.
Caswell, Judson, and family, 76, 93, 307, 474.
Caswell, William, and family, 84, 94, 122, 128, 307, 473.
Cat-and-clay chimneys, 55.
Cattle, 140.
Cat-vaughan, or Catamount, 408.
Censuses, 73.
Cents and dollars, 264.
Chadwick, Emily, 444.
Chaffin, 194, 196, 469.
Chain on the North River, 328.
Champlain explores the Penobscot, 20.
Chapman, 216, 327, 438, 495, 500.
Charles I., places named by, 2, 21.
Chase, 79, 111, 233, 347, 512, 516.
Cheney, Jonathan, Rev., 219.
Child and Childs, 197, 464.
Chimneys, 52, 55.
Churches organized, 172, 188.
Clark and Clarke, 76, 87, 129, 192, 194, 196, 197, 209, 433, 440, 460, 468, 490, 500.
Clark, Asa, and family, 441.
Clark, Benjamin, and family, 94, 513.
Clark, Nathan, and family, 95.
Clark, Nathaniel, family of, 92, 504.
Clark, Walter W., family of, 93, 308.
Clary, 88, 466, 515.
Cleaveland, 458.
Clough, Jeremiah, 194.
Clouse, 84, 443.
Cloyce and Cloyes, 455, 475.
Cobb, 76, 83, 127, 481.
Cobb, Ebenezer, 75, 116, 139, 223, 225, 226, 306, 307, 453. Family of, 75, 82, 83, 452. In office, 124, 126. Builds a town-house, 141, 142. Licensed, 230. Justice, 253. Lieutenant, 342, 371, 372.

GENERAL INDEX.

Cochran, Thomas, Rev., 170.
Coffin, Uriah, 146, 441.
Coggan, William, and others, 76, 92, 119-121, 307, 308, 333, 445, 510.
Coggswell, 491.
Colby, 438, 507.
Cole, 90, 308, 367, 456, 478.
Collamore, 75, 93, 194, 196, 440, 442, 458.
Collectors, 123.
College-graduates, 163, 167-170, 318, 471, 479.
Collier, 93, 482.
Collins, 82, 135, 430, 437, 456.
Collins, Zuinglius, and family, 82, 117, 227, 447, 454.
Colored persons, 96, 272, 484, 485.
Comet, Wm. Dické and the, 26.
Comings. See Cummings.
Commissioners, highway, 280.
Common, the, 1, 19, 136.
Concord and Lexington battle, 33, 34, 328, 331, 332.
Congress, votes for members of, 239.
Conklin, 465, 481.
Constables, 121.
Consumption, remedy for, 17.
Cony, Daniel, 363.
Cook, Dr., 323. Peggy, 507.
Coolidge, Abraham, 330.
Coombs, 56, 88, 92.
Cooper, Sally, 76, 80.
Copeland, 469, 481.
Copp, Susan, 441.
Copperas, 97.
Corduroy roads, 277.
Coroners, 254.
Cotterell, 479.
Councils, 177, 181, 205, 215, 216.
Court-martials, 362, 364, 366, 375, 378.
Covenant, 175.
Cox, 91, 220, 449.
Crabtree, 90, 461.
Craft, Samuel, and family, 472.
Cranberry Island, 330, 494.
Crane, 470, 505.
Crawford, 6, 28, 445.
Crawford's Meadow, and Pond and River, 3, 4, 6, 19, 334, 335, 416, 424.

Creed, 173.
Cressey, Anna, 507.
Croad, 501.
Crockett, 2, 4, 5, 96, 489.
Cromett, or Crommett, 83, 91, 121, 490.
Crooks, 455.
Crosby, John and Polly, 499.
Crowell, 82, 85, 453.
Crows, 416.
Croxford, Lydia, 452.
Cummings, David, 54, 152, 223, 306. Takes bread, 54. Family of, 75, 96, 441.
Cummings, George, and family, 95, 223, 225, 226, 253, 307, 441.
Cummings, Joseph G., and family, 96, 441.
Cummings, Richard, 38, 115, 152, 195, 258, 259, 347. Settler, 38. His grain burnt, 44. His family, 64, 69, 441. Tanner, 110. In office, 123, 126, 127. His dog, 388, 394. Hunts, 400.
Cummings, Samuel, family of, 83, 308, 441.
Cummings, Suell, and family, 75, 88, 307, 442.
Cunningham, 251, 442, 457.
Currier, Sarah, 464.
Curtis, 82, 88, 451, 466, 493, 512.
Cushman, 75, 88, 305, 443.
Cut-downs, burning of, 98.
Cutler, Manasseh, Rev., 170.
Cutler, Nelson, 83, 224-226. Family of, 83, 320. In office, 121, 122, 124, 280, 307. Licensed, 230. Representative, 250. Justice, 253, 254. Lawyer, 320. Captain, 377.
Cutter, 216, 505.
Cutting, Jane, 192, 209.

D.

Daggett, 50, 66, 176, 430, 433, 438, 482, 508, 510, 516.
Daggett, Aaron, and family, 66, 443.
Daggett, Brotherton, and family, 66, 76, 94, 111, 133, 444.
Daggett, Ebenezer, 158, 445.
Daggett, Ebenezer, and family, 75, 89, 96, 445.

GENERAL INDEX.

Daggett, Ebenezer, Mrs., 65. Her letter, 70. Her family, 470.
Daggett, Edmund, and family, 76, 327, 446.
Daggett, Elijah, Dr., and family, 443.
Daggett, John, of Attleborough, 69, 471.
Daggett, Jonathan, and family, 129, 444.
Daggett, Matthew, 443, 445.
Daggett, Mayhew and Chloe, of Attleborough, 470.
Daggett, Samuel, 75, 117, 120, 127, 133, 168, 169, 267, 303. His bewitched horse, 228. In the Jersey prison-ship, 329. His family, 444.
Daggett, Samuel, and family, 76, 95, 122, 133, 307, 445.
Daggett, Thomas, 66, 126, 144, 145, 152, 158, 162, 163, 166, 176, 445.
Daggett, Thomas, 66, 129, 194, 195, 197, 445.
Daggett, William, and family, 75, 209, 307, 444.
Dakin, Dr., 215.
Dam, Nancy Nelson, 462.
Daniels, F. A., and family, 80, 308, 447.
Daniels, Joseph, and family, 80, 308, 447.
Daniels, Milton, and family, 81, 225, 307. 447.
Daniels, Nathan, and family, 74, 80, 154, 201, 446. In office, 118, 120, 306, 307.
Daniels, Nathan, 29. Family of, 77, 78, 447.
Daniels Brook, 3.
Davis, 14, 79, 81, 82, 85, 93, 333, 387, 430, 453, 454, 462, 472, 488, 495, 505.
Davis, Isaac, Capt., of Acton, 328.
Davis, Jason, and family, 76, 80, 81, 227, 280, 306, 308, 470.
Davis, Mark, family of, 81, 447.
Davis, Pond, and family, 91, 308.
Davis, Sterling, and family, 76, 114, 120, 127, 194, 195, 447.
Davis, Sterling, and family, 80, 81, 307, 448.

Davis, Wilber, and family, 80, 307, 448.
Day, 74, 304-307, 432.
Dean, 79, 438, 450, 500, 501.
Dearborn, Henry, Gen., 73.
Death, Caleb and Abigail, 476.
Decker, Capt., 30.
Decoster, 88.
Dedman, 441, 514.
Deed of land to Taylor, 32.
Deer, 388, 389.
Delusions, 227.
Demerritt, Hannah, 437.
Demuth, 84, 475.
Devereux, Nathaniel, Rev., 219.
Dické, 6, 24, 26, 28, 59, 387.
Dickey, 75, 84, 90, 95, 113, 464.
Dike, 497, 498.
Dillingham, 465.
Dix, Sally, 476.
Dodge, 320, 511.
Dods, John Bovee, 75, 223, 304.
Doe, Samuel, 249.
Dogs and dogwhippers, 159, 387, 392, 394, 403, 411.
Dole, 34, 494.
Dollars and cents, 264.
Door [Dorr, or Duer?], 449.
Dorman, 86, 254, 433.
Doty, 485, 510.
Dougherty, William, Dr., and family, 201, 321, 469.
Douglas, Mass., 34, 48.
Douglass, Hannah, 491.
Dow, 77, 93. Rev. Mr., 171. Sarah, 502.
Dowry, bride's, 53, 503.
Dows, Joseph, 330.
Drake, Amos, and family, 78, 250, 453. In office, 126, 304, 305, 307.
Drake, Jesse, and family, 74, 82, 95, 196, 223, 306, 453, 493.
Drake, John, and others, 74, 82, 122, 123, 154, 194, 196, 223.
Drummond, Alexander, 364.
Drury and wife, 455.
Ducks, 413.
Dudley, Albion S., Rev., 224-226, 305.
Dunbar, 482, 483.
Dunham, 448.
Dunning, John A., 376.

GENERAL INDEX. 525

Dunster, Henry, President, 389.
Dunton, Chloe, Mrs., and family, 25, 39, 82, 414, 427, 452, 488, 489.
Durgin, Joseph, 81.
Dutton, Louisa, 491.
Dwinell, Andrus, 435.
Dyer, 127, 129, 141, 149, 159, 194, 196, 448, 507.

E.

Eagles, 421.
Eames, Anna, 455.
Eastman, 75, 84, 129, 154, 194, 196, 227, 307, 317, 464, 466, 471, 504, 507.
Eaton, 24, 507.
Ecclesiastical History, 161.
Eddy, Caroline, 430.
Educational History, 294.
Eels, 421.
Eley, Josiah, and family, 514.
Elkins, John, 499.
Elliott, Charles, 465.
Ellis, 177, 209, 446, 482.
Embargo, 232.
Emerson, Noah, Rev., 204, 207, 209.
Emerton, 511.
Emery, 320, 499.
Emmons, Nathaniel, Rev., 57, 190.
Erskensa, 434.
Esensa, 194, 196, 228, 449.
Estabrook, J. H., Dr., 323.
Esty, Reuben, 476.
Evans, Enoch B., 95.
Everett, Erastus D., and family, 471.
Everton, Zeph., 450.
Eves, Emily, 466.

F.

Factories, 109.
Fairbanks, 46, 79, 84, 325, 330, 450, 452, 474, 476, 508, 516.
Fairfield, Lois, 501.
Fales, 32, 37, 38, 42, 195, 197, 281, 451, 456, 459, 460, 479, 484, 487.
Fanning, 505.
Fargo, George W., Rev., 214.
Farley, Joseph, 407.
Farnham, Dudley, 87.
Faux, 455.

Felt, Joseph B., Rev., 496, 497.
Ferguson, Hannah, 433.
Fessenden, S. C., Rev., 216, 217.
Field, B. P., 319.
Filer, 88.
Finnegan, John, Rev., 219.
Fires in the woods, 99.
Fish, Susan, 458.
Fish Wardens, 129, 420. Laws, 418. Hawks, 421.
Fisher, Eliza, 434. Rev. Jabez P., 168. Nancy, 453. Mary, 459. Peter, 463.
Fiske, Jemima, 432.
Flagg, S. A., Rev., 220.
Flanders, 507.
Fletcher, 442, 465, 493.
Flies, annoying, 56.
Flint, 459, 497.
Flitner, Isaac, Dr., 83, 305, 322, 511.
Flucker, Thos., 28, 29, 33, 50, 61.
Fobes, Perez, Rev., 167, 169.
Fogler, John, 77, 154, 201, 223. Ann, 79. Mary, 192. Miranda, 483.
Fogler, Charles, and family, 54, 84, 227, 318, 439. In office, 121, 122, 307.
Follansbee, Leonard, 77, 306.
Follet, Susanna, 497.
Food, scarcity of, 44, 45, 54, 55, 67.
Foote, Col., 344.
Fossett, 16, 84, 93, 94, 122, 458, 495.
Fossett, Henry, 16, 76, 93, 133, 223, 305, 306.
Fossetts' Mills, 3, 111, 256, 469.
Foster, Edward, loyalist, 333.
Foster, Robert, 77, 111, 154, 201, 231, 237, 248, 249, 304, 305, 333, 345.
Foster, Robert N., 317.
Fourth-of-July celebrations, 236.
Fox, Mary Esther Jane, 461.
Foxes, 408.
Fox Islands, named by Pring, 20. Abandoned, 47, 487.
Framingham, Mass., 109, 320, 321, 456.
Franklin, Mass., settlers from, 41, 46, 50, 54, 430, 453, 460, 486.

45

GENERAL INDEX.

Frary, Jeanette Kingsley, 461.
Frazer, 501.
French, James, 320. Polly, 502. Polly, 503. Daniel and Sarah, 506.
French war expected, 336.
Freshets, 9.
Frogs, 12.
Fruit, 107.
Frye, Benj., and family, 93.
Fuller, 220, 221, 470. Albert, and family, 89. Amelia, 84. Edmund, and family, 505. Esther, 470. Henry D., and family, 80. Isaac, 308, 441. James, and Givens, 442. John, 339, 378. Jonathan, 505. Rhoda, 91. Rosanna, 87. Samuel, and family, 76, 91. Samuel C., 308. Sarah, 469. Simon, 76, 127, 193, 306. Susannah, 433.
Funerals, 130, 135, 231.
Furbush, Keziah, 474.

G.

Gage, 506.
Gallop, 78, 253, 435.
Gannett, Benj. and Deborah, 478.
Gardiner, Robert H., 424.
Gardner, 76, 80, 305, 306, 447.
Gary, George, Rev., 219.
Gay, 459, 460, 477. Abiel and family, 74, 135, 223, 306, 451. David, 74, 436. Elijah, 74, 223, 451. Elizabeth, 85. James, in the army, 347, 451. John C., and others, 82. Jonah, and family, 65, 71, 101, 451. Martha H., 82. Mary, 194, 195, 197. Mary F., 82. Richard, 223, 452. Willard, 76.
George, 466, 503.
Getchell, 506.
Ghentner, Reuben, 445.
Gibbs, Daniel, 434. John, 455.
Gilchrist, Eliza, 512.
Gillett, E., Rev., 177, 182, 215.
Gillmor, David, 54.
Gillmor, David, and family, 129, 136, 138, 149-152, 328, 338, 452.
Gillmor, Marcus, and family, 74, 326, 342, 424, 454.
Gillmor, Millard, 339, 454.

Gillmor, Robert, 491.
Gillmor, Rufus, 54, 65, 115, 137, 138, 147, 152, 154, 201, 225, 226, 237, 347, 364. His family, 74, 82, 453. Offices held by, 118, 122, 123, 129, 131. On committees, 146, 149, 151, 164, 288. To purchase ammunition, 337. Military officer, 339. Buys beef, 346. Has tame cubs, 397. Takes fish, 420.
Gillmor, Rufus, 339, 453.
Gilman, 87, 501.
Gilmore, Jonathan, 168.
Giraldman, Margaret, 432.
Glass, 509.
Gleason, Aaron, 197, 456.
Gleason, Calvin, and others, 76, 95, 120, 127, 132, 133, 222, 250, 253, 306, 308, 441, 455.
Gleason, John, Col., and family, 177, 209, 329, 455. John, of Thomaston, 62.
Gleason, Joseph, 28, 223, 227, 308, First settlement near, 31, 39. Family of, 85, 90, 456.
Gleason, Joseph M., family of, 94, 455. In office, 120-122, 124, 280.
Gleason, Micajah and Polly, and family, 77, 154, 201, 306, 324, 455. His fulling-mill, 109. Offices held by, 118, 203. On committees, 134, 292, 304. Military, 340.
Gleason, Nathan M., and family, 92, 455.
Gleason, Wm., 77, 132, 225, 226, 306, 307. Censuses taken by, 77. Family of, 85, 456. His factory, 109. In office, 121, 122. Justice, 253, 254. On fish, 420, 422, 423.
Goodridge, 501.
Goodspeed, Rebecca, 440.
Goodwin, 254, 446.
Gordon, 91, 128, 404, 430.
Gordon, William, cited, 23.
Gore, Thomas, Dr., 304, 322.
Gough, Athelinda, 434.
Gould, 79, 364, 497.
Gove, 92, 503.
Governors, votes for, 232, 242.

GENERAL INDEX. 527

Gowen, Asa, and family, 93, 504. Benjamin, 307, 473, 517. Cyrus, 121. Elizabeth H., 94. John, 76, 93, 120, 254, 280, 306. John H., and family, 308, 504. Nathaniel B., 94. Rebecca H., 93, 209. William H. and Louisa A., 81, 454.
Graduates. See College-graduates.
Grafton, 196, 339, 347, 442, 509, 516.
Grain, 30, 35, 105.
Grant, Elizabeth, 505.
Graves, Bathsheba, 437.
Gray, Mary, 436.
Greeley, 219, 505, 509.
Greene, David, 33.
Greene, Joshua S., and family, 82, 251, 256, 305. His high-school, 316.
Grinnell, Bailey, and family, 75, 126, 152, 194, 196, 457.
Grinnell, Hannah, 465.
Grinnell, James, and family, 75, 86, 227, 307, 458.
Grinnell, Mace S., and family, 196, 457.
Grinnell, Philip, and wife, 133, 457.
Grinnell, Richard, 129, 194, 196, 329.
Grinnell, Royal, 55, 68, 129, 194, 196, 276, 329, 510. His family, 56, 64, 75, 458. Takes salmon, 420.
Grist-mills, 41, 55.
Groton, 378, 443.
Guild, Joseph, 65, 117, 145, 267, 459, 481.
Guns, on setting, 395.
Gurney, Kingman, 465.
Gushee, 165, 443, 453, 489.

H.

Hadley, 434, 506.
Hagar, Ezekiel, and others, 77, 129, 327, 453. Hunts, 397.
Hagar, John, and family, 89, 308.
Hagar, Reuben, and family, 90, 227, 469.
Hagar, Samuel, 77, 305-307, 495.
Hagar, Sewell, and family, 89, 305, 307.

Hagar, Thomas, and others, 90.
Hahn, 479.
Hail, 11.
Hall, 76, 307, 515.
Hamlin, 215, 250, 470.
Hammond, Dimmis, 485.
Handay [Hendee?], 83.
Hanson, 321, 478, 479, 497, 500.
Harding, Daniel F., and family, 74, 78, 177, 227, 318, 432. In office, 126, 127, 206, 304, 306. Candidate for representative, 249, 250. Justice, 253, 254. Lawyer, 319.
Harding, Elisha, Dr., 74, 223-225, 227, 304, 305, 307, 380, 452. Senator, 247. Road commissioner, 280. Lecturer, 316. Physician, 322, 324. At the muster, 356, 360. His family, 463.
Harding, Phillips C., 77, 135, 223, 227, 250, 270. Family of, 77, 85. In office, 118-120, 306. Justice, 254.
Hardy, Seeth, 500.
Harriman, 86, 509.
Harris genealogy, 482.
Harris, from England, 483.
Harris, Elizabeth, 488.
Harris, Obadiah, and family, 75, 87, 127, 128, 225, 250, 482.
Harris, Thaddeus William, on insects, 56.
Hart, 77, 84, 85, 129, 430, 479.
Hart, Fisher, 26, 77, 83, 154, 201, 223, 225, 227, 305-307, 463.
Hart, John F., and family, 26, 29, 65, 77, 85, 306, 308, 327, 423, 459. His dogs, 411.
Hart, Miriam, Mrs., 148, 459. Caught in a bear-trap, 405.
Hart, Stephen, escapes from Indians, 26.
Hart, William, Lieut., 14, 65, 66, 101, 129, 201, 338, 412, 448, 513. His family, 77, 85, 459. Enlists men for the French war, 336.
Hartford, 447.
Harthhorn and Hathorne, 435, 468.
Harvard University, 20, 64, 389.
Harwood, 488, 508.

Haskell, 79, 83, 122, 466.
Hastings, 81, 467.
Hatch, George, 444.
Hathaway, Elizabeth, 438.
Hathorne or Harthhorn, 435, 468.
Haverhill, Mass., 498, 503.
Hawes, 464, 482.
Hawes, Abijah, Deacon, 41, 121, 127, 152, 176, 201, 210, 211, 259. Settles, 41. His family, 64, 75, 459. On committees, 143, 162, 168. In the army, 328.
Hawes, Charles A., and family, 78, 122, 463, 511.
Hawes, Galen, and family, 306, 317, 462.
Hawes, Herman, 8, 47, 62, 201, 223, 249. His family, 75, 96, 463. Offices held by, 118, 120, 122, 124, 280, 305, 306. On committees, 198, 292. Military officer, 340. On eagles and fishhawks, 421.
Hawes, Madison, cited, 219, 459. Family of, 462.
Hawes, Matthias, 7, 152, 305. His account-book cited, 7, 50, 51, 58, 107, 161. His barn struck by lightning, 15. Land bought by, 42. His settlement, 46. Marriage, 51. Log-house, 51. His family, 64, 75, 460. Offices held by, 118, 119, 126, 129. On committees, 130, 143, 164, 290, 302, 303. Methodist, 194, 196, 218. Exposure of, 273. In the revolutionary army, 328.
Hawes, Matthias, Mrs., 51, 55, 67, 460. Her dowry, 53. Visiting, 278.
Hawes, Moses, 25, 152, 157, 258, 259, 294, 325. Settles, 47. Town-officer, 60, 61, 117, 118, 119, 121, 122, 129. On committees, 60, 143, 144, 164, 231, 268, 302, 303. His family, 64, 462. In the army, 328.
Hawes, Moses, and family, 87, 121, 463.
Hawes, Noyes P., 7, 304, 315, 317. His notices of the town cited, 45, 74, 103, 107, 130, 309. His family, 462.

Hawes, Otis, and family, 88, 250, 251, 307, 317.
Hawes, Silas, and family, 84, 462.
Hawes, Stephen S., and family, 38, 96, 120, 121, 225, 227, 251, 307, 352, 463, 514.
Hawes, Whiting, and family, 42, 96, 201, 306, 317, 460.
Hawes, William G., and family, 96, 119, 121, 225, 226, 307, 463, 493.
Hayden, Angela, 457.
Heald, Abigail, 430.
Healey, Sally, 435.
Hearses, 135.
Heaton, Isaac, 248, 249.
Hedding, Elijah, Bishop, 466.
Heisler, John, and family, 80.
Hemenway, 76, 79, 127, 177, 195, 197, 306, 433, 456, 513.
Henderson, Gavinus, 225, 322.
Hewes, Solomon, 76, 127, 194, 196.
Hewitt, Hannah, 463.
Heywood, Mary, 505.
Hibbard, C., and family, 92, 307, 513.
Hichborn, Charles, 75, 223.
Higgins, Joshua, Rev., 220.
High-schools, 315.
Highways, 61, 273, 440. Surveyors, 279. Compensation for work, 282. Breaking, in winter, 284.
Hill, Mary, 457.
Hilliard, 503.
Hillman, Samuel, Rev., 219.
Hills, 85, 96, 127, 128, 464, 471.
Hills, Benj. B., and family, 78.
Hills, Cyrus, Dr., 322, 464.
Hills, Edward, and family, 83, 122, 254, 255, 305, 453.
Hills, Isaac, 112, 124, 128, 196, 306, 307, 317, 464, 515.
Hills, Jabez Fisher, 321, 464.
Hills, Joel, and family, 317, 464.
Hills, Josiah, and family, 75, 84, 464.
Hills, Nathan, and family, 75, 84, 194, 196, 223, 225, 230, 290, 292, 464, 490, 515. In office, 119, 120, 122, 124, 280, 306–308. On committees, 132, 156.
Vinal, 307, 315.

GENERAL INDEX.

Hills, Reuben, 75, 134, 194, 196, 288, 289, 291, 464.
Hills, Reuben, and family, 75, 194, 196, 223, 317, 464.
Hills, Samuel, 8, 152, 209, 289, 321, 400. His journal, 8. In want, 55. Blacksmith, 56, 58, 464. His arrival, 58. On committees, 60, 136, 144, 162, 164, 166, 231-233, 251, 267, 303, 304. His family, 64, 77, 464. In office, 119, 121, 123, 126, 127, 129. His opposition to Mr. True, 172-214. Writes, for Esensa, to Germany, 449.
Hills, Samuel, and family, 75, 83, 194, 196, 225, 226, 462, 464. Representative, 250.
Hills, Sanford, and family, 77, 83, 86, 96, 306, 464.
Hills' Mills, 2, 101, 291, 420, 510.
Hills Point, 58, 69, 388.
Hilt, 4, 80, 467.
Himes, 511.
Hoar, Cyrena, 214.
Hobart, Peter, Rev., and Jael, 478, 479.
Hobbs, Josiah, of Hope, 63.
Hodge and Hodges, 320, 475, 500.
Hogs and hogreeves, 136.
Holbrook, Susanna, 476.
Holman, Betsey Barr, 500.
Holmes, 57, 64, 464, 484, 487, 517.
Hook, Charles, 471.
Hopkins, 163, 220, 254, 305.
Hopkinson, Lydia, 499.
Hopkinton, N.H., 107, 417, 495, 503.
Horse, bewitched, 228.
House, 450, 513.
Houses, first built, 35, 39. See Log-houses.
Hovey, Isaac C., and family, 84, 327, 462.
How, Elizabeth, 455.
Howard, 43, 76, 80, 89, 195, 479, 495.
Howland, S. M., and family, 85, 128.
Hoyt, 502, 506.
Hubbard, Daniel, 33. Rev. R., 219.
Hudson, 371.
Hull, David, and family, 79.

Humphrey and Humphreys, 164, 219, 279, 376.
Hunnewell, 77, 490.
Hunt, 34, 430, 488, 490.
Hunter, Lithgow, 318.
Hunting, 386. Matches, 417.
Hunting, Timothy, 472.
Huse, Jonathan, Rev., 171, 206-208, 212. His letter, 171.
Huse, Stephen, and family, 458.

I.

Ide, 469.
Ilsley, Horatio, Rev., 215, 305.
Incorporation of the town, 60.
Indian doctor, 323.
Indians, carried off by Weymouth, 2. Names given by, 2, 4, 21. Notices of, 23. Hart's and Boggs's escape from them, 26.
Infantry and officers, 338. At the muster, 355.
Ingraham, John H., Rev., 207.
Irish, Cornelius B., Rev., 46, 68, 127, 194, 196, 218, 249, 250. His family, 75, 88, 465.
Irish, Ichabod, and family, 67, 195, 248, 268, 465.
Irish, Ichabod, and family, 76, 466.
Irish, Joseph, family of, 88, 466, In office, 127, 250, 251, 305, 308.
Irish, Milton, in the Texan war, 348. His family, 466.
Iron-works, 111.
Isense, John Andrew, 450.

J.

Jackson, 87, 446, 512.
Jacobs, 201, 347.
James, Mrs., doctress, 321.
Jameson, Samuel, 75. Eliza B., 83. Ellen, 87. Maria, 94. Silence, 437. Brice, 441. Lydia, 445. Mary K., 457. Henry, and family, 472. Deborah, 474. Priscilla, 482.
Jefferson, Thomas, President, 232.
Jellard, Betsey, 488.
Jennison, Ebenezer, 62, 149, 294, 325, 466. Offices held by, 118-120, 123, 252, 303.

Jennison, Timothy L., Dr., 32.
Jennison, William, Dr., and family, 47-50, 61, 64, 275.
Jewett, 219, 364, 375, 490, 503.
Jews, 110.
Johnson, Alfred, Rev., 170.
Jones, Benjamin, Rev., 219, 220.
Jones, 250, 489. Benjamin L., 327. Daniel, 495. Elizabeth, 434. George H., and family, 85. Hannah, 449. Lucy L., 78. Mary, 110. Mary, 481. Mary S., 470, 492. Melicent, 512. Michael, 495. Sally, 434.
Jones, Edward, and others, 110, 111, 115, 466. Town-officer, 117-119, 123, 126, 127, 129. On committees, 145, 163, 164, 195, 231, 303-304. Pew-owner, 152, 218. Methodist, 194, 196. Representative, 247. Justice, 251, 252. To purchase stores, 336.
Jones, John, and family, 75, 82, 308, 327, 416.
Jones, John, family of, 93.
Joy, Emery Franklin, 491.
Judd, 454.
Justices of the Peace, 251.

K.

Kahler, 128, 490.
Kastner, 472.
Keene, 84, 446.
Kellar, 441, 492. See Kelloch.
Kellerin, 459.
Kelloch, Adam, 435. Alexander and Mary, 462. Eliza, 436. Elizabeth Libbey, 472. Lory, 459. Margaret, 441. Rosanna, 441. Silas, 453. William, 442.
Kellogg, Ezra, Rev., 219, 220, 249.
Kellogg, Samuel E., 433.
Kendrick, 469.
Kennedy, Henry, 375.
Kenniston, 504.
Kieff, 90, 127, 194, 196, 466.
Kilgore, Eveline, 430.
Kimball, Daniel, and family, 500. George, 199, 237, 319. John and family, 86. Sarah, or Sally, 444.
Kinney, Harriet, 438.
Kirkpatrick, Jane, 192.

Knapp, 463.
Knight and Knights, 488, 500.
Knowlton, 93, 509.
Knox, Henry, Gen., 8, 113, 171, 214, 266, 414.
Kuhn, Jacob, 443.

L.

Labadea, 348, 349.
Labor and money compared, 286.
Lair or Lehr, 83, 444, 458.
Lakin, 100, 279.
Lamb, Elizabeth, 467.
Lambert, Sarah, 500.
Lambricht, Dr., 324.
Lamson, Mary, 481.
Lanfest, 87, 94.
Law, 76, 77, 89, 90, 176, 209, 306, 307, 442, 494.
Lawrence, 76, 81, 126, 510.
Lawyers, 318.
Lea, Robert, 476.
Leach, Ambrose, and family, 78, 307. Samuel, and family, 449. Waterman, 470. William A. J., 91.
Leathers, Patty, 439.
Leavitt, 127, 500.
Le Brocke, Bathsheba, 478, 479.
Le Doit, 197, 456, 466.
Lee, Jesse, Rev., 217.
Lehr or Lair, 83, 444, 458.
Leland, 65, 67, 276, 456.
Lennan, 216, 470.
Lermond, 13, 82, 197, 308, 468, 514.
Lermond, Elbridge, family of, 81, 467. In office, 119, 121, 122, 307. Senator, 247. Representative, 251.
Lermond, John, and family, 101, 467.
Lermond, John, 76, 114, 134, 195, 223, 231, 305. Family of, 76, 81, 467. Offices held by, 118, 269, 280. On committees, 203, 270, 292, 304. Representative, 247.
Lermond, John, and family, 81, 227, 308, 467.
Lermond, John W., and family, 80, 307.
Lermond, William, 13, 76, 195.

GENERAL INDEX. 531

Lewis, 148, 152, 219, 450, 467.
Lexington fight. See Concord.
Libbey, 87, 463, 468, 481.
Libbey, Andrew, and family, 82, 117, 305.
Libbey, Wm., 75, 226, 305-307.
Libraries, 317.
Light, 443, 458.
Light-infantry, 237, 340.
Lightning, damage by, 13.
Lime-casks, 102.
Lincoln, 11, 16, 87, 430, 490.
Lindall, 61.
Lindley, John, and family, 87, 280, 468.
Lindley, John W., 62, 201, 227, 248. His family, 75, 88, 468. Offices held by, 118-120, 203. On committees, 134, 290, 304, 306. Justice, 253, 254. Military notices of, 340, 347.
Linniken, 76, 85, 248, 485, 510.
Linscott, 504.
Litchfield, Benjamin, and family, 47, 75, 88, 305, 307, 481.
Litchfield, Zaccheus, and others, 74, 127, 306, 441, 472, 511.
Lithgow, 59, 364.
Little, John, 74, 84, 102, 111, 114, 115, 134, 154, 201, 215, 304. Town-officer, 117, 120, 126. Inn-holder, 158. Justice, 253.
Little, John M., 84, 492.
Littlehale, George S., and family, 81, 473.
Littlehale, James, 76, 196, 197, 226. In office, 118, 120.
Livermore, Abigail, 455.
Locke, John, 64.
Log-houses, built, 35, 39, 54. Described, 35, 40, 51, 55, 294. Crowded, 40.
Long, John, Capt., 335.
Looms, 52, 108.
Loons, 415.
Lord, 82, 500.
Loring, Judith, 437.
Lothrop, 81, 90, 458.
Loup-cervier, 412.
Loyalists, 333, 334.
Lucas, 75, 87, 91, 194, 458, 473.
Luce, Abigail, 479. Edmund, 195, 497. George, and family, 95. Jeremiah, 196, 468. Joseph and Lydia, 435. Lot, 516. Moses, and family, 89, 510. Prince, 127, 436, 468. Rebecca, 445. Remember, 89. William S., 307.
Luce, Seth, and family, 67, 76, 126, 145, 152, 169, 176, 201, 209, 468, 489.
Luce, Thaddeus, and family, 76, 90, 127, 128, 194, 196, 306, 308, 456, 468.
Ludwig, William, Col., 353.
Lumber, Eliony, 459, 460.
Lummus, Elizabeth, 491.
Lunt, 480.
Lyceum, 316.
Lyon, Maria, 460. R. E., 227.

M.

McAllister, 96, 493.
McClellan, John, 471.
McClintock, Robert, 318.
McCurdy, 84, 159, 249, 449, 469.
McDowell, 170, 248, 250, 482, 492.
McGray, William, Rev., 219.
McGregor, 334.
McGuier, Robert, and family, 29, 78, 308, 470.
McIntyre, 30, 256, 257.
McKinney, Caroline, 95.
McLean, 11, 92, 163, 377.
McLellan, Nancy, 481.
McPheters, 481.
Maddocks, 75, 87, 113, 196, 328, 483, 510.
Maidman, Martha, 446.
Maine, separation of, 231.
Malcom, James, 27.
Mallard, Edmund, 111, 198, 232, 304, 325, 340, 347.
Mann, Beriah, 460.
Mansfield, Daniel H., 450.
March, 117, 164, 166-168, 176, 186, 202, 252, 303.
Marriages, 158.
Marsh, Jeremiah, Rev., 219.
Marshall, Emily, 444.
Martha's Vineyard, 66, 67, 516.
Martin, Adam, 75, 196, 402, 481. Betsey, 444, 485. Frances, 455, Isley, and family, 88, 120, 128, 308, 481. Leander, 512. Mar-

532   GENERAL INDEX.

garet, 436. Mary, 493. Samuel, 58, 401.
Mason, John, 459.
Mass. Provincial Congress, 34.
Matthews, 436, 489, 513.
Maxcy, Benjamin, and his family, 65, 69, 469.
Maxcy, Hervey, and family, 70, 154, 194, 196, 341, 405, 471.
Maxcy, Joseph, 65, 66, 69, 116, 293, 405. Offices held by, 118, 119. On committees, 144, 149, 170, 264, 302, 303. Military officer, 338. His family, 469.
Maxcy, Josiah, 65, 194, 405. Offices held by, 117, 120, 129. On committees, 163, 251, 303, 304. Family, 470.
Maxcy, Josiah A., 80.
Maxcy, Sally. See Daggett, Ebenezer, Mrs.
Maxcy, Ward, and family, 223, 372, 470, 492.
Maxfield, 75, 127, 194, 196, 510.
May, Dorothy, 478.
Mayhew, 438.
Maynard, Jonathan, 455.
Medomac River, 1, 3, 62, 390, 407.
Meduncook, 4.
Meeting-houses, 139, 143, 215, 218, 221, 226.
Megunticoock, 4.
Meredith, N.H., 502, 503.
Mero, Amariah, 54, 144, 147, 152, 201, 278, 412, 485. His family, 54, 64, 75, 471. Offices held by, 117, 118, 121-123, 129, 159. On committees, 131, 136, 145, 149, 150, 251, 264, 288, 290, 292. Agent to court, 201, 336. In the army, 329. Takes fish, 420.
Mero, Hermon, and family, 87, 306, 472, 492.
Mero, John, 291, 491.
Mero, Sanford, 94.
Mero, Spencer, 75, 120, 225, 227, 306, 307. Family of, 88, 471. Selectman, 118. Military officer, 342.
Mero, Susan, Mrs., 37, 40, 177, 278, 398, 427, 471, 494.
Merrifield, Asaph, 476.

Merrill, J. G., Rev., 216.
Merritt, Timothy, Rev., 219.
Merry, Prudence, 467.
Mesarvy and Meservey, 29, 404, 487, 494.
Messer, Alice, 494.
Messer, Asa, and family, 76, 472. Seizes a fox, 410.
Messer, Asa, and family, 83, 225, 254, 305, 463, 473.
Messer, Ebenezer S., family of, 94, 473.
Messer, Minot, family of, 94, 473.
Messer, Parker, family of, 90, 473.
Messer, Thomas, and family, 76, 196, 473.
Metcalf, 85, 93, 322, 328, 463, 491.
Methodists and Meeting-house, 116, 194, 196, 217.
Miles, Nathan, Capt., 455.
Military History, 327.
Mill Farm, 5, 55. First settlement there, 28.
Miller, Abijah, 467. Alvitia C., 431. Betsey, 448. Charles, and family, 81, 225. George, 93. Godfrey and family, 514. Hannah, 512. Horace, and family, 81, 459. Joanna, 452. Johnson, 83. Joseph, and family, 76, 81, 154, 196, 305, 306, 307, 408. Margaret and Salome, 445. Nancy, 447. Noah, 346. Oliver, 334. Seth and family, 88, 512. Sarah Catharine, 504.
Miller's Brook, 3. Landing, 30. Rocky Point, 26.
Mills, 2, 41, 55, 101.
Mills, Emeline Amanda, 514.
Minerals, 97.
Minks, 412.
Minott, 431.
Mirick, 498.
Mitchell, 154. A., and family, 445, 474. Christiana, 89. Rev. David M., 190, 207. Henry, 89. Jabez N., and family, 122, 123, 474. Jane W., 475. Jeremiah, and family, 76, 123, 129, 177, 201, 209, 474. Jeremiah W., 94. Rev. M., 220. Mary and Mercy, 177, 209. Rachel, 76, 474.

GENERAL INDEX.   533

Mitchell, Thomas, Thomas, jun., and others, 76, 127, 131, 133, 164, 167, 168, 176, 177, 201, 212, 249, 250, 304–306, 474. In office, 118, 120, 122–124, 253.
Mitchell, Thomas A., 76, 317, 474.
Money and labor compared, 286.
Monhegan, 2.
Montgomery, 69, 70, 257.
Moody, 94, 465, 492, 516.
Moore, Tryphena and Albert D., 81.
Moose, 31, 388, 389, 396.
More, Bailey, 120, 339, 433.
Morrill, 220, 479.
Morse, Abner, Rev., 477.
Morse, Asa, and family, 47, 308, 481. Barnard, and family, 317, 479. Calvin, and family, 129, 177, 201, 475. Catherine, 457. George W., and family, 65, 78, 225, 480. James, 455. James B. and Mary A., 85. Jedidiah, and family, 88, 481. Jeremiah, 455. Jonathan, and family, 76, 133, 306, 475. Lavinia, 516.
Morse, Joseph, and family, 57, 76, 118, 127, 199, 249, 292, 305, 306, 340, 455, 476.
Morse, Joshua, and families, 76, 83, 226, 307, 308, 457.
Morse, Levi, 64, 126, 129, 201, 227, 303, 432. His family, 74, 476. In the army, 329.
Morse, Levi, 65. Family of, 78, 480.
Morse, Micajah, G., family of, 84.
Morse, Moses, 14, 201, 305, 451. Family of, 77, 78, 477.
Morse, Obadiah, and family, 14, 57, 75, 194, 196, 480.
Morse, Walter, and family, 317, 464, 478.
Morse, William B., and family, 327, 480.
Morton, 76, 95, 455, 481.
Mosquitos, 56.
Moss, as a guide, 273.
Moulton, Batt, 498.
Mount Pleasant, 1, 20.
Mowry, B. R., and family, 74, 84, 111, 126, 511.
Muddy Pond, 5, 402, 411.

Murphy, Charles, 81.
Murray, 194, 475, 502.
Muscongus Patent, 22.
Muscongus River, 406.
Music, 325. At the muster, 359.
Musquash, 412.
Musters, military, 352. At Waldoborough, 354. At Warren, 371. At McLean's Mills, 377. Description of, 385.
Muzzey, 461.

N.

Nash, Mary Ann, 442.
Nason, Abram, 488.
Needham, Thomas and Ruth, 497.
Neptune, Governor of the Penobscot Indians, 2, 5.
Nevans, 505.
Newbit, 14, 334, 435, 443, 482, 488, 510, 511.
Newcomb, 80.
Newhall, James, 251, 482. Jonathan, and family, 115, 192, 195, 302, 481. Roderic G., 93. William, 248, 249.
Nichols, John S., and family, 486.
Nicholson, 158, 176, 192, 347.
Nolen, Patrick, 510.
Non-resident proprietors, 61, 266.
Norwood, 76, 93, 440.
Noyes, 79, 436, 448, 489.
Nurse, Mehetabel, 475.
Nye, Cyrus Crocker, and family, 75, 483. Edward T., 483. Stillman, and family, 87, 482. Thomas, and family, 23, 75, 129, 198, 482. Thomas C., and family of, 86, 483.

O.

Oakes, 92, 94, 129, 444, 475, 483.
Oath for town-officers, 116.
Odlin, Elisha and Mary, 501.
Olney, 272, 484.
O'Meira, 95, 96.
O'Neil, John, 435.
Orchards, 107.
Ordway, 507.
Overlock, Sally, 450.
Owen, Susan B., 316.
Owl's Head, 20, 21.

Oxton, William, 92.

P.

Packard, 517. Benjamin, 35, 38, 39. Joanna, 438. Reuben, 76.
Packard, Hezekiah, Rev., 170, 206. Mr. Huse's letter to him, 171.
Packard, Marlboro', and their families, 75, 88, 118, 193-195, 197, 227, 280, 304, 306, 307.
Page, 90, 430, 454, 469.
Palmer, 480, 512.
Paper-mills, 109.
Pardoe, John, and family, 85, 111.
Parker, 472. Rev. Freeman, 170, 214.
Parks, 351, 509.
Partridge, 50, 57, 64, 130, 404, 464, 484.
Patch, Daniel, 434.
Patten, Hugh, Capt., 364.
Patterson, 499, 506.
Paupers, 270.
Payne, Elizabeth, 431.
Payson, Jesse W., and family, 83, 122, 225, 255, 327, 463.
Payson, John, 74, 225, 226, 389. His family, 80, 446. In office, 118, 280, 306.
Payson, Madan K., and family, 95, 327, 464.
Payson, Nathan D., and family, 78, 327.
Payson, Samuel and Sarah, 51, 460.
Payson, Eunice, 450.
Peabody, 80, 84, 197, 443, 460, 466, 481, 484, 485, 515, 517.
Peace, 346.
Peaches, 107.
Peale, Elizabeth, 498.
Pearce or Pearse, 490.
Pearson, Rachel, 474.
Pease, 16, 63, 90, 93, 410, 432, 437, 448, 466, 468, 505, 508.
Peck, Capron, 471.
Pelton, Moses, 249-251.
Pendleton, Abby, 441.
Penny, William, and family, 473.
Penobscot, 20, 334. Explored by Champlain, 20. See Biguyduce.

Pentecost Harbor, 2.
Perham, Samuel, and family, 442.
Perkins, 220, 485, 502.
Perry, 330, 347, 436, 455.
Pettengill Stream, 2, 391.
Pevee [Peavey ?], Jacob, 474.
Philbrook, 89, 465, 504.
Phippen, 500, 507.
Phipps, 330.
Physicians, 320.
Pickerel, 423.
Pickering, 447, 470.
Picket, Anna, 500.
Pickworth, 497.
Pigeons, 413.
Pike, 319.
Pilsbury, 76, 127.
Pinkham, 93.
Piper, 456.
Pitcairn, 332.
Pitcher, 85.
Pitkin, J. B., Rev., 315.
Pitman, 95, 339.
Pitts, Abner, 74.
Plantation organization, 59.
Plums, 107.
Politics, 230.
Pomeroy, 476.
Pond, 446, 460, 463, 484.
Ponds in Union, 4.
Poor, Betsey, 478.
Pope, 111, 116, 195, 232, 233, 304.
Popham, George, 2, 20.
Population, 73.
Porterfield, 44.
Post, 78, 85, 307.
Post-offices, 115, 254.
Potatoes, 106.
Potter, Mary, 431.
Pound, 140.
Powder and Powder-house, 153, 337.
Pratt, 193, 195, 305, 485, 510.
Preaching, the first, 162.
Preble, Martha, 450.
Prescott, Rufus, 83.
Preston, John, 493.
Priest, John Baxter, 470.
Prince, 216, 271, 464, 485.
Pring, Martin, Capt., at Fox Islands, 20.
Prior, 476, 514.
Proctor, John, family of, 92.

GENERAL INDEX. 535

Publishments, 158.
Putnam, town of, 62.

Q.
Quakers, 67, 192, 195.
Quantabacook, 389, 392.
Quiggle, 76, 79, 293, 304, 485, 488.

R.
Raccoons, 411.
Rackliffe [Radcliffe?], Isaac, 90.
Rains, 9.
Raisings, 39, 147.
Raizor, Dolly, 474.
Ransom, Olivia, 487.
Rawson, Avery, Col., 353, 357, 361, 365, 369.
Read, 505.
Reed, 34, 50, 101, 134, 266, 432, 454, 471.
Remely, Matthias, Journal of, 24.
Revolution, incidents in the, 258, 334.
Revolutionary soldiers, 41, 327.
Rice, 96, 225, 227, 342, 455.
Rice, Elisha E., and family, 122, 127, 254, 319, 320.
Rice, Franklin, family of, 92, 492.
Rice, Isaac, family of, 506.
Rice, James, 114, 129, 177, 201, 204, 209, 210. His family, 320.
Rice, Nathan D., 46, 141, 194, 196, 218, 306, 442. Family of, 75, 90, 320. In office, 122, 124, 128, 129, 253, 254, 305.
Rice, Noah, 14, 75, 201, 280, 291, 304, 306, 307, 479, 480. Military officer, 338, 339. At the muster, 356, 360, 374. Re-elected captain, 374. Court-martialled, 375.
Rice, Noah S., and family, 86, 225, 479.
Rice, Richard D., and family, 320.
Rich, 76, 220-222, 446.
Richards, 74, 510.
Richardson, John W. and Abigail, 462.
Ricker, 192, 219.
Riddel, and family, 163.
Rifle Company, and officers, 341, 351. At the muster, 355. Disbanded, 377.

Ring, Jacob, 127, 194, 195, 197.
Ripley, 88, 89, 347, 439, 440, 443, 445, 474, 508.
Ripley, Ezra, Rev., 169, 189.
Rising, 79, 439.
Rivers, 1.
Roads, 61. See Highways.
Roakes, 334. Robert and John, 16. Marcus, 78. James, and family, 93. Sarah and E. P., 93. Margaret, 434. Daniel, 437.
Robbins genealogy, 486.
Robbins, 76, 79, 80, 84, 92, 95, 96, 262, 339, 374, 380, 445, 452, 489.
Robbins, Augustus C., 253, 318, 319. Cited, 315. Information from, 425. His family, 493.
Robbins, Bela, 47, 64, 75, 127, 145, 194, 196, 302. In the army, 330. Deer-reeve, 389. His family, 486.
Robbins, Cyrus, and family, 76, 90, 91, 280, 307, 339.
Robbins, David, 37, 130, 152, 154, 201, 209, 258, 259, 279, 403, 484. An early settler, 38, 39. Distressed for food, 45. His family, 75, 488. In office, 119, 121, 123, 127, 129, 159. On committees, 136, 168, 170, 290. Church-member, 177. Hunter, 387, 397. Pigeon-catcher, 414.
Robbins, David, and family, 75, 96, 201, 223, 305-308, 489.
Robbins, Ebenezer, 38, 330, 494.
Robbins, Ebenezer, and others, 47, 64, 75, 80, 87, 145, 146, 196, 258, 259, 306, 347, 445, 469, 475, 487.
Robbins, Jacob, 331, 334, 494.
Robbins, Jason, and others, 50, 75, 95, 226, 306-308, 400, 488, 491.
Robbins, "Aunt Mima," 176, 321, 493.
Robbins, Jessa, 25, 37-39, 47, 50, 54, 69, 126, 129, 152, 154, 159, 201, 258, 259, 331, 337, 425. On going to mill, 56. His family, 64, 75, 95, 490. A hunter, 390, 396, 408. Oldest person in town, 427.

Robbins, Jesse, and family, 226, 227, 491.
Robbins, John C., and family, 75, 122, 124, 306, 490. His military performances at musters, 358, 370.
Robbins, John P., 42, 201, 225, 227, 400. Family of, 75, 95, 491. Military officer, 339. At the muster, 355, 356. Court-martialled, 366. Proposition to re-elect him, 373.
Robbins, Joseph, and family, 76, 489.
Robbins, Josiah, 7, 131, 146, 152, 176, 274, 413, 420. Early settler, 54. His family, 57, 64, 65, 176, 491. In office, 117, 119, 123, 129. On committees, 136, 143-145, 150, 162, 166, 167, 198, 267, 290. In the army, 330.
Robbins, Lewis, and family, 75, 83, 292, 493.
Robbins, Nathan B., and family, 83, 254, 493.
Robbins, Nathaniel, 56, 152, 154, 201, 226, 279, 416, 419, 467. On black flies, 56. Storekeeper, 111, 112, 114. Moderator, 116. In office, 117, 118, 120, 123, 126, 129, 252-254. Monument to, 132. Takes jobs, 155, 291. On committees, 170, 192, 199, 232, 233, 288, 289, 302, 304. Of the legislature, 247-249. A hunter, 400, 407. Catches pigeons, 414. Information from, 425. His family, 491.
Robbins, Nathaniel, and family, 79, 226, 307, 415, 492.
Robbins, Oliver, and others, 58, 436, 437.
Robbins, Philip, 7, 25, 59, 114, 115, 130, 152, 258, 259, 275, 397, 420. Builds, 40. His family, 64, 487, 493, 504. Raises rye, 105. In office, 117, 129. On committees, 143-147, 162, 163, 198, 267. First preaching at his house, 162. Licensed, 230. Agent, 257. In the revolution, 331, 334, 335. Hunts, 394.

Robbins, Willard, 54, 63, 225, 226, 307. Family of, 84, 492. In office, 119, 121, 254, 280. Burying-ground and, 131, 132.
Robbins Neck, 24, 318. Taken possession of, 28. Settled, 54. Moose and bears on the, 392, 401.
Robbins's Point, 130, 388.
Robertson, Paulina Pottle, 441.
Robinson, 75, 95, 306, 320, 437, 442, 444, 448, 450, 488, 501, 503, 511.
Rogers, 129, 293, 494, 501.
Rogue's March, 359, 365.
Rolfe, 450.
Rollins, 80, 82, 96.
Ropes, John, 499.
Rosier's account of Weymouth's voyage, 2, 3, 20.
Round Pond, 5. Beaver-dam at, 411. Meadows, 45, 387.
Rowell, Ruth, 436.
Ruggles, John, 364.
Russ, Jane Houston, 436.
Russell, 48, 459.
Rust, 248.
Ryan, Daniel R., and family, 85.
Rye, 7, 30, 35, 39, 105.

S.

Sables, 393, 412.
Sagadahoc, 2, 20.
St. Clair, 80, 127.
St. George's Island Harbor, 2.
St. George's River, 1, 19, 105. Proposed as a boundary, 22.
Salmon, 419.
Sambo, the dog, 403.
Sampson, 320. Deb., 478.
Sanford, 512.
Sargent, 127, 317, 507.
Sargus, 482.
Savage, 320.
Sawin, Phares and Mary, 476.
Saw-mills, 41, 101.
Sawyer, 177, 182, 498, 501.
Sayward, 78, 88, 305, 451, 495.
Schenck, Capt., 449.
Schools, 294. Districts, 302. Houses, 303. Committees, 303. Agents, 305. Children, 308. Money, 310. State-grants for,

GENERAL INDEX. 537

311. High schools, 315. For writing, 315.
Scott, 182, 467.
Searles, Stephen, 30.
Seaton, James and Abigail, 502.
Seavey, David, and wife, 481.
Segocket, the river, 1, 2, 20.
Seiders, Henry, 38. Family of, 96.
Selectmen, 117.
Senators, 247.
Sennott, Francis, 88.
Setting guns for bears, 395.
Seven Brook, 3, 19.
Seven-tree Pond, 5. Persons drowned in, 69. Bear in, 397. Loons in, 415. Eagles there, 421.
Severance, Severing, or Sevrance, 194, 196, 483, 515.
Sewall, and the Hills' party, 172, 177.
Seymour, Ri:, 3.
Shattuck, 479, 480, 494.
Shaw, 457, 499, 511.
Shepard, 76, 89, 90, 92, 95, 176, 195, 201, 209, 280, 292, 448, 451, 471, 494.
Shepard, Chloe, 451. Eunice W., 471.
Shepard, Prof., 216.
Shepherd or Shepard, Wm., 75, 128, 249, 250. Justice, 253. Lieutenant, 342.
Shepherd, of Stratham, 501.
Sherburne, Mass., 64, 65.
Sherman, 475, 510.
Sherror or Sherrod, 444.
Shibles, James, 75.
Shingles, 100.
Shorey, 506.
Sibley genealogy, 495.
Sibley, Jacob, 16, 195, 197, 306. Struck by lightning, 16. Family of, 76, 87, 504.
Sibley, John L., 318, 409, 497.
Sibley, Jonathan, Dr., 9, 107, 314, 412, 413, 439, 453. Cited, 9, 11, 13. Family of, 75, 84, 134, 476, 495. Town-clerk, 117. On committees, 198, 199, 303, 304. Justice, 252, 253. His lyceum-lectures, 316, 426. Physician, 321, 324.
Sidelinger, 77, 88, 89, 306-308.

Sikes, O., Rev., and family, 214, 304.
Silloway, George, 75, 84, 464.
Simmons, 75, 83, 87, 93, 94, 120, 194, 195, 197, 306, 443, 454, 455, 463, 472, 481, 504.
Simulium molestum, 56.
Simulium nocivum, 57.
Sinclair, James, 76, 197.
Singer, Jane, 437.
Singing-schools, 325.
Skidmore, 93, 251, 280, 306-308.
Skinner, 76, 81, 339, 380.
Sleds, 278.
Sleeper, Albert, 438.
Small, 307, 497.
Smelts, 422.
Smith, 95, 129, 320, 436, 491, 493, 499.
Smith, Rev., 207, 215, 219.
Smith, John, Capt., explores the coast, 2. His books and map, 2, 20. His attempt to form a colony, 21.
Smith, S. E., Governor, 156, 375.
Snell, 126, 157, 194, 196, 506.
Snow, 431, 452, 508.
Somes, 485, 486.
Southworth, Alice, 478, 479.
Spalding and Spaulding, 434, 516.
Spear, 81, 201 [?], 436, 457, 513.
Speed, Benjamin, 100.
Spencer, Mass., 111.
Spinning-wheels, 108.
Spooner, Reliance, 457.
Spurr, Samuel, 196, 201 [?].
Standish, Eliza, 513.
Stanley, John, 450.
Stanwood, 511.
Staples, Mariah, 471.
Starr, Rev. Mr., 325.
Starrett, 114, 192, 209, 304, 448, 480.
Staunton, Paul, and family, 503.
Stearns, Charles, 84.
Sterling, 83, 308, 489.
Sterling, in Warren, 24, 27.
Stetson, 86, 445, 483.
Stevens, 76, 83, 90, 93, 95, 307, 308, 502, 503, 512.
Stewart, Holmes, 508.
Stewart, I. D., Rev., 500, 502, 506.
Stewart, O. O., 87, 128, 491, 508.

538 GENERAL INDEX.

Stewart, Timothy, 76, 152, 194, 196, 412. Family of, 87, 508. In office, 120, 129, 136, 252, 253.
Stewart, W. D., family of, 87, 508.
Stimson and Stimpson, 75, 219.
Stinson, 506.
Stirling, Lord, 27.
Stirlington, 27. A plantation, 59.
Stoddard, Abby Maria S., 442.
Stone, Allen, and family, 75, 508. Caroline F., 78. Eben, 341, 509. Jonas, 347, 509. Micah, 456. Rachel, 76. Rufus and Silvia G., 94.
Stone, Samuel, 76, 223, 250, 251. Family of, 76, 94, 509. Offices held by, 118, 120, 132, 256, 280, 306, 308, 341.
Stone, Waldron, and family, 119, 136, 152, 303, 433, 508.
Storer, Horatio Robinson, 419.
Stores, 111.
Stoughton, Mass., settlers from, 38, 54.
Strachey manuscript, 2, 20.
Stratham, N. H., 440, 490, 498.
Stratton, 477, 506.
Stuart, Anna, 501.
Stubbs, 127, 194, 196, 347, 430.
Suchfort, 11, 43, 44, 92, 449, 514.
Sullivan, James, Governor, 2, 7.
Sumner, 86, 448.
Sunnybec Pond, 1, 4, 43, 424.
Superstitions, 227.
Surplus revenue, 269.
Surveyors of highways, 279.
Sutton, Mass., 439, 498.
Swain, John and Abigail, 499.
Swan, 77, 483.
Sweetser, Olive, 468.
Swivel, 347.
Symonds, 500.

T.

Tanneries, 110.
Taxes, 256. Petitions to the Legislature respecting, 257, 262. In other towns, 260. Tables of, 261, 262, 281. Paid in produce, 261, 310. Time for paying, 265. Reed's case, 266. Highway, 280. For schools, 310.
Taxes, parish or ministerial, 164, 165, 193. Remission of, 145 146, 193-197.
Taylor, 78, 91, 92, 219, 447, 467 470.
Taylor, J., Dr., 29, 101, 266, 436. Purchases the township, 29, 61. His arrival, 30. Deed to, 32. His life, character, and family, 34, 48. Purchases made of, 36, 42, 45, 50. His trade and quarrel with Jennison, 47. His death, 48. His conveyance to Reed, 50.
Taylortown, 28. Organization of, 59.
Temperance, 230.
Tenney, 75, 502.
Tew, Elethan, 482.
Texas and Texan War, 348, 441.
Thatcher, Ebenezer, 214.
Thayer, 128, 454.
Thing, Nancy, 499.
Thomas, Waterman, 63. Emery, and family, 81. James, 90. Mary, 451. Catherine and Mary, 457.
Thomaston, 1, 2, 347.
Thompson, 75, 76, 81, 86, 89, 92, 122, 127, 194, 196, 305-307, 320, 392, 443, 454, 465, 509, 510, 513.
Thorndike, 77, 82, 154, 227, 459, 491, 492.
Thurrell, Patience, 501.
Thurston, 216, 305.
Thurston, Nahum, 50, 66, 75, 307. Family of, 95, 133, 483, 484.
Thurston, Philo, and family, 57, 75, 85, 91, 227, 306, 449, 489. Military notice of, 339, 377.
Thwing, James, Rev., 220. Josiah, 453.
Tibbets and Tibbetts, 486, 500.
Tifft, 517.
Tilson, 448.
Timber, 97.
Tinkham, 479.
Tithingmen, 126.
Titus, 75, 91, 128, 129, 152, 194, 196, 223, 278, 510.
Tobey, Cecilia and George, 442.
Tobey, John, Capt., 57, 152, 201,

GENERAL INDEX. 539

228, 281, 292, 401, 402. Family of, 76, 95, 133, 177, 512. Assessor, 120.
Tobey, Nathaniel, and family, 76, 223, 306, 307, 339, 512.
Tolman, 79, 434, 438.
Tombs, 134.
Toothaker, 438.
Tories, 333, 334.
Town histories, 2, 24.
Town-house, 141.
Town-lines perambulated, 62.
Town-meetings, 114.
Townsend, 76, 94, 95.
Trade, 111.
Trask, 500.
Travelling, early, 257, 273, 277.
Treasurers, 126.
Trees, felling of, 98.
Tripp, Charles, 90.
Trout, 423.
True, Ezekiel, of Montville, 106.
True, Henry, Rev., 17, 249, 326, 344. Notices deaths, 17. Family of, 75, 169, 432. Offices held by, 117, 253, 304. Settled as a clergyman, 169. Opposition to him, 170, 177. Dismissed, 203, 204, 208.
True, H. Rev., Methodist, 219.
True, Henry A., Dr., 25, 316, 318, 322, 432. Cited, 25, 493.
Tuck, 88, 90.
Tucker, 47, 129, 192, 194, 195, 197.
Tuner, the dog, 387.
Turner, 364, 367, 498.
Twining, Mary, 452.
Twins, exemption from taxes for, 262.
Tyler, 431, 517.

U.
Ulmer, Sally, Catherine, and Elizabeth, 437. Dr. Charles, 452. James A., 57, 439, 481.
Underwood, Joshua, 455.
Universalists, 222.
Upham, 76, 93, 94, 306, 444, 480.
Urine doctor, 324.
Urquhart, 161.

V.
Valpey, 499.
Vaughan or Vaughn, Joseph, 29, 74, 112, 139, 154, 201, 289, 291, 305, 307, 469. Family of, 78.
Vaughan, Joseph, and family, 85, 111, 120, 307.
Vaughan, Stetson, and family, 456.
Vaughan, William, family of, 78.
Vaughan's Iron Works, 111.
Vaughn for Vaughan, 305.
Vinal, Phebe, 473.
Visiting by early settlers, 277.
Vose, Elijah, and family, 83, 325, 432. In office, 121, 126. On committees, 132, 305. Justice, 254. Lawyer, 319.
Vose, Joanna E., 432.

W.
Wade, 75, 95, 306, 320, 445, 504.
Wadsworth, Peleg, Gen., 258, 335.
Walcott, Jona., and family, 497.
Walcott, Manning, family of, 96, 514.
Walcott, Pente, and family, 76, 304, 473, 513.
Walcott, Spencer, and family, 74, 86, 492, 513. In office, 120, 122, 123, 126, 127, 129, 305. Baptist, 193, 195, 197. Votes, 247.
Walcott, Spencer, and family, 87, 226, 307, 514.
Waldo, 6, 33.
Waldo patent, 22.
Waldoborough, 1, 62. Military difficulty with, 350.
Walker, Abel, 76, 127-129, 194, 195, 197, 306. Family of, 79, 470.
Walker, Amos, 74, 127, 306, 307, 459. Family of, 82, 447. Of the Hill's party, 177, 209.
Walker, Asa, 308, 514. Benjamin and family, 76, 86, 127. Daniel and family, 76, 91, 127, 194, 209-212, 307, 514. John and family, 76, 91, 127, 305-307, 514. Dr. John B., 323. Mercy, 476. Nathan and others, 128, 514. Silas and family, 76, 79.
Walpole, Mass., settlers from, 36.

Walton, J. H., and family, 466.
War of 1812, 343.
Ward, 476, 499.
Ware, Jason, 15, 114, 259, 264, 275, 328. Struck by lightning, 15. Buys land, 42. Settles, 46, 51. His family, 64, 75, 511, 515. Offices held by, 117, 119, 121, 126, 127, 304. Methodist, 194, 196, 218. A hunter, 403. His dog Sambo, 403.
Ware, Vinal, 46, 75, 198, 307, 411. Family of, 90, 515.
Ware, Warren, 248.
Warning out of town, 270.
Warren, Eaton's History of, 24. Controversy with, 256.
Warren, Cyrus, Rev., 220.
Washington, town of, 1, 100. First team to, 279.
Waters, 325, 443.
Weasel, 412.
Weaver, Polly, 487.
Webb, 69, 268, 456, 499, 500, 516.
Webster, 81, 220, 305, 454, 512.
Wedding, the first, 49.
Weeks, 490.
Wellington, 127, 168, 177, 328, 332, 433, 493.
Wellman, 69, 82.
Wells, Sarah, 498, 501.
Wentworth, Lemuel, 14, 15, 333. Joshua W., and family, 80. Warren, 83. Mary, 87. Rev. Daniel, 219. Freelove, 447. Lewis, 451.
West, George, 115, 126, 149, 152, 288, 401, 441, 467. On committees, 145, 146. His family, 516.
West, George W., 129, 195–197, 222, 516.
Weston, 219, 445.
Wetherbee, 482, 509.
Weymouth, George, Capt., 2, 20.
Weymouth, Timothy, 508.
Wheaton, Mason, Col., 45, 47, 49, 51, 60, 66, 251, 275, 484.
Whedon, 76.
Whipple, 49.

Whitcomb, 465.
White, 78, 219, 454.
White, William, writes a petition, 233. His Fourth-of-July Oration, 236. Postmaster, 255. On a committee, 304. Lawyer, 318.
White Hills visible, 20.
Whiting, 236. Thurston, and family, 79, 122, 227, 439. B. G. and Nancy, 85. Nathan, 122. John, 197, 253. Hervey, 452.
Whitney, 79, 86, 127, 128, 197, 444, 476.
Whittemore, 85, 327.
Whittier, 226, 470.
Wight, 129, 461, 516.
Wilder, Lydia, 506.
Wiley, 443, 489.
Williams, John, and family, 85. Martha, 176, 192. Capt. Nathan, 340. Sarah Elizabeth, and others, 431. John, 456. Lucy, 468. Roger, 482. Elijah, Elizabeth, and Eunice, 485.
Williamson, 219, 472.
Wing, 444.
Wingate, 77, 83, 95, 197, 512.
Winslow, 33, 471, 488, 489.
Witchcraft, 228.
Witham, 514.
Witt, William, 249, 251.
Wolves and wolf-hunt, 406.
Woodcock, 114, 126, 129, 130, 144, 162, 302, 490, 516.
Woodhull, R., Rev., 216, 217.
Woodman, Charlotte, 434.
Woodward, Nathan, 46.
Worth, 457.
Wright, Thos., 30, 34. Eliab, 460.
Writing-school, 315.
Wyman, 30, 517.

Y.

Yellalee, Robert, Rev., 219.
York, Thomas and Mahala, 493.
Young, 74, 79, 86, 92, 127, 194, 196, 250, 251, 491.
Young, Christopher, 76, 225. Family of, 82, 454. In office, 120, 122, 251, 306–308.

www.ingramcontent.com/pod-product-compliance
Lightning Source LLC
Chambersburg PA
CBHW060907300426
44112CB00011B/1379